Dwight W. B...

Text for class — Dr. Huber
Drumright

# THE EVANGELICAL COMMENTARY
## ON THE BIBLE

*This Commentary is Volume IV in*

THE EVANGELICAL COMMENTARY ON THE BIBLE

*Other volumes now published:*

THE GOSPEL ACCORDING TO ST. MARK
RALPH EARLE

THE ACTS OF THE APOSTLES
CHARLES W. CARTER
RALPH EARLE

# THE GOSPEL ACCORDING TO JOHN

GEORGE ALLEN TURNER, Ph.D.
Professor of Biblical Literature
ASBURY THEOLOGICAL SEMINARY

AND

JULIUS R. MANTEY, Th.D.
Professor Emeritus
NORTHERN BAPTIST THEOLOGICAL SEMINARY

WILLIAM B. EERDMANS PUBLISHING COMPANY
GRAND RAPIDS, MICHIGAN

# The Evangelical Commentary on the Bible

This volume is the third to appear in a projected twenty-volume commentary on the entire Bible. It is "evangelical" in the historic sense, being sympathetic to the principles of the Evangelical Revival within Protestantism, the effects of which have been felt from the 18th century to the present. As such this volume seeks to maintain the combination of sound scholarship and spiritual insight for which the commentaries of Adam Clarke and Matthew Henry are justly famous. Since the days of these great commentators the Biblical world has been rediscovered. Now, in addition to the classical Greek and Latin authors upon which the scholarship of that day was based, we have access to civilizations of the Near East contemporary with the Bible. As a modern commentary, this volume seeks to utilize this additional Biblical knowledge including the rapidly multiplying data from recent manuscript discoveries in Palestine and Egypt.

This commentary addresses itself to the Christian minister in particular and to the alert layman as well. The authors seek to place in the reader's hand a volume characterized by sound exegesis, wide perspective, up-to-date scholarship, spiritual discernment, and contemporary relevance.

The Editorial Committee which initiated this volume assumes general responsibility for the scope and format, but the views expressed herein are those of the authors alone. The editors and their advisors are representatives of several denominations, schools, and nationalities. It is to be hoped that this cooperative endeavor will "serve the present age" by making its contribution to the current revival in Biblical studies.

# Preface

To live long and intimately with a book of the Bible is a profound and vitalizing experience. This is especially true when the book is as full of life and fire as the Gospel according to John. The minds and lives of the authors of this commentary have been permanently affected as the result of this experience. As J. B. Phillips once said of a study of the Pauline letters, it is like exploring an old house and touching one of the wires only to find that it is still charged with electricity (*Letters to Young Churches*, Macmillan, 1951, p. xii).

This is third volume in a series of Bible commentaries launched as *The Evangelical Bible Commentary*; the two previous volumes are *Mark*, by Ralph Earle, and *Acts*, by Charles W. Carter and Ralph Earle. Like these previous volumes this present one seeks to provide the Bible student with an up-to-date, practical commentary in the evangelical tradition of Adam Clarke, John Wesley, Matthew Henry, and their spiritual successors. The main purpose of the authors, however, has been to discover the meaning and relevancy of the Bible text rather than to follow a particular theological tradition.

This commentary is exegetical in that it seeks to exhibit the nuances of the Greek text in a manner useful to readers unacquainted with the Greek. It is expository in that it endeavors to interpret the Bible text in language which is clear and convincing. The Greek text followed is Nestle's, but frequent reference is made to other texts for comparison. The English text is the American Standard Version, but comparison is made constantly with other English versions public and private, from the time-tested King James Version to the lucid New English Bible.

Anyone who presumes to add another to the hundreds of excellent volumes on the Fourth Gospel is under obligation to justify his presumption. Most of the best commentaries on this Gospel are by German and English authors. Many of these are not likely to be superseded. However, the major contributions were written too early to take advantage of the bearing on the interpretation of this Gospel of the new scroll discoveries in Palestine and Egypt. These finds are particularly relevant to Johannine studies. The abundance of recent articles on the Fourth Gospel in religious journals bears witness to the ferment which these finds are making. It is unfortunate that the great volumes of C. H. Dodd and C. K. Barrett were unable to take cognizance of these manuscript discoveries. Perhaps the chief justification for the present volume is the perennial interest in this Gospel, the book considered by many to be the most important volume in the Biblical "library" of sixty-six books.

The writers have discovered this cooperative endeavor to have been very worthwhile. Dr. J. R. Mantey provided the exegesis of chapters six through twenty-one and contributed to other portions. Dr. G. A. Turner provided the balance of the exegesis, the exposition and the introduction. The expositor used in college the *Greek Grammar* published in 1927 by the exegete, and at Harvard University used in class *A Hellenistic Greek Reader*, edited by Colwell and Mantey. The method of procedure was for the expositor to take the exegesis provided by his colleague, occasionally modifying and supplementing it by his own exegesis, and use it as the basis for the exposition. The exegete then read the typescript and made suggestions for improvement.

In a project of this scope an author incurs many obligations. The staffs of the libraries of Asbury Theological Seminary, Drew Theological Seminary, Princeton Theological Seminary, and New York Public Library were most helpful and efficient in making available the resources of their respective domains. Several students in Asbury Theological Seminary rendered valuable assistance in various phases of research. These include Frank Thompson, Harvey Bailey, Umsted Pitts, Frank Zink, and Henry James. The assistance of these men, extending over a period of several years, included compilation of bibliographies, exegetical word studies, notes on periodical articles, and help with the index. The efficiency of the typist, Mrs. Betty Chow, has often evoked admiration. Dr. Wilber Dayton, former student of the exegete and present colleague of the expositor, gave expert assistance in reading the first draft. Dr. J. Harold Greenlee, Professor of New Testament Greek in Asbury Theological Seminary, rendered invaluable service by his critical reading of the entire typescript. The index was prepared by Mr. Charles Strawn. We are especially grateful to authors and publishers who have granted permission to quote from their printed works.

For the convenience of the user of the volume the page format is divided into four sections. At the top of each page is a portion of the Bible text in the American Standard Version (ASV), a text which mediates well between the King James Version and modern versions and which also follows rather closely the Greek idiom. Below the Bible text is the verse-by-verse exegesis, based upon the Greek text but arranged so that those who read only English will have no difficulty. Beneath the exegesis is the exposition which normally handles the material by paragraphs, rather than by verses. The exposition is designed to be practical and to indicate the relevancy of the Biblical material to contemporary life; it seeks to give perspective. An outline-analysis of John's Gospel is distributed throughout the exposition to provide a clearer perspective. The footnotes at the bottom of the page provide explanatory details and indicate source materials which need not detain the rapid reader. The first citation of a bibliographical reference is given in full, afterwards frequently cited sources are abbreviated and placed within parentheses rather than cited in footnotes — see the list of abbreviations. Thus, on each page the reader has the Bible translation, an elucidation of the original language, insights which emerge from the detailed study, and sources for further investigation.

If the users of this volume receive a small part of the inspiration and challenge which has come to the authors, their labors will have been amply rewarded.

JULIUS R. MANTEY                                    GEORGE ALLEN TURNER
*New Port Rickey, Florida*                              *Wilmore, Kentucky*

# CONTENTS

*Preface*                                                           vii

*Abbreviations*                                                       x

*Maps*                                                             xiii

INTRODUCTION

    I. The Influence of the Fourth Gospel          1
   II. Distinctive Features of the Fourth Gospel         3
  III. Problems in the Fourth Gospel                          5
   IV. Background                                         6
    V. The Book Itself                              16
   VI. Distinctive Emphases in Johannine Thought        26
 VII. The Text                                                   43
VIII. Outline of the Gospel                                          45

COMMENTARY

Chapter I                                                            53
Chapter II                                                           78
Chapter III                                                          88
Chapter IV                                                          104
Chapter V                                                           129
Chapter VI                                                          153
Chapter VII                                                         173
Chapter VIII                                                        188
Chapter IX                                                          202
Chapter X                                                           212
Chapter XI                                                          225
Chapter XII                                                         242
Chapter XIII                                                        260
Chapter XIV                                                         279
Chapter XV                                                          295
Chapter XVI                                                         312
Chapter XVII                                                        332
Chapter XVIII                                                       351
Chapter XIX                                                         367
Chapter XX                                                          384
Chapter XXI                                                         402

*Selected Bibliography*                                             417

*Index*                                                             419

# ABBREVIATIONS

| | |
|---|---|
| ASV | American Standard Version (1901) |
| ASVm | American Standard Version margin |
| BV | Berkeley Version |
| KJV | King James Version |
| Knox | R. A. Knox, The New Testament |
| JRM | J. R. Mantey, Translation of the New Testament |
| Moffatt | James Moffatt, The New Testament |
| NEB | New English Bible (1960) |
| Phillips | J. B. Phillips, The New Testament in Modern English |
| RSV | Revised Standard Version |
| Wesley | John Wesley, The New Testament |

## GENERAL REFERENCE WORKS

| | |
|---|---|
| A-G | W. F. Arndt & F. W. Gingrich, eds. *A Greek-English Lexicon of the New Testament.* Chicago: University of Chicago Press, 1957. |
| Cremer | Herman Cremer. *Biblico-Theological Lexicon of New Testament Greek.* Tr. by Wm. Urwick. 4th edit. Edinburgh: T. T. Clark, 1895, 1954. |
| D-M | H. E. Dana & J. R. Mantey. *A Manual Grammar of the Greek New Testament.* New York: Macmillan, 1927. |
| GA-S | G. Abbott-Smith. *A Manual Greek Lexicon of the New Testament.* New York: Scribner's, 1922. |
| HDB | James Hastings, ed. *Dictionary of the Bible.* New York: Scribner's, 1900. |
| IB | G. A. Buttrick, ed. *The Interpreter's Bible.* Nashville: Abingdon, 1952. |
| IDB | G. A. Buttrick, ed. *Interpreter's Dictionary of the Bible.* Nashville: Abingdon Press, 1962. |
| ISBE | James Orr, ed. *International Standard Bible Encyclopedia.* Chicago: Howard Severance Co., 1930. |
| JHT | J. H. Thayer. *Greek-English Lexicon of the New Testament.* New York: American Book Co. |
| Jos. *Ant.* | Flavius Josephus. *Antiquities of the Jews. Loeb Classical Library.* |
| Jos. *War* | Flavius Josephus. *War of the Jews. Loeb Classical Library.* |
| L-S | Liddell and Scott. *Greek-English Lexicon.* American Book Co., n.d. |
| M-G | W. F. Moulton & A. S. Geden. *A Concordance to the Greek Testament.* Edinburgh: T. & T. Clark, 1897. |
| M-M | W. F. Moulton & G. Milligan. *Vocabulary of the Greek New Testament.* Grand Rapids: Eerdmans, 1949. |
| MRV | Marvin R. Vincent. *Word Studies in the New Testament.* New York: Scribner's, 1906. |
| RCT | R. C. Trench. *Synonyms of the New Testament.* London: Macmillan, 1871. |
| S-B | H. L. Strack and P. Billerbeck. *Kommentar zum Neuen Testament aus Talmud und Midrasch.* München: C. H. Beck, 1922-8. |
| TWNT | G. Kittel, ed. *Theologisches Wörterbuch zum Neuen Testament.* Stuttgart: 1933. |
| WPNT | A. T. Robertson. *Word Pictures in the New Testament.* New York: Harper, 1932. |

## PERIODICALS

| | |
|---|---|
| ATR | *Anglican Theological Review* |
| BA | *Biblical Archaeologist* |
| BASOR | *Bulletin of the American Schools of Oriental Research* |
| CBQ | *Catholic Biblical Quarterly* |
| ET | *Expository Times* |
| HTR | *Harvard Theological Review* |
| JBL | *Journal of Biblical Literature* |
| JTS | *Journal of Theological Studies* |
| NTS | *New Testament Studies* |
| RB | *Revue Biblique* |

## COMMENTARIES

| | |
|---|---|
| Bauer | Walter Bauer. *Das Johannesevangelium* (H. Leitzmann, ed. *Handbuch zum Neuen Testament*). Tübingen: J. C. B. Mohr, 1933. |
| BFW | B. F. Westcott. *The Gospel According to St. John.* Greek Text with Introduction and Notes. 2 vols. London: J. Murray, 1908. |
| Bultmann | Rudolph Bultmann. *Das Evangelium des Johannes* (*Kritisch-exegetischer Kommentar über das Neuen Testament*). Göttengen: Vanderhoeck & Ruprecht, 1953. |
| CGT | A. Plummer. *The Gospel According to St. John* (*Cambridge Greek Testament*). Cambridge: The University Press, 1938. |
| CHD | C. H. Dodd. *The Interpretation of the Fourth Gospel.* Cambridge: The University Press, 1953 |
| CKB | C. K. Barrett. *The Gospel According to St. John.* London: S.P.C.K., 1955. |
| EFS | E. F. Scott. *The Fourth Gospel, Its Purpose and Theology.* Edinburgh: T. & T. Clark, 1906. |
| EGT | Marcus Dods. *The Gospel of St. John* (*Expositor's Greek Testament*). Grand Rapids: Eerdmans, n.d. |
| Godet | F. Godet. *Commentary on the Gospel of John.* Translated by T. Dwight. 2 vols. New York: Funk & Wagnalls, 1886. |
| Hoskyns | Edwin Hoskyns. *The Fourth Gospel.* Edited by F. Davey. London: Farber & Farber, 1947. |
| JHB | J. H. Bernard. *The Gospel According to St. John* (A. H. McNeile, ed., *International Critical Commentary*). 2 vols. Edinburgh: T. & T. Clark, 1949. |
| MJL | M. J. Lagrange. *Evangile selon Saint John.* Paris: J. Gabalda, 1936. |
| RHL | R. H. Lightfoot. *St. John's Gospel, A Commentary.* Edited by C. F. Evans. Oxford: The Clarendon Press, 1956. |
| RHS | R. H. Strachan. *The Fourth Gospel, Its Significance and Environment.* London: Student Christian Movement Press, 1941, 46. |
| WFH | W. F. Howard, John. "Exegesis," *The Interpreter's Bible.* Vol. VIII. Nashville: Abingdon Press, 1952. |
| WmH | Wm. Hendriksen, *New Testament Commentary, John.* 2 vols. Grand Rapids: Baker Book House, 1953. |

## DEAD SEA SCROLLS

| | |
|---|---|
| IQS | Rule of the Community or Manual of Discipline |
| IQH | Hymns |
| IQM | War of the Children of Light Against the Children of Darkness |

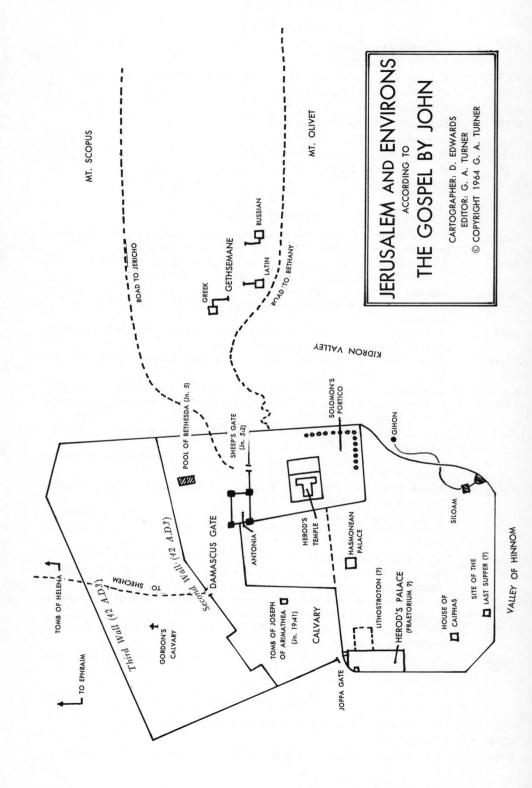

JERUSALEM AND ENVIRONS

ACCORDING TO

THE GOSPEL BY JOHN

CARTOGRAPHER: D. EDWARDS
EDITOR: G. A. TURNER
© COPYRIGHT 1964 G. A. TURNER

MT. SCOPUS

MT. OLIVET

ROAD TO JERICHO

GETHSEMANE

GREEK

LATIN

RUSSIAN

ROAD TO BETHANY

KIDRON VALLEY

POOL OF BETHESDA (Jn. 5)

SHEEP'S GATE
(Jn. 5:2)

SOLOMON'S PORTICO

GIHON

Third Wall (42 A.D.?)

TOMB OF HELENA

TO EPHRAIM

Second Wall (42 A.D.?)

TO SHECHEM

DAMASCUS GATE

ANTONIA

HEROD'S TEMPLE

HASMONEAN PALACE

SILOAM

GORDON'S CALVARY

TOMB OF JOSEPH OF ARIMATHEA
(Jn. 19:41)

CALVARY

LITHOSTROTON (?)

HEROD'S PALACE
(PRAETORIUM ?)

HOUSE OF CAIPHAS

SITE OF THE
LAST SUPPER (?)

VALLEY OF HINNOM

JOPPA GATE

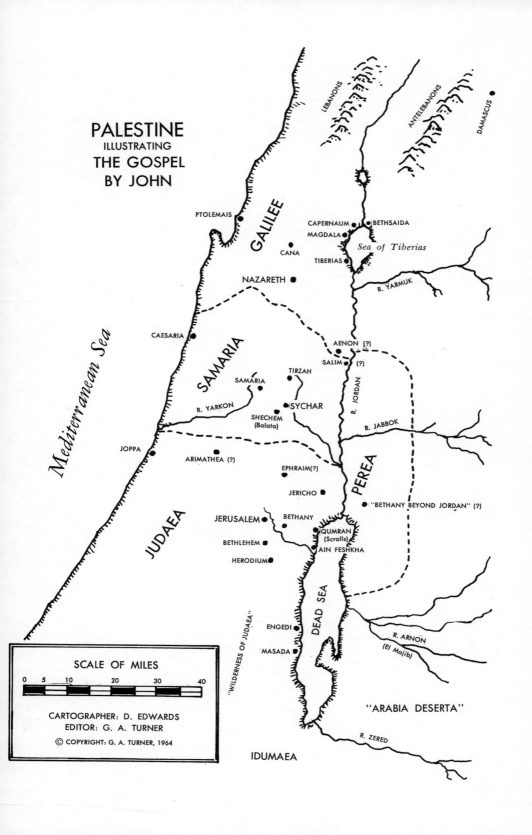

PALESTINE
ILLUSTRATING
THE GOSPEL
BY JOHN

*Mediterranean Sea*

GALILEE

PTOLEMAIS ●

CANA ●

NAZARETH ●

CAPERNAUM ● ● BETHSAIDA
MAGDALA ●
*Sea of Tiberias*
TIBERIAS ●

LEBANONS

ANTELEBANONS

DAMASCUS ●

R. YARMUK

CAESARIA ●

SAMARIA

SAMARIA ●

TIRZAH ●

R. YARKON

SHECHEM
(Balata)

● SYCHAR

AENON (?)

SALIM (?)

R. JORDAN

R. JABBOK

JOPPA ●

ARIMATHEA (?) ●

EPHRAIM(?) ●

JERICHO ●

PEREA

"BETHANY BEYOND JORDAN" (?) ●

JUDAEA

JERUSALEM ●

BETHLEHEM ●

HERODIUM ●

BETHANY ●

QUMRAN
(Scrolls)
AIN FESHKHA

"WILDERNESS OF JUDAEA"

ENGEDI ●

MASADA ●

DEAD SEA

R. ARNON
(El Majib)

"ARABIA DESERTA"

R. ZERED

IDUMAEA

SCALE OF MILES

0  5  10    20      30      40

CARTOGRAPHER: D. EDWARDS
EDITOR: G. A. TURNER

© COPYRIGHT: G. A. TURNER, 1964

# INTRODUCTION

The Gospel According to John has been the most praised and also one of the most maligned books of the Bible. During the first century of the Christian Era some Christian took time to record an interpretation of the Christian message. He did so with the burning conviction that the eternal destiny of every person was bound up with his attitude towards Jesus of Nazareth. In a general letter he put the issue succinctly: "This is the record, that God hath given to us eternal life, and this life is in his Son. He that hath the Son hath life; and he that hath not the Son of God hath not life" (I John 5:11, 12). It was just that simple, just that important; those were — and are — the alternatives. The overarching issue with which this book deals is LIFE. The conception of life with which this author operates is that of existence which originated before time and extends beyond time. This life finds its most concrete and explicit expression in a Person, a Person discernible to the inhabitants of the planet Earth in a human life. As this author contemplated the appearance of this Life among men he compressed his awareness of it in one sentence of wonder, love, and praise. Said he, "The Word became flesh and dwelt among us and we beheld his glory, glory as of the only Son from the Father full of grace and truth" (John 1:14). While the theme of belief is prominent, belief is regarded as a means to an end (John 20:31): the discovery of Life as available in Christ.

## I. THE INFLUENCE OF THE FOURTH GOSPEL

### A. EXTENT

With the possible exception of the Psalms and the Epistle to the Romans it is likely that the Fourth Gospel has exerted a greater influence on more people than any other book of the Bible. The Roman Emperor called Julian the Apostate, the one who tried his best to bring the empire back to paganism, said,

" 'It was this John who (by declaring that the Word was made flesh) wrought all the mischief' " (Cyril G. *Julianum*, x. 335).[1] This Gospel has appealed to the most diverse natures. Numerous missionary societies testify to the reception given to this Gospel by primitive people hearing of Christ for the first time. It is not by accident that this book is often selected for translation first since it serves as the most effective means of introducing Christ to non-Christians. Albert Schweitzer found that in tropical Africa the natives responded very readily to this Gospel's presentation of Jesus Christ. It deals with such elemental and universal concepts as bread and water, life and death, love, light and darkness — the most profound truths expressed in the simplest vocabulary. More specifically it may be said that no other book of the Bible matches this one in its ability to present in simple, familiar monosyllabic words the most sublime concepts.

This Gospel has challenged the most sophisticated minds as well as the simplest. In this generation alone it has challenged the best efforts of such scholars as Bultmann, C. H. Dodd, Edwin Hoskyns, W. F. Howard, C. K. Barrett, and R. H. Lightfoot. In another generation Wm. Sanday, W. F. Westcott, and J. H. Bernard each devoted a major portion of their productive lives to understanding and explaining this one book. Few can ponder the stark simplicity and beauty of sentences such as "I am the bread of life" without being aware that beneath the plain exterior are unplumbed depths which challenge investigation. The simple diction borders on the "numinous," or the spiritual, on the sublime. By the middle of the second century A.D. it was accepted as equally authoritative with the three earlier Gospels. "The Church has never been aware of any fundamental incompatibility between the portrait of the Lord in this gospel and that in the other three" (RHL, p. 1). No book of the Bible played a larger part in shaping the creedal foun-

---

[1] Cited by Hoskyns, p. 23. Cf. Julian, *Contra Christianos*, ed. C. J. Neumann, 233-35, cited by B. J. Kidd, *Documents Illustrative of the History of the Church* (London: SPCK, 1938) II, 66.

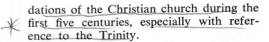

dations of the Christian church during the first five centuries, especially with reference to the Trinity.

Many have testified to the vast influence of this book upon them personally and upon the world. Origen, greatest Biblical scholar of the third century, called this "the consummation of the Gospels as the Gospels are of all the Scriptures." Jerome, leading Latin Biblical scholar of the ancient church, agreed that "John excels in the depths of the divine mysteries."[2]

The most eloquent preacher of the ancient church was John Chrysostom, Bishop of Constantinople. While pastor in Antioch, about 390 A.D., he preached a series of eighty-eight homilies on John's Gospel. In introducing the series he eulogized the author of the Fourth Gospel as having "blotted out and obliterated all the teachings of the pagans," including the Greek philosophers Pythagoras and Plato, while "the whole world — Syrians, Egyptians, Indians and Persians — has become a theatre" for John the Apostle.[3] Christianity's most influential theologian after St. Paul appreciated John's above the other Gospels because of its emphasis on the deity of Christ.[4] In Luther's judgment this Gospel is "the unique, tender, genuine, leading Gospel, that should be preferred by far to the others."[5] He added that if all of the Bible would be lost except this Gospel and the letter to the Romans "Christianity would be saved." From a writer with no ordinary acquaintance with literature and the Bible comes the judgment that "The Gospel according to John is the most original, the most important, the most influential book in all literature. . . . It is simple as a child and sublime as a seraph, gentle as a lamb and bold as an eagle, deep as the sea and high as the heavens."[6]

That one book could call forth such unqualified praise is probably due to the fact that, under the inspiration of the Holy Spirit, the author gazed intently, lovingly, and thoughtfully on the "event of Christ," never ceasing to marvel that "the Word became flesh and dwelt among us."

In Christian art and architecture the symbol of John the Evangelist is the eagle. Doubtless this came originally from Ezekiel 1:10; 10:14; and Revelation 4:10. The fact that in these scriptures the "living creatures" numbered four probably suggested to some medieval artist that these four corresponded to the four Evangelists. In these three passages the only one of the four which has the same symbol in each instance is the fourth — the symbol of the eagle. It fits the fourth Evangelist well because the eagle can soar into the heavens. Appropriately, a large eagle surmounts the Cathedral of St. John the Divine in New York City. In Christian art John is usually pictured as rather youthful, in notable contrast to Peter.

### B. CURRENT INTEREST

In recent years there has been a revival of interest in the Fourth Gospel. The new manuscript discoveries in Palestine and in Egypt have a special relevance to the study of this Gospel. But these are only a part of the reason for this revival of interest. Two generations ago Protestant liberalism was inclined to look askance at the Gospel of John because it was too theological. It was assumed that the book could not be both historical and theological. Recently, however, there has been a revival of Biblical theology and the New Testament scholar no longer shrinks from being considered theological in his approach to the scriptures. Archaeology has done much to rehabilitate the Fourth Gospel during the second quarter of this century. The oldest extant portion of the New Testament is considered by the paleographers to be a fragment from John, dating back to the first quarter of the second century.[7] The effect of this, as well as the discovery of the Bell and Skeat papyrus in 1935, has been to place the composition of the Fourth Gospel well into the first century A.D., the traditional date. This has led to fresh investigation into the

[2] Cited in D. A. Hayes, *John and His Writings* (New York: Methodist Book Concern, 1917), p. 77.
[3] Saint John Chrysostom, *Commentary on St. John the Apostle and Evangelist*, tr. by Sister Thomas Aquinas Goddin, S.C.H. (New York: Fathers of the Church, Inc., 1957), p. 16.
[4] Augustine, Bishop of Hippo, *Tract.* 36 *In Johannes*.
[5] M. Luther, "Preface" to the N. T. (A.D. 1539). Cited in P. Schaff in "Special Introduction" in J. P. Lange, *John, Commentary*, tr. by P. Schaff (Grand Rapids: Zondervan, reprint) p. vii.
[6] Philip Schaff, *History of the Christian Church* (New York: Scribner's, 1912) I, 688.
[7] The fragment contains John 18:31-33, 37, 38. It was discovered in 1931 with the remainder of the Chester Beatty Biblical papyri and published by Mr. C. H. Roberts, "An Unpublished Fragment of the Fourth Gospel," *Bulletin of the John Rylands Library;* Jan., 1936; 20:45-55.

purpose and date of the Gospel. In short the Gospel is at the center of the current revolution in New Testament studies.

## C. THE AUTHOR'S ARTISTIC SKILL

Scholars have always appreciated the artistic manner in which the Gospel is composed, for it contains not only truth but beauty as well. As in many of the classical tragedies of Homer, Aeschylus, and Sophocles the catastrophe is announced in the beginning and is kept in view until the climax. In this Gospel likewise the shadow of the cross lies across every page, from the identification of the Lamb of God until the offering of the Lamb as a vicarious sacrifice. The dramatic quality of the narrative is outstanding; it is a classic. In John's record a "sign" is performed resulting in mixed reactions, with the parallel trends toward acceptance and rejection continuing until their climax. Also characteristic of this Gospel is dialogue in which Jesus' views are set forth in contrast to those of the perplexed (Nicodemus) or the unbelieving. This theological or Christological tension is seen throughout the twenty-one chapters.

The hand of a master craftsman is apparent also in the selection and arrangement of materials for maximum effect. Only those events in Jesus' life are mentioned which bear upon the subject of belief and life. Much that is of great human interest is omitted. Attention is focused upon the doctrine of the person of Christ and the proper response by the reader to this presentation. The importance of the struggle between light and darkness, belief and unbelief is kept in mind as the "signs" are reported in chapters 2-12. In chapters 13-20 the offering up of the Son of God is stressed by means of compressing the events of three days in these eight chapters, as compared with three years and more in the balance of the book.

The author employs the law of contrast with great effect. He highlights the contrast between friend and foe, light and darkness, good and evil, God and the devil, physical blindness and spiritual blindness, water that does not quench thirst and water that does, bread which affords only physical relief and spiritual bread from heaven. These are a few of the evidences that the author is an artist as well as an author.[8]

## II. DISTINCTIVE FEATURES OF THE FOURTH GOSPEL

### A. WITNESSING

One of the most distinctive features of this Gospel is the emphasis on *witnessing*. Many have called attention to the prominence of this theme.[9] The term "witness" occurs thirty-four times in verb form and thirteen times as a noun in John, a total of forty-seven occurrences as compared with only sixteen in all of the other three Gospels (M-G). The author himself does not assume the role of an instructor, as does Luke. Rather, he is a witness of the things he has seen and heard. He places himself at the side of John the Baptist and the other witnesses to the truth listed in 5:30-47. These attestations of "the witness" are not limited to the notation in 21:24 but appear throughout the book.[10] The author is at pains to present, like an attorney, a convincing argument to the "jury," i.e., the readers, but he does more than marshall evidence and argue the case; he is also witnessing to a life he has experienced. He writes in the conviction that while it is a great privilege to be a first-hand witness, an even greater blessing is in store for those who believe on the basis of the testimony of these apostolic witnesses (20:29). As these believe they share fully in the gift of life.

### B. BELIEF

Another distinctive feature of this Gospel is the kindred idea of belief or faith. John does not use the noun "faith" (*pistis*) except on one occasion (I John 5:4). But he uses the verb "believe" (*pisteuein*) many times.[11] Thus the emphasis is on the act of believing rather than on having faith (*pistis*) as in the Synoptics. Not only is John distinctive in the stress placed

---

[8] See D. A. Hayes, *op. cit.*, pp. 92-97.
[9] E.g., E. A. Abbott, *Johannine Vocabulary* (London: A. & C. Black, 1905), pp. 19-79. W. W. White, *Thirty Studies in the Gospel by John* (New York: Revell, 1895), *passim*. M. C. Tenney, *John, The Gospel of Belief* (Grand Rapids: Eerdmans, 1948), *passim*.
[10] E.g., 1:14, 16; 19:35; cf. I John 1:1-3.
[11] The verb occurs about 96 times in this Gospel; about 34 in the three Synoptics.

on "believe," he is also distinctive in the connotation given to belief. It is not in contrast to works, as it so often is in Paul, nor faith as a conviction of unseen reality, as it is in Hebrews, but rather the term connotes committal to a Person, to the Lord Jesus Christ.[12] It goes beyond the acceptance of testimony as to the truth of a proposition. A choice against the world and for the light as seen in Jesus is involved. This is a belief which calls for renunciation of trust in self-sufficiency and committal to God's incarnate Son.[13] Faith is paradoxical in that it is a divine gift yet available to all. While in Paul it is the cross which is scandalous and proves an obstacle to belief, in John the cross is a part of Jesus' glorification. In John the center of tension is not so much the cross but the Incarnation and the resurrection. In the Synoptic accounts it is hard to believe that the Messiah must die; in John it is hard to believe that "The Word became flesh and dwelt among us."[14] The emphasis is on belief in a person, i.e., belief in Jesus as Son of God and Savior. As with all writers of the New Testament, the intimate connection between the Old Testament and the new evidence jointly provides the basis for belief.

## C. LITERARY STYLE

In literary style as well as ideas the Fourth Gospel is distinctive. Instead of a swift-moving narrative of major events as remembered by the apostles, there is a rather leisurely and dramatic treatment of a relatively few events. The tempo of chapters 1-4 is unhurried and features extended conversations: with the Galilean disciples, with Nicodemus, and with the Samaritans. Missing is the intense activity about the Sea of Galilee with scarcely enough time to eat (Mark 3:7-21). In John, by contrast, relatively little attention is given to the Perean ministry which bulks so large in Luke's account; instead, the early Judean ministry and the later Jerusalem ministry are emphasized. The approximate proportions by chapters, outlining the contrast between John and the Synoptists, are these:

| Chapters | Galilee | Jerusalem | Total |
|----------|---------|-----------|-------|
| Matthew  | 18      | 10        | 28    |
| Mark     | 9       | 7         | 16    |
| Luke     | 13      | 11        | 24    |
| John     | 4       | 17        | 21    |

Even in the feeding of the 5000, the only miracle common to all four Evangelists, the stress is placed upon the discourse following, rather than the event itself.

## D. VOCABULARY

The vocabulary of John is distinctive for its brevity and simplicity. The words are more simple and are fewer in number — light, life, world, darkness, truth, glory, believe, know, hour, and the like. Each of these terms, as used here, conveys a heavy load of freight; in Johannine usage they are pregnant with meaning above and beyond their normal secular connotations.

## E. HABIT OF THOUGHT

Another characteristic of the Fourth Gospel is the author's habit of thought. It is essentially Hebraic and oriental rather than Hellenistic and occidental. Paul, in contrast, reflects the influence of his Gentile environment in his mode of thought. His concepts were Hebraic, but his mode of expressing them was Hellenistic.[15] In the Galatian and Roman letters, for example, he arranges his material like the typical westerner. He states all he has to say about a subject before moving on to the next topic. In Romans, for another example, the subjects of condemnation, justification, sanctification, Israel's destiny, and practical Christian living are treated in that order. In Johannine thought, by contrast, several main ideas are carried simultaneously. An idea comes into focus, then recedes to recur later. This has been compared to a spiral staircase. One ascending such a staircase appears then disappears to reappear later at a higher level. In John, for example, light is mentioned in 1:5-9 where "light" is in the Incarnate Word. In 3:19-21 the principle is stated

---

[12] But see John 6:29; Cf. 10:32; 17:4; Gal. 3:2; Heb. 11:1.
[13] Bultmann, p. 172. See John 6:44, 45.
[14] John 1:14; 20:31; 1 John 4:10-12. See also R. Bultmann and Arthur Weiser, *Faith*, tr. by D. M. Barton from Kittel, ed., *Theologisches Wörterbuch zum Neuen Testament: Bible Key Words* (London: A. & C. Black, 1961), pp. 100-105.
[15] Cf. James Barr, *Biblical Words for Time* (Naperville, Ill.: Allenson, 1962), p. 148.

explicitly that everyone is confronted with the necessity of making a decision with reference to the light. Jesus is said to be the Light of the world in 8:12 and in 9:38-41 the consequences of rejecting the light are stated. Finally, in 11:8-10 the necessity of walking in the light is stressed (cf. I John 1:7). This is one of many themes which, like the musical themes or motifs in an oratorio, become dominant and then recessive several times during the composition.

## III. PROBLEMS IN THE FOURTH GOSPEL

The book which contains the most precious truths, presented in terms universally understood, is the one which has suffered the severest attacks from its critics. There are many problems associated with a study of this Gospel which cannot be easily brushed aside. The problems of authorship are not in the forefront of historical research to the extent that they were seventy-five years ago; these are treated later in this introduction.

### A. OMISSIONS

One of the problems encountered in studying this Gospel is that of explaining the omission of things mentioned in the other Gospels. A most meticulous comparison of this Gospel with the other three, so far as vocabulary is concerned, is that of Edwin A. Abbott. His conclusions may thus be summarized: (1) in words common to all four evangelists John's use is often metaphorical, theirs literal; (ii) John's vocabulary is much smaller than that of the other three; (iii) John has more in common with Mark than with either Matthew or Luke so far as parallel passages are concerned; (iv) from the standpoint of vocabulary, however, the greatest degree of correspondence is between John and Luke.[16] In short, John is more influenced by Mark than by the other two, something on which scholars generally are agreed.[17]

There are many important things omitted in John's Life of Jesus:

(i) There is no mention of Jesus' birth or his first thirty years.

(ii) Nothing is told of the birth or death of John the Baptist.

(iii) Neither the story of Jesus' baptism nor that of the temptation is reported by this Evangelist.

(iv) Although the apostle John was a participant, the Fourth Gospel makes no mention of the Transfiguration.

(v) This Gospel does not describe the institution of the Eucharist.

(vi) John omits Jesus' prayer in Gethsemane but includes the Lord's intercessory prayer.

(vii) John omits the trial before Caiaphas in which the accusation was blasphemy.

(viii) There is no account of the ascension in this Gospel although it is frequently predicted therein.

(ix) In this Gospel no mention is made of the exorcism of devils although Jesus was accused three times of being demon-possessed.

(x) Children, lepers, p u b l i c a n s, scribes, or Sadducees, so prominent in the Synoptics, are not mentioned in this Gospel.

(xi) The list of the twelve apostles is omitted.

(xii) The Sermon on the Mount, as reported by Matthew and Luke, is omitted.

(xiii) The calling of sinners to repentance, so conspicuous in the Synoptics, especially in Luke, is omitted by this Evangelist.

(xiv) Apocalyptic and eschatological themes, including the mention of hell, also prominent in the first three, are omitted from the Fourth Gospel.

(xv) Jesus' method of teaching by parables, emphasized in the Synoptic reports, is lacking in this Gospel. (The analogies of water, bread, shepherd, vine, and the like are metaphors and not true parables.)

(xvi) John omits all of the characteristic apothegms and proverbs of Jesus such as "a city set on a hill cannot be hid," and "ye are the salt of the earth."[18]

### B. MATERIAL PECULIAR TO JOHN

To compensate for what this Gospel

[16] Edwin A. Abbott, op. cit., pp. 349f.
[17] W. F. Howard, The Fourth Gospel in Recent Criticism and Interpretation (London: The Epworth Press, 1931), p. 144.
[18] For a convenient summary of these omissions see D. A. Hayes, op. cit., pp. 82-88.

omits is the fact that about ninety percent of the material is peculiar to John.

(i) Only John records Nicodemus (three times) and the New Birth.

(ii) John alone reports the details of the calling of five disciples.

(iii) Only John tells of the wedding at Cana.

(iv) The conversion of the Samaritan woman is peculiar to John.

(v) Only John records the miracles associated with the pool of Bethesda, the pool of Siloam, and Lazarus.

(vi) Only John reports some fourteen dialogues which normally include a question, Jesus' enigmatic answer, the misunderstanding of the question, and finally Jesus' clarification of the issues (EFS, p. 20).

(vii) This Gospel alone gives special attention to Nathaniel, Thomas, Nicodemus, Judas, Philip, Caiaphas, and Pilate.

(viii) Only here do we find Jesus comparing himself to water, bread, shepherds, truth, vines in a series of great "I am" affirmations.

(ix) Only this Gospel mentions the *Paraclete,* the Holy Spirit.

(x) Jesus' appearance by the Sea of Galilee after the resurrection is mentioned only in this Gospel.

In short, the view that John was acquainted with the other biographers and sought not to duplicate their efforts but rather to supplement them, seems very plausible (EFS, p. 32-43). In so doing this author was not content to give the bare facts, as Mark often does; rather, he put these facts into a relationship. He lets the reader catch the significance of the facts, and thus he is both reporter and interpreter.

## C. Parallels to the Synoptic Records

An even greater problem is that of explaining how and why this author reports events and sayings similar to the Synoptic writers in such a way as to leave the reader wondering whether he is recording a separate event, not mentioned elsewhere, or whether he is presenting a different account of what is reported in the Synoptics. These include several diverse items:

(i) Did the cleansing of the temple occur once or twice?

(ii) Were Jesus' feet anointed by a woman once or twice?

(iii) Did Jesus' ministry extend over three Passover seasons (i.e., three years) or was it limited to one year as the Synoptists imply?

(iv) Did Peter make one or two confessions of faith (cf. Matt. 16:16; cf. John 6:69)?

(v) Why is there no mention of the Lord's Supper in chapter thirteen while words appropriate only to the Lord's Supper are used in ch. 6.

(vi) Did Jesus' prayer, "Father, save me from this hour" (John 12:27), have any connection with his prayer in Gethsemane, "Father . . . remove this cup from me" (Luke 22:42; cf. John 18: 11, "Shall I not drink the cup which the Father has given me?" RSV)?

These are samples of the problems encountered when one seeks to relate the data given in the Fourth Gospel with what he finds in the other three.

## D. Distinctive Terminology

Another series of problems confronting the interpreter of John involves the subtle and often enigmatic use of terminology. It has been said that there are more ambiguities in this Gospel than in the other three combined. Many of these ambiguities are deliberate. They are apparently designed to be provocative, to stimulate inquiry. Examples include the instruction about the birth from above, about blindness (9:38), about genealogy (1:13; 3:3; 8:37-56; I John 3:8-10), and about the Master's departing and returning. Often the simplest diction "disturbs with the presence of elevated thoughts," leaving the reader conscious that beneath the obvious lies a deeper meaning which he can only vaguely grasp but which entices him on to further investigation. This is the challenge to the student of the "spiritual Gospel."

## IV. BACKGROUND

### A. Importance

Every standard commentary on the Fourth Gospel gives much attention to the ideological background. To a greater extent than is true of the other three, a knowledge of the intellectual milieu out of which this Gospel came is indispensable to the serious student. True, the reader can find ample material in this evangel for "life more abundant" without such knowledge, but the Gospel impinges at so many points upon contemporary thought that sooner or later the curious reader will want to ascertain more of this possible interaction. Two generations ago, it was regarded as almost axiomatic by critical scholars that the Synoptic Gospels, especially Mark, presented the most authentic portrait of Jesus available with a minimum of theological and ecclesiastical coloration. By contrast, John's account was considered more theological than historical and hence less trustworthy. Of the factors which accounted for John's alterations and additions the major one was Greek thought. They pointed to the terms *logos* (word), truth, light, and life to prove that primitive Christianity had been given "an acute Hellenization" (Harnack) by John and his successors. This view no longer prevails. Even before the recent manuscript discoveries certain scholars were emphasizing the dominant influence of the Old Testament on the Fourth Gospel.[19] This judgment is sound when only the Gospel itself is considered; it is confirmed by recent external evidence.

## B. SEMITIC INFLUENCE

### 1. THE OLD TESTAMENT

The case for the predominantly Hebraic background and ideology of the Fourth Gospel may now be summarized. The prologue, including the logos concept, has only superficial affinities with Stoic and Philonic concepts (see exegesis *ad loc.*). On the other hand the connection between the Word of God in John 1:1 and the Word of God in creation is apparent in Psalm 33:6 — "By the word of the Lord were the heavens made." The passage in John which begins with the words "in the beginning" is obviously influenced by the Genesis account of creation including the reference to light (John 1:1-5). The background of ch. 1 of John includes creation (Gen. 1-3), the Passover (cf. John 1:29, 36), and Jacob's ladder

(John 1:51). In chs. 3 and 8 can be seen the Old Testament emphasis on the covenant with Abraham (generation and regeneration), the work of the Spirit (Ezek. 20:25-27; John 3:5-8), and upon God as light and as love. Behind ch. 4 with its emphasis on water, lies the wilderness of Sin and water emerging from the rock (Exod. 17:2-7). Beneath ch. 5 (vv. 30-46) is the witness of the Old Testament to the Christ. Beyond ch. 6 one glimpses again the Israelites' dependence on the manna from heaven. Ch. 7 recalls the Feast of the Tabernacles (Lev. 23:34-36) and the water from the rock (Num. 20:10-13). The analogy of the Good Shepherd reminds one of Psalm 23; Isaiah 40:11; Jeremiah 23:1-4 and Ezekiel 34. The analogy of the vine and branches takes one back to Isaiah 5:1-7; Jeremiah 2:21; Psalm 2:21; Psalm 80:8-13. In the above the influence of the Old Testament is not explicitly affirmed. There are many other passages in which the Old Testament influence is explicitly stated by the citation of quotations. There is little in the Fourth Gospel which does not have some background in the canonical Scriptures. Indeed, like the other Evangelists, John was eager to demonstrate the fulfillment of the Scriptures in the work and words of Jesus.[20]

The influence of Hebrew ideas, other than those of the Old Testament, is no less impressive, especially in the light of recent manuscript discoveries. These contemporary Jewish writings, whether within or without Palestine, reflect in varying degrees influences other than from the Old Testament, but they are predominantly Hebraic in orientation. The Odes of Solomon were viewed by Harnack as affording an important source of ideas for the Fourth Gospel, but subsequent research has modified this judgment and virtually annulled it. Likewise, the discovery of Mandean writings, with numerous alleged parallels to Johannine thought, was hailed as a major contribution to source materials and background. A second look, however, brought second thoughts until now it is widely recognized that these are much later than John and

[19] W. F. Howard, *op. cit.*, pp. 169-177. W. F. Howard, *Christianity According to St. John* (Philadelphia: Westminster, 1946), pp. 30ff. Hugo Odeburg, *The Fourth Gospel in Contemporary Religious Currents* (Uppsala, 1929), *passim*.
[20] For an effective presentation of O. T. influence, see JHB, I, cxlvii-cv.

may have been the borrowers rather than the borrowed.

## 2. RABBINIC INFLUENCE

The literature of orthodox or "normative" Judaism, i.e., the religion of the rabbis, is later than the New Testament, and its influence must be assessed with great caution. Attention has been called to John's use of "Law" (Heb. *Torah;* LXX *nomos*). By using it in its more inclusive sense (i.e., as embracing both the written revelation and authoritative exposition) John is closer to the rabbinic usage than either Paul or James (CHD, pp. 75ff.).

More specifically, as Dodd points out, this Evangelist is acquainted with rabbinic casuistry. Jesus had been criticized for healing on the Sabbath (5:16). He defended himself by reminding his detractors that this was consistent with the rabbinic sanction of circumcising a child on the Sabbath. Rabbi Eliezer ben Azariah (c. A.D. 100) maintained that if circumcision and ensuing healing of one of the 248 members of the body are lawful on the Sabbath, how much more is the healing of the whole body commendable.[21] In other words, when Jesus is quoted as saying, "Why are you indignant with me for giving health on the Sabbath to the whole of a man's body?" (John 7:23), there is reflected a familiarity with the subtleties of rabbinic exegesis. Jesus is pictured as employing the same exegetical methods his critics employed, thus exposing their inconsistency in condemning his action.

Additional evidence for the thesis that the Evangelist knew rabbinic lore intimately is the fact that the statement in the Prologue about the "true light coming into the world" has many parallels in rabbinic Judaism. The rabbis often spoke of the Torah as the light of the world. Says Dodd, "We are justified in concluding that the doctrine of Torah as the pre-existent thought of God revealed in time, which we find in the Talmud and Midrash, is by no means a late creation, even though many of the *testimonia* may be relatively late. In its main outlines it formed a part of rabbinic teaching at the period of the Fourth Gospel, and we may safely infer that the author of that word was acquainted with it" (CHD, p. 85).

Other evidences of Jewish influence in the Fourth Gospel include the use of the term "Messiah" (*messias*) found in John 1:41; 4:25 and nowhere else in the New Testament. Here and elsewhere it is translated by the term "Christos" ($\chi\rho\iota\sigma\tau\delta s$), a translation of the Hebrew term "Messiah" (משח) meaning "anointed one," and applied in the Old Testament to the king (I Sam. 26:9), to Cyrus (Isa. 45:1) and to the Christ (Is. 61:1). The rabbis taught that when the Messiah came he would be hidden during his childhood and suddenly appear as a mature man ready to take over control.[22] Familiarity with this rabbinic doctrine is reflected in John 7:27 where the people quote the rabbis as saying, "When the Christ cometh, no one knoweth whence he is." Jesus answers that he is from above, from God. Thus the Evangelist shows familiarity with the concepts of rabbis in Palestine during the first century, since there is reason to believe that the Mishnah (c. 100 A.D.) preserved the oral traditions prevalent in Jesus' day.[23]

The Johannine emphasis on the unity of Father and Son may also reflect familiarity with rabbinic thought of the first century (CHD, p. 93-96).

## 3. THE ESSENES

The New Testament is strangely silent about the Essenes. Until recently little was known about this sect of the Jews. Josephus devotes more space to them than to both Sadducees and Pharisees together, and they are mentioned by both Philo and Pliny. Christian scholars have noted the similarity between certain ideas and words in the New Testament and what little is known about the Essenes and have wondered why the Scriptures are silent about them.

The discovery of the Dead Sea Scrolls has opened up new vistas of study con-

[21] Joma 85a-b, cited in S-B, II, 48. See also CHD, p. 79.
[22] Some rabbis thought he would be hidden in Rome, or the North, or Paradise, or in the sea. S-B, II, 340, 489.
[23] G. F. Moore, *Judaism* (Cambridge: Harvard University Press, 1927), I, 87, 132-134. The judgment of Moore, however, needs to be revised in the light of recent discoveries of literature contemporary with the New Testament and antedating the Mishnah. We must now recognize that Tannatic Midrash may not be as "normative" as Moore surmised. See Noel Freedman, "The Scrolls and the New Testament, (Review)," *Journal of Biblical Literature*, Dec., 1959, pp. 327f.

cerning the Palestinian environment of the Gospels. The parallels between the Scrolls and the Fourth Gospel are particularly striking, as several Christian scholars were quick to recognize.[24] In the judgment of most scholars "one of the most important results of Qumran research has been to prove the Jewish origin of the Gospel of John conclusively."[25] While the Scrolls have a bearing on most books of the New Testament, it is with the Fourth Gospel that the parallels are most noticeable. In the first flush of new discoveries, judgments are apt to be exaggerated and conclusions reached which careful scrutiny does not sustain. This has been demonstrated, for example, in the case of the Mandean writings.[26] In the case of the Scrolls, however, the parallels are more obvious and the material is of such a nature that controls can be more easily established. Of utmost importance is the date of the Scrolls of Qumran, and a date in the first century B.C. is now well established. It is certain that none were written after 70 A.D. when the site was destroyed and made into a Roman fortress. Thus, the scroll material almost certainly antedates the New Testament. Neither can it be successfully maintained that the ideas of the early Christians came from the Qumran Essenes; while the parallels are striking, the differences are even more marked. In particular the Scrolls reflect no belief in a Redeemer who died for the sins of the world, the central tenet of Christianity. The Scrolls are invaluable, however, for proving that it is not necessary to posit Gospel material gathered from outside of Palestine after the Jewish War of 66-70 A.D. Instead it shows that during the life of Jesus there existed in Palestine a group of pious Jews who believed themselves to be "children of light" and members of the "new covenant" who were preparing in the desert for the coming of the Lord as predicted in Isaiah 40:

1-5. Both they and John the Baptist were influenced by this passage in Isaiah. It is not unlikely that John lived with these Essenes at Qumran for he was "in the deserts until the day of his showing unto Israel" (Luke 1:80).

The similarities are most impressive in four areas: (i) The authors of the Scrolls were members of the New Covenant or the "new alliance." The Qumran community in their poverty, their repudiation of the world, their sharing of common property, and their emphasis on repentance paralleled many of the distinctive features of the early Christian community in Jerusalem. (ii) Like John the Baptist the Essenes practiced baptism, but not a rite of initiation. (iii) Their sacramental meal together has certain affinities in the Lord's Supper in the church. (iv) Both had a modified dualism, i.e., a universe dominated by opposing forces of good and evil; in John the victory over evil is presently in effect, in the Scrolls it is still future.[27] (v) Their Teacher of Righteousness exerted an influence upon them in a unique and unprecedented manner with some points of similarity to Jesus of Nazareth.[28]

More remarkable, and with special relevance to the Fourth Gospel, are the verbal similarities. Phrases characteristic of both the Scrolls and the Johannine writings include "life eternal," "darkness and light," "truth and error," "wrath of God," "light of life," "spirit of truth," "sons of light," and "Spirit of Truth."

There are many passages in the Fourth Gospel with verbal similarities to the Scrolls thus far published. In the "Hymn of the Initiants" we read, "Only through His knowledge have all things come to be, and all that is, is ordained by His thought: and apart from Him is nothing wrought."[29] The similarity in thought to John 1:3 is obvious; however, instead of the Logos the Scroll has God's knowledge as the creator. In the Manual of Discipline

[24] R. E. Brown, "The Qumran Scrolls and the Johannine Gospel and Epistles," CBQ XVII (1955), pp. 403-19; 559-74. W. H. Brownlee, "John the Baptist in the New Light of Ancient Scrolls," *Interpretation*, IX (1955), pp. 71-90. K. G. Kuhn, "The Lord's Supper and the Communal Meal at Qumran," in K. Stendahl, *The Scrolls and the New Testament* (New York: Harper, 1957), p. 69. F. M. Braun, "L'arrière-fond judaïque du quatrième évangile et la Communauté de l'Alliance," RB LXII (1955), pp. 5ff. Lucetta Mowry, "The Dead Sea Scrolls and the Background for The Gospel by John," BA XVII (1954), pp. 78-97. W. F. Albright, "Recent Discoveries in Palestine and the Gospel of St. John," in W. D. Davies and D. Daube, editors, *The Background of the New Testament and Its Eschatology* (Cambridge: The University Press, 1956), pp. 153-171.

[25] Kurt Schubert, *The Dead Sea Community* (London: Adams & Black, 1959), p. 152.

[26] W. F. Albright, *From the Stone Age to Christianity*, 2nd edit. (Garden City: Doubleday, 1957) p. 364-367.

[27] Raymond Brown, *op. cit.*, p. 411.

[28] F. F. Bruce, *The Teacher of Righteousness in the Qumran Texts* (London: Tyndale Press, 1957), pp. 1-36.

[29] Tr. by T. H. Gaster, *The Dead Sea Scriptures* (Garden City: Doubleday, 1956) p. 121.

3:20f. it says, "All who practice righteousness are under the domination of the Prince of Lights, and walk in ways of light; whereas all who practice perversity are under the domination of the Angel of Darkness and walk in the ways of darkness." With this compare John 8:12 — "I am the light of the world; he who follows me will not walk in darkness, but will have the light of life" — and John 12:35 — "Walk while you have the light, lest the darkness overtake you; he who walks in the darkness does not know where he goes." Again, in the Manual of Discipline cleansing by the spirit is promised: "God will purge all the acts of man in the crucible of His truth, and refine for Himself all the fabric of man, destroying every spirit of perversity from within his flesh and cleansing him by the holy spirit from all the effects of wickedness. Like the waters of purification He will sprinkle upon him the spirit of truth, to cleanse him of . . . all pollution . . . to the end that . . . being made blameless in their ways, they may be endowed with inner vision. For them has God chosen to be the partakers of His eternal covenant, and theirs shall be all mortal glory."[30]

Not even the New Testament so specifically links cleansing with the Holy Spirit as does this passage (cf. Acts 15:9); in the Scrolls, however, the cleansing is often ceremonial cleansing and the "spirit" is not personal as in John's Gospel. Among the main areas of agreement between the Johannine literature and that of Qumran is that of the Spirit as truth and as the vehicle of divine revelation.[31] Only here and in John is the Spirit designated as the Spirit of truth; only in John, however, is the term "Paraclete" used.

The Qumran and Johannine literature are alike also in their emphasis on unity in the community. In both cases they were not "of the world" and were dedicated to God. Because of the sharp disjunction between them and the world their sense of unity was intensified.[32] Also, in both there was a strong emphasis on brotherly love, a strong sense of community.

Gaster has tabulated some twenty-seven passages in the Johannine writings which have similar statements in the Qumran literature thus far published,[33] a greater number by far than in any other New Testament work. It is clear, therefore, to many scholars that one does not need to go outside of Palestine to discover the ideological background of the Fourth Gospel.[34]

## C. HELLENISTIC INFLUENCE

### 1. PHILO

Since the Fourth Gospel was intended for the widest possible audience, "that the world may believe," it is safe to assume that the writer had in mind the Jews of the Dispersion — people of Jewish background and belief who were scattered throughout the Levantine countries. These Jews and their descendants were influenced by their intellectual environment and an effective evangelist, or author of a Gospel, would have to establish rapport with them. He could be expected to present the *kerygma* (message) to them in meaningful nomenclature and relevant idiom. For an acquaintance with what might impress thoughtful Jews of the Dispersion one can learn much from Philo of Alexandria, a Jewish philosopher contemporary with Jesus and St. Paul. In the use of symbolism, Philo and the Fourth Gospel have several things in common (CHD, 55). These include such concepts as light, water, shepherd, and love.

(i) Both John and Philo emphasize light as symbolizing God. The worship of the sun prevailed in the Mediterranean world from about the sixth century B.C. until the third century A.D., as witnessed by the rise of Zoroastrianism and the worship of the sun at such places as Tel el Amarna and Heliopolis in Egypt, and Baalbek in Syria. There is much in the Old Testament which equates God with light (e.g., Psa. 27:1; 36:9; Isa. 2:5; 60:3), although there is no sun-worship in the Old Testa-

    30 1QS 4:20-23, Gaster, *op. cit.*, pp. 45f.  Cf. Ezek. 36:26; John 3:5; 14:17, 26; 17:24.
    31 1QH 14:1-27 cf. John 14:26; 16:13-15.  See also G. A. Turner, "The Doctrine of the Spirit in the Dead Sea Scrolls," *The Seminary Tower* (Kansas City, Mo.: Nazarene Theological Seminary) Summer, 1960, pp. 12-15.
    32 Cf. 1QS 5:2, 7 and John 11:52; 17:11, 21, 23.  See also F. M. Cross Jr., *The Ancient Library of Qumran and Modern Biblical Studies* (Garden City: Doubleday, 1958), pp. 155f.
    33 T. H. Gaster, *op. cit.*, pp. 348f.
    34 A. M. Hunter, "Recent Trends in Johannine Studies," *Expository Times*, May, 1960, pp. 164-67.

ment. In Philo the light of God is said to be the archetype of every other light,[35] in a sense similar to that in which the Logos is the true light (John 1:9). Especially significant is the fact that both Philo and John emphasize the eternal antagonism between light and darkness (cf. John 1:5-11; 3:19-21). Philo in commenting on creation (Gen. 1:1-5) remarks, "After the kindling of the intelligible light, which preceded the sun's creation, darkness its adversary withdrew: for God, in His perfect knowledge of their contrariety and natural conflict, parted them one from another by a wall of separation. In order, therefore, to keep them from the discord arising from perpetual clash, to prevent war in place of peace prevailing and setting up disorder in an ordered universe, He not only separated light and darkness, but also placed in the intervening spaces boundary-marks, by which He held back each of their extremities; for, had they been actual neighbours, they were sure to produce confusion by engaging with fierce and never-ceasing rivalry in the struggle for mastery. As it was their assault on one another was broken and kept back by barriers set up between them. These barriers are evening and dawn."[36] John, and later the authors of the *Didache* and the *Epistle of Barnabas,* also emphasized this struggle of light and darkness. The same emphasis was held by the Essenes of the Qumran community as the Manual of Discipline and the War Scroll testify.

(ii) Another emphasis common to John and to Philo is the symbolism of water as a source of life. Philo spoke of God as the fountain of immortality (*anastasis*) (*De Somn.* II. 245) while John speaks of the fountain welling up into everlasting life (John 4:10, 14). Philo, commenting on Jeremiah 2:3, speaks of God as the Fountain of life (*De Fuga,* 197-8), suggesting that this concept was not unknown among his contemporaries. Thus both Philo and John testify to their common heritage in the Old Testament.

(iii) Because of this common heritage both John and Philo employ the symbol-ism of the shepherd as typifying the Lord as the leader. Said Philo, with the twenty-third Psalm before him, "For like a flock . . . all . . . are led according to right and law by God the Shepherd and King, who has set over them His true Logos and first-begotten Son, who takes over the care of this sacred flock like the vicegerent of a great king."[37]

(iv) Like the author of the Fourth Gospel, Philo placed chief emphasis on love. As a Jew Philo was greatly influenced by the Shema (Deut. 6:5) and its summons to love God with all the heart. It is good to fear God, he says, but it is better to love him (*De Spec. Leg.* 1. 299-300). Likewise John said, "Perfect love casteth out fear" (I John 4:18; cf. John 15:15).

While these parallels are interesting and informative, the differences between John and Philo are much greater. With the latter there is an amalgamation of Platonism, Stoicism, and Old Testament religion. It is neither Greek philosophy nor the Old Testament but a mixture of both. In the Fourth Gospel, however, we find an independent and distinctive Christian witness, built on and growing out of the Old Testament, and employing some modes of expression designed to "speak to the condition" of Greek-speaking and even Greek-thinking people. John was a witness, not *of* Greek ideas but *to* Greek ideas.

## 2. HERMETIC LITERATURE

There were many religions of salvation employing rites of initiation which permeated the older civic religions of the Near East from the sixth century B.C. onwards. These were called the mystery religions because only those properly initiated by secret rites could experience personal communion with the deity. They testify to a desire on the part of some for a more intimate and personal religious experience than was afforded by the conventional religious functions of society. On Egyptian soil emerged a synthesis of mystery religions and Gnosticism in the form of literature dedicated to Hermes, i.e., the

---

[35] Philo, *De Somn.* 1, 75, tr. by F. H. Colson and G. H. Whitaker, *Loeb Classical Library* (London: Wm. Heinemann, 1934), V, 337.
[36] Philo, *On the Creation,* IX, 33-34, tr. by F. H. Colson and G. H. Whitaker, *Loeb Classical Library* (London: Wm. Heinemann, 1929), I, 26-27.
[37] Philo, *De Agr.,* 51; *Loeb Classical Library* (London: Wm. Heinemann, 1930), III, 135.

god Thoth.[38] While these writings have little relevance to the Fourth Gospel they are worth noting for their contribution to our understanding of the world for which this Gospel was written. Unlike Gnosticism, the primary concern in these writings was not speculative philosophy but religion. "The writers in question taught philosophic doctrines, but valued those doctrines only as means or aids to religion."[39] The stress was upon knowledge as the way of salvation, but it was linked with a certain asceticism; there was little ethical or social concern (CHD, p. 13). As in John 17:3, the eternal life consisted in the knowledge of God. As in Plato, but not as in the Bible, sin was ignorance, knowledge was virtue. The dualism of soul and body was prominent as in Gnosticism and asceticism generally. Like the Fourth Gospel, the concepts of light and life are prominent in these writings. As in Gnosticism, and in antithesis to Christianity, the great gulf fixed between the spiritual and the physical man is bridged by aeons. Man can know God and have life by becoming an *aeon*. By possessing the divine *nous* (mind) man can become divine. The *logos* (articulate thought) is said to be the *nous* of God and the image of God. *Logos* is closely associated with *nous* or mind. In one dialogue between Hermes and his son Tat it is stated that "the Creator made the whole world, not with hands, but by logos" (CHD, p. 29).

Certain parallels between the Incarnation and the *anthropos* (generic man) in the tract called the *Poimandres* are noteworthy. As Dodd puts it, "The Son of Man is God's Son, beloved by His Father, and like Him; He is the light of the world and the life of men; He descends and takes on a material body. He ascends again to His Father, and those who are united with Him have knowledge of God and enter into life and light" (CHD, p. 43).

While the subject of regeneration is common both to the Fourth Gospel and to the Hermetic literature, the differences are as striking as the similarities. In the *Poimandres,* to become divine one needs to be born again. The father explains to his son Tat that the father is God's

will, the womb is wisdom, the seed is the real Good and the offspring a child of God (CHD, p. 44). Rebirth in this literature (*De Regeneratione*) is the deliverance of the soul from the passions of the flesh, not unlike the rebirth in certain forms of Buddhism. This parallel is not indicative of borrowing from Christian sources, as even Dodd admits (p. 52), but at least it shows that the idea was not unknown in the Middle East and the author of the Fourth Gospel may have emphasized Jesus' discourse with Nicodemus (3:5-10; cf. 1:13) to catch the attention of those exposed to this influence in Gnosticism. The significance of the Hermetica is that although they were written long after the composition of the Fourth Gospel they reflect a religious vocabulary at the disposal of the Christian evangelists. (WFH, VIII, 453). A comparison of these literatures with the New Testament cannot fail to impress the reader with the superiority of the latter, especially with reference to freshness, originality, and power.

## 3. GNOSTICISM

Gnosticism was a very widespread religio-philosophical system which exerted as much pressure on the church internally as the persecutions did externally. The system or systems were so vague and complex that it is difficult to understand them and assess their influence. In general they were based upon the conviction that knowledge is virtue and matter is evil. They emphasized "salvation," i.e., that "emancipation came through knowledge, gnosis, the possession of which saved the initiates from the clutch of matter."[40] most of these systems were concerned with the deliverance of the soul from matter rather than with salvation from sin. Salvation was by a superior knowledge, or, in some post-Christian systems, by a gnostic redeemer, and it was only for the "elect," those who possessed the divine spark of life. The fact that a redeemer was unknown in gnostic hierarchy until the rise of Christianity implies that this idea was borrowed from Christianity.[41]

---

[38] A. J. Festugiere, *Hermes Trismegiste,* Vol. 1; also *L'Hermestism,* Lund, 1948, and A. D. Nock and A. J. Festugiere, *Corpus Hermeticum,* Paris, 1945, are the best primary sources for the Hermetic literature. See also Walter Scott, *Hermetica* (Oxford: Clarendon Press, 1924), Vols. I-IV.
[39] Walter Scott, *op. cit.,* I, 1.
[40] *Webster's Collegiate Dictionary* (Springfield, Mass.: G. & C. Merriam Co., 1938), p. 427.
[41] R. M. Grant, editor, *Gnosticism* (New York: Harper, 1961), p. 18.

The chief sources of our knowledge of Gnosticism are the Church Fathers of the second century. Until recently critical scholars tended to treat these sources with reserve. In their judgment the Church Fathers were so prejudiced that they pictured the Gnostics as worse than they really were. But recent discoveries near Nag-Hamadi, Egypt, in 1945 now provide scholars with materials which enable them to study these systems at first hand rather than looking at them through the eyes of the apologists. These discoveries tend to confirm the judgment of the Fathers as to the evil nature and the danger to the church.[42] The Gnostics in general considered themselves superior to ordinary Christians. They regarded ordinary Christians as dependent upon the Bible for their knowledge of God while they professed direct revelations from God; while others were saved by faith, they were "saved" by gnosis or knowledge. Some Gnostics classed all worshippers in three groups: the *auditori* who only listened, the *credenti* who were believers, and the *perfecti*, or the Gnostics, who were saved not by faith but by knowledge. It was the latter group perhaps against which John protested when he said, "If we say we have no sin we deceive ourselves" (I John 1:8). These Gnostics were complacent and haughty because "superior" (cf. I Cor. 1:21; 2:5; 8:1; 13:2), much the same as the Sophists of Athens who drew the scorn of Socrates, and some Pharisees of Jerusalem who called forth Jesus' condemnation (Matt. 23:1-36).

Little is known of pre-Christian Gnostic systems. The earliest post-Christian Gnostic system is described by Irenaeus (c. A.D. 180), and perhaps by a lost work of Justin Martyr (c. A.D. 150), as that of Simon of Samaria. Claiming to have come down from heaven, he was to appear among the Jews as the Son, among the Samaritans as the Father, and among the nations as the Holy Spirit.[43] It is in John's Gospel that we encounter an emphasis upon Jesus' descent from heaven and ascent "unto the Father" (cf. 1:51; 3:13; 6:38; 16:28; 20:17).

In the Coptic tract "The Secret Book of John" the Logos followed Will "for through the Logos, Christ created all things."[44] There is a stress on light as well as upon knowledge. Barbelo (foreknowledge) "looked intensely into the pure Light and . . . gave birth to a blessed Spark of Light; . . . the Monogenes, who revealed himself to the Father, the divine Self-born. . . ."[45] Quispel argues successfully that the Barbelo-Gnostics made their appearance before the end of the first century. Therefore, the thesis that because Gnosticism was little known until the middle of the second century John must have been a second century work, lacks support.[46]

The most important of the Coptic papyri discoveries in 1945 in Upper Egypt was "The Gospel of Truth." In it there are several rather remote parallels to the Fourth Gospel. The "power of the Logos" enables the believer to know the Father. The Logos is called "the Saviour" because his work is to redeem those who have not known the Father.[47] He redeems them from error, rather than from sin. Among the prominent ideas are unity, truth, wisdom, judgment, light, and the revelation of Truth. The relationships among these concepts are not specific; there is fusion and confusion of ideas related to illumination and salvation. There are many verbal similarities but few ideological similarities between this "Gospel" and the Gospel by John.

Unlike the works of the Church Fathers and the authors of II Peter and Jude, the texts of the Fourth Gospel, the First Epistle, and the Pauline Epistles do not openly describe and condemn the Gnostic systems. Instead, they reflect an awareness of them and attack them indirectly. In John's Gospel and First Epistle there is much stress on knowledge and knowing the truth. As if to refute false gnosticism, John sets forth the true gnosticism. Like Clement of Alexandria (*Stromata*, c. A.D.

---

[42] W. F. Albright, "Discoveries in Palestine and the Gospel of St. John," in W. D. Davies and D. Daube, editors, *The Background of the New Testament and Its Eschatology* (Cambridge: The University Press, 1956), p. 162.

[43] Irenaeus, *Adversus Haereses*, cited by Robert Grant, *op. cit.*, p. 24. Confirmed by Gilles Quispel, *Gnosis als Weltreligion* (1951) cited by W. F. Albright, in Davies and Daube, *op. cit.*, p. 163. See also Jean Doresse, *The Secret Books of the Egyptian Gnostics* (New York: Viking Press, 1960), pp. 15-19, 329-332.

[44] W. Till, *Die Gnostischen Schriften*, cited by R. M. Grant, *op. cit.*, p. 73.

[45] *Ibid.*, p. 72.

[46] W. A. Albright, *op. cit.*, p. 163.

[47] W. W. Isenburg, *The Gospel of Truth*, cited by R. M. Grant, *op. cit.*, pp. 146f.

200) John believes himself to be the true Gnostic who knows he has passed from death unto life (I John 4:6; 5:11, 13, 18-20). His knowledge is the assurance of having received eternal life.

Because of the belief that matter was evil, the Gnostic stressed the transcendence of God. Good and bad, matter and spirit, God and man cannot come into direct contact. This basic conviction led to many ramifications in early doctrinal beliefs and its influence is reflected in the New Testament and in the ancient Church. It led to asceticism, the effort to be free from the desires of the flesh by repressing the body, by abstinence from all but the necessities for physical life. It led also to heretical views of the Person of Christ. The true Gnostic did not believe that God could actually become man for that would necessitate the union of Eternal Spirit with mortal flesh. Therefore they were known as Docetists, those who refused to believe that Jesus Christ actually came in the flesh (I John 2:22; II John 7). For this reason John insists that "the Logos became flesh and dwelt among us" (John 1:14), one of the most trenchant affirmations of the New Testament, one that cut across the main tenet of Gnosticism. This background helps explain John's emphasis on Jesus' real humanity (John 1:14; 4:6; 11:35; I John 4:2). He pictures Jesus as weary, thirsty, sorrowful, and as shedding blood copiously while upon the cross; he was not a phantom who temporarily assumed human form and departed at the crucifixion as the Docetists affirmed. An awareness of the main principles of this incipient Gnosticism is essential to a full appreciation of these emphases in the Johannine literature.

### 4. THE MANDEANS

An obscure Mesopotamian sect caught the attention of German scholars in the 1920's. These Mandeans professed to be disciples of John the Baptist and scholars sought eagerly for relationships to the New Testament. Many parallel passages in their writings were cited by Walter Bauer and Rudolph Bultmann and their resemblances to passages in the Fourth Gospel were noted. According to a theory developed by Wilhelm Boussett[48] and others, a group of disciples of John the Baptist migrated to the lower Euphrates valley, bringing with them Jewish-Gnostic beliefs mixed with Phoenician polytheism, and some Christian influences. This was gradually transformed by amalgamation with Parsiism. The Mandean religion is still practiced by a small community in Iraq. Three of their sacred books have now been published and translated from Aramaic into German. These are The Ginza ("Treasure"), the Book of John, and the Qulasta, a volume of liturgies for baptism and burial services (WFH, 455). Rudolph Bultmann has theorized that the Fourth Gospel is based upon an Iranian or Mandean myth in which a divine Messenger descends and later ascends for the salvation of mankind.[49] In support of this theory Bultmann calls attention to passages in the Fourth Gospel which emphasize John's inferiority to Jesus (John 1:8, 27; 3:28-30), similarities of language and imagery, and statements about Jesus paralleled in the Mandean literature. These include the coming of the Redeemer to dwell in the soul (cf. John 14:23 and Man. Lit. 198) and a parallel to John 14:1 in which there appears the statement "I go now to the house of life, then I will return and free you from the evil and sin of this world" (Bultmann, op. cit., p. 463). Other parallels include the unity of the Father of Majesty and his Son. The Son is entrusted to give life, pronounce judgment, and to lead men out of darkness into light. He knows his own disciples and chooses them but is hated by the world. Some passages recall the "I am" affirmations of the Fourth Gospel, such as the following: "A shepherd am I who loves his sheep; I keep watch over my sheep and my lambs; Around my neck I carry my sheep and they wander not from the village. I bring them into the fold, the good fold, and then with me they find pasture. . . . No wolf leaps into our fold, and of fierce lions they need not be frightened" (WFH, VIII, 455).

[48] W. Boussett, Das Religion des Judentums (Berlin: Reuther & Reichard, 1903), pp. 348f.
[49] R. Bultmann, article in ZNTW, XXIV (1925) pp. 100-146; Bultmann, pp. 25, 482, et passim; See C. H. Dodd, pp. 121f.

The evidence cited by Bauer and Bultmann is impressive until the contexts of the passages are consulted. The contexts indicate that these passages are not arranged in any system. There is no consistency in designating which is Father and which is Son; they come from a variety of sources and there are many messengers (*loc. cit.*). Bultmann assumes two things which cannot be proven: that the Mandeans came from Palestine and that their traditions antedate Christianity. F. C. Burkitt, C. H. Dodd, and others have proven conclusively that neither of these assumptions is justified. The Mandean literature tells us nothing new about John the Baptist, their alleged founder, nor does it provide evidence that the Fourth Gospel is directed against Mandean tenets. Mandean baptism is not a once-for-all act of initiation as in the New Testament, but a repetitive lustration (as at Qumran). The evidence shows rather that this Mandean literature came into existence after the rise of Islam (since John the Baptist is spelled the same as in the Koran). It is best viewed as an eclectic Gnosticism which has borrowed from both eastern and western sources, including Christianity and Islam. It is more helpful to an understanding of the rise of Islam than to any understanding of the New Testament (CHD, pp.129f.). Such was the judgment of discerning scholars prior to the evidence of the Dead Sea Scrolls. Since the publication of the Qumran literature the fallacy of assuming a Mandean influence upon the Fourth Gospel is even more obvious. The dualism of the Fourth Gospel (light vs. darkness, etc.) is not cosmological and metaphysical as Bultmann assumes. Mandeanism is eclectic dualism predominantly Iranian and post-Gnostic, with no written literature prior to the fifth century A.D.[50]

## D. THE INDEPENDENCE OF THE FOURTH GOSPEL

While there is much evidence of "communication" between the Fourth Gospel and its intellectual-religious environment, there is also abundant evidence of the author's independence and originality. There is evidence that he is acquainted with the Synoptic Gospels and yet is free to utilize material common to all four or to present material which is quite independent of the others.[51] This has been mentioned in the section dealing with the relation of the Fourth to the other three Gospels (pp. 5, 6). John has much in common with Paul but presents the material in a manner independent of but not in contradiction to the Apostle to the Gentiles. Both, for example, emphasize the radical change which occurs when a person becomes a Christian. John speaks of it as regeneration while Paul calls it justification, the former using biological phraseology, the latter the nomenclature of jurisprudence.

There is no evidence of literary borrowing on the part of the Evangelist from the Stoics, or Philo, or the Mandeans, or from the Dead Sea Scrolls. There is evidence of borrowing from the Fourth Gospel by the Gnostics and the Mandeans. Borrowing by the Gnostics is obvious, as, for example, in the Gospel of Philip.[52] The abundant parallels between the Fourth Gospel and the literatures of Philo, the Qumran Scrolls, and the Gnostics is best explained as the result of the work of authors who employ the vocabulary and idioms which were common property to residents of the Near East during the first century.

In a monograph published in 1938 a Cambridge scholar argued with great effectiveness that the author of the Fourth Gospel may not even have known the Synoptics, much less have been influenced by them.[53] This author is convinced that once the assumption that John knew the first three Gospels is abandoned many of the problems relative to similarities and differences become clearer. He believes that the relatively "advanced" Christology may be due not to a lapse to time but rather to a different place of origin — in some quarters advance was more rapid than in others. An increasing

[50] W. F. Albright, *op. cit.*, pp. 365f.
[51] D. M. Smith, "John 12:12, and the Question of John's Use of The Synoptics," JBL. LXXXII, 1, March, 1963, pp. 59ff.
[52] R. McL. Wilson, *The Gospel of Philip* (New York: Harper & Row, 1962), "If you know the truth, the truth will made you free" (cf. John 8:31), p. 60.
[53] P. Gardner-Smith, *Saint John and the Synoptic Gospels* (Cambridge: University Press, 1938), *passim*.

number of scholars think of the Johannine theology as having matured at about the same time as that of Paul, i.e., by about A.D. 60, and hence as having arisen from an independent "tradition."[54] Some who do not regard John the son of Zebedee as the author, nevertheless agree with the book itself that the author was an eyewitness who was dependent not on other written documents, but rather on his "Spirit-inspired memory."[55]

### E. SUMMARY

Out of this complex religious background of the first two centuries as it relates to the Fourth Gospel the following conclusions may be drawn:

(i) The background of the book is now generally recognized as predominantly Semitic; in fact it has been called "the most Jewish book of the New Testament" (Albright) in spite of the Jewish background evident in Matthew, Hebrews, James, and Revelation.

(ii) The linguistic background of Aramaic and the historical background of Palestinian Essenism argue convincingly for a Palestinian origin of the author.

(iii) The apocalypticism of the Dead Sea Scrolls and pseudepigrapha such as Enoch is not a part of the Fourth Gospel.

(iv) The Dead Sea Scrolls have a greater affinity with the Gospel by John than with any other New Testament book. There is no evidence of direct borrowing, but both draw upon a common vocabulary and viewpoint in many respects.

(v) Literary parallels in the Fourth Gospel and the writings of the Mandeans show only that the latter borrowed extensively from earlier ideas of many kinds.

(vi) The Hermetic writings contain passages pointing to a common background of ideas, but again without evidence of direct borrowing.

(vii) The Gnostic writings of Chenoboskion in Upper Egypt reflect the influence of the Fourth Gospel and show the deviations of Gnostic Christians from orthodoxy.

## V. THE BOOK ITSELF

### A. DATE

#### 1. TRADITIONAL VIEW

The traditional date of the Fourth Gospel is the last decade of the First Century. This is based upon the tradition of the early church that the Apostle John lived to an old age in Ephesus.[56] Irenaeus of Lyons (c. A.D. 180), a disciple of Polycarp (Bishop of Smyrna c. A.D. 140), claimed to have a knowledge of the Apostle John through Polycarp. After noting the books of Matthew, Mark, and Luke, Irenaeus remarks, "Afterwards, John, the disciple of the Lord, did himself publish a Gospel during his residence at Ephesus in Asia."[57] Another witness to John's residence in Asia is Polycrates, (Bishop of Ephesus A.D. 189-198). He relates that "John, who leaned on the Lord's breast, who was a priest wearing a mitre, and martyr and teacher, . . . sleeps at Ephesus."[58] Clement of Alexandria, in his treatise concerning a rich man's salvation, endorses a story "which is not a story but a true tradition of John the Apostle preserved in memory," of the aged apostle's efforts in winning a backslider to Christ and the church. These traditions of John's long residence at Ephesus are among the reasons for assuming this date for the Gospel. As summed up by Eusebius, John knew of the existence of the Synoptic Gospels but "used all the time a message which was not written down, and at last took to writing for the following cause."[59]

Another reason for dating the Gospel at this time is the fact that this Gospel appears to be more reflective and more theological than the rather matter-of-fact narratives in the Synoptics. It is widely assumed that a lapse of time and meditation accounted for this more meditative and interpretive presentation of the Fourth Gospel. Thus the content of the Gospel itself is in accord with the statement by Eusebius that the fourth was composed

[54] J. A. T. Robinson, "The New Look on the Fourth Gospel," *Studia Evangelica*, ed. by Aland, Cross, Danielou, Riesenfeld and van Unnik, (Berlin: Akademie Verlag, 1959), p. 346. See also E. R. Goodenough, "John, A Primitive Gospel," JBL 64 (1945), pp. 145-182.

[55] E.g., R. M. Grant, *Earliest Lives of Jesus* (New York: Harper, 1961), pp. 7-9. On rather precarious ground he thinks Nicodemus was the author.

[56] Irenaeus, *Adv. Haer.* II, xxii, 5; III, iii, 4; Eusebius, H. E., IV, xiv, 3-8.

[57] Irenaeus, *op. cit.*, III, i, 1.: A. Roberts & J. Donalson, editors, *The Ante-Nicene Fathers* (New York: Scribner's, 1903) I, 414.

[58] Eusebius, *H.E.*, III, xxxi, 3: tr. by K. Lake, *Loeb Classical Library* (London: Wm. Heinemann, 1926) I, 271.

[59] Eusebius, *H.E.*, III, xxiv, 7 (K. Lake, *op. cit.*, I, 251).

some time after the other three Gospels toward the end of the first century.

## 2. LATE DATE

This view was gradually replaced in many quarters by the view that this Gospel must be dated at about the middle of the second century and hence could not be apostolic. Several German scholars, from Bauer to Bultmann, dated the book from A.D. 110 to A.D. 160. This was based upon the assumption that the Christology of this Gospel would take time to develop and hence it must have been formulated long after the completion of the Synoptic accounts, which are relatively factual with a minimum of interpretation. It was also assumed that the Gospel either reflected the influence of Gnosticism or was designed to combat it. Since Gnosticism did not come to full power until the middle of the second century the Gospel was dated to coincide with this development. This point of view was ably championed by B. W. Bacon and E. F. Scott in Britain and the United States and by Loisy in France. The result of this was to discredit the author as a historian, and, as a consequence of abandoning Johannine authorship, it was fashionable to call it "The Fourth Gospel."[60] Typical of this view is the comment of F. C. Grant: "He is also determined to make Jesus as un-Jewish, even as anti-Jewish, as possible. . . . As a consequence he mingles fact and theological interpretation so thoroughly that we can scarcely separate them, even with the help of the Synoptics."[61] Because of the general acceptance of this point of view by critical scholars, Mark, with the least interpretive material, was the most highly regarded of the four because more primitive and hence supposedly nearer to the "Jesus of history." John was regarded with great reserve and suspicion because he emphasized the "Christ of faith," and because this Gospel is allegedly partly fact, partly legend, and partly pagan ideology. Such is the view of Bultmann today.[62]

## 3. EARLY DATE

A revolt from this second century dating of John's Gospel was led by C. C. Torrey who emphasized the Aramaic and hence Palestinian element in the Gospels and F. C. Burney (*The Aramaic Origin of the Fourth Gospel*, Oxford, 1922). E. R. Goodenough was also a pioneer in advocating an early date.[63] Others favoring an early date include Gardner-Smith, W. F. Albright and J. A. T. Robinson. This recent trend is well summed up in these words: "The most likely solution of the problem seems to be that John's Gospel is actually independent of the synoptics; he did not use them among his sources. To date his gospel, however, is practically impossible. It probably comes from a time considerably before the end of the first century."[64]

There is another consideration favoring an early date which should receive more attention than is given to it. The Fourth Gospel, especially chs. 2-12, is largely dominated by Jesus' controversy with "the Jews." This would seem to favor a date prior to A.D. 70 for several reasons. Before the fall of Jerusalem and the migration of the Sanhedrin to Jamnia (A.D. 70), it may be assumed that Judaism was much more potent than later. The crucial issue prior to the fall of Jerusalem — and the termination of the Sadducees, the high priesthood, and the sacrificial system — was the relation

---

[60] Compare "I frankly think that 'Fourth Gospel' is a scholastic affectation. Why not the First, Second and Third Gospels? Are we sure of their authors? Any tyro knows that Deuteronomy is not 'the Second Giving of the Law,' but are we obliged to make constant profession of our critical attainments by calling that document the Fifth Book of Pseudo-Moses?" James Montgomery, *The Origin of the Gospel According to John* (Philadelphia, 1923); cited by J. A. T. Robinson, *op. cit.*, p. 339.
[61] Frederick C. Grant, *The Gospel of John: Harper's Annotated Bible Series* (New York: Harper, 1956), p. 7.
[62] Cf. R. Bultmann, *Theologie Des Neuen Testaments* (Tübingen: J. C. B. Mohr, 1953), pp. 350-361. However, on the basis of the Roberts fragment (P 457) and the Egerton Papyrus No. 2, Bultmann believes that this Gospel was known in Egypt by 100 A.D., *Johannes Evangelium*, p. 204, note 4.
[63] E. R. Goodenough, "John, A Primitive Gospel," JBL LXIV (1945), pp. 145-182.
[64] R. M. Grant, *The Earliest Lives of Jesus* (New York: Harper, 1961), p. 7. In 1877 a critic of Baur's views wrote, in defense of apostolic authorship, "It is inconceivable that the Gospel should have been composed in the second century. . . . The spirit of the century does not harmonize with that of the book. That spirit had already become traditional and ascetic . . . . only a previous knowledge of the personality speaking in the Gospel, only the notorious *authority of the eye-witness and Apostle*, from the first moment appealing on behalf of the book, could have opened the way for the acceptance and recognition of a Gospel, departing so much from all tradition, and that in an age so careful of tradition and already in possession of the Synoptists." W. Beyschlag, "The Gospel of John and Modern Criticism II," *The Contemporary Review* (London: Strahan & Company, Nov. 1877), p. 943. Thus, after nearly a century, New Testament criticism has almost completed a full circle!

of Jesus Christ to Judaism. This is reflected in the earliest of Christian documents. Paul writing to the Thessalonians before the middle of the first century reflects the intensity of this struggle: "The Jews . . . killed the Lord Jesus, and their own prophets, and have persecuted us; and they please not God, and are contrary to all men; Forbidding us to speak to the Gentiles that they may be saved, to fill up their sins always: but wrath is come upon them to the uttermost" (I Thess. 2:15, 16).

These words, and others like them in Galatians, were written when Christianity was on the defensive. Justin Martyr wrote to Trypho the Jew a century later, at a time when Christianity was in the ascendency and Judaism on the defensive. The Fourth Gospel seems more appropriate in this respect to a time prior to the Jewish revolt when the controversy with Judaism was keenest as reflected in Paul's letters and in *Acts*. By the end of the first century the central issue was the relation of the Church to Rome and to pagan ideologies, rather than to Judaism.

It is difficult to imagine a situation in the Diaspora after the Jewish Revolt in which the central conflict would be between church and synagogue. This must have been the case, however, prior to the destruction of the temple. It would have been particularly acute in Palestine where Judaism was the dominant element in the culture rather than a somewhat isolated series of colonies, as in the Diaspora. All of these considerations point to a possible if not probable date contemporary with the Pauline Epistles.

"When we look to the background, strictly speaking, rather than to the eventual environment, of the Evangelist and his tradition, I detect a growing readiness to recognize that this is not to be sought at the end of the first century or the beginning of the second, Ephesus or Alexandria, among the Gnostics or the Greeks. Rather, there is no compelling need to let our gaze wander very far, either in space or in time, beyond a fairly limited area of southern Palestine in the fairly limited interval between the Crucifixion and fall of Jerusalem."[65]

## B. PURPOSE

### 1. "THAT THE WORLD MAY BELIEVE"

In recent times more attention has been given to the purpose and destination of the Gospel than to the question of authorship. On the purpose of the four Gospels Luke and John are the most explicit. Luke wrote to a believer to confirm him in his faith (Luke 1:4). John wrote to unbelievers that they might be convinced and in Christ find life (John 20:31). In this sense Luke's Gospel is *didache,* or instruction for the believers, while John's is *kerygma,* or proclamation of the good news to all who will hear. The purpose of the Fourth Gospel is thus "good news" for everyone in the truest sense of the word. By inference there is ground for the generalization that Matthew wrote primarily for the Jewish world because he was careful to note fulfillment of O. T. predictions, that Mark had Roman readers in mind and therefore was terse, dramatic and practical, that Luke wrote with Greeks in mind because of his interest in the lower classes, while John wrote with the whole world in mind. It is true that the universal note is clearer and stronger here than in the other three; the horizon is wider, the vista extends farther into the future and the themes of the Fourth Gospel have a wider and more general relevance.

### 2. "TO REHABILITATE THE HELLENISTS"

Scholars are currently preoccupied with the less explicit and less obvious purpose or purposes of this Gospel. Oscar Cullmann believes the Fourth Gospel was designed to "rehabilitate the Hellenists."[66] The "Hellenists" are those described in Acts (6:1—8:40; 9:29; 11:20) as Palestinian Jews who either spoke Greek or lived, in Cullmann's words "according to the Greek manner." The argument that the Fourth Gospel is especially interested in these Hellenists and seeks to "rehabilitate" them, is based on these considerations: (i) John's Gospel, the Hellenists and the Qumran Essenes were opposed to the Temple and its worship (cf. Acts 7:48; John 2:13-22; 4:20-24). (ii) This opposition led to the departure of the Hel-

[65] J. A. T. Robinson, "The New Look and The Fourth Gospel," *Studia Evangelica,* p. 342.
[66] Oscar Cullmann, "The Significance of the Qumran Texts for Research Into the Beginnings of Christianity," JBL, Dec., 1955, pp. 213-226.

lenists from Jerusalem; they went to the Samaritans who also opposed worship in the Temple (Acts 8:5; cf. John 4:1-42). (iii) The Shekinah, symbolizing God's presence in the Temple, becomes in John the "glory" residing in Jesus Christ (John 1:14; 17:1, 24). (iv) The term "Son of man" is common to the Hellenists (Acts 7:56) and to the Fourth Gospel (but not to Acts). Cullmann concludes that the Synoptic Gospels reflect the ideas held by the Hebrew Christians while the Fourth Gospel reflects the ideas prized by the Hellenists, both of which existed simultaneously from the beginning. John's Gospel therefore seeks to defend and define the Hellenists.

This thesis is yet to be proven; some of it rests upon rather dubious evidence, such as the item dealing with the term "Son of man," a title which occurs also in the Synoptic Gospels and not in John and Acts 7:56 alone.

### 3. "FOR JEWS OF THE DISPERSION"

A very plausible thesis has recently been presented by W. C. van Unnik of the University of Utrecht. He argues that this Gospel was designed primarily for Jews of the Dispersion. It aimed at convincing these Jews who attended the synagogues that Jesus of Nazareth was their Messiah. It also aimed to convince the Gentile God-fearers also that this Jesus was the Son of God and Savior of the world. It was not an apology for the Christian church (only chapters 13-17 were primarily for believers), but rather a missionary book designed to convince the unbelievers. He bases this conclusion upon the Johannine use of the term Messiah which agrees with the missionary message of Paul, Apollos, and other evangelists working with the synagogue congregations in the *Diaspora* (Acts 17:2; 13:26; 18:5,28; 9:20,22). Such a view explains why the Evangelist does not condemn pagan practices such as idolatry, a prominent feature of Paul's letters, but deals exclusively with sins of the Jews, e.g., wrong belief and unbelief, spiritual blindness, etc.[67] This is confirmed by the similarities between this Gospel and Justin's debate with Trypho the Jew. The Christian evangelists had to convince their hearers of the theological position that the Messiah must be the same as the Suffering Servant and that the Messiah was Jesus of Nazareth. It was the same task that confronted Jesus himself, as reported by the Synoptists (Mark 8:31). While the Synoptists told many things about Jesus, John concentrated on one theme — that Jesus is the Anointed One and that he alone gives LIFE.

### 4. OTHER PURPOSES

One British scholar, after surveying the arguments advanced by Gardner-Smith, C. H. Dodd, W. F. Howard, Albright, Cowley, Cullmann, and J. A. T. Robinson concludes that the purpose of the Fourth Gospel is to make its contribution "not only to those who wish to grasp the eternal significance of Jesus Christ, but also to those who wish to gain a clear insight into the historical personality of Jesus of Nazareth."[68] In other words, the Evangelist is not a copyist but probably used unwritten Aramaic sources originating in Palestine prior to 70 A.D. and later put them in written form designed to convince Jews and others of the Levant that Jesus is the Christ. Therefore the Fourth Gospel is not to be understood as history contrary to the Synoptics, nor theology unconcerned with history, but rather as history plus theology independent in treatment and yet supplemental to other contemporary sources. Thus, much in contemporary scholarship, chastened and informed by archaeological discoveries, is essentially in agreement with the early traditions preserved in Eusebius to which reference has already been made.

### C. THE AUTHOR

#### 1. A SECOND CENTURY MYSTIC

For about two generations many New Testament critics have dated the Fourth Gospel in the second century. This view precluded apostolic authorship and for that reason the book came to be called "The Fourth Gospel" rather than the Gospel by John. According to some proponents of this view, this Gospel is a literary composition in which theological interests so

---

[67] W. C. van Unnik, "The Purpose of St. John's Gospel," *Studia Evangelica*, ed. Aland, Cross, Danielou, Risenfeld & van Unnik, (Berlin: Akademie-verlag, 1959), p. 398.

[68] C. Leslie Mitton, "Modern Issues in Biblical Studies — 'The Provenance of the Fourth Gospel,'" *Expository Times*, Aug., 1960, p. 340.

far outweigh the historical that there is little history in the Gospel. Such a view dismisses details which are attributed to any eyewitness as the fabrication of a gifted writer. "The picturesque detail in John's narrative can be set down, not to the accurate memory of the eyewitness, but to the fine instinct of the literary artist" (EFS, p. 19). Some who take a less extreme position argue that the book, as we now have it, is the work of three authors, including the "Witness," probably a resident of Jerusalem of the high priestly family. This would account for the neglect of Galilee and the detailed knowledge of Judea and Jerusalem evident in the work. If the "Witness" were a Sadducee, this would account for the lack of any reference to demon-possession. This "Witness" was the anonymous "Beloved Disciple" who had been a secret disciple, perhaps Nicodemus or the "rich young ruler." Such a person, rather than the rough and unlettered son of Zebedee, would be the disciple whom Jesus loved and in whom he confided.

## 2. JOHN THE ELDER

The actual writing of the Gospel was then done by John the Elder, a disciple of "The Beloved Disciple" who wrote down the memories of the "Witness" and composed the Prologue of the Gospel. This Elder John lived at Ephesus and composed the Gospel here.

The third member of the team was the Redactor who reworked some of the material and harmonized it with the Synoptic Gospels by adding chs. 4, 6, and 21, all dealing with Galilee.[69] On this assumption the Palestinian background would be reflected in the report of the "Witness" who is the same as the "Beloved Disciple," the literary style and Prologue would reflect the influence of the anonymous writer, perhaps the Elder at Ephesus, and the Redactor is given credit for the harmonization with the other Gospels, chiefly by the portions in which the locale is Galilee. For twenty-one reasons against apostolic authorship see Pierson Parker, "John The Son of Zebedee and The Fourth Gospel," JBL, 81:35-43 (1962).

## 3. THE APOSTLE JOHN

The view that the Apostle John wrote the Gospel which bears his name has been stated with great effectiveness by B. F. Westcott, Alfred Plummer, and William Sanday. This position proceeds by the process of elimination to the Apostle John. (a) That the author was a Jew is proven by his familiarity with Jewish ideas (1:19,51; 4:25; 6:14,15; 7:26), his acquaintance with Jewish customs (2:6; 3:25; 11:55; 18:28; 19:31), and his familiarity with the Old Testament (e.g., the "Lamb of God," the serpent in the wilderness, manna and water in the wilderness, the Shepherd, the vine, etc.). (b) That the author was a Jew of Palestine is evident in his knowledge of its topography (11:18; 2:1; 3:23; 4:5; 6:22), of Jerusalem before A. D. 66 (5:2; 9:7; 10:23; 18:1,28; 19:13,17-20,41,42), his use of the Hebrew O. T. and his Palestinian treatment of the *logos* concept (CGT, p. xxix). (c) That the author was an *eye-witness* is seen in his vivid delineations of Nicodemus, Thomas, and Peter, his attention to seasons, days and hours, and the details of such events as the conversation with the Samaritan woman, the healing of the blind man, the raising of Lazarus and the resurrection. (d) The author was an apostle as is evident in the report of conversations known only to the inner circle of disciples (2:11,17,22; 14:27; 6:19,60; 4:31; 11:54; 18:4). (e) If the foregoing points are true, it follows that the author of the Fourth Gospel was John the son of Zebedee, who was also the "Witness" and the "Beloved Disciple." This view is the one which prevailed in the ancient church; there are no rival claimants and no one denied apostolic authorship. Among the modern champions of this view are William Hendriksen (1953); R. C. H. Lenski (1942); P. Beeckman (1951); A. C. Headlam, *The Fourth Gospel as History*, (1948); A. H. N. Green-Armytage, *John Who Saw*, (1952), H. E. Edwards, *The Disciple Who Wrote These Things*, (1953); R. A. Edwards, *The Gospel According to St. John*, (1954). This traditional view "has never been shown to be impossible" (RHL, p. 2).[70]

The view that presently enjoys a num-

---

[69] See G. H. C. Macgregor, *op. cit.*, pp. l-lxvii; A. E. Garvie, "John," *Abingdon Bible Commentary* (New York: Abingdon Press, 1929).

[70] See also J. A. T. Robinson, "The New Look at the Fourth Gospel," *op. cit.*, pp. 348ff., and especially W. Scott Holland, *The Fourth Gospel* (London: J. Murray, 1923) pp. 45-134.

ber of responsible adherents is that the Fourth Gospel preserves the memories and "witness" of the Apostle John as recorded by the Presbyter John or some other disciples of the Apostle. Among the adherents of this view are Harnack, J. H. Bernard (1928); Wm. Barclay (1955); R. H. Lightfoot (1956); W. F. Albright (1957); and perhaps Edwin Hoskyns (1940); J. A. T. Robinson (1957) and Alan Richardson (1959). The present trend, however, appears neither to affirm or deny apostolic authorship but to ascertain the authority and purpose of the writing as based upon internal evidence. All of these questions have become alive within the last decade largely because of manuscript discoveries in Palestine (at Qumran) and in Egypt, some of which may be contemporary with this Gospel.

### 4. EXTERNAL WITNESSES OF AUTHORSHIP

*Primary Witnesses.* For convenience the witnesses to the authorship and authority may be listed in chronological order. We have manuscript evidence for the Gospel of John which is earlier than any other New Testament book.[71] On paleological grounds the Rylands Papyrus fragment No. 457 has been dated between 125 and 150 A.D.[72] This fragment contains only a portion of the Fourth Gospel (18:31-33,37,38) yet it testifies to the circulation of this Gospel, as part of the New Testament, hence a date toward the end of the first or beginning of the second century. Also, the Egerton Papyrus 2, dated A.D. 140-160 gives evidence for the existence of the Gospel by John at the beginning of the second century.[73]

Among the earliest witnesses to the Fourth Gospel is the Jewish-Christian apocalypse called *Rest of the Words of Baruch* (4 Baruch). Dated by J. Rendal Harris as soon after A.D. 136 because of probable reference to the edict of

Hadrian against the Jews, it contains "unmistakable allusions" to John 1:9.[74] Ignatius of Antioch, writing about 110 A.D., gives evidence of acquaintance with the Gospel by John.[75] In addition to these parallels is the emphasis, common to Ignatius and the Johannine Gospel and Epistles, on Jesus Christ as being in the flesh, a refutation of Doceticism (cf. Ign. *Trall.* 10 and John 1:14; I John 4:2). This would seem as cogent an argument for a similar date as the argument that Galatians and Romans were both written at a time when circumcision and justificaion by faith were live issues. Ignatius of Antioch therefore may well have been dependent on John and hence John available before 100 A.D.[76]

The newly discovered *Jung Codex* of the "Gospel of Truth" is dated by the editors at about A.D. 150.[77] In this Coptic translation of the original Greek "Gospel" there is evidence that the Fourth Gospel was known and, as Quispel says, "was already old and held in high repute."[78] The newly discovered manuscript evidence for the antiquity of the Fourth Gospel cannot be easily dismissed; it greatly reinforces the view of the Gospel's apostolic origin which held undisputed sway among the Church Fathers.

In the same Codex containing the Gospel of Truth is the Gospel of Philip, the composition of the original Greek dated, according to Puech, at about 150 A.D.[79] In this Valentinian Gnostic "Gospel" there are a total of about twelve passages where the influence of the Fourth Gospel is apparent. There are at least two direct quotations from John.[80] There are more allusions to John than to all other books of the New Testament together. The conclusion may be drawn that here is another newly discovered witness to the authority and antiquity of the Fourth Gospel. It witnesses to the acceptance of the Fourth, along with the other three Gospels, as apostolic before the middle of

[71] Alan Richardson, *op. cit.*, p. 17.
[72] C. H. Roberts, "An Unpublished Fragment of the Fourth Gospel," *Bulletin of the John Rylands Library* (1935).
[73] H. I. Bell and T. C. Skeat, *Fragments of the Unknown Gospel* (1935); C. H. Dodd, *Bulletin of the John Rylands Library,* XX (1936), 56-92.
[74] JHB, I, lxxii, 13. Cf. R. H. Charles, *op. cit.*, II, 529.
[75] Cf. Ign. *Mag.*, 7:1 and John 5:19; *Mag.* 8:2 and John 1:1; 8:29; *Philad.* 7:1 and John 3:8; 16:8.
[76] T. E. Pollard, "The Fourth Gospel — Its Background and Early Environment," *Australian Biblical Review,* Dec., 1959, pp. 41-54.
[77] Kendrick Grobel, *The Gospel of Truth* (London: A. & C. Black, 1960), p. 28.
[78] T. E. Pollard, *op. cit.*, p. 43.
[79] H. C. Puech, in Hennecke-Schneemelcher, *NT Apokryphen* (Tübingen, 1959), p. 199. Cited by R. McL. Wilson, *The Gospel of Philip* (New York: Harper & Row, 1962), p. 3.
[80] R. McL. Wilson, *op. cit.*, pp. 33, 60.

the second century. In view of this new evidence the position of Bultmann that the Fourth Gospel is a Gnostic gospel is increasingly untenable.

The new-found Gospel of Thomas is also Gnostic in orientation. It is the second in the thirteen-volume library discovered at Chenoboskion, the first being The Gospel of Truth and the third, The Gospel of Philip. The Gospel of Thomas, which perhaps goes back to the middle of the second century, contains many passages parallel to Matthew and Luke, several parallels to Mark and a few which reflect the influence of John. In common with the Gospel by John it identifies Thomas as "The Twin" (John 11:16; 20: 24; 21:2). Research at the present time is still fluid as to the origin of this work, still undecided as to whether it comes from an independent source or is dependent on the Synoptics. It is significant that the Apostle Thomas is featured only in the Fourth Gospel. "It may be noted that several passages of the *Gospel According to Thomas* are reminiscent of John's doctrine. . . . The parallels with *John*, though fairly numerous, are found only in short formulas."[81] While the Gospel of Philip has more in common with John than with the Synoptics, the opposite is true of the Gospel of Thomas which consists mostly of statements attributed to Jesus, similar to those reported in Matthew and in Luke.

Another witness to apostolic authorship of the Fourth Gospel is the apocryphal Acts of John, dated "not later than the middle of the second century."[82] This work gives details of the Apostle's ministry at Ephesus. It gives evidence that about A.D. 150 Christians believed John spent his last days in Ephesus. All that can be said concerning the present state of investigation (1963) is that we now have additional witnesses to the antiquity and authority of the Fourth Gospel. There are a few witnesses who assert that John the son of Zebedee died a martyr's death along with his brother James, but these are not of sufficient worth to be taken seriously.[83]

Justin, writing about A.D. 150, explains Christian baptism by quoting from John 3:5 and follows it by explaining the nature of the New Birth.[84] His manner of using the text indicates that its apostolic authority was unquestioned. In his argument with Trypho the Jew, Justin refers to the descent of the Spirit on Jesus at his baptism "as the apostles wrote." Justin also quotes from John 1:20-27; "Men supposed him to be the Christ; but he cried to them, 'I am not the Christ, but the voice of one crying; for He that is stronger than I shall come, whose shoes I am not worthy to bear.' " Justin must have had John 1:20-27 in mind when he quoted from what he called "our apostles."[85] Other evidences of Justin's dependence on the Gospel by John include Trypho 63 cf. John 1:13 and Trypho 91 cf. John 3:14, a reference to the brazen serpent. Justin's doctrine of the Logos apparently is indebted to the Fourth Gospel (cf. *Second Apology,* X).

The writings of Melito, Bishop of Sardis (c. A.D. 165), show unmistakable evidence of the influence of John's Gospel (*CKB,* p. 94). The Odes of Solomon, dating from the first half of the second century, contain several parallels of disputed significance; Lagrange has listed five of these parallels. (*MJL,* p. xxviii).

Polycarp, Bishop of Smyrna (c. A.D. 156), quotes I John 4:2-4 almost verbatim in his letter to the Philippians (vii). It is generally recognized that the same person wrote both the Fourth Gospel and the First Epistle of John.[86] According to Irenaeus (c. A.D. 180) Polycarp personally knew the apostle John and learned carefully what he had to say about Jesus.

Even Marcion (c. A.D. 140), who rejected all of the New Testament except Luke and ten letters of Paul, apparently knew the Fourth Gospel. He has passages which closely resemble the wording of John 6:33; 13:34; 15:19. The significance of this is that the Fourth Gospel must have been acknowledged as by the Apostle John as early as A.D. 140 (MJL, p. XLVII).

The earliest exegesis of John's Gospel presently known is that of Ptolemaeus

[81] Jean Doresse, *The Secret Books of the Egyptian Gnostics,* tr. by Philip Maret (New York: The Viking Press, 1960), pp. 339, 342.
[82] M. R. James, *The Apocryphal New Testament* (Oxford: Clarendon Press, 1924), p. 228.
[83] Cf. CKB, p. 87 and JHB, I, xlv.
[84] Justin Martyr, *The First Apology,* lxi., in *Ante-Nicene Fathers* (New York: Scribner's, 1903), I, 183.
[85] Justin Martyr, *Dialogue with Trypho,* 87, *ibid.,* L, 243.
[86] But not by CHD, p. 203.

of the school of Valentinus, the date of which is approximately A.D. 150. He speaks of the Fourth Gospel as having been written by "John the Lord's disciple."[87]

Another early commentary of the Fourth Gospel was that of Heracleon, another Gnostic who flourished in the latter half of the second century. In his comment on John 1:18 he implies that the one who wrote this verse was a disciple of the Lord, i.e., John. He used this Gospel as authoritative Scripture (JHB, I, lxxiii).

Tatian, a disciple of Justin Martyr, composed his harmony of the four Gospels about A.D. 160 (Kruger). In addition to including the Fourth Gospel in his *Diatessaron,* his opening verses are from John. It is certain that he, like his teacher Justin, regarded the Gospel by John as having apostolic authority.

The *Epistle to Diognetus,* dated by Lightfoot at the middle of the second century, indicates in several passages a familiarity with the language and ideas of the Fourth Gospel. The author professes to be a "disciple of the apostles" and uses language which indicates an acceptance of the Johannine Prologue. It also contains some eleven allusions to texts in the Gospel and Epistle.[88]

Melito of Sardis (c. A.D. 165), recognized both Luke and John as equally authoritative as he undertook to harmonize their chronologies (MJIL, p. 2).

The foregoing indicates a recognition of the apostolic authority of the Fourth Gospel which goes back to the first quarter of the second century, i.e., back to Ignatius of Antioch. In addition, the fragments of the Fourth Gospel now extant are earlier than any of the Synoptic Gospels. There seems little room for doubt that the Fourth Gospel was generally acknowledged to be apostolic and authoritative during the entire second century of our era, at least after the first decade. This implies a date of composition several years earlier, well within the first century. This recognition is attested to both by heretics and by the orthodox writers.

*Secondary Witnesses.* The witness of Irenaeus (c. A.D. 180) to the Johannine authorship of the Fourth Gospel is clear and unequivocal. Irenaeus claimed to be a disciple of Polycarp, who in turn was said to be a disciple of "John and others who had seen the Lord."[89] In refuting those who said Jesus died in his thirtieth year Irenaeus appealed to the authority of John: "The Gospel and all the elders testify; those who were conversant in Asia with John, the disciple of the Lord, (affirming) that John conveyed to them that information. And he remained among them up to the times of Trajan. Some of them, moreover, saw not only John, but the other apostles also, and heard the very same account from them."[90] The trustworthiness of this testimony is jeopardized by the context, which seeks to prove that Jesus was about forty years of age when he died.

Later Irenaeus appealed against the heretics to the teaching of the apostle John as related by Polycarp and the church at Ephesus where John resided. Said he, "Polycarp also was not only instructed by apostles, and conversed with many who had seen Christ, but was also, by apostles in Asia, appointed bishop of the church in Smyrna, whom I also saw in my early youth, for he . . . always taught the things which he had learned from the apostles, and which the Church has handed down, and which alone are true . . . . Polycarp . . . caused many to turn away from the aforesaid heretics to the Church of God, proclaiming that he had received this one and sole truth from the apostles, — that, namely, which was handed by the Church. There are also those who heard from him that John, the disciple of the Lord . . . perceived 'Cerinthus . . . the enemy of the truth,' and fled . . . . The Church in Ephesus, founded by Paul, and having John remaining among them permanently until the times of Trajan, is a true witness of the tradition of the Church."[91] Irenaeus also testified to his personal acquaintance with Polycarp, emphasizing that Polycarp had learned the Gospel from "John and with the others who had seen the Lord." Irenaeus fur-

---

[87] Irenaeus, *Adv. Haer.* I. 8. 5.
[88] See K. Lake, ed., *The Apostolic Fathers, Loeb Classical Library* (London: Wm. Heinemann, 1930), II, 348-379.
[89] Eusebius, *Eccl. Hist.* V. xx. 6 (K. Lake, tr. *Loeb Classical Library*) I, 497.
[90] Irenaeus, "Against Heresies," II. xxii. 5; in *Ante-Nicene Fathers,* I, 392.
[91] Irenaeus, *op. cit.,* III. iii. 4; in *op. cit.,* 416.

ther based his authority as a teacher of truth on the claim that he had learned directly from Polycarp who in turn had learned directly from John the apostle. From this we learn the importance of oral tradition in the early church and also of Irenaeus' conviction that the Apostle John lived in Asia until the times of Trajan (A.D. 98-117). Irenaeus adds that after the three Synoptic Gospels had been written, "John the disciple of the Lord, who also had leaned upon His breast, did himself, publish a Gospel during his residence at Ephesus in Asia."[92]

Polycrates, bishop of Ephesus, A.D. 189-198 also believed John lived, died, and was buried in Ephesus: "John, who leaned on the Lord's breast, who was a priest wearing the mitre, and martyr (witness) and teacher, and he sleeps at Ephesus."[93]

Clement of Alexandria (c. A.D. 200) also believed that John the apostle resided at Ephesus until extreme old age as evidenced by his report of an anecdote concerning John's success in winning an outlaw back to the Lord and the Church.[94]

Eusebius (c. 325) accepted and quoted most of this evidence as indicating John's authorship of the "undoubted writings of this Apostle." He states that after John's banishment to Patmos during the persecution under Domitian he came to reside at Ephesus (*Eccl. Hist.*, III, xx. 8). He represents John as living to very old age contemporary with the emperors Domitian, Nerva, and Trajan, and also with Bishops Clement (Rome), Ignatius (Antioch), and Simeon (Jerusalem). This John, he concludes, wrote the Fourth Gospel, "read in all the churches under heaven" as an "undoubted" writing of the Apostle. He explains that it was fourth because the first three lacked something in "persuasive or artistic language" and because he wanted to supplement the material found in the first three, especially at the beginning and the end "of the preaching" (*Eccl. Hist.* III, xiv. 3-8). John began, he says, "with the description of his divinity since this had been reserved for him by the Divine Spirit as for one greater than they," i.e., the

Synoptists. In other words, John was privileged to perform the most important task, that of emphasizing Christ's divinity. He then adds that while the Fourth Gospel and the First Epistle are unquestionably the works of John the Apostle, the Second and Third Epistle and the Apocalypse are not unchallenged and may be the work of another John (*Eccl. Hist.* III, xxiv, 13 —xxv. 3).

Of the objections to these witnesses for John's residence in Asia and authorship of the Gospel none seems to carry much weight except the silence of Ignatius concerning John. This, however, is offset by the fact that Ignatius is concerned, as was John, with Doceticism, and the language is often similar. Parallels in the writings of Ignatius have been noticed in at least twenty verses of the Gospel by John (JHB, I, lxxi).[95]

Papias is said by Irenaeus to have known John but Papias himself denies it (Euseb., *Eccl. Hist.* III, xxxix, 1-3). In his five books he is quoted as saying, "If ever anyone came who had followed the presbyters, I inquired into the words of the presbyters, what Andrew, or Peter or Philip or Thomas or James or John or Matthew, or any other of the Lord's disciples, had said, and what Aristion and the presbyter John, the Lord's disciples, were saying."[96] It appears here either that "presbyter" and "disciple" are synonymous or that the term "disciple" as applied to the first list means something different from the same term associated with the second list. Eusebius interprets Papias as saying that there were two Johns in Asia, one the apostle and the other the Elder, each of whom had a tomb at Ephesus. Eusebius concludes from this that the Presbyter wrote the Apocalypse which carries the name John, but observes that Papias was not a careful or well-informed writer — "he was a man of very little intelligence" (III, xxxix, 13). It seems precarious to conclude on the basis of ambiguous statements of as unreliable a witness as Papias that there were two men of the same name at Ephesus, especially since they were both called disciples by Papias and since Irenaeus knew

[92] Irenaeus, *op. cit.*, III. i. 1; in *op. cit.*, 414.
[93] Cited in Eusebius, *Eccl. Hist.*, III. xxxi. 3.
[94] Clement of Alexandria, *Quis Dives salvetur?*, 42; *Euseb. Eccl. Hist.* III. xxiii. 6-19.
[95] See also WmH, I, 26; CKB, p. 93.
[96] Eusebius, *Eccl. Hist.*, III. xxxix. 4.

of only one John. If the Apostle did write one book rather than both it appears likely that he wrote the Apocalypse and that his secretary penned the Fourth Gospel and First Epistle. Nevertheless, the interpretation of Eusebius, that two men by the name of John lived in Ephesus, one the apostle and the other the presbyter, is not to be discounted. Even if this be true, it is significant that Papias believed, according to Eusebius, that what he learned from "Aristion and the presbyter John, the Lord's disciples" was the authentic teaching of Jesus. Eusebius adds the further note that Papias quotes other of the Lord's sayings reported by Aristion and "John the Presbyter." Aristion may have been one of the many who saw and heard Jesus yet was not among the Twelve.

### D. Summary

(i) The question of authorship is receiving less emphasis recently than questions of date and purpose.

(ii) Largely because of recent manuscript discoveries and a better acquaintance with literary and religious milieu of the first and second centuries, an increasing number of experts are inclined to date the Fourth Gospel within the first century.

(iii) There is an increasing degree of evidence that John's Gospel is not simply the result of long meditation over the more factual reports of the Synoptists; instead it may well come from an independent source or sources. This means that John is even more unique than previously assumed.

(iv) The evidence now seems decisive in favor of a Palestinian origin of the Gospel.

(v) Internal and patristic evidence lead to the conclusion that the Fourth Gospel is the "witness" of the Beloved Disciple, John the son of Zebedee, while the actual writer may have been John the Presbyter or an unnamed disciple. Apostolic authorship of the Gospel and Epistles has not been disproved, however, in any case. Even if the writing was done by another, the reminiscences and the interpretations of them come from the mind and heart of the Apostle. This Apostle, the son of Zebedee, was both a "Son of Thunder" and the meekest of saints. This apparent paradox can be explained on the likelihood that beneath the surface of the Apostle of Love was a fiery nature which abhorred sin, deception, and falsehood. Could this be the same person who sought a seat at Jesus' right hand in the kingdom and wanted to call down fire upon the inhospitable Samaritans? The experiences of the Lord's passion, the power of his resurrection, and the transforming baptism in the Holy Spirit could make a saint out of a "son of thunder." John was like Jesus in that in him was combined an intense love for God and truth with an intense hatred of sin and falsehood. It was Jesus who told of the Father who loved his enemies, sought for lost sinners, and sent the blessing of rain on both deserving and undeserving. It was also Jesus to whom is attributed the most scathing denunciations of sin and hypocrisy to be found in either Old or New Testament (Matt. 23). For this reason "John" could emphasize love of the brethren and warn against loving the world. He could consistently portray sympathetically Jesus' "love-feast" with his disciples (ch. 13-17) and yet be intolerant of heretics (as when he reportedly fled from the bath house after learning of Cerinthus' presence there, and when he forbade hospitality to heretics (II John 11). Was pride his besetting sin?[97] It is doubtful.

One of the most assured results of the massive research concerning the author of this Gospel is that he was a religious genius of first rank. The natural aptitudes of insight, sensitivity, forthrightness, and passion for truth were so inspired by the Spirit of the Lord that the resultant Gospel contains the highest expression of truth in the Bible. It has been well said that Peter left his influence on the church as the chief spokesman for the first millennium and a half, that with the Reformation Paul's influence became dominant and that John's influence will be dominant in the future.[98] It might be more accurate to say that in the post-Reformation age of the Evangelical Awakening (18th-20th centuries) John became the most influential. It is noteworthy that to the leader of this awakening, John Wesley, the favorite book of the Bible was

---

[97] James Stalker, *op. cit.*, p. 80.
[98] *Ibid.*, p. 20.

the First Epistle of John. It has also been observed that on the continent Reformation theology and Pauline influence is dominant. In English-speaking countries the Fourth Gospel came into its own in the twentieth century. Probably the best commentaries on John, certainly the best *modern* commentaries on the Fourth Gospel are by British writers — Plummer, Westcott, Bernard, Howard, Hoskyns, Dodd, Lightfoot and Barrett, to mention a few.

The three greatest apostles of the New Testament are Peter, Paul, and John. In the earliest writings of the New Testament we see the great doctrine of faith which the Apostle Paul was first to articulate. In Peter's influence, as reflected in the Second Gospel and in the Epistles which bear his name, we see the emphasis on hope (I Pet. 1:3-13; 3:15-22; 4:12-5:4). In the Johannine writings the emphasis is upon love. Thus, the three greatest apostles emphasize in sequence faith, hope, and love, "and the greatest of these is love." Both Paul and John were theologians. To Paul was committed the formation of the doctrines of salvation: justification and sanctification. John's task was to provide the doctrines of Christ and of the Holy Spirit and to lay the foundation for the doctrine of the Trinity. Not until the fifth century did the Church catch up to the Fourth Evangelist, correctly termed by Origen, "The Theologian."

## VI. DISTINCTIVE EMPHASES IN JOHANNINE THOUGHT

### A. The Logos

By his introduction to his Gospel, the Evangelist apparently seeks to establish rapport with both his Jewish- and Gentile-oriented readers. The term "Word," or *Logos,* is the word that bridges the gap between these two worlds — the world of the Jew and of the Greek. Nearly six hundred years before the Fourth Gospel was written, Heraclitus of Ephesus (c. 500 B.C.) was saying "All human laws are nourished by the divine law. Though this Word (Logos) — this fundamental law — existeth from all time, yet man-

kind are unaware of it."[99] The famous philosopher thus recognized, in common with the Hebrew prophets, that the world is essentially monistic, that it is a unity, and that basic to all human institutions is a spiritual, all-pervasive principle with which, sooner or later, every man must deal. This principle or law he called the Logos or the Word. The thought of a supreme intellectual principle active in the world was strengthened by Athenagoras who emphasized the transcendence as well as the immanence of this universal principle or Logos.[100] Both Plato and Aristotle thought of the Mind or God as being above the material creation and having no dealings with it since mind and matter cannot merge. The Stoics, as a school of philosophy flourishing between the classical age of Athens and the Christian Era, revived the Logos concept of Heraclitus and made it divine. They believed that the impassible gap between matter and spirit, Creator and creature, God and man is bridged by the Logos, the divine Word. This Logos, said Cicero, is the soul of the world, it pervades the universe as honey fills the honey comb, and links time with eternity.[101] It was believed that man is linked to the gods by reason (*logos*), and that Zeus gives to rational man a part of himself. Later the Stoics distinguished between *logos* as thought (*endiathetos*) and as speech (*prophorikos*) (CHD, p. 263). But at first there was no need to distinguish between thought and the expression of thought. This merging of the two concepts, of thought and word, was habitual among Greek-thinking persons as is reflected in Origen's commentary on the Fourth Gospel.[102] The influence of Stoicism on Alexandrian philosophy is reflected in the idea of Hermes, as the messenger of the gods, who acts as a mediator between the gods and men and was termed the Logos by some thinkers.[103] This concept was the Stoics' answer to the gulf between the Supreme Being and the material universe, and the Platonists accepted it. Passages which at first seem remarkably close to the Prologue of the Gospel, on closer inspection reveal their

[99] Heraclitus, "Fragment," 94. Cited in *Elegy and Iambus*, I, *Loeb Classical Library* (London: Wm. Heinemann).
[100] E. K. Lee, *The Religious Thought of St. John* (London: S.P.C.K., 1950), p. 79.
[101] Cicero, *De Natura Deorum*, II. 20ff.; 45ff.
[102] Origen, *Commentary on John*, 42, cited in *Ante-Nicene Fathers*, IX, 319.
[103] Lee, *op. cit.*, pp. 82f.

dissimilarities. The Stoic Logos is impersonal; in John personal. In Stoicism the Logos is a lesser deity, in John deity itself. In the former the Logos communicates messages from the gods to men; in the latter the Logos becomes flesh and dwells among men. Stoicism retains much of the belief that matter is intrinsically evil; the Gospel does not.

In the writings of the Jewish philosopher Philo (c. 20 B.C.), there is greater affinity with the Fourth Gospel. Philo was closer to John because they shared in common the heritage of the Old Testament. For Philo, the Logos was the medium through which God created and governed the universe; it was both transcendent and immanent (CHD, p. 68). The Logos in Philo is the medium of communication between God and the world. Because man can participate in the Logos of God, he can find immortality.[104] In the Logos God and man can meet. Philo's Platonism is reflected in his idea that the true is not the opposite of the false but rather of the phenomenal.

In Philo the Platonic-Stoic concept of the logos was modified by the Jewish concept of wisdom (Sophia in the LXX). "Philo used the term 'Logos' to express that personalized activity of God in creation and revelation which was represented in later Judaism by the semi-personalized figure of wisdom. With him this term . . . was a bridge to span the gulf between the conception of the absolute and transcendent God of Plato and Aristotle and the idea of the divine immanence which was taught by the Stoics" (WFH, VIII, 452). Philo was not consistent, however; sometimes he wrote that the Logos was "a second God, bridging the begotten and the unbegotten." At other times he said, "He used no assistant (*paraklētos*) — for who was there but himself alone?"[105] Philo's inconsistency was due to his failure to integrate fully his Jewish heritage of monotheism with his philosophical ideas borrowed from the Greeks.[106]

While the parallels with the Fourth Gospel are remarkable, the contrasts are equally so. In John the Logos becomes incarnate, not merely dwelling in men's thoughts but suffering and dying with them. The logos of Philo is never personal (CHD, p. 73).

Bultmann's argument that the source of the Logos idea in John comes from Iranian Gnosticism is unconvincing because of insufficient evidence and because he ends by attributing the distinctive elements in John's use to the influence of the Old Testament (*op. cit.,* pp. 5-19).

In the LXX the *Logos* is the creative agent (Gen. 1:3,6,9; Ps. 33:6,9). This usage is analogous to Jeremiah 1:4; Ezekiel 1:3; and Amos 3:1 — "the word of Jehovah came" — hence revelation and creation are linked by the creative *logos* of God. In the creation story God's word is the same as his act as is true in several of the Psalms (e.g., Ps. 33:4,9; 105:19; 106:12,13). But the *logos* is never personified; it means in the LXX the expression of God's mind.

Closer to the Johannine usage is the concept of "wisdom" (Heb. *hochmah*), especially in Proverbs 8:22,34. Here Wisdom is personified as the one standing beside God and sharing in creation. It is probably the closest known literary parallel to the Johannine usage.[107] The linking of *wisdom* (*hochmah*) with the *word* (*deabar*) is seen in Wisdom 9:1,2 — "O God of the fathers . . . Who madest all things by thy *word;* And by thy *wisdom* thou formedst man." From this O. T. concept therefore John finds in the Logos that which creates the world and reveals God. In addition to this revelation the Logos remains among men in contrast to Wisdom which previously had been so inaccessible (Job 28:12-28; cf. John 1:14).

Part of the O. T. background for the Logos-concept is to be found in the term "Name" (*Memrah*) which often stands for God.[108] But this is never personalized in the LXX and is often over-emphasized as a contributor to the Logos-concept.[109]

Basically, *logos* means the *expression* of a *thought*. Among its varied shades of meaning are these: "word, subject

---

[104] Philo, *De Spec. Leg.* IV. 14.
[105] Philo, *De Opif. Mund.* 6 and *Leg. All.* 2. 86.
[106] Cf. E. M. Sidebottom, *The Christ of the Fourth Gospel* (London: S.P.C.K., 1961), p. 45.
[107] In John 1:4 from the Logos comes first life and then light as in Genesis 1. See also G. Vos, "The Range of the Logos-Name in the Fourth Gospel," *Princeton Theological Review,* Oct., 1913, p. 565.
[108] E.g., Deut. 16:2; cf. Gen. 16:13; Deut. 16:2, 6, 11; 26:2; II Chron. 33:7; Ps. 5:11; Isa. 42:8; Ezek. 20:9; John 17:6, 11; Rev. 19:12, 13.
[109] Sidebottom, *op. cit.,* p. 38.

under discussion, speech, divine revelation, computation, reckoning, reason and logic" (A-G). The Word of God is personalized, not only in John's Prologue but also in Wisdom 18:15 and Revelation 19:12 where the rider of the white horse has a Name which only he knows, "the Word of God."

Thus, there were three precedents for John's use of the term: the creative word of Psalm 33:6 and Genesis 1:2, the personification of Wisdom in Proverbs 3:1, and Philo's impersonal logos. In John the Logos-concept becomes personal and incarnate, a concept strikingly original and unique, but with the main influence from the Old Testament.[110] He took a term meaningful to his readers, both those with a Jewish background and also those with a Greek background, and gave it a new and distinctively Christian connotation. He borrowed an available container and into it placed a new content so that the world might more readily come to believe. Such is the significance of the "Word" as used in the Fourth Gospel.

## B. LIGHT

Since the theme of spiritual "Light" is so prominent in this Gospel an elaboration of it seems indispensable to a proper understanding of the "Spiritual Gospel." The kinship between light and life is everywhere demonstrated in nature. This connection is also present in the creation-hymn of Genesis. As the sun is the light-life of nature, so is the Logos in the world of human beings. God is likened to light several times in the O. T.[111] Physically light connotes "splendor" or "glory"; intellectually it connotes "truth"; morally it connotes "holiness." The implication here is that holiness is God's nature and that his nature is to impart this quality to believing men.

In Genesis, God is the source of all things, including light — "God said, 'Let there be light'" (Gen. 1:3). In the accounts of the wilderness sojourn and in the temple God's presence was represented by OR ("light") with a variety of meanings ranging from the light of the sun to "lightning" (Job 36:32), "dawn" (Job 24:14), "spiritual illumination" (Ps. 43:

3), the "law" (Prov. 6:23; Ps. 119:105), the "light of life" (Ps. 56:14), the "light of the Lord" (Isa. 2:5). Thus the meaning of physical illumination from the sun passes readily into the metaphysical and metaphorical meaning of mental and spiritual illumination and truth. The concepts of light and life are often joined in the Old Testament also: "I may walk before God in the light of the living" (ARVm — life Ps. 56:13); "with thee is the fountain of life; in thy life shall we see light" (Ps. 36:9).

There is a Messianic meaning attached to some of these Old Testament passages in which the concept of light occurs, and it will be important to examine them for a clue to a possible Messianic connotation in Jesus' assertion at the passage in question. Passages in which the Messianic significance is recognized by a New Testament writer include Isaiah 9:2, where the child-king's birth dispels the environing darkness (Isa. 5:30; 8:22) and Isaiah 42:6; 49:6 (Acts 13:47) where the "servant of the Lord" will be a "light to the Gentiles." In Isaiah 60:1-3 the nation is told, "Thy light is come," and as a consequence it is to be a center of light to which the nations shall be attracted. Elsewhere the latest of the prophets refers to the Messianic hope as "sun of righteousness" (Mal. 4:2).

Obviously the sun in the solar system is both the source of life and light. Likewise Jehovah is recognized as the source of light and life in such passages as Isaiah 60:20 — "Jehovah will be thy everlasting light."[112] In the Bible, however, the Creator and creation are clearly distinguished so that God is spoken of as replacing the sun (Isa. 60:19; Rev. 22:5. cf. Rev. 1:16). The Bible writers, while never giving a suggestion of sun-worship, nevertheless made bold to use the metaphor freely in the midst of sun-worshippers.

Parallels with other religious ideas of the Near East are numerous. In Platonic thought, the sun is the intermediary being which "links sight and visibility";[113] In other words, the eye, unlike the ear, cannot function without "a third nature" (genos), which is light. The sun, as Plato

---

[110] See Eric May, "The Logos in the Old Testament," CBQ, Oct., 1946, pp. 334-347.
[111] E.g., Ps. 4:6; 27:1; 37:6; 43:3; Isa. 2:5; 60:1, 3, 19, 20; Mic. 7:8.
[112] Likewise Ps. 27:1; cf. Ex. 13:21, 22.
[113] Plato, Republic, VI, 508, a, I, J. Burnet, ed. (Oxford: University Press, 1938).

noted, gives life as well as light and yet is distinct from both.[114] So likewise "the Good" is distinct from knowledge, from being, and from essence (*physis*) and yet is indispensable to them all. Seen thus the Christ is the link which unites the believer to God as the sunlight links the viewer and the view. To Plato, however, reason (*noēsis*) is the highest faculty; to John it is faith (*pistis*).

It is from Plato, thinks C. H. Dodd (who perhaps more than any other has explored the ramifications of these ideas in the contemporary culture of the Near East) that the thinkers of the Hellenistic world derived the religious symbolism of light. Or at least they rationalized their mythology with the help of Plato (CHD, p. 202).

Philo, commenting on Psalm 27:1, says God is not only light but the archetype (*archetypos*) of light, indeed He is prior to all archetypes.[115] In John the "archetype" might be compared to God the Father (cf. I John 1:9 — "God is light") while the Messiah himself would be comparable to the light (John 1:4-9). The "true light" (John 1:9 — *phōs to alēthinon*) would, contrary to Dodd, be not the archetype but rather the light which reveals truth, or the real light as distinct from the false.[116] In John we encounter the simple moral dualism between light and darkness rather than the metaphysical dualism between mind and matter, or the plurality of hierarchies, as in Gnosticism.

The same may be said for the Essenes of Jesus' day as reflected in the literature of the Qumran community. There the antagonism between light and darkness is even more pronounced than in John. Among the Covenanters of the Dead Sea Scrolls, there is the stern and absolute tension between light and darkness viewed in an eschatological context. The Hebraism of the Fourth Gospel is now much more obvious, in the light of these scrolls, than when Dodd and Barrett were writing their superb volumes on John. The significance of the scrolls for Johannine studies is that they confirm the position of scholars like W. F. Howard, reflecting a reaction away from the Hellenistic to the Hebraic background of this Gospel.[117] The Brethren of Qumran called themselves "Sons of Light" and considered all others "Children of Darkness" (IQS i,9; iii, 13,24; War IQM i,3). They comprised an army of salvation ready to fight in the apocalyptic battle of the last days against the Children of Darkness. The chief difference between this literature and the Fourth Gospel is that the men of Qumran had no Messiah, no one whom they acknowledged as the "Light of the world." It is understandable that John, writing in the first century, would be alert to acknowledge in Christ the "true light" which illuminates everyone in the world. In a world longing for "light" or assurance of salvation, of belonging to the divine, Jesus' message, as reported by the Fourth Evangelist, made the grandest claims in the simplest language. The message was couched in terms universally meaningful, throughout the solar system.

The theme of light is prominent both in John's Gospel and in the First Epistle. In the Gospel, as in the book of Genesis, it is introduced "in the beginning" (John 1:4-9) as the "true light" which brings life to all believing men. The linking of this light with judgment is elaborated in 3:17-21 where one of the main theses of the Gospel is stated: "men loved darkness rather than light." This theme is resumed in 8:12 in the declaration that Jesus is the "Light of the world." The following chapter is an object-lesson in the consequences of accepting — and rejecting — this Light. The necessity of walking in the light is mentioned casually in 11:9, 10; (cf. I John 1:7) and pressed home with vigor in the summation of Jesus' challenge at the close of the public ministry (12:46-50) where it is again linked with judgment — with life and death.

The Greek word "to judge" (*krinein*) means "to separate," or "to discriminate." It is usually used to translate the Hebrew *shaphat* which means "to decide," "to judge," "to establish, or govern" and "to condemn."[118] The recognition of Jesus Christ as the Light of the world, along with the related ideas of judgment (*krisis*)

---

[114] *Ibid.*, 509, b, l.
[115] Philo, *De Somn.*, 1. 75.
[116] Dodd does not think the author of the Gospel is the author of I John (CHD, pp. xlvii-lvi).
[117] W. F. Howard, *Christianity According to St. John* (Philadelphia: Westminster, 1946), p. 30.
[118] Cf. Gen. 19:9; I Sam. 3:13; 8:20.

and hence the issues of life and death, is one of the cardinal ideas of this Gospel and a key to an understanding of its message.

## C. LIFE

Probably the one most important word in John's Gospel (other than names of deity) is the word "Life." It is more basic than "love" for love cannot exist without life. John's emphasis on belief is important only as a means to an end: this end is life (John 20:31). The importance of Christology in Johannine thought is heightened by the affirmation that life is equated with Jesus Christ (John 14:6) for "in him was life" (1:4; I John 4:11, 12).

John built on the Jewish concept of life inherited from the Old Testament. This concept was that of physical life and well-being, except in Daniel 2:2 where the term "eternal life" occurs. Originally the Greek *aeon* and its Hebrew equivalent *olam* indicated an indefinitely long rather than an infinite period, the indefinite prolongation of the present life (CHD, p. 144). In the intertestamental age and later, the rabbis distinguished "this age" from the "age to come," a contrast not only in time but in quality.[119] Later Jewish usage therefore distinguished simple "life," as contrasted with death, from "life of the age to come."

In New Testament Greek three words were employed to convey the idea of life. Physical life, shared by humans and animals, was expressed by *bios,* from whence comes the term "biology."[120] Included in the connotations of this term are *duration* (I Pet. 4:3), *source* (Mark 12:44), and *manner* (I Tim. 2:2).

The second word is *zōē.* In classical Greek *bios* had an ethical quality which *zōē* lacked, but in the New Testament it is reversed; *bios* becomes life on a lower level, and it is *zōē* which has the ethical connotation. In the New Testament *zōē* connotes all that is highest and best in the association of the saints with God.[121] It it this term which is usually associated by contrast with death. The ethical content of *zōē* derives from the fact that it is the opposite of death. Since, in the Bible, death is linked with sin, life implies victory over sin and freedom from its power (RCT, pp. 29f.). The term thus often means spiritual life.

The third synonym for life is *psychē* (ψυχή). Its meanings are complex. These include (i) the animating principle in physical organisms (Gen. 9:4; Acts 20:10; Luke 12:20; (ii) earthly life as distinct from spiritual life (Matt: 20:28; Mark 10:45; John 10:11,15,17; 13:37; Rev. 12: 11); (iii) the soul as center of the inner life that transcends the earthly (Matt. 16: 26; Mark 8:37; II John 2); (iv) that which possesses life (I Cor. 15:45; Rev. 16:3; I Pet. 3:20) (A-G). The contrast between *psyche* and *zōē*, both of which are translated "life," is well illustrated in John 12:25: "he that loves his life (*ho philōn tēn psychēn*) shall forfeit it, but he that hates his life (*psychēn*) shall keep it unto life eternal (*zōēn aiōnion*)." The choice of the synonyms cannot be accidental; the latter speaks of a higher type of life than the former (cf. Luke 12:15,22).

It is in the concept of eternal life that John's contribution is most distinctive and important. In the LXX the term "eternal" (*aiōnios*) occurs some 150 times and usually means "age-lasting" rather than "endless."[122] In Daniel life is said to be eternal (Dan. 7:14; 12:2). The rabbis believed that eternal life comes as a result of obedience to the Torah or Law; a belief to which Jesus gave conditional endorsement (John 5:39), the condition being that it be recognized that the source of life is not in the writings *per se* but in Him of whom the Scriptures bear witness. The rabbis thought of eternal life in quantitative terms, in terms of duration. The contribution of the Fourth Gospel is that life eternal is thought of in qualitative terms, not merely as a continuation but rather as a superior quality of life which begins in the believer now (John 5:24-26; 6:54; 17:3).[123] In the account of Lazarus the popular conception of a general resurrection is contrasted with Jesus' teaching concerning a spiritual resurrection in Christ (11:24-26). The point seems to be that "eternal life"

---

[119] Enoch 48:7; cf. 71:15; IV Esdras 7:12, 13; 8:52, 54.
[120] Cf. Luke 8:14, 43; 15:12, 30; 21:4; I John 2:16; 3:17; I Tim. 2:2.
[121] E.g., Matt. 7:14; Rom. 5:17; Eph. 4:18; II Tim. 1:10; II Pet. 1:3; Rev. 2:10; 21:6.
[122] E. K. Lee, *op. cit.,* p. 196.
[123] G. B. Stevens, *The Johannine Theology* (New York: Scribner's, 1900), pp. 319-324.

is not a matter of time alone but is a new kind of life, different in nature, which, if begun here through faith, will last on after the dissolution of the body. Unlike the teaching of the Sadducees, it was more than physical life; unlike the Greek notion, it was not an intrinsic quality of the soul; unlike the idea of Philo it was more than timelessness; rather it was "life from above," from God, and given only through Christ (John 3:5; 5:26; I John 5:19); cf. CHB, pp. 146-150. This life becomes available to the believer as he enters into an experiential "knowledge" of God through the Son (John 17:3; I John 3:14; 5:11,12). The issues of life and death are settled not simply as a final day of reckoning, therefore, but are determined momentarily according as one believes or disbelieves (5:24).

## D. LOVE

"Love" is one of the most important words in the vocabulary of the New Testament and especially in that of the Beloved Disciple. The concept of "love" is a characteristic emphasis in both the Gospel and the First Epistle of John. While the trilogy of faith, hope, and love is characteristically Pauline, it may be said of John that a corresponding trilogy is life, light, and love (I John 1:2,5; 2:5).

Of the three Greek words for love, the noun *eros,* and the verbs *phileō* and *agapaō,* the former is predominant in classical Greek, and the latter in the New Testament. Perhaps the three English words which most nearly approximate the meaning of these Greek terms respectively are, infatuation, friendship, and love.

It is significant that *eros* does not occur in the New Testament. In classical Greece sensuous songs were sung in honor of the sensual, demonic deity Eros. This god was uncontrollable and yet all-controlling; the ultimate in religious ecstasy was to lose one's self-control in maddening devotion to this deity with fertility rites which often included sacred prostitution.[124] In its higher levels of expression Eros was regarded as the urge by which the individual could merge his individuality

with the divine in something akin to mysticism.[125] Although the term is not used in the New Testament, Ignatius used it in language borrowed from St. Paul — "my passionate love (for material things) has been crucified."[126]

The term for friendship, affection of gods for men or men for each other, is usually *philein* or *philia* in pre-Biblical Greek. It is the normal love experienced by humanity, a natural, spontaneous affection which can be offered but not commanded. Occasionally in the LXX it is the translation of the Hebrew *aheb.* In the literature of pre-Christian Judaism, however, it tends, like *eros,* to disappear. In the New Testament it occurs occasionally, sometimes used almost synonymously with *agapaō.* Its normal N. T. usage is to express affection among men, as when Jesus is described as a friend of publicans and sinners and as one who loved Lazarus (John 11:3,36) and John (John 20:2). *Phileō* means "to love," "to be friendly to one" (Matt. 10:37; John 5:20; 15:19; 16:27; I Cor. 16:22; Rev. 3:19— JHT, p. 653). It also means "to kiss" (Gen. 27:26; Matt. 26:48; Mark 14:44; Luke 22:47; and "often in Greek writers" —JHT). Places where this term appears to be used interchangeably with *agapaō* include John 14:23; 16:27b; 21:15-17 (A-G). In the Vulgate it was regularly translated by *amo*: "to love from inclination or passion" (rather than by *diligere* which means "to love from esteem"), a term which apparently combined the meanings of the two Greek terms *eros* and *philia, phileō.*[127]

The noun *agapē* was a colorless word in secular Greek and very seldom used.[128] This word (verb and noun forms) was chosen by the translators of the Old Testament rather than *eros* because the latter was associated with sexual practices. In the LXX, therefore, *agapaō* and *agapē* are regularly used to translate the Hebrew term *ahabah,* which stands for the Election-love which led Jehovah to select Israel from all the nations (Deut. 7:7,8; Exod. 33:19; Jer. 31:20).[129] The other Hebrew term for

---

124 G. Quell & S. Stauffer, Love: *Bible Key Words* from TWNT.
125 Cf. Plato, *Symposium,* 211; *Phaedrus,* 55; Dio Chrys. *Or.* xii. 60.
126 Ignatius, *Ep. to the Romans* VII. 2; cf. Gal. 6:14.
127 J. R. V. Marchant & J. F. Charles, *Cassell's Latin Dictionary* (New York: Funk and Wagnalls, n.d.), p. 35.
128 Only three known occurrences — M-M, p. 2; A-G, p. 5.
129 Stauffer, *Agapaō,* in TWNT.

love is *chesed* which denotes the Covenant-love of God which led him to favor his chosen people in spite of their repeated apostasies (Jer. 31:3; Hos. 2: 19).[130] This term is usually translated by the Greek *eleos,* meaning "mercy." In the Septuagint the Hebrew *chen* ("favor") was rendered normally by *charis* ("grace"). In the New Testament, the LXX meanings of "steadfast love" (RSV) and "favor" combine to designate God's favor or grace given to undeserving man freely. In John 3:16, I John 4:9 and elsewhere the Covenant-love which led God to choose and bestow favor upon Israel is extended to the entire world. Thus the O. T. "limited atonement" becomes the N. T. "universal atonement," not in the sense of being unconditioned but rather in being conditioned only upon man's acceptance of this free gift of life in the Son.

The Hebrew term *ahabah* combines something of all three Greek terms for love except the element of religious eroticism, which characterized not only Greek religion but the surrounding fertility cults in Canaan as well.[131] In contrast to *eros, agapē,* as the LXX rendering of *ahabah,* is not undiscriminating, undisciplined, and promiscuous but selective, deliberate, and steadfast — the exact opposite. It is a jealous love like that of a true marriage bond rather than of promiscuous mating; it is a love which involves self-giving, self-sacrifice. At its best, *eros* is a man's quest for the divine while *agapē,* at its best, is God's love for man, for those of low degree.

*Agapaō* and *agapē,* because of usage as well as spelling, seem to have been derived from two Greek words: *agan* meaning "very much" and *paos,* meaning a relative or "kinsman." (The last consonant of *agan* was dropped since *paos* began with a consonant.) The word thus derived beautifully expresses the N. T. concept of Christian love — to treat others as beloved kin. Similarly, we are to think of God as a dearly beloved Heavenly Father and obey him as such (I John 5:3). We are likewise to regard fellow Christians as spiritual brothers and sisters and serve with them as such. This connotation of *agapaō* survives in modern Greek.[132] Similar to this is Philo's use of *agapaō*: "These have learned to kiss it, not to like it (*philein*), but those to love (*agapān*) it exceedingly and to consider it most desirable"; also, "Love (*agopaō*) God and obey and cleave to him."[133] *Agapē* is a love which can be commanded; it includes the element of choice. It is the normal term, especially in the New Testament, to describe love in which volition is involved, such as God's love for man.[134] The element of proving one's love by deeds is also an important element in this term (Test. Gad 6:1; I Clem. 15:4; cf. John 13:1,34; I John 3: 19). The element of choice, constancy, sacrifice seems rather characteristic of the word. The Vulgate rendering of this term is consistent with the foregoing. It is translated by *diligere* which means "to choose; to prize, love, esteem highly."[135]

The extent to which *phileō* and *agapaō,* as used in the N. T., are synonymous is a matter of dispute. One of the most thorough and objective treatments is that of Wm. Hendriksen, who concludes there is a slight distinction in the meaning as used in John's Gospel, particularly in chapter twenty-one (Wm. H, II, 494-500). The trend appears to lie in the direction of minimizing the distinctions formerly held. Bernard, after listing many passages in which the terms appear to be used without distinction, observes that in John 21:17 the author says Jesus had asked the third time whether Peter loved (*phileis*) him, whereas the two previous questions had used *agapaō* as if synonymous (*op. cit.,* II, 703). Other evidences cited to support this position are that the Syriac versions made no distinction and also that Peter's answer was regarded as affirmative even though he used a different word in his reply. These last two reasons are less than convincing. More

[130] N. P. Snaith, *Distinctive Ideas of the Old Testament* (Philadelphia: Westminster Press, 1946), p. 223.
[131] Quell and Stauffer, *op. cit.,* p. 32.
[132] As defined by a Greek university graduate this term describes the love which leads a man to take a wife and be willing to sacrifice for her.
[133] Philo, *Who is Heir to Divine Things,* sec. 8 and *Posterity of Cain,* sec. 4.
[134] E.g., Rom. 8:37; 9:13; John 14:21; cf., Test. Naph. 8:4, 10; Test. Benj. 3:1; 4:5; I Clem. 56:4; Shep. Herm. 9, 12, 5.
[135] Marchant & Charles, *op. cit.,* p. 172.

plausible is the judgment that other synonyms in the chapter appear to be used without distinction, such as words for "feed" (A-G). Barrett, agreeing with this conclusion, notes that both terms are applied to the Beloved Disciple and that both words occur in Proverbs 8:17, LXX, as translations of *ahebh* (CKB, p. 486).

There seems to be little doubt that the terms are often used synonymously. It does not necessarily follow, however, that no distinction is discernible. In the overall background and N. T. usage there does seem to be a valid distinction such as that reflected in the Vulgate. Such a distinction, to recapitulate, includes the following: (i) *agapaō* never means to kiss, *phileō* does (Gen. 27:26; Matt. 26: 48 *et al.*); (ii) *phileō* is used of Jesus' love for Lazarus (John 11:3,36) and *agapaō* of his love for the family (John 11:5); (iii) For ordinary human friendship and affection the *normal* term to use is *phileō* (Matt. 10:37; Titus 3:15; cf. Matt. 11:19; Luke 7:34) — Jesus was scornfully called a "friend (*philos*) of sinners"; (iv) The love connoted by *phileō* is spontaneous and involuntary while *agapaō* indicates a love that arises from discrimination, esteem and choice; hence God loves (*agapaō*) the world (John 3:16) but his children are not to love (*phileō*) the things pertaining to this life (John 12:25; but cf. I John 2:15). Disciples are commanded to love (*agapaō*) their enemies as well as their friends (Matt. 5:44); (v) Normally God's love for man and man's love for God is expressed by *agapaō* while *phileō* usually describes man's love for his fellowmen, thus the greatest commandment employs the former term (Luke 10:27); (vi) *agapaō* calls for a response from the entire being — body, mind and soul — while the other term has the more limited emotional connotation; (vii) influenced by the LXX, Origen concluded "*agapan* is the more divine and, so to speak, the more spiritual meaning, but *philein* is bodily and savours of men;"[136] John can affirm "God is love" (*agapē*) but it would seem inappropriate to use the other synonym in such a context because the former is more universal, the latter more particular.

It seems that Cremer is essentially correct in concluding that "*philein* denotes the love of natural inclination, affection, — love, so to say, originally spontaneous, involuntary (*amare*); *agapan*, on the other hand, has the direction of will, *diligere*" (Cremer, p. 11). With particular reference to John 21:15-17 the observation of Moulton and Milligan seems sustained by the evidence surveyed: "In so severely simple a writer as John it is extremely hard to reconcile ourselves to a meaningless use of synonyms, where the point would seem to lie in the identity of the word employed" (*op. cit.*, p. 2). The use of *agapaō* and *agapē* in the LXX and especially in the New Testament is another conspicuous example of a colorless word becoming the supreme vehicle of a fresh divine revelation. "In John especially the world of light and love break through into this world in the form of love."[137]

### E. THE HOLY SPIRIT

It may be said that in the present generation the doctrine and experience of the Holy Spirit has been receiving more attention than in most other generations. It has been stated with considerable insight that the current emphasis on the Spirit-filled life among many Christian groups constitutes a third major group in Protestantism, the other two groups being the liberals and the conservatives. The doctrine of the Spirit is one of the most distinctive features of John's Gospel. It was not without cause that Clement of Alexandria called this "The Spiritual Gospel."

In chs. 1-12 of John's Gospel the Holy Spirit is primarily the source of divine *life*. Jesus was anointed by the Holy Spirit (1:32), and thus John the Baptist was able to recognize him as the Lord's anointed, the Christ, the Messiah. The Holy Spirit is also mentioned as the one by whom divine life is given to the believer. Animal life can only reproduce its own kind; spiritual life must come from above, from God (3:5); hence the Spirit is the regenerative principle in human life.[138] Worship of the true God, who is

[136] Cited by E. A. Abbott, *op. cit.*, p. 434.
[137] Quell & Stauffer, *op. cit.*, p. 62.
[138] H. B. Swete, *The Holy Spirit in the New Testament* (London: Macmillan, 1910), p. 351.

a spiritual Being, is impossible apart from the Spirit of God (cf. 4:25). The Spirit is linked with life, not only by way of water, but also by way of Jesus' words.[139] In contrast to food which nourishes only the physical phase of life, the Spirit nourishes the divine life through the words of Jesus — "It is the spirit that giveth life . . . the words that I have spoken unto you are spirit, and are life" (6:63). The Spirit provides not only life on the level of the divine but also causes that life to flourish and flow out (7:38). This is a mirraculous gift of life, comparable to the water which gushed out in the desert of Sinai (Exod. 17:6) and to the river of life which was predicted to emerge from the temple area and fill the Arabah with fresh water teeming with life (cf. Ezek. 47:1-12). Thus the "book of signs" (chs. 2-12) presents the Holy Spirit as the source, the nature, and the center of divine life.

### 1. THE ADVOCATE

In chs. 13-20 the Spirit is designated as the *Paraklētos,* a term in contrast to *katēgoros,* the accuser. One way of ascertaining the meaning of a term is to define its antonym. The term *katēgoros* is used seven times in the N. T.; in John 8:10; 12:31; Revelation 12:10; Acts 23: 30,35; 25:16,18 (TWNT, cf. M-G). The accuser is man in most of these instances, as when the Jews sent an accuser to Caesarea to testify against Paul. He served as a prosecuting attorney. Only in Revelation 12:10 is "the accuser of the brethren" a malignant spirit, in this case Satan. In contrast to this is the Paraclete who stands as the accuser of the world according to John 16:8-11, although a different word for "accuse" is used here (*elengchō*); "he will confute the world, and show where wrong and right and judgment lie. He will convict them of wrong" (NEB).[140]

Among N. T. books, the term *paraklētos* is found only in John (John 14:16,26; 15:26; 16:7; I John 2:1). There is no English equivalent of the term, or rather there are several, no one of which takes in the full meaning. In the LXX the cognate verb (*parakaleō*) is used several times in the general meaning of calling to one's

side with the view of giving comfort. The comfort may be human (Job 2:10; 29:25; II Kings 10:2) or divine (Isa. 57:18; Job 21:34 — TWNT). The term is frequent in the N. T. but neither this term nor the noun *paraclēsis* ("comfort, consolation") appears in this Gospel. The synonym *synēgoros* was a loan word with the rabbis and means "advocate in the sense of attorney." (S-B, II, 560-562).

In the N. T. the verb *parakaleō* occurs frequently (except in Johannine writings) and has at least five meanings: (i) "to call to one's side or to summon," (ii) "to appeal, to urge, exhort, encourage," (iii) "to request, implore, entreat," (iv) "to comfort, encourage, cheer up," and (v) "to console or conciliate" (A-G). Of these the primary meaning is to "call along side," the other meanings being derivative. The noun *paraklēsis* means (i) "encouragment or exhortation" (ii) "appeal or request" and (iii) "comfort or consolation" (A-G).

In the LXX the cognate verb form *parakalein* appears 138 times; in 61 of these it is used to translate the Hebrew term (*nachim*) for "comfort or console."[141] Both Davies and Barrett conclude that the meaning of *parakletos* is to be sought in the verb *parakaleō.* The former concludes that the basic meaning is "comfort," the latter decides that "exhortation" is basic.[142] The point made by Davies is that although the form in John is passive — "one called to the side of" — the major factor in interpretation is that the contexts in both LXX and the Fourth Gospel, specifically Isaiah 40-66 and John 14-16, are sufficiently similar to warrant the conclusion that "comfort" is the dominant meaning (cf. Isa. 66:13; John 16: 22). Although originally passive in form, the active meaning of "comforter" seems the meaning in John, Davies concludes. Agreeable to this conclusion of Davies is the statement, "In our literature the active sense of helper, intercessor is suitable in all occurrences of the word" (A-G, p. 626). Mandean parallels lead Bultmann also to the conclusion that "Helper" is the best equivalent. This is the term chosen by J. B. Phillips for his translation of the New Testament. The New English Bible has "Advocate."

[139] John 6:63; cf. 3:5; 4:14; 7:38, 39.
[140] Cf. Luke 6:7; John 18:29; I Tim. 5:19; Titus 1:6.
[141] J. G. Davies, "The Primary Meaning of ΠΑΡΑΚΛΗΤΟΣ," JTS, IV, Part I. (April, 1953), pp. 35ff.
[142] C. K. Barrett, "The Holy Spirit in the Fourth Gospel," JTS (1950) Vol. I, Part 1, pp. 1-16.

The word "comfort" has now become ambiguous. It comes from the Latin *cum fortis* ("with strength") and had this connotation in English when Wycliffe used it in his translation. In modern English, however, it has the connotation of "console" more than of "strengthen." Too much, however, should not be made of these distinctions, for that which strengthens at the same time consoles.

All have agreed that the primary meaning in John is "advocate." Latin translators rendered it "advocatus."[143] In the context which is least ambiguous, the Johannine meaning is clearly that of "Advocate" (I John 2:1). The meaning of advocate or defense counsel is clear in several passages in the Synoptics and Acts where the Holy Spirit assists the believer in the defense of this faith.[144] In John also the prediction of excommunication from the synagogues is followed immediately by the assurance that the Paraclete will be at the believer's side accusing the world of sin, righteousness, and judgment (16:1-13). There seems good reason, therefore, both from Johannine usage in Gospel and Epistle and the work of the Spirit in the Synoptics and Acts, to consider the basic meaning of the term as "Helper," with Bauer (*op. cit.,* pp. 182f.) and Bultmann (*op. cit.,* 437-440), "Intercessor" (cf. Rom. 8:26,27), and "Advodate." "*Paraklētos* is properly a forensic term."[145] The Paraclete in these passages is an Advocate and a Helper because he assists in thought and utterance in times of emergency. This is the same role Jesus played during his ministry. While the term includes the meanings of Comforter, Intercessor, and Helper, the basic meaning, and one which includes the others, appears to be Advocate. Deissmann suggests that this meaning was probably initiated by Paul (Rom. 8:26-34), developed in the Gospels (Mark 13:11; Matt. 10:20; Luke 12:12) and "grew to full maturity and received classical formulation in the Johannine writings" (*loc. cit.*). Many translators have fol-

lowed the precedent of the Vulgate in translating the term "Advocate" at I John 2:1 and paraphrasing rather than translating it where the term occurs in the Gospel. The picture of an attorney or counsel appears to best describe the primary function of the Paraclete as given in John and elsewhere in the N.T. since an Advocate also helps and intercedes and in so doing brings comfort, strength and consolation. This is a more active mediatorial role than is conveyed by "Comforter."

In this Gospel five distinct Paraclete passages have been identified by Hans Windisch, supported by W. F. Howard.[146] These five are identified as (i) John 14:15-17; (ii) 14:25,26; (ii) 15:26,27; (iv) 16:5-11 and (v) 16:12-15. Actually these are only four in number since 16:5-15 is a literary unit: the antecedents of the personal pronoun "he" in vv. 8, 13 go back to the Paraclete mentioned in v. 7. Therefore with Barrett and Dodd it seems best to conclude that there are four, rather than five, distinct references to the Paraclete in the Gospel (plus one in the Epistle).

14:16 — "He shall give you another Paraclete . . . the Spirit of Truth."

15:26 — "The Paraclete, even the Holy Spirit, whom the Father will send in my name."

15:26 — "When the Paraclete is come, whom I will send unto you for the Father, even the Spirit of Truth which proceedeth from the Father."

16:7-13 — "If I go not away the Paraclete will not come unto you; but if I go, I will send him unto you . . . . when he, the Spirit of Truth is come."

I John 2:1 — "We have an Advocate with the Father, Jesus Christ the Righteous."

## 2. THE SPIRIT OF TRUTH

Three times in this Gospel the Holy Spirit is equated with the "Spirit of Truth,"

[143] Tertullian, *Prax*, 9; Cyprian, *De Domin. Orat.* 3; Novation, *De Trin.* 28.
[144] Matt. 10:20; Luke 12:12; Acts 4:8, 31; 6:8; 13:9; Mark 13:11.
[145] CHD, p. 414. In support of this see H. W. Swete, *op. cit.,* p. 149; II, 188.; Liddell & Scott, *Lexicon;* A. Deissmann, LAE, 336; W. F. Howard, *Christianity According to St. John,* pp. 74f., RHS, p. 285.
[146] WFH, p. 72-79. Windisch endeavors to show that these five sayings form a unity and could be removed from the respective contexts without injury to the Gospel as a whole. Without these sayings a return of Christ is taught; by their inclusion the coming of the Spirit is substituted for the return to Christ. H. Windisch, "Five Johannine Sayings About the Paraclete" in *Festgabe,* for Adolf Jülicher (Tübingen, 1927). See S. Schulz, *Untersuchungen zur Menschon-christologie im Johannesevangelium* (Göttingen: Vandenhoeck & Ruprecht, 1957), p. 150.

and only in John is the Holy Spirit thus designated among N. T. books.[147] The term is comparable to the "spirit of righteousness" which, according to Jubilees 25:14, inspired Rebecca as she blessed her son Jacob.[148] A closer parallel is found in the New Testament of the Twelve Patriarchs (c. 115 B.C.) where the divine Spirit is called the Spirit of Truth (*pneuma tēs alētheias*).[149] It reads "Two spirits wait upon man — the spirit of truth and the spirit of deceit . . . . (*to tēs alētheias kai tēs planēs*) And the spirit of truth testifieth all things, and accuseth all" (*to pneuma tēs alētheias martyrei kai katēgorei pantōn*).[150] The parallel to John 16:13 and I John 4:6 is very remarkable, especially to the latter — "the spirit of truth and the spirit or error" — *to pneuma tēs alētheias kai to pneuma tēs planēs*. While in John 16:8 the Spirit "convicts (*elengchei*) the world," in Test. Jud. the Spirit "accuses" (*katēgorei*) all (cf. Rev. 12:10).

The Dead Sea Scrolls (c. 125 B.C. — A.D. 50) afford even more remarkable parallels to the idea of the Spirit of Truth, viz., The "Spirit of Truth" and the "Spirit of Error" or deceit. The term "Holy Spirit," which occurs only three times in the O. T. (Ps. 51:13; Isa. 63:10, 11; cf. LXX, Exod. 31:3), and seven times in the Apocrypha, occurs some twenty times in the Qumran literature published before 1960. This compares with the eighty-eight times the terms occur in the N. T. Thus the Scrolls may be viewed as a literary and ideological link between Old and New Testaments, at least with respect to the doctrine of the Spirit. In the Manual of Discipline (IQS) the "Spirit of Truth," the "Spirit of Knowledge," the "Holy Spirit," the "Fountain of Light," the "Prince of Lights," the "Angel of his Truth" are terms used almost synonymously. As with the rabbinic doctrine of the "Evil Imagination" (*yetzer hara*), God is represented as the Creator of these two opposing spirits and man is continually subject to one or the other of them, depending upon his personal reaction to them (cf. Gal. 5:17; Rom. 8:5).

"Between the two categories God has set an eternal enmity. Deeds of perversity are an abomination to Truth, while all the ways of Truth are an abomination to perversity; and there is a constant jealous rivalry between their two regimes, for they do not march in accord. Howbeit, God in His inscrutable wisdom has appointed a term for the existence of perversity, and when the time of Inquisition comes, He will destroy it for ever. Then truth will emerge triumphant."[151] The destiny of each individual, at the final judgment, will be determined by his choice of which of the two spirits he will follow.

The source of the truth is the "Fountain of Light" under the dominion of the "Prince of Lights" while the "Angel of Darkness" dominates those who walk perversely. The "sons of light" are helped by the "Angel of Truth." God will sprinkle upon man "the spirit of truth" to cleanse him from "abominations of falsehood" and sin (IQS *passim*). A Qumran poet prayed thus: "I would put into words . . . my constant search for Thy spirit, the inner strength which is mine through the holy spirit, my devotion to the truth of Thy covenant, the truth and sincerity in which I walk."[152] In these Scrolls the "spirit of truth" is not personal as in John, but is linked with the Holy Spirit and with the "Prince of Lights" and opposed to the "spirit of darkness." A strong ethical dualism is present, as in the Johannine writings, but it is more ceremonial and less moral than in John. The association of holy living with the Holy Spirit is as prominent in these Scrolls as in the Old Testament. The linking of *cleansing* with the Spirit is emphasized more *explicitly* in the Scrolls than even in the New Testament.[153] The chief significance of these pre-Christian Jewish sources is to show that they have, in common with the Johannine Gospel and Epistles, a strong emphasis on moral dualism and that they both recognize a "Spirit of Truth" as the antithesis to error and evil.

A newly-published Gnostic writing from the second century A.D., called *The Gos-*

---

[147] John 14:17; 15:26; 16:13.
[148] R. H. Charles, *Apocrypha and Pseudepigrapha of the Old Testament* (Oxford, 1913), II, 51. The date of this work is about 107 B.C. according to Charles.
[149] W. Bousset, *op. cit.*, p. 343.
[150] Test. Jud., 20:1-5, cited in R. H. Charles, *op. cit.*, II, 322 (the Greek from W. Bousset, *op. cit.*).
[151] IQS iv. 20-26 cf. Test. Asher I. 3-9; Levi 5:30; Judah 20:1; Barn xiv. 3ff. See T. H. Gaster, *The Dead Sea Scriptures* (Garden City: Doubleday, 1956), p. 45.
[152] 1QH, XVI, 8, Gaster, *op. cit.*, p. 195.
[153] Cf. 1QS IV, 15ff.; cf. Acts 15:9.

*pel of Truth,* a document mentioned by Irenaeus and Tertullian but now for the first time available to scholars, links the Holy Spirit with Truth. It states that when the Logos appeared from the Father, Error was disturbed and every person came under judgment. "Everyone who loves the Truth . . . attaches himself to the Father's mouth by means of His tongue as he receives the Holy Spirit."[154] The parallel to John's teaching about the Spirit of Truth is remote. It reflects only the Gnostic-Christian school of Valentinus (c. A.D. 150) with its syncretism of the philosophical concepts of truth and the Biblical view of the Holy Spirit and the Father. Only John, among the N. T. writers, links the Holy Spirit and the Spirit of Truth and sets them in contrast to evil and error. The similarities of both Jewish and Gnostic writings to the Fourth Gospel are verbal and superficial. The chief significance of indicating the parallels is to underscore the fact that John is unique in his stress upon the deity and personality of the Spirit. The parallels indicate also that the "Spirit of Truth" is a concept native to Palestinian soil of the first century and not necessarily indebted to Gnosticism of the second century as many N. T. scholars have previously concluded.[155]

The emphasis on the Holy Spirit in the Fourth Gospel is greater than the emphasis in the Synoptics. Indeed, John, Acts, and the letters of Paul stress the Spirit more than do the first three Evangelists. This has been interpreted as a result of the Fourth Evangelist's determination to read back into the life and words of Jesus an emphasis which the church later acquired but which was lacking in the Master's own teachings.[156] Much more appropriate is Swete's conclusion that it is well to assume that the sayings attributed to the Lord are essentially his and that the Evangelist had not the genius to create these discourses free hand.[157] An emphasis on this phase of the Lord's teaching would be appropriate in preparing the "Spiritual Gospel." E. F. Scott further concludes that for John the doctrine of the Holy Spirit was superfluous and could not easily be harmonized with his doctrine of the Logos. As Scott interpreted the Fourth Gospel, there was no Holy Spirit until after Jesus' resurrection (cf. John 7:39). The giving of the Spirit after the resurrection was John's equivalent of the Pentecostal effusion stressed in Luke and Acts. Consequently the Johannine doctrine of the coming of the Spirit to replace Jesus means that for John there is no second bodily *parousia* of Christ at the end of the age as taught in other parts of the New Testament. Instead, as Jesus' coming did not occur when expected, John revised the Synoptic-Acts story of Pentecost and the Second Advent so that the idea of Jesus' *parousia* simply gave way to the teaching that the Holy Spirit is identical with the Spirit of the Risen Christ and that no sudden coming of the Spirit of Christ is expected other than that reported in John 20:22 (see commentary *ad loc.*).[158] This interpretation not only places the Fourth Gospel at variance with the rest of the New Testament but even contradicts I John 2:28; 3:2; 4:17, passages by the same author in which the Second Advent of Christ is anticipated. The conclusion seems warranted that, contrary to Scott, John's doctrine of the Logos does not render superfluous the doctrine of the Spirit and that the Evangelist does not present his doctrine of the Spirit as a substitute for the historical Pentecostal effusion or the Parousia of Christ in power and glory at the end of this aeon. He simply supplements these events; the day of judgment for John is not only ever present (John 3:19), *but also* a future event in time (I John 4:17).

### 3. JOHANNINE EMPHASIS—THE PARACLETE

It is in his doctrine of the Holy Spirit that John makes one of his most important contributions to Christian thought. "John lays greater stress than any other Evangelist upon the work of the Holy Spirit, and more clearly than any other Evangelist he shows what constituted the distinctive operation of the Holy Spirit" (RHS, p. 212). Agreeing with this is E. F. Scott who states, "No other John-

---

[154] Kendrick, Grobel, *op. cit.*, p. 108.
[155] E.g., F. C. Grant, *op. cit.*, p. 17.
[156] Thus E. F. Scott, *The Spirit in the New Testament* (New York: Geo. Doran, 1923), pp. 193ff.
[157] H. B. Swete, *op. cit.*, p. 130.
[158] E. F. Scott, *op. cit.*, pp. 189-212 and EFS, pp. 332-352. Similar views are set forth in CHD, pp. 403-415 and W. R. Hutton.

nine doctrine has exercised a profounder influence on the whole course of theological development" (EFS, p. 320). Among other things John stresses the *personality* of the Spirit. In the ancient writings concerning the Holy Spirit, with the exception of the New Testament, the distinct personality of the Holy Spirit is not explicit. In most instances the Spirit is thought of as an impersonal divine influence. In John, by contrast, "the term *paraklētos* is a personal name, and the personal pronoun 'he' is consistently employed, even where the neuter would be naturally demanded by *pneuma*" (EFS, p. 342). In function the Paraclete is likewise referred to in language appropriate to a person. In addition he is said to serve in the same capacity as Jesus himself.

Another characteristic stress in John is the relation of the Spirit to Father and the Son. Although we do not find a fully articulated doctrine of the Trinity here, we do find the chief materials from which the early church councils defined their understanding of the Trinity. These Paraclete sayings in particular "carry us farther than any other writing in the development of the New Testament doctrine of the Godhead" (WFH, p. 80). John's reports say that the Paraclete will perform several specialized services after his arrival.

(i) The Paraclete will bear witness to the Truth (14:16). The Incarnate Truth (14:6) is to be replaced by the Spirit of Truth (14:16).[159] This links the Holy Spirit with one of John's distinctive themes — truth. Three times in this context the term "Spirit of Truth" occurs, making this a major contribution to the N. T. teaching concerning the Spirit.[160] As the Spirit of Truth the Holy Spirit comforts the saints (14:16,17; 16:13) and disturbs the sinners (16:8-11; cf. 5:45).

(ii) The Paraclete will console or comfort the believers (14:16-18). The Paraclete is not merely another Holy Spirit but another "Counsellor," distinct from Jesus and yet his *alter ego*. The intimate connection with Jesus is indicated in 14:18 when, after saying that he will send "another Comforter," Jesus adds, "I will not leave you desolate, I will come unto you." The one who makes the request and the one sent in answer to the request appear to be the same. With this may be compared Romans 8:9 where the Spirit of God and the Spirit of Christ appear to be synonymous and Acts 16:6, 7 where the Holy Spirit and the Spirit of Jesus have identical functions — that of guidance. As Jesus' bodily presence was a source of strength and consolation to the disciples so the presence of the Paraclete will compensate for the absence of Jesus' bodily presence.

(iii) The Paraclete will also serve as instructor or tutor (14:25,26). The subject matter of the Spirit's teaching will be "all things" but especially things pertaining to Jesus (cf. 16:14). His teaching is not so much that which is new and unprecedented but rather the recalling and clarifying of the Scriptures and of the sayings of Jesus. Again the intimate connection between the two Paracletes is indicated for the Spirit will not speak of himself but shall glorify Christ (16:13, 14). This promise was fulfilled when the New Testament was written by the apostles; under the instruction of the Holy Spirit they were able to recall the words and deeds of Jesus and report them accurately. It was also fulfilled when after the resurrection they were able to interpret the Old Testament so convincingly. After being endowed with the Holy Spirit, the Old Testament became to the apostles a "revised version."

(iv) The Paraclete will reinforce the disciples' witness to Christ (15:26). As the official emissary of both Father and Son, the Paraclete will interpret and apply the divine message to the believers and through the believers to the world. The idea of a joint witness of the Spirit and the believers is carried forward in Acts 1:8 ("ye shall be witnesses unto me") in Acts 15:28 ("It seemed good to the Holy Spirit and to us") and in Revelation 21:17 ("The Spirit and the bride say, Come").

(v) The Paraclete will serve as the believer's Advocate or defense attorney when he is attacked by the world (16:7-11). He not only defends the believer from the accusations of the enemy, but also takes the offensive against the hostile world by convicting it of the sin of un-

---

[159] F. J. A. Hort, *The Way, The Truth, and the Life* (New York: Macmillan, 1893), p. 57.
[160] John 14:17; 15:26; 16:13; cf. I John 4:6; 5:7.

belief and warning it of future judgment. Previously, Jesus had defended his disciples (Mark 2:24); afterwards this role of defense counsel was continued by the other Advocate (Luke 12:12; Acts 6:10—7:60).

(vi) The Holy Spirit will serve also as the voice of prophecy in the sense of predicting future events (16:13). Again he does not initiate the message but repeats what he hears. Thus the subordinate status of the Paraclete is kept constantly in mind. This verse is appealed to by those who argue that the Paraclete is synonymous with the risen Christ and distinct from Jesus of Nazareth.[161] The predictive element in the Spirit's ministry is seen in the prediction of a famine (Acts 11:28), of a shipwreck (Acts 27:10,21), and of heresy (I Tim. 4:1).

(vii) The Spirit will also serve as official interpreter of the words and acts of Jesus — "he shall take of mine and shall declare it unto you" (16:14,15). A good interpreter seeks not to call attention to himself but rather to faithfully convert the ideas and words of one into symbols intelligible to another. In this function is seen again the intimate connection and yet distinction of Father, Son, and Holy Spirit. For the role of interpreter in the Palestine synagogue see A. Edersheim, *Life and Times of Jesus the Messiah* (New York: Longmans, Green, 1899) I, 445. The apostles and their spiritual successors have served as interpreters of Jesus through both words and actions in many ways (Acts 4:8-13). Both Paul and John left the relationship of the Father, the Son, and the Holy Spirit unresolved, but from their words, especially from the Paraclete sayings of John, the Church Fathers formulated their understanding of the relationship in the first ecumenical creeds, culminating in the Creed of Chalcedon (451 A.D.). In spite of this there arose the "Filoque controversy" of the eighth and tenth centuries which became the major theological factor in the split between the Roman Catholic and the Eastern Orthodox churches. The Western churches believe that the Spirit proceeds from the Father *and* the Son (John 15:

26a; 16:7) while the Eastern churches believe it is from the Father *through* the Son (John 14:16,26; 15:26b). The Roman position thus stresses the *coordinate* status of the Son while the Orthodox emphasis is upon the Son's *subordinate* status. John was apparently content to leave the matter unresolved, his stress being placed upon the intimacy and yet distinction among the three Persons of the God-head.[162]

### 4. SUMMARY

In the perspective of the New Testament as a whole, the Gospel and Epistles of John make a unique and important contribution to the doctrine of the Holy Spirit. In the Synoptics and Acts the stress is upon the work of the Spirit as inspiring the witnesses by guiding and *empowering* their utterances.[163] In the four Gospels and in Acts, the baptism of the Spirit is stressed as the distinctive baptism of Jesus in contrast to that of John.[164] In Paul, the *ethical* effects of being filled with the Spirit are stressed (Gal. 5:16-23). His concern was that the gifts of the Spirit be matched and balanced by the disciplines of the Spirit, by sanctity of motive and conduct; hence his exhortation — "If we live by the Spirit let us also walk by the Spirit" (Gal. 5:25 RSV). The Johannine doctrine of the Holy Spirit stresses his role as Interpreter, Counsellor, Comforter, Advocate or, more precisely, the *intellectual* aspect of the Spirit's work. In short, the Synoptics and Acts stress the *energy* of the Spirit, Paul the *ethics* of the Spirit, and John the *illumination* of the Spirit, or his work of revealing Christ. These three aspects present a full-orbed picture of the Spirit with verbal similarities to the Qumran scrolls and with many roots into Old Testament teaching.[165] As under the Old Covenant the Spirit mediated God to believing men, so in the New Covenant the Spirit mediates Jesus Christ to believers.

### F. GLORY

One of the key-words in the vocabulary of the Fourth Gospel is the term "glory"

[161] W. R. Hutton, "The Johannine Doctrine of the Holy Spirit," *The Crozier Quarterly*, Vol. XXIV, No. 4, Oct., 1947, pp. 33-343.
[162] For a helpful discussion see G. S. Hendry, *The Holy Spirit in Christian Theology* (Philadelphia: Westminster, 1956), *passim*.
[163] Matt. 10:20; Luke 12:12; Acts 4:8, 31; 13:9; I Cor. 2:4; II Cor. 13:3.
[164] Cf. Matt. 3:11; Mark 1:8; Luke 3:16; John 1:33; Acts 1:5.
[165] E.g., Joel 2:28; Ezek. 36:25-27.

($\delta\delta\xi\alpha$ - *doxa*). It is closely allied to the term "light." The importance of the term in this Gospel is underscored by the frequency of its occurrence. The noun form occurs 19 times and the verb form (*doxado* - $\delta o\xi\acute{\alpha}\zeta\omega$) 22 times; the verb occurs more times in John than in the first three Gospels combined (M-G). Strangely, neither is found in the Johannine Epistles.

The background of the term is to be sought primarily in the Old Testament where the LXX term *doxa* is the translation of the Hebrew *kabod* (כבוד) meaning "heavy." It is a synonym of "holiness" (Heb. *qadosh* — קרש), and is especially prominent in Isaiah (6:1-5; cf. John 12:41) and in Ezekiel 1:28. The connection between "weight" and "honor" in Hebrew may be somewhat analogous to the English idiom — "threw his weight around" — meaning to exert one's influence, to use one's prestige to gain a desired end (RHS, p. 104). God's glory flashed forth in the wilderness (Exod. 16:10), in the temple (I Kings 8:11), in poetry (Ps. 8:1) and in prophecy (Hab. 3:3; Hag. 2:6-8). In the Old Testament therefore, the "glory" of God means (a) his *presence,* as on the mount (Exod. 24:16) or in the sanctuary (Exod. 40:35) (b) his *power* (Ps. 63:2; Exod. 16:7 cf. Isa. 8:7), and his *honor* (Ps. 102:16; Ezek. 39:21). The most characteristic of these is Jehovah's *presence* (Exod. 33:22; Ezek. 10:4), and it is this which characterizes the Johannine use of the concept.

In secular usage *doxa* means "opinion" (Plato), "judgment," "worth" (*geltung*), or "renown (*ruhmes*) (TWNT). The characteristic usage in classical Greek ("opinion") is not as such found in the Bible (MRV, II, 417). The development of this idea, however, appears in the Bible in the sense of "the opinion in which one stands to others" (Cremer, p. 207). Thus, God's "honor" means the "opinion" of him held by the nations (Isa. 66:19). From the analogy of *dokeō,* used intransitively, ("to appear, to seem") there comes a meaning of "appearance" in contrast to the "truth" (*alētheia*), hence the heresy known as Doceticism.

In the New Testament its primary meaning is "brightness, splendor, or radiance" (A-G). The term is used to describe the light of the sun (Acts 22:11) and of the radiance around the throne of God

(II Thess. 1:9; Rev. 15:8). A secondary meaning is "majesty" or "honor," e.g., the majesty of God in contrast to his creatures (Rom. 1:23). The verb "to glorify" is a variation of this meaning and involves a *recognition* of God's power and holiness (Phil. 1:11; I Pet. 1:7). It is seen also in John 9:24 — "give God the praise," by telling the truth, in contrast to the honor which is given to men (John 12:43). Other meanings include "splendor" and "magnificence" such as that of a king (Matt. 6:29) or of angels (II Pet. 2:10).

The use of "glory" in John's Gospel is more complicated and forms a distinct characteristic of the Gospel. At times it appears to be deliberately ambiguous or enigmatic, to include a deeper meaning which is not readily apparent. In John "glorify" means a *revelation* of God's nature, particularly in Jesus Christ. Jesus is said to glorify the Father by his obedience (17:1,4), and the Father is glorified in the Son (13:31; 14:13). The radiance or splendor of the most high God could not be fully revealed in the Old Testament because it was too dazzling (Exod. 33:20; 34:30-35; cf. II Cor. 3:7-13). The witness reports, however, that in the incarnate Son of God, "we behold his glory . . . full of grace and truth" (1:14; cf. 2:11). In the Synoptic accounts this was experienced only by those on the mount of transfiguration (Luke 9:32; II Pet. 1:17). The distinctive emphasis in John is that the glory which was evident in Jesus, even during the "days of his humiliation," was not confined to one mountain-top experience but was apparent to the discerning throughout his ministry (WFH, p. 67). The "Shekinah" of God's presence, which the rabbis associated only with the temple, now is to be seen in the Incarnation, as a new "temple" (cf. 2:21) (RHS, p. 106).

Also characteristic of John's emphasis is the contrast between the "glory" of God and that of men as a factor in belief. On the one hand, Jesus seeks the "glory of him that sent him" and hence is entitled to be heard as God's representative. On the other hand, those who seek their own glory find it impossible to judge righteously and objectively because they lack sincerity (5:44; 7:18; 8:54; 12:43). Self-glorification, or the glorification of the creature rather than God, amounts to spiritual suicide as both Paul and John agree (Rom. 1:21; John 5:41-44).

The most distinctive and most important connotation of "glory" in the Fourth Gospel is a "glory" emerging paradoxically out of the ignominy of death (11:4; 12: 33; 21:19). This connotation of "glory" includes the complex of death, resurrection, ascension and session of the Son. It is the glory of bringing triumph out of tragedy, honor out of disgrace, lasting victory out of apparent defeat.[166] Perhaps the best illustration of this distinctively Johannine concept is seen in the prayer "glorify thou me" with the emphasis on the ascension and session of the Son (17: 5). With this is linked Jesus' prayer in the shadow of the cross, "Father, glorify thy name" (12:27,28). When the Father answered that he would glorify his name, Jesus interpreted it as a prediction of his death on the cross as the means by which he would "glorify God" (12:28-33). Likewise death by martyrdom is spoken of as glorifying God (21:19).

While Paul places in contrast the sufferings of Christ and the glory that shall result (Phil. 2:5-11), John puts the two together. Peter, like Paul but in contrast to John, contrasts suffering and "glory" (I Pet. 1:11; 4:13). In John, suffering and humiliation are not a prelude to glory but a part of the glory. The death on the cross was not in contrast to but consistent with "the glory that should follow." Perhaps a longer perspective permitted this concept to coalesce in the Fourth Gospel. "Glory" in this Gospel is presented as the climax in the redemptive process when the Savior and the redeemer share the divine glory in the presence of the Father (17:24-26).

## G. TIME

John's is the most time-conscious of the Gospels. With the exception of the recording of the hour of the crucifixion, his is the only Gospel which takes note of the time of day. References to the time of day in the Fourth Gospel include John 1:39; 4:6, 52; 11:9 and 19:14. Scholars are not in agreement as to whether John followed the Synoptists and others in the Middle East by reckoning the day as beginning at dawn, whether he followed the Roman *legal* custom of beginning the day at midnight (as we do), or whether he followed a system entirely independent. The problem, as it occurs in 1:39; 4:6, 52; 11:9, is dealt with at the appropriate places in the exegesis. The problem appears at its most acute form in 19:14 ("about the sixth hour") where it apparently is in conflict with Mark 15:25 ("the third hour"), with reference to the hour when Jesus was crucified. According to the Synoptists Jesus was brought before Pilate about 7 A.M. (Edersheim), sentenced at 9 A.M. and crucified soon afterwards. Darkness covered the land from the 6th to the 9th hours (noon until 3 P.M.) at which time Jesus expired (Luke 23:44). The entombment would be about 5 P.M., "when the even was come" (Matt. 25:57). They had to hurry and did not complete the embalming of the body before the beginning of the Sabbath at sundown. If John used the Roman *legal* reckoning of time, as is stated by many eminent authorities including A. T. Robertson, B. F. Westcott, Edersheim, and Hendriksen, the sixth hour would be either 6 A.M. or noon (cf. 4:6). Hendriksen, who believes the sentencing occurred at about 6:30 A.M. has no explanation for the two or three hour lapse of time between the sentencing and the crucifixion (*op. cit.*, II, 421) although it would take some time to proceed from the Praetorium to Golgotha. It would have been psychologically impossible for the frenzied mob and their fanatical leaders to have remained inactive for two hours under these circumstances. The suggestion has been made that this interval could have been filled with "the scourging, mockery, and preparations for the execution.[167] But this overlooks the fact that all four evangelists report that these events *preceded* the sentencing. If John employed the customary "Jewish" reckoning, according to his report the sentencing would have occurred at noon and the crucifixion soon afterwards. In either case, whether John's "sixth hour" occurred at 6:00 A.M. or noon, it is difficult to harmonize with Mark's "third hour." As Lenski observes, the early hour does not leave enough time for the trial while the noon hour does not leave

---

[166] John 12:16, 23, 28; 13:31, 32; 17:1, 5, 24; 21:19.
[167] Ralph Earle, *The Evangelical Bible Commentary*: Mark (Grand Rapids: Zondervan, 1957), p. 183.

enough time for the crucifixion.[168] It should be borne in mind that the time, especially at mid-day, was difficult to ascertain with precision without a sundial, and, in the absence of clocks, the "hour" was only an approximation. The problem, in a large measure, is that of adjusting the precision of a mechanical age to a less complicated one.

What did John mean by "the sixth hour"? What do the primary sources say? The usual method of reckoning time appears to be that of numbering the hours from dawn. Matt. 20:1-12 describes a typical working day. Most laborers began at the first hour, some did not start work until the "third hour" or 9 A.M., others at the "sixth hour" (noon), still others at the "ninth hour" (3 P.M.) and one not until the "eleventh hour" (5 P.M.).

In Acts the hours of the day began at dawn. This is clear in Acts 2:15 where the "third hour" indicates mid-morning, before there was time to become inebriated. In Acts 3:9; 10:3,30 the "ninth hour" indicates 3 P.M. (A-G). In Acts 23:23 the "third hour of the night" indicates 9 P.M. Thus the Synoptics and the Acts agree that the mode of reckoning was to number the hours of the day beginning at dawn and the hours of the night from sunset.

. Evidence shows that in everyday usage the Greeks and Romans also followed the same method of reckoning the hours. Josephus (c. A.D. 90), accustomed to Roman ways, used the same method of computation, the "ninth hour," for instance, meaning 3 P.M.[169] Suetonius, the Roman historian (c. A.D. 95), repeatedly used the same method of noting time.[170] Aristides (c. A.D. 140), Livy, Aristophanes, and Horace are among other secular writers who employ this method of measuring time (MRV, II, 718).

After an exhaustive survey of the situation Ramsay concludes that "the numbering of hours in popular usage always started from the beginning of the natural day."[171] Dodd agrees. "It seems that

at this time throughout the Graeco-Roman world one system of reckoning the hours prevailed. There is indisputable evidence that while the Romans calculated their civil day, by which leases and contrasts were dated, as extending from midnight to midnight, the hours of each day were reckoned from sunset to sunset. Thus, on the Roman sun-dials noon is marked VI" (EGT, I, 699).

Jesus' statement that there are "twelve hours in the day" (John 11:9) Westcott finds irrelevant to this question because "we commonly use the same phrase though we reckon from midnight to noon" (BFW, II, 326). But Westcott fails to note that in this passage Jesus was talking about hours of daylight as was the case in Matthew 20:1-12. Furthermore, when we refer to the number of hours in a day we say twenty-four rather than twelve. Origen's commentary on John gives no evidence that he considered John's mode of reckoning time unusual. "It is antecedently improbable that St. John should in this point vary from the rest of the N. T. writers: and we ought to require strong evidence before accepting this theory, which has been adopted by some in order to escape from the difficulty of xix.14."[172]

The suggestion that John employed a method of reckoning different from all others is both improbable and lacking in any evidence; it should therefore be discounted.[173]

Alone among the four evangelists John is careful to note such details of time as the hour of his own conversion (1:39) the time when Jesus was left alone at the well (4:6), and the hour when the servant's fever subsided (4:52). In 19:14 he takes particular note of the day and of the hour as one of great significance.[174] The fact remains that none of the attempts to harmonize Mark 15:25 and John 19: 14 have been fully satisfactory, even to their respective proponents. If no reconciliation is possible, we do well with Meyer and Plummer to conclude that "prefer

---

[168] R. C. H. Lenski, *The Interpretation of St. John's Gospel* (Columbus, Ohio: Lutheran Book Concern, 1942), p. 1273.
[169] *War*, VI. 68. 79. 147.
[170] Suetonius, *Lives of the Caesars* (New York: Modern Library, 1931), pp. 14, 46, 50, 82.
[171] Wm. Ramsay, "Numbers, Hours, Years and Dates," *Hastings' Dictionary of the Bible*: Extra Volume, (New York: Scribner's, 1903), p. 478.
[172] A. Plummer, *Cambridge Greek Testament* (Cambridge: The University Press, 1938), p. 84.
[173] For an excellent survey and summary, R. G. Bratcher, "Reckoning of Time in the Fourth Gospel," *Review and Expositor*, April, 1951, pp. 161-168.
[174] "St. John also in the N. T. stands out as habitually careful and accurate in this respect." Ramsay, *op. cit.*, V, 499.

ence in point of accuracy must be given to the report of the Evangelist who stood beneath the cross" (CGT, 326). In any case, complete unanimity among witnesses is not necessary since slight discrepancies are inevitable when each witness is independent. And since time-keeping was not habitually exact in any case (they went by the "watch" or quarter-day more than by an hour of sixty minutes), "the hour" in this case could have been toward the middle of the second watch, or between 9 and 12 A. M.

## VII. THE TEXT

The exegesis in this commentary is based upon the Nestle text in the twenty-third and twenty-fourth editions. These take into account the newly-published Papyrus Bodmer II (P[66]), collated by the help of Kurt Aland. The witness of this new text, earlier by far than any other complete text of this Gospel (c. A.D. 200), has frequently been consulted with profit by the authors. This papyrus text affords additional evidence that codices (bound volumes) were used much earlier than had once been assumed.[175] It is noteworthy that several passages of dubious authenticity in the Fourth Gospel are missing from this most ancient of the witnesses, including John 5:4 and 8:1-11. This papyrus text, 125 years older than any (complete) text of John previously known, serves to verify the results of New Testament criticism as reflected in the Nestle text.[176]

Since the monumental work of Westcott and Hort, on which the Revised Versions of 1881 and 1901 were based, much progress has been made in textual criticism. Recent commentaries on the Fourth Gospel, including Dodd, Bultmann, and Barrett, reflect an unwillingness to adopt any one text as definitive. Dodd, for example, at John 10:29 adopts a reading which is in violation of the W-H principle that the "harder" (most unlikely) reading is generally to be preferred; he decides on an alternative reading on the basis of contextual rather than textual evidence (CHD, p. 433). Bultmann likewise often makes a decision on a disputed text on exegetical grounds, thus showing a preference for an eclectic text.[177] Like Dodd, he often decides the matter on the basis of which reading makes the best sense and is most in conformity with the general Johannine usage elsewhere.

C. K. Barrett's critical commentary on John is based upon the Westcott and Hort text. Yet he follows procedures very similar to those of Dodd and Bultmann, deciding each variant on what he believes is its own merit and "on the basis of other aspects of the Evangelist's language, thought and style" (CKB). These three scholars thus share in common the tendency to regard no one text as the ultimate authority but rather to prefer a somewhat fluid and "eclectic" text.

It is remarkable that, whereas C. H. Dodd declared in 1936 (*The Present Task in New Testament Studies*) that the age of textual criticism was past and the present task was that of New Testament theology, Kurt Aland recently stated that the present condition of New Testament textual criticism is anything but satisfactory. Aland calls for a great new effort in quest of a definitive text, one which takes cognizance of the abundance of new material now for the first time available. The present text is therefore not static and absolutely fixed. The prestige of the *Textus Receptus*, which formed the basis of the great English and German translations prior to a century ago, is now accepted only in the Russian and Eastern Orthodox Churches. The stability which the pioneer work of Westcott and Hort gave to the text is no longer unchallenged. The next great achievement may well be that of establishing a more definitive text. Relevant to this is the International Project to Establish a New Critical Apparatus of the Greek New Testament. The American Bible Society is also working on a new text which uses the text of Westcott and Hort as a convenient point of departure and takes seriously into account some three thousand variants "corresponding to our present state of knowledge."[178] The best all-around text presently available re-

---

[175] Victor, Martin, "Introduction," Papyrus Bodmer II (Cologny — Genève: Bibliothèque Bodmer, 1956-58), p. 8.
[176] R. Schipper, "New Johannine Manuscript," *Christianity Today*, June 10, 1957, p. 17.
[177] J. N. Birdsall, "The Text of the Fourth Gospel," *The Evangelical Quarterly*, Oct.-Dec., 1957, p. 197. E. C. Colwell, "The Interpretation of a Gospel," *Encounter*, Winter, 1964, 1964, pp. 21-33.
[178] Kurt Aland, "The Position of New Testament Textual Criticism," *Studia Biblica*, p. 727.

mains the Nestle text, now in its twenty-fourth edition and so strengthened by the collaboration of a number of scholars that it now has an international character.[179]

Comparison of the Fourth Gospel with the Synoptics will now be greatly facilitated by the new "Synopsis Quattuor Evangeliorum," (Stuttgart: Württembergische Bibelanstalt), which differs from Huck's synopsis in that it includes the Fourth Gospel, a reversal from early tendencies to think this impractical.

For the Bible student, this generation, with new manuscript discoveries, with new critical editions of the text in the making, and with its revival of Biblical theology, is an exciting time to be alive. It is challenging, but at times frustrating for the one who aims at perfection and finality. One must therefore be content to make his own contribution and await hopefully the result of the labors of his contemporaries. It is unlikely, however, that current research will greatly upset the results of past labors. Instead, the current trend is in the direction of confirming the soundness of the textual critic's work. The same is not likely to be said of the work of many students of Biblical theology who seek to interpret the text.

Nothing in the accumulating evidence tends to justify the bold rearrangements of order of the text as done by Bernard, Macgregor, and Bultmann. Instead, evidence supports the order of the extant texts. A recently published major commentary defends the existing order by suggesting that the author may have more interest in logical order than chronological order (RHL, pp. 8ff.). He notes, for example, that the passage in 5:23-30 is presented as if for the first time, while the parallel passage in 6:38-40, 57 assumes prior acquaintance. Much of the demand to reconstruct the text arises from the assumption that the author's mode of thought should be occidental rather than oriental. Finally, the attempts to "improve" the text by rearrangement have thus far created more problems than they have solved.

Several hold that the alleged displacement is attributable to the text's having been written on separate sheets of papyrus which were not placed in proper sequence before being pasted together in a scroll.[180] Others suggest that pages in an original codex became displaced (JBL, I, xxviii-xxx). To refute the former hypothesis it has been pointed out that "the writing frequently runs over the junction of the two sheets," hence the sheets were joined before the writing.[181] The latter hypothesis overlooks the fact that "if leaves in a codex became displaced the length of each passage so dislocated, and the space between its 'original' and its present position, would in every case be equivalent to a multiple of two pages (i.e., sufficient to cover one or more complete leaves of two pages each)."[182]

Both church tradition and the evidence within the Gospel itself testify to a concern on the part of the author to be accurate in his report. The exegete therefore needs to take cognizance of "the extreme care with which this Gospel appears to have been composed as a complete and coherent whole, with each section playing its part in the whole . . . ." (RHL, p. 11). As he does so, his confidence in the integrity of the text and its arrangement is likely to be enhanced.

[179] *Ibid.*, p. 729.
[180] F. R. Hoare, *The Original Order and Chapters of St. John's Gospel* (London: Burnes, Castes and Washburne, 1944), p. 9.
[181] F. G. Kenyon, *Books and Readers in Ancient Greece and Rome*, p. 53.
[182] W. G. Wilson, "The Original Text of the Fourth Gospel," JTS, Jan.-April, 1949, p. 59. Cf. D. Moody Smith, "The Sources of the Gospel of John," NTS, April, 1964, pp. 336-51.

# OUTLINE

## I. INTRODUCTION (1:1-51)

### A. PROLOGUE (1:1-18)

1. THE PRE-INCARNATE WORD-LIGHT (IN ETERNITY) — 1:1-4
   a. Before Creation (vv. 1, 2)
   b. After Creation (v. 3, 4)

2. THE REVELATION OF THE LIGHT (IN TIME) — 1:5-9
   a. John as Witness to the True Light (vv. 5-7)
   b. The True Light Revealed (vv. 8, 9)

3. THE RECEPTION OF THE LIGHT — 1:10-13

4. THE INCARNATE WORD-SON — 1:14-18
   a. "We Beheld His Glory" (vv. 14-16)
   b. "Grace and Truth Came" (vv. 17-18)

### B. THE WITNESS OF JOHN (1:19-36)

1. JOHN'S SELF-IDENTIFICATION — 1:19-28
   a. "A Voice" (vv. 19-23)
   b. A Servant (vv. 24-28)

2. JOHN'S IDENTIFICATION OF THE CHRIST — 1:29-36

### C. JESUS' FIRST DISCIPLES (1:37-51)

1. THE CALLING OF ANDREW AND PETER: TO COME IS TO SEE — 1:37-42

2. THE CALLING OF PHILIP AND NATHANAEL: TO SEE IS TO BELIEVE — 1:43-49

## II. PUBLIC MINISTRY: MANIFESTATION OF GLORY IN THE "SIGNS" (2:1 — 12:50)

### A. THE INITIAL ENCOUNTERS (2:1 — 4:54)

1. THE FIRST "SIGN" — 2:1-11
   a. The Occasion (vv. 1-5)
   b. The "Sign" (vv. 6-11)
   c. The Reaction: Belief (vv. 9-12)

2. EVENTS AT THE FIRST PASSOVER (2:13-3:21)
   a. The Temple Cleansed (2:12-22)
   b. The Result: Many Believe (2:23-25)

c. Interview with Nicodemus (3:1-21)
  (1) The New Birth (vv. 1-12)
  (2) Salvation Is by Faith (vv. 13:17)
    (a) The Ascent of the Son of Man (vv. 13-15)
    (b) The Descent of the Son of God (vv. 16, 17)
  (3) Responsibility for Acceptance (vv. 18-21)

3. THE WITNESS OF JOHN (3:22-26)
  a. The Occasion for the Witness (vv. 22-26)
  b. The Witness Itself (vv. 27-30)
  c. The Rationale of the Witness (vv. 31-36)

4. INTERVIEW WITH THE SAMARITAN WOMAN (4:1-42)
  a. The Occasion (vv. 1-6)
  b. The Woman's Awakening (vv. 7-15)
  c. The Woman's Conversion (vv. 16-26)
  d. The Woman's Witness (vv. 28-30)
  e. The Disciples Challenged (vv. 31-38)
  f. The Samaritans Believe (vv. 39-42)

5. THE SECOND "SIGN" (4:43-54)
  a. Introduction: Galileans Believe (vv. 43-45)
  b. A King's Officer Believes (vv. 46-54)
    (1) Initial Belief Demonstrated (v. 47)
    (2) Belief Tested (vv. 48-50)
    (3) Belief Confirmed (v. 53)

B. MOUNTING HOSTILITY (5:1-12:50)

1. THE THIRD "SIGN" (5:1-47)
  a. The Cripple Healed (vv. 2-9)
  b. Jesus Accused (vv. 10-18)
    (1) Sabbath Desecration (vv. 10-16)
    (2) Blasphemy (vv. 17, 18)
  c. Jesus' Defense (vv. 19-47)
    (1) Father and Son Co-workers (vv. 19-30)
      (a) In Raising Dead (vv. 21, 25, 29)
      (b) In Judging (vv. 22, 23, 27, 29, 30)
      (c) In Giving Life (vv. 21, 24, 26)
    (2) Witnesses (vv. 31-47)
      (a) The Witness of Jesus (v. 31).
      (b) The Witness of John (v. 31-35)
      (c) The Witness of "The Works" (v. 36)
      (d) The Witness of the Father (v. 37)
      (e) The Witness of the Scriptures (vv. 39-47)

2. THE FOURTH "SIGN" AT THE SECOND PASSOVER (6:1-71)
  a. Five Thousand Fed (vv. 1-15)
  b. Jesus, Master of the Storm (vv. 16-21)
  c. Works or Faith? (vv. 22-29)

    d. The Bread of Life (vv. 30-59)
      (1) Life Available (vv. 30-40)
      (2) Real Manna (vv. 41-51)
      (3) "A Hard Saying" (vv. 52-59)
    e. The Words of Life (vv. 60-71)
      (1) Disciples Offended (vv. 60-65)
      (2) Peter's Profession (vv. 66-71)

3. AT THE FEAST OF THE TABERNACLES (7:1-52)
    a. Confusion Concerning Jesus (vv. 1-13)
      (1) His Brothers' Skepticism (vv. 1-9)
      (2) Perplexity in Jerusalem (vv. 10-13)
    b. Jesus Teaches in the Temple (vv. 14-24)
    c. Jesus' Origin, They Say, Proves He Is Not the Messiah (vv. 25-36)
    d. Jesus' Invitation to Partake of the Spirit (vv. 37-44)
    e. Nicidemus Calls for Justice (vv. 45-52)

4. THE WOMAN TAKEN IN ADULTERY (7:53-8:11)
    a. Textual Problem
    b. The Test Question (vv. 1-6)
    c. The Answer (vv. 7-11)
    d. Significance

5. THE LIGHT OF THE WORLD (8:12-9:41)
    a. Its Source in God (vv. 12-20)
    b. Its Destination: "to the Father" (vv. 21-30)
    c. Its Mission: Freedom Through Truth (vv. 31-38)
    d. Its Antiquity:
      (1) Abraham's True Children (vv. 39-47)
      (2) Jesus' Priority to Abraham (vv. 48-59)
    e. Its Remedy for Physical Blindness: The Fifth "Sign" (vv. 1-34)
      (1) The Blind Man Healed (vv. 1-12)
      (2) Opposition Encountered (vv. 13-17)
      (3) Parents Non-committal (vv. 18-23)
      (4) The Man's Witness Rejected (vv. 35-41)
    f. Its Exposure of Spiritual Blindness (vv. 35-41)

6. TRUE AND FALSE SHEPHERDS (10:1-39)
    a. The "Parable" of the Good Shepherd (vv. 1-6)
    b. The "Parable" Explained (vv. 7-18)
    c. The Sheep Heed Only the Good Shepherd (vv. 19-30)
      (1) Divisions Again (vv. 19-21)
      (2) The Security of the "Sheep" (vv. 22-30)
    d. Jesus Escapes Stoning for Alleged "Blasphemy" (31-39)

7. RETIREMENT TO JUDAEA AND BETHANY (10:40-12:11)
    a. "Beyond Jordan" Many Believe: (10:40-42)
    b. Recalled to Bethany (11:1-53)
      (1) "Lazarus is sick" (vv. 1-4)
      (2) "Lazarus is Dead" (vv. 5-16)

    c. The Sixth "Sign" (vv. 17-53)
      (1) Jesus Greeted by Martha (vv. 17-27)
      (2) Jesus Welcomed by Mary (vv. 28-37)
      (3) Lazarus Lives Again (vv. 38-44)
      (4). Divided Reaction: Many Believe: Some Report to the Pharisees
        (vv. 45-53)
    d. The Retirement of Jesus near Ephraim (vv. 54-57)
    e. The Anointing at Bethany (12:1-11)
      (1) Mary's Lavish Devotion (vv. 1-8)
      (2) Lazarus' Witness Threatened (vv. 9-11)

  8. JESUS' LAST PUBLIC APPEARANCE (12:12-50)
    a. His Triumphal Entry (vv. 12-19)
    b. The Rationale of Jesus' Death (vv. 20-36)
      (1) The Greeks' Inquiry (vv. 20-22)
      (2) The Relationship of Death to Life (vv. 23-26)
      (3) The Lifting Up of the Son of Man (vv. 27-36)
    c. Explanation of Unbelief (37-43)
    d. Jesus' Summary of His Relationship to the Father (vv. 44-50)


III. PRIVATE CONFERENCE WITH THE DISCIPLES (13:17-26)

  A. THE PASSOVER MEAL (13:1-38)

    1. INTRODUCTION (vv.1-3)

    2. THE FOOT WASHING (vv. 4-11)

    3. THE MEANING OF THE WASHING (vv. 12-20)

    4. THE PREDICTION OF BETRAYAL (vv. 21-30)

    5. THE NEW COMMANDMENT (vv. 31-35)

    6. THE PREDICTION OF DENIAL (vv. 36-38)

  B. PREPARATION FOR JESUS' DEPARTURE (14:1-16:26)

    1. REUNION ASSURED (vv. 1-3)

    2. THE TRUE WAY (vv. 4-6)

    3. UNION OF FATHER AND SON (vv. 7-11)

    4. OBEDIENCE, THE TEST OF DISCIPLESHIP (vv. 12-17)
      a. The Power of Prayer (vv. 12-14)
      b. The Mission of the Paraclete (vv. 15-17)

    5. THE UNION OF FATHER, SON, PARACLETE AND DISCIPLES (14:18-15:11)
      a. The Tri-unity of Father, Son and Believer (vv. 18-24)
      b. The Relationship of Son, Spirit and Believer (vv. 25-31)
      c. The Parable of the Vine (15:1-8)

    6. LOVE, THE DISTINCTIVE QUALITY OF DISCIPLESHIP (15:9-17)

    7. THE HOSTILITY OF THE WORLD (vv. 18-25)

8. THE WORK OF THE PARACLETE (15:26-16:15)
   a. In Bearing Witness to Christ (vv. 26, 27)
   b. Warning (16:1-6)
   c. The Paraclete Accusing the World (vv. 7-11)
   d. Guiding the Believer (vv. 12-15)

9. JESUS' DEPARTURE AND RETURN (16:16-33)
   a. Sorrow Turned to Joy (vv. 16-24)
   b. The Disciples Enlightened (vv. 25-33)

C. THE MASTER'S PRAYER OF INTERCESSION (17:1-26)

1. CHRIST'S PRAYER FOR HIMSELF (vv. 1-5)

2. JESUS PRAYS FOR HIS DISCIPLES (vv. 6-11)

3. FOR FUTURE BELIEVERS (vv. 20-24)

4. SUMMARY (vv. 25, 26)

IV. THE PASSION NARRATIVE (18:1 — 19:42)

A. THE ARREST (18:1-14)

1. THE BETRAYAL (vv. 1-5)

2. PETER'S ILL-ADVISED DEFENSE (vv. 6-11)

3. ARRAIGNMENT BEFORE ANNAS (vv. 12-14)

4. PETER'S DENIAL (vv. 15-18, 25-27)

B. THE TRIAL (18:19-19:16)

1. BEFORE ANNAS (18:19-24)

2. BEFORE CAIAPHAS (18:24, 28)

3. BEFORE PILATE (18:29-19:16)
   a. Pilate Denies Jurisdiction (vv. 29-32)
   b. Pilate Interviews Jesus about Kingship (vv. 33-38)
   c. The Mob Prefers Barabbas (vv. 38-40)
   d. Jesus Mocked as False King (19:1-11)
   e. Pilate Abandons Jesus to the Mob (19:12-16)

C. THE CRUCIFIXION (19:17-42)

1. THE VICTIM IDENTIFIED BY PILATE (vv. 17-22)

2. THE GARMENTS DISTRIBUTED (vv. 23-25)

3. THE VIGIL (vv. 25-27)

4. "IT IS FINISHED!" (vv. 28-30)

5. BLOOD AND WATER (vv. 31-37)

6. BURIAL (vv. 38-42)

## V. THE RESURRECTION (20:1-21:19)

### A. THE FIRST EIGHT DAYS (20:1-31)

1. THE FIRST DAY (vv. 1-18)
   a. Mary's Discovery (vv. 1, 2)
   b. Peter and John Investigate (vv. 3-10)
   c. Jesus' Appearance to Mary (vv. 11-18)
   d. Jesus' Appearance to the Ten Disciples (vv. 19-23)
      (1) Their Joy at Seeing Jesus (vv. 19, 20)
         (a) The Miraculous Entrance (v. 19)
         (b) Verification (v. 20)
      (2) Their Commission (vv. 21-23)

2. THE FIRST WEEK (vv. 24-31)
   a. Thomas' Demand for Tangible Evidence (vv. 24, 25)
   b. Jesus Appears to the Disciples with Thomas (vv. 26-29)
   c. The Author's Summary of Purpose (vv. 30, 31)

### B. JESUS' APPEARANCE IN GALILEE (21:1-19)

1. FISHING (vv. 1-8)
   a. The Night of Failure (vv. 1-3)
   b. The Morning of Success (vv. 4-8)

2. THE THIRD APPEARANCE (AT BREAKFAST) (vv. 9-14)

3. JESUS' INTERVIEW WITH PETER (vv. 15-23)
   a. Questions Addressed to Peter by Jesus (vv. 15-19)
   b. The Question Concerning the Beloved Disciple (vv. 20-23)

## VI. FINAL ATTESTATION (21:24, 25)

### A. WRITER'S AFFIRMATION OF THE WITNESS (v. 24)
   a. His Identity
   b. His Veracity

### B. "OTHER THINGS" NOT MENTIONED (v. 25)

# THE EVANGELICAL COMMENTARY
## ON THE BIBLE

# CHAPTER I

In the beginning was the Word, and the Word was with God, and the Word was God.

---

## EXEGESIS

1 The Prologue (John 1:1-18) of John's Gospel reflects in almost every line the influence of the Old Testament. Here the phrase **in the beginning** (*en archē*) is paralleled by the same phrase in the LXX of Genesis 1:1 and is similar to the *ap' archēs* — "from the beginning" — of I John 1:1. In Genesis 1:1 the "beginning" is with reference to creation, in the Epistle it apparently refers to the Incarnation of the Word (*Logos*), while here the "beginning" goes back of history into eternity. This phrase occurs only twice elsewhere in the N. T. (Acts 11:5; Phil. 4:15) where it is associated with the origin of the Gospel.

A striking contrast is noticeable between the verbs for *being* and *becoming* of vv. 1-4. The fourfold **was** (*ēn*) of vv. 1, 2 (the imperfect expressing continuous, timeless existence) is in contrast to the **made** (*egeneto*) of vv. 3, 4, cf. 6, 10, 12, 13, 14, (the aorist denoting a specific event in time). These phenomena highlight the fact that the Logos is eternal while everything created is temporal. The contrast is between that which always *was* in existence (the Logos) and that which *came* into existence (*egeneto*). This verse, in association with vv. 14, 18, 34, indicates that the Son of God is eternal and yet has the status of sonship. Sonship implies a beginning in time. Origen recognized the paradox and resolved it with the phrase "eternal generation of the Son."

The important word in this passage is **Word** (*Logos*). While the term occurs forty times in this Gospel (M-G) and usually indicates an expression of thought either by God or man, it has a specialized meaning in John 1:1, 14; I John 1:1; Revelation 19:13, where it is a title of the Christ. As used here it does not merely denote an attribute of God, nor is its origin to be found in Gnostic sources as Bultmann contends (Bultmann, pp. 5-15). Rather, as Bultmann correctly says, it is

---

## EXPOSITION

In simple, majestic sentences, reminiscent of the Genesis account of Creation, the Fourth Gospel raises the reader's anticipation of the message which is to follow. The Prologue (1:1-18) of the Gospel according to John is actually a preview of the entire Gospel. This Prologue has analogies in Luke 1:1-4; Acts 1:1-5; Romans 1:7; I John 1:1-4 and Hebrews 1:1-4. The closest parallels are the latter two: I John 1:1-4 because of similarity of style and vocabulary; Hebrews 1:1-4 because it also is an epitome of all that follows. As in Luke and Hebrews, the language is more formal than is true of the remainder of the book. "The Gospel of the 'Son of Thunder' (Mark 3:17) opens with a peal."[a]

Unlike that of Matthew's Gospel, this introduction is intended to attract a wide audience. In this respect it is similar in purpose to the *protreptikos* or introduction with which Plato began his dialogues. The purpose of the *protreptikos* was twofold: to lead into the subject, and to arouse interest. This Prologue does both in an admirable manner.

Many of the characteristics of the Gospel and Epistles bearing the name of John are apparent in this Prologue. These include the bold contrasts between light and darkness, truth and error, time and eternity, the world and heaven, God and the devil, and others. All colors become black and white in these writings; there are no neutral grays. With a relatively limited vocabulary John's style achieves

[a] A. Plummer, *John, The Cambridge Bible* (Cambridge: University Press, 1899), p. 59.

53

## 2 The same was in the beginning with God.

the Word which lies at the source of all the particular words of God (*op. cit.,* p. 7). The "Word of God" may mean the "written word" (Rom. 9:6), it may mean the "creative word" (Ps. 33:6), it may mean the "recreative" (or regenerating) word (Jas. 1:18, 21), it may mean the "Living Word" (Heb. 4:12) or, as here, it may mean the "Incarnate Word" (John 1:14). The *power* of the Word of God is manifest in creation, the *wisdom* of the Word of God is displayed in the illumination which comes to man with the advent of God's Word, but it is the *love* of God which is demonstrated in the Incarnation (John 1:14).[1] The closest known literary parallel for the *Logos,* as used here, appears to be the personification of wisdom in Proverbs 8:22-30 (cf. Wisd. 18:15, 22).[2] God's word and wisdom are said to create and sustain the world (Ps. 104:24; Pro. 3:19; Wisd. 9:1, 2). The *Logos* here is more than reason, more than word; it is more than wisdom personified. The term designates a Person, distinct from and yet co-eternal and identical in essence with God — "all that God is the Logos is."

The Logos was with (*pros*) God. With the accusative of person *pros* expresses

"close proximity," the normal idea of direction being weakened here (JHT). The idea of motion or aspiration toward the Father is not entirely absent, however, and the translation "face to face" is appropriate (WmH). The stress is upon the fellowship within the Godhead and a reminder of the plural in Genesis 1:26, "Let *us* make man in *our* image, after *our* likeness." *Pros* has a close parallel in I John 1:2, "the eternal life which was with the Father" (*pros ton patera*), or, "in the presence of the Father" (cf. Mark 6:3; 9:19; 14:49; Luke 19:41).

**The Word was God** (*theos ēn ho logos*). Here **God** is placed first (in the Greek), indicating that the stress is on the deity of the *Logos* (cf. John 4:24). The omission of the article before *theos* indicates that the Logos is not identical with God and that stress is placed, not on the person, but on the nature of God, i.e., upon his deity. By the grammatical structure, therefore, stress is placed upon the fact that the Logos is divine, viz., is actually God and yet distinct in person (EGT, I, 684).

**2 The same** (*houtos,* "this one") **was in the beginning with God** is a reaffirmation of verse one, in a manner character-

a most profound effect by the paradox of simplicity of diction and profundity of thought. In this basic vocabulary are certain "key-words," an understanding of which is fundamental to an understanding of the Johannine literature. These include light, life, belief, sign, darkness, witness, world, glory, truth, and love. Thus, throughout the Prologue three of the main characteristics of the Gospel — simplicity, subtlety and sublimity are especially noteworthy. This simplicity of diction accentuates by contrast the richness of the ideas conveyed.

Consistent with the announced purpose of the writer (John 21:31), the opening verses reflect a world-wide perspective. The author-artist spreads his canvas over a vast area in time and in eternity. One gains the impression that the Synoptic

writers, especially Mark and Luke, wrote to confirm the faith of persons already committed to the Christian way (Luke 1:1-3). John, on the other hand, wrote to "the world" in order that unbelievers might join believers and have life. He wrote not so much to strengthen faith as to initiate it. It is significant that in modern missionary strategy the portion of the Bible most often selected to win first converts is this "universal" or "spiritual" Gospel.

Upon closer examination the Prologue is seen to consist of several segments. Among the better analyses are those of Barrett, Bultmann, and Westcott.

### JOHN: THE PROLOGUE IN PERSPECTIVE

The relation of the parts to the whole in the Prologue may conveniently be pre-

---

[1] A. Alexander, "Logos," ISBE, III, 1915.
[2] Wisdom assisted in creation (Prov. 3:19; Jer. 10:12; Wisd. 7:22; 8:6;).

**3** All things were made through him; and without him was not anything made that hath been made.

---

istic of this writer (cf. 1:7; 3:2; 6:46; 7:18). But it is more than a repetition; it signifies that the Logos and the Father existed contemporaneously from eternity. This emphasis is set in contrast to the forthcoming assertion that the eternal word became flesh in time. The contrast is between being and becoming. Having stated the *nature* of the Logos as being eternal, personal, and divine, the author now proceeds to show the *work* of the Logos; he moves from Creator to creation, from eternity into time.

**3** All things were made (*egeneto*, "came into existence") through him. The verb *egeneto* occurs ten times in the remainder of the Prologue and in most instances can be appropriately translated "came into existence, or into being." In contrast to the "was" of v. 1, it stresses change, timeliness, becoming. Did the eternal Logos create all things or did God create all through the *Logos*? In Genesis 1:3 and Psalm 33:6 the Word of God appears to be the creative agent: "he spake and it was done" (Ps. 33:9). In Proverbs 8:30

---

sented in the form of a diagram or chart. The segments may be labelled differently depending upon one's standpoint. A differ-

ent standpoint presents a different perspective, as it does when one views a distant mountain peak from different angles.

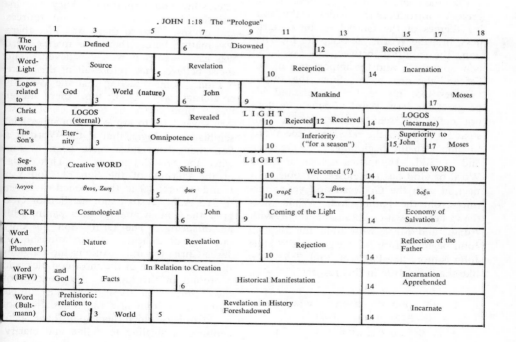

JOHN 1:18 The "Prologue"

| | 1 | 3 | 5 | 7 | 9 | 11 | 13 | 15 | 17 | 18 |
|---|---|---|---|---|---|---|---|---|---|---|
| The Word | Defined | | | 6 Disowned | | | 12 Received | | | |
| Word-Light | Source | | 5 Revelation | | | 10 Reception | | 14 Incarnation | | |
| Logos related to | God | 3 World (nature) | | 6 John | 9 Mankind | | | | 17 Moses | |
| Christ as | LOGOS (eternal) | | 5 Revealed | L I G H T | 10 Rejected 12 Received | 14 | LOGOS (incarnate) | | | |
| The Son's | Eternity | 3 Omnipotence | | | 10 Inferiority ("for a season") | | 15 Superiority to John | 17 Moses | | |
| Segments | Creative WORD | | 5 Shining | L I G H T | 10 Welcomed (?) | 14 | Incarnate WORD | | | |
| λογος | θεος, Ζωη | | 5 φως | | 10 σαρξ 12 βιος | 14 | δοξα | | | |
| CKB | Cosmological | | 6 John | 9 Coming of the Light | | 14 | Economy of Salvation | | | |
| Word (A. Plummer) | Nature | | 5 Revelation | | 10 Rejection | | 14 | Reflection of the Father | | |
| Word (BFW) | and God | 2 Facts | In Relation to Creation | 6 Historical Manifestation | | | 14 | Incarnation Apprehended | | |
| Word (Bultmann) | Prehistoric: relation to God | 3 World | 5 | Revelation in History Foreshadowed | | | 14 | Incarnate | | |

Wisdom shares in the creative process (cf. Gen. 1:26). In I Corinthians 8:6 Paul "distinguishes between the Father as the primal source of all things and the Son as the actual Creator" (EGT, I, 685). Here, as in Hebrews 1:2 the *dia* with the genitive designates the agent through whom the work of creation was done. So it seems clear that God the Father created the world through the agency of his Son, the Father being the *efficient* cause, the Son the *instrumental* cause.[3]

The first two verbs of this verse are in the aorist tense, thus signifying decisive or "punctiliar action," a definite completed act, in contrast to the continuing action of the imperfect tenses of vv. 1, 2. The verb *ginomai* (here translated **made**) occurs 12 times in this chapter. In the ASV it is translated "made" 4 times (vv. 3, 10),

"became" 4 times (vv. 12, 14, 15, 30) "came" 2 times (vv. 6, 17). Once the term is rendered by "born" (v. 13) and once by "done" (v. 28). In nearly all of these instances the phrase "came into existence" expresses the thought very well. The texts in which this term occurs are historic events in which the idea of "becoming" is apparent. The contrasting verb "was," occurring 7 times in this chapter, is here applied to the uncreated Logos in eternity and the idea of "being," i.e., "continuing existence" is dominant.

3b For the sake of emphasis John repeats the assertion "no single thing was created without him" (NEB). In other words there is nothing in existence which does not owe its existence to the Word. In making this sweeping claim the author may have had in mind incipient Gnos-

---

# I. INTRODUCTION (1:1-51)

A. PROLOGUE (1:1-18)

Like the overture of a great oratorio the prologue introduces the reader to the leading themes of the Gospel — light, darkness, life, the Word, the Son, the Incarnation, the contrast between the old and new covenants, and the importance of belief and the new birth. Since the author assumes that his readers understand his usage of the term **Word** (*Logos*), he does not define it (see "Introduction"). Instead he indicates the *relation* of the Word to time ("in the beginning"), to creation, and to God. He makes it clear that the Word of God has the closest possible connection with the Godhead and yet is distinct from the Father-God. While Matthew begins with Abraham, Luke with Adam, and Mark with John the Baptist, John begins before the "beginning." Thus John is more like Paul (cf. Phil. 2:5) than like the Synoptists in this respect.

1. THE PRE-INCARNATE WORD-LIGHT IN ETERNITY (1:1-4)

a. Before Creation (vv. 1, 2)

Here is the most daring Christology of the Bible, and it is expressed in almost poetic form. The reader is taken back of the preaching of John (Mark 1:1),

back of the birth of Jesus (Matt. 1:1), back of the creation of the universe (Gen. 1:1), back to eternity. Origins are both interesting and important. They are interesting because they deal with sources and causes. Before there was life, there was matter, before there was matter there was gas — so it is widely believed. The theist believes that before all of this there is God. John is saying that the Word is co-eternal with God, that there never was a time when the Son did not exist. Arius was later to argue, with a superficial semblance to logic, that if the Word is a Son then there must have been a time when the Son did not exist. This denial of the eternity of the Son of God was branded heretical at the Council of Nicea in 325 A.D. Jesus is not the Son of God after the human analogy of a parent with an offspring. The term "Son" is only one way of indicating the relationship of Jesus Christ to God. Among the religions of the world, one of the most complex and profound of theologies is the concept of the Trinity. In these short and simple affirmations John lays the foundations of a Christology which theologians have spent centuries struggling to define and clarify. The term "Word" or *Logos* is a designation of the Christ which would appeal to both Jews and Greeks. To the latter it would probably connote a creative and life-

---

[3] P. Schaff, ed., in J. P. Lange, *John, Commentary,* tr. by P. Schaff (Grand Rapids: Zondervan, reprint), p. 57.

4 In him was life; and the life was the light of men.

---

ticism which had begun to make its influence felt toward the end of the first century. Some Gnostics believed that angels shared in the work of creation and others that matter is eternal.[4] This statement would refute both of these doctrines. The idea that Christ is the sole agent of creation and sole mediator between God and creation is also expressed in Colossians 1:9-20 and Hebrews 1:2-14. Thus, creation was the direct result of the One who declared that "as the Father hath life in himself, even so gave he to the Son also to have life in himself" (5:26).

4 Two alternative punctuations have an important bearing on the interpretation of these verses. Most of the earliest (uncial) manuscripts were without punctuation. But during the third and fourth centuries the sentence was punctuated so as to end with the verb "was" (*autō zōē ēn*, i.e., "in him life was") as in the ASV and RSV margins: "without him was not anything made. That which hath been made was life in him."[5] Against this reading, and in favor of our standard versions are the "mass of secondary uncials and later manuscripts" and the consideration that the

---

giving principle in the universe. To those with an Old Testament background, the term would evoke associations with the origin of life and would not be in conflict with monotheism. The term combines the aspects of thought (to the Greek) and action (to the Hebrew). It would suggest the sequence of thought-word-deed.

The simple and yet breath-taking affirmation here is three-fold. The Word was in the beginning; the Word was in the beginning with God; the Word actually was God. The sentence structure is not unlike that of a first grade reader; it uses the same technique of limited vocabulary, simple sentences, and repetition. Yet this studied simplicity is what gives John's beginning such an arresting and provocative quality. He makes it clear that the birth of Jesus was an Incarnation. There can be no Incarnation without pre-existence. This is John's distinctive way of affirming the existence of the Son of God before he was born as a helpless babe. He does so in such a way as to lift it above the level of fruitless speculation about details.

b. After Creation (vv. 3, 4)

3 In a manner similar to that of Semitic parallels, the Evangelist twice affirms that the Logos created all things. He says simply (i) everything owes its existence to the Logos and (ii) there is nothing which did not originate with the creative

work of the Logos. Paul makes the same affirmation when writing to the Colossians, "for in him were all things created . . . and he is before all things, and in him all things cohere" (Col. 1:16, 17). With the increasing secularism of this scientific age it requires real faith to affirm, "I believe in God Almighty, Maker of heaven and earth." But scientific investigations to date have failed to account for the origins of life apart from a creative intelligence.

4 Here, and later in this Gospel, the Evangelist categorically states that the only source of life is the Son of God. It is a bold affirmation, but no bolder than some of Paul's statements concerning Christ (Col. 2:9, 10; cf. Eph. 1:10). It has been said that in the space age a new Christology is needed, one in which Christ's jurisdiction over other planets is acknowledged. One who reads from John and from Paul will recognize that such a Christology has been in existence from the middle of the first century. The New Testament writers did not have to await the coming of the age of space travel to envision a Christ whose jurisdiction embraced all of creation. The prayer which astronaut Cooper recently dictated into his tape recorder during his twenty-two orbital flights and repeated before both houses of Congress on May 21, 1963 is evidence that the "faith of our fathers" can survive the age of space exploration.

---

[4] Irenaeus, *Against Heresies*, II. ii. 1; IV. xx. 1.
[5] A reading supported by the Old Latin and other MSS. and by Irenaeus, Clement, Origen, Tertullian, and recently by Westcott, Bernard, and Howard. For the documentary evidence see BFW, I, 59-63.

5 And the light shineth in the darkness; and the darkness apprehended it not.

alternative reading "would destroy the absolute idea of life" which the context demands.[6] The NEB paraphrases "in him was life" to read "all that came to be was alive with his life." In other words, not that the life in the Logos was created, but rather, all created life derived its being from the life of the Logos as its source. The *immediate* source of life for the creation was the Logos; the *ultimate* source was God (5:26).

5 The darkness, in John's writings, always stands in direct antithesis to light. There is a continual tension between the light and the darkness, the good and the evil.[7]

In Johannine literature the contrast is stark and emphatic:

| LIGHT | DARKNESS |
|---|---|
| God | Satan |
| Truth | Falsehood |
| Holiness | Sin |
| Life | Death |

The term darkness (*skotia*) is one of the key words of this Gospel and also of I John where it stands in contrast to

As in the Genesis account of creation, so here light follows life. The author here means not only that physical life from the Creator came into being "at the beginning," but he means that "this life is spiritual life as well. The ease with which the meaning changes from the physical to the spiritual is seen in v. 4. Light and Life are two important "key-words" in this Gospel (see Introduction). His word for "life is *zōē*, a synonym which usually means spiritual life as distinct from merely animate life or *bios* (see Introduction). While the Synoptic Gospels usually stress spiritual life in an eschatological context (e.g., Matt. 7:14; 19:16, 17, 29), in the Fourth Gospel spiritual life is a quality of existence available now.[b] John does not speak of light in an entirely metaphorical sense. When he thinks of light, he thinks of it as embodied in a person, the Lord Jesus Christ. His life among men was the light of the world. He embodied in his person the qualities of love, courage, truth and obedience. Judaism correctly recognizes that the greatest asset of Christianity is the fact that virtue was incarnate in Jesus. As Schleiermacher expressed it, "The fruits of the Spirit are the virtues of Christ." What the best Greeks sought in vain was an embodiment of their highest ideals. The Gospel states that man's highest ideas and much more were embodied in Jesus. Into a darkened world this Light came in due time and the world has never been the same since. The emphasis on this light-in-a-life as a picture or a foretaste of the life to come[c] is characteristic of John.

## 2. THE REVELATION OF THE LIGHT IN TIME (1:5-9)

5 To readers influenced by the Persian emphasis on the struggle between light and darkness John can say that the only one who can successfully cope with the problem of darkness and evil is the Son of God; indeed he has already overcome darkness. Everyone who believes and obeys him can also be a "son of light" who overcomes the darkness. Men whose deeds are evil love darkness and avoid the light (3:19, 20). Jesus said later that those who follow him shall not walk in darkness (8:12; 12:35).

The present tense shineth (v. 5) is in contrast to the was of v. 4. The progression of thought is not historical but logical, i.e., from the general to the specific. The world at creation was dependent on the *Logos* as the source of light (general) while the present world of dark-

[6] Lange, *op. cit.*, p. 57. See also Westcott, Meyer, Alford, and Barrett. As the latter points out, redundancy is characteristic of John (e.g., 1:1); he also begins sentences with *ēn*. The simple, direct explicitness seems more consistent with the immediate context and with John's style generally. The marginal reading in the ARV and RSV implies that the life in the Logos was not eternal, but created.
[7] John 8:12; 12:35, 46; I John 1:5; 2:8; cf. I John 1:6; John 3:19.
[b] A. Feuillet, "La Participation Actuelle a la Vie Divine," *Studia Evangelica*, p. 300.
[c] Hermann Strathmann, *Das Evangelium nach Johannes* (Göttingen: Vandenhoeck & Ruprecht, 1959), p. 32.

**6 There came a man, sent from God, whose name was John.**

---

light.[8] The conflict is presently in progress as the present tense of **shines** (*phainō*) indicates. John is constantly alert to couch his message in phrases calculated to arrest and convince his contemporaries. Zoroastrianism has been prominent in the Near East since the sixth century B.C., and movements stemming from this kept alive the concept of the eternal struggle between light and darkness, as the Qumran sect now testifies.[9]

**The darkness apprehended it not.** The meaning of apprehend (*katelaben*, aor. ind.) is debatable here. Its basic meaning is "to take," or "to seize." It is translated "comprehended" (KJV), "overcome" (RSV), "quenched" (NEB), "put out" (Phillips) or "extinguished." The Greek fathers generally read it "overcome." The Latin fathers, following the Vulgate *comprehenderunt*, favored the reading "apprehended" or "comprehended," as does the KJV. The evidence

seems to support the reading "overcome" or "extinguish" for the following reasons: (i) the parallel passage in 12:35 reads "that the darkness overtake you not" (cf. 6:17) — in this figure the darkness overtakes the pedestrian, envelops him, and eclipses the light.[10] This interpretation is in harmony with the basic N. T. conception of the continual moral struggle between light and darkness as is reflected in I Thessalonians 5:4, "not in darkness, that that day should overtake you." (ii) The meaning "comprehend," to the English reader, implies "understanding" or "comprehension" and obscures the basic meaning of conflict which both the term and the context demand.

**6 There was a man** (*egeneto anthrōpos*). The verb *egeneto* ("came" or "was"), as in v. 3, is in direct contrast to the *ēn* of v. 1, a contrast between the eternity of the Logos and the temporal setting of John's coming. The distinction

---

ness is dependent on the *Logos* for spiritual light (special).[d]

**6 The name John** means "Jehovah is merciful" and was given the Baptist by divine direction (Luke 1:13). The name was certainly appropriate in view of the general emphasis on the "Good News." The **sent** (*apostalmenos*) indicates one with delegated authority, rather than simply one sent (*pempo*) with no special sense of authority. It follows that the one sent by God confronts men, not only with a message, but a message from God. In John, and to a greater extent in Jesus, men were confronted not merely by a prophet or rabbi but by God himself (cf. 1:18). Among both Jews and Greeks the idea of man sent directly from God was current.[e]

The dominant factor in the background, however, is the Hebrew prophet. John's prophetic voice broke the silence of four hundred years. He was a majestic, lonely, transitional figure — last of the prophets (Mal. 4:5) and first of the evangelists — almost as unique as Melchizedec (cf. Heb. 7:3).

**7** The Fourth Gospel always stresses the subordinate position of John as compared to that of Jesus. This is probably to counteract a tendency to think of John as having a separate ministry significant in itself. Acts 19:1-5 indicates a separate movement of John's disciples unrelated to the disciples of Jesus. The fact that *some* of John's disciples left him

---

[8] John 1:5; 6:17; 8:12; 12:35, 46; I John 1:5; 2:8, 9, 11. The term occurs only four times elsewhere in the N.T. With the exception of two passages all of the Johannine occurrences employ the term in a moral sense, in the opposition of light and truth.

[9] Among the closest extant literary parallels to John's emphasis on the contrast between light and darkness is the apocalyptic book among the Dead Sea Scrolls entitled the "Book of the War Between the Children of Light and the Children of Darkness." The moral conflict of John 1:5; 3:19-21 has, in this scroll, its counterpart in a cosmic struggle at which time the "Sons of Darkness" will suffer complete and final defeat. "For they are of the portion of darkness, while the portion of God is everlasting light. . . . They follow only the laws of darkness. . . . But we are in the portion of Thy truth." "Wars," xiii, xiv. trans. by T. H. Gaster, *The Dead Sea Scriptures in English Translation* (Garden City: Doubleday, 1956), p. 298.

[10] Wm. Barclay, *The Gospel of John* (Philadelphia: The Westminster Press, 1956), I, pp. 25-28. WmH (I 73, 74) favors "appropriate."

[d] See G. Vos, "The Range of the Logos-name in the Fourth Gospel," *Princeton Theological Review*, Oct., 1913, p. 583.

[e] Cf. Moses (Exod. 3:10), Isaiah (Isa. 6:8), Jeremiah (Jer. 1:5), Diogenes (Epictetus, I, XXIV, 6), Menander, (Eusebius, *H. E.*, III, 1).

7 The same came for witness, that he might bear witness of the light, that all might believe through him.

8 He was not the light, but *came* that he might bear witness of the light.

9 There was the true light, *even the light* which lighteth every man, coming into the world.

---

is between uncreated, timeless existence and the beginning in time of what was previously nonexistent (cf. 8:58, "Before Abraham was, I am"). The came of the ASV is better than the "was" of the KJV and RSV. A still more precise English equivalent of *egeneto* is "came into existence." The suddenness with which the Baptist is introduced lends to this lonely figure an awesome grandeur. He is the only John named in this Gospel.

7 The same (*houtos*) came for witness. The *houtos* is parallel in construction to the same term in v. 2: "this one" or "the same," and is also parallel to the *ekeinos* (He or "that one") of v. 8. The ASV rendering is preferable to the KJV here as the *eis martyrian* is properly translated for witness rather than "as a witness," the *eis* here meaning not "into" as normally, but to denote purpose or goal as in Matthew 8:4 (A-G, p. 228). The RSV "for testimony" is also accurate; perhaps more precisely, "for the purpose of bearing witness." The term witness is repeated for emphasis, the first giving the

*purpose* of the witness, the second the *subject* of the witness. The first purpose clause (*hina*), with the aorist subjunctive, signifies the purpose of witnessing to the one true light. The second *hina* clause also indicates purpose — that all might believe through him. The last two words through him (*di' autou*) indicate agency. The phrase occurs also in vv. 3, 10.

7 That all might believe through him. The *him* refers to John the Baptist, the thought being that John's witness is calculated to appeal to all men. The relation of John to Jesus is explicitly and emphatically spelled out. John was not the light himself; he was only the witness to the light. The statement is repeated twice for emphasis (vv. 7, 8).

9 Two interpretations depend on the grammatical construction of this verse. Is the verb coming (*erchomenon*) to be joined to man (KJV, ASV) or to light (RSV)? The first alternative would read with Phillips "That was the true light which shines upon every man as he comes into the world." The second alternative

---

to follow Jesus implies that not all of them did (John 1:37).[f]

The purpose of John's mission is expressed in a three-fold series of purpose clauses. The general objective was witnessing, the specific objective was witnessing to the Light, and the ultimate objective was that all might believe thereby (BFW).

8 Again for the sake of clarity and emphasis John repeats that the Baptist was not the light but the witness to the light.

9 This is the favorite text of the Quakers. Followers of Fox and Barclay stress direct revelation of God to the individual under the Johannine figure of *light*. Similar to the conception of *wisdom* in the Wisdom of Solomon, their notion was of a divine illumination shed upon every person alike.[g] While followers of

Luther and Calvin stress the written Word and the Pietists, including Methodists, stress the work and witness of the Spirit, the Friends stress spiritual illumination. All need proportionate emphasis. This verse has important implications for the pagan without the written Word of God. The implication is that since the Light has entered the world they who now have the Light are responsible and hence guilty because of sin (cf. Rom. 2:12).

According to the accepted reading the coming of the Light into the world is alluding to the Incarnation rather than implying that every man receives the illumination at birth. But if this is the meaning, what about those who lived before the Incarnation?

To what extent do all men have a

---

[f] The existence of a group of John's disciples simultaneous with Jesus' followers is also indicated in Matt. 9:14; 11:2; 14:12; John 3:25; 4:1.

[g] Wis. Sol. 7:22-27; Cf. Test. Levi 14:4 — "light of the law for all men."

10 He was in the world, and the world was made through him, and the world knew him not.

11 He came unto his own, and they that were his own received him not.

---

reads, "the real light which enlightens every man was even then coming into the world." In other words, does the participial phrase, **coming into the world**, modify **light** or **man**? The latter seems preferable because it is in line with John's use of the phrase elsewhere.[11] The true **light** stresses the real in contrast to the symbolic, the substance not shadow, the perfect in contrast to the imperfect (Bultman, p. 32). The same light illuminates believers and blinds unbelievers.[12]

10 **He was in the world.** With great pathos the writer reports that the creation did not welcome her Creator and Benefactor. The key-word here is *cosmos*. The New Testament uses four words for "world": *gē*, meaning the land, *oikoumenē*, meaning the inhabited earth, *aeon*, the time element in human existence, and *cosmos* which means (a) "order," (b) "adorning" (I Pet. 3:3, 8) (c) "sum total of all life above animals," (d) "the world

as mankind," (e) "the inhabited world alienated from God." The latter is the usual meaning in John's Gospel and Epistle, where the term occurs a total of about 102 times. In most instances the usage reflects the moral tension, in the Johannine writings, between God and the world, light and darkness, good and evil. In this verse "world" obviously means the inhabitants of the earth. The last word of this verse **knew him not** is the second aorist indicative active of *ginōsko,* a verb meaning "to know, to learn, to comprehend, to perceive, to realize, to recognize or to acknowledge." In this passage the word seems best rendered as "acknowledge" in the sense of recognition and acceptance as Lord. This verb is used in the same sense in 17:3 — "this is eternal life, that they might *know* thee."

11 The tragedy of the world's lack of response continues in v. 11 to a still more tragic fact. "He came to his own home

---

knowledge of the truth and are thus responsible to the Judge of all the earth? Does the statement in v. 9 apply to the heathen who have never read a verse from the Bible or even heard the name Jesus Christ? Recently in Japan, this writer asked several Japanese if they had ever heard of Jesus Christ. Several replied in the negative; one said with great emphasis that a person by that name had never been in that vicinity. Not only here, however, but also in Romans 2:15, is a "natural revelation" that is given to all men set forth. If it is suggested that this "light" is too dim to involve its recipient in much moral responsibility, it may be stated in reply that "those who sinned without the law shall be judged without the law and that those who sinned under the law will be judged by the law ("special revelation" — Rom. 2:12). Also relevant to this point is Luke 12:48 — "that servant, who knew his Lord's will . . . shall be beaten with many stripes; but he that knew not, and did things worthy of

stripes shall be beaten with few stripes." Thus, while all are responsible and hence are subject to condemnation, the punishment will be in proportion to the responsibility, which in turn is proportionate to "light" and opportunity.

### 3. THE RECEPTION OF THE LIGHT (1:10-13)

10 The hostility of "the world" to the Savior, and especially the unbelief of the Jews in their Messiah, was a constant source of embarrassment to the early Christian evangelists and later to the apologists. Here John expresses the two-fold unresponsiveness of "the world" to the Light: the general mass of humanity — "the world" — did not acknowledge the Light, and even the Jewish nation — "his own" — did not accept him.

11 There was a process of selectivity at work in Biblical history. God chose from the nations the Semitic line, narrowed it to the family of Abraham, and selected the

---

[11] 3:19; 6:14; 11:27; 12:46; 16:28; 18:37. (See MRV, II, 43.)
[12] John 9:39-41; Wisdom Sol., 7:22-27; cf. Test. Levi. 14:4, "light of the law for all men."

12 But as many as received him, to them gave he the right to become children of God, *even* to them that believe on his name:

---

(*idia*) and his own people (*idioi*) received him not" (RSV). The verb *paralambanō* ("receive," "accept") is to be compared with the *katalambanō* ("overtake") of v. 5. The general meaning is "to take" or "receive," and here has the special significance of "approve" or "accept" (A-G, p. 625).[13]

12 In contrast to the nation which did not accept or receive the Light, a remnant did "receive" him. The meaning of the verb *lambanō* is essentially the same as *paralambanō* (v. 11) but stresses the possession gained (M-M). The verb right (*exousian*) is best rendered "authority." There are six synonyms for "power" in the New Testament. The contrast between this term and its most important synonym is illustrated in Acts 1:8 — "It is not for you to know the times or the seasons which the Father has placed in his own *exousia* (authority), but ye shall receive power (*dynamis* — intrinsic force)." The thought here is that faith in Jesus as Son of God bestows upon the believer the right or privilege of sonship, analogous to a legal adoption of a son. This means that genealogical descent from Abraham is no longer the criterion of true sonship, as the argument with Nicodemus makes clear (3:5-13; cf. 8:44).

John's use of *tekna* is significant here.

*Huios* may mean "son of adoption," *Tekna* means "son by biological descent" (cf. A-G). The latter is John's favorite way of viewing the "new birth" or citizenship in the Kingdom. With Paul *huios* is the preferred concept since it stresses the extension of grace to the Gentiles: they are "adopted." Here, in line with his emphasis on new life, the biological term is used by John. All the privileges of Jewish nationalism and far more are transferred to the simple believer. The *eis* (*into*) denotes something more than faith in the Jesus of history. It means here an individual appropriation and participation in the divine nature, in line with the basic idea of motion into something. The *object* of faith is Jesus as the revealed Word of God and Savior. The *nature* of faith is reception, trust, obedience to Jesus Christ in his redemptive capacity. The NEB expresses it succinctly — "those who have yielded to him their allegiance." Where the Word is welcomed, where credence and loyalty are given, there follows the bestowal of the divine nature and privilege of sonship. To believe on his *name* is to believe on his unique divine-human nature, the "name" meaning the nature of the person. This is in line with O. T. thought as when Jacob demanded of the angel "what is thy name?" (Gen. 32:27).

---

lineage of Isaac, Jacob, and Judah. Later this was narrowed to the righteous remnant envisioned by Isaiah and embodied in the repatriated exiles under Ezra. Even this remnant as a whole rejected the revealed Logos; the real remnant became the believers in Jesus Christ who constitute the New Covenant. This is the theology of the New Testament.

Hostility to the "light of the world" is a major concern in this Gospel as it is in the New Testament as a whole. As Plato found it difficult to explain why the people of Athens put to death their best citizen (Socrates), so the early Christian evangelists found it difficult to explain why God's chosen people did not accept as

their Messiah a "man who sent about doing good, healing all who were oppressed by the devil" (Acts 10:38) and claiming to be the Lord's anointed. But John sees the context as larger than the rejection of Jesus by the Jews; he sees the context as the basic hostility of the world as a whole. In Pauline writings the stress is upon the rejection of Christ by the Jews and his acceptance by the Gentiles (Rom. 10:20, 21), but in John the rejection by "the world" includes both Jews and Gentiles whose "deeds are evil" (John 3:19, 20).

12 Strange as the doctrine of spiritual regeneration was to those of Jesus' day, it is no less strange today. What a reformation would take place in the majority

---

[13] Cf. I Cor. 15:1; Phil. 4:9.

**13** who were born, not of blood, nor of the will of the flesh, nor of the will of man, but of God.

---

**13** Here, as in the conversation with Nicodemus (ch. 3), and in the discussion with the Pharisees (ch. 8), an important distinction is made in regard to "spiritual birth." Birth is more than being in the genealogy of Abraham; it is a different order of birth. The threefold contrast is designed to stress the distinction between generation by the flesh and regeneration by the Spirit. "Birth" of which John speaks is "not of blood"; the plural is idiomatic (CGT) and does not refer to the two sexes. A. T. Robertson argues for the singular of "blood" and believes it to be a reference to the Incarnation.[14] Neither is it the result of "the will of the flesh," i.e., the sex impulse or human desire. It is not the result of man's will or conniving, not of human purposes. The Old Testament recounts many instances of schemes to assure the continuity of a family lineage, among them the law of Levirite marriage (Deut. 25:5-10). Such a threefold repudiation of the idea that membership in the kingdom of God is a matter of human genealogy was diametrically opposed to the typical Jewish attitude of racial exclusiveness. This idea that citizenship in the kingdom is a matter of personal faith, rather than racial ancestry, is one of the cardinal doctrines of the New Covenant. Paul, John, and Peter emphasized this great truth with difference of terminology but in the same spirit. In Pauline phraseology it is "justification," a legal term; in Johannine literature it is "regeneration," a biological term; in Petrine nomenclature it is being made "partakers of the divine nature" (II Pet. 1:4). With citizenship on this basis, the Christian people were, in Harnack's apt phrase, "a third race."[15] It is not surprising that reactionary Jews viewed this as a revolutionary idea which "turned the world upside down" (Acts 17:6; 22:21, 22).

**13** The phrase **out of God** is another Johannine characteristic. (The phrase *ek tou theou* occurs some sixteen times in the First Epistle alone.) It connotes "intimate connection" or "source" rather than merely "from" or "of." John is again stressing here that sonship is not a matter of generation but of regeneration, a theme to be elaborated later in chapters three and eight.

---

of Christian churches today if being "born of the Spirit" were made the condition of becoming and remaining a member! In the middle of the seventeenth century in New England, the Half-way Covenant provided that unregenerate children of church members could be included in the Christian church. Since then the majority of Protestant churches have been content if their members can affirm a confession of faith even though they are not consciously born of the Spirit or have not become "partakers of the divine nature" (II Pet. 1:4). Even in many of the larger evangelical denominations, it is widely accepted that it is appropriate to accept one on a profession of faith in the hope that later, under the influence of the Gospel, he may become "a new creation in Christ Jesus" (cf. II Cor. 5:15). Following this strategy, the church is not a fellowship of those redeemed by the blood of the Lamb (Rev. 1:5) but a group of auditors who need to be evangelized. The New Testament concept of the church is not that of merely a group of kindred spirits drawn together by a common aspiration but a group of those who by repentance and faith have been incorporated into the body of Christ by the baptizing work of the Holy Spirit (I Cor. 12:13) and "sealed with the Spirit" (Eph. 1:13).

The Moslem sect of Shiites, followers of the Aga Khan, stress that they possess in Aga Khan a direct descendant of Mohammed, hence laying little stress on the Koran. They need not face Mecca when they pray; they only need to face a picture of their current leader. Thus they exemplify a stress on the physical rather than the spiritual, on the person rather than the teaching.

---

[14] "The Meaning of John 1:13," *The Bibical Review*, Oct., 1925, pp. 569ff.
[15] A. Harnack, *Mission and Expansion of Christianity*, II, 240.

14 And the Word became flesh, and dwelt among us (and we beheld his glory, glory as of the only begotten from the Father), full of grace and truth.

15 John beareth witness of him, and crieth, saying, This was he of whom I said, He that cometh after me is become before me: for he was before me.

16 For of his fulness we all received, and grace for grace.

---

It is not a matter or human devising or initiative; it is divinely inwrought.

14 **The Word became flesh.** The *egeneto,* as in vv. 3, 10 marks the contrast between the *being* of the eternal Logos and the *becoming* in time of the man Christ Jesus. "In becoming, He did not cease to be the Eternal Word. His divine nature was not laid aside. . . . Retaining all the essential properties of the Word, He entered into a new *mode* of being, not a new being" (MRV, II, 31).

The **flesh** (*sarx*) means more than a physical body, which would be rendered *sōma.* It means human nature, including man's body, mind, soul and moral nature.[16] This change was not an alteration but an addition. Moreover, the assuming of human nature was more than a temporary episode — "God did not merely lend his Son, he *gave* Him."[17]

The term **only begotten** is used in John only of Christ (1:18; 3:16, 18; I John 4:9) to indicate uniqueness. The term does not refer to birth (*gennaō*) but to uniqueness of kind (*genē*). It is also proper to translate it simply "only" as does the RSV. The term is applied also to an only child in Luke 7:12; 8:42; 9:38

and Hebrews 11:17, where Isaac was not the only son but the "only one of his kind."[18]

15 **Grace** (*charitas*), from whence comes "charity," means (1) "attractiveness, comeliness, winsomeness" in classical Greek, (2) "kindness" and "good will" in the Greek of the N. T., and (3) "God's favor" toward undeserving men. The latter usage is most characteristic of the N. T., especially of Paul. Its spiritual ancestry is less with classical precedents than with the O. T. doctrine of divine good will, favor, lovingkindness, or steadfast love.[19]

**Truth,** a characteristic word in this Gospel, has much affinity with Greek thought. It occurs more than thirty times in this book. In this context it means that "from the life of God . . . an activity of love has entered human history and brought the gift of eternal life . . ." (WFH, VIII, 474).

16 **Out of his fulness** is a reference to the preceding statement **full of grace and truth.** As wonderful as it is to have God in human form, it is still more amazing that he should share the richness of this divine nature with sinful humanity. This is possible, not because God became sinful

---

4. THE INCARNATE WORD-SON (1:14-18)

a. "We beheld his glory" (vv. 14-16)

14 With this striking declaration the reader is carried from eternity into time. This is John's way of describing the Incarnation, the details of which are re-

corded in Matthew and Luke. This was not a statement likely to find sympathy among those influenced by Greek thought. To Hellenized Jews like Philo the mingling of spirit and flesh was not good. This affirmation was a direct refutation of one of the main tenets of Gnosticism[h] and the kindred heresy of Docetism.[i]

---

[16] E. DeWitt Burton, *Spirit, Soul, Flesh in Pauline Thought* (Chicago: U. of Chicago, Press, 1918).

[17] A statement attributed to the Rev. Joseph H. Smith, evangelist.

[18] The RSV rendering of "only" here and elsewhere in John is supported by A-G and Dale Moody, JBL, 1953, pp. 213-19. That its meaning in John and I John is heightened to mean "begotten of the Only one" to parallel "born of God in John 1:13; I John 3:9 *et al.* is supported by Bauer, p. 26.

[19] Heb. *chen, e.g.,* Gen. 18:3; Exod. 3:21; Num. 11:11; Deut. 24:1; I Sam. 20:29 and *chesed,* e.g., Job 10:12; Esther 2:17; Dan. 1:9; Hos. 2:19. See H. P. Snaith, *Distinctive Ideas of the Old Testament* (Phila.: Westminster, 1946), pp. 118f.

[h] Gnosticism was a religious-philosophical system which flourished in the second century A.D., a prominent feature of which was a dualism between spirit and matter. Salvation was not so much deliverance from sin as deliverance from flesh (by ascetic practices in this life and especially by death). This led to a denial of the Incarnation and to an exaltation of knowledge at the expense of faith. For new data see R. M. Grant, ed., *Gnosticism, A Source Book of Heretical Writings from the Early Christian Period* (New York: Harper, 1961).

[i] Docetism was a view that the Incarnation was only a "seeming incarnation" — but not real, that Jesus Christ was divine but not actually human (cf. II John 7).

17 For the law was given through Moses; grace and truth came through Jesus Christ.
18 No man hath seen God at any time; the only begotten Son, who is in the bosom of the Father, he hath declared *him*.

---

in consequence of the Incarnation, nor because man is naturally like God, but only because the grace of God bridges the "impassable gulf" between a holy God and sinful, perverted man. The term "fulness" (*plērōma*) is suggestive of the complete richness and adequacy of God's nature in Christ. The concept is elaborated with great emphasis when Paul warns the Colossians against substitutes for an implied impoverished revelation in Christ (Col. 2:9, 17, 19).

**We all received.** The plural is an allusion to the Christian community of which both John the Baptist and John the Evangelist were members. Paul often wrote with an awareness that he and his readers were sharers alike of a common grace. The primitive Christians were participants, not spectators or auditors, in the church of the living God. The historical as well as the personal is prominent here. Collectively, believers share in the fulness of God mediated through Jesus Christ; personally, they gain access to the privileges of the kingdom by individual spiritual birth (v. 12). **Grace for grace** (*charin anti charitos*) means literally "Grace in the place of grace, one grace succeeding another and as it were taking the place," not the latter displacing the former, but the consequence and reward of the former" (CGT, 74).[20] "For" (*anti*) may mean

"instead of," or (as here) "in view of" (cf. Heb. 12:2).

17 Like other writers of the New Testament John does not present the Gospel (*evangelium*) as displacing the Law (*Torah*), but rather implementing and fulfilling it. Nevertheless the contrast is striking in favor of the Gospel. None denied the grandeur of the Law and the Lawgiver. But with astonishing confidence the early Christian witnesses asserted the superiority of the evangel over the greatest institution of Judaism. Perhaps this was what John meant when he used the phrase **grace upon grace** — the giving of the Law was an act of grace but the giving of the Son was a greater favor.

The *dia* (through) occurs four times in the prologue with the genitive of agent (vv. 3, 7, 10, 17). Since it is agent, not source, it is best translated in each of these instances by "through" rather than "by" as in KJV.

In saying that "no one has ever seen God" (RSV) John may have had in mind the account of Moses, hidden in the cleft of the rock, seeing God pass by (Deut. 33:20, 23). Here it is said, "my face shall not be seen."[21] Jesus Christ not only sees, but "is in the bosom of the Father," a phrase suggesting closest intimacy.[22] The **hath seen** (*heōraken*) is a perfect tense, implying a condition resulting from having

---

From the standpoint of the New Testament writers the Incarnation is one of the cardinal doctrines of the Christian faith. There is an aura of mystery and of wonder about this simple declaration, a statement which ends in adoration. Plato said that philosophy begins in wonder; the same is true of religion (cf. Ps. 8:1-4). The idea is that the Logos, as the expression of God's thought and will, temporarily assumed human form for the purpose of redemption, even redemption of those hostile to the Light.

14 **The Word became flesh and dwelt** ("tabernacled") **among us.** The word "tabernacled" (*skēnoō*) has rich connotations to the reader of the Old Testament. Here the author has in mind the Tent of Meeting during the wilderness sojourn with the Shekinah presence of God filling the tabernacle (Exod. 40:34). The tent, with the glory of God as a bright cloud filling and covering it, was the visible symbol of God's abiding presence. A similar idea is reflected in the Roman Catholic doctrine of "the Presence" in

---

[20] Cf. A-G, p. 73: "*grace after or upon grace* (i.e., grace pours forth in ever new streams; cf. Philo, Poster. Cain. 145 . . . , Theognis 344 . . .) . . . ."
[21] This is difficult to harmonize with Deut. 34:10; Exod. 24:11; Judg. 13:23.
[22] Cf. Lazarus in Abraham's bosom (Luke 16:22) and the disciple in Jesus' bosom (John 13:23).

19 And this is the witness of John, when the Jews sent unto him from Jerusalem priests and Levites to ask him, Who art thou?

20 And he confessed, and denied not; and he confessed, I am not the Christ.

seen God (cf. D-M, p. 203). The best Greek texts, including Bodmer, II P[75] (c. 200 A.D.), read "only God" rather than "only Son." The former is probably the more authentic because it is in the best manuscripts and because it is "the harder reading," and therefore the reading least likely to be the result of editorial changes or scribal error.[23] However, the context justifies the rendering son because of the relation to the following phrase in the bosom of the Father. In any case the Son is actually God because the Word is said to be God and equated with Son. The NEB rendering is good, "God's only Son, he who is nearest to the Father's heart, he has made him known."

19 John's witness was three-fold: (a) to the delegation from Jerusalem (vv. 19-28), (b) to a group of disciples (vv. 29-34), and (c) to two of his disciples (vv. 35-37). Here, as in the Synoptics and Acts, the Gospel begins with the witness of John. The birth stories of Matthew and Luke, with the Prologue of John, are introductory. More precisely, the Gospel does not begin with John; it begins

with John's witness to the Christ (cf. Acts 1:22).

20 John's reply was prompt and categorical, I am not the Christ. The phrase egō ouk eimi ("I am not") is intriguing because of its possible contrast to Jesus' use of egō eimi ("I am"). Jesus used this emphatic affirmation several times in this Gospel: "I am the bread of life," the "light of the world," the "good shepherd," the "true vine," etc.[24] John's negation is equally emphatic. The self-abnegation of John the Baptist is extraordinary, exceeding that of Jonathan with reference to David. The Evangelist emphasizes that John quickly rejected the temptation to accept the status of Messiah and stressed instead his own subordinate role. A certain reticence on John's part is implicit in the specific questions with which they plied him before he identified himself. With Malachi 4:15 in mind they inquired whether he were Elijah, the Messiah's forerunner. Even this John denied, in spite of Jesus' assertion later that this was essentially John's role (Luke 7:27; Matt. 11:14; Mark 9:11-13). The point is that

the consecrated "host" on the altar. Ezekiel saw the "glory of God," or this luminous Shekinah, leave the temple of Solomon because of the sins of the people, visible evidence that God had left his people to their own destruction (Ezek. 10:18, 19; 11:23). The climax of the drama of redemption is seen in Revelation 21:3 "behold, the tabernacle of God is with men. . . ." The word skēnoun ("to tabernacle") appears only five times in the N. T., here and in Revelation 7:15; 12:12; 13:6; 21:3; possibly a hint of common authorship. Thus in the incarnate Son of God, the divine glory, or Shekinah, returned to abide with humanity, a testimony to "God's eternal solicitude for man." The glory of God did not make a hidden, occult, clandestine rendezvous with man; it came openly for all to see and welcome. This divine radiance, giving both light and

the assurance of God's presence, was that of an only Son of the Father. While all are "sons" of God by creation and all believers are spiritual sons by adoption (v. 12), the Sonship of Jesus Christ is utterly unique. In this sense there is only one Son of God.

Aside from John 3:16 there is probably no more important statement in the Fourth Gospel than the affirmation "the Word became flesh." If it is remarkable to state that "the Word was God," it is even more amazing to state "the Word became flesh." Not only did the Son of God create the universe directly, without working through intermediate beings as the Gnostics taught, he actually clothed himself in human form. The Gnostics believed that, since matter was evil, God would not come into direct contact with matter. The most direct refutation of

[23] Ezra Abbot, "On the Reading Only Begotten God in John 1:18," *Bibliotheca Sacra*, 1861, pp. 840-72; J. H. Goodwin, *On the Reading Only-begotten God: John 1:18* (London: J. Clark, 1883).
[24] John 4:26; 6:35; 8:58; 10:7, 11; 11:25; 14:6; 15:1.

21 And they asked him, What then? Art thou Elijah? And he saith, I am not. Art thou the prophet? And he answered, No.

22 They said therefore unto him, Who art thou? that we may give an answer to them that sent us. What sayest thou of thyself?

23 He said, I am the voice of one crying in the wilderness, Make straight the way of the Lord, as said Isaiah the prophet.

---

John was not Elijah in the literal sense, but was Elijah in the figurative sense (CGT, p. 78).

21 Their next question was Are you the prophet? This is an allusion to the passage in Deuteronomy 18:15, where it is predicted that a "prophet" like Moses will be raised up, one of the clearest O. T. predictions of a Messiah.

22 After learning what John was not, they "put him on the spot" by demanding who he did claim to be. They did not wish to return to Jerusalem with their fact-finding mission a failure. The author's interest here is in John's witness rather than with the purpose and methods of the committee, since he dwells so little upon the latter.

23 At length John did make his own identification. In the eloquent passage cited, "the voice" is that of a herald stationed along a super highway from Mesopotamia to Jerusalem passing along the message that God is coming to Jerusalem for the purpose of giving pardon, salvation and comfort. John's modesty is apparent here. He is less than a prophet, only a "voice," yet his was the voice that heralded the Lord's historic advent.

Similarity with the Qumran sect which produced the Dead Sea Scrolls is apparent here. Influenced by this same passage in Isaiah the Covenanters of Qumran went into the desert to prepare the way for the Messiah. It has even been suggested that John the Baptist was a member of the community until he turned from asceticism to evangelism.[25] In any case the similarity of place, imagery, and sense of mission is striking. The Scrolls, especially the *Manual of Discipline* and the *Book of Wars,* reflect the apocalyptic hopes and excitement of the period before and during the ministry of the Baptist.

---

dualism is the affirmation that the Word became flesh. The chief reason for rejecting Docetism — the idea that Jesus' humanity was not real (II John 7) — was its denial of the truth of the Incarnation. Unlike the Gnostic Redeemer, Jesus did not come to bring gifts to souls imprisoned in matter.[j] He came to give himself, that is, his life, in order that mankind could be free from sin and find real life. Only John points up the paradox involved in becoming flesh and reflecting God's glory at the same time.[k] Paul stressed the self-emptying which this involved (Phil. 2:7) while John stressed the attendant "glory." Who is sufficient for these things for "great is the mystery of godliness" (I Tim. 3:16)?

15 For the second time John is introduced to identify the incarnate *Logos.* The greater accuracy of the ASV (and NEB) as compared to the RSV is in evidence here: the RSV changes the tense of the verb *martyrei* from present to past. Although "crieth" (*kekragen*) is the perfect tense in this unusual construction, both verbs have the force of the present and indicate John's influence as being contemporary (CKB, p. 140). There is another paradox here. Jesus was before John (in time) but came after him (in public presentation). Because of this priority in existence Jesus has pre-eminence over the herald of his advent. As in the Synoptics, John comes in the role of announcer or herald, similar to the "voice crying in the wilderness" (Isa. 40:3).

b. "Grace and Truth came" (vv. 17-18)

Revelation is a prominent theme here and throughout the Gospel. The Prologue ends as it began with the theme of reve-

---

[25] G. Lancaster Harding, *London Times Supplement,* Sept., 1955. W. H. Brownlee, "John the Baptist in the New Light of Ancient Scrolls," *Interpretation,* Jan., 1955, pp. 70ff.
[j] R. Bultmann, *Theology of the New Testament,* tr. by K. Groebel (New York: Scribner's, 1955), 40.
[k] *Ibid.,* II, 50.

24 And they had been sent from the Pharisees.

25 And they asked him, and said unto him, Why then baptizest thou, if thou ar
not the Christ, neither Elijah, neither the prophet?

26 John answered them, saying, I baptize in water: in the midst of you standeth
one whom ye know not,

27 *even* he that cometh after me, the latchet of whose shoe I am not worthy to
unloose.

28 These things were done in Bethany beyond the Jordan, where John was baptizing

24 The delegation was sent by the Pharisees probably because they had more interest in the Messiah and the fulfillment of Scripture than the opportunistic Sadducees or the fanatical Zealots and Herodians. Their question was "Why conduct a sacramental rite, such as baptism, when you have no official status or authority?"

26 In reply John minimized the importance of his own baptism by contrasting it with the greater baptism with the Spirit and a greater Baptizer. In the Synoptic accounts John's baptism with water is set in striking contrast to Jesus' baptism with the Spirit. Here, although implied in v. 26, the contrast does not appear until v. 33. Barrett suggests that the baptism with the Spirit was not revealed to John until the Spirit descended upon Jesus.

27 The figure John used was the familiar act of a servant in removing the sandals of a visitor, preparatory to washing his feet. Then, as now, the customary footwear in Palestine was a leather sol with enough straps to hold it to the foot This type is inexpensive and does not retain gravel to chafe the foot. John claimed to be unworthy of even being Jesus' servant.[26]

28 The oldest manuscripts have "Bethany." After Origen visited Palestine he could not find any Bethany near the Jordan an decided that a Jordan ford named Bethabara was the place (cf. Josh. 15:6, 61; 18

lation. The climax of divine revelation is that effected by Jesus the Christ. His revelation "in the flesh" is not contradictory to the O. T. but rather implements, fulfills, completes it. This is the consistent theme of the N. T. (cf. Matt. 5:17; Rom. 4; Gal. 4; Heb. 1:1-5; I Pet. 1). With full appreciation of the O. T. revelation John enthusiastically presents Jesus as the one who does to complete satisfaction what the old covenant did only in part.

B. THE WITNESS OF JOHN (1:19-36)

1. JOHN'S SELF-IDENTIFICATION (19-28)

a. "A Voice" (vv. 19-23)

For the third time the witness of John about Jesus is presented, this time in greater detail. It is characteristic of the Johannine literature to treat several themes simultaneously rather than in sequence. The presentation is cyclical, or spiral — a theme stated briefly then reiterated and expanded. This is characteristic of the style of both the Gospel and the Epistle In Paul's letters and in Hebrews, on the other hand, one subject at a time is treated before moving to the next. In structur therefore, the Johannine literature is like an oratorio in which several motifs or themes are introduced and continued with varying emphases throughout the composition. Among the motifs introduced in ch. 1 are light, life, truth, grace, belief sonship, and witness. The remainder of ch. 1 is characterized by a pastoral, idyll charm, a calm before the storm which breaks out in the polemical sections following.

19 The mission was evidently an official delegation from the ruling body of the Jews — the Sanhedrin, a group of seventy elders with civil and religious authority dating from the time of Moses (Exo 18:13-26). Unlike most of the late hecklings (cf. Luke 20:20, 21), this inquiry was probably a sincere search for the truth concerning the now famous evan

[26] The third century Rabbi Joshua ben Levi is credited with the statement, "Every service which slave performs for his master a pupil will do for his teacher, except loosing his shoe." — S-B, I, 12

29 On the morrow he seeth Jesus coming unto him, and saith, Behold, the Lamb
of God, that taketh away the sin of the world!
30 This is he of whom I said, After me cometh a man who is become before me:
or he was before me.

21), a reading which afterwards prevailed
in western texts. This Gospel apparently
distinguishes two Bethanys, one near Jeru-
alem, the other "beyond Jordan" — John
:28; cf. 10:40; 11:28.[27]

29 The morrow probably means the
day after the visit of the delegation from
Jerusalem (vv. 19-28). This naturally
created excitement among John's disciples
and it would remain fixed in memory as
a time of crisis. Prior to this time had
come the baptism and temptation of Jesus.
John's language on this occasion strongly
implies that he had recognized Jesus as
the Messiah before answering the Jeru-
alem delegation. Jesus was probably
coming directly from his temptation (Westcott). It was appropriate that this recognition by John should precede his Galilean
ministry (Mark 1:14).

The one bearing the sin of the world
was a present active participle which comes
from the verb airo meaning "to take up,
lift, bear, carry, take away, remove, destroy, kill." Here the preferred reading is
"to bear" or "to carry away." The meaning of removal and expiation are combined

and the meaning is "bear away." The
present tense indicates that the "taking
away" is not only historical, at Calvary,
but continuous. The singular hamartia
(sin) indicates something more than the
sum total of all individual acts of sin. "It
is the sin of the cosmos which knew not
Jesus (v. 10) that is in view in this tremendous phrase" (JBL, I, 47).

Verse 30 is related to vv. 6 and 15
where the same statement occurs. Obviously John had been referring to the
Messiah in his earlier preaching. Now
he points out the one for whose coming
he had been preparing his hearers. It
was the historic moment of identification.
In paraphrase John's paradoxical statement means, "this man, whose public
ministry is later than mine in time, is
actually before me in importance because
he existed before me in time." The use
of aner (man) rather than anthropos
(man) is probably to suggest the virility
and commanding presence of Jesus;
anthropos is the generic term which includes man and woman (MRV, II, 67).
The phrase who was before me is another

---

elist of the Jordan valley. To inquire
concerning the authenticity of an alleged
Messiah was the Elders' prerogative
Deut. 18:21).

### b. A Servant (vv. 24-28)

These passages give rise to many questions, some of which have caused endless
theological controversy. Was Jesus' baptism with the Holy Spirit designed to replace water baptism? Acts and the Epistles
indicate a negative answer.[1] An opposite
conclusion could easily be drawn from the
Gospels. What form of baptism was employed? John 3:23 and Romans 6:4 are
said to imply immersion and Acts 2:41;
10:47; 16:33 to imply some other mode.
The scanty evidence suggests that immersion may have been the preferred but

not the only method. The N. T. does
make it clear that the mode was less important than the spiritual transformation
to which the rite bore witness.[m] Does the
"Baptism with fire" connote fire as a
purifying agent (Isa. 4:4) or an agent of
judgment and destruction (Lev. 10:12;
Luke 3:16, 17; 12:46, 50)? Is the Spirit
given in connection with the water baptism
(Acts 2:38; 10:47; Gal. 3:2) or later
(Acts 8:16; 19:5, 6)? Some of these
questions remain as living issues today.

### 2. JOHN'S IDENTIFICATION OF THE CHRIST (1:29-36)

This chapter abounds in designations or
titles of Jesus of Nazareth: the "Word of
God" (v. 1), the "Light of the World" (v.
5), the "Christ" (vv. 25, 41), the "Lamb

---

[27] P. Parker, "Bethany Beyond Jordan" (JBL, Dec., 1955), argues for only one Bethany, the one near
Jerusalem.
[1] Acts 2:38; 10:47; 19:5, 6; Heb. 6:2; I Pet. 3:21.
[m] I Cor. 1:17; Eph. 2:8, 9.

31 And I knew him not; but that he should be made manifest to Israel, for thi[s] cause came I baptizing in water.

32 And John bare witness, saying, I have beheld the Spirit descending as a dov[e] out of heaven; and it abode upon him.

allusion to the pre-incarnate existence of the Logos. It is in harmony with John 8:58, "before Abraham was, I am."

31 **And I** is from *kago,* crasis for the two words *kai* (and) and *ego* (I), here an emphatic "even I." **I knew** is *ēdein,* the pluperfect of *oida,* which means (a) "to perceive" and (b) "to know;" it is the knowledge resulting from insight and perception. John and Jesus were cousins (Luke 1:36), and John knew of Jesus before the baptism (Matt. 3:14). It seems therefore that John is not saying that he had no prior knowledge of Jesus as a man, but rather that he did not previously know him to be the Messiah. John is saying that he knew only that this work was to prepare the way and that in the appropriate time and manner God would make clear the identity of the real Messiah John had been sent to announce.

32 **I have beheld the Spirit descending.** With great solemnity John makes his pub-

lic identification of Israel's messianic king. The *tetheamai* (**I have beheld**), is th[e] perfect tense of *theaomai,* signifying tha[t] the effects of the vision still remain. Th[e] verb means more than a quick glanc[e] (*blepō*), more than perception (*eidō*) it means "to scrutinize, to inspect, to gaz[e] upon intently." The verb is normally use[d] of physical, not mental vision. The imager[y] of the Spirit, as a dove, recalls the lan[g]uage of Genesis 1:2 — "The Spirit o[f] God brooded (hovered) over the face o[f] the waters." The Talmud comments: "Th[e] Spirit of God was borne over the water a[s] a dove which broods over her young."[28] In Palestine the dove has always been re[-]garded as a sacred bird.[29] It appear[s] therefore that a dove actually alighted o[n] Jesus at his baptism and that at least Joh[n] and Jesus recognized this as the visibl[e] evidence of the God-sent anointing of th[e] Spirit. The incident is analogous to th[e] phenomenom of tongues at Penteco[st] (Acts 2).

of God" (vv. 29, 36), the "Messiah," the "Son of God" (vv. 34, 49), and the "King of Israel" (v. 49). What did John mean by the "Lamb of God"? What connotation did this designation have for his contemporaries? Four meanings are possible: (i) the lamb of the sin offering, (ii) the paschal lamb, (iii) the vicarious lamb (*amnos*) of Isa. 53:7, and (iv) the warlike lamb (*arnion*) of the apocalypses including Revelation 5:6, 8, 12, 13; 6:1, 16; 7:9; 12:11; 13:11; 17:14; 22:1, 3.[n] Dodd thinks that here the "lamb" is the militant Messianic leader of the apocalypses, that "taking away the sins of the world" is not by vicarious sacrifice but by leading the flock of God, the armies of God, to victory.[o] He notes that the

context supports this in that the state[-]ment of the Baptist is followed by An[-]drew's designation of Jesus as "the Mes[-]siah" (1:41) and Nathanael's as "Kin[g] of Israel" (1:49).

John's thought is admittedly comple[x] and "extremely subtle" (Dodd, p. 236) Is it not probable that in the Baptist[s] designation of Jesus there were thre[e] connotations: sin-offering, paschal laml[b] and the vicarious "suffering servant" o[f] Isaiah 53:7? The "lamb" of the Gospel [is] *amnos.*[p] The "lamb" of the Apocalyps[e] is a different word — *arnion.* Even i[n] the latter usage the idea of the Lamb a[s] vicarious sacrifice is as prominent as th[e] idea of Lamb as Messianic warrior.[q] I[n] Revelation there seems to be not tw[o]

[28] Chagiga, 15a, cited in BFW, I, 21.
[29] Xenophon (*Anab.* I, iv. 9) says it was unlawful to hunt doves in Syria. Philo (*Euseb. Praep. Evange[l.]* viii. 14. 64) notes the large number of tame doves in Ascalon because it was forbidden to eat ther[.] In Song of Sol. 2:12 "the voice of the turtle dove" is translated in Chaldee as "the voice of the Spirit." See Bernard, *loc. cit.*
[n] CHD, pp. 230-38. See also *Enoch* lxxxix ff.; *Test. Twelve Patriarchs: Joseph.* xix. 8.
[o] I John 3:5 ("to make an end of sin is a function of the Jewish Messiah, quite apart from an[y] thought of a redemptive death." — CHD, p. 237). Test. Levi. xviii: 9; Ps. Sol. xvii; 29; Apoc. Baruc[h] lxxiii: 1-4; cf. Acts 5:31; 3:26; Matt. 1:21; cf. Isa. 16:1.
[p] Also in Acts 8:32; I Pet. 1:19; cf. Heb. 9:14; Acts 20:28.
[q] E.g., Rev. 5:6, 12; 7:14; 12:11.

33 And I knew him not: but he that sent me to baptize in water, he said unto me, Upon whomsoever thou shalt see the Spirit descending, and abiding upon him, the same is he that baptizeth in the Holy Spirit.

34 And I have seen, and have borne witness that this is the Son of God.

35 Again on the morrow John was standing, and two of his disciples;

36 and he looked upon Jesus as he walked, and saith, Behold, the Lamb of God!

---

**33 I myself did not know him** (as the Messiah). The **I** (*kagō*) again is emphatic. John did not recognize Jesus as the Messiah by any human acquaintance; it was a supernatural revelation to him. As God alerted Samuel and told him beforehand the signs by which he would be able to recognize the Lord's anointed (I Sam. 9:15-17) so John was given some objective manifestation. See is the verb *horaō* which suggests physical vision in which a spiritual significance is seen. John uses five synonyms for seeing in this chapter. Here, in describing the descent of the Spirit two are used. As noted in v. 32, *theaomai* is the physical act of seeing with emphasis on the abiding significance of what is seen. In vv. 33 and 34, in recounting the vision the sense of spiritual perception (*horaō*) is uppermost. The last significant conviction to which John bore witness is that the individual from Nazareth whom he baptized, the one on whom the Spirit descended in the form of a dove, is none other than the Son of God.

**36 He looked upon Jesus as he walked.** The verb **looked upon** (*emblepsas*) here means "to scrutinize, to fix one's gaze upon, to consider in a spiritual sense." After this scrutiny, he spoke out of divine revelation and deep conviction — "There goes the Lamb of God!" Upon hearing this exclamation, the two disciples of John left their master and walked off with Jesus. The verb *peripateō*, used to describe Jesus' walk, is a reminder of the Athenian Peripatetics, disciples of Plato and Aristotle. Like these great Greek teachers whose "school" was the market place, or a home, or a place of seclusion (any place in particular), so Jesus had his "school." The only elements in this "school" were teacher and pupils, master and disciples. There was no classroom; they learned as they walked with the mas-

---

concepts of the role of the "Lamb" but one; the difference in the Lamb's role is temporal. In retrospect "the Lamb" is acknowledged as the one through whose vicarious death the saints are made citizens of the kingdom (Rev. 5:6, 8, 12, 13; 7:10, 14, 17; 12:11). In prospect "the Lamb" is the judge of the world and the saints' king and leader (Rev. 14:1, 10; 17:14; 19:7, 9; 21:9, 22; 22:1, 3). Throughout the New Testament there are not two Christs (one of Isaiah 53 and the other of Jewish apocalypticism) but one; the emphasis is on his suffering-servant role (Mark 10:45) but the factor of his future as judge and king is seldom lost sight of — the difference is only a temporal one.

There are many evidences that John's use of the title "Lamb of God" has the central meaning of vicarious sacrifice in harmony with Isaiah 53 — a chapter which had greater influence on the writers of the New Testament than any other O. T. chapter. The suffering-servant motif of Isaiah 41-53, adopted by the Synoptists, appears also in John in a wealth of analogy.[r] In I John 1:2 Christ is the "propitiation (*hilasmos*) for the sins of the whole world." John 3:16 clearly asserts that salvation is dependent on the death of God's Son. In John 11:50 Caiaphas acknowledges the appropriateness of one dying for the people. In John 10: 11 the Good Shepherd lays down his life for the sheep. In John 6:50-58 eternal life is conditioned upon "eating the flesh" of the Son of God. The emission of blood with water from the side of the crucified Christ is regarded by John as vastly significant (John 20:34; cf. I John 5:6). It seems clear therefore, especially in the light of the qualifying clause "takes away the sins of the world," that the connotation of the title "Lamb of God" was that of a substitutionary death, a vicarious

---

r Cf. J. H. Farmer, "The Gospel by Mark," ISBE, III, 1994.

37 And the two disciples heard him speak, and they followed Jesus.

38 And Jesus turned, and beheld them following, and saith unto them, What seek ye? And they said unto him, Rabbi (which is to say, being interpreted, Teacher), where abidest thou?

39 He saith unto them, Come, and ye shall see. They came therefore and saw where he abode; and they abode with him that day: it was about the tenth hour.

---

ter. The world has never witnessed more effective teaching than that done in Athens and in Palestine by walking teachers.

There are some problems here. Why did the Synoptists give the impression that Jesus went immediately from his temptation to Galilee and to preaching when a quiet interlude near the Jordan is indicated in John? Also, how may the calling of the four in Judea be reconciled with the calling of the four near Galilee as reported by the Synoptists? Unless the accounts are irreconcilable (CKB), John reports their introduction to Jesus while the Synoptists describe their formal commission as apostles.

38 **Jesus turned** (cf. 21:20) **and saw them following.** He gazed intently on them — the third occurrence of the verb *theaomai* (aor.), here meaning a penetrating scrutiny. They addressed him as "Rabbi," an Aramaic word for teacher

or master which John translates into *didaskale* ("teacher") for his Greek readers.

39 **They abode with him.** The verb for "abide" is *menō* (cf. "remain") and suggests its deeper meaning in John 15:3. The author notes that **it was about the tenth hour.** In the New Testament the Greek and Jewish system of time was in practice. The day was twelve hours long (John 11:9) and began about 6 A.M. or at sunrise. As the length of the days varied with the season, so the length of the hours varied accordingly. The "tenth hour" thus was about 4 P.M. In ancient times, with little artificial illumination, only limited activity was planned after this hour. Since activities were limited to daylight hours, the force of the numerous exhortations in Gospels and Epistles to "work while there is daylight" (John 9:4; 11:9; Rom. 13:13) is apparent.

---

sacrifice, "an amalgamation of Old Testament ideas" presenting Jesus as the "new and better sacrifice."[s]

## C. JESUS' FIRST DISCIPLES (1:37-51)

### 1. THE CALLING OF ANDREW AND PETER: TO COME IS TO SEE (vv. 37-42)

This is the fifth mention in this chapter of John as a witness (viz. vv. 7, 15, 19, 29, 35). He is reported as witnessing to Jesus' being the "light," the pre-historic one, and the "Lamb of God" (vv. 29,35). He himself was only "a voice." This witnessing is specifically mentioned on three separate occasions: (i) when he witnessed to representatives of the Pharisees (v. 19), (ii) when he witnessed to a group of his disciples (v. 29), and (iii) on the second day after the visit of the delegation from Jerusalem (v. 35).

When Jesus asked **what seek ye?** (v. 38), the disciples probably were somewhat embarrassed and confused. Perhaps their reply — "where do you live?" — was evasive. Probably what they really wanted was to get better acquainted. In any case that was the outcome. In his reply **come and see** one may note a characteristic of Christianity and especially of John's Gospel. That is the correct sequence: "Come and you will see;" spiritual insight and knowledge is a condition of obedience, a characteristic thesis of this Gospel.[t]

The expression **come and see** (or better, "come and you will see") in vv. 39 and 46 is echoed by the invitation and challenge to the Samaritan woman. One senses here the excitement of venture and discovery. Jesus' place of abode may have been the same as that stated in 10:40, the place "across the Jordan" near the scene of John's baptizing. The evening interview

s CKB, p. 147; l.c. See also "The Lamb of God," *New Testament Studies*, Feb. 1955, pp. 210ff.
t E.g., "If ye continue in my word . . . ye shall know" — John 8:31.
"He who receives" knows that "God is true." — John 3:32.
"If any man will to do his will, he shall know . . . " — John 7:17. See also John 1:46; 4:29; 11:34; cf. 20:8.

40 One of the two that heard John *speak,* and followed him, was Andrew, Simon Peter's brother.

41 He findeth first his own brother Simon, and saith unto him, We have found the Messiah (which is, being interpreted, Christ).

42 He brought him unto Jesus. Jesus looked upon him, and said, Thou art Simon the son of John: thou shalt be called Cephas (which is by interpretation, Peter).

---

40 Who was the unnamed companion of Andrew on this initial encounter with Jesus? Most commentators think it refers to John the son of Zebedee, brother of James. There is little basis for a confident conclusion and the question must rest on the basis of probability. In this Gospel only one "John" is named, and that is John the Baptist. Many believe the author of the Gospel to be the son of Zebedee and that this accounts for his reticence about naming himself. Andrew is more prominent in this Gospel than in the others. He has been called "the contact man" since on three occasions he is shown bringing others to Jesus: On various occasions he brought his brother Simon (1:41), a lad with lunch (6:8), and some Greeks (12:22) to Jesus, twice in association with Philip.

41 The first (*prōton*), found in the best manuscripts, indicates that he turned his attention first to his brother. An alternate reading found in Old Latin and a few other versions has *mane* (Gk. *prōi*), suggesting the beginning of another day. This would allow additional time for the events recorded and make v. 43 mark the fifth day after the delegation from Jerusalem (JHB). Available evidence seems to favor the first alternative (CKB, 151).

42 Jesus looked (*emblepsas*) upon Simon with a searching gaze; looked him "through and through." The verb signifies a careful scrutiny and is found also in v. 36 and in Matthew 19:26; Mark 10:27 (Jesus looked at his disciples), Mark 10:21 (Jesus looked into the "rich young ruler's" mind), and Luke 20:17 (Jesus looked at the Pharisees before predicting their doom). While *blepō* often suggests a quick glance, *emblepō* here denotes a penetrating gaze (L-S).

On the morrow means the fourth or fifth day after the mission from the Pharisees to John, depending on the reading of v. 41.

---

gave them an opportunity to learn more about the travelling teacher whom John has just called "Lamb of God."

Coming and seeing led to the great discovery. The narrative conveys the undertone of excitement with which Andrew breaks the news to his brother. When one considers the background of Messianic expectation which had prevailed for almost a century among the devout Jews beginning with the Maccabbean period and which John had fanned into expectancy, Andrew's enthusiasm is understandable.

41 We have found him is *heurēkamen* from whence comes "eureka," the word Archimedes is reported to have used when he excitedly announced his discovery of a solution to the problem of ascertaining the amount of gold in King Hiero's crown. The thrill and excitement of discovery is still important in personal evangelism. An old Gospel song expresses it well: "Hallelujah, I have found Him whom my soul so long has craved! Jesus satisfies my longings; through his blood I now am saved" (C. T. Williams).

Two Aramaic words are used here and translated into Greek. Simon was Peter's Jewish name. Jesus gave him the Aramaic name Cephas or its Greek equivalent *petros* (rock). The giving of this surname was a prophecy of Peter's strength as leader of the twelve. The term *Messias* is Aramaic for "the Anointed one." In the Old Testament prophets, priests and kings were anointed with oil typifying the bestowal of the Spirit of God for service to the community.[u] One of Andrew's greatest recorded deeds was that of leading his brother to Jesus, the Christ.

Some of the best lessons in personal evangelism are to be found in the first and fourth chapters of this Gospel. Worth

---

[u] I Sam. 10:1; 16:13; I Kings 1:39; 19:15, 16. The role of "The Lord's Anointed" is best set forth in Isaiah 61:1-4, the passage by which Jesus introduced himself to his townspeople in Nazareth (Luke 4:17-19).

43 On the morrow he was minded to go forth into Galilee, and he findeth Philip: and Jesus saith unto him, Follow me.

44 Now Philip was from Bethsaida, of the city of Andrew and Peter.

45 Philip findeth Nathanael, and saith unto him, We have found him, of whom Moses in the law, and the prophets, wrote, Jesus of Nazareth, the son of Joseph.

46 And Nathanael said unto him, Can any good thing come out of Nazareth' Philip saith unto him, Come and see.

47 Jesus saw Nathanael coming to him, and saith of him, Behold, an Israelite indeed, in whom is no guile!

48 Nathanael saith unto him, Whence knowest thou me? Jesus answered and said unto him, Before Philip called thee, when thou wast under the fig tree, I saw thee

49 Nathanael answered him, Rabbi, thou art the Son of God; thou art King of Israel

---

Into Galilee: a new shift in geography is noted here. From the "wilderness of Judea," probably the upper Jordan region where John was baptizing, Jesus moved northwest in southern Galilee, a distance of perhaps thirty miles. Attention is again called to the word "find" — Jesus "found" Philip and Philip in turn "found" Nathanael (v. 45).

Nathanael is mentioned only in the Fourth Gospel, a fact which leads some to identify him as Bartholomew, on the assumption that his last name was Bar-Tholmai (son of Tholmai). In permitting Philip to designate Jesus as "son of Joseph" our author does not thereby subscribe to Philip's inadequate understanding of Jesus whom John believes to be the unique "son of God" (1:18). He lets the characters express their own thoughts without editorial corrections. This gives a much more authentic note than would have been the case had all expressed a mature Christology at this stage (JHB, I, 62).

48 Whence knowest thou me? Nathanael's surprise at Jesus' prior acquaintance with him was similar to that of the Samaritan woman (4:19, 29) and led to a similar response — an acknowledgment of Jesus' supernatural insight. In the mention of the fig tree there is probably more significance than is apparent. The fact that the rabbis recommended a fig tree as a good place to study the Torah is hardly adequate to account for Nathanael's reaction (S-B, II, 371). Nor is it likely that it refers to Nathanael's infancy, as some have asserted. It seems probable that a short time previously (before Philip called) Nathanael had been meditating under a fig tree about Israel's messianic hope and his own involvement. Jesus knowledge of this time of soul-searching would be to Nathanael evidence of Jesus supernatural insight. This insight is mentioned later in this Gospel (e.g., 2:25).

49 Completely convinced at this, like Thomas later (20:27), Nathanael made the most complete confession of faith

---

noting here is the fact that the emphasis is upon investigation and experience rather than upon indoctrination. The disciples were invited to get acquainted with Jesus before they were asked to declare their faith. This acquaintance was the basis for the commitment which came to a decisive climax after the feeding of the five thousand (John 6:66-69; Mark 8:28-30).

One is unavoidably impressed by the naturalness and charming simplicity of John's account of the initial acquaintance between Jesus and his earliest disciples. The readiness with which these men left their occupations to follow Jesus must have been due to their expectation of a

Messiah and the influence of John the Baptist. In John's report a full expression of their faith in Jesus as the predicted Messiah (1:41, 45), Son of God and King of Israel (1:49) came much earlier in their experience than in the reports of the Synoptics (cf. Matt. 16 13-20).

Some ground-rules for successful recruiting, derived from this chapter, include:

(i) Call attention to the person of Jesus (1:36).

(ii) If possible, invite those with whom you have had some previous association (1:41).

50 Jesus answered and said unto him, Because I said unto thee, I saw thee underneath the fig tree, believest thou? thou shalt see greater things than these.

51 And he saith unto him, Verily, verily, I say unto you, Ye shall see the heaven opened, and the angels of God ascending and descending upon the Son of man.

---

voiced thus far (except the Baptist's). The title "Son of God" is the more surprising statement coming from Nathanael. It would be harder for a Jew than for a Greek thus to designate any man. The latter title "king of Israel" would be more in line with the conventional conception of the Messiah as son of David. In any case, Nathanael's conversion was quick and complete.

50 **Greater things than these.** In Nathanael's case "seeing was believing." Pleased with this use of evidence presented, Jesus promised him more evidence and greater privileges. A rabbinic proverb states that the reward of keeping a commandment is another commandment or duty. So here, the reward of faith is a better basis for faith.

51 **The angels of God ascending and descending.** The allusion here is to Jacob's ladder (Gen. 28:12), as St. Augustine was perhaps the first to observe. It is connected to v. 47 and its reference to a guileless Israelite. Two events of Jacob's life are thus recalled: at Peniel where his guile was exposed, then removed, and his name changed to Israel (Gen. 32); also at Bethel where Jacob saw the ladder reaching to heaven (Gen. 28). In Genesis 28:12 the Hebrew *be* ("upon it" or "upon him") may refer to Jacob rather than to the ladder, and thus read "upon him." Hence Jesus may be the true patriarch.[30] The "Son of Man" now becomes the "ladder" which reaches from earth to heaven. In John's characteristic manner he is using O. T. background to suggest another facet of Jesus' person and ministry. In Johannine usage it is not the "one like unto a son of man" of Jewish apocalypses. Hellenistic notions are reversed: the Incarnation is a descent, not an ascent.[31] The thought of mediatorship seems prominent here. Heaven has come to earth, the Shekinah has come down and heaven and earth are united in the unique heavenly Son of Man. In John 3:13 also Jesus presents himself as one who ascends to and descends from heaven.

**Upon the Son of man.** The title "son of man" means the prophet in Ezekiel; in Daniel 7:13 the title is messianic and apocalyptic. In Jesus' usage both these

---

(iii) Invite people when you have had the thrill of personal discovery (1:45).

(iv) Meet resistance not by argument but by a challenge to investigate (1:46).

(v) Be sure to experience yourself what you recommend to others.

(vi) Lose no time in setting about winning souls; begin at once.

2. PHILIP AND NATHANAEL: TO SEE IS TO BELIEVE (vv. 43-49)

Here Jesus takes the initiative in searching out Philip and inviting him to follow. It is not unlikely that Philip had been a disciple of John, for it is difficult otherwise to account for the readiness with which he not only followed but immediately recruited Nathanael. Probably the example of his neighbors Andrew and Simon conditioned his decision as well. It is likely that theirs was a warm, enthusiastic response which was impulsive and genuine but not a considered and final decision. This initial acquaintance, however, prepared them for their final decision, as reported by the Synoptics, to leave their fishing nets and kinfolk and accept Jesus' formal invitation at the Sea of Galilee. Bethsaida, the home town of the three, was located on the north shore of the lake, just east of the mouth of the Jordan. Even its ruins have now all but disappeared, as if in literal fulfillment of Jesus' prediction (Matt. 11:21).

Philip's announcement to Nathanael was similar to that of Andrew — "we have found him." In his summary of the Old Testament witness to the Messiah, Philip apparently had no particular proof texts in mind. It was a broad assertion that

[30] Ed. Schweizer, "The Son of Man," JBL, 1960, p. 126.
[31] E. M. Sidebottom, "The Ascent and Descent of the Son of Man," *Anglican Theological Review*, April, 957, pp. 119ff.

meanings are apparently combined. He was truly a man who took the nature of the children of Abraham (Heb. 2:16) and yet was the Lord from heaven. Why did Jesus use the title so frequently, the disciples almost never?[32] The phrase "son of man" occurring in Psalm 8:5 is applied to Christ in Hebrews 2:6-9 as the "second Adam" (cf. Rom. 5:12ff.; I Cor. 15:45). The same term in Daniel 7:13, in the context of apocalypse, is quoted in Mark 14:62. The frequent use of the term in Ezekiel as the prophet's designation of himself probably influenced Jesus' use of the term also.[33] As such it would connote universal humanity and Jesus' real humanity. The church fathers avoided the term perhaps because of the fear that it might suggest that Jesus had a human father. The influence of Daniel 7:13 with its apocalyptic context is seen in Matthew 26:64; Matthew 16:27, 28; II Esdras 13; Luke 22:69; Mark 8:38; 13:26, 27; Matthew 24:30; Luke 21:27; Zechariah 12:10; Revelation 7:1.

A review of these and other passages in which the term "son of man" occurs indicates a frequent eschatological and apocalyptic setting, quite understandable in the light of Daniel 7:13. It is also clear that the term itself did not necessarily have a Messianic connotation as evidenced in such passages as Matthew 16:13, 16, where it is used in contrast to the Messiah or at least is non-committal and neutral.

In summary it seems clear that in some circles at least, the term "son of man" had a definite apocalyptic and hence messianic connotation. It also implied a homogeneity with the human race equivalent to "son of Adam." In the light of Ezekiel it stood for God's representative among men. The use of the definite article, when the term is applied to "Son" (huios), is unprecedented, hence the term is really a new one (Westcott) and gives it a mark of distinction and uniqueness. Consistent with Jesus' strategy elsewhere, the title was probably appropriated to suggest two concepts: the humanity of Jesus and also his heavenly origin.[34] The former would emphasize his ascent from humanity to the Father; the latter his descent from heaven in the Incarnation. This supposition is strengthened by John 3:13 where the descent is mentioned and John 14:3; 16:28; 20:17 where the ascent is stressed. With Deuteronomy 30:11ff. in mind, Paul in Romans 10:6-8 speaks of Christ's ascent and descent; the same theme is mentioned in Ephesians 4:8 where Christ's descent at the Incarnation is paired with his ascent at his resurrection. In John's treatment, as in Paul's, the descent of Christ makes possible the believers' spiritual resurrection and ascent with Christ at the general resurrection "so shall we ever be with the Lord" as Paul expressed it (I Thess. 4:17).[35]

---

he had met one who fulfilled the messianic hopes of Israel, as delineated in the Scriptures. But Nathanael was skeptical when the alleged Messiah was said to come from neighboring Nazareth. "Familiarity breeds contempt," and this familiarity with Nazareth made the acceptance of Jesus by his neighbors more difficult.

46 In reply to Nathanael's skeptical query Philip did not argue but simply invited him to investigate. The implication was that Nathanael should not judge the case before getting the evidence. Philip called for a first-hand investigation. Again one notes the emphasis on response as the condition for discovery and verification.

The sequence is not understand and then respond, but the reverse. Nazareth was not mentioned in the Scriptures as being the home town of the Messiah (Micah 5:2), and this doubtless added to Nathanael's surprise. Whether his exclamation was skepticism or only surprise, Jesus did not condemn it. Instead, as Nathanael approached him, Jesus welcomed him as a guileless Israelite. The Psalmist praised the man without guile (Ps. 32:2) and prayed for deliverance from it (Ps. 34:13). Before his name was changed to Israel, Jacob was not without guile, his name meaning and nature being that of a "supplanter" (Gen. 27:35). Probably

*good!!*

---

[32] John and the Synoptists agree in this; the term occurs in Matthew 27 times, in Mark 14 times; in Luke 27, and in John 13 times. It occurs only once elsewhere in the N. T. (Acts 7:56).

[33] In Ezekiel the term, as a designation of the prophet (Heb. "son of Adam"), occurs about 100 times.

[34] Agreeable with the conclusion is E. M. Sidebottom, *Expository Times*, June, 1957, p. 283; see also op. cit., May, 1957, pp. 231ff.

[35] John 5:25-29; 6:41, 44, 50, 51; 12:26, 32 (cf. I Pet. 3:19; John 20:17).

with this background in mind, Jesus sees in Nathanael a worthy son of Israel, open, guileless, and sincere, in contrast to his ancestor Jacob-Israel.

The word guile (*dolos*) appears on a tombstone described by Deissmann, containing an eloquent imprecation on an Israelite (?) in whom there was "guile," one who murdered two Jewish girls of Delos (LAE, pp. 422-424). Guile is related to the idea of cunning, treachery, and enticement, a quality exemplified in the patriarch Jacob. The opposite quality of sincerity or blamelessness Jesus saw in Nathanael. Sincerity is also the opposite of hypocrisy. (The latter term is said to have originated among Greek actors who wore masks to conceal their true identity and were thus called "hypocrites" [under the mask]. The words they spoke and the roles they played were those of others.) In both Old and New Testaments a synonym for the quality of unaffected simplicity and sincerity is "blamelessness" (Heb. *tamim;* Gk. *amemptos*). Such men were said to be "just and perfect" in their generations (cf. Gen. 6:9; 17:1; Job 1:8). Christ can do more with simple unaffected men without guile than with men who are merely clever.

With this chapter as an introduction, the reader of this Gospel is led on to the chapters which deal with a series of miracles or signs, each of which presents a different facet of Jesus' person and work. This introductory chapter has taken the reader from the eternal verities of the Prologue to the details of Jesus' recruitment of some of his earliest adherents. The witness to Jesus, inaugurated by John, is climaxed by the witness of Nathanael, who, like Thomas, compensated for his initial reserve by an unequivocal and emphatic affirmation of faith.

# CHAPTER II

And the third day there was a marriage in Cana of Galilee; and the mother of Jesus was there:

2 and Jesus also was bidden, and his disciples, to the marriage.

3 And when the wine failed, the mother of Jesus saith unto him, They have no wine.

---

## EXEGESIS

2:1 **On the third day** — By John's counting it is the fifth day since the deputation from Jerusalem to John, but it is the third day from the calling of the first two disciples (1:35) and apparently 2:1 is to be understood in that sense. If one day is allowed for travel this would be the sixth day after the events of 1:19ff. (CHD, p. 158). If the day on which Andrew and John "abode with him" (1:39) was the Sabbath, as seems most probable, the wedding would be on Wednesday in accordance with Talmudic direction (JHB, I, 12).

3 The *oinos* (wine) was of the ordinary kind. Attempts to show that this was a special type of unfermented wine have not been convincing.[1] The implication of v. 10 is that normally at such a feast the wine consumed was such that the guests could be slightly intoxicated so that they would be unable to distinguish good wine from bad. In the ancient Near East there was no method of refrigeration and no known chemical process by which milk could be kept from souring or wine from fermenting.[2] Wine was often regarded as a gift from God and was almost as common as food.[3] It was a prominent part of the wedding ceremony. The higher Christian ethic of later times, however, called for moderation and even, at times, for complete abstinence.[4] The influence of a Christian upon others was also a major concern (cf. I Cor. 8:9; 9:12; 10:23, 24, 32, 33; Rom. 14:7, 8, 21).

---

## EXPOSITION

### II. PUBLIC MINISTRY: MANIFESTATION OF GLORY IN THE "SIGNS" (2:1-12:50)

#### A. The Initial Encounters (2:1-4:54)

##### 1. the first "sign" (2:1-11)
###### a. The Occasion (vv. 1-5)

In the light of v. 11, as Bultmann has observed, this chapter begins a section dealing with the revelation of "glory" to the world (*op. cit.*, pp. 77). This section, embraced in chs. 2-12, is devoted to Jesus' *public* ministry. The events of this period revolve around a series of seven "signs" (*sēmeia*), beginning with the changing of water to wine and ending with the raising of Lazarus. Usually the "sign" comes first and a discussion then follows showing the significance of the "sign" as it is related to belief.

The scene was probably Kefr Kanna, five miles east of Nazareth.[a] Nazareth and this "Cana" occupy similar topographical sites on the high plateau just north of the plain of Esdraelon. The distance from the Jordan would be thirty miles or more. Jesus' mother may have been a relative of the bride or groom,

---

[1] E.g., B. R. Palmer, *The Bible and The Use of The Word "Wine"* (Signal Press) and *The Temperance Bible Commentary*, edited by J. R. Lees and D. Burns.
[2] Easton, "Wine," ISBE, V, 3087.
[3] Gen. 14:18; Isa. 55:1; Amos 9:14; Ps. 104:15; I Tim. 5:23.
[4] I Cor. 6:19; Eph. 5:18; Gal. 5:21, 25; Rom. 8:4. Temperance was sought by several means: wine was forbidden to priests when in service (Lev. 10:9) and to those serving as judges (Prov. 31:4, 5); wine was weakened with water (II Macc. 15:39; Justin Martyr *Apol.* i. 65); inebriation at a feast was controlled by a governor (Ecclus. 32:1, 2; John 2:9, 10); warning (Gen. 9:21; Isa. 5:22; Heb. 2:5; Prov. 21:17); and by condemnation of drunkenness (I Sam. 1:14-16; Isa. 5:11-17; I Cor. 5:11; 6:10; Gal. 5:21; Eph. 5:18; I Pet. 4:3).
[a] Other possible sites are Qanat el Gelil and 'Ain Qana (CKB, p. 158).

4 And Jesus saith unto her, Woman, what have I to do with thee? mine hour is not yet come.

5 His mother saith unto the servants, Whatsoever he saith unto you, do it.

6 Now there were six waterpots of stone set there after the Jews' manner of purifying, containing two or three firkins apiece.

7 Jesus saith unto them, Fill the waterpots with water. And they filled them up to the brim.

---

4 In addressing his mother as "woman" (gynai) rather than "mother" (mētēr) Jesus meant no disrespect. Such greetings were common at that time and betokened affection and respect. He used the same term when addressing his mother at the cross and commending her to the care of the beloved disciple (19:26). The significance here may be that Jesus thus indicated that he was independent of maternal control. In other words, "We stand on different grounds" (Trench), or "Leave me in peace" (W. Bauer, Das Johannes Evangelium, 1933).

The expression my hour is not yet come is more puzzling. It occurs a total of six times in this Gospel.[5] In each case the "hour" is a reference to the "hour" of his passion. Here the meaning is less lucid but seems to say, "The time of my self-revelation is in the future; leave this situation to my judgment" (cf. v. 11). The "hour" here then would mean the time for revealing his identity through a miracle. At the same time he was dependent on his Father in Heaven.

5 His mother's statement is intriguing. Did she expect him to work a miracle? Her advice to the servants (diakonai) implies that she believes that with Jesus in command of the situation all would be well. "Between the lines of His refusal her faith reads a better answer to her appeal, and she is content to leave all to Him" (CGT, p. 91).

6 Six waterpots (hydriai) of stone. The stone waterpots would hold about twenty gallons each and hence are not the same as the common earthen wine jars which held about four gallons. As John explains to his non-Jewish readers, these jars held water for ceremonial washing of the hands before meals (cf. Mark 7:3) and were not used for carrying water; they were storage vessels. Apparently the servants drew water from the well or cistern and filled the six pots. As they drew out the water to serve the tables it turned to wine in the smaller jars; otherwise the quantity of wine left over would be prodigious.[6] It was only enough wine for that particular occasion.[7]

---

but it is not necessary to assume this. An Oriental wedding was and is an elaborate affair, and a large gathering of wellwishers was quite customary.[b] The sponsors were generous so Jesus' disciples were also included among the invited guests.[c] From the fact that Joseph is not mentioned one may assume that Joseph was now deceased. Jesus' presence at the feast was a testimony to the sanctity of marriage. He was not an ascetic or a recluse

like John the Baptist. Consequently, his conviviality may have been a particular problem to John's disciples, and confusing to the neutrals (Luke 7:33, 34). Because John drank little or none he was called a fanatic; because Jesus did so he was called self-indulgent.[d]

Weddings in every culture are among the most joyous occasions which a community experiences. In the Old Testament the Song of Solomon gives expression to

---

[5] John 7:30; 8:20; 12:23; 13:1; 17:1.

[6] Westcott's view that the command *draw out now* indicates that they were commanded to draw water from the well, rather than from these stone jars, although recently supported by P. A. Illingworth ("The Miracle of Cana," *Expository Times*, 1954, pp. 289ff.), has not won wide acceptance. Such an interpretation renders useless any mention of the waterpots and ignores instances when this verb (antlein) means "to draw out of" another vessel (A.M.G., Stephenson, "The Miracle at Cana," *Expository Times*, 1955, p. 177).

[7] Dods, among others, thinks the number and capacity of the jars indicates that the entire contents (120 gallons) was changed to wine as a lasting witness of God's generosity (EGT, I, 704).

[b] At an Oriental wedding in Jerusalem in 1958, to which the writer was invited, a distant relative or a guest could invite other guests. It was a festive occasion with the wedding ceremony following the feast.

[c] The practice of *inviting* the guests is also alluded to in the parable of the wedding garment (Matt. 22:3).

[d] The suggestion that the Cana miracle was influenced by Isaiah 9:1-3 (LXX) is possible but not probable. See H. W. Montefiore, *Journal of Theological Studies*, July-Oct., 1949, pp. 183ff.

8 And he saith unto them, Draw out now, and bear unto the ruler of the feast
And they bare it.

9 And when the ruler of the feast tasted the water now become wine, and knew
not whence it was (but the servants that had drawn the water knew), the ruler of th
feast calleth the bridegroom,

10 and saith unto him, Every man setteth on first the good wine; and when
men have drunk freely, then that which is worse: thou hast kept the good wine unti
now.

11 This beginning of his signs did Jesus in Cana of Galilee, and manifested hi
glory; and his disciples believed on him.

---

9 The ruler of the feast (architriklinos, superintendent of the dining room) comes from the word "ruler" compounded with a term meaning "room with three couches" (JHT). His responsibility was not supervision of the ceremonies, i.e., he was not the "toastmaster," but rather his job involved the arrangement of the room and the food — the job of a wine steward or headwaiter. One of his responsibilities was probably to "taste" and approve of the beverages used. The word for "taste" is geuo meaning "to taste, try the flavor, enjoy, experience, or to take nourishment." Obviously the bridegroom or his friends were responsibile for furnishing the beverages. Since he did not know the source of the new wine, the architriklinos was able to judge impartially. Addressing the bridegroom privately, or perhaps before the assembly, he jocularly generalized on common practice and noted this unusual situation. Usually the inferior wine was reserved for the time when the guest were too intoxicated to distinguish goo wine from bad.

10 The word translated drunk freel (methysko) is a stronger term than th English translation suggests; it means "t become intoxicated." It was a generali zation applicable to all such feasts, no necessarily to this one in particular. Th entire Mediterranean area is excellent fo grape culture and the use of wine wa practically universal then as now, and it value seldom questioned. Under circum stances such as obtain today, however, i seems that Jesus might not have partake of wine, much less provided it.

11 The first of Jesus miracles, or won ders, or signs according to John, is thi one at Cana. One of John's key words i sēmeion (sign), his favorite term fo miracle.[8] Miracles in the New Testamen were an important factor in apologetics an important factor in the Christian faith.[9]

---

the joy of romance and marriage. In the New Testament this episode indicates that the religion of the Bible has room for wholesome joy. This story of the wedding feast provides a lighter side to the Fourth Gospel, a Gospel dealing mostly with the grim realities of light versus darkness. This story, found only here, presents an other interesting facet in Jesus' life an ministry.

b. The "Sign" (2:6-11)

This "sign" or miracle is found only in John and is different from all other mentioned in the New Testament. I was not, like all of the others, done t

[8] There were seven such miracles in John, each with significance for the matter of belief; six o them manifested his glory before the world, and one of them (walking on the sea 6:17-21; cf. Luke 8:24 Matt. 14:26) was known only to the Twelve.

[e] The author was invited in the fall of 1961 to a typical oriental wedding in Old Delhi, India, on which had many things in common with the wedding to which Jesus was invited. In the early evenin the guests met at the home of the bridegroom. The groom was seated, clothed in brightly-colored garments a headdress all but covered his face. He greeted the guests graciously and stated that he was highl honored to have a non-Indian among his guests. A band, hired for the occasion, played for about thirt minutes before the procession started. At the appointed time the bridegroom was seated on a burro wit a small boy (his nephew) seated in front of him, and the procession began. Hired torchbearers, numberin about two dozen, marched in front of and beside the procession while friends of the bridegroom followe behind. After a march of about a mile, the party stopped for twenty minutes while friends of th bridegroom, most young business and professional men, danced in the streets in celebration of the event (In the city of Agra, a few nights previously, the street dancing was performed by a young woman and a dwarf man — each dancing alone, of course.) Upon arrival at the bride's home, food was serve to the 200 men present in an open-air pavilion that had been set. Later the women, friends of th bride, ate also. The marriage ceremony itself was not conducted until almost 2 a.m. It was nearl dawn before the guests departed. Only those fairly wealthy could afford an affair of this scale, bu even the poor have celebrations costing far more than they can afford, as is common in Western land today.

[9] Cf. Heb. 2:4; Acts 4:16; John 5:36; Rom. 1:4; II Cor. 12:12; I Pet. 1:3.

12 After this he went down to Capernaum, he, and his mother, and *his* brethren,
and his disciples; and there they abode not many days.

The purpose of this "sign," or at least of
its effect, was to manifest the "glory" of
Jesus. The noun "glory" (*doxa*) occurs
twenty times in this Gospel; the verb "to
glorify" occurs twenty-two times, far more
than in the other Gospels. It was a favorite term of Paul, also. It is the usual
LXX translation of the Hebrew term
*kabod* (glory) which means "heavy," or
"severe," or "in honor" (Job 1:14-21),
or "to be glorious" (Isa. 66:5). It is a
synonym for *qadosh* (holiness). This last
quotation is the most relevant here. Indeed the closing chapters of Isaiah (60-
66), with their emphasis on God as the
light of his people, almost certainly have
influenced John's expression here. The
glory or Shekinah of God shines through
Jesus Christ as anticipated for the reader
in 1:18 where Jesus is said to be "full
of grace and truth."

12 After this (*meta touto*), lacking in
the Synoptics, occurs 4 times in John
11:7, 11; 19:28) and denotes passage of
time. The author deems it worthwhile to
mention the short stay in Capernaum, although it is not clear just why. Some
suggest that Jesus wished to go over the
details with his family in preparation for
his separation from them to his public
ministry. Others think it was a stop-
over enroute to Jerusalem for the Passover; but since Capernaum would be somewhat out of the way, this suggestion is,
while plausible, less probable. Capernaum
was the Jewish "capital" of Galilee on the
north shore of the lake, while Tiberias on
the southwest shore was the Roman center.
The fact that the Sea of Galilee is almost
700 feet below sea level makes it an ideal
winter resort, a good place to sojourn before the spring pilgrimage to Jerusalem
for the Passover.

The verb **went down** (*katebē*) is appropriate since the Sea of Galilee is some
2500 feet lower than the plateau on which
Cana and Nazareth are located. Because
of Roman Catholic insistence on the virginity of Mary, some interpreters have
assumed that Jesus was Mary's child

relieve distress. Unlike all of the other
"signs" mentioned in this Gospel, this
one alone has no discourse resulting from
it; there is no opposition, and no defense
or explanation is necessary. It lacks the
obvious moral justification which is apparent in the other miracles. For this
reason there has been a widespread effort
to allegorize and to spiritualize it and thus
guarantee its beneficent influence. As
might be expected, one of the earliest expositors to allegorize this event was Origen.
He saw in the six waterpots the symbol of
the six days of creation and thought the
two or three firkins represented the psy-
chical, spiritual, and corporeal senses
(Origen, *De Princ.* iv. 1. 12). To Origen
the main significance of the account is
in its symbolizing that to the Christian
Jesus is the source of joy.[f] Others in the
Alexandrian School saw in this event a
prophecy that the water of Judaism
would be transformed by Christ into the
new wine of the Gospel.[g] Clement adds,
"If He made water wine at the marriage,
He did not give permission to get drunk."
He notes that "The Scripture accordingly, has made wine the symbol of the
sacred blood."

In modern commentators there is also
a strong tendency to find in this event a
spiritual significance through symbolism.
Hoskyns sees in this "beginning of signs"
a parable of the inadequacy of the Jewish
waterpots for purifying and the need for
the better beverage which comes later and
is fully satisfying — the adequacy of the
Gospel as compared to the Law (*op. cit.*,
p. 186). Other modern commentators
stress the idea of Christ's love for the
Church and see in this "sign" a prelude
to the entire Gospel.[h]

f Origen, *Works*, ed. A. E. Brooks (Cambridge, 1896) 10, 12; 13, 57; 13, 62. Cited in M. F. Wiles, *The Spiritual Gospel* (Cambridge: The University Press, 1960), p. 43; cf. John 16:22, 24; 7:13. Said Origen, "Before Jesus the Scripture was indeed water, but after Jesus it has become wine for us" (13, 62).
g See Clement of Alexandria, *The Instructor*, II, ii, 29, *Ante-Nicene Fathers* (New York: Scribner's, 1903, II, 245).
h Alan Richardson, *The Gospel According to St. John* (London: SCM Press, 1959), p. 59. H. P. Patton, "Marriage at Cana," *Methodist Review*, 110; 597-602, July, 1929, p. 600.

13 And the passover of the Jews was at hand, and Jesus went up to Jerusalem.

---

and that the "brethren" were cousins. There seems to be no foundation for this assumption. The record calls them Jesus' "brethren" and there is no reason to believe that they were not so in fact. Later it is recorded that these brothers did not believe in Jesus (7:5), but "James the Lord's brother" later confessed his faith, in the Epistle which bears his name.[10]

13 The passover of the Jews was at hand, and Jesus went up to Jerusalem. Characteristic of John's chronology is the grouping of events around the various sacred festivals of the Jewish calendar.[11] Most of them are specifically mentioned — the Passover, the Feast of Dedication (Hannukah) which originated in the Maccabbean period as a result of the cleansing and reconsecration of the temple after the Syrian profanation (I Macc. 4:50; John 10:22), and the Feast of the Tabernacles (7:2). Except for the Fourth Gospel, one would suppose that during Jesus' public ministry only one trip was made to Jerusalem for the Passover. This chronology represents one of the chief

points of difference between the Synopt Gospels and John.

A generation ago most critical schola were inclined to think the Synoptic a counts the more nearly accurate; recentl however, the trend has been to return the traditional view, to a greater respe for John's accuracy. The most satisfa tory view, on the whole, is to accept th evidence from each of the four Gospe and thus to recognize Jesus' ministry extending over a two or three-yea period.[12] The chief difficulty of this tr ditional view, however, is the inherent in probability of two similar cleansings, th first with no recorded after-effects whi the second speedily led to Jesus' exe cution. A deliberate transfer for theolog cal reasons seems to present the fewe difficulties: Matthew apparently trans ferred elements in chapters 5-7 to mak one continuous "sermon," a topical a rangement; John does have a marke theological rather than a strictly chrono logical interest, and the transfer woul have the benefit of presenting at the ou

---

The fact that at Corinth and at Gerasa so-called "miracles" of the changing of water to wine are recorded, together with the prevalence of the worship of Dionysius and Bacchus, has led some scholars to assume that this account is not historical and that John borrowed this theme from pagan sources.[i] Bultmann suggests also that the ignorance of the "ruler of the feast" and the bridegroom as to the source of the wine is symbolic of the blindness of the world to Jesus, in spite of his signs.

It should be kept in mind that not all

who regard the event as symbolical deny i historicity. Many who regard it as hi torical think John included it because c its symbolic meaning. Most of the churc fathers interpreted it thus.[j] Any attemp to make practical use of the story fo edification virtually compels resorting t symbolism and allegory. But such us should be practiced with caution her because the event is not presented wit the same obvious symbolism as that of th blind man whose restoration of sight be came the occasion of a greater blindnes on the part of "the Jews" (John 9:39).

[10] See JHB, "Additional Note," I, 84-86.

[11] THE HEBREW CALENDAR

MONTH — NAME OF MONTH — FESTIVALS

1. New Year — NISAN — Passover (14th day).
2. April, May — IVYAR — (ZIV)
3. May, June — SIWAN — Pentecost (50 days after Passover)
4. June, July — TAMMUZ
5. July, Aug. — ABH
6. Aug., Sept. — ELUL (Neh. 6:15)

7. Sept., Oct. — TISHRI — Trumpets, Atonemen Tabernacles
8. Oct., Nov. — HARHESHWAN
9. Nov., Dec. — CHISLEV — Hannukah
10. Dec., Jan. — TEBET — Esther 2:16
11. Jan., Feb. — SHEBAT — Zech. 1:7
12. Feb., Mar. — ADAR — Purim

[12] For discussions of Johannine and Synoptic chronology see Godet, pp. 68-81; RHS, pp. 27-37 CKB, p. 163; and JHB, I, cii-cviii. The problem of consistency in chronology leaves one with severa choices (a) there were two cleansings, one at the beginning and the other at the close of Jesus' ministry (b) John deliberately corrected Mark's chronology; or (c) John deliberately transposed the incider to another chronological setting for theological reasons.

[i] Bultmann, p. 83; Estlin Carpenter, The Johannine Writings (London: Constable & Co., 1927), 380; Bauer, pp. 46, 47.

[j] John Chrysostom, Homilies on the Gospel of John, in Fathers of the Church (New York: 1957 pp. 218ff.

14 And he found in the temple those that sold oxen and sheep and doves, and the changers of money sitting:

15 and he made a scourge of cords, and cast all out of the temple, both the sheep and the oxen; and he poured out the changers' money, and overthrew their tables;

---

set of the public ministry a prophecy of what was to follow.[13] As many recognize, however, there is no compelling reason for denying two cleansings.[14]

The verb **went up** is in contrast to the "went down" of v. 12. Since Jerusalem is nearly 2600 feet above sea level, it is a climb of some 3300 feet from Capernaum. The route could have been either the shorter one through Samaria and the "hill country of Judea," or the longer one through the Jordan valley, thus avoiding Samaria.

14 **In the temple.** The word used (*hieros*) indicates the Court of the Gentiles, or the temple precincts, rather than the sanctuary itself (*naos*). Pilgrims were required to offer a sacrifice — a bullock, a sheep, or, in the case of the poor, a dove. Since it was inconvenient to bring livestock for a long distance, local enterprising businessmen provided sacrificial victims for the convenience of the pilgrims — at a price. It is probable that those who offered their merchandise in the temple area paid a high rental to the temple authorities for their concessions. This,

plus the fact that they had a monopolistic advantage, led them to exact high prices from the devout. Jesus saw and condemned both the merchandising in the holy place and the exploitation of devotion by the profiteers. "Money changers" (*kermatistas*) is derived from a term meaning "to cut up," hence the meaning of "small change." Changers of money still are numerous in the old section of Jerusalem. They operate a quasi-legal "black market" where one can usually find a more favorable rate of exchange than in the banks. In Jesus' day they were the only "bankers" available. They often used their familiarity with foreign currency to cheat the "tourists," and pilgrims.

15 **The scourge** (*phragellion*) is recorded only by John and the term is used only here in the N. T.[15] This happened not far from the present "Chapel of Flagellation" on the so-called "Via Dolorosa." The scourge consisted of a short handle to which were bound several lengths of rope or cord. The word *scheinos* means a "rush," hence a "cord" of twisted rushes (Vincent). The term

---

c. The Reaction: Belief (vv. 9-12)

One lesson the "sign" teaches is the importance of obedience. Jesus' mother urged obedience; Jesus commanded obedience as the condition of the miracle, and the miracle took place as the servants obeyed. There is in the narrative an undertone of expectancy which helps account for the servants' unquestioning compliance with the strange command of Jesus: that they carry "water" to the winesteward at the feast.

John's purpose in telling this story is to record the reaction it produced in his disciples: they believed in him. In his command over "the fruit of the vine" Jesus had let his "glory shine forth," a faint prophecy of greater things than these" to be revealed later. The reader's expectancy

is raised as to the other signs and resulting belief which are here envisioned.

2. EVENTS AT THE FIRST PASSOVER (2:13-3:21)

a. The Temple Cleansed (2:12-22)

The cleansing came by means of a scourge. Why did Jesus use force rather than persuasion? Is this resort to force in keeping with the gentle nature of Jesus as presented elsewhere in the Gospels? This is the only instance in the records in which Jesus used force. The episode serves as a reminder that often God resorts to a scourge in disciplining both individuals and nations. "Whom the Lord loveth he chasteneth, and scourgeth every

---

[13] CKB, p. 163; JHB, I, 88, 89.
[14] W. A. Stevens, & E. D. Burton, *A Harmony of the Gospels* (New York: Scribner's, 1904), p. 37.
[15] The Latin form is *flagellion* (whip or sourge). The Greek verb (*phragelloō*) occurs twice in the N. T. (Matt. 26:26; Mark 15:15).

16 and to them that sold the doves he said, Take these things hence; make not my Father's house a house of merchandise.

17 His disciples remembered that it was written, Zeal for thy house shall eat me up.

is used by Herodotus to describe the "rope" used by the Ephesians to enclose the temple of Diana in their city, thus avoiding destruction at the hand of Croesus (Herod., ii, 6). The word commonly denoted a whip used to flog offenders condemned to death like Jesus by a Roman tribunal. The Egyptian Pharaohs of the New Kingdom Period were usually sculptured holding across the chest a similar scourge as a symbol of their authority. The usage perhaps resulted from the practice of a master asserting his authority by flogging his slave. In its use by Jesus, therefore, the scourge would not only be a useful weapon but also an evidence of Jesus' authority (cf. Westcott, ad loc.).

The *pantas* (all) implies that he cast out of the temple not only the livestock but also the vendors. The bird was a *peristera* (dove, pigeon), a favorite bird for sacrifice and the same as was seen at the baptism of Jesus (1:32). The dove was often used as a symbol of Christian virtues and also used to symbolize the soul (A-G). One can readily imagine the noise, stench and filth which greeted the pilgrim as he entered the temple precincts. The temple "market" was indefensible whether from the standpoint of aesthetics, reverence, hygiene, or justice. "It was a scene

of violence: the traders trying to protect their property, cattle rushing hither and thither, men shouting and cursing, the money changers trying to hold their tables as Jesus went from one to another upsetting them. It was indeed so violent a scene that the disciples felt somewhat scandalized until they remembered, then and there, not afterwards, that it was written, "the zeal of thy house hath eaten me up" (Dods, EGT).

The take (aorist imperative *arate*) is more solemn and "more authoritative than the present imperative, which may denote continuous action.[16] In using the possessive pronoun in **my Father's house** Jesus implies his unique relation to God. He does not say "our Father" or "your Father," and his use "my Father" is an indirect claim to Messiahship. This in turn is the basis for his authority for the drastic action. The remark is similar to the audacious claim of Luke 2:49 — "my Father's business."

17 **His disciples remembered.** The quotation is from Psalm 69:9, "For I am become a stranger unto my brethren and an alien unto my mother's children. For the zeal of thy house hath eaten me up; and the reproaches of them that reproach thee are fallen upon me." One cannot

son whom he receiveth" (Heb. 12:6). It was this prophetic insight during the dark days of the American Civil War which caused a poetess to see above the grim statistics a divine purpose in this "scourging." She expressed it thus:

Mine eyes have seen the glory of the coming of the Lord.
He is trampling out the vintage where the grapes of wrath are stored.
He hath loosed the fateful lightning of His terrible swift sword:
His truth is marching on.

I have seen Him in the watchfires of a hundred circling camps;
They have builded Him an altar in the evening dews and damps.
I can read His righteous sentence by the dim and flaring lamps.
His truth is marching on.[k]

Out of this divine "scourging" came the emancipation of four million slaves. A warning against a divine scourging was voiced by England's foremost poet at the peak of Great Britain's power and prestige. Said this "prophet,"

[16] E. A. Abbott, *Johannine Grammar*, London, 1906, p. 318. The authoritative (aorist) imperative is addressed to Christ's mother (2:5), here (2:16, 19), to the Samaritan woman (4:16), to the blind man (9:7), and to Lazarus (11:44). John avoids the use of the aorist imperative with *pisteuo* (believe); instead the present imperative of "believe" is used, thus "allowing time for reasonable examination" (*ibid.*, p. 319).
[k] Julia Ward Howe, "Battle Hymn of the Republic."

18 The Jews therefore answered and said unto him, What sign showest thou unto us, seeing that thou doest these things?

---

say with confidence whether some or all of the disciples remembered this, or whether it came to their minds at that occasion or later. In general, the disciples related these words and this deed to the Old Testament only afterwards (cf. John 14:26; 2:22; 12:16; cf. Acts 11:16; Jude 17).

Psalm 69 is the psalm most frequently quoted in the N. T. (JHB, I, 91). Often attributed to Jeremiah, its frequent references to vicarious suffering give it a distinctive messianic connotation, and it apparently was so regarded by the early Christians. That Jesus' fiery zeal for the Kingdom impressed itself upon close observers is indicated also in Mark 3:21 where his friends said, "He is beside himself." The past tense of the Psalm is here changed to the future — shall consume me. Jesus' earnestness caused his enemies to accuse him of fanaticism — of having a demon, like the accusation made against John the Baptist (John 8:48; cf. Luke 7:33).

18 What sign . . . ? A demand for a "sign," or some objective evidence of supernatural power, was characteristic of the Jews. They made a similar demand after witnessing a series of miracles (Matt. 12:38), a demand which Jesus said was not justified since they already had sufficient evidence for faith. Later, after witnessing the feeding of the five thousand, they made a similar demand (John 6:30). Their position stated that if Jesus could perform some prodigy on demand they would have a basis for believing his claims. Jesus' response was to say that they already had so much evidence that more of the same would not change their attitude (John 6:36; Matt. 12:39ff.; Luke 16:31). In John especially, the point is made that what the people need is not so much spectacular miracles as spiritual discernment to detect the supernatural in what was going on at the time (John 6:47-51; Matt. 4:5, 6). The latter portion of the verse gives the reason for their challenge. Their position is summarized: "Since you have asserted authority in cleansing the temple, prove to us by some miracle that your authority is from God." Jesus' reply here is markedly different from that

---

Far-called our navies melt away;
On dune and headland sinks the
    fire;
Lo, all our pomp of yesterday,
Is one with Nineveh and Tyre.[1]

Sometimes the "scourge" of God is administered to his children personally in order to bring forth good fruit unto perfection. No chastening at the moment seems joyous, "nevertheless afterwards, it yieldeth the peaceable fruit of righteousness unto them who are exercised thereby" (Heb. 12:11 KJV). He sits "as the refiner and purifier of silver" (Mal. 3:3) to prepare for himself a bride "holy and without blemish" (Eph. 5:27).

The temple and its unholy commerce represented what are now called "vested interests." The custodians of the temple no doubt received a commission from the temple merchandise and thus had a financial interest in maintaining the concession This did not deter Jesus from a frontal attack upon those who were trespassers in his Father's house. John the Baptist, in a similar manner, did not shrink from declaring to Herod Antipas the sin of living in adultery. God's prophets have certain occupational hazards that make their way of life extremely precarious.

The central truth of this paragraph is that Jesus is greater than the temple. In the third temple was focused the religious nerve-center of world-wide Judaism. In response to the challenge to show his authority in the temple precincts he predicted that if they destroyed "the temple" (his body) he would erect it in three days — a prediction of his death, burial, and resurrection. Here, as elsewhere, the Jews were uncomprehending and materialistic while Jesus spoke in symbols. Elsewhere he had spoken of himself as greater than Solomon and as one greater than Jonah. Now he says in effect that he is greater than the temple with all that it represented

[1] R. Kipling, "Recessional."

19 Jesus answered and said unto them, Destroy this temple, and in three days will raise it up.

20 The Jews therefore said, Forty and six years was this temple in building, and wilt thou raise it up in three days?

21 But he spake of the temple of his body.

22 When therefore he was raised from the dead, his disciples remembered that he spake this; and they believed the scripture, and the word which Jesus had said

---

given in answer to a similar question reported in the Synoptics (Matt. 21:23— 22:46; Mark 11:27-12:37; Luke 20:1-47).

19 Jesus frequently, especially in John's account, answered the Jews in terms of symbols, notably in conversing with Nicodemus and after the feeding of the five thousand (John 3:3; 6:41). In other words, he invested material picture with spiritual meaning. In this case his hearers naturally assumed that he was speaking of the nearby temple sanctuary. This was the third temple. The first had been destroyed in 586 B.C. The second temple had been begun in 536 B.C. and was dedicated twenty years later. The present temple, according to Josephus, had been begun in 20 B.C. by Herod the Great. Like the great cathedrals of the Middle Ages, it was not completed in one generation. It had then been under construction forty-six years, and was not finally completed until 64 A.D., shortly before its total destruction in 70 A.D. by the soldiers of Titus (Jos. *Ant.*, xx. 219).

20 The Jews' question was obviously asked with a skeptical sneer. The word temple here is *naos* (sanctuary), referring to the temple proper, not the surrounding court, which was referred to in v. 15 Evidence that Jesus made some prediction about the destruction of the temple is seen in the accusation of his enemies at his trial (Mark 14:58). Actually, the temple was "destroyed" by three factors: the prevalence of synagogue worship made the sacrificial system unnecessary; the Romans destroyed the building; and Christianity transferred the temple idea to the body of believers in Jesus (Eph. 2:21; I Cor. 6:19; I Pet. 2:4). The *idea* which the temple represented ("God with us") survived the destruction of the *building*.

21 The Christian individually and the church collectively are both referred to as shrines, as "temples" (I Cor. 6:19; Eph. 2:21). The husk of the temple sacrifices passed away like a discarded wineskin (cf. Mark 2:22), but the kernel remained in the Shekinah-filled church of Christ (Eph. 5:18; Rev. 21:3; cf. II Chron. 7:1).

22 Does this verse represent the disciples' insight at the time of Jesus' utterance, or did they gain this insight only after the resurrection? Probably the latter was the case; at this time they must have reacted in a manner similar to the others. After the resurrection, however, this sensa-

---

— the full flower of Old Testament religion. As Jesus' contemporaries had difficulty in recognizing him for what he was, so today we need to be alert to recognize God's messengers, his "incarnations."

To the casual observer Miss Effie Southworth was a woman who had given her best years to service in India. To the Indians of Berar province, who had been either recipients or witnesses of her labors of love, she was a "goddess." To the average newspaper reporter the Wright brothers, with their flying machine, were "crazy"; to history they were pioneers in the age of space.

b. The Result: Many Believe (2:23-25)

By a series of acts and deeds Jesus exhibited his true nature and destiny. The cumulative effect upon the disciples and many other close observers was seen in their response of belief, their placing of trust in him. They came to share his vision, his dedication, and his enthusiasm. First there was the conversation in Judea, then the display of his creative power in Cana, and finally his actions and words in the temple. Their faith was not yet made perfect, but they did place credence in him as far as the level of their understanding and insight.

23 Now when he was in Jerusalem at the passover, during the feast, many believed on his name, beholding his signs which he did.

24 But Jesus did not trust himself unto them, for that he knew all men,

25 and because he needed not that any one should bear witness concerning man; for he himself knew what was in man.

---

tional challenge was actually seen to be fulfilled, in a spiritual sense. This is given as another reason for belief, an addition to the accumulation of evidence on which their faith was based. Jeremiah had predicted the destruction of the first temple (Jer. 7:4-15) as had Micah before him (Mic. 3:12; cf. Jer. 26:9, 18), and it is not unlikely that Jesus had this whole precedent in mind as he spoke. In the final analysis it was not Jesus who destroyed the temple but the unbelieving Jews themselves (Mark 12:9).

The passive voice was raised implies the Father's agency in the resurrection (cf. Rom. 1:4). The scripture, in the singular, probably refers to a specific passage rather than to the Old Testament as a whole, in which case the plural (hai graphai) would be used. In the light of apostolic usage it is likely that Psalm 16:10 is the passage referred to (Acts 2:31; 13:35).

23 The reference is to v. 13 and the Passover occasion. While the cleansing of the temple occupies an entire paragraph of ten verses, the overall effect of Christ's other miracles and the belief which resulted are here summarized in three verses. This illustrates John's method of selecting from a vast number a few events on which he dwells at some length (cf. 21:25).

Miracles were regarded correctly as God's "mighty acts." In the Old Testament God revealed himself through these "mighty acts" as well as through the Law and the Prophets (Ps. 106:2; 105:2; II Chron. 20:6-12). Miracles had long ceased to be prevalent in Judaea. No miracle is recorded in the Maccabean crisis (see I Macc.). With the possible exception of Isaiah's day, one would have to go back to the time of Elisha to find a comparable concentration of miracles. The last O. T. miracle prior to this is reported in the Book of Daniel. John's preaching was so sensational that many accepted him as a prophet. Now Jesus came in the same spirit as John but performing miracles as well. The evidences of his Messiahship were accumulating, and hence many believed.

The phrase of 1:14 is here repeated in the sense of believing "into" his name, i.e., placing their faith into. The preposition eis (into) here implies not merely credence but participation in the life of the Son of God. If this belief was actually saving faith, why was Jesus so reserved (v. 24)?

25 In spite of apparent popular endorsement, Jesus was wary and somewhat skeptical. John indicates that Jesus knew enough about human nature to anticipate the alternations of favor and disfavor which would characterize the multitude.[17] He apparently placed little confidence in mass conversions at this time. In the light of this Jesus was not surprised that the people of Jerusalem applauded his "triumphal entry" and a few days later demanded his death. Today the same instability is too frequently in evidence, in Palestine, as elsewhere. Paul encountered this fickleness in Lystra (Acts 14:11, 19) and in Galatia (Gal. 1:6). Jesus manifested similar skepticism with reference to human nature after the burst of approval which resulted from his feeding of the five thousand (John 6:26). It is heartening to realize that Christianity's initial triumphs were made in spite of much human shallowness and instability. It was this instability which caused Paul to travail until Christ was formed in his converts (Gal. 4:19).

Jesus' penetrating knowledge of human nature is indicated several times in the Fourth Gospel (1:48; 13:1, 3; 16:33; 17:14). In John's picture of Jesus he consistently represents him, as do the other evangelists, as having complete command of every situation because he knew human nature and was constantly aware of his Father's assistance. Normally belief — and hence life — will come not by mass movements but by "winning them one by one."

[17] Luke, however, reports Jesus as surprised at the unbelief of his neighbors of Nazareth (Luke 6:6).

# CHAPTER III

Now there was a man of the Pharisees, named Nicodemus, a ruler of the Jews:
2 the same came unto him by night, and said to him, Rabbi, we know that thou
art a teacher come from God; for no one can do these signs that thou doest except
God be with him.

## EXEGESIS

1 This paragraph is linked to the preceding one by the word "man." There (2:25) the definite article denotes the generic noun, *anthrōpos* (mankind as a whole). In contrast, in 3:1 "a man" is without the article. The significance of the omission of the article is that Nicodemus was one of "the many" who believed (2:23), a "sample of the humanity whose inmost thoughts Jesus could read" (EGT). The same could be said for John the Baptist (cf. 1:6). Of the Pharisees, literally, "out (*ek*) of the Pharisees." The same phrase is used of the children of God (i.e., "out of God") in I John 3:8, 9 and elsewhere. Thus, the phrase implies more than adherence, or membership; it implies origin, hence similarity of nature or disposition. The name Nicodemus (*nikē* — victory and *dēmos* — people) means "conqueror of the people." Possibly this man was of the family of that name which joined the diplomatic mission from Aristobulus to seek the help of Pompey in the civil struggle of 63 B.C.[1] He was a rabbi and a member of the Sanhedrin, that governing body of the Jews which had evolved from the seventy associate justices of Moses' time (Exod. 18:13-27).

2 The RSV's "this man" is a better rendition of the Greek pronoun here than the same. The construction is the same as in 1:7.

## EXPOSITION

### c. Interview with Nicodemus (3: 1-21)

#### (1) *The New Birth* (vv. 1-12)

Now there was a man of the Pharisees. Thus begins the first of the series of discourses which characterize the Gospel of John. In most of them a miracle or "sign" is followed by a discourse which usually involves a dialogue between Jesus and "the Jews." This discourse is of more than ordinary importance. Says Hoskyns, it is "not a discourse, but The Discourse, the subject-matter of which is repeated in all subsequent discourses" (Hoskyns, p. 203). He further defines the main themes of "The Discourse" as four in number: Repentance — Jesus himself; God's love in giving his Son — Judgment and Salvation; Works; and Faith. On looking closer one may fairly conclude that the main themes of the chapter are five, and in this order: Regeneration (vv. 1-9), Revelation (vv. 10-13), Life through Death (vv. 14-18), Judgment (vv. 19-21), John's Witness (vv. 22-36).

Little is known of Nicodemus. He is mentioned only in this Gospel, and even here he soon fades out of the picture unnoticed because the author is more interested in what Nicodemus represented than in the man himself. But he reappears in 7:26 to courageously champion Jesus' right to a hearing before he was condemned. His courage is again in evidence when, with Joseph of Arimathaea, he requests custody of the body of Jesus (19:39). The view that he represents the religious leaders of the day has much to commend it. As well as being an individual in quest of spiritual life, he is a representative of the Pharisaic party. The Pharisees in turn reflect and give definition to the prevailing religious view of the generation. Whether Nicodemus was a typical Pharisee

[1] Josephus, *Ant.,* XIV. iii. 2.

3 Jesus answered and said unto him, Verily, verily, I say unto thee, Except one be born anew, he cannot see the kingdom of God.

4 Nicodemus saith unto him, How can a man be born when he is old? can he enter a second time into his mother's womb, and be born?

---

**3** The repetition of "amen, amen" (**verily, verily**) introduces a statement of extraordinary importance. It apparently was characteristic of Jesus' speech. Why did Jesus not wait for the visitor to explain his mission? Perhaps the evangelist simply failed to report it. More probably, however, Jesus discerned Nicodemus' query before he had time to formulate it (cf. John 1:48; 2:25).

The word **anew** (*anōthen*) has at least three distinct meanings: (a) *location* — "from the top" (Matt. 17:51; Mark 15:38; John 19:23) or "from above" (John 3: 31; 19:11; Jas. 1:17; 3:15; 17); (b) *time* — "from the beginning" (Luke 1:3; Acts 26:5); and (c) *repetition* — (Gal. 4:9) — where it is accompanied by the adverb *palin* (again).[2] In this context the meaning is limited to "from above" and "anew" or "again"; that is, either direction or <u>repetition</u>. In support of the latter

is the clear indication that Nicodemus so understood it (v. 4). In support of the reading "above" is the larger context: cf. vv. 10, 13, 31 where credibility is based on the source of authority from above. Also this is the basic meaning of the term (*ana* means "above" or "up"); it is the meaning in most of its N. T. occurrences (John 3:27; 19:11). In John 3:5, 6, 8, it is equated with birth by the Spirit of God. In this context, therefore, all three connotations of the term are in evidence: "again," as Nicodemus understood it, "from above," since God is the source (cf. 1:12-14; 3:31) and "of the Spirit." The one English term which seems best to fit this text is "anew." The NEB renders it "over again," or repetition, as Nicodemus misunderstood it.

**To see the kingdom of God** is the equivalent of citizenship or participation in the kingdom (cf. Matt. 5:8 — "the pure in

---

is another question. It is fairly clear that he was representative of that considerable group who were as neutral as any contemporary could well be, the group of whose members it is said, "many of the rulers believed in him, but . . . failed to confess him lest they be put out of the synagogue" (John 12:42; cf. 9:22).

**2** Why did Nicodemus come by night? Is there some reason why John mentions this specific detail? Since data is lacking the answer must rest upon conjecture. The usual answers include these: (i) More leisure would permit a more thorough discussion; (ii) The rabbis recommended the study of the Torah at night (S-B, II, 420); (iii) His daytime duties necessitated a night interview; (iv) He wished to escape detection; (v) Jesus was busy with the crowds during the day. The theory that he was prompted by a desire for secrecy is highly probable since many believers at this time made no open profession for fear of the consequences (John 9:22; 19:38). Nicodemus had more to lose than most by overt adherence (John 7:

50). The fact that in this Gospel "night" has a moral connotation (John 11:10) adds additional plausibility to this theory. That Nicodemus was a man of courage and conviction, however, is borne out by the two later references to him (John 7: 50-52; 19:39).

Nicodemus began the interview by indicating his recognition of Jesus as a God-sent teacher-prophet on the basis of the miracles attending his ministry. This conclusion was based upon a premise universally held by Jews and pagans — that miracles are of supernatural origin and hence are a divine endorsement of the human instrumentality. The invocation of this principle by the man born blind implies its acceptance even by Jesus' enemies (John 9:30-33; cf. Acts 4:16; Heb. 2:4). In none of the other Gospels is the correlation between miracles and belief more prominent than in John. The "works" (*erga*) of God (4:54; 5:36; 9:3) are often equated with "signs" (*sēmeia*). The view attributed to Nicodemus is the same as that reflected in

---

[2] Also Jos. *Ant.*, 1. 263; Epict. 2. 17. 27.

5 Jesus answered, Verily, verily, I say unto thee, Except one be born of water and the Spirit, he cannot enter into the kingdom of God.

6 That which is born of the flesh is flesh; and that which is born of the Spirit is spirit

---

heart" shall "see God"). In the background is an eschatological meaning: he will be able to enter heaven, but he will not be able to immediately "see" God — something impossible according to John 1:18. The phrase "kingdom of God" (or "heaven") is as rare in the Fourth Gospel as it is frequent in the Synoptics.

5, 6 In most of the discourses recorded in John the Old Testament background is emphatic and obvious. Here, while less obvious, there seems little question but that the association of regeneration with "water" and "Spirit" goes back to Ezekiel 36:25-27, where one of the most gracious promises of the Old Testament is recorded: "I will sprinkle clean water upon you, and you will be cleansed from all impurities; from all your idols I will purify you. 26 A new heart, too, I will give you, and a new spirit, I will put within you. I will take the heart of stone out of our flesh, and I will give you a heart of flesh. 27 I will put My Spirit within you and cause you to walk in My statues . . . ." (BV)

In these words Ezekiel describes the New Covenant which was first announced

through Jeremiah (31:31-34). The language is that of the sanctuary and the ceremonial washing to which is added the evangelical note of inner renovation by the divine Spirit (cf. Jer. 4:14). The "high water mark" of the Old Testament teaching concerning the ministry of the Spirit of God is reached here in Ezekiel.[3] Thereafter the subject is neglected until revived in the New Testament.[4]

The reference here is possibly another allusion to the creation account where "the Spirit of God moved upon the surface of the water" — there a creative Spirit.

Why are "water" and "Spirit" combined in this verse? For dogmatic reasons some have argued from it that water baptism is essential in becoming a Christian. Others, on the opposite extreme, have argued that "water" here refers to the water accompanying physical birth and hence the "water" refers to physical birth in contrast to the birth by the Spirit. Both are examples of forced "exegesis" (or "eisegesis") to support a pre-determined theology. To gain perspective it should be noted that water is mentioned here only once, while the Spirit of God is

---

2:23, where faith is said to result from the seeing of miracles. The plural "we" indicates that others shared his view.

4 The whole idea of a *new* birth was shocking to Nicodemus, accustomed as he was to thinking that a descendant of Abraham would automatically inherit the promises (cf. Gen. 22:17, 18). John the Baptist had sought to shatter this illusion by addressing his countrymen as "off-spring of vipers" and assuring them that God was able to make the very stones at their feet "children of Abraham" (Luke 3:8). It was a telling blow against Jewish exclusiveness, a touchy subject to the Jews (Acts 22:22) but a major theme of the New Testament.[a] This was a radical idea which "turned the world [of the Jews] upside down" (Acts 17:6). Nicodemus

was typical of his countrymen who soon would reject the revolutionary idea that entrance to the Kingdom was by faith, and hence available to all on an equal basis, because it undercut the advantages of being in Abraham's lineage (cf. Rom. 2:28-3:4; 10:1-4).

To Nicodemus, as to most Jews, who, according to John, thought in physical rather than spiritual concepts (John 6:26, 52), the idea of a second birth was an absurdity. The verse indicates that he interpreted Jesus' words in terms of repetition. Did his question voice skepticism or perplexity? Was his perplexity due to disbelief or to uncertainty as to how this could be done?

In rabbinic tradition proselytes were spoken of as newborn children. Rabbi

---

[3] I. F. Wood, *The Spirit of God in Biblical Literature*, pp. 52ff.
[4] The Apocrypha contains only seven references to the "Holy Spirit." In the Dead Sea Scrolls, however, the Spirit is more prominent, the term "Holy Spirit" occurring at least twenty times.
[a] E.g., Eph. 3:6; Gal. 2:7, 8; 3:14; Rev. 4:13.

mentioned in this context three times as being essential in regeneration (vv. 5, 6, 8). Elsewhere in the New Testament the linking of water and the Spirit is not infrequent. John contrasted his own intiatory rite of baptism with Jesus' baptism of the Spirit (Matt. 3:11; Mark 1:8; Luke 3:16; cf. John 1:33). In Acts water baptism is often linked with the bestowal of the Holy Spirit (2:38; 10:47; 11:16; 19:5, 6).[5]

Perhaps the closest Biblical parallel to this verse is Titus 3:5, which links "the washing of regeneration and renewing of the Holy Spirit." Westcott expressed it tersely: "Water purifies, the Spirit renews."

Odeberg argues that "water" as used here is "a term for celestial *sperma* (or semen), viewed . . . as an *efflux* from above, from God." Hence the citizen of the kingdom "owes his existence as such to the procreative power of the efflux from God, the *sperma* in the spirit."[6] This conclusion is based upon the observation that the whole passage presents a contrast between flesh and spirit, the earthly and the heavenly, the human and the divine. Rabbinic parallels are cited to demonstrate that water (*tephah* — ("drop") is sometimes associated with se-

men as having procreative power.[7] Psalm 48:7 and Isaiah 45:8 were cited by Rabbi Levi as implying that the rain out-poured from heaven is the male principle and the receptive earth the female principle; the offspring is the vegetation resulting from this union of water and soil. From III Enoch 6:2 comes the implication that one born of woman and a "white drop" (of semen) has no right to enter the highest heaven (Odeberg, *op. cit.*, p. 51). Several Mandean texts may be cited as witnesses to the idea that water was regarded by them as engendering life. On the basis of these literary parallels, many of which are much later than the New Testament, Odeberg concludes that Nicodemus is not thinking of a *babe* re-entering his mother's womb but rather of the generating *sperma* or semen. Hence, Odeberg concludes, the water is equivalent to the generating *sperma* from above as the condition of spiritual life in contrast to earthly *sperma*. Parallels are to be noted in I John 3:5 and in John 1:13 (cf. 8:44).

Since the baptism of John was so well known to the Pharisees of Jerusalem (John 1:19, 22, 25), Jesus here appears to have been alluding to John's baptism with

---

Jose, at the middle of the second century said that a proselyte who is converted to Judaism is as a child by nature (S-B, II, 423). However, Barrett thinks the O. T. and rabbinic precedents cited by Strack and Billerbeck are not relevant since the rabbis were speaking only of the new legal status of the proselyte rather than a change of nature (CKB, p. 172).[b] However, the analogy in both rabbinic and Christian usage is appropriate in that it stresses discontinuity between the old life and the new, the necessity of a drastic emergence into the new.

5 The nature of entrance into a vital fellowship with God the Father through Jesus Christ is voiced by the New Testament writers with a surprising degree of unanimity. Paul speaks of the necessity of being a "new creation" in Christ (II

Cor. 5:17). He also uses legal terminology when describing the effect of change Christ makes in the believer, calling it "to justify," or "to make righteous." In II Peter reference is made to the same as being made "partakers of the divine nature" (1:4). Whether in the nomenclature of jurisprudence or that of biology, the central point is that a change of nature is necessary as a condition of participation in the kingdom of heaven, contrary to the position of Jewish orthodoxy that genealogy automatically determines kingdom status (cf. John 8:33-47; Rom. 2:28, 29).

6-8 The assertion that birth from the flesh is distinct from birth in the spirit is characteristic of John's writings, and particularly similar to the earlier contrast between those born of God and those born

---

[5] But cf. Acts 8:16; 16:33; 8:38; etc.
[6] Hugo Odeberg, *The Fourth Gospel* (Uppsala: Almquist & Wiksells, 1929), pp. 63f.
[7] "The angel that is appointed over the conception is called Laila and he takes the *tephah* ΩGЦ) — semen) and brings it before the Holy one, and says before him: 'Lord of the universe! what shall arise out of this σπερμα (sperma), a strong man or a weak man, a wise or a fool, a rich or a poor?'" —TB Nid. 16b, cited by Odeberg, *op. cit.*, pp. 49f.).
[b] Cf. G. F. Moore, *Judaism* (Cambridge: Harvard University Press, 1927) I, 328.

7 Marvel not that I said unto thee, Ye must be born anew.

"water unto repentance."[8] To argue, however, that water is indispensable in salvation would be to repeat the Jewish error of equating the Kingdom of God with physical ceremonials, an error which Jesus so emphatically denounced (Mark 7:8; cf. Rom. 3:24ff.; Gal. 5:2-6; Col. 2:16-3:1). It has been noted that it is not probable that the meaning is baptism because this would break the continuity of the discourse and because baptism is not implied elsewhere in the section.[9]

After taking the relevant Old and New Testament passages together the conclusion seems justified that the linking of water with the Spirit appears to signify the negative and positive phases of regeneration. The washing with water symbolizes the cleansing from the old life — "not as removal of dirt from the body but as an appeal to God for a clear conscience,

through the resurrection of Jesus Christ" (I Pet. 3:21 RSV). As in John's baptism the water connotes repentance from the former manner of life.[10] The birth with the Spirit is the positive side of regeneration; the bestowal of the divine nature the "renewal of the Holy Spirit," the positive phase of sanctification which continues in the life of the believer.[11]

7 The assertion of v. 3 is here repeated by way of summary and also for emphasis. In using the plural ye, Jesus implies that it is not Nicodemus alone but also the class he represents who must be born anew. The contrast continues between the natural and the supernatural, the fleshly and the spiritual, the human and the divine. Paul had the same contrast in mind when he remarked that "the natural man receiveth not the things of the Spirit of God . . ." (I Cor. 3:14).

of the flesh (1:12, 13). It is also in line with the insistence in ch. 8:37-47 that a genealogical link with Abraham is less important than a spiritual affinity with Abrahamic ideals. It is consistent also with the emphasis in I John 3:7-10, in which the children of God and the children of the devil are contrasted. Prominent, therefore, in Johannine theology is the idea that there are only two contrasting genealogies, one of the flesh the other of the Spirit; one of them merely human (or of the devil), the other of God. There is no neutral ground, just as there is no middle ground between light and darkness. It is akin also to Paul's contrast between "flesh" and "spirit" in Romans 8:5-9, in which sonship to God is determined by whether one is dominated by the flesh or by the Spirit. In this statement Jesus answers by saying that the new birth of which he speaks is not a mere repetition of physical birth but a birth in a different sphere of existence; it is a birth not so

much "new" in the sense of being additional as "new" in the sense of being qualitatively different and distinct. To Nicodemus, as the typical Jew, the concept of a "birth" other than a physical one was exceedingly difficult to grasp. The Samaritan woman more easily grasped the idea of spiritual water than the Jews the idea of spiritual bread. So the contrast between the physical and spiritual is a dominant motif with this Evangelist. The surprising thing to Nicodemus was the linking of birth with spirit. Birth is associated with Life. Life is on four levels: vegetable, animal, spiritual, and divine. To man life is available from the animal realm below and from the divine above. Only in man do animal and divine meet, in spirit.

9, 10 The idea of regeneration is a cardinal doctrine of the New Testament. Whether expressed in biological terms as in John, or legal terms (justification) as in Paul, whether called partaking of the

[8] As J. Wesley expressed it, the water refers to baptism "as the outward sign and means of spiritual birth." *Explanatory Notes on the N.T.* (London: Epworth Press), p. 312. Modern evangelicals would object to Wesley's inclusion of "and means" as it could imply baptismal regeneration. Wesley apparently taught "baptismal regeneration" in his younger years and later modified his position. The English Methodist Church repudiated baptismal regeneration at the Annual Conference of 1882; E. H. Sugden, *Standard Sermons of John Wesley* (Nashville: Lamar & Barton, n.d.), I, 280-282.
[9] Odeberg, *op. cit.*, p. 65.
[10] As Josephus reported it, John's baptism was administered only *after* repentance had "purified the soul" (*Ant.*, XVIII. 5. 2).
[11] "Initial" (I Cor. 1:2) and "progressive" (I Cor. 1:30) sanctification as distinct from "entire" (I Thess. 5:23) sanctification.

8 The wind bloweth where it will, and thou hearest the voice thereof, but knowest not whence it cometh, and whither it goeth: so is every one that is born of the Spirit.

A Jew, such as Nicodemus, classified man into two classes: Jew and Gentile, circumcised and uncircumcised. In Paul, as in John, the division is between the carnal and the spiritual, the natural man and the man in Christ, the generate and the regenerate (Rom. 8:1; II Cor. 5:17). Since Nicodemus is a leader in Israel, Jesus tells him he should not be surprised at this. But this classification of humanity was different from that to which Nicodemus was accustomed; it seemed quite beyond him. There is reason to believe that in selecting this episode for elaboration John considered Nicodemus not merely an isolated case, but as representative of his race.

Ye must: the *dei* (it is necessary) has several variations in meaning; here it signifies "the compulsion of what is fitting" (A-G), a necessity in view of the end (JHT).[12]

8 The word *pneuma* (spirit) is the Greek term normally used to translate the Hebrew word *ruach* (spirit). This Hebrew term is translated equally well by three English words: "wind," "breath," and "spirit." This is illustrated in Psalm 33:6 "By the word of Jehovah were the heavens made, and all the host of them by the breath of his mouth." In this parallelism "word" and "breath" are synonymous. The psalmist had in mind the Genesis passage — "And God said, Let there be a firmament in the midst . . ." (Gen. 1:6, 9, 14, 20, 24, 26). It is the same in Ezek. 37:9 — "come from the four winds, O breath, and breathe upon these slain, that they may live." When the wind-breath-spirit inbreathed (inspired) the dry bones, they lived anew. This is in agreement with Acts 2:2 where the bestowal of the Holy Spirit was accompanied by a "rushing, mighty wind." Thus there is a double significance in the comparison of spiritual birth with the movement of wind: the word itself is the same for "wind" and "spirit," and both are non-physical, spontaneous, and unpredictable. The point is that a wind can-

divine nature (II Pet. 1:4), or receiving of the "wisdom from above" (James 3:17), the language of the New Testament emphasizes the contrast between the natural man and the man "in Christ." The confusion which Nicodemus exemplified is not limited to his time or his countrymen. It is difficult even today among Protestants to define with precision what is meant by becoming a Christian. To Horace Bushnell it meant, primarily if not entirely, the nurture of Christian tendencies into maturity of character. To the liturgist it means primarily conformity to religious practices. To the neo-orthodox it means the "existential confrontation" of man with the living Word resulting in a somewhat esoteric "faith." To the literal fundamentalist it means acceptance of belief in Jesus and in the Bible. To the evangelical it means a new level of life, issuing from Christ enthroned within, following repentance and "saving faith." Then, as now, it is more easily explained by analogy than by analysis. Many can witness to Christ's transforming power but cannot explain it.

A laboring man, who had been converted, was taunted by his fellow workmen. "Surely," they asked the new convert, "you don't believe in miracles like turning water into wine." Replied the workman, "I do know that in my own house and home He has turned beer into furniture."[c]

Jesus was saying to Nicodemus that one does not doubt the existence of the wind even though he cannot explain it or determine its origin and destination. So also the new birth is not less real because it cannot easily be explained.

The noted church historian Adolph von Harnack speaks of the early Christians as those who considered themselves to be "a third race." They were not distinguished by geographical region, or race, or political alliance, or ancestry, or any of the normal distinctions among ethnic

[12] As compared with its synonym *chrē, dei* "is suggestive of moral obligation, denoting especially that constraint which arises from divine appointment" (JHT).
[c] John Hutton, cited by Wm. Barclay, *The Gospel of John* (Philadelphia: Westminster Press, 1956), I, 122.

9 Nicodemus answered and said unto him, How can these things be?

10 Jesus answered and said unto him, Art thou the teacher of Israel, and understandest not these things?

---

not be seen nor can its course be predicted, yet its reality is evident in its effects. Similarly, spiritual birth is not less real because many, even professed Christians, are as mystified as Nicodemus over the necessity and nature of regeneration.[13]

**9, 10 Are you a teacher of Israel . . . ?** The significance here of the definite article (*ho didaskalos*, "the teacher") appears to stress that we have here not only one of several teachers but a specific teacher who is distinguished. Macgregor reads it "Is it you, O Teacher of Israel, who does not recognize even this?" W. F. Howard anticipated the rendering of NEB by saying "Are you that famous teacher in Israel?"[14] The NEB rendering is thus to be preferred: "Is this famous teacher of Israel ignorant of these things?"

In certain Hellenistic circles it was believed that a man may attain knowledge and become perfect through baptism in a crater (bowl) which God has filled with *nous* (mind) or spirit.[15] One of the Hermetic writings is entitled "Regeneration." In it, too, "become divine" means to be "born again." Sired by the will of God in the womb of wisdom the "real good," which is the sperm, issues as a child of God. To be regenerated one must cleanse his soul from the pollution of matter. "Rebirth in fact, is the identification of man with God through the indwelling of the logos" according to this Hermetic tractate.[16] In both these Hermetic writings and the Johannine thought "the status of 'child of God' is attained through the *logos*."[17]

Although there are more than twenty close parallels of expression between the Hermetic dialogue on regeneration and John (Dodd, pp. 50, 51) one must beware of assuming literary dependence. The significance of the Hermetic writings is that although they were written long

---

or national religions. They were neither Jews nor Gentiles, as such, but included both. The idea of a new supra-national religion was something novel for that day, and to a large extent it is novel even today.

A second-century Christian expressed a similar conviction — that a Christian was not distinguished by the usual criteria of race, language, clothing, color, or nationality, but rather by the inner qualities of joy, peace, love, etc. They were *possessed* of a new nature.[d]

**12** A basic principle in good pedagogy is to proceed from the known to the unknown. Jesus is saying that the Jews, as represented by Nicodemus, do not accept his teaching in the more mundane and obvious spheres; how then can they expect to understand the higher things of the kingdom? The "earthly things" are an apparent reference to matters concerning the birth of the Spirit, like the movement of wind about which Nicodemus has just expressed bewilderment (v. 9). This assertion is intimately associated with the doctrine of the Incarnation which, with the exception of Philippians 2:5-11, reaches its highest development in this Gospel. It is also characteristic of this Gospel that response to present light is the condition of further light (cf. John 8:31, 32). The contrast between the past condition (**I have told**) and the future contingency (**if I should tell**) suggests that Jesus had not yet told them of **heavenly things.** Godet believes that **earthly things** has reference to things pertaining to man's moral nature while **heavenly things** refers

---

[13] "The allusion to wind does not refer to the mystery or freedom of the Spirit's action in the New Birth, but rather, to the independent and unconventional character of the conduct of the man who has been Spirit-born. Such a man will not consent to run in well-oiled grooves of social convention, ecclesiastical programs and church programs as a matter of dictation or a mere matter of course. . . . He is impelled by the free Spirit of God which is in him." R. E. Neighbor, "The New Birth and the Conversation with Nicodemus," *The Review and Expositor*, Jan., 1923, p. 31.

[14] E. F. Bishop, "The Authorized Teacher of the Israel of God," *Biblical Translator*, VII (2, 1956), pp. 81-83.

[15] *Corpus Hermetica*, IV, cited in CHD, p. 304.

[16] *Ibid.*

[17] *Ibid.*, p. 49.

[d] Epistle to Diognetus, K. Lake, edit., *The Apostlic Fathers*, II, 350ff.

11 Verily, verily, I say unto thee, We speak that which we know, and bear witness of that which we have seen; and ye receive not our witness.

---

after the Fourth Gospel they reflect ideas current at an earlier time. While some of the language is similar, there is a basic divergence of thought. The most one can say is that the similarities reflect "a religious vocabulary . . . . at the disposal of a Christian missionary" which he could utilize to introduce his message but which he invested with an entirely new and independent content (WFH, VIII, 453). As one specialist in the religious environment of the New Testament expresses it: "The thought of this Gospel is so original and creative that a search for its 'sources' or even for the 'influence' . . . . may easily lead us astray. Whatever influences may have been present have been masterfully controlled by a powerful and independent mind" (CHD, p. 6). The facts

compel the conclusion that the idea of regeneration herein set forth is one of the most independent and revolutionary in the religious world.[18]

11 Since Nicodemus seems unable or unwilling to grasp what Jesus has set forth by argument and analogy, Jesus says to him in effect, "Since you cannot see the reason for this then take my word for it, accept it on my authority." Jesus goes from assertion to explanation and now back to assertion. Why did Jesus use the plural "we" here? Perhaps it refers to the joint witness of Father and Son as in 8:18, "I am he that beareth witness of myself, and the Father . . . . beareth witness of me."

The fact that the object in each clause stands first justifies this translation: " 'that

---

to matters of regeneration and redemption for the individual. It is perhaps analagous to the instance of the paralytic, (Mark 2:3-12) when Jesus' authority to forgive sins was linked with his authority over disease; if one acknowledged the physical healing he would be more ready to acknowledge Jesus' claim to spiritual healing.

(2) *Salvation is by Faith* (vv. 14-17).

(a) The Ascent of the Son of Man (vv. 14-15)

The assertion ascended . . . . descended needs to be considered in the light of several parallel passages. In Deuteronomy 30:12, quoted in Romans 10:6,8, the Word of God (cf. Logos) is not found by ascending into heaven or descending into the deep but is near at hand, accessible, available (by faith). Paul also speaks of Christ ascending and descending with the view of bringing grace to men, in Ephesians 4:9,10. Even more relevant is John 1:51, where the Son of man bridges the difference between heaven and earth. The passage has as its background the statement in the Prologue that the Incarnation makes possible re-

generation (1:11,12). His descent and ascent in 1:11,12 makes possible eternal life, and here make authoritative and trustworthy his witness concerning regeneration. Contrary to Bultmann, the ascending and descending Son of man is not that of Jewish apocalypses nor of paganism; it is that of a divine person coming to give life. "The Hellenistic notions are completely reversed: His incarnation is not a gradually ascending process but a fall."[e] Here in John the descent (Incarnation) is the condition of the ascent (ascension).

14 The episode of Moses and the serpent is found in Numbers 21:5-9. There the episode is the fourteenth and last of a series of murmurings or complaints lodged by the Israelites against Moses or against God or both. In each of the other cases the sin of complaining was punished without an opportunity for repentance. In this case, however, provision was made for them to escape the penalty for their sin without suffering the punishment which their sin deserved. It is an anticipation of the doctrine of repentance which looms so large in the prophets, in the inter-testamental period (e.g., the Prayer of Manassas) and in the New

---

[18] Strachan suggests that the "new birth" idea may also include a demand that the old world of Judaism be re-born into the new world of the Gospel (RHS, p. 135.).

[e] E.M. Sidebottom, "The Ascent and Descent of the Son of Man," *Anglican Theological Review,* XXXIX, April, 1957, p. 119.

12 If I told you earthly things and ye believe not, how shall ye believe if I tell you heavenly things?

13 And no one hath ascended into heaven, but he that descended out of heaven, even the Son of man, who is in heaven.

14 And as Moses lifted up the serpent in the wilderness, even so must the Son of man be lifted up;

---

which we know, we speak; and that which we have seen, we witness' " (Westcott). The stress is placed on the certainty of the knowledge which lies back of the witness. The knowledge is that of intuition and insight, the stress being upon personal and immediate knowledge, a subjective but certain assurance. The second assertion is a parallelism for emphasis, similar to I John 1:1: "that which we have seen (perfect tense) with our eyes . . . we . . . bear witness . . . ." The rejection of the witness (v. 11) is a prominent theme in this Gospel. It is introduced in 1:10 and is dwelt upon climactically in 12:37-43, where the unbelief of the Jews is analyzed in the light of Isaiah 6:10.

13 There is a textual variant here; the best textual evidence omits the words "who is in heaven," while the ancient versions favor its retention. It is probable, therefore, that the clause was not in the original and should be omitted. To assume that some copyists inserted these words as a marginal gloss, in order to provide a more balanced sentence, presents fewer objections than alternative views.[19]

14 The lifted up (hypsōsen) of this verse is parallel with the ascension (anabēsis) into heaven of v. 13. Does this lifting up refer to the ascension of Jesus or to his crucifixion? That it means the latter is suggested by 12:32, "And I, if I be lifted up from earth, will draw

---

Testament. It is also an anticipation of the doctrine of vicarious suffering. It is this, rather than the idea of "lifting up" as such, which probably caused Jesus to use the analogy. The serpent analogy is appropriate because there was physical elevation of the victim as a public spectacle in the case of both Jesus and the serpent. Even more important was the effect upon the spectators. To those who looked with eyes of faith, the sentence of death, of both those who looked at the uplifted serpent and those who believed on a crucified Messiah, was changed. The ancient Israelites had the alternatives of either refusing to look and dying, or of combining obedience and faith by looking and hence living. In both cases it was "life for a look." It is possible that a double meaning is implicit here. The serpent was both the agent of death and of life. The person bitten by a serpent and faced with death could avert death by looking in faith upon the uplifted bronze serpent. Likewise Jesus Christ is the basis on which God condemns the unbeliever (3:18) but also the basis on which God gives life to the believer (3:16). Jesus Christ is both man's judge (5:22) and the one who

delivers man from judgment (5:24). Verse 15 is a reminder of 1:12, "to all who receive him . . . he gave power to become children of God." Thus Nicodemus is told that salvation is not necessarily limited to those privileged to be born in the posterity of Abraham but anyone who qualifies by repentance, faith, and obedience. It is the same idea which Paul elucidates, in a different frame of reference, by contrasting circumcision in the flesh and that in the spirit (Rom. 2:25-29).

(b) The Descent of the Son of God (vv. 16, 17)

God so loved (houtōs ēgapēsen ho theos), an emphasis so characteristic of John's Gospel and Epistles, is here introduced for the first time. The verb is characteristic of John's writings since it occurs some 36 times in the Gospel and 32 times in the three Epistles, nearly half of the total occurrences in the New Testament. The word is rare in secular sources where the usual term for love is phileō or eros (see the "Introduction").

The term used for love is used elsewhere to designate the nature of God (I John

---

[19] The words are omitted by Aleph, B, L and 083, 33. See Westcott, op. cit., I, 140.

15 that whosoever believeth may in him have eternal life.

---

all men unto myself." The following verse (12:33) explains that this is a reference to the crucifixion. The similarity of the "lifting up" of the serpent and Jesus' elevation on his instrument of death is apparent. The ascension is never spoken of as an act of "lifting up" although Luke refers to it as being "received up" (Luke 9:51). That the bystanders interpreted the "lifting up" as the crucifixion is indicated also in 12:34, where it is viewed as antithetical to "abiding forever." The ascension, on the other hand, would be consistent with "abiding forever" (12:34a). In 8:28 Jesus spoke of the time when his enemies would lift him up, a reference to the passion rather than to the ascension. The verb *hypsoō* then means "to exalt" or to "lift up on high." It is done by another, while *anabainō* (ascend) is done by the person himself. The Evangelist pictures Jesus as seeing the humiliation of the cross and the ascension beyond as one event, the total effect of which is to glorify God, both the Father and the Son.

With v. 14 the Evangelist introduces another cryptic statement which will receive fuller elaboration later (e.g., 8:28; 12:32). The sequence of thought has been up to this point: in 1:51 the ascent and descent of angelic messengers is associated with the Son of man. In 3:12 the Son of man is he who ascended and descended out of heaven and hence is qualified to speak authoritatively about heavenly things. In 3:14 the same Son of man is to be "lifted up" vicariously for the redemption of the world. In this case the contrast is between the earthly and the heavenly, between the human and the divine, and ultimately between life and death.

15 The textual variants are: *en autō, ep autō* (P66), *ep auton* and *eis auton*. In this verse the *en autō* (Nestle) — **in him** — should be joined to "eternal life"

---

4:8-10) and God's love for the human race (Rom. 5:8) as well as his love for his Son (John 18:26). It normally includes the element of suffering for the object of one's love. The idea of God loving men and suffering for them is peculiar to the Bible. It is unknown in paganism. Homer has Juno say to Vulcan:

"Dear Son, refrain; it is not well that thus

A god should suffer for the sake of men"

(Iliad xxi. 379, 380 — MRV, II, 100).

A great number of important affirmations are contained explicitly or implicitly in this verse, the "golden text" of the Bible. (i) God's attitude, even toward those under the sentence of death, is one of benevolence, or redemptive love. (ii) The measure of God's love is so exhaustless that he gave his only Son; God did not *lend* his Son, he *gave* him. (iii) The object of God's love is the sinful world; God loves the unlovely and unloving. (iv) All men are included in the scope of God's redemptive plan — a universal atonement. (v) The only beneficiaries of this love are those who choose to accept it. (vi) The alternative to acceptance is perpetual exclusion from God's presence and hence from life.

17 This verse appears designed to counteract any impression which some might draw that the Savior's advent brought additional guilt and punishment to many. Although Jesus Christ is responsible for judgment of the world (John 5:27) and although the light he brings exposes the darkness (John 1:5; 9:39), his coming is redemptive rather than punitive in purpose. The primary purpose is to redeem, but the necessary consequences of those who refuse this privilege is greater condemnation and hence judgment. The accent seems to be on condemnation rather than judgment as such, for the righteous will be judged along with the wicked. In John's use of the term, however, the condemnation of the wicked seems to be predominant (John 5:24; 16:8). Every man is presented with a crisis (judgment, v. 19). The common apocalyptic idea of the Jews was that the Messiah would save the Jews and judge all non-Jews. Jesus (or John) affirms that the Gentiles as well as Jews are to be included in the great salvation.

16 For God so loved the world, that he gave his only begotten Son, that whosoever believeth on him should not perish, but have eternal life.

17 For God sent not the Son into the world to judge the world: but that the world should be saved through him.

18 He that believeth on him is not judged: he that believeth not hath been judged already, because he hath not believed on the name of the only begotten Son of God

---

rather than to "believe." It would thus read with the ASV (and not with KJV, RSV, etc.) *may in him have eternal life* (CKB). The "in him" is repeated twice in the NEB. In v. 15 the Son of Man is the source of eternal life; in v. 16 "he is the object of faith" (WFH).

16 This verse is the very heart of the Gospel by John and indeed a summary of the Christian faith. Whether these are the words of Jesus or the Evangelist is not easy to determine, but it is of little importance if one believes that the Evangelist was given divine guidance in his insights and utterances. It is true regardless of whether they are the words of Jesus or of the Evangelist. The tenses, however, as Dods observes, "forbid us to refer the passage directly to Jesus" (EGT). The present tense "loves" rather than aorist "loved" might have been more natural had Jesus been the speaker. But God's solicitude for the world is indicated in 1:9-11. Here the assertion is repeated with much greater emphasis. The pregnant phrase "so loved" indicates that God's love is infinite and immeasurable. The so (*houtōs*) is an adverb of degree which points toward the clause which follows and here serves to express the idea of infinity, a love that is limitless, that is fully adequate. **Only begotten** (cf. 1:17) is better rendered "only" as in RSV and NEB.

The giving of the "only son" may be intended to suggest a similarity to the divine command to Abraham in Genesis 22:2 to give up his son — "thine only son, whom thou lovest." The term "only begotten," which occurs in this Gospel and four times elsewhere in the N.T., means

---

### (3) Responsibility for Acceptance (vv. 18-21)

18 It is characteristic of John's thought to merge the present and the future. Those who will have eternal life are viewed as already possessing its firstfruits. Eternal life is regarded as having quality as well as extent. It is more than a continuation of the present life. Those who will be condemned at the final judgment are under the sentence of death already — because they refuse to believe that Jesus is the Son of God.

19-21 The Evangelist now continues to explain, on psychological grounds, the theme introduced in the Prologue and declared in 3:18. The judgment of the unbeliever is not an arbitrary fiat of God but a result which one brings on himself inevitably. It is the nature of light to expose darkness. The comparison of light with goodness and of darkness with evil is a common one. Evildoers do not wish to have their deeds known and hence desire the cover of darkness. Lovers of truth, on the other hand, welcome scrutiny in the confidence of vindication. In the nature of the case, therefore, the coming of light and truth confirms goodness and exposes evil for what it is. Thus light, instead of being judged, becomes the judge and sifter of men's motives and deeds. It is reported that a visitor in an art gallery, after viewing some ancient masterpieces, concluded, "I don't like those old pictures." The guide replied, "Those pictures are no longer on trial; those who view them are."[f]

### 3. THE WITNESS OF JOHN (3:22-36)
#### a. The Occasion for the Witness (vv. 22-26)

22 **Into the land of Judea.** After visiting Jerusalem at the Passover season, Jesus and his followers moved north into the country of Judea, not far from the scene of John's ministry and Jesus' baptism. It has been conjectured that this Gospel was written in Ephesus where there were disciples of John the Baptist (Acts 19:1). At any rate this Gospel takes great pains to show that the superseding

---

f W. Barclay, *op. cit.,* I, 130.

19 And this is the judgment, that the light is come into the world, and men loved the darkness rather than the light; for their works were evil.

20 For everyone that doeth evil hateth the light, and cometh not to the light, lest his works should be reproved.

21 But he that doeth the truth cometh to the light, that his works may be made manifest, that they have been wrought in God.

22 After these things came Jesus and his disciples into the land of Judaea; and there he tarried with them, and baptized.

23 And John also was baptizing in Aenon near to Salim, because there was much water there: and they came, and were baptized.

24 For John was not yet cast into prison.

25 There arose therefore a questioning on the part of John's disciples with a Jew about purifying.

---

the "only one of its kind." The "only" of this term is in contrast with the "all" of the same verse: *one* vicarious sacrifice provides for *all* men. In the New Testament, when belief is said to lead to eternal life, as is the case here, the tense expressing continuous action is always used while the tense expressing a single action is never used.[20] The stress is thus placed on continuous faith rather than on an isolated moment of faith.

19 John has much to say about judgment (*krisis*). The word originally meant "to separate."[21] While the context supports the meaning of condemnation as it is used in KJV, the word for "condemn" is *katakrinō;* thus the better word here is "judgment" as in the RV and RSV. *Krinō*

means to distinguish, to pick out, to be *of opinion,* hence, to judge.[22]

25 The question of purifying may be related to John 11:55, "many went up to Jerusalem out of the country before the passover, to purify themselves." The question about purification is not central in the author's mind; it is only the *occasion* of the discussion concerning the relationship of John and Jesus. This passage, together with 4:1, implies that many had the impression that John and Jesus were rivals since they were doing similar work in the same general area. This erroneous assumption is dealt with in vv. 25-36.

The "therefore" (*oun*) is not a particle of time but of consequence (Westcott); the baptismal activities of Jesus and John

---

of his own movement by that of Jesus was consistent with John's own emphasis. The relationship between John and Jesus is the subject of thirty-nine verses in this Gospel.[g] In each instance the subordination of John to Jesus is stressed. This theme is not peculiar to John, however; it is consistent with the emphasis in the Synoptics. Why did John not merge his labors with those of Jesus and become a follower? Why did his ministry continue separate and independent? The Bible gives no answer, but it may be that by background and temperament John considered his ministry to be rural rather than of the villages. He also may have felt that they could exert greater influence laboring in

separate spheres with the same spirit and purpose.

The place of John's labors is not known for certain. But most archaeologists now believe that it was further north in the Jordan valley and probably west of the river (see accompanying map). Of this area it could be said that there was "much water" there; the Greek says "many waters." In the lower Jordan valley, on the other hand, with the exception of Elisha's Fountain at Jericho, the Jordan itself is virtually the only source of water. The reference to an abundance of water perhaps implies immersion as John's preferred method of baptism. If he had baptized by sprinkling, or even by pouring, the

---

[20] Thus never in these passages expressing belief in eternal life is one's eternal security said to be guaranteed by a single, isolated act of faith. (E. A. Mills, "Terms for Belief in John's Gospel"; thesis in Asbury Theological Seminary, 1952.)

[21] Homer reports Ceres (god of cereals) *separating* grain from chaff (Iliad, v. 501).

[22] The synonym "hypocrite" is compounded from the same stem; "to separate gradually, to separate truth from falsehood, to speak, to simulate or pretend."

[g] E.g., 1:7, 8, 15, 19-37; 3:22-4:1; 5:33-36; 10:39.

26 And they came unto John, and said to him, Rabbi, he that was with thee beyond the Jordan, to whom thou hast borne witness, behold, the same baptizeth, and all men come to him.

27 John answered and said, A man can receive nothing, except it have been given him from heaven.

28 Ye yourselves bear me witness, that I said, I am not the Christ, but, that I am sent before him.

29 He that hath the bride is the bridegroom: but the friend of the bridegroom, that standeth and heareth him, rejoiceth greatly because of the bridegroom's voice: this my joy therefore is made full.

30 He must increase, but I must decrease.

31 He that cometh from above is above all: he that is of the earth is of the earth,

---

were the occasion for the question. The better textual evidence supports a Jew rather than "Jews" as in the KJV. The noun *zētēsis* ("question") indicates a "disputation" rather than an inquiry (Lange). The purifying was perhaps the purifying effect of baptism which Josephus mentions.[23] Or perhaps it was ceremonial purification (cf. John 2:6; Mark 7:1-5). If the dispute arose over Jesus' threat to John's prestige, as v. 26 implies, it seems strange that the subject would be introduced as involving purification, especially since the connotation of this term is cere-

monial purification (cf. 2:6; 11:55). Also, it is unlike John to refer to Jesus' disciples as "Jews." (In Johannine usage "the Jews" are usually unbelievers, hostile to Jesus.) The question could also be, "Why baptize if you are already purified as Moses specified?" (Bultmann, p. 123).

31 As is the case earlier in this chapter, dialogue here merges into monologue. In this paragraph the Evangelist, from his perspective, summarizes in general principles the relation of John to Jesus and of the relation of Father to Son. Some scholars regard these verses as a con-

---

place would have been less significant.[h] Another possible reason for ministering in an area where there was "much water" was that it would be a populated place. If Salim were south of Bethshan it would also be near the trade routes and additional crowds. On the other hand the records imply that the crowds sought John "in the wilderness" rather than that John sought the crowds.

John appears to have been placed in prison shortly after this, at about the midpoint of Jesus' public ministry. This Gospel gives no reason for the imprisonment as such as those of the Synoptists and Josephus.[i]

26 It is John's disciples who come to their teacher with a question that amounted to a complaint. With great respect they address John as "Rabbi." Avoiding the mention of the name Jesus, they point out that his popularity is such

that men are coming over to his side. Not only that, but Jesus was practicing the rite of baptism the same as John. "He with regard to whom you witnessed is baptizing." The competition, they feel, is aggravated by the fact that Jesus had joined with John's movement months before and that John had borne witness with regard to him (John 1:19ff). In short, John's followers were worried about Jesus' fame at John's expense. Their concern was comparable to those who reported to Moses that he had rivals in the camp — men who also prophesied (Exod. 11:26-29). Like Moses, John was too magnanimous to worry about an infringement of his spiritual prerogatives. John's reply is in harmony with all that is known about the man, a selfless humility comparable only to Jonathan in his deference to David (I Sam. 18:1-5).

---

[23] Jos. *Ant.,* XVIII. v. 2; I Pet. 3:21.

[h] The numerous large cisterns at Qumran (Dead Sea Scrolls) may have been used for the purpose of "baptism." But this is not certain. Nor is it certain that John the Baptist spent some time here as has been suggested — W. H. Brownlee, "John the Baptist in the New Light of Ancient Scrolls," in *The Scrolls and the New Testament,* K. Stendahl, ed. (New York: Harper, 1957), p. 35. There is however, nothing improbable in this suggestion, especially in the light of Luke 1:80.

[i] See Matt. 14:1-12; Mark 6:14-29; Luke 9:7-9; Jos. *Ant.,* XVIII. v. 2.

and of the earth he speaketh: he that cometh from heaven is above all.

32 What he hath seen and heard, of that he beareth witness; and no man receiveth his witness.

33 He that hath received his witness hath set his seal to *this,* that God is true.

34 For he whom God hath sent speaketh the words of God: for he giveth not the Spirit by measure.

---

tinuation of v. 21, and consider vv. 22-30 as a misplaced segment. But even if v. 31 followed v. 21 immediately, some critics would notice a break and wonder what had been left out (CHD). It is unlike this Evangelist to say all he has to say on a subject before moving on to another topic; instead he usually treats a subject in installments, like a spiral staircase.

These words from above recall 3:13 and indicate that he is contrasting Jesus who came from above with John who came of the earth. The writer has in mind primarily all his contemporaries who are confronted with God's revelation in his Son. The authority with which the one "from above" speaks is stressed in 3:11-

13, while the rejection of this witness is first described in the Prologue (1:5-11). Thus, by repetition, this author makes clearer and more emphatic the nature and extent of the heavenly witness. It was not easy for the Gospel writers to explain the authenticity of the messianic witness and its rejection by the majority of those for whom it was intended. But to those who accept it a divine confirmation follows (cf. 8:31).

34 Still speaking of Jesus, the Evangelist continues to emphasize that he spoke as God's messenger. It is true that the Baptist was also God's messenger, but Jesus was both the message and the messenger. He not only spoke the truth; Jesus was and is the Truth. In line with

---

### b. The Witness Itself (vv. 27-30)

27 John considers his relation to Jesus in the light of the general principle that all spiritual gifts come from God, in the same spirit as Paul's declaration (I Cor. 4:7), "What hast thou that thou didst not not receive?" This is the true basis for humility. Humility must of necessity be unconscious; it comes not so much by bemeaning oneself as from acknowledging dependence upon God. Thus John declared that any differing in degree of spiritual power and influence is due to God's distribution of gifts. It follows then that no one has any basis for jealousy since the gift is not really his but is of God. John was not interested in building up a reputation or a spiritual dynasty to be perpetuated in his name. His concern was to fulfill his own distinctive mission as God's gift to him.

28 John professed to be consistent. He reminded his anxious disciples that the current developments were in line with his own avowed purpose. He had said all along that he was not the Messiah but rather his forerunner. John's success in

fulfilling his mission was to facilitate subordinating his ministry to that of Jesus. Thus John resisted the temptation, to which many leaders succumb, of confusing the means with the end. Selfishness could easily have led John to be loath to relinquish his power, prestige, and influence and to regard Jesus as a usurper. One of life's severest tests comes with the consciousness of waning power and influence and its resultant insecurity of fame, status and livelihood.

29 In further defining his relationship to Jesus the Christ, John used an effective analogy. The typical oriental wedding was familiar to John's hearers. In such the bridesmaids adorn the bride at her parental home. Meanwhile the friends of the bridegroom congregate at his home to share in his joy. At the proper time they accompany the groom to the bride's home. The bridegroom, who may not have seen his betrothed before, goes to the bride's apartment and lifts her veil to see her face, perhaps for the first time. If pleased with her the groom reports to his well-wishers his delight with his bride.[j]

---

[j] Trumbull, *Studies in Oriental Life,* cited in Peloubet, *Suggestive Illustrations on the Gospel of John,* 1898, p. 101.

35 The Father loveth the Son, and hath given all things into his hand.

36 He that believeth on the Son hath eternal life; but he that obeyeth not the Son shall not see life, but the wrath of God abideth on him.

---

the Father's policy of giving the Son "all things," he gave the Spirit without restriction. This is a theme which the Evangelist will take up and enlarge upon later (5:20).

35 **The Father loveth the Son,** a theme much stressed in John, is the explanation for the Father's generosity of v. 34. He **hath given all things into his hand** so that they are now *in* his hand. The point is that the relation of Father and Son is most intimate. Jesus enjoys the full confidence of the Father and has unlimited access to the Father's exhaustless resources.

36 **He that believeth** (*ho pisteuōn*) stresses the continuing act of believing, not merely one who once believed. The matter of practical importance is that men accept the Son's testimony and therefore accept Him. The connection between belief and life, announced in the Prologue (v. 12), is again emphasized. The fearful alternative to belief is eternal death. The disbeliever is not merely destined to destruction but is already under the sentence of death (cf. v. 18). By simplicity of

language and by emphasis John seeks to drive home by repetition the all-important bearing of belief upon life and death.

**Obeyeth not** (*apeithōn*). This Greek verb was never used in first century Greek to mean "believe not" as it is translated in the KJV. Rather, it always had the meaning of disobedience. Philo in his book on "Drunkenness" used the verb again and again to denote disobedience of a son to his father. The fact that John used it as the opposite of "believe" suggests that to him saving faith in Christ also included obedience to Christ. The person that did not believe to the extent of *becoming* obedient was not born again and naturally did not have eternal life. The present participles for both believing and disobeying imply continuance in: not a single act of life, but rather a procedure in and a relationship to. Thus the one that ignores the mission and claims of Christ remains disobedient to him, and the wrath of God "remains upon him."

---

The "friend of the bridegroom" (like the "best man" in our culture) has general responsibility for the wedding celebration, including the supper usually held in the home of the bridegroom.ᵏ This friend, of the groom, who as the "go-between" may have selected the bride, is concerned solely with the successful consummation of the nuptial arrangements. His joy is made full only if the bridegroom is pleased. He then knows that his concern· and labor have not been in vain. Thus did John describe his satisfaction at Jesus' widening influence even at the expense of his own. John's conclusion, **He must increase but I must decrease** was a hard lesson for his admirers to learn. It was perhaps John's most noble utterance. It was climactic also, especially in view of the fact that it was John's last recorded public utterance before his imprisonment and death. Thus, philosophically and with noble self-effacement, he welcomed the prospect of being eclipsed by Jesus.

### c. The Rationale of the Witness (vv. 31-36)

This paragraph appears to be a summary of the entire chapter. The contrast between the one whose authority is only human and the one from above, whose authority is from God, is reaffirmed (cf. vv. 11-13). Since it follows the comparison of Jesus and John the Baptist, it appears that the Evangelist is saying that Jesus' authority is greater than that of John. The Baptist, however, was also sent by God, as is stressed in 1:6. Since both John and Jesus were sent from God (1:6; cf. 3:34), wherein does their authority differ? Both were in the categories of prophets in that they were both bearers of a message from God (1:6, 15, 23; cf. 3:11, 34). John, however, was a prophet in the unique and special sense of being a forerunner, and witness of the Messiah as well. Jesus was a prophet, as well as having the status of Sonship (3:35). John

ᵏ Geo. B. Eager, "Marriage," ISBE, III, 199.

had a prophetic consciousness (1:23), while Jesus had a messianic consciousness (4:25,26).

The paragraph contains four great affirmations:

(i) God has revealed himself; this revelation is conveyed through the Spirit-anointed Son (3:31, 32, 34).

(ii) This revelation meets with a mixed reaction; some believe while others disbelieve (3:32, 33)

(iii) Confirmation of the truth comes to those who accept the message and act upon it (3:33).

(iv) Only those who believe and obey this message have life; upon all who refuse falls the wrath (*orgē*) of God (3:18, 19, 36).

# CHAPTER IV

W hen therefore the Lord knew that the Pharisees had heard that Jesus was making and baptizing more disciples than John

## EXEGESIS

1 **When therefore the Lord knew** (2nd aorist of *ginōskō*) in NEB is rendered "when the Lord learned." The context implies a knowledge acquired by ordinary means (BFW). That Jesus learned or experienced things by ordinary means is indicated also in Luke 2:52 and in Hebrews 5:8 (cf. Heb. 2:10). There is no hint of docetism in this Gospel. The meaning here is apparently different from the connotation of the same verb in 2:25, where intuitive insight is implied.

The title **Lord** appears also in 6:23; 11:2; 20:2, 28; 21:7. Several ancient manuscripts have "Jesus" instead, and this may be the preferred reading (JHB, Bauer,

Hoskyns, CKB). Evidence is inconclusive: NEB adopts Nestle's marginal reading, and translates it "Jesus." After the resurrection this was the title normally given to Jesus Christ (John 20:2, 28 21:7; Acts 1:6, 21, 24; Rom. 1:4 *et al.*) The same term with the connotation o. respect and translated "Sir" is found in John 4:11, 15, 19, 49; 5:7; 6:34, 68 *et al.*) Other passages in this Gospel have *Kyrios* as the translation of *Yahweh* (e.g. 1:23, a quotation from Isa. 40:3; 12:38; cf Isa. 53:1). Thus *Kyrios* may refer to God, to Christ, or to a man.

**The Pharisees had heard.** This is per haps the same group that had earlier sen a delegation to John (1:24). Normally the

## EXPOSITION

4. INTERVIEW WITH THE SAMARITAN WOMAN (4:1-42)

### a. The Occasion (vv. 1-6)

Only John has preserved this fascinating episode in our Lord's ministry. It follows a successful ministry in Judea, probably in the Jordan valley north of Jericho. So successful was Jesus in winning disciples through his teaching that he became concerned about its reaction upon John. He did not want to do anything that would create rivalry with the Forerunner, whom he so greatly admired (Matt. 11:11). The times were exciting with old political and new religious movements stirring the countryside into an atmosphere of expectancy. To the south, the Essene Community at Qumran, west of the Dead Sea, was registering a silent but effective protest to the religious pretentions and

monopolies of both the large party o Pharisees and the influential party o Sadducees in Jerusalem. These ascetic had been considering themselves men o the New Covenant preparing a highway in the desert for the new dispensation (cf Isa. 40:3). It may be that John was once a resident of the Essene Community her at Qumran. If so he later turned from asceticism to evangelism.[a] There i enough similarity to the Essene com munities in the message and ministry o John the Baptist to suggest that the similarities between the tenets of the Essenes and early Christianity may hav been due to the association of John's disci ples with the men of Qumran.[b] John the Baptist was the link between the Ol Testament and the Christian Church. The Essenes, as represented by Philo, Josephus and the Qumran literature, were the chie sources and custodians of the Apocalypse

[a] W. H. Brownlee, "John the Baptist in the New Light of Ancient Scrolls," *Interpretation* 9, 195. pp. 71-90.
[b] O. Cullmann, The Significance of the Qumran Texts for Research into the Beginnings of Christianity, *JBL*, IV, 1955, pp. 213-226.

2 (Although Jesus himself baptized not, but his disciples),
3 he left Judaea, and departed again into Galilee.
4 And he must needs pass through Samaria.

---

Evangelist refers to the religious leaders — whether Pharisees or Sadducees — collectively as "the Jews." Apparently they were keeping in close touch with events in the valley of the Jordan; they may have been suspicious, but were not openly hostile as yet.

**More disciples than John.** Jesus' departure from Judea may have been due either to a desire to avoid rivalry with John (see John 3:22-26) or to avoid arousing the jealousy of the Pharisees. The possibility of rivalry with John is seen only in the Fourth Gospel; in Matt. 4:12 and Mark 1:14 it is stated that Jesus went from Judea to Galilee only *after* learning of John's imprisonment. From Josephus (*Ant.* XVIII. v. 2) we learn that it was jealousy which led Herod to arrest John, and jealousy could easily have motivated the religious leaders. In these tense days the people were easily stirred up, and all popular leaders were regarded with apprehension by those desiring to maintain the *status quo.* To harmonize these three Gospel accounts one must assume that John's arrest coincided with Jesus' decision to leave for Galilee, probably to avoid further trouble. **More disciples** is clarified by the statement in 3:26 that "all men" were coming to Jesus.

2 **Jesus baptized not** is a parenthetical note to explain that, in spite of the statements in 3:22 and 4:1, Jesus did not perform the mechanics of baptizing; the disciples did it in his name. It was customary for the rabbis to have their pupils baptize proselytes.

4 Why must Jesus **pass through Samaria?** He could have gone around the longer route east of the Jordan and thus avoid Samaria as did many of the Jews. He may have wanted to defy popular

---

of the intertestamental period, which were rejected by normative Judaism and appreciated by the Christians.[c] The silence of the N. T. with reference to the Essenes has puzzled scholars for years, and there is perhaps no better explanation to date than that the Christians were in greater rapport with the Essenes than with the Sadducees or Pharisees.[d] Thus they were not in conflict as with the other three religious sects — Sadducees, Pharisees and Herodians. In any case history records that Essenism as such faded from history with the coming of the Roman armies to occupy the site of Qumran in A.D. 70. The passage before us gives an early intimation of John's lessening influence and the vigor of Jesus' movements, a prophecy of the conquest of Christianity. Jesus appears here to permit John to have a monopoly in the Jordan valley while he concentrates on Galilee and Jerusalem. This may have been a comity arrangement by which they divided the field to avoid duplication.

There is today a road leading northwest from the Jordan valley to Shechem. It follows a small stream which descends into the Jordan valley, the stream affording irrigation for the tiny gardens which flourish alongside the road. Josephus states that it took three days to go from Jerusalem to Galilee through Samaria (*Vita* 269). Jesus may have reached this well by noon of the second day of travel. Even in his weariness, as he sat in these pleasant surroundings, he must have been moved to contemplation and prayer. From the top of nearby Mt. Gerizim to the southwest Jotham had uttered his famous fable to Abimelech and the assassins of his brethren, the posterity of Gideon (Judg. 9:1-21). The Master may have recalled that here at Shechem originated the rebellion of the ten tribes after learning from Rehoboam that his tyranny would be more severe than that of Solomon (I Kings 12: 1-20). Here they stoned Adoram when he came to enforce the decrees of Rehoboam, and the kingdom became perma-

---

c F. M. Cross, Jr., *The Ancient Library of Qumran and Modern Biblical Studies* (Garden City: Doubleday, 1958), pp. 147-151.
d J. E. H. Thomson, "The Essenes," ISBE, II, 1004f. F. M. Cross, *op. cit.*, pp. 149f.

5 So he cometh to a city of Samaria, called Sychar, near to the parcel of ground that Jacob gave to his son Joseph:

6 and Jacob's well was there. Jesus therefore, being wearied with his journey, sat thus by the well. It was the sixth hour.

---

prejudices against the Samaritans, as he did with the Parable of the Good Samaritan (Luke 10:29-37). The Samaritans were descendants of ancient Israelites and displaced persons from Mesopotamia; hence they were a religious as well as racial mixture (II Kings 17:24-41). Animosity between these people and the descendants of Judah who returned from Babylonia is reported in the books of Ezra and Nehemiah. Later this animosity was increased when Sanballat, governor of Samaria under Darius, built a temple on Mt. Gerizim to rival that of Jerusalem (Jos. *Ant.* XI. viii. 2). Hatred was further inflamed by the destruction of Samaria, Shechem, and Gerizim by John Hyrcanus about 128 B.C. (Jos. *Ant.* XIII. x. 2; *War.* I. ii. 7). The fact that the way was shorter and more convenient, however would seem sufficient explanation of this decision. Josephus reported that "it was the custom of the Galileans, when they came to the holy city at the festival, to take their journey through the country of the Samaritans" (*Ant.* XX. vi. 1).

5 A city of Samaria called Sychar is usually identified with 'Askar, a village which today lies about one mile north of Jacob's Well. Recent archaeological evidence, however, tends to support the view that this "Sychar" is really Shechem. The Syriac version reads "Shechem" and may well represent an older tradition. Shechem has now been identified with Balata, which is much nearer the well than either Nablus (Neapolis) or Askar.[1]

The parcel of ground that Jacob gave to his son Joseph had a remarkable history. Jacob purchased a camp-site there (Gen. 33:19) and gave it to Joseph (Gen. 48:22), and it was here that Joseph's remains were buried (Josh. 24:32). The name Shechem comes from the former owner (Gen. 33:19) or from the fact that it was a mountain slope or "shoulder" (Gen. 48:22).

6 Jacob's well was there, one of the most authentic sites in Palestine, because wells, like rivers, seldom "migrate" as do many ancient holy places! The well itself is about 100 feet in depth and 6 feet in

---

nently divided as a consequence of the apostasy of Solomon. Near where Jesus sat, Jereboam I had erected his palace (I Kings 12:25) and only a few miles to the west, the city of Samaria had fallen to Sargon II in 722 B.C. after a seige of three years. Soon Jesus and his disciples would walk past either the site of Samaria, now crowned with the city Herod had built in honor of Augustus, or, more likely, journey north on the other fork of the road past the site of Tirzah, first capital of the Northern Kingdom of Israel (I Kings 14:17; 15:33; 16:23). Before him were the survivors of a series of tragedies which could have been avoided had the people of Israel remained loyal to their God. Jesus did not share the animosity of his Jewish contemporaries towards these Samaritans; he yearned to befriend them, to bring them the good news. As George

Whitefield expressed it before preaching his last sermon, Jesus was weary *in* well doing, not *of* well doing.

They had probably left very early in the morning, and it is not surprising that by noon they were weary. But Jesus never permitted the legitimate demands of the body to keep him from an opportunity to minister to the physical and spiritual needs of others. He conversed with Nicodemus at night instead of relaxing; he left his place of security and retirement to respond to the call "Lazarus is sick"; he neglected sleep and food in order to meet human need, as in Capernaum (Mark 1:28-39). Here he was alert to the opportunity of winning one convert and even took the initiative in so doing. Personal evangelism is one of the most important and yet one of the most neglected of Christian duties. An attitude

[1] W. F. Albright, *Archaeology of Palestine* (Penguin, 1954), p. 247.

7 There cometh a woman of Samaria to draw water: Jesus saith unto her, Give me to drink.

8 For his disciples were gone away into the city to buy food.

---

diameter, and at the bottom is clear, cool water. The term for well or "spring" (*pēgē*) occurs in v. 14 and in Rev. 7:17; 8:10; 14:17; 16:4; 21:6 but rarely elsewhere in the N. T. It is distinct from "well," (*threar*) which occurs in vv. 11, 12; Rev. 9:1, 2; Luke 14:5. The former term connotes a spring or fountain of flowing water as in Rev. 21:6; the latter a pit, shaft, or dug well, as in Luke 14: 5. It was, therefore, not a cistern for the collection of water but a spring-fed well that never ran dry, a priceless blessing, especially in the semi-arid area of Samaria.

6 **Jesus, being wearied . . . sat thus by the well.** This Gospel, like the Epistle to the Hebrews, places side by side the most daring affirmations of Jesus' deity and the most emphatic assertions of his real humanity. Only this Gospel notes that Jesus was weary and that he wept. **Jesus . . . sat,** or better, "just as he was, was sitting" (imperfect tense). **The sixth hour** was noon according to Jewish reckoning, a good time to rest, but an unusual time to be coming for water.[2]

Perhaps the woman was despised by the other women of the village and avoided coming in the morning or the evening when the women usually came for water.

7 **Give me to drink.** By this means Jesus placed himself beneath her in status. He took the position of a dependent, asking for a favor. This was a disarming approach. The request was a natural one, however, as there was not enough community spirit to leave rope and bucket for the convenience of wayfarers. This is often true today from Samaria to India. Had a rope and bucket been left a thief would probably have taken it in short order. The influence of Christianity makes possible a more honest moral climate in a community. This visiting rabbi had no disciples present to minister to his needs for they had all gone away to purchase food. So Jesus broke protocol and asked the favor of a strange woman.

8 **A Jew askest drink of me?** She registered great surprise. Her surprise was due to the fact that he was a Jew; the disciples later were surprised because she was a woman (v. 27).

---

of professionalism and of specialization often results in a neglect of many such opportunities for effective witnessing. The professional religious worker tends to limit his energies to his stated rounds and is not alert and resourceful when an evangelistic opportunity is presented. The specialist may feel that this duty is not expected of him because his specialty is missions, or preaching, or administration rather than that of responding to novel situations with faith and love.

Some women were holding a committee meeting on missions in a restaurant. While they were concentrating on their business at hand, the father of one of the committee women was busy talking to one of the waiters about Christ. As a result, the waiter became converted; the women were embarrassed that their pre-

occupation with foreign missions had led them to overlook an opportunity for personal evangelism. Although weary, Jesus was alert to this opportunity for evangelism which was presented by the approaching woman intent on her daily chore of fetching water. What follows is one of the most detailed examples of effective evangelism in the New Testament. This story of the water and the woman's conversion is one of the best demonstrations of technique in personal evangelism.

### b. The Woman's Awakening (vv. 7-15)

In this paragraph it is profitable to trace the change of attitude on the part of the woman and Jesus' strategy in inducing it.

---

[2] Did John reckon the days as beginning at sunset (as the Jews then and now), or at midnight (as today) or at dawn? It was probably the last (cf. Mark 15:25, 33, 34, 42; Acts 2:15). Westcott (*Speakers' Bible*, p. 282) believed John's day began at midnight, hence 6 P.M. is meant here. Most (e.g., MRV, II, 113) believe John followed the usual practice of beginning the day at dawn and cite John 1:39; 4:6, 52; 19:14 in support. See "Introduction."

9 The Samaritan woman therefore saith unto him, How is it that thou, being a Jew, askest drink of me, who am a Samaritan woman? (For Jews have no dealings with Samaritans.)

9 **To buy food:** We know little about how Jesus and his disciples secured their food while traveling. We learn that certain women followed them to Jerusalem on pilgrimages to the festivals "ministering to him of their substance" (Luke 8:3). We know also that they had a common purse and from it bought food as needed (John 13:29). That the purchase of food was common from this purse is implied in the questions of Philip when Jesus asked him to feed the multitude (John 6:5). Here in Samaria they were not in hospitable country and hence could expect no "handouts" or free meals; they would have to purchase food and possibly even water. There is nothing to suggest that they "fared sumptuously."

9 **How is it . . . ?** This woman had curiosity, hence her questions, and hence her discovery of *life*. In the Orient, as elsewhere, "losing face" is something worse than losing life. The code of the medieval warriors in Japan made it commendable to commit suicide if one "lost face" by a political or military defeat. Here Jesus broke caste by asking a favor of a despised Samaritan, thus placing himself subordinate to her rather than "standing on his dignity" or superiority. He did not command her to give him a drink; he only requested it as a favor. She was astonished at his unconventional behavior.

**The Jews have no dealings** (*Synchrōntai*). A rabbinic statement of A.D. 65 specified that all Samaritan women were ritually unclean and that using the same vessels with them rendered the user unclean. The practice probably preceded the formal adoption of the rule, and if this was so it would account for the surprise of the woman and of the disciples at Jesus

| Jesus' Strategy | The Woman's Reactions |
|---|---|
| | v. 9 Wonders *why*, registers SURPRISE |
| v. 7 Requests water | |
| | v. 11 Wonders *how: Whence?* |
| v. 10 Offers "living water" | |
| | v. 12 Wonders *who* Jesus is, registers CURIOSITY |
| v. 13, 14 Offers "eternal life" | v. 15 Requests better water, registers sense of NEED |

The paragraph begins with a request by Jesus and ends with a request by the woman. The role of Jesus changes from petitioner for water to dispenser of life. The woman's role changes from dispenser of water to petitioner for a "water" which will permanently satisfy. In the interval it is noteworthy that Jesus establishes rapport by a natural and yet unconventional request that was hard to ignore or refuse. Trumbull relates a story from the victory of Saladin over the Christian knights at the battle of Hattin the most decisive battle of the Crusades lost largely by the lack of water. Saladin offered water to one of the defeated Christian leaders but refused it to the other the latter he had marked for destruction while the former he permitted to live. The giving of water indicated a truce. Even today in Palestine, especially among the Bedouins, the offering of a drink of water is a pledge of friendship and of hospitality. The woman was virtually compelled by the mores of hospitality to comply with the request of this "Stranger of Galilee."[f]

The woman could not conceal surprise that Jesus ignored the current folkways which maintained a policy of strict exclusiveness towards Samaritans. Normally the more religious Jews were the most scrupulous in maintaining this barrier Jesus was apparently religious and yet not at all strict in this regard. It often happens that the most strict and disciplined in the externals of religion are the most flagrant transgressors in the "weightier

e H. C. Trumbull, cited in F. N. Peloubet, *Suggestive Illustrations on the Gospel of John* (New York, 1898), p. 106.
f The demand of hospitality to strangers was and is one of the most compelling in the mores of the Orient. A citizen of Gilbeah offered to sacrifice the virginity of his own daughter rather than having a guest embarrassed even though only a stranger (Jud. 19:24).

10 Jesus answered and said unto her, If thou knewest the gift of God, and who it is that saith to thee, Give me to drink; thou wouldest have asked of him, and he would have given thee living water.

---

disregard of these scruples.[3] Arguments for the former, more inclusive, meaning rest upon historic tensions which originated in the post-exilic period of Ezra and Nehemiah. At that time a policy of exclusiveness was due to a desire to avoid a mixture of faith and blood. Many Jewish men had taken non-Jewish wives thus endangering not only the purity of Jewish stock but also the purity of their faith, as had happened under Solomon (Ezra 9:1—10:42; Neh. 13:23-30). As G. F. Moore observed (*Judaism,* I, 21), this exclusiveness was probably the price of survival as a distinct religious and ethnic entity and hence was justified historically. That they had some business dealings with the Samaritans is evidenced by the fact that the disciples bought food nearby. But on the level of cordiality there was no fellowship, as the Parable of the Good Samaritan implies (Luke 10:29-37).

**10 If thou knewest the gift of God.** Jesus, as was his custom, did not answer the question directly but lifted the questioner's thought to a greater question. From an attitude of inferiority to her he now assumes the role of a dispenser of favors rather than that of one in need of a favor. The gift (*dōrean*) has the connotation of a free and generous offering, usually from God, such as the gift of the Holy Spirit (Acts 2:38; 8:20; 10:45; 11:17; cf. Rom. 5:15, 17; Eph. 3:7; 4:7). Its synonym (*dōron*) is usually employed to designate the gifts man makes (Matt. 2:11; Heb. 8:4). Jesus thus conceals his identity, implies his superior resources, and excites her curiosity both as to the gift and the Giver.

---

matters" of such fruits of the Spirit as "love, joy, peace, patience, kindness, goodness, faithfulness, gentleness and self-control" (Gal. 5:23 RSV). The parables of the Good Samaritan and the Prodigal Son were occasioned by such people.

After the woman's expression of surprise at the stranger's request she listened to his rather tantalizing exposure of her ignorance — "if you knew the gift of God." Such a challenge aroused her curiosity about both the gifts of living water and the Giver. Her reply shows her increasing respect for Jesus, since she now addresses him "Sir." She also betrays her increasing perplexity and curiosity both as to the source of the superior water and of the speaker's identity.

As the conversation develops, Jesus elaborates on the inward and spiritual nature of the "gift of God." In terms she could understand so well he assured her that this "gift of God" would be so satisfying that further trips to this well would be unnecessary. Jesus was speaking in terms of her experience and yet sufficiently above her experience to whet her desire for better water. It has been said that this narrative has been studied intensively by effective salesmen as they have noted Jesus' skill in getting attention, arousing curiosity, exposing the inadequacy of present possessions, presenting the image of something better, and then urging its acceptance by a commitment. Whether in salesmanship, pedagogy, or evangelism, it is important to communicate by accommodating oneself to the other's experience, at the same time showing the way to something better, enough superior to be wanted and near enough to be accessible.

The barriers which Jesus penetrated in the discussion up to this point were very formidable. There was the barrier of *race* of which the woman was painfully aware. She appreciated the fact that Jesus did not treat her as a second-class citizen, as one beneath his caste. She was not made to feel inferior because of her pedigree or lack of one. The attitude of superiority assumed by many religious leaders was felt keenly by the common people of Jesus' day.[g] The Samaritans

---

[3] D. Daube, "Jesus and the Samaritan Woman: The Meaning of συγγράομαι," JBL, June, 1950, pp. 137-147.

[g] Louis Finklestein, *The Pharisees, The Sociological Background of Their Faith* (Philadelphia: Jewish publ. Soc., 1940), I, 197.

11 The woman saith unto him, Sir, thou hast nothing to draw with, and the well is deep: whence then hast thou that living water?

12 Art thou greater than our father Jacob, who gave us the well, and drank thereof himself, and his sons, and his cattle?

---

**Living water.** This is water of a gushing spring or stream, running water. This would be in marked contrast to water deep in the well which must be laboriously lifted in small quantities. Such language to a Jew would evoke Jeremiah's description of God as "the fountain of living waters" (Jer. 2:13; 17:13) and Zechariah's prediction of future blessings (13:1; 14:8). "Living water" or running water was preferred for baptism (*Didache* vii. 1, 2). But John's employment of "life (zoē) elsewhere as "eternal life" strongly implies more than literal running water as the woman naturally interpreted it. The same term which normally designated only running water here means the water of life (cf. Gen. 26:19; Lev. 14:5; Rev. 7:17; 21:6).

11 **Whence then hast thou that living water?** Was the woman curious, skeptical, or scornful? Commentators, as usual, differ in their analysis of the woman's attitude at this point of the conversation.

Hoskyns considers her attitude one of indignation (*op. cit.,* p. 236) and scorn (p. 242). Westcott thinks her question reflects wonder at what lies deeper in Jesus' meaning, a quest for a fuller understanding. Her mode of addressing him and the sequel indicates an attitude of respectful inquiry. She noted the absence of any physical means by which Jesus could avail himself of the water and naturally wonders how he could dispense "living water." Her curiosity is aroused, an important factor in personal evangelism, or in a learning situation.

12 **Art thou greater than our father Jacob?** The *thou* (*sy*) is emphatic — "Surely *Thou* art not greater" (CGT)! The interrogative particle *mē* expects a negative answer. Her belief that she and her countrymen were descendants of the patriarchs was probably more than presumption. It is true that her ancestors were displaced persons from Mesopotamia as indicated in II Kings 17:23-41. On

---

were considered by the strict Jews as even inferior to the despised "people of the land."

Race prejudice, or the myth of racial superiority, is one of the most pervasive and tenacious social evils of our times. Often the Bible is cited in a vain effort to sanctify such unhallowed presumptions. There are those who appear unaware that assumptions of racial superiority are a hindrance to the evangelization of so-called "inferior races." Jesus was aware of this and made it clear that he did not downgrade this woman simply because of her ancestry, over which she had no control. He always treated people as individuals rather than as merely representative of a group. In his dealing with individuals he judged them not so much on the basis of what they had been, or even what they were, but rather on the basis of what they could become under grace.

Another barrier which Jesus penetrated in this conversation was that of *creed.*

Rather than arguing about the relative merits of Mt. Zion or Mt. Gerizim, he called attention to what was at once self-evident — that the object of worship is more important than the place. He stressed that the manner and spirit of worship are also more important than the place. Instead of permitting historical differences of opinion and tradition to hinder communication he set these aside and concentrated on matters they held in common, such as the worship of one God rather than idols. He also pointed out something unique about the true God — that he is the seeker as well as the sought. The pagan deities did not seek out worshippers. God seeking out and saving the sinner is one of the most distinctive features of the Christian faith as defined by its Founder. But in bridging the gap of faith Jesus did not compromise on essentials; he did not seek a common denominator by eliminating distinctives. He said that the Samaritans worshipped in ignorance and that salvation was of the Jews, but

13 Jesus answered and said unto her, Every one that drinketh of this water shall thirst again:

14 but whosoever drinketh of the water that I shall give him shall never thirst; but the water that I shall give him shall become in him a well of water springing up unto eternal life.

---

the basis of II Kings 17:6, 24-41; 18:11, 12, Josephus concludes that *all* of the Israelites were removed and only heathen dwelt there thereafter (*Ant.* IX. xiv. 1). This is borne out by the necessity of bringing back a deportee to teach the immigrants the law of Jehovah (II Kings 17:27). But many texts cannot be pressed too literally. It seems likely that a few Israelites of the hinterlands either eluded deportation or were ignored in the mass exodus and Israelites from Judea probably would have intermingled with the newcomers in the centuries following. Furthermore, the immigrants would naturally have respect and perhaps reverence for the local traditions and holy places they had come to occupy (II Kings 17:28). Later the Moslem invaders of the Holy Land revered the places associated with the patriarchs and built their mosques on the sites of Jewish temples and Christian churches. It is not improbable therefore, that the woman of Samaria had some tenuous blood ties with the patriarchs as well as an ideological kinship.

**Cattle** (*thremmata*) is found only here in the N.T. It is from *trephō* meaning "to nourish" or "to feed" and means primarily domesticated animals such as sheep or goats. It indicates that the traditions of nomadic patriarchal life were still strong in Shechem. The inhabitants then, as now, were rooted in the past.

13 **Shall thirst again** — the possession of Jacob's well was not only a great economic asset; it was also a matter of supreme historical value which lent prestige to the community. But Jesus boldly contrasts the water that Jacob gave with the "water" which he had to give.

14 **Whosoever drinketh** (*hos an piēi*) is in contrast to the **everyone that drinketh** of v. 13. In v. 13 the article and the participle **drinking** indicate habitual and continued drinking. In v. 14 the aorist indicates a single act that is done once for all. The contrast, there-

---

he coupled that with the appeal to experience, to the pragmatic test of performance — "he that drinks of this water shall never thirst again." To the needy woman this sounded better than contending over ancient traditions simply because of local pride, partisan prejudice, or venerable precedents.

Another barrier to evangelism penetrated by Jesus at the well was that of *sex*. Then, as now, the Orient was a "man's world." Women, simply because they are women, are often considered inferior. It is said that even today, in certain rural sections of a major country of the East, women give to their husbands a reverence like that they render to their gods. In many major religions of the Orient, women's attendance at public worship is not encouraged, and if they do choose to come they are segregated from the men and the boys. The prophecy of Joel stated that in the latter days God would pour out his Spirit upon *all* flesh, the young and the old, the men and women alike. This was historically fulfilled on the day of Pentecost and may be witnessed throughout Christian history when the Spirit of God has been much in evidence. Today certain major Christian groups ordain women as clergy on the same basis as men, but they have come to this action only after long delays during which time they conveniently forgot that Miriam, Deborah, and others were among the Lord's anointed and became the most effective charismatic leaders of their generations.

### c. The Woman's Conversion (vv. 16-26)

The woman's desire for superior water has been gradually increasing and she has become convinced that Jesus can give her something she needs, although she would have found difficulty in defining what she expected to receive. The crucial

15 The woman saith unto him, Sir, give me this water, that I thirst not, neither come all the way hither to draw.

16 Jesus saith unto her, Go, call thy husband, and come hither.

---

fore, is between water that relieves thirst only temporarily and water that satisfies permanently, between repeated drinking and one decisive act of partaking.

**Shall never thirst** — the significance of the double negative is a strong statement: "never again, in nowise, by no means" (MRV). The reason for not thirsting is that the source of "water" is not *without* as in a well, but *within*. Since it is **within** him, it shall be a "fountain (*pēgē*) gushing up (*hallomenou*) into life everlasting." The RSV rendering is an improvement over both the KJV and ARV versions — "a spring of water welling up." The NEB is good also — "an inner spring always welling up for eternal life."

**15** **Sir, give me this water.** The **Sir** is, in this context, the correct translation of *kyrie*, a term which in many other contexts means "Lord" (cf. 4:11, 49; 20: 28). The conversation began with Jesus saying, "give me to drink," and now the woman says "give me this water." She

has heard enough to make her aware of the inadequacy of ordinary water, even from this venerable source, and to desire something better. Had Jesus' approach been more direct and dogmatic he would probably have incurred her hostility and placed her on the defensive at the outset.

In this paragraph we find the climax of the conversation and one of the highest expressions of the Christian religion. The woman's request, **give me**, now enables Jesus to present her with a command, "go . . . come hither" (v. 16). Until she had come to the place of admitting need there was little likelihood that she would respond favorably to a command. Now Jesus is in the role of an expert giving a prescription for soul satisfaction.

**16** **Call thy husband** is the condition of further enlightenment in her quest for the water of life. By this apparently casual remark Jesus touched a sore spot, a place at which she was particularly vulnerable.

---

decision is faced when she is confronted with the condition of receiving **the gift of God: go call thy husband.** She now learns that her relation to God is conditioned by her relations with others, as the prophets from Amos to Isaiah had so eloquently stressed. Many isolate religion from ethics and assume that our relations with others have little bearing on our relation to God. Would this woman become negative as the light sought to overcome the darkness, and shrink from the light because her deeds were evil? At first she tried to profess innocence: "I have no husband." When Jesus showed that he knew her marital history, she tried to evade the issue by reverting to a theological problem. In response, Jesus finally convinced her that the important thing was not place but Person. Instead of a concern for a holy place, she was now confronted with a Holy Person. One of the greatest assets of Christianity, in its task of world-evangelism, is the person of Christ. His unique and sinless life has no parallel among the

founders of world religions. Jesus Christ attracts not only because of what he says and does but also because of what he is.

The emphasis here on worship in *spirit* is based on the fact that God is Spirit. This states God's nature rather than his personality, and it also emphasizes that man is basically spiritual in nature. Man's partly spiritual nature is suggested by the beautiful account of creation in which "God . . . breathed into his nostrils the breath of life; and man became a living soul" (Gen. 2:7). ("Breath" and "spirit" come from the same Hebrew word *ruach*.) Because of this kinship God and man can come closest together in the realm of the spirit. The Spirit of God represents the immanence of God — his nearness. Thus it is that on the basis of *worship in spirit* atonement between man and God is possible. Although he was enslaved by a parasitic habit, few expressed a clearer spiritual insight than Robert Burns as he described the family worship of the Scottish peasant of his day.

17 The woman answered and said unto him, I have no husband. Jesus saith unto her, Thou saidst well, I have no husband:

18 for thou hast had five husbands; and he whom thou now hast is not thy husband: this hast thou said truly.

19 The woman saith unto him, Sir, I perceive that thou art a prophet.

17 **Well** (*kalōs*) means "aptly, truly, indeed," cf. Acts 28:35; Matt. 15:7; Luke 20:39. The woman has spoken the truth, but not the whole truth. Further probing is necessary before the whole truth comes out. But the Master commends her for telling the truth up to a point; then he tells her more.

18 **Thou hast had five husbands.** Jesus spoke with both courtesy and candor. The suggestion that the five husbands symbolize the five nations from which the Samaritan colonists came (II Kings 17:24; Jos. *Ant.* IX. 14. 3) was put forth by Pfleiderer (*Primitive Christianity*, IV, 30), favored by Hoskyns, and considered credible by Barrett, but it is rejected in favor of a literal interpretation by Bernard, Howard, Plummer, Lange, and most others. While there is symbolism in the Fourth Gospel, there is no justification for assuming it when a plain literal historical meaning is more natural.

19 **Sir, I perceive** (*theōreō*). This verb occurs 24 times in this Gospel as compared with 16 times in the three other Gospels (M-G), and is a preferred term with John. It means to scrutinize critically, to behold, to investigate, "to give intelligent attention."[4] Here it means that the woman is gaining increasing discernment as to Jesus' real nature.

**Thou art a prophet,** that is, one who is possessed with supernatural discernment and information (cf. I Sam. 9:9). The closest parallel is the conclusion drawn by Simon the Pharisee: "if this man were a prophet, he would have known who and what sort of woman this is" (Luke 7:39 RSV). In the light of vv. 20-25, it seems

Then kneeling down to Heaven's
   Eternal King,
The saint, the father, and the hus-
   band prays;
Hope 'springs exulting on trium-
   phant wing,'
That thus they all shall meet in
   future days.

Compared to this, how poor Religion's pride,
In all the pomp of method and of
   art;
When men display to congregations
   wide
Devotion's every grace except the
   heart![h]

There is a sense in which Marx was correct in saying that "religion is the opiate of the people." But this is true only of false religion. Certainly the externals of religion sometimes blind one to its inner spirit, and involvement in the paraphernalia of worship can inoculate one against what Jesus called being "born of the Spirit." By virtue of granting the status of sanctity and acceptance to those who accept the form but have not experienced the Spirit, a false sense of security is created which will make more difficult finding the true water of life. The Christian religion is no exception to this tendency; Protestantism is no exception; and even the more "spiritual" and informal segments of Protestantism at times succumb. "It is possible to know about Christ so well that, satisfied with that, we never come to know him; possible to haunt the holy place, and bustle about its precincts, yet catch no vision of the Holy One."[i]

The woman had heard enough to be prepared for Jesus' climactic announcement of his identity. She now concluded that he was even more than a prophet — perhaps even the Messiah. Hers was the attitude of a receptive learner. Because receptive she was responsive. The time was ready for the announcement: "you are now hearing the Messiah speak." Jesus

[4] For the difference between *theorein*, *horaō*, *optomai*, *blepō*, see exegesis on John 20:7; and MRV, I, 59; J. H. Bernard, *op. cit.*, I, 99.
[h] Robert Burns, "The Cotter's Saturday Night."
[i] A. J. Gossip, *John* in *The Interpreter's Bible* (Nashville: Abingdon-Cokesbury Press), VIII, 527.

20 Our fathers worshipped in this mountain; and ye say, that in Jerusalem is the place where men ought to worship.

---

unlikely that the woman was thinking of "*the* Prophet" or the Messiah of Deut. 18: 15 (cf. John 1:25).

**20 Our fathers worshipped in this mountain.** She abruptly changed the subject. "Convinced that He can read her life she shrinks from inspection and hastily turns the conversation from herself. In seeking a new subject she naturally catches at one absorbing interest to every Samaritan" (Plummer, *CB,* p. 111). Either she wanted to avoid further investigation of her past and present or because of her interest in the current controversy as to the preferred place of worship she grasped at the opportunity to get the opinion of an "authority." Probably both factors influenced her change of subject. Jesus did not press accusations further but answered her as though her interest in worship were sincere. By **our fathers** she doubtless referred to the ancestors of the Samaritans, who built the temple on Mt. Gerizim in the time of Nehemiah. But in view of her reference to Jacob as "our father" she doubtless included the patriarchs in her

reference. It was here at Shechem that Abraham set up his first altar in the land of Canaan (Gen. 12:7). When Jacob returned to Canaan after twenty years in Syria, his first altar was also erected here at Shechem (Gen. 33:20). In Deut. 11: 29; 27:12 this site was designated as the place where the covenant would be ratified by the people, the blessings being recited on Mt. Gerizim and the curses recited on Mt. Ebal just to the north. Here Joshua assembled the people and carried out this mandate (Josh. 8:30-35). Prior to this time Shechem was a great sanctuary for the religion of the Canaanites, the importance of which is becoming increasingly apparent to archaeologists in charge of current excavation.[5]

About 400 B.C. the local inhabitants, descendants from the eighth century, and immigrants from Mesopotamia (II King 17:24-41) built their temple on Mt. Gerizim. (Joshua's cairn was erected on Mt Ebal — Josh. 8:30 — as commanded in Deut. 27:4, even though Mt. Gerizim was the mount of blessing — Deut. 11:29

---

could reveal more to her than to Nicodemus because, in spite of her background, she was more receptive.

Why was it that Nicodemus with his superior spiritual advantages proved so difficult to convince when this ignorant woman was won so easily? He was learned, she unlearned; he was a man, she a woman; he was an Israelite, she a Samaritan; he a ruler in Israel, she a peasant in Sychar; he was in a formal interview, she in a casual conversation; he in a place and time conducive to meditation, she by the roadside; he was "righteous," she a sinner. The Evangelist apparently had a purpose in placing these two conversations so close together. Was it not to show by contrast the fact that it is often more difficult to reach those who possess much and have more to give up? Paul was an exception to this rule. In his case he came to the place where he reckoned all his assets as "refuse" in order to have Christ (Phil. 3:8). This Nicode-

mus found difficult to do. The Samaritan woman, with less to lose, was more easily won, in spite of deepseated prejudices and a guilty conscience. "If with all your heart ye truly seek Me, Ye shall ever surely find me" (cf. Jer. 29:13).

On this occasion, and in such parable as the Lost Coin, the Lost Sheep, and the Lost Son (Luke 15:3-32), Jesus presented a picture of God such as is found in no other religion. In other religion man seeks God; in Christianity God seek man. Few have expressed this distinctive doctrine of the Christian faith more eloquently and poignantly than the author of "The Hound of Heaven."

> Now of that long pursuit
> Comes on at hand the bruit;
> That Voice is round me like a
>     bursting sea;
> "And is thy earth so marred,
> Shattered in shard on shard?
> Lo, all things fly thee, for thou
>     flyest me!

---

[5] L. E. Toombs and G. E. Wright, "The Third Campaign at Balatah (Shechem)," BASOR, Feb. 1961, pp. 28-39. G. E. Wright, "Archaeological Fills and Strata," BA, May, 1962, pp. 34-40.

21 Jesus saith unto her, Woman, believe me, the hour cometh, when neither in this mountain nor in Jerusalem, shall ye worship the Father.

---

26:12.) Thus Shechem had a religious history for the Israelites much older than the temple in Jerusalem.

**Jerusalem is the place where men ought to worship.** The designation of Jerusalem as the only legitimate sanctuary of Jehovah is based upon Deuteronomy 12:5, 11, 13, 14. The original purpose of this regulation was to discourage idolatry, the practice of worshipping at local shrines revered by the Canaanites. The monopoly of Jerusalem over worship was then justified by the necessity of excluding worship of all "gods" except Jehovah. Because of this Old Testament concern with monotheism, and the relation of *one* sanctuary to this ideal, the importance attached to the temple in Jerusalem is understandable.

**21 Believe me** — As the conversation progressed Jesus became increasingly affirmative and positive, even dogmatic, as in the conversation with Nicodemus, which ended by Jesus asking that his interrogator learn from one who came down from heaven (3:11). **The hour cometh** — this expression is characteristic of the Gospel. It sounds an apocalyptic note, probably in the tradition of the O. T. phrase "the day of the Lord." The "hour" cannot be pinpointed but probably the climactic "hour" of its fulfillment was that described in Acts 2:1ff. **Neither here . . . nor in Jerusalem.** For the woman to hear the visitor say that in the future there would be no worship either on Mt. Gerizim or in Jerusalem must have occasioned an initial shock of surprise. Jesus was emphasizing that the *place* of worship is not what is important but rather the One being worshipped. That the place or house of worship was not the most important thing was clearly taught in the Old Testament: in the dedicatory prayer of Solomon (I Kings 8:27), in the visions of "new heavens and a new earth" (Isa. 66:1, 2), and in the time of the Second Temple (Mal.

---

*Whom wilt thou find to love ignoble*
*thee*
    *Save only Me, save only Me?*
*All which I took from thee, I did*
    *but take*
*Not for thy harms,*
*But just that thou mightst seek it*
    *in My arms.*
    *All which thy child's mistake*
*Fancies as lost, I have stored for*
    *thee at home:*
    *Rise, clasp My hand and come!"*

        .    .    .

*Halts by me that footfall:*
    *Is my gloom, after all,*
*Shade of His hand, outstretched*
    *caressingly?*
    *"Ah, fondest, blindest, weakest,*
*I am He Whom thou seekest!*
*Thou dravest love from thee, who*
    *dravest Me."*[1]

The manner in which the Master sought to win this woman differed from his method with Nicodemus, as Chrysostom and others have noted. With the teacher in Israel he appealed to the Scripture and to logic; to woman he used the appeal of water and promised her some of the same which was better. But in both the objective is the discovery and experience of real life.

### d. The Woman's Witness (vv. 27-30)

At this climax of the interview, when Jesus said "I am he," the disciples returned to marvel at his conversing with a woman. She left her waterpot in the excitement of her discovery and hurried back to the village to bear witness. So convincing was her testimony and so obvious was the transformation that without hesitation the villagers came to see for themselves. As they were coming, the disciples were urging (both verbs imperfect) Jesus to eat.

**27 They marvelled that he was speaking with a woman,** not because she was a Samaritan but because she was a woman. The rabbinic writings advised, "Rather burn the sayings of the law than teach them to a woman " (MRV, II, 124).

[1] Francis Thompson, "The Hound of Heaven."

22 Ye worship that which ye know not: we worship that which we know, for salvation is from the Jews.

23 But the hour cometh, and now is, when the true worshippers shall worship the Father in spirit and truth: for such doth the Father seek to be his worshippers.

---

1:11). But in the subsequent times of war and resulting sectarian prejudices this noble vision had been obscured. What Jesus said, therefore, sounded like a new Gospel.

22 **Ye worship that which ye know not.** Jesus was in agreement with the O. T. evaluation of the religion of the Samaritans. In II Kings 17:33 this worship is described as one of fearing Jehovah and worshipping their own gods. Apparently they were awed by the realization of living under the jurisdiction of the God of the land, but their heart and soul belonged to the gods they had brought with them from their homelands. They were never converted as Ruth had been (Ruth 1:16; 2:12). Worship (*proskyneō*) is the common N. T. term for devotion, in contrast to classical Greek where the common verb is *eusebeō* ("to revere"). The latter is rare in the N. T. (Acts 17:23; I Tim. 5:4). *Proskyneō* may include showing obeisance to a ruler, worshipping God, or idols, or devils, or Jesus the Christ (A-G).

23 **The hour . . . now is.** This affirmation of Jesus indicates the vast extent and influence of the New Covenant, the Christian religion. In announcing this new day in the worship of God, Jesus' role becomes, in the woman's understanding, much more than that of a prophet. He comes to usher in this new era of worship, as its High Priest. **Worship the Father in spirit and truth.** The sequence is from the *place* of worship (v. 21). to the *Object* of worship (v. 22) to the *manner* of worship (vv. 23, 24). In saying that the forthcoming worship will be in "spirit," the Master was stressing the fact that worship in its highest and essential nature is inward and spiritual rather than outward and ceremonial. Although there are many passages in the Old Testament which speak of this higher worship of the true God, this statement is outstanding and almost unique in its affirmation both of the nature of God and of true worship. In Deuteronomy 6:4 ("the Shema") the affirmation of mono-

---

Jesus was remarkable in his transcendence over tradition and his subordination to the will of the Father as expressed in the Law and the Prophets (cf. Matt. 5:17; cf. Mark 7:8). Jesus kept the commandment of God and ignored the tradition of men; "the Jews" did the opposite, leaving the commandment of God and holding fast to the traditions of men.

The fabulously rich diamond fields of South Africa, according to one story, were discovered by chance. A visitor approached the door of a settler and noticed a boy throwing stones for a pastime. The stranger picked up one of the stones, saw it sparkle strangely, examined it closely, and discovered a diamond. This stone, which had been trodden under foot, held a priceless treasure and led to still further discoveries.[k]

Jesus saw in the least promising citizen of Sychar far more than the disciples had seen. When the famous English artist

Turner finished painting one of his sunsets, a woman stood gazing at it. Said she, "Mr. Turner, I can't see all in that sunset that you do." The artist replied, "Madame, don't you wish that you could?"

Thus, this unnamed woman of Samaria was one of the most effective evangelists in Biblical history because she was a receptive, perceptive, and enthusiastic witness.

### e. The Disciples Challenged (vv. 31-38)

Between the time of the woman's departure to Sychar and her return with other inquirers Jesus had opportunity to preach to his disciples a sermon on missions and evangelism. As elsewhere in this Gospel, the contrast between the physical and the spiritual is prominent. There is a contrast also between Jesus' weariness and thirst, reported in v. 6, and the enthusiasm which overcomes his natural appetite now. Any-

---

k From James Stalker, *Imago Christi.*

24 God is a Spirit: and they that worship him must worship in spirit and truth.

25 The woman saith unto him, I know that Messiah cometh (he that is called Christ): when he is come, he will declare unto us all things.

---

theism is joined to an admonition to "love Jehovah thy God with all thy heart." Saul was advised that "to obey is better than sacrifice" (I Sam. 15:22). Joel advised the people to "rend your heart, and not your garments" (Joel 2:13). Amos scorned any externals in worship apart from inward righteousness (Amos 5:20-24) as did Isaiah (1:11-20). Micah voiced one of the most eloquent pleas for spiritual worship coupled with righteousness (Mic. 6:6-8). Psalms 50:7-15 and 51:1-17 express the insight that real worship is not in animal sacrifices but in a worship of the mind and heart. Similar ideas may be found in Philo, and the Stoics expressed like ideas about the spiritual nature of God and true worship (Bauer, p. 71).

24 **God is a Spirit.** There is no article in the Greek, and the reading of the ASV, RSV, and NEB is to be preferred — "God is Spirit" or God is spiritual in nature. This is the basis for the oft-quoted definition of God in the *Westminster Catechism*: "God is a Spirit with-out body or parts." This statement about God is one of three found in the Johannine literature; the others are "God is light" (I John 1:5) and "God is love" (I John 4:8). The same emphasis on the Spirit is found also in John 6:63 where the contrast between flesh and spirit is stressed (cf. II Cor. 3:17). **Must worship** (*dei proskynein*) does not mean that worship is compulsory, but that if worship is to be effective, to be real worship, it must be spiritual in nature. This is a continuation of the consistent emphasis on the superiority of the spirit over the flesh voiced thus far in 1:13, 51; 2:19; 3:6; 4:14.

25 **The woman saith unto him I know,** (*oida*) using the same word for "know" that Jesus had just used (v. 22), a word which includes both information and insight. She was so impressed by Jesus' statement about the true God and true worship that she almost wistfully expressed the desire and expectation of a fuller revelation.

---

one who is truly human has experienced similar moments of physical exhaustion and then mental or spiritual exhilaration which makes physical wants seem trivial. The disciples felt that it was of utmost importance that the Master partake of the food they had just purchased. After experiencing the thrill of having someone accept his offer of "living water," Jesus felt this was quite a "let-down." When told that he already possessed "food" they were perplexed in the same manner as Nicodemus and the Samaritan woman had been perplexed. They thought in physical terms, Jesus in spiritual terms; the words were the same but the concepts entirely different. Dialogue cannot be carried on successfully through the medium of words alone. "A man who is unspiritual refuses what belongs to the Spirit of God; it is folly to him; he cannot grasp it, because it needs to be judged in the light of the Spirit" (I Cor. 2:14 NEB). Again and again Jesus sought to teach his disciples to be more spiritually-minded by speaking to them enigmatically to provoke them to inquiry and discovery. The parable of the Soils (Mark 4:1ff.) is a good example of this.

Perhaps he was thinking of his current mission and the need for urgency in pursuing it when Jesus remarked that the "field" is now ready to be harvested. On numerous other occasions Jesus is quoted as sensing the urgency of winning the lost. Once, after early morning prayer in solitude, he said, "Let us go . . . into the next towns" (Mark 1:38). Later, upon seeing the multitudes "he was moved with compassion for them, because they were distressed and scattered, as sheep not having a shepherd" (Matt. 9:36). On another occasion, after hearing the report of his evangelists, Jesus "rejoiced in the Holy Spirit," a moment of elation and gratitude not unlike that recorded here by John (Luke 10:21). The consistent pattern of Jesus' ministry is that of one zealous of preaching to the world, teaching

26 Jesus saith unto her, I that speak unto thee am *he*.

---

**Messiah cometh . . . he will declare unto us all things.** In contrast to the construction in 1:41, the article is omitted before Messiah, thus indicating a proper name (Bauer). What was the common messianic expectation of the Samaritans; how did it differ from that of the Jews? There is little information on this subject.[6] Josephus mentions an uprising which may have been inspired by messianic expectations, possibly associated with Simon Magus (*Ant.* XVIII. iv. 1; Acts 8:9-24). It is safe to conclude that as the average Samaritan shared with Israel the traditions going back to patriarchal times so he also shared the essentials of a messianic hope. The woman's confession of this hope is a reminder of Martha's belief in a general resurrection "at the last day" (11:24). In both cases the accounts make clear that this general acceptance of a creed is not enough. Christian discipleship involves an individual decision and commitment to Christ. The creedal background is good as far as it goes, but it is in itself inadequate. James agreed when he said, "Even the demons believe — and shudder" (2:19 RSV).

**He will declare unto us all things.** This expectation was as basic in the messianic

hope of the Samaritans, as it was in that of the Jews. Since the Samaritans did not accept the prophets, it is likely that this belief was inferred from Deuteronomy 18:15, a passage which presents the Messiah as the only medium of divine revelation.

In Jewish messianic expectations the Messiah will teach the Gentiles (Isa. 11:10). There is nothing to indicate that the Teacher of Righteousness of the Qumran Scrolls fits into this messianic expectation of the Samaritans or of the Jews.[7]

**He will tell us all things.** The verb *anangelei* (will tell) is used in 5:15 of a report of officials and in 16:13 of the Spirit's work in revelation of future events. The term, compounded as it is with the prefix *ana,* implies "from bottom to top." In her view the Messiah's function was similar to the work Jesus said the Spirit would perform. "The Samaritan idea was less worldly and political than the Jewish" (MRV, II, 112).

**26 I that speak unto thee am he.** This is the climax of the dialogue! The woman was apparently convinced of the truth of this statement and yet speechless. The statement **I am** (*egō eimi*) appears here

---

the disciples, healing the sick and casting out demons with a great sense of urgency.

The situation is essentially the same today. Ours is not a static but a dynamic world. Christianity now faces in atheistic materialism, linked by the Marxists with political and military zeal for conversions, its greatest threat since the Moslem invasions of the seventh century. World power, in terms of *potential* in manpower and raw materials, has recently shifted from nations with a Judeo-Christian culture to nations with an atheistic ideology. The challenge to gather sheaves in-

to life eternal has never been more imperative.

Jesus, here and in Luke 10:23, 24, indicates an awareness that he was in the midst of a harvest season for which the people had been prepared by the Law and the Prophets. The "fulness of time" (Gal. 4:4) had now come and the Master's nourishment consisted mostly in witnessing and implementing this fulfillment. He was eager that the disciples be aware of the high privilege that was theirs in witnessing and participating in what the patriarchs and saints of the past would

---

[6] Most of the sources in W. Bousset, *Die Religion des Judentums* (Berlin, 1903), pp. 224-229, relative to the messianic expectations of the Samaritans are later than the composition of the Fourth Gospel. The Samaritan Messiah was referred to as the "Taheb," meaning "he who returns," or "converts" (SB, II, 438). That the beliefs of Samaritans and Jews were similar is implied in Justin, I *Apol.* 53.
[7] For a full discussion of the Teacher of Righteousness of the Dead Sea Scrolls see F. M. Cross, Jr., *The Ancient Library of Qumran and Modern Biblical Studies* (Garden City: Doubleday, 1958), pp. 95-119; F. F. Bruce, *Second Thoughts on the Dead Sea Scrolls* (Grand Rapids: Eerdmans, 1956), pp. 85-98; F. F. Bruce, *The Teacher of Righteousness in the Dead Sea Scrolls* (London: Tyndale Press, 1956); K. Schubert, *The Dead Sea Community* (London: A. & C. Black, 1959), pp. 113-121. In support of the position that the Teacher of Righteousness is essentially the Biblical Messiah see Dupont — Somer, "Le Testament de Levi (XVII — XVIII) et la secte joive de l'alliance," *Semitica* IV, pp. 33-53. The conclusion Cross draws — that present data is insufficient to justify the identification of the Righteous Teacher of the Qumran Scrolls with the Jewish Christian Messiah — seems convincing: *op. cit.,* pp. 164-173.

27 And upon this came his disciples; and they marvelled that he was speaking with a woman; yet no man said, What seekest thou? or, Why speakest thou with her?

28 So the woman left her waterpot, and went away into the city, and saith to the people,

---

with a definite messianic connotation in itself, apart from its context. It is thus in 8:58; 18:37; Mark 14:62 and by implication is true here also (see exegesis of 6:35; 8:24, 58). Jesus' answer here is similar to his self-disclosure to the man born blind (9:37). In both of these instances the self-disclosure is the reward of sincere inquiry in contrast to the self-identification given to legal authority (Matt. 26:64).

**27 They marvelled that he was speaking with a woman.** There were at least two unconventional things about this dialogue. The woman was surprised that Jesus would talk with her, because she was a Samaritan. Now the disciples were surprised because he was talking with a woman. Judaism shared in common with paganism a low estimate of women. Part of this attitude goes back to The Pentateuch with its laws of ceremonial uncleanness (Lev. 18:19). Part of it also goes back to Eve's transgression (Gen. 3:6; I Tim. 2:11-15; Ecclus. 25:24). Jesus Ben Sirach admired virtuous women but was distrustful of many (cf. Ecclus. 42:12-14). The rabbis

said that a man should not talk with a woman in the street, even his own wife, because of the possibility of gossip (SB, II, 438). Jose ben Jochanan of Jerusalem warned, "Do not converse much with a woman." To do so, said another rabbi, might cause one to end in hell (Bauer, p. 72). Jesus, and his disciples in subsequent centuries changed all of this. The age of chivalry in medieval Europe assumed man's superiority but treated women with respect. Today equality between the sexes is common-place in the western world and, to an increasing extent, in the Orient. This is one of many instances in the Gospels where Jesus' attitude is set in contrast to that of his disciples, who to large extent, especially before Pentecost, were "conformed to this age" (Rom. 12:2). In spite of their surprise none of the disciples dared question the propriety of the conversation.

**28 So the woman left her waterpot.** Barrett agrees with Daube that she left her waterpot in order that Jesus might drink from it. This is based upon the rabbinic belief that a Samaritan would

---

like so much to have experienced. This sense of the immanence of the Kingdom of God pervades the Synoptic Gospels and appears occasionally in the Fourth Gospel, as this passage indicates. The important thing here is the note of historical fulfillment.

The practical lesson to be noted here is that in the history of the kingdom, of the church, there are periods of seedtime and later periods of harvest. There are a multitude of complex factors involved. Just as there are "seasons of the soul" so there are harvest times of churches and nations. The church in India illustrates this. Individual missions had sown "seed" for a generation or even two with little outward result, then came the "harvest season" with hundreds, even thousands accepting Christ. About two generations ago whole villages in south India were converted at a time. Similar "mass move-

ments" occurred in west India a generation later. The ancient Syrian church of south India was static for centuries. When the Bible was translated into the language of the people a revival resulted which in a relatively few years welcomed two hundred thousand into Christian fellowship. This area remains the most evangelistic segment of the Christian community of India, which now includes eight million believers. Ultimately sower and reaper, prophet and apostle, will rejoice together, not in professional competition but in satisfaction of a task jointly completed.

### f. The Samaritans Believe (vv. 39-42)

There were two types of believers in Samaria. The first group **believed on him because of the word of the woman who testified.** They may have been impressed by Jesus' reported supernatural insight and

29 Come, see a man, who told me all things that *ever* I did: can this be the Christ
30 They went out of the city, and were coming to him.
31 In the mean while the disciples prayed him, saying, Rabbi, eat.
32 But he said unto them, I have meat to eat that ye know not.

---

pollute even the drinking vessels. The leaving of the vessel therefore symbolized that Samaritans were no longer unclean to Jesus and his disciples.[8] A more natural interpretation, that her new-found joy made her forget the original purpose of her visit and rush back to the city to bear witness to her discovery, has much to commend it, as many ancient and modern expositors agree.[9] It may also have been due to her plan to return soon (Westcott).

29 **Come and see . . . can this be the Christ?** The woman uses an expression rather characteristic of this Gospel. The question (*mēti*) expects a negative answer. It is similar to the invitation issued by Jesus (1:39) and later by Philip (1:46), and it is consistent with the Johannine conviction that obedience is the condition of insight and spiritual discovery. By asking a question rather than by making an assertion the woman's report aroused curiosity and encouraged investigation. Inquiry into the truth, rather than blind credulity, is the basis for belief in the

New Testament generally and in this Gospel particularly. They probably went out expecting to see a sooth-sayer, one who could work wonders, like Simon, "the great" (cf. Acts 8:9, 10). These people were more responsive than those of the other cities of Galilee and Judea. On one occasion Jesus said that Tyre, Sidon and even Sodom would fare better in the Day of Judgment than cities like Chorazin, Bethsaida, Capernaum, and perhaps even Nazareth, which had their opportunity and did not respond (Matt. 11:20-24 Mark 6:5). Since it was more alert and responsive, this village of Sychar (or Shechem) was the first to give a generally favorable response to the Good News.

32 **I have meat to eat.** The RSV is better here in translating *brōsin* as "food" rather than as "meat" (cf. Col. 2:16; I Cor. 9:10). The term "meat" in this context is archaic, since the term itself is more inclusive than a menu of flesh. Here again is another instance of the contrast between the physical and the spiritual which is so characteristic of this Gospel.

knowledge, like that of a soothsayer. Daniel was representative of those whose knowledge was a gift of God. For every genuine thing there is usually a counterfeit. Simon of Samaria was the counterfeit who impressed his contemporaries with alleged supernatural powers. These Samaritans may have been simply curious and credulous, but they did register initial belief. Others may have believed because they thought Jesus "had her number," that is, he had been able to find her out. They had found satisfaction in having the woman exposed and changed. In any case, like those of Antioch (Acts 13:42), they were eager to investigate, to learn more. Their responsiveness, their "opportunism," resulted in their welcoming one who was "greater than Solomon," an opportunity which Jerusalem and Capernaum missed. This is the right kind of "opportunism."

The second group of believers in Sychar were those who believed on the firsthand evidence of hearing Jesus in person. This larger group included the initial believers whose faith was now confirmed together with those who believed only after hearing Jesus themselves. These believers did not base their faith on miracles. They were more noble in this way than many in Galilee (v. 48 cf., 20:29). Theirs was a full assurance of faith. If quoted correctly they were then convinced that Jesus Christ was Savior not only of the Jews but of the Samaritans and of the whole world. They deserve much credit for so all-embracing a statement this early in Jesus' career. This was Jesus' most successful "harvest" up to that point, and it was among the despised Samaritans, a link between Jewish and Gentile Christianity. There is reason to believe that John's con-

---

[8] D. Daube, *op. cit.*, pp. 137-147.
[9] Among the ancients, Chrysostom; among the moderns, R. C. H. Lenski, *The Interpretation of St. John's Gospel* (Columbus, 1942), p. 329.

33 The disciples therefore said one to another, Hath any man brought him *aught* to eat?

34 Jesus saith unto them, My meat is to do the will of him that sent me, and to accomplish his work.

35 Say not ye, There are yet four months, and *then* cometh the harvest? behold, I say unto you, Lift up your eyes, and look on the fields, that they are white already unto harvest.

---

In most cultures then and now the inclusion of flesh in the menu is common only among the more affluent people. For most people in most parts of the world today meat is considered a luxury, too expensive except for special occasions.

**34 My meat is to do the will of him that sent me.** Probably Jesus was so enthusiastic over the success of his interview that he felt no hunger. But the deeper meaning is clear — Jesus' real concern was not physical nourishment but the doing of the will of God. In the Gospels Jesus is repeatedly pictured as obsessed with the idea of obedience to the Father's will. To solicitous kinfolk on one occasion he said that those who "do the will of God" are closer to him than those of his immediate family (Mark 3:35). He could truthfully say, "I do always those things that please him" (John 8:29 KJV). Later, he would consistently emphasize to disciples that obedience is the mark of true discipleship (15:14).

As Jesus repeatedly affirmed, he was to **accomplish his work,** the work of the Father who had sent him.[10] The word **accomplish** (*teleiōsō*) means "to perfect, to carry on to completion, to consummate." The term occurs five times in John with the meaning of "complete, fulfill, or finish" (5:36; 17:4; 23; 19:28).

**35 Then comes the harvest.** The *harvest* is mentioned frequently in the Gospels.[11] This statement may have been made as he viewed the men of Sychar advancing while he spoke (Hoskyns). To the disciples, who may have been looking away from the direction of Sychar toward the fields of grain extending over the broad plain of the east, he said, "Do you not say, 'There are yet fourth months, then comes the harvest'?" (RSV). The *hymeis* is emphatic and means, "Is it not *your* saying . . . ?" (CKB).

Does the **four months** refer to the normal interval between seedtime and harvest or does it indicate the season of

---

cern in telling the story at such length was to underscore this idea of the link. A little "world" in themselves, these Samaritan villages were the first fruits of a world harvest.

### 5. THE SECOND "SIGN" (4:43-54)

#### a. Introduction: Galileans Believe (vv. 43-45)

Even Jesus Christ had "no honor at home." On numerous occasions Jesus indicated that he was in the tradition of the prophets, especially when it came to persecution. There have been many contemporaries who failed to recognize prophets or what they were. Majority votes and popularity polls are no sure source of truth. Plato, who saw the Athenians execute their best citizen, had little confidence

that the "will of the people" was best in the long run. Julius Caesar evoked resentment and even scorn in the eyes of some contemporaries who were blinded by prejudice and selfish ambition to his true greatness. Cassius, as depicted by Shakespeare, recalled saving Caesar's life from drowning, then seeing him shake with fever. He remembered that "the same eye whose bend doth awe the world" once lacked its luster, that the tongue that dictated speeches to the Romans once cried pietously for water. He cried out:

> Ye gods it doth amaze me
> A man of such a feeble temper
> should
> So get the start of the majestic world
> And bear the palm alone
> .    .    .    .

---

[10] The idea of being sent by the Father is also characteristic of this Gospel (see 5:23, 30, 37; 6:38, 4; 7:16, 18, 26, 29; 9:4; 12:44, 49; 13:20; 14:24; 15:21; 16:5).

[11] Matt. 13:30, 39; Mark 4:29; 13:25, 29; Matt. 25:26; Luke 19:21, 22; Rev. 14:15.

36 He that reapeth receiveth wages, and gathereth fruit unto life eternal; that h
that soweth and he that reapeth may rejoice together.

37 For herein is the saying true, One soweth, and another reapeth.

38 I sent you to reap that whereon ye have not labored: others have labored, and y
are entered into their labor.

---

the year when this episode occurred? If the latter then the conversation took place in November, at the beginning of the winter rainy season. Although Hoskyns, Barrett and others believe the reference is simply to the *interval* between seedtime and harvest, the contrast between "you commonly say" (*hymeis legete*) and "I am saying to you" (*legō hymin*) added to the contrast between *four months* and *already* would seem to support the view that the disciples were thinking of the calendar, thus setting an autumn date for the interview (Lenski, *op. cit.*, pp. 333f.).

**36 He that reapeth receiveth wages . . . unto life eternal.** In this sentence Jesus makes a rapid transition from the temporal to the eternal, from the material to the spiritual. The emphasis seems to be upon the conditions of the harvest, upon immediate personal responsibility — he that reapeth is the only one who enjoys the rewards of labor.

**37 One soweth and another reapeth.** Whether the saying of v. 35 is proverbial is by no means certain, but there is no uncertainty here. It is plainly stated t be a proverb.[12] Failure to reap what on has sown was regarded as a calamity (Deut. 28:30, Job 31:8; Mic. 6:15). O the other hand to harvest what others hav sown is regarded as a great privilege, cause of thanksgiving, (Deut. 6:11; Josh 24:13). The analogy was a favorite on of Paul also (Rom. 6:22; Gal. 6:8) Normally the servant sows and his em ployer takes the harvest (cf. Matt. 25:26) but here Jesus, as Lord of the Harvest is the sower and his servants, the disci ples, are the reapers (JHB). In the par able of the Soils Jesus is also the sowe of the seed (Mark 4:1-20). Paul though it commendable that sower and reape should co-operate creatively, each regard ing his part as a segment in the complete cycle of planting, watering, and harvesting under the divine providence (I Cor. 3 6-9; 4:6).

**38 I have sent you to reap.** Again an again in the Gospels it is emphasized tha the disciples are God-sent men.[13] The noun *apostolos* was used in Judaism t

---

*He doth bestride the narrow world
Like a Colossus, and we petty men
Walk under his huge legs and peep
    about
To find ourselves dishonorable
    graves.
Men at some time are masters of
    their fates:
The fault, dear Brutus, is not in our
    stars,
But in ourselves, that we are under-
    lings*

        .        .        .

*Upon what meat doth this our
    Caesar feed,
That he is grown so great?*[1]

One of the saddest verses in the Bible is John 1:11, "He came unto his own home and his own people received him not" (RSV).

b. A King's Officer Believes (vv. 46-54)

(1) *Initial Belief Demonstrated* (v. 47)

That "the just shall live by faith" is one of the greatest affirmations of the Bible. There is a sense in which everyone lives by faith. Without faith daily life in society would be paralyzed. The paper, milk, and bread are delivered on faith, the traveller buys his ticket on faith, and the parents send children to school on faith. The nobleman who came from Capernaum to Cana to get help from Jesus came on an imperfect faith, but he came.

---

[12] The analogy of sowing and reaping is used also in Plato, *Phaedrus*, 276 (B. Jowett, tr. *Dialogues of Plato*, Random House, p. 279). See also Bauer, p. 74.
[13] E.g., Matt. 10:5; Mark 3:14; 6:7; Luke 9:2; John 17:18. Cf. Philo, *Migration of Abraham*, 22 (AG).
[1] Wm. Shakespeare, "Julius Caesar," Act I, Scene II, 100-105.

39 And from that city many of the Samaritans believed on him because of the word of the woman, who testified, He told me all things that *ever* I did.
40 So when the Samaritans came unto him, they besought him to abide with them: and he abode there two days.
41 And many more believed because of his word;

---

designate one sent out from the temple in Jerusalem to collect the temple tax from the Jews of the Dispersion.[14] The disciples were not simply called to be learners; they were called to work, to perform a mission.

39 **Many of the Samaritans believed.** This is the third report of groups believing in Jesus; the disciples' faith was confirmed after the miracle of Cana (2:11), at the Passover in Jerusalem "many believed on his name (2:23), and now many of the inhabitants of Sychar believe. To the credit of the Samaritans it may be noted that the basis for their belief was different from that of the Jews in Jerusalem. The Jews believed because of the *"signs* which he did"; these Samaritans believed because of the *word* of a witness (cf. 20:29). Even here, however, the element of miracle was not wholly lacking, for it was Jesus' knowledge of her past that convinced the woman that Jesus possessed supernatural powers. Her conviction and enthusiasm were contagious and conveyed

themselves to the villagers with the result that they also were convinced.

40 **They besought him to abide with them.** They were hospitable here, in contrast to another Samaritan village on a different occasion (Luke 9:52-56). Doubtless the Evangelist is not concerned with probing their motives or measuring the extent of their belief; he is simply reporting that here was an outstanding example of responsiveness to the light. It will be recalled that the first two disciples recruited became believers after they abode (*emeinan*) with Jesus (1:39). A similar result of living together occurred here — **many more believed** (v. 41). The significance of the "abiding," in addition to being an expression of hospitality, is that further acquaintance permitted fuller evidence that in turn led to belief. Faith is based upon fact; belief arises out of evidence — such is the emphasis in this Gospel. Because the *kerygma* ("proclamation") is true, it welcomes scrutiny, confident that the incoming of light will

---

His faith, though imperfect, was sufficient to lead him to decisive action. Many times extreme urgency will activate a very feeble faith. In desperation men "believe" and act when under other circumstances they would wait and see. The desperate father came in faith because of Jesus' fame and because of the urgency of his need. He believed Jesus could and would help.

> *The healing of the seamless robe*
> *Is by our beds of pain —*
> *We touch Him in life's throng and*
> *press,*
> *And we are whole again.*[m]

### (2) *Belief Tested* (vv. 48-50)

As Jesus apparently rebuffed the seeker he only increased the urgency of his petition. He was in no position to argue but rather "to urge in trembling self-dis-

trust, a prayer without a claim" (Whittier). We pray best when we are most helpless. Charles Wesley thus interpreted Jacob's experience of wrestling with an angel (Gen. 32:25-28).

> *Yield to me now, for I am weak,*
> *But confident in self-despair;*
> *Speak to my heart, in blessing*
> *speak,*
> *Be conquered by my instant prayer:*
> *Speak, or thou never hence shall*
> *move,*
> *And tell me if thy Name is Love.*[n]

Paul expressed the same paradox by saying "when I am weak then am I strong" (II Cor. 12:10).

The second stage in the father's faith came when he believed Jesus' word before seeing any visible evidence that it was true. The story is told that while Napoleon

---

[14] See G. F. Moore, *Judaism* (Cambridge: Harvard University Press, 1946), I, 109.
[m] J. G. Whittier.
[n] C. Wesley, "Come, O Thou Traveller Unknown."

42 and they said to the woman, Now we believe, not because of thy speaking, for we have heard for ourselves, and know that this is indeed the Saviour of the world
43 And after the two days he went forth from thence into Galilee.

---

expel darkness and falsehood (cf. 3:19-21).

42 **We have heard for ourselves and know.** "Heard" (perfect tense) stresses the abiding results of hearing. The faith of the men of Sychar had a normal, healthy, gradual growth. First they gave credence to the woman's testimony; then, in response to her invitation, they came to the well to investigate at first hand; there they invited him to their village; and finally they became believers on the basis of first-hand experience. Here the Evangelist chooses the word *oida* to express the fact that they now **know,** the same word used earlier in the conversation (vv. 22, 25, 32). The association here of *oida* with belief is an exception to the general practice of linking *ginōskō* with belief.[15] Whether or not the Evangelist wished to maintain a distinction between the two words for knowing or used them synonymously is not easy to determine.[16]

**This is indeed the Saviour of the World.** The best texts omit the words *ho Christos,* "the Christ." This confession of faith may have been a verbatim quotation of the

Samaritans or "the evangelist's own adaptation to Christian ends of a title that was widely used in the Hellenistic cults of the contemporary world" (WFH). The idea was not uncommon in the world of the first century and could well have come from the Samaritans themselves. It is one of the earliest expressions of its kind in the history of New Testament times. The term *Savior of the World,* found here and in I John 4:14, was applied to Julius Caesar, Augustus, Claudius, Nero, Vespasian, Titus, Trajan, and especially to Hadrian (117-138 A.D.).[17] This, of course, coincided with the rise of the cult of emperor-worship which was encouraged by Augustus and expanded greatly by Nero and his successors. But in the Old Testament the idea of a world savior was expressed a number of times. The God of Israel is called "Savior" several times, especially in Isaiah.[18] The idea of extending to include the world is found in several O. T. passages.[19] There is therefore no necessity for assuming that the idea of a world savior is an importation from paganism (cf. WFH).

---

was reviewing his troops he lost control of his horse. A private soldier stepped from the ranks and secured the steed. The Emperor, greatly pleased, said, "Much obliged to you, captain." The soldier, quick to notice the word "captain," said "Which regiment, sire?" Napoleon replied as he rode away, "of my guards." The soldier left his musket and walked to the officers' quarters and announced that he was now a captain of the guards.

Incensed at this apparent presumption, the chief officer demanded to know on whose authority he made his claim. Pointing towards the Emperor the soldier replied confidently, "*He* said it, sir!"[o] He took the Emperor at his word.

**The man believed the word that Jesus spake.** In the summer of 1962 video messages were relayed from Europe to the U.S.A. and back for the first time by way of outer space. By the turn of

---

[15] M. C. Tenney, *John, the Gospel of Belief* (Grand Rapids: Eerdmans, 1953), p. 309.
[16] In classical usage, *ginōskō* indicated the acquiring of knowledge, with emphasis on the means, i.e., philosophical knowledge. *Oida,* on the other hand, indicated direct knowledge, intuitive vision (cf. Plato, *Res Publica,* VI. 510 A.D., J. Burnet, ed., Oxford, 1927). This distinction is evident in non theological uses in John (e.g., 1:48; 4:53; 8:52; 10:33; 12:9; 13:35). In the Fourth Gospel *ginōskō* (12 times) seems always to emphasize Jesus' human empirical knowledge (4:1; 5:6; 10:14; 21:17). *Oida* (22 times) is used of Jesus' absolute, non-acquired, knowledge of God (7:29; 8:55) and of his "hour" (13:1; 18:4; 19:23). To the disciples *ginōskō* indicates a learning process. This is progressive knowledge and is implicit in "eternal life" dwelling in him with deepening faith. *Oida,* on the other hand, is used negatively of a lack of spiritual apprehension (4:22, 32; 20:9, 14; 21:4). It is used positively of an inner, instant, hyperconscious knowledge of the significance or symbolism of a witnessed fact (4:42; 19:35; 21:24). See Jean de La Potterie, "Oida et Ginōskō, les Deux Modes de la Connaissance dans le Quatrième Évangile," *Biblica* 40:3, 1959, pp. 709-725.
[17] A. Deissmann, *Light From the Ancient East,* tr. by L. R. M. Strachan (New York: Harper, 1928), p. 364.
[18] E.g., Ps. 106:21; Isa. 19:20; 43:3, 11, 15, 21; 49:26; 60:16; 63:8; Hos. 13:4.
[19] E.g., Amos 9:11, 12; Jer. 12:15; Isa. 45:21 (cf. Acts 15:16-18); Isa. 49:6 (cf. Acts 13:47); Isa. 11:10 (cf. Rom. 15:12); Isa. 65:1 (cf. Rom. 10:20).
[o] Cited by F. N. Peloubet, *op. cit.* p. 133.

44 For Jesus himself testified, that a prophet hath no honor in his own country.

45 So when he came into Galilee, the Galilaeans received him, having seen all the things that he did in Jerusalem at the feast: for they also went unto the feast.

46 He came therefore again unto Cana of Galilee, where he made the water wine. And there was a certain nobleman, whose son was sick at Capernaum.

47 When he heard that Jesus was come out of Judea into Galilee, he went unto him, and besought *him* that he would come down, and heal his son; for he was at the point of death.

---

**44 No honor in his own country.** This is a proverbial saying cited in all four Gospels (Matt. 13:57; Mark 6:4; Luke 4:24). In John it seems somewhat out of context, for here it appears in connection with his movement into Galilee and away from a scene of success. In the Synoptic records it appears in connection with his rejection at Nazareth and in Galilee. The suggestion that John changed the meaning of "his own country" to Jerusalem is at least plausible (Origen, Plummer, WFH, CKB). It is more likely, however, that the Evangelist inserted here a remark of Jesus spoken on another occasion, or perhaps several occasions (JHB). Its location here may have been occasioned by the contrast between the cordial reception in Samaria and the apathy he anticipated as he moved into Galilee. Hendrikson thinks he went to Galilee to avoid popularity and a premature crisis.

**45 The Galilaeans received him.** This reception was an exception to the generalization that "his own" did not receive him (1:11). The reason given for this favorable reception is what they saw Jesus do in Jerusalem (cf. 2:23). The connection between miracles and belief is again under-

scored. It is understandable that "signs" produced in Jerusalem might well have been more influential on the visiting Galilean pilgrims than if they had witnessed them at home. This may shed light on the proverb just quoted.

**46 There was a certain nobleman.** The nobleman (*basilikos*) was perhaps one of the courtiers of Herod the tetrarch. The word means "a princelet, or one in the service of the king" (Jos. *War.* I. 45).

This account has many points of similarity with the healing of the centurion's servant reported in Matt. 8:5-13 and Luke 7:1-10. Most modern commentators consider them different versions of the same event (e.g., JHB, WFH, Barrett, Gardner-Smith, *St. John and the Synoptic Gospels*, p. 23, Bultmann, Macgregor, Lightfoot). Others conclude that they are two different events (e.g. Origen, Chrysostom, Plummer, Tasker, Dods, Lange, Stevens and Burton, *A Harmony of the Gospels* (New York: Scribner's, 1904). Some are non-committal (e.g., Hendriksen, Hoskyns, Westcott). The decision of each scholar is likely to be determined by *a priori* considerations, theories as to the freedom with which the evangelists treated their source materials. The two events are

---

a dial man can control the artificial satellite Telstar in orbit about the earth. By his word Jesus instantly healed a sick child twenty miles away in Capernaum. It should be easier to believe in miracles now than it was then.

### (3) Belief Confirmed (v. 53)

After learning from the messengers that his son was actually healed at the hour Jesus had spoken the word, the father evidenced a third level of faith. The first level was general faith that led to his decision to ask Jesus' help. The second

was the faith that appropriates the promise for special answers that effect a change. The third was the full assurance of faith, the vindication of the venture of faith which caused him to journey to Cana in quest of Jesus. Faith is a venture into the unknown. We walk by faith and not by sight. For "hope that is seen is not hope" (Rom. 8:24). Abraham earned the title "Father of the faithful" because his faith was strong enough to cause him to venture into the west "not knowing where he was to go" (Heb. 11:8 RSV).

Like the harassed but grateful noble-

48 Jesus therefore said unto him, Except ye see signs and wonders, ye will in no wise believe.
49 The nobleman saith unto him, Sir, come down ere my child die.
50 Jesus saith unto him, Go thy way; thy son liveth.  The man believed the word that Jesus spake unto him, and he went his way.

---

sufficiently similar that the assumption that they are three accounts of the same event has appealed to readers from Irenaeus to the present.  On the other hand, the differences between this event and that reported in the Synoptics are quite extensive.  They are well summarized by Plummer:

(i) Here a nobleman pleads for his son; there a centurion for his servant.

(ii) Here he pleads in person; there Jewish elders intercede for him.

(iii) Here the petitioner is a Jew; there the centurion was a Gentile.

(iv) Here the healing words are spoken at Cana; there at Capernaum.

(v) Here the malady is fever; there it is paralysis.

(vi) Here the father asks Jesus to come; there the centurion asks him not to.

(vii) Here Jesus remained in Cana; there he went almost to Capernaum (Luke 7:6).

(viii) Here the father's weak faith is rebuked; there the centurion's faith commended.

Although this data is not necessarily decisive it argues strongly for two separate occasions of healing.  We know that more miracles were performed than were reported.

48 **Signs and wonders** (*sēmeia,* and *terata*).  The former were miracles with a spiritual message, the latter emphasized the physical aspect (BFW).  The terms appear frequently in the LXX for the equivalent O. T. expression.[20]  This combination occurs at least 14 times in the N. T., especially in the book of Acts.  Of six such synonyms in the N. T., *sēmeia* has the most spiritual significance and *terata* the least, the latter often designating heathen portents (RCT, p. 323).

**Ye will in no wise believe** (*ou mē*) signifies the strongest possible negation (cf. v. 14; 18:11).  The father's faith was weak in at least two points: he believed Jesus' presence was necessary to effect healing and he felt that if death came, Jesus' help would be too late.  The Master's initial rebuff here is similar to that which greeted the Syrophoenician woman's request (Matt. 15:26).  It may have been designed to test faith and make it more articulate.

49 **Sir, come down ere my child die.** The father uses the affectionate term *paidion* rather than the more formal *huios* (son).  The father's concern led him to implore help in desperation rather than struggle in self-justification.

50 **The man believed.** The father left assured that because of what Jesus had said his son would recover.  This was not the type of belief that would make him a Christian; it was simply taking Jesus'

---

man of this story, Alfred Lord Tennyson had his struggles with faith and doubt.  He advised:

*Cleave ever to the sunnier side of doubt,*
*And cling to Faith beyond the forms of Faith!*
*She reels not in the storm of warring words,*
*She brightens at the clash of 'Yes' and 'No.'*

*She sees the best that glimmers through the worst,*
*She feels the sun is hid but for a night,*
*She spies the summer through the winter bud,*
*She tastes the fruit before the blossom falls,*
*She hears the lark within the songless egg,*
*She finds the fountain where they wailed 'Mirage!'*[p]

---

[20] "Signs" (*othoth*) and wonders" (*mophethim*) as in Deut. 4:34; Neh. 9:10; Isa. 8:18.
[p] Alfred Tennyson, "The Ancient Sage."

51 And as he was now going down, his servants met him, saying, that his son lived.

52 So he inquired of them the hour when he began to amend. They said therefore unto him, Yesterday at the seventh hour the fever left him.

53 So the father knew that *it was* at that hour in which Jesus said unto him, Thy son liveth: and himself believed, and his whole house.

54 This is again the second sign that Jesus did, having come out of Judaea into Galilee.

---

statement at face value. This gave him the assurance he craved. It is noteworthy that he **believed** on the basis of Jesus' word alone *before* witnessing the change.

**51 His servants met him.** The **servants** (*douloi*) were bond-servants or slaves, indicating something of the man's affluence. The distance from Cana to Capernaum was a day's journey (about 20 miles) so that it is likely that they met at about the half-way point. The *douloi* came to relieve the father's anxiety, not waiting for his arrival at Capernaum. **Thy son liveth** (*zē*) in the sense of recovering from disease (cf. Num. 21:8).

**52 Yesterday at the seventh hour.** The accusative case indicates duration: "during the seventh hour" (KJV). Westcott and Hendriksen agree that the Roman (and modern) method of reckoning of time is to be followed here. Thus, if the cure was effected at 7 P.M., the servants started out immediately for Cana, stayed overnight enroute, and on the following day met the returning father.[21] If John reckoned the day as beginning at dawn the cure would have been effected at 1:00 P.M., the two could have met after sunset when a new day (according to Jewish reckoning) would have begun, and an afternoon healing would have occurred "yesterday." If the event occurred in the short days of December (as 4:35 implies), the "hour" was only about 45 minutes in length (Ramsay) and, contrary to Lenski, the two parties could not have met until well after the sun had disappeared over the Galilean hills (about 5:00 P.M.).

**53 The father knew . . . and himself believed and his whole house.** Yesterday he had believed that what Jesus said about his son's health was true. Today his faith was confirmed by finding that the healing had occurred at the moment Jesus had spoken. This apparently was "saving faith" by which the man and his household became avowed disciples of Jesus, or Christians. The conversion of his household was comparable to that of the Philippian jailer (Acts 16:31-33). In the patriarchal type of home the example of the father was usually followed. This was not the second miracle of Jesus' ministry (2:23; 4:45) but only the second in Galilee.

**54 The second sign.** The first, of course, was at Cana. This verse gives the clue that this section of John's Gospel (chs.

---

Chapters one through four together form a phase of our Lord's ministry which was essentially like that presented in the Synoptic Gospels, especially in its emphasis on initial success and popularity. The following chapters stress the note of strife. The light seeks to overtake the darkness and those who feared the light resist it. These first chapters of quiet, exciting discovery make clear to the reader that Jesus Christ is indeed, as the Samaritans were first to recognize, "the Saviour of the world." Before this central point was clearly and convincingly established the reader would have been unprepared for the conflicts in which Jesus soon found himself. Assertion, witness, and demonstration are now to be challenged and cross-examined. In the process the ultimate issues are brought out with increasing clarity.

---

[21] WmH, p. 183. JHB, (pp. 56, 57, 170) disagrees with Westcott and cites the parable of the laborers (Matt. 20:5, 6) and other evidence to support the view that in the N. T. the system of counting time from dawn to sunset was followed. W. M. Ramsay (HDB, V, 475-479) shows that the N. T. followed the common practice of counting hours of the day from dawn (cf. Matt. 20:5, 6; John 11:9). Bernard ignores the problem of explaining why, if the cure occurred at 1 P.M., it was not until the following day that the servants met the father with the news. He does, however, suggest that the "seventh hour" means not the time of day but the duration of the fever. This, however is inconsistent with "that hour" of v. 53 (see "Introduction").

2-12) is the "book of signs." John was careful to select certain miracles for special mention of their relevance to the theme of his book — belief in the Lord Jesus Christ. Thus far, as in the Synoptic Gospels, the early portion of his public ministry was relatively free from hostility. From this point on the "signs" will cause not only additional faith but also increasing opposition and unbelief.

# CHAPTER V

After these things there was a feast of the Jews; and Jesus went up to Jerusalem.
2 Now there is in Jerusalem by the sheep *gate* a pool, which is called in Hebrew Bethesda, having five porches.

---

## EXEGESIS

The chapter begins with the healing of a long-time cripple. Because the healed man was carrying his bed on the Sabbath he was criticized. In defense he reported that the miracle-worker had commanded him to do so. When the Jews turned their wrath upon Jesus for breaking the Sabbath Jesus said he only was doing his Father's bidding. This assumption of divine prerogatives further infuriated the Jews and the ensuing discussions reveal Jesus stating his cooperation with the Father, a relationship attested by the witness of John, the miracles, and the Scriptures.

1 **After these things** probably refers to the healing of the official's son reported in 4:46-54 and called by the author "the second sign." The suggestion that the sequence of chs. 5 and 6 be reversed is based in part on the difficulty of geographical transition from ch. 5 to ch. 6; 6:1 seems to follow 4:54 more naturally than it follows 5:47. The order will be discussed at greater length in connection with ch. 7.[1]

**A feast of the Jews** involves a disputed reading. Some texts have the definite

article and it would then refer to the Passover, as elsewhere in John (e.g., 2:13; 23; 6:4; 11:55; 12:1). The better witnesses, however, in the judgment of most scholars, omit the article.[2] Since the article is used elsewhere when John refers to the Passover, its omission here implies that some other feast is indicated. Apparently John did not regard the specific feast important; he only wanted to account for Jesus' presence in Jerusalem. Some authorities, on the assumption that ch. 6 precedes ch. 5, hold that it is the Passover of A.D. 28 (JHB). Others, pointing to John 4:35 as indicating a date in December and to 6:4 as an April date, conclude that the feast of 5:1 is Purim, in February (EGT). Others hold that it was the Feast of Trumpets (Lev. 23:24) in September, a feast of which the keynote was the giving of the Law and universal judgment; this would be consistent with the emphasis of the discourse which follows (BFW). This latter view has much to commend it.

2 **By the sheep gate a pool . . . having five porches.** It is generally believed that the reference here is to the ancient gate near the northeast corner of the city. It

---

## EXPOSITION

### B. Mounting Hostility (5:1-12:50)

Chapters 5 through 12 are often described as "the conflict between the church and the world."[a] These chapters illustrate the tension that is a prominent feature of these discourses between the Jewish leaders and Jesus. The same illustrations, however, are also characteristic of the con-

flict later between synagogue and church. The synagogue is not identical with "the world" but the same principles have a universal application.

### 1. THE THIRD "SIGN" (5:1-47)

In this, the major section of the Fourth Gospel, the basic theme of un-

---

[1] A helpful discussion may be found in JHB, I, xvii-xix and in A. Power, "The Original Order of John's Gospel," CBQ, Oct., 1948, pp. 399ff.
[2] The article precedes "feast" in some ancient MSS. including Aleph and C. The article is omitted in a greater number of ancient witnesses including Bodmer II (P66), Vaticanus, and Bazae — 3rd, 4th, and 5th centuries respectively.
[a] R. H. Strachan, *The Fourth Gospel* (London: SCM Press, 1946), p. 166.

was here that sheep were brought into the temple area for sacrifice. The present Stephen's Gate is on or near this site. The "pool" here connotes a place for bathing (cf. John 9:7; II Esd. 13:15). Near this cistern or spring a large group of invalids languished in Jesus' day. Even today waters believed to have healing properties are hopefully patronized by the sick, both in the Christian and non-Christian worlds. It must be borne in mind that there were no hospitals in those days and little sense of social responsibility for the relief of the distressed. Modern organizations for social service are largely the result of the Christian spirit. The lack of a social conscience in that day is reflected in the invalid's explanation of the length of his misery — there was no one who cared enough to assist him into the pool.

2 The texts vary as to the name of this pool. Some of the texts read Bethesda, others Bethsaida, others Bethzatha.[3] The better critical texts favor Bethzatha and this seems to be confirmed by the fact that this is the name given by Josephus to this section of the city.[4] It is still applied to that portion of the Old City between Stephen's Gate and Herod's Gate. The five "porches" are *stoa*. This term was used in many cities of the Near East, espe-

cially those of Grecian character. Indeed, porches or arcades are characteristic of Moslem architecture in that area today. We can therefore imagine a covered arcade of five arches bordering the pool to afford shelter from sun and rain, such as may still be seen in opulant homes in the Levant that have interior courtyards.

The location of the pool is also uncertain. Five locations have been suggested: the Twin-pools near the Antonia, Birket Israel (north of the temple area), the Twin-Pools at St. Anne's Church, Gihon, and Siloam.[5] Eusebius and Cyril describe a twin pool near the present Crusader Church of St. Anne and northwest of St. Stephen's Gate as having five porticoes. Over it were built two Christian churches. The site was unknown until the time of the Crusades, when the buildings were destroyed and the site forgotten. After the thirteenth century, the large fosse, or ditch, north of the temple area (Birket Israel), regarded by Robinson as protecting the Antonia, was pointed out as the "Pool of Bethesda." In 1888 the traditional pool was rediscovered.[6] It consists of two cisterns lying about twenty feet below the present level of the street. The roof of the ancient church over this pool (55' by 12') rests on five arches com-

---

belief is developed at length. Here the light of the world encounters the increasing hostility of the world of darkness, as presented in the prologue.[b] This chapter sets forth in detail an analysis of the nature

of and basis for the hostility of the Jewish leaders to Jesus and sets the stage for ensuing debates. A panoramic view of the chapter may thus be sketched in outline form.

| MIRACLE | | DISCOURSES | |
|---------|------|------------|------|
| vv. 1-9 | vv. 10-18 | vv. 19-29 | vv. 30-47 |
| Healing | Jesus Accused | Jesus' Defense: | Witnesses |
| Problem | of Sabbath Desecration | Father & Son Co-workers, (19) | Jesus (v. 31) John (v. 33)    WORDS |
| Command | | | |
| Obedience | of Blasphemy | Raising Dead (21,25,29) | "signs" (v. 36) Father (v. 37)    WORKS |
| | | Judging (22,23,27,29,30) | |
| Faith | | Giving Life (21,24,26) | Scripture (v. 39) Moses (v. 46)    WRITINGS |

    [3] The term Bethesda means "house of mercy," an appropriate name for the place.    (The NEB retains "Bethesda.")
    [4] Jos. *War*, V. iv. 3 (where the meaning is given as "New City").
    [5] G. A. Smith, *Jerusalem*, II, 566.
    [6] By Schick, Vincent and van de Vliet; see Kraeling, *Bible Atlas* (Chicago: Rand McNally, 1956), p. 392; J. Jeremias, *Die Wiederentdeckung von Bethesda* (Göttingen, 1949); WmH, I, 190.
    [b] See Bultmann's suggestive analysis, *op. cit.*, pp. 185ff.; also Lange, *op. cit.*, pp. 176ff.

3 In these lay a multitude of them that were sick, blind, halt, withered*

---

memorating the five porches or arcades. It appears that the pools were originally surrounded by the four covered porticoes or colonnades, one on each of the four sides and another through the middle between the pools — thus making the five porches. A fading fresco on the walls shows an angel "troubling the waters."[7] Since this rediscovery, scholars are generally agreed that the early Christians believed this to have been the site; they could hardly be sure, however, for the Jerusalem of Jesus' day had twice been destroyed (by Titus and by Hadrian) before any Christian churches were built in the area. Also there is no natural spring in this area, and it is difficult to believe that healing properties would have been attributed to the waters of a cistern. Edward Robinson, P. Schaff, and G. A. Smith favor the identification with Gihon, the one source of "living water" in Jerusalem. Only at Gihon is there any intermittent action of the water (due to syphon action) which could have been attributed to the "troubling of an angel." If Robinson's conjecture is to find support, the location of the

sheep gate or pool must be changed from the site of Stephen's Gate to a location southeast of the temple area.[8] The one certain thing about the authentic site is its uncertainty. It is also certain that the imporant thing is *what* happened there, not *where* it happened.

3, 4 The most important of the ancient texts omit the last of v. 3 and all of v. 4, and they are therefore placed only in a footnote in Nestle's latest text and in the RV and RSV. The portion omitted reads (RSVm) "Waiting for the moving of the water; 4 for an angel of the Lord went down at certain seasons into the pool, and troubled the water: whoever stepped in first after the troubling of the water was healed of whatever disease he had."

The most probable explanation for the appearance of these verses is that they were first inserted as a scribal note to explain v. 7, or to record a popular interpretation of an intermittent spring; later the explanation became a part of some texts. It may be that v. 7 is to be regarded as the man's explanation to Jesus of an

---

The "sign" and the discourse which follows bring into sharper focus the major themes of the relation of Father and Son, witnessing, belief, and judgment.

### a. The Cripple Healed (vv. 2-9)

At the feast many pilgrims, hucksters, and soldiers were gathered together in an excited throng. In the absence of hospitals, clinics, and any organized effort to relieve disease, any place which promised health was deluged with sick people hopeful of a cure. Today, even in the more progressive parts of Palestine, people will still gather at the traditional "tomb of David" in Jerusalem or the grotto of Elijah on Mt. Carmel, hoping that a miracle of healing will occur in them, and religious healing shrines are also found in Europe and the New World. This ill-

kempt, foul-smelling, pathetic group of patients were assembled near the northwest gate of the city because of the presence of a pool believed to have healing properties. Healing is often associated with water in the Middle East, Europe, and the West. To many pilgrims and traders, no doubt, a crowd of invalids, with hands outstretched for alms, was an annoyance, and to the residents of Jerusalem a source of embarrassment. Many probably thought, "The sick are always with us," and made little effort to give relief.

In the midst of this unpleasant and pitiable situation Jesus' attitude was different from that of the others. He was moved with compassion. His sympathy was particularly aroused by a cripple who had lain helpless for nearly forty years. The man did not live and enjoy life; he simply

---

*Many ancient authorities insert, wholly or in part, *waiting for the moving of the water: 4 for an angel of the Lord went down at certain seasons into the pool, and troubled the water: whosoever then first after the troubling of the water stepped in was made whole, with whatsoever disease he was holden.*

[7] Masterman, "Bethesda," *ISBE*, I, 445.

[8] E. Kraeling, *Bible Atlas* (Chicago: Rand McNally, 1956) thinks the John 9:6, 7 reference to Siloam rules out this possibility, ignoring the fact that Gilhon and Siloam are not identical; thus the healing of John 5 could have taken place at Gihon and that of John 9 at Siloam.

5 And a certain man was there, who had been thirty and eight years in his infirmity

intermittent flow of water, a view which John reported without necessarily endorsing. It seems rather strange that such *regular* phenomena would be attributed to the work of angels, but one is often amazed today at the credulity of certain people. It has been suggested also that the verse was a part of the original text and later deleted to avoid comparison with pagan practices associated with sacred springs.[9] Tertullian, Chrysostom and other patristic writers saw in this episode a prophecy of the efficacy of baptism, the physical healing being a figure of the spiritual healing which comes to the believer.[10] C. H. Dodd suggests that the water symbolizes the impotence of the Law in contrast to the Gospel; but the healing was typical of the ministry of Jesus as reported in all four Gospels, and the relief of suffering needed no further justification in John's thought (CHD, p. 319).

3 In these lay a multitude, that is, within the shelter of these five stoa or porches were gathered a throng of weak and sick people including the blind, the

crippled, and the emaciated. It is a vivid picture of pathos. Here were the unfortunate ones, miserable and yet living in hope that somehow, sometime, healing would come. The belief that certain mineral waters have healing properties is almost universal. Sickness was taken for granted with an attitude of resignation. Where the Church has kept in touch with her Head, she has remained compassionate and responsive to human need. Jesus, unlike his contemporaries, could not look upon suffering with indifference.

5 A certain man was there. After giving the background, John relates the actual event which constituted the third great "sign" of Jesus' ministry. Jesus selected from the multitude a man apparently much more helpless and hopeless than the others. He was a middle-aged man who had suffered from his affliction for almost forty years. It was to this one, perhaps the most hopeless of the lot, that Jesus now turned. It is significant that the Savior did not avoid this unpleasant sight or so occupy himself with things exclusively religious that he neglected the humani-

existed. Jesus knew, of course, that the man wanted to be made whole and his question "Wilt thou . . . ?" was probably designed to have this *desire* articulated. The second step in the healing process therefore was *petition*. In replying to Jesus' question the man was slow to realize the significance of the questioner or the question; instead he remained preoccupied with his *problem*, that of reaching the pool. Such response is typical of the many who are more aware of the difficulties confronting them than of the Lord's presence and power. The third step in his healing was *obedience* to the command of the Lord to arise and walk, something that must have seemed out of the question to one who had been unable to walk for thirty-eight years. Whether the man was conscious of a restoration of his body before he made the attempt is not clear. It may be that, inspired by faith in Jesus' word, he made the effort

before being actually conscious of the healing. If so, it would be consistent with the healing described in Luke 17:14: "as they went they were cleansed." Faith is always the condition of divine blessing, and faith usually requires demonstration by action, by obedience. In this account the element of *faith* is not mentioned specifically, but in the light of similar reports of healing, it is at least implicit.

Strange as it may seem, there are some who acquire a preference for ill health. They have a masochistic satisfaction in their own suffering. This man could have abandoned hope after nearly four decades of waiting. But his presence at the pool testified that he was not without hope. He could have indulged in bitterness and resentment at those who stepped down before him; he could have blamed God for limiting healing to the *first* who entered the water. Instead he stood ready to embrace what the Lord of life had

[9] Cf. W. R. Smith, *The Religion of the Semites*, pp. 159, 167, 182.
[10] Tertullian, *De Bapt.*, V. (Water was not involved in the actual healing, however).

6 When Jesus saw him lying, and knew that he had been now a long time *in that case,* he saith unto him, Wouldest thou be made whole?

---

tarian. The healing was designed as a "sign," as evidence of his divine nature and mission.

6 "Do you want to be healed?" (RSV). This question of Jesus' must have shocked and irritated the crippled man. He had waited thirty-eight years and daily had sought healing and now such a question, the answer to which was so obvious! The directness of the question is similar to that addressed to the blind man at Jericho who was crying for help, the one to whom the Master said, "What do you wish me to do?" (Mark 10:51 Berkeley). In that instance Jesus apparently wanted the man to be specific as well as loud and insistent. Here the man's expectancy needed to be aroused. After thousands of defeated efforts the man was in danger of losing even the desire to become well; he seemed about to lose the capacity to believe. Some expositors think the man had become so habituated to his helpless condition that, like many sinners, he acquiesced in his condition and did not expect or even want to be made whole.[11] Jesus seemed to be inviting him to ask for help. Why cannot the Lord give us help without asking? One of the mysteries of

prayer is that while our Father knows our needs before we ask (Matt. 6:8) we need to direct our attention to him and to make explicit and articulate our needs. Asking implies dependence, an essential condition for the reception of grace. His reply was an explanation of his plight and a rebuke to his associates, I have no man to help me. Unlike the cripple whose four friends lowered him through the roof into Jesus' presence (Mark 2:4), this man had no one to assist him. Apparently only one person could be healed at a time and it was a case of every man for himself. The ones most in need were the least likely to get help. Nietzsche criticized Christianity for assisting the weak at the expense of the strong and in protest created the cult of the "super man" which an infamous politician later exploited to his own destruction and that of his nation. Jesus, in harmony with the spirit of Ezekiel 34, determined to help the weak in their unequal competition with the strong.

The word "whole" or "sound" or "healthy" (*hygiēs*) is in contrast to the weakness or "infirmity" (*astheneios*) of v. 5. The word is used of persons (Matt. 15:

---

for him. Had he been paralyzed in mind and soul as he was in body, he would not have been able to accept the gift of health.

### b. Jesus Accused (vv. 10-18)

#### (1) *Sabbath Desecration* (vv. 10-16)

The Torah forbade the carrying of burdens on the Sabbath day. This was emphasized in the Haftorah or prophetic writings. In a pastoral economy the keeping of the Sabbath was comparatively simple. With the coming of the industrial revolution and a closely-integrated and interdependent society it is now much less simple to have one specific day in seven for rest and worship. Travel on public transportation is necessary for many in

urban areas to gather for public worship. The Negro evangelist Amanda Smith tells of her own struggle in deciding whether to use public transportation in order to meet speaking engagements on the Lord's Day; she concluded that it was justifiable in view of the purpose. In the modern section of Jerusalem and many other sections of Israel today, there is no public transportation on Saturday. There are many so-called "blue laws" on the statute books in the United States which make it unlawful to open a store on Sunday, some of which recently (1963) have been upheld in the Kentucky courts. These laws were originally passed because the majority of the people felt that it was important to comply with the letter of the Biblical injunction to keep the Sabbath Day holy.

---

[11] C. R. Erdman, *The Gospel of John* (Philadelphia: Westminster Press, 1942), p. 54; A. J. Gossip, *Interpreter's Bible*, VIII, 541.

7 The sick man answered him, Sir, I have no man, when the water is troubled, to put me into the pool: but while I am coming, another steppeth down before me.
8 Jesus saith unto him, Arise, take up they bed, and walk.

---

31), of things (Herm. *Simul.* 8:1, 3) and of doctrine (Titus 2:8). The Vulgate has *sanus* or "sane." Here, and in v. 9, it has been rendered whole (ASV), "healed" (RSV), "recover" (NEB), and "well" (Berkeley).

Jesus is pictured as active and decisive here. He *saw* him lying helpless, he *knew* he had been helpless for a long time, and then he *spoke* the healing word. This reaction to human need is similar to that reported in Exodus 3:7 when, in response to the affliction of the Hebrew slaves, Jehovah "saw" their condition, "took knowledge" of their sufferings, and "came down" to deliver them. The "seeing" here is a reminder also of Mark 10:21, "Jesus looking upon him loved him." It affords a clue to the Master's basic response to human suffering; he ignored the fact that no one else had concerned himself with the man's plight and did an unconventional thing — he responded with sympathy and recreative energy.

7 I have no man . . . to put me into the pool. The "put" is emphatic; in some contexts *ballō* means "to throw." Here it is best translated "take" (A-G). One can easily imagine the sense of defeat and frustration one might have if he

hoped in vain for health for thirty-eight years. The question of Jesus implied a mild rebuke (v. 6) and now the man's answer implies a measure of self-defense, as if to say, "I am here, not because I want to be but because I have no friends to help me." The length of his suffering entitled him to no preferential treatment, it seemed, in the selfish view of his companions in misery. Suffering in itself is not redemptive; suffering linked with Christian love is redemptive because it can sympathize and also effect changes.

8 Rise . . . and walk. The tense (pres. imp.) here is decisive. It was a command which the man was powerless to obey. Jesus had commanded the impossible! But "God's commands are his enablings." In the healing of the ten lepers (Luke 17: 14) "as they went they were cleansed." The point seems to be that the sequence is important: the *word* of the Lord, the *response* in faith, and then the miracle of *deliverance*. The man did not remain there skeptical and point out the impossibility of rising; he believed Jesus' word and as he responded in faith healing came. He arose (aorist), began to walk, and continued walking. As additional evidence of his cure, and in response to Jesus'

---

Industrialization has imposed serious hindrances to a strict keeping of this law. Factories, hospitals, public utilities, and similar operations cannot be closed down on one day of the week. And many people no longer have any religious scruples about complying with the Biblical injunction. They buy groceries, automobiles, houses, and almost any available commodity on the Lord's Day without inhibition. The percentage of grocery stores and merchandise marts open seven days a week is increasing. Sporting events, commercial broadcasts, and elections are held on the Lord's Day to an increasing degree. The effects on public worship are painfully obvious.

How may one avoid casuistry on one hand and keep the essential spirit and purpose of the Sabbath in an industrial society

on the other hand? Even in the conditions obtaining in the twentieth century, it is possible to limit Sunday work to the essentials. It is also possible to purchase only necessary meals (not groceries) and emergency medicinal needs on the Lord's Day. The basic peril faced is that of secularism. The need for recognizing that this is a theistic universe, under a universal moral law, becomes increasingly acute as the "acids of modernity" and overt atheism challenge our entire Judaeo-Christian heritage.

The basic problem of Sabbath observance in Jesus' day was an exaggerated emphasis on legalism that blinded many to the need for the relief of suffering. In the modern world the peril is not so much legalism as antinomianism; this is a time of moral anarchy, which "every man does

9 And straightway the man was made whole, and took up his bed and walked. Now it was the Sabbath on that day.

---

command, he rolled up his pallet or mat and carried it with him. It is characteristic of Jesus and of true Christianity not only to advise and sympathize, but to effect relief at the source of trouble. Certain Eastern (and Western) religions seek to give relief by insisting that matter is not real and hence not important; pain must be endured. Jesus' method is not to minimize the trouble but to remove it. It is the *"fait accompli"* of God in both Old and New Testaments that reveals his true character. God's redemptive acts in history are the source of faith for the present and of apocalyptic hopes of the future.

In this Gospel, as in the Synoptics (Mark 3:6), the first expressions of overt hostility to Jesus were occasioned by his alleged desecration of the Sabbath. Here also, as in the Synoptics, the next expression of hostility was in connection with the charge of blasphemy, the former provoked by Jesus' actions, the latter by his explanation of the authority for his actions. The distinctive feature of John's presentation is in the relatively few miracles compared to the relatively large amount of space given to the controversies aroused by them.

9 **It was the sabbath.** Sabbath desecration was a major concern of the prophets. Jeremiah, before the Exile (Jer. 17:21-27), Ezekiel, during the Exile (Ezek. 20:12-24; 22:8, 26), and Nehemiah, after the Exile (Neh. 10:31-33; 13:15-22) protested against the secularization of the Sabbath in the strongest terms. In the centuries between the exilic period and the first century of our era the Hasadim (pious ones) and their successors, the Pharisees, had elaborated in great detail the things not to be done on the Sabbath. The keeping of the Sabbath, even more than circumcision, was the distinctive mark of a Jew, since it was kept by an individual voluntarily.[12] Because of this universally known characteristic of the Jews, Julius Caesar had exempted them from military service, the only ones in the Roman Empire thus privileged. For a time the Jews would not even fight in self-defense on the Sabbath (I Macc. 2:29-41). After the religious crisis of the second century B.C. had passed, Sabbath observance remained as one of the touchstones of fidelity to the faith of their fathers, distinguishing a real Jew from an "assimilated" one. During the next century Sab-

---

what is right in his own eyes." There is a vast difference between using the Lord's Day for personal gratification and using the day for the relief of suffering. The Pharisees considered only the external legal aspect; Jesus considered the motive. They were concerned with an institution, he with the man.

13 There is something touching in the fact that the man did not know the identity of his benefactor. Behind the gospel hymn entitled "Tell Me His Name Again" lies a true story from China. An aged Chinese woman walked eight miles over dusty roads to attend a gospel service. She responded to an invitation to accept Christ and was converted, and she returned home a "new creature in Christ Jesus." A few days later she walked back over the long miles to the mission church with the request, "Tell me his name again." She

had forgotten the name of Jesus Christ. The woman had experienced the power of Christ in her life even though her knowledge of Christianity was next to nothing. She had experienced new life in the Son without learning the identity of the Lifegiver; her heart-knowledge exceeded her cognitive knowledge.

The sequence is interesting. The Jews blamed the man for carrying his pallet on the Sabbath day. He, in turn, placed the blame on his benefactor. When the Jews turned their wrath on Jesus, he put the responsibility on his Father (v. 17). This was not a case of evading guilt as Eve had done after her sin; it was simply the stating of the facts.

16 Of the thirty-six miracles of Jesus reported, seven were done on the Sabbath day to relieve suffering. In all four Gospels his breaking of the Sabbath is given

---

[12] G. F. Moore, *Judaism* (Cambridge: Harvard University Press, 1927), II, 24.

10 So the Jews said unto him that was cured, It is the sabbath, and it is not lawful for thee to take up thy bed.

11 But he answered them, He that made me whole, the same said unto me, Take up thy bed, and walk.

bath observance was fortified by further definitions and modifications, notably the thirty-nine prohibitions. The Biblical background for these lay in the fact that in Exodus 35, immediately after the prohibition of Sabbath work, there follows a description of tabernacle construction. Hence each of these activities mentioned was construed as an infraction of the Sabbath. Each of the thirty-nine had thirty-nine subdivisions, a total of 1521 in all.[13] These prohibited activities included lighting a fire (quite a chore then), clapping the hands, and carrying a burden through the door of a house.[14] Jesus did not inveigh against such casuistry in his teaching, but ignored it in his actions.[15] To the watchful Pharisees it may have appeared that Jesus, whose Galilean origin would in itself make him suspect, was encouraging carelessness in Sabbath observance.

10 **The man who was cured.** The word *therapeuō* is frequently used in the other three Gospels but only this once in John. The word itself, with a root meaning of "serve," has both spiritual and physical connotations; it means to serve a divinity (Acts 17:25) and to "care for," "heal,"

"restore" (Sir. 38:7; Mark 1:34). Its usage here suggests that the man's healing may have been more than physical. From this word come the many modern terms such as "therapy"; this man was one who had received therapy from Jesus. It is an indictment of the casuistry of that day that the interrogators showed little interest in the man himself or in his sudden and complete cure. A distortion of perspective is a common characteristic of a legalism which has a perverted sense of values. To Jesus the man was a person; to his critics he was an object, a case in point.

11 **The man who healed me said . . . walk.** The man's answer may have been simply an explanation of his action, spoken in self-defense. Or it may have been more — "defiance in the first flush of his recovered health is very natural" (CGT). The man was simply obeying an order from the One who had just demonstrated the fact that he was Lord over disease. It now appears that he is also Lord of the Sabbath (cf. Mark 2:28). It had not occurred to him to question the authority of his healer.

as the cause of the initial opposition to Jesus. The tragic thing is that the main issue was obscured by a subordinate one; false sanctity had the effect of combatting true sanctity. The manner in which basic values are obscured by secondary values is illustrated in the Byzantine church at Daphnae, Greece, near Athens. For centuries the beautiful mosaic portraits of Christ were covered with plaster. When the plaster was removed, it seemed to be a destructive act, but the underlying figure of Christ was then unveiled. It remains one of the best extant examples of the devotion and artistic skill of the middle ages. Likewise, the Pharisees feared that

Jesus was destroying the Sabbath when actually he was restoring it to its true meaning and beauty.

### (2) *Blasphemy* (vv. 17, 18)

The statement **My Father worketh hitherto and I work** (v. 17) is something calling for reflection. It sums up not only the substance of this chapter but of the Gospel as a whole. The NEB rendering is felicitous: "My Father has never yet ceased his work and I am working, too." It was the bold use of "my Father" as applied to God which caused the Jews to shift their charge from Sabbath desecra-

[13] Jer. Shabbat 9 b-c, cited in Moore, *op. cit.*, II, 28.
[14] One might carry a burden within a house, or between houses if they were joined by a rope and thus in theory becoming one house. Today, among the orthodox, smoking and cooking are prohibited if striking a match is involved.
[15] In Sabbath observance Jesus was aligned with the school of Hillel; but on the subject of divorce with the stricter school of Shammai.

12 They asked him, Who is the man that said unto thee, Take up *thy bed,* and walk?

13 But he that was healed knew not who it was; for Jesus had conveyed himself away, a multitude being in the place.

14 Afterward Jesus findeth him in the temple, and said unto him, Behold, thou art made whole: sin no more, lest a worse thing befall thee.

15 The man went away, and told the Jews that it was Jesus who had made him whole.

16 And for this cause the Jews persecuted Jesus, because he did these things on the sabbath.

---

12 **Who is the man . . . ?** There was an air of contempt implicit in their question. These Jews considered themselves the official custodians and interpreters of the Torah and were ready to challenge the right to private interpretation. They might have challenged anyone carrying a bundle on the Sabbath as even today in Jerusalem their descendants protest the appearance of public conveyances such as taxis on *Shabbat* (Sabbath). They continued to show no interest in the miracle or in the man, only in their "hedge about the law."[16] It is not clear whether Jesus deliberately did something provocative to bring the issue of proper Sabbath observance out into the open, or whether the order to carry his couch was simply to demonstrate the completeness of the cure.

13 After the cure Jesus did not wait for the adulation of the onlookers. He "slipped away" (NEB) or, as the Greek *ekneuō* suggests, "turned aside" or "withdrew" and "made himself invisible" (cf. A-G). This is the first of four such instances, recorded by John, when Jesus made a quiet and hasty departure from the crowds (cf. 8:59; 10:39; 12:30). This time the man is addressed as "the cured" (*iatheis*), that is, the recipient of a completed act of healing.

14-16 "Afterward Jesus found him . . ." (RSV). The Lord obviously desired the man's soul as well as his body, hence he sought him out. The verb (*heuriskō* — to find) indicates that it was no chance encounter; Jesus sought him. The man's presence in the temple suggests his gratitude to God for the healing. Jesus' warning in the light of the larger context does not imply that the man's affliction had been the consequence of his exceptional sins. It is made clear in John 9:3 that there is no necessary correlation between one's physical and moral conditions.[17] It is clear that Jesus is concerned that the man's inner spiritual change be as marked as the outward physical change. Probably Barrett is correct in relating the warning of a **worse thing** to v. 29 — the general judgment. The forgiveness of sins is clearly implicit here as it is explicit in Mark 2:5. In this instance, however, the man reports back to the Jews rather than continuing in Jesus' presence. Whether he returned to the Jews to testify to them

---

tion to blasphemy. Both offenses were punishable by death under Mosaic law (Lev. 24:16; I Kings 21:23; Num. 15: 32-36). Their anger therefore, is understandable.

Why did not Jesus move more cautiously so as not to incur their hostility? Why did he not content himself with healing the man without instructing him to bear his pallet? Did not Paul later advise the avoidance of all appearance of evil and the use of Christian liberty if it offended a brother whose conscience was "weak" and misguided (Rom. 14:15-23; I Cor. 10: 23-33)? Could not Jesus have extended his life and usefulness by avoiding a head-on collision with religious prejudice? It ill becomes one to insist on answers to these questions. But it does provoke the practical question of whether the Christian minister today should adjust his message to the mores of the time or "take on" the opposition even if it means a shortened ministry. Henry Lyte was asked to leave his pulpit because his parishioners could not tolerate the rugged truths of the Gospel. After prayer and reflection he testified to the world:

---

[16] A reference to the oral traditions with which the Pharisees hedged about the written law as a double precaution against transgressing the latter. The unwritten law or tradition was a buffer zone to protect the written law of Moses (Mark 7:8; G. F. Moore, *op. cit.,* I, 259).

[17] Cf. Ps. 38:5; 107:17; I Cor. 11:30; Mark 2:5-10; John 2:24, 25.

17 But Jesus answered them, My Father worketh even until now, and I work.

18 For this cause therefore the Jews sought the more to kill him, because he not only brake the sabbath, but also called God his own Father, making himself equal with God.

because he was less interested in Jesus than was the blind man of ch. 9 is not clear. John's interest in the man himself is less than in the issues which the cure exposed. The imperfect tenses of v. 16 indicate that the Jews were continuing to persecute Jesus on this issue of Sabbath desecration; this was no isolated instance. The NEB suggests that the persecution began at this time — "it was works of this kind done on the Sabbath, that stirred the Jews to persecute Jesus."

**17 My Father worketh . . . and I work.** In this rejoinder Jesus made two astounding assertions. He implied that the miracle-cure was really God's work, not his, and also that as the Son he worked in cooperation with the Father. The miracle was from God. The question concerned working on the Sabbath. Here Jesus excused himself for the action by saying that he was only doing what God is continually doing (*arti* — "at the present time" or "until now"). As Judge, God works continuously. Thoughtful Jewish leaders acknowledged that in his capacity as Judge, God did not and does

not cease his activity even on the Sabbath. Philo believed that "as it is the property of fire to burn and snow to chill, so it is the property of God to make . . . . He causes to rest that which . . . he is apparently making, but He Himself never ceases making."[18] The rabbis distinguished between God's work as Creator which ceased on the seventh day (Gen. 2:2) and his work as Judge and Law-giver which never ceases (S-B, II, 460; WFH, VIII, 545). This helps to explain why later in the chapter Jesus stressed the work of judgment which the Son shares with the Father (vv. 22, 27, 29).

This verse is probably the key verse of the entire chapter and also one of the major emphases of the Fourth Gospel. The remainder of the chapter supports the thesis of the Father and Son working together in three supporting assertions: in raising the dead (vv. 21, 29), in judging (vv. 22, 27, 29), and in giving life (vv. 21, 24, 26) as already noted.

**18 He . . . called God his own Father, making himself equal with God.** He was equal with God because he did the "same

---

*Jesus, I my cross have taken,*
*All to leave and follow thee.*
*Destitute, despised, forsaken,*
*Thou from hence my all shall be.*

        .    .    .

*Let the world despise and leave me,*
*They have left my Saviour, too;*
*Human hearts and looks deceive me;*
*Thou art not, like man, untrue;*
*And while thou shalt smile upon me,*
*God of wisdom, love and might,*
*Foes may hate, and friends disown me;*
*Show thy face, and all is bright.*

John Wesley was forbidden to preach in the church his father served as a rector, but he used his father's tomb-stone as a podium and preached outside to the by-

standers. Later he was forbidden to preach at Oxford because he had told his learned audience that they were Christians in name and not in reality.[c]

The opposite type of clergyman, who sought the praise of men rather than the glory of God, is well-described by Timothy Dwight, President of Yale College.[d]

c. Jesus' Defense (vv. 19-47)
  (1) *Father and Son Co-workers* (vv. 19-30)
    (a) In Raising the Dead (vv. 21, 25, 28)

As in most of these discourses, Jesus, as reported by John, does not move from one topic to another but keeps several themes in view with frequent repetition

---

[18] Philo, *Allegorical Interpretation*, I, 3: (Loeb).
c J. Wesley, "Scriptural Christianity," in E. H. Sugden, ed., *Standard Sermons of John*, I, 87-111.
d T. Dwight, "The Smooth Divine," C. Hill, ed., *World's Great Religious Poetry* (New York: Macmillan Co., 1938), p. 369.

19 Jesus therefore answered and said unto them, Verily, verily, I say unto you, The Son can do nothing of himself, but what he seeth the Father doing: for what things soever he doeth, these the Son also doeth in like manner.

---

kind of work" (*kagō ergazomai,* v. 17). To Paul the fact that Jesus considered Himself "equal to God" (*isa theōi*) (Phil. 2:6) was evidence of his *kenōsis,* or self-emptying at the Incarnation; to the Jews here the same expression (*ison heauton . . . Theōi*) was rank blasphemy (cf. II Thess. 2:4). "His *own* Father (*idion*) in the ASV and NEB seems more accurate than the omission of "own" in the KJV and RSV. While in the Old Testament God was spoken of as the Father of Israel, the manner in which Jesus used the term caused his hearers to see it in a relationship quite unique, in a manner which no ordinary man could claim. Jesus was affirming that God was his Father not only in the sense of His being tribal head but in a personal sense as well. There is here the clear implication of Jesus' equality with God the Father, although the Savior does not bluntly say so. There is here, and throughout the remainder of the chapter, a remarkable combination of Jesus' equality with and subordination to the Father. The subordination of the Son is indicated in vv. 19, 20, 26, 27, 30, 31, 36, 37, 38 and 43 — about twelve different expressions of his subordination.

In contrast are assertions of equality with the Father in vv. 17, 18, 19, 21, 23, 26, 27 and 43 — about nine statements in which equality is asserted or implied. This paradox is sometimes called an antinomy, in which two apparently contradictory affirmations are placed side by side. One of the most striking of these is in John 10:17 — "I have power to lay it down, and I have power to take it again [equality], this commandment have I received from my Father [subordination]." In this Gospel, as nowhere else in the New Testament except the Epistle to the Hebrews, the most unqualified expressions of Jesus' deity are placed beside the most unqualified expressions of his humanity with no attempt at rational harmonization. It took the church four centuries to harmonize these two concepts and even then the decision was not unanimous. Indeed, the Christological controversy has never yet been fully settled: "great is the mystery of godliness." What we are dealing with in the New Testament is not systematic theology but the raw material out of which systematic theology is developed.

Westcott's judgment is probably sound when he declares of 5:19-47, "These are

---

and cross references. In his defense, the first affirmation Jesus makes relative to the work performed jointly by the Father and the Son in cooperation is that of raising the dead. Is the Master here referring to those dead physically, or spiritually, or both? It is Paul who makes most extensive use of the analogy of life and death in describing the Christian life (e.g., Rom. 6:1-6; Col. 3:1ff.; Eph. 2:1-8). Here, however, the primary meaning is apparently physical resurrection at the last since it is an eschatological rather than evangelistic setting (v. 28, 29). This underscores the fact that as the greatest enemy of man is death so the greatest possible miracle is giving life to those who have experienced death in any form.

In the section dealing with the cooperation between Father and Son (vv. 19-30), we note the subordination of the Son in

vv. 19, 30, in the statement that the Son can do nothing without the Father. Later Jesus will tell his disciples that they can do nothing without him (John 15:4). This theme supports the "key-verse," v. 17; Father and Son are co-workers (vv. 17, 19) because of the love (*philia*) which the Father has for the Son (v. 20). To the Christian this description of the intimate relations between God and Father and Son in God-head sounds both good and true. To the bystanders who listened it seemed like two gods, and more like paganism than the religion of the Old Testament. But Jesus Christ is the expression of the Father's thought and will; he is the *Logos,* the Word expressing the Father's thought.

Arising from this cooperation between Father and Son are the greater works which will follow the recent healing of the foundations of all later teaching in the Gospel" (BFW, I, 181). The solemnity of the statement is reinforced by the formula "verily, verily" (NEB; "in truth, in very truth") which occurs 25 times in this Gospel. The relationship of the Son to the Father is not only prominent in this paragraph but throughout the chapter. Jesus' sense of mission, of subordination to the Father as Son of man, is reflected in many statements of the chapter: **The Son can do nothing of himself** (v. 19); the Father shows the Son (v. 20); the Father gave life and authority to the Son (vv. 26; 27), Jesus does nothing on his own authority, but rather seeks to follow the Father's will (v. 30); the Father gave the Son work to do (v. 36); the Father sent the Son (vv. 37, 38); and he came to do the Father's will (v. 43). At the same time his sense of equality as Son of God is reflected in the following assertions: Father and Son work together (v. 17); the Son is equal with God (v. 18); the Son works "in like manner" with the Father (v. 19); the Son gives life (v. 21); all should honor the Son as the Father (v. 23); the dead hear the voice of the Son and hence live (v. 26); both Father and Son have life (v. 26); the Son executes judgment and those who

come to the Son find life (v. 40). In this paragraph specifically the assertions of Jesus are linked with four propositions:

(1) for the Son does what the Father does (v. 19);

(2) for the Father reveals all his activity to the Son (v. 20);

(3) for the Son gives life as does the Father (v. 21);

(4) for the Father commits all matters of judgment to the Son (v. 22).

19 The statement that the Son does only what is in harmony with the Father's will and action is a defense against the charge of blasphemy, and also of "loosening" (*lyō*: i.e., "breaking") the bonds of the Sabbath (v. 18). Later Jesus can say to the Father, "I have completed the task thou gavest me to do" (John 17:4 Berkeley), and assert "I do invariably what pleases Him" (John 8:29 Berkeley). This was the basis of the Master's confidence when he lifted his voice in prayer to the Father, and the believer's confidence in prayer has a similar basis: e.g., I John 3:22, "We can approach God with confidence, and obtain from him whatever we ask, because we are keeping his commands and doing what he approves" (NEB).

---

the cripple. Among the **greater works** mentioned is the raising of the dead. The listeners would not actually witness that, except as pre-figured in the raising of Lazarus, but they would see people raised from spiritual death in unbelief unto spiritual life. Connected with resurrection is the judgment which follows it. Since the Sadducees did not believe in the resurrection of the dead, many of those listening would not have been sympathetic. But the statement should have pleased the Pharisees in any other context. Paul was able to gain many sympathizers in an otherwise hostile audience by professing his acceptance of the doctrine of the resurrection (Acts 23:6-9). The doctrine of the resurrection is perhaps the major theme of the New Testament.

(b) In Judging (vv. 22, 23, 27, 29, 30)

Related closely to the theme of a general resurrection of all the dead and of a

spiritual resurrection of the believer is the theme of Jesus as the Judge. In the famous frescoes in the Sistine Chapel of the Vatican the artist Michaelangelo made his painting of the Last Judgment dominate the whole. His portrait of a stern Christ on the throne is world-famed. The pictures of Christ in many Byzantine icons, such as the mosaic of Christ at Daphne, Greece, portray him as Judge. It was perhaps this emphasis on Christ as Judge which assisted the rise of the cult of the Virgin Mary. Where Christ's sternness and remoteness is emphasized to the exclusion of his priestly role as a compassionate intercessor, it is understandable that men would seek the help of Mary in gaining the attention of her august Son.

John's Gospel has much to say about judgment. It is characteristic of this Gospel to stress that in his role of Judge Jesus is better qualified because of his experience of humanity. The author of Hebrews agrees with this when he says

20 For the Father loveth the Son, and showeth him all things that himself doeth: and greater works than these will he show him, that ye may marvel.

21 For as the Father raiseth the dead and giveth them life, even so the Son also giveth life to whom he will.

22 For neither doth the Father judge any man, but he hath given all judgment unto the Son;

---

20 The partnership between Father and Son is brought out in the next four assertions introduced by "for" (*gar*). Four things are included in this sweeping statement of the cooperation between Father and Son. It is on the level of affection ("The Father loves the Son"), and of information ("shows him all"), and of power ("greater works"). The verb **show** (*deiknymi*) means "to point out, make known, explain or prove something" (cf. 2:18; 3:13). The love of the Father for the Son is expressed by the term *phileō*, meaning "affection resulting from personal relationship."[19] The promise of **greater things** was voiced earlier to Nathanael (1:50) and is repeated to the disciples (14:12).

21 **The Father raises the dead.** This is the second explicit statement in John relative to the basic doctrine of the early church — the doctrine of the resurrection (cf. 2:22). The raising of the dead as a joint action of Father and Son is in harmony with other passages which speak of the Father working with or through the Son (cf. John 1:3). Paul speaks of the resurrection as primarily the act of God (Rom. 1:4; Acts 17:31). Peter's sermons have the same emphasis (Acts 2:32; 3: 15). In this passage as reported by John, Jesus avoids two extremes. On the one hand Jewish monotheism was to be conserved. So Jesus asserts his equality with God, which goes beyond the conventional Jewish concept of a Messiah, without the sacrifice of monotheism. On the other hand is the danger of lapsing into the polytheism of the surrounding pagan culture. The assertions of Jesus' humanity and his deity are laid side by side with precision and repetition, and the reader is left to reflect upon them (CHD, p. 328). The alleged Gnostic source of some of these facets of Jesus' relation to the Father is a theory which becomes increasingly untenable as new evidence emerges.[20] Rather, John is articulating a distinctively Christian evangel built on the background of the Old Testament, aware of the thought

---

that because of his humanity Jesus can be "touched with the feeling of our infirmities" (Heb. 4:15; 2:14-18; 5:8). Only those under the power of darkness and guilt need fear the judge. It is a paradox that Jesus Christ is both the Judge and the Defense Attorney or Advocate, but such he is. As Savior he bears our sins and in response to repentance and faith frees us from the sentence of death. As Judge he passes sentence on the basis of whether or not we believe and obey. Seldom has Jesus in this dual role of Judge and Savior been grasped more clearly or expressed more powerfully than in the lines of Thomas of Celano.

*The Judge ascends his awful throne;*
*He makes each secret sin be known,*
*And all with shame confess their*
*   own.*

*Oh, then, what interest shall I make*
*To save my last important stake,*
*When the most just have cause to*
*   quake?*

*Thou mighty, formidable King,*
*Thou mercy's unexhausted spring,*
*Some comfortable pity bring!*

*Forget not what my ransom cost,*
*Nor let my dear-bought soul be lost*
*In storms of guilty terror tost.*

[19] *Agapaō* "denotes affection resulting from deliberate choice" (CGT, 137).
[20] Bultmann holds that the pre-existent Son as portrayed in the Fourth Gospel draws heavily upon Gnostic mythology of a pre-Christian heavenly Man, made in the image of God, who is made an intermediary between God and man, comes from heaven to do God's work, then returns to heaven in glory. (Cf. Bultmann, pp. 188-190.) Against this it may be noted that Gnosticism followed rather than preceded Christianity and that recently discovered Gnostic texts reflect a theology quite unlike that of John. See R. M. Grant and D. N. Freedman, *The Secret Sayings of Jesus* (Garden City: Doubleday, 1960), p. 113.

23 that all may honor the Son, even as they honor the Father. He that honoreth not the Son honoreth not the Father that sent him.

24 Verily, verily, I say unto you, He that heareth my word, and believeth him that sent me, hath eternal life, and cometh not into judgment, but hath passed out of death into life.

25 Verily, verily, I say unto you, The hour cometh, and now is, when the dead shall hear the voice of the Son of God; and they that hear shall live.

currents in the Mediterranean world at large, but convinced that Christ alone has the answer.

25 The hour cometh and now is . . . Does this refer to the future apocalyptic day of judgment or does it mean that at the present moment it is possible to live anew? The meaning here is related to "the dead." Does he mean his living contemporaries who are "dead in trespasses and sins," or does he refer to those who have departed from this life? The "greater works" of 5:20 apparently refers to the raising of the dead. In reading John, one learns to expect that behind and beneath the obvious literal meaning is a more spiritual connotation, e.g., 4:10. Here the words now is indicate that those spiritually dead may now have a resurrection. Two conditions for eternal life are here given: hearing and believing, knowing the content of Jesus' message and accepting it. The emphasis on hearing and responding is consistent with that in chs. 1, 3, 6, and elsewhere. To hear and see and not to heed leaves one the worse for having heard. No one ever confronted Christ and remained the same; he was left better or worse. The resurrection of those physically dead was prominent in New Testament theology. In I Thessalonians 4:16 Paul writes, "The Lord himself shall descend from heaven with a shout, with the voice of the archangel, and with the trump of God: and the dead in Christ shall rise first." Paul speaks only of the resurrection of the dead "in Christ." But here Jesus says all in the tombs shall hear his voice and come forth, implying a general resurrection at the last day, which was generally believed in among the Pharisees (cf. John 11:24; Acts 23:6-8). In v. 29 the contrast is between the resurrection of life and that of judgment. Likewise in v. 24 the contrast is between judgment and death on the one hand and belief and life on the other. Two kinds of resurrection are surely envisioned here. Vv. 21-25 refer to a spiritual resurrection immediately available to the believer and resulting in eternal life beginning at once; the resurrection is a figurative expression. Such a resurrection is, of course, only possible to the believer in Jesus. In vv. 25-29 a future literal resurrection in which all shall participate is envisioned. This belief in a future judg-

*Thou who for me didst feel such pain,
Whose precious blood the cross did stain,
Let not these agonies be in vain!*[e]

In this majestic poem the author moves swiftly from addressing Christ as Judge to addressing Christ as Redeemer. A similar idea of the combination of Law and Gospel is echoed in the 18th century hymn of John Newton, "Amazing Grace":

*'Twas grace that taught my heart to fear,
And grace my fears relieved;
How precious did that grace appear
The hour I first believed.*

(c) In Giving Life (vv. 21, 24, 26)

Out of resurrection and judgment comes life. Dodd finds in v. 21 "the dominant theme" of the discourse (CHD, p. 318) — "the Son gives life to whom he will," as does the Father. As we learn in v. 24, this life comes through the Word of God. This Word is declared to be the Voice of the Son of God (v. 25). The ultimate source of this life is in the Father, but he shares it freely with his Son, who in turn gives it to the believers. The basis for the bestowing of life on the believers is said to be good works (v. 29). This is in accord with many passages in the Synoptic Gospels, and the

e Thomas of Celano, "Dies Irae," (tr. by W. Dillon) C. H. Hill, ed., op. cit., p. 758.

26 For as the Father hath life in himself, even so gave he to the Son also to have life in himself:

27 and he gave him authority to execute judgment, because he is a son of man.

28 Marvel not at this: for the hour cometh, in which all that are in the tombs shall hear his voice,

---

ment forms a prominent eschatological feature of the Synoptic Gospels, Acts, the Epistles and the Apocalypse. The important point here is that Jesus, under attack as a blasphemer, makes the stupendous claim that he is not only uniquely divine but shall, under the Father's sanction, have the authority to give spiritual life to those spiritually dead now and eternal life at the general resurrection. The picture of the last assize is consistent with the parables of judgment and Synoptic portrait generally.

28, 29 **Those in the tombs** is perhaps a prophecy of the resurrection of Lazarus as the "firstfruits" of general resurrection. The emphasis on the resurrection in the Fourth Gospel is probably greater even than in the Synoptics. The *come forth* (*ekporeuomai*) of v. 29 is a strong verb often used to describe the exorcism of demons (Matt. 17:21; Acts 19:12). Here it is linked with the *goal* of the resurrection. Matthew records such a resurrection at the time of the crucifixion (Matt. 27: 52, 53), but it is only an isolated event which apparently was overshadowed by the

death of Jesus. While in vv. 21, 24, 25 the emphasis was upon those spiritually dead, here the mention of "tombs" (*mnēmeiois*) indicates that physical death is meant. The author does not labor to make clear the transition from the spiritual to physical aspects of death; Jesus apparently here deliberately used language with a two-fold meaning, as he did elsewhere.

The term **voice** merits attention. John the Baptist had been a "voice" in the wilderness summoning men to emerge from spiritual darkness into the light. Jesus' "voice" at the end of the era or aeon will summon all men to receive the final disposition of their respective cases, even though they already have the status of either life or death (John 3:18; 5:24). In many of the other pictures of the last time the voice of God is an important feature. The concern of Jesus here is that they will not wait until the last day to hear that Voice, but will hear and heed it now so that they may escape out of the tomb of spiritual death and find eternal life.

---

Epistles.[t] The manner in which salvation by good works is harmonized is best stated by James 2:14-26 and by Martin Luther in his classic treatise, "The Liberty of the Christian Man," written in A. D. 1520.

Life is perhaps the main concern of the Fourth Gospel. This theme constantly recurs in various contexts but in this context it appears as the gift of God, the greatest gift of Father and Son jointly. Here it is associated with the resurrection of life (*anastasin zōē*) and contrasted with the **resurrection of judgment.** These two resurrections may be compared to the "first resurrection" and the "second death" of Rev. 20:5, 6. The reference here, however, seems to be to one general resurrection from which some enter into

life and others into death (cf. Matt. 25: 46).

### (2) *Witnesses* (vv. 31-47)
#### (a) The Witness of Jesus (v. 31)

Throughout this Gospel the theme of witness is linked to the major theme of belief. In this section the subject of witness is concentrated. The witness of Jesus in the Fourth Gospel consists in a large part of his words, such as the discourse reported in 5:17ff., the gist of which was that Jesus of Nazareth is both the Messiah of the Jews and the Savior of the whole world and is in the closest conceivable relationship to the one Supreme God of Creation. The testimony of Christ to him-

---

[t] Matt. 25:31-46; John 9:4; Gal. 6:7-10; II Thess. 3:11-13.

29 and shall come forth; they that have done good, unto the resurrection of life; and they that have done evil, unto the resurrection of judgment.

---

22, 23, 27, 29, 30 The concept of judgment and judge forms a large place in the literature and theology of the Bible. Moses was a judge, and the heads of the tribal confederacy after the conquest of Canaan were judges. The greatest and last of the judges was Samuel. Solomon was famed for his God-given wisdom in the capacity of judge. The messianic king of Israel was envisioned as one who functioned as a righteous judge (Isa. 11:3, 4). Absalom gained the throne of Israel because he promised to be a better judge than his father (II Sam. 15:2-6). The judges were under a sacred obligation to avoid bribes and to let their judgments be according to God's righteousness. In stating that he was responsible for judgment, Jesus was filling the role of Moses, Samuel, David, and of God himself. In ancient Israel future judgment had reference to God's punishment of the nation for national sins. Judgment is the prerogative of God, the all-knowing one (Deut. 1:17). The idea of a future judgment seems to be post-exilic, Daniel 12:2, 3 being the earliest expression of such a view. Later apocalyptic literature greatly elaborated on the theme of a final judgment, as in Enoch 46:3, "When the Lord shall send a great light, then there shall be judgment for the just and the unjust, and there shall no

one escape notice."[21] The "day of the Great Judgment" is also mentioned in Jubilees (23:11). Most of the text alluding to a future judgment are parts of apocalypses in which the messianic Son of Man figures prominently. In most of them, however, the judging is done by God Almighty. In Baruch 50:3, 4; 51 the resurrection precedes the final judgment as it does in the major Christian apocalypse (Rev. 20:11-15).

The linking of the Son of Man with judgment goes back to Daniel 7:27 and is common in the Synoptics (Mark 14:61; Matt. 26:63; Luke 22:67). Here the reason is given: "because he is son of man." That is, Jesus' real humanity gives him insight and sympathy. This is like the principle in modern jurisprudence: one is entitled to a jury of his peers, his equals. The same idea is characteristic of the Epistle to the Hebrews where Jesus' real humanity is given as the qualification of his high priestly office of intercession (Heb. 2:18; 4:15; 5:8).

23 The second reason for committing all judgment to the Son is that he may thereby be glorified. The Son's equality with the Father, their unity in the Godhead, is indicated by the sharing of honor. Here Jesus is in the role of ambassador. An insult to the ambassador is really an

---

self in the Synoptic accounts consists mostly of deeds. When John sent messengers to inquire of Jesus as to his identity, Jesus did not answer directly but continued doing "good works" after which the delegation was advised to report to John the things they had seen and heard (Matt. 11:2-6). These things that they had "seen and heard" included miracles of healing of the blind, the lame, lepers, and the deaf, and the raising of the dead. They had heard the Gospel preached to "the poor." In other words, the things they had seen Jesus do and say were precisely those which the "Lord's Anointed" was supposed to do according to Isaiah 61:1-4, the passage Jesus said was being fulfilled

in himself (Luke 4:16-22). Later Jesus was remembered as one who "went about doing good" (Acts 10:38). Thus he witnessed both by his good works (10:32) and by his words of life (6:63), such as had never been heard before (7:46).

(b) The Witness of John
(vv. 31-35)

In this Gospel John the Baptist is mentioned 19 times, always by the name "John" without other identification; he is mentioned seven times in Matthew, and four times each in Mark and in Luke. This gives some idea of the importance of John as a witness in the composition

[21] R. H. Charles, *Apocrypha and Pseudepigrapha of the Old Testament* (Oxford: Clarendon Press, 1913), II, 458.
g W. W. White, *Thirty Studies in the Gospel by John* (New York: Revell, 1958), p. 77.

30 I can of myself do nothing: as I hear, I judge: and my judgment is righteous; ecause I seek not mine own will, but the will of him that sent me.

---

ısult to the one who commissioned him. he consciousness of Jesus, as being niquely and unprecedentedly God-sent, is onsistently prominent in all the Gospels. his consciousness is powerfully reflected 1 the Parable of the Vineyard (Mark 12: -9) where the rejection of the prophets nd later of the Son is defiance of the ord and punishable by death.

27 Here the ARV text correctly says son of man — the article is missing in 1e Greek text. As such it refers to uality and is not a personal title.[22]

30 Another basis for Jesus' authority s a judge is the fact that his motive is ood. He does not seek to forward his wn selfish purposes, as did Absalom in is role as judge (II Sam. 15:4-6). He 1akes it clear that his authority as judge not inherent but delegated: "I can of 1yself do nothing." His authority comes om the Father. It is also clear that his 1dgment is not capricious or arbitrary — as I hear I judge." His judgments, there- ore, are in conformity with and subordi- ate to the canons of right and wrong. hings are not right because he does or 1ys something; he says or does so because is right. His sovereignty is "limited" y righteousness. For practical purposes

Christ's way and the way of righteousness are identical.

The Christian faith holds out hope for the eventual redress of grievances. Mar- tyrs, suffering to the death for their faith, were and are sustained by the con- viction that their case is in the hand of a Judge who judges righteously (Rev. 19:2). Saints suffering from exploitation know that "their redemption draweth nigh," and can afford to be patient (Jas. 5:7). Victims of injustice and oppression have as their example one who himself endured harassment with patience (I Peter 3:23). A righteous judge is a terror to the evil- doer but a comfort to the righteous.

21 The resurrection, whether physical, spiritual, or both, is preliminary to life. In ch. 3, it is birth from above which makes spiritual life possible. The resur- rection can be the prelude either to life, or to exclusion from life, that is, to a resurrection of judgment (v. 29). The Father and Son together bestow life on those whom they will. Life is not some- thing to which one is inherently entitled; it is a gift of God which disobedience can forfeit. If life comes, it will be always on the basis of grace, not by achievement or merit. As giver of life and dispenser of

---

f this Gospel. John the Baptist's sole urpose was not to establish a church but ɔ bear witness to the light (1:7, 31; 3:26, 8). This he did to the delegation from 1e Pharisees (1:19-28), later to the public 1:29-34), and on the day following his ublic witness to his disciples privately 1:35-40). He called himself the bride- room's friend and not a rival (3:22-30).

John, like his predecessor Elijah, must ave seemed to his contemporaries like strange and bizarre figure, accustomed ɔ "secret fasts and midnight vigils . . . om which he comes with a divine mes- ıge to his followers."[h]

Like Amos, he had learned in the soli- tude of the "wilderness" to think God's thoughts after him. So great was John's influence among the common people that the Jewish leaders dared not deny that he was God's messenger (Mark 11:29-33). Ascetics were not admired as much then as they were during the fourth century but "all took him to be a prophet." His moral stature made such an impression on the people that, according to Josephus, the defeat of Herod's armies was attributed to divine retribution for the murder of this prophet of God (Ant., XVIII. v. 2). The witness of John therefore could not easily be disregarded.

---

[22] In words attributed to Jesus he calls himself Ho huios tou anthrōpou (the son of the man); when e writers speak of him it is always huios anthrōpou. As "Son of man" Jesus is both homogeneous with e prophets (cf. Ezekiel as "son of man") and with the heavenly "Son of man" of the apocalypses. 1e title thus suggest his humanity (like a prophet) and his deity (the Lord from heaven).

[h] James Stalker, The Two Johns of the New Testament (New York: American Tract Society, 1895), 202.

judgment, Christ is here placing himself at the level of the Godhead. So stupendous are his claims that Jesus is either the Son of God or the most reckless of blasphemers.

**24 He that heareth . . . and believeth . . . hath eternal life.** In the cyclic style, characteristic of this writer, the theme of life, introduced in v. 21 as one of the **greater works,** continues. The power of the Son to make alive **whom he will** goes beyond the children of Abraham and extends to all the sons of men. The emphasis here on hearing and believing relieves v. 21 of any suggestion that the giving of life is a "limited atonement" or capricious (Hoskyns, p. 270). We have here what has been termed a "realized eschatology," that is, the cosmic themes of judgment, second advent, and attendant cataclysms are merged with the inward, personal, spiritual crisis of the individual before God. Eternal life becomes something not for the future age only, but it may begin immediately within the heart. It is faith in the Son which enables one to meet the crisis of the last judgment that, as John 3:19 explains, is due to the rejection of God's light.

The Gospel of Thomas, a recently discovered Gnostic document which had been rejected by the Church, is characterized by a neglect of the future life and a stress on the present; it stresses salvation by knowledge rather than by grace, and hence is in contrast to John's Gospel and the New Testament as a whole.[23] As stated here, belief leads to life and freedom from condemnation (cf. 3:16). The converse is also implied here: to him who does not heed and believe, the light becomes darkness. Grace is always accompanied by judgment for those who reject it. The prepositions here are noteworthy: "passed out of (ek) death" and passed "into (eis) life." With these words Jesus rises far above the argument over the cripple and his healing. As the "second Adam" he presents himself as related to the entire human race in the role of Savior. "As in Adam all died, so also in Christ shall all be made alive" (I Cor. 15:22).

The source of this life is God. It is mediated by Christ and received by faith. The means by which its life-giving contact is established are hearing Jesus and believing in his mission. This involves personal surrender and commitment as the human basis or condition for receiving the universally desired gift of life. Again it connotes quality of life rather than merely duration, a characteristic distinction and

---

### (c) The Witness of the Works (v. 36)

The works are the same as the miracles or signs in John. All are cited not so much as evidence of Jesus' good character as evidence that he had the sanction of God for all that he said and did. Jesus appealed to this several times in an effort to gain acceptance of his message and ministry (5:36; 10:25, 37, 38; 14:11). In John's Gospel "sign" (*sēmeion*) is used 17 times to describe these miracles and "work" (*ergon*) 23 times. Behind the deed itself, especially in John, was the message or significance of the deed. The healing of the cripple, for instance, strengthened Jesus' claim that he, in association with the Father, could give life to whom he would. In addition to the miracles recorded by John are many to which an allusion is made without a description of the nature of the "good work."[1] These the early Christians remembered and related in much the same manner that the ancient Israelites recalled God's "mighty acts" in delivering and preserving their nation (Ps. 78 *et al.*). The greatest of these mighty works was, of course, the resurrection, which was the nucleus of the earliest creeds (Rom. 10:9), and which, if accepted, included all of the lesser miracles.

### (d) The Witness of the Father (v. 37)

The Father's witness was given verbally three times during Jesus' ministry. The first time was at the baptism when the Voice said, "Thou art my beloved Son in thee I am well pleased (Luke 3:22) The second voice from heaven was hear at the Transfiguration with a similar en

---

23 R. M. Grant & D. N. Freedman, *op. cit.*, p. 14.
1 John 2:23; 3:2; 6:2; 7:31; 9:16; 11:47; 12:37; 20:30.

emphasis in this Gospel. In John "eternal life" is both temporal, as with Philo, and qualitative, as with Plato (CHD, p. 150).

**26 The Father gave to the Son also to have life in himself.** The fact that the Father shares with the Son the principle gift of life is an emphatic way of affirming the equality of Son and Father. Yet even here the Son's subordination is glimpsed in the phrase "the Father hath . . . and gave." Jesus is truly God and yet is not identical with the Father nor separate from him; there are not two Gods. The Son does not keep the gift of life but comes to men, tabernacles among us, to make the gift available. The concept is infinitely greater than the myth of Prometheus, the Greek god who gave man the gift of fire. The Son, like the Father, gives life. He is not exactly the *ultimate* source of life, but is at least the bestower of life. Life is a gift of God, not something one earns, or something to which one is inherently entitled. Life comes only on the basis of grace and not by merit. It is not an inherent quality of the soul which one is entitled by virtue of being human. Survival is intrinsic in human nature, but not life as such.

While the theme of *belief* is the major one of this Gospel, the concept of *witness,* because of its bearing on belief, is also of paramount importance. The theme of witnessing comes to focus in ch. 5. The material on the subject of witnesses may thus be summarized:

(1) The witness of the Father (5:37; 8:18). The Father bore witness in three ways: (i) by direct public testimony at least three times (Mark 1:11; 9:7; John 12:28), (ii) indirectly through miracles (John 5:17), and (iii) by the inner voice of assurance and guidance to Jesus personally (John 11:41, 42).

(2) The witness of Jesus to himself (John 5:31; 8:14, 18). Jesus bore witness of himself in such statements as "I am the good shepherd."

(3) The witness of John (1:7, 8; 5:33-35).

(4) The witness of the works of Jesus (5:36; 10:25; 14:11; 15:24). It was widely accepted by both Jesus' friends and enemies that "no one can do a miracle ex-

dorsement of Jesus (Luke 9:35). This experience apparently made a deep impression on the apostles (II Pet. 1:17). The third such Voice occurred at the close of the public ministry (John 12:28-30). Not only this but the miracles which Jesus performed were the most incontrovertible proof that "God was with him" (Acts 10:38).

Jesus' dependence on the Father is a prominent theme of John and also of the Synoptists. His early morning and all night vigils of prayer were a testimony to this dependence "in the days of his flesh" (Heb. 5:7). In such times as these his dependence on the Father was very personal and real. At other times his calling on the Father was for the purpose of publicly acknowledging divine intervention, as in the short prayer before the resurrection of Lazarus (John 11:41).

**37 In saying Ye have neither heard his voice at any time, nor seen his form** (*eidos*) Jesus apparently meant that the Jews had no first-hand knowledge of the Father on which they could refute his own claim of intimacy with Him. They neither have immediate knowledge of God, as did Moses nor have they mediate knowledge of God through the Scriptures since they have rejected the Scriptures' testimony.

As the evidence accumulates later in the narrative, Jesus' hearers were even then rejecting the Living Word and in so doing also rejecting the Written Word. They were dishonoring the "Impress of God and the Father by refusing to hold his true form."[1] That the leaders of the nation, past and present, rejected the testimony of God was as prominent a theme of the N. T. evangelists as it had been of the O. T. prophets (e.g., Acts 7:51; 13:40-41, 46).

(e) The Witness of the Scriptures (vv. 39-47)

The witness of the Old Testament to Christ was the chief arsenal of the Christian apologists during the early centuries. The early Christians faced the problem

---

[1] Cyril of Alexandria, *Commentary on the Gospel According to John* (Oxford: James Parker & Co. 1847), I, 300.

31 If I bear witness of myself, my witness is not true.

32 It is another that beareth witness of me; and I know that the witness which he witnesseth of me is true.

33 Ye have sent unto John, and he hath borne witness unto the truth.

34 But the witness which I receive is not from man: howbeit I say these things, that ye may be saved.

35 He was the lamp that burneth and shineth; and ye were willing to rejoice for a season in his light.

---

cept God be with him" and thus endorses his life and words.

(5) Jesus also witnessed by the superior quality of his life.

The greatest miracle of all was the moral life, the sinlessness of Jesus. His betrayer and his judge (Pilate) and his executioner agreed with his friends that "this was a righteous man."

(6) The Scriptures bear witness of Jesus (John 5:39; 46; 1:45; Luke 24:27).

(7) The witness of acquaintances (John 4:39; 9:25, 38; 12:17).

(8) The witness of disciples (John 15:27; 19:35; 21:24).

(9) The Witness of the Holy Spirit (John 15:26; I John 5:6).

The subject of this multitude of witnesses is, of course, Jesus the Christ. It is Christ who unifies this book; all lines of investigation converge on him.

31 **My witness is not true.** This statement apparently contradicts 8:14 where Jesus states, "my witness is true." There the Jews were accusing him of falsehood because he was an interested party. They were saying in effect, "your witness has no value because it is not independent and disinterested; furthermore, there is no collaborating witness." In protest Jesus affirmed that whether acceptable to the people or not what he says is in accordance with truth. In this context Jesus seems to say, "If I were the only one witnessing to my claim it would be unconvincing be-

cause I am a party to the case; I am the defendant." Jesus was not saying that he was less truthful than John but simply that John's witness is more convincing because from an independent source. Jewish law required more than one witness for testimony to be acceptable (Deut. 19:15; cf. Matt. 18:16; II Cor. 13:1; I Tim. 5:19).

33 **Ye have sent unto John** is a probable reference to the delegation from Jerusalem reported in 1:19. The other witness of this verse could refer either to John or to the Father. John's witness is presented in the Fourth Gospel as an important factor in belief. In the prologue (1:6-8, 18), in John's discussion with his own disciples (3:27-30), and now here, great importance is given to his witness. The use of perfect participle of "witness" (*martyreō*) indicates that not an isolated incident is in mind, but the continuing effect of John's witness.

In 1:7 it is stated of John that "he was not the light" (*phōs*). Here it states that he was "a light" (*lychnos*), the latter word meaning a flickering oil lamp (Mark 4:21; Matt. 5:15) as compared with the light like that of the sun (*phōs*). John was the candle; Jesus the sun.

35 The witness of John should have been convincing to them, but Jesus does not place reliance upon this witness alone, even though it is true and should be sufficient. The fact that Jesus has other wit-

---

of what to do with the Jewish Bible. Should they reject it *in toto* as did Marcion and other radicals, or should they retain it *in toto* as the conservatives urged. The compromise retained the essentials, the portions with universal relevance, and rejected the non-essentials, the portions pertaining only to the Jewish nation (Acts 15). Even among the Jews there was in

practice, if not in theory, a distinction made between laws binding on all men and those for Israelites only.[k] The surprising thing is not the portions of the Old Testament which Christians felt irrelevant but the extent to which they accepted the entire O. T. Indeed, in many instances, they accepted it more literally than did "normative" Judaism, especially

---

k G. F. Moore, *op. cit.*, II, 6-10.

36 But the witness which I have is greater than *that of* John; for the works which the Father hath given me to accomplish, the very works that I do, bear witness of me, that the Father hath sent me.

37 And the Father that sent me, he hath borne witness of me. Ye have neither heard his voice at any time, nor seen his form.

38 And ye have not his word abiding in you: for whom he sent, him ye believe not.

39 Ye search the scriptures, because ye think that in them ye have eternal life; and these are they which bear witness of me;

---

nesses is no reflection upon John's veracity. **He was a lamp that burneth . . . for a season.** The metaphor recalls Sirach 48:1 where, in a reference to Elijah the author says, "There arose a prophet like fire, whose word was like a burning furnace" (cf. Mal. 4:1, 5). The mutual admiration between Jesus and John is frequently voiced (John 11:28; 3:29; cf. Luke 3:16; 7:28; 20:4). John's popularity with the people was extensive but short-lived. When he was imprisoned they considered him a closed chapter in Jewish history (Hoskyns). The past tense here, as compared with 3:24, indicates that John is now in prison or dead. The consistent picture of John in all four Gospels is that of a transient personage whose sole task is to prepare the way for Another. The measure of John's success was the extent to which he "worked himself out of a job." Even a flickering candlelight is relatively brilliant in dense darkness; such was the relation of John to his contemporaries.

36 The evidential or apologetic value of miracles is rather consistently voiced not only in John but throughout the New Testament. When Peter tried to convince his hearers in Jerusalem, his climactic argument was the *fait accompli* of the resurrection (Acts 2:32, 33; 3:15; 4:10). In Hebrews 2:4 it is stated that God the Father endorsed the preaching of the apostles by means of miracles. In the Old Testament also, God's mighty acts in history constitute one medium of divine

revelation (Ps. 105:5; 150:2). Some scholars see in the retelling of God's "mighty acts" in history the genesis of the creeds. It is certain that God did reveal his nature and purpose by deeds as well as words. And these acts, as well as the words, sustained the faith of subsequent generations. Here, as elsewhere, the acts demonstrate and reinforce the truth of the words. Hence, in apostolic preaching the word was confirmed by the "signs." It is not the miracle *and* the Father as separate witnesses, therefore, but the Father expressing his will *through* miracles or "signs."

John is associated with the Christ in the matter of the *spoken word* of witnessing. The Father is associated with the Son in the matter of *deeds*. And Moses is associated with the Son with reference to the *written word*. It might well be asked why, if the Scriptures bear witness to the Christ, and if the Jews know and believe the Scriptures, these Jews are still unconvinced that Jesus' claims are true and valid? One of the reasons is given in this paragraph.

39 **Ye search the Scriptures.** Is this a command or a declaration; is the verb imperative (as in KJV) or indicative? Here the context seems determinative in favor of the indicative as in the ASV, RSV and NEB. "Only this interpretation makes sense of the *dokeite* which follows, and of the whole context" including the parallel description of John as the other

---

those portions believed to be anticipatory of the messianic age.

Christians today have the practical problem of knowing how binding upon them the precepts of the O. T. are. Some cite the Old Testament in justification of capital punishment; others believe the N. T. supercedes the O. T. at this point. Some find justification for war in the Old Testa-

ment; other Christians are convinced that the N. T. ethic makes it mandatory for them to abstain from all participation in modern warfare. For some earnest Christians the O. T. law of the tithe is mandatory; others think this too legalistic or too inadequate for one who should dedicate not only his tenth but his entire income to the Lord. A good principle to follow is

40 and ye will not come to me, that ye may have life.
41 I receive not glory from men.

witness (CKB). The *dokeite* ("think") here represents a mistaken opinion.[24] The term translated "search" connotes a wide number of synonyms such as "trace," "explore," "ransack." This the Pharisees of Jesus' day did. Indeed they conceived of religion as primarily the study of the Torah, the law of God's total revelation, especially the written Torah preserved in the twenty-two books of the Hebrew canon.

The preoccupation with the Scriptures goes back to the books of Moses where Israelites are exhorted to study the Torah night and day (Deut. 6:4-9). After the destruction of the temple and the return from the captivity in the sixth century B.C., the people realized that the temple sacrifices were not indispensable and they turned with still greater diligence to the Scriptures (Neh. 8:3ff.). The study of the law was a delight to the true son of Israel and not a burden (Ps. 19, 119). Thus the religion of the Jews became increasingly nomistic — legalistic and bookish. To a greater extent than has been the case with any other religious group except the Mohammedans they had become the "people of the book." Jesus did not disparage their perusal of the Scriptures; he was only saying that such study should lead them to find Him to whom the Scriptures bear witness. The Scriptures in themselves do not give life, but they do lead to the Life-giver. To use the metaphor of Paul, they are not the teacher, but

they are the pedagogue, the one who leads to the Christ (Gal. 3:24). The Jews believed that the Bible itself was the chief means of man's salvation, much the same as some liturgical churches think of the mass or the sacrament as the means of salvation. Jesus' point is that their problem is not a lack of diligence in Biblical study, nor any deficiency in knowledge of the Scriptures. The source of life is not in the parchments or even in the truth revealed therein. The source of life is in God, who even now was incarnate in their midst.

40 The Jews' search failed because of a lack of obedience — "ye will not come to me." Prejudice against an unauthorized Galilean "prophet," as they viewed him, had blinded their eyes. Evidence which should have been sufficient was blurred and dulled by an unresponsiveness on their part. They were not objective in their searching of the Scriptures and hence did not give its message opportunity to mold their thinking. Prejudice — deciding on emotional rather than logical grounds — still keeps the multitudes from the Source of Life.

41, 44 There are two kinds of "glory" (*doxa*) which most men seek. Jesus disclaimed any interest in the "glory," honor, rank, status, or prestige which men might bestow. His view of human nature was such that he believed that what is "highly esteemed among men is an abomination in the sight of God" (Luke 16:15). Like Paul, he esteemed men's judgment of

that of keeping in focus the emphasis of this passage, namely, that the Scriptures testify of Christ Jesus and should be consulted in that light. Another matter of practical helpfulness is to keep in mind that the O. T. is still binding except where modified by the N. T. The Gospel does not abrogate the Law for that would lead to antinomianism; instead the Gospel implements and thus fulfills the basic principles and purpose of the Law. It is the "law of the Spirit of Life" which fulfills the "Law of Sin and death" rather than abrogates it. In the O. T., obedience is the

important thing. In the N. T., love, demonstrated by obedience, is the fulfilling of the Law; there is no substitute for obedience even under grace.

As this chapter ends, Jesus successfully shows that the Law, the Pentateuch which both Sadducees and Pharisees profess to revere, instead of being an alternative to acceptance of the Son actually compels them to recognize the Son and his claims. It is Moses, rather than Jesus, who will judge them for rejecting the evidence God himself provides for their acceptance of life.

[24] Cf. John 5:45; 11:13, 31; 13:29; 16:2; 20:15.

42 But I know you, that ye have not the love of God in yourselves.

43 I am come in my Father's name, and ye receive me not: if another shall come in his own name, him ye will receive.

44 How can ye believe, who receive glory one of another, and the glory that *cometh* from the only God ye seek not?

45 Think not that I will accuse you to the Father: there is one that accuseth you, *even* Moses, on whom ye have set your hope.

46 For if ye believed Moses, ye would believe me; for he wrote of me.

47 But if ye believe not his writings, how shall ye believe my words?

---

relatively little consequence (I Cor. 4:3). This estimate of the relative worth of man's scale of values has its basis in such insights as those voiced in Isa. 55:9.

42 Unbelief, then, does not have its origin in any lack of convincing evidence. The problem is not external and objective; it is internal, personal, and subjective. The prophets attributed it to an innate perversity, an "evil imagination" which expressed itself generation after generation in a stubborn refusal to walk in God's ways.[25] Jewish writers of the inter-testamental period and into the first century A.D. were even more incisive and pessimistic in their appraisal of basic human nature.[26] The rabbis were impressed by the "evil imagination," which accounts for the chronic disposition to deviate from God's commandments, as reported in repeated apostasies in the Old Testament period and which continues to the present.[27] A similar appraisal of human nature, particularly of the prevailing disposition of Jewish leadership, is reflected in various parts of the New Testament, including Paul's characterization of his countrymen (Rom. 2). Stephen's indictment of Israel's leadership (Acts 7:51) reflects this as well: "How stubborn you are, heathen still at heart and deaf to the

truth! You always fight against the Holy Spirit" (NEB). It has been stated that such violent opposition to Jewish leadership, attributed to Jesus here and in ch. 8, could not have been possible in the first century and reflects instead the bitter hostility between church and synagogue of the second century.[28] But is this expression more hostile than that in Paul's letters and the book of Acts, both of which were composed before the Fourth Gospel?[29]

43 **I am come in my Father's name.** Jesus' sense of mission is again reflected in this statement, which stresses the source of his authority in the Father whom he represents as an ambassador. Reference to the "Father's name" occurs seven times in this Gospel (John 10:25; 12:28; 17:6, 11, 12, 26), making it a basic evidence of Jesus' messianic self-consciousness.

45 **Think not that I will accuse you to the Father.** This statement is in harmony with the earlier statement, "God sent not his Son into the world to condemn the world" (John 3:17 KJV), indicating that they stand self-condemned. Here, likewise, they are condemned by the very Scriptures to which they profess supreme allegiance. The authority of the Scriptures is accepted without question; Jesus simply

---

The list of five or six witnesses is basically only three: the *witness* (of John and Jesus), the *works* (of Father and Son), and the *word* of Scripture (Moses and the O. T.). The case made here is that the testimony of these is adequate ground for

belief and that nothing remains to be done but to accept or reject this testimony. The reader is thus confronted by John with the necessity of an "existential decision." They must, as Jesus' hearers, choose life or remain under the sentence of death.

[25] Reflected in the Heb. word *avah* and its synonyms, e.g., Jer. 3:21; cf. Gen. 6:5; 8:21.
[26] E.g., "O Adam, what hast thou done . . . all this multitude are going to corruption" (II Bar. 48:42); cf. IV Ezra 3:30; 4:30, 31; 7:118.
[27] Schechter, *Aspects of Rabbinic Theology*, p. 130; F. C. Porter, "The Yeser Hara," *Yale Biblical and Semitic Studies* (1901), p. 108.
[28] F. C. Grant, *John* in *Harper's Annotated Bible* (New York: Harper, 1956), p. 11.
[29] I Thess. 2:14-16 (probably the earliest Christian writing extant); Acts 13:45; 14:2, 19; 17:5, 13; 18:6; Matt. 23:1-36 (Matthew, Mark, and Luke are the criteria on the basis of which Grant thinks Jesus, as portrayed in John, is not historical!).

says that he, rather than they, is supported by the Pentateuch. The conviction that the Scriptures alone, apart from any supplemental evidence, are adequate as a basis for repentance and faith is also voiced in the parable of the rich man and Lazarus (Luke 16:29-31). It is in harmony also with Jesus' claim that he did not come to destroy the law or the prophets but rather to fulfill or implement them (Matt. 5:17). In the light of the Pharisees' devotion to the Torah it is difficult to imagine a more stinging rebuke than accusing them of not believing Moses.

To what extent did Moses testify of Jesus? "Since Moses bears witness to the mission of the Son (Luke 24:44; Acts 3:21ff; II Cor. 3:13-16), there is an essential unity between the work of the lawgiver and the work of the giver of life" (Hoskyns, p. 275). Hoskyns is probably correct in observing that the reference is not to a collection of messianic predictions only but to the entire Old Testament witness to the coming of the Righteous One, whom these very leaders should have been the first to recognize.

The discourse therefore does more than report the discussion which followed the cure of the cripple at the pool. It also analyzes "in depth" the basic issues that resulted in Jesus' being condemned rather than commended for performing a merciful act on the Sabbath. His answer probes the reasons for ancient Jewish unbelief and at the same time sets forth the reasons for unbelief in all ages. The clear inference is that unless one can bring himself to renounce the environing influence of his contemporaries, unless he refuses to conform to the present age, unless he values the favor of God more than the prestige among his fellows, in short, unless he repents, he cannot believe on the Son and find the secret of life.

# CHAPTER VI

$A$fter these things Jesus went away to the other side of the sea of Galilee, which is *the sea* of Tiberias.

2 And a great multitude followed him, because they beheld the signs which he did on them that were sick.

3 And Jesus went up into the mountain, and there he sat with his disciples.

4 Now the passover, the feast of the Jews, was at hand.

---

## EXEGESIS

1 **After these things** (*Meta tauta*). This phrase does not denote with John an immediate sequence of events. A whole year may have intervened between the events of ch. 5 and those in ch. 6. **Of Tiberias** is a second genitive construction in apposition with **of Galilee**. There are textual variants which relieve the awakwardness of the two genitives but Barrett thinks that "clumsy text" was as originally written (CKB, p. 227). Tiberias was the Roman name for the lake of Galilee and was given in honor of the Roman emperor Tiberias (A.D. 14-37). The city by that name, located on the southwest shore of the lake, was built by Herod Antipas about A.D. 22 to 26 (Jos., *Ant.*, XVIII. ii. 3).

2 The verb **followed** (*ēkolouthei*, imperfect tense) presents a graphic picture of the crowd in action, given in greater detail than elsewhere (cf. Mark 6:32; Matt. 14:13). The reason given for the following of such a large group was their **seeing the signs** (miracles). Whether they also wanted to be healed or were attracted to his words because of the healing ministry is not stated (cf. v. 26).

3, 4 **Into the mountain** is rendered "hillside" (NEB) or "hills" (RSV) in some newer versions because there are no real "mountains" bordering the lake. It is, however, surrounded by what one might call steep hillsides. The lake is nearly

---

## EXPOSITION

### 2. THE FOURTH "SIGN" AT THE SECOND PASSOVER (6:1-71)

Ch. 6 brings before the reader another Old Testament picture. In the first chapter one could catch a glimpse of Jacob, in flight from Esau, learning in a dream that Bethel was at "the gate of heaven" (cf. Gen. 28:12-17; John 1:51). In Ch. 3 an episode from the Sinai desert foreshadowed the cross which gives life (Num. 21:8; cf. John 3:14). In ch. 4 the lesson on the Water of Life was placed against the background of the patriarchal struggle for water (Gen. 26:15-22; 33:19; cf. John 4:5). There was an echo of Moses, the judge and lawgiver, in ch. 5. Here the presentation of Jesus as the Bread of Life is placed against the background of the Israelites' struggle for survival in the Sinai desert and the miraculous manna which sustained life.

#### a. Five Thousand Fed (6:1-15)

Jesus' popularity was now at its height. It was about the middle of his public ministry, after his initial successes and before hostility became prevalent in the north. Jesus' leading his disciples into a solitary place indicates that he needed time for rest and recuperation. Such an inference is consistent with the portrait in the Synoptic accounts, which quote Jesus as saying, "come apart into a deserted place and rest awhile" (Mark 6:31; Matt. 14:13; Luke 9:10). In each of the Synoptic accounts this retirement to a deserted place and the feeding of the crowd follow immediately after the beheading of John the Baptist. It may well be that Jesus felt

153

5 Jesus therefore lifting up his eyes, and seeing that a great multitude cometh unt
him, saith unto Philip, Whence are we to buy bread, that these may eat?

6 And this he said to prove him: for he himself knew what he would do.

---

700 feet below sea level, set in a deep basin surrounded by hills. The town of Safed, fifteen miles distant and visible from the lake, is about 4000 feet above the surface of the water. The hills "on the other side" (from Capernaum) would be at the eastern side and are quite steep. The traditional site of the feeding, however, is on the northwest edge of the lake, perhaps because it is more conveniently reached by pilgrims. The northwest shore of the lake, however, was then thickly populated; there would have been no need of a miracle of feeding there since they could have gone home or to a nearby hamlet for food.[1]

The Passover was at hand. Unless the "feast" mentioned in 5:1 is also the Passover, this is the second of the three Passovers of Jesus' public ministry (John 2:13; 11:55).

5 Therefore (oun) is a conjunction which always serves to alert the reader to look backward and forward. John's use of this conjunction merits careful study In the first century it was often used as somewhat colorless conjunction, merely t connect the thought of one sentence wit that of another. Here, however, it is use in an explanatory sense and is best trans lated "now." In the phrase cometh unt him (erchetai pros auton) the verb is i the present tense, denoting action in prog ress. The same crowd that previousl was following him is now described a gradually reassembling towards (pros him.

6 Jesus asked the question not for h own information but to prove him (peir zōn auton); this verb is used primarily i the gospels to mean "to tempt." It is use here in its general, neutral sense meanin "to test," as in II Cor. 13:5, "examin yourselves." It was a common practic with Jesus to "lead out," that is, "to edu cate" his disciples rather than drilling in formation into them. This testing wa

---

the need of retirement in order for him and his disciples to think through and pray over the implications of this tragedy and to chart their future course. But the opportunity for rest and reflection was denied them by the popular demand for his services. This opportunity did not come until later, when they retired to Caesarea Philippi (Mark 8:27).

Luke places the area near Bethsaida (Luke 9:10) while Mark and Matthew indicate that it was a desert area (Mark 6:31-35; Matt. 14:13-15). The most probable site appears to be near the northeast shore of the lake, a few miles south of Bethsaida Julias and north of Wadi es Samakh.[a] Today the place is virtually inaccesible except by boat. This seems to have been the case in Jesus' day, since the people then came on foot and by boat.

Several lessons can be drawn from the incident. Even Jesus and his disciples

needed times of retirement for rest an reorientation. Human nature is such tha an alternation between activity and rest between publicity and privacy seems im perative. It indicates that Jesus was reall human and needed to take "time out" fo prayer, reflection, and rest. Another les son is in the apparent paradox betwee divine plenitude and economy. Jesus gav generously of the multiplied food but late carefully gathered the fragments.

To what extent does the narration re flect the eucharistic practices of the churc at the time? Many think it is not s much an historical account as an histori cal kernel around which the author elabor ates a story designed to justify sacramenta practices of his day. If John's were th only account, this widely held interpreta tion might be very plausible. But th other three accounts present essentiall the same picture of the event. In fac this is the only miracle recounted by al

---

[1] E. Kraeling, Bible Atlas (Chicago: Rand McNally, 1956), p. 386.

[2] See J. R. Mantey, "John's Use of Oun" (Th. D. Thesis, Southern Baptist Theological Seminary Library, Louisville, Kentucky).

[a] E. Kraeling, Bible Atlas (Chicago: Rand McNally, 1956), p. 387; International Standard Bible Encyclopedia, V, Plate, 14.

7 Philip answered him, Two hundred shillings' worth of bread is not sufficient for them, that every one may take a little.

8 One of his disciples, Andrew, Simon Peter's brother, saith unto him,

9 There is a lad here, who hath five barley loaves, and two fishes: but what are these among so many?

10 Jesus said, Make the people sit down.   Now there was much grass in the place. So the men sat down, in number about five thousand.

11 Jesus therefore took the loaves; and having given thanks, he distributed to them that were set down; likewise also of the fishes as much as they would.

---

to prepare the disciples for the forthcoming lesson.   John notes again that he himself knew the outcome and was not seeking information.   The author thus creates the image of Jesus as one who was never surprised at a turn of events because he knew in advance how things would develop (cf. v. 64).   Jesus was always in command of the situation.

7 **Two hundred shillings** is translated in the NEB as "twenty pounds."   The Greek "denarius," as stated in the RSV, is today worth about twenty cents.   The denarius was the usual pay for one day's labor (Matt. 20:2, 9, 13).   The cost of feeding this congregation would have been almost as much as a year's pay for a common laborer.   This amount, said Philip, would barely suffice for a lunch, much less a full meal.

9 One hero of the day was an unnamed boy who had either brought his lunch or

something to sell, a **lad** (*paidarion,* diminutive form of *pais*).   This diminutive word does not occur elsewhere in the New Testament but is found in the LXX (II Kings 4:38-41) where it describes Elisha's servant.   Thus it did not always denote extreme youth (CKB, p. 229).   **Barley** (*krithinous*) was considered an inferior type of bread eaten by poor people.   Accompanying it were **fishes** (*opsaria*), cooked fish (cf. John 21:9-13).

10 **Make the people sit down** (*anapesein*); actually "lie down" or recline, as the people customarily did when eating.

11 **Jesus therefore** (in this context "then" is better) . . . **distributed** (*diedōken*, aor., act.), a simple report of action completed.   In the synoptic accounts imperfect and present tenses emphasize the process of breaking that the disciples might continue distributing the food to the large crowd.[3]

---

four of the Evangelists.   One is justified, therefore, in concluding that the narrative itself rests on solid factual grounds.   It is in the discourse growing out of this miracle that John's distinctive interpretation is in evidence.   Two important lessons are underscored by this episode; they are somewhat paradoxical.   The first lesson is that man's physical needs are a matter of concern to our Lord.   The second is that "man shall not live by bread alone"; his need for spiritual food is far greater than the desire for physical satisfaction.   Both of these messages are relevant to the present: on the one hand they stress the importance of "the social implications of the gospel" — that the church should concern itself with the cry of mankind for "bread."   On the other

hand the message of this chapter is a protest against secularism, against political philosophies that assume that man's only needs are material and against a purely economic interpretation of history.

The problem of food distribution is still, after two millenia, very acute.   In the United States the major problem is that of having too much to eat.   In many of the populous older areas of the world, such as China and India, the problem is the opposite, that of insufficient food supply. It is not by accident that in our Lord's model prayer there is the petition, "give us our daily bread."   Christ and his true church are not insensitive to the worldwide cry for sufficient nourishment.   The combination attributed to the Salvation Army — "soap, soup, and salvation" —

---

[3] The Greek word behind "having given thanks" is *eucharisteō* rather than *eulogeō* as in the Synoptic parallels. . . .   The two words seem to be used synonymously in the N. T.   In partristic writings, however, *eucharistia* was the preferred term for the sacrament of the Lord's Supper.   This is one of the few instances in the N. T. in which a grace before meals is reported, although it was a well-established Jewish custom. Whether its mention here has sacramental significance is not certain.   See JHB, II, 180, 181.

12 And when they were filled, he saith unto his disciples, Gather up the broken pieces which remain over, that nothing be lost.

13 So they gathered them up, and filled twelve baskets with broken pieces from the five barley loaves, which remained over unto them that had eaten.

14 When therefore the people saw the sign which he did, they said, This is of a truth the prophet that cometh into the world.

15 Jesus therefore perceiving that they were about to come and take him by force, to make him king, withdrew again into the mountain himself alone.

16 And when evening came, his disciples went down unto the sea;

---

12 **They were filled** (*eneplēsthēsan* aor. pass.); the prepositional prefix denotes completeness or fulness — "to fill in," "to fill completely." The **broken pieces** (*klasmata*) were "not crumbs or scraps on the ground, but pieces broken by Jesus (Mark 6:14) and not consumed" (ATR, V, 99). Jesus did not do things halfway — the people were fully satisfied.

13 The **twelve baskets** (*kophinous*, cf. "coffin") were large wicker baskets mentioned in each of the four Gospel accounts (viz., Mark 6:43; Matt. 14:20; Luke 9:17). It is significant that in the feeding of the *four* thousand (Mark 8:19, 20; Matt. 16:9, 10) another term for basket (*sphyris*) is used, attesting two separate miracles of feeding. This latter was a flexible, mat basket coming in various sizes.

14, 15 John, like the Synoptists, usually reports the reaction of the people to Jesus' words and works. **This is the prophet** was probably an allusion to Deuteronomy 18:

15, a passage with messianic connotations (cf. John 1:21; 11:27). The phrase is peculiar to John and Acts (Acts 3:22; 7: 37), but it was a political rather than a spiritual leader that they expected. Then, as now, deliverance was sought in the external realm of politics, rather than in the inner realm of the spirit. **Therefore** (or "now") introduces not a conclusion but an exploration (D-M, p. 253). **To make him king** (*hina poiēsōsen basilea*), a purpose clause with aorist subjunctive, denotes immediacy of intent on the part of the freshly-fed multitude. Jesus met the crisis by sending the disciples away and withdrawing himself from the multitude. Unlike most people, who seek honor and power, Jesus refused to accept the highest office his nation could give him. Instead he went off alone to pray.

This account is similar to that recorded in Mark (6:47-52) and Matthew (14:23-33), but more concise. John gives just

---

and the modern agricultural missionary are consistent with the Spirit of Christ. It is because the church has too often deliberately catered to the middle and upper classes that it has to a large extent lost rapport with the masses whose major concern is "daily bread." It seems likely that Jesus would have performed this miracle for no other reason than to relieve distress, to prevent their "fainting by the wayside." The miracle was not designed merely to set the stage for the eucharistic discourse which followed, however important this discourse is.

### b. Jesus, Master of the Storm (6: 16-21)

Was the episode of the storm at sea one of the "signs" or miracles of this Gospel? In the Mark account, as in John's, he enters the boat. In Matthew's

account, Peter joins Jesus, also walking on the water. John does not report the cessation of the wind but it is implied. In all three instances the arrival of Jesus puts an end to their trouble. It appears probable that John wanted to suggest the factor of human response to the Master, as he did elsewhere — when they willed to receive Jesus (cf. 1:12) their objective was reached. It is obvious that John's account, like that of others, intends to report a miracle, or rather two. Jesus walked on the water, and he stilled the storm. But unlike the other "signs" mentioned by John this one evoked no discussion and no new expression of faith on the part of the disciples, even though the Synoptists report the profound impression created by the miracle. This miracle was not performed publicly like the other "signs" listed by this Evangelist. It seems

17 and they entered into a boat, and were going over the sea unto Capernaum. And it was now dark, and Jesus had not yet come to them.

18 And the sea was rising by reason of a great wind that blew.

19 When therefore they had rowed about five and twenty or thirty furlongs, they behold Jesus walking on the sea, and drawing nigh unto the boat: and they were afraid.

20 But he saith unto them, It is I; be not afraid.

---

enough of the background events to set forth Christ as master even of the elements of nature.

**17, 18** The imperfect tense **were going** (*ērchonto*) indicates what the disciples were attempting to do. John states that darkness overtook them in the process and that Jesus was not with them; they were alone in the dark! As sometimes happens on the Sea of Galilee, a **great wind that blew** (*anemou megalou pneontos,* a genitive absolute construction) caused destructive waves. The wind not only caused giant waves, but it was coming from the wrong direction (Mark 6:48). It was a terrifying situation even for these experienced fishermen; their lives were in danger. Anyone who has experienced a sudden storm on an inland lake can well understand their fright.

**19 When therefore** (*oun*) here means "now" (D-M, pp. 235f.). **Thirty furlongs** (*stadia*); the *stadion* was 606 ¾ feet in length and the lake about 40 stadia wide in this area. Thus they were about three fourths of the way across when Jesus appeared to them. **They behold** (*theōrousin*) is graphic historical present, followed by present active participles, *peripatounta* ("walking") and *ginomenon,* ("coming"), all denoting a moving picture scene.

**20 Be not afraid** (*mē phobeisthe*) is a present middle imperative form meaning "stop being afraid." Jesus commanded them to fear no more (cf. v. 19) and he also removed the source of their fear. John does not mention Peter's walking on the water or the stilling of the storm (cf. Matt. 14:28-33; Mark 6:51-52). **They were willing** (*ēthelon*) or "they were wishing to receive him into the boat . . ." (JHB). They became willing to receive the Savior, and the adverse circumstances of the situation were reversed. With Christ aboard they quickly reached their destination.

In v. 20 there is to be noted another instance of the expression "I am" (*egō eimi*). Here it simply identifies the speaker as Jesus, rather than a spectre, and, as in the identical phrase in Mark 6:50, means "It is I, fear not."

In the extended discourse which followed the two recorded events near the lake, Jesus, using the manna in the wilderness as a background, states that he is

---

unlikely therefore that John intended this even to be listed in the same category as these "signs." To John, a "sign" appears to have been both the miracle *and* the reaction to it in terms of belief and unbelief.

At the very height of the crisis the Lord of life suddenly appears. He who had demonstrated his authority over disease (John 4:50), over evil spirits (Mark 1:26, 34), over sin (Mark 2:5), in exposition of the Scriptures (Mark 1:22), and in the multiplying of food (John 6:11), now shows his authority in the realm of nature. This miracle was three-fold: walking on the water (overcoming gravity), stilling the storm (ordering the cosmos), and conquering space: ("immediately" [eutheōs]) they were at land.

The picture is a vivid one. One can envision Jesus alone on the mountain as darkness deepens, engaged in earnest prayer to God his Father. The disciples were on the water rowing back toward the friendly western shore. At this point of the culmination of his Galilean ministry Jesus faces the same temptation to the kingship, which according to the Synoptic accounts he had also faced after his baptism (cf. Matt. 4:1). It is a reminder that at our times of crises, times when basic decisions must be made, times when we have little or no leisure, we should take time out for concentrated prayer.

21 They were willing therefore to receive him into the boat: and straightway the boat was at the land whither they were going.

22 On the morrow the multitude that stood on the other side of the sea saw that there was no other boat there, save one, and that Jesus entered not with his disciples into the boat, but *that* his disciples went away alone

23 (howbeit there came boats from Tiberias nigh unto the place where they ate the bread after the Lord had given thanks):

24 when the multitude therefore saw that Jesus was not there, neither his disciples, they themselves got into the boats, and came to Capernaum, seeking Jesus.

25 And when they found him on the other side of the sea, they said unto him, Rabbi, when camest thou hither?

---

the true and only bread from heaven that can satisfy the soul's deepest needs.

**22, 23 The multitude that stood on the other side** (*ho ochlos ho hestēkōs*). The perfect tense, here translated "stood," implies that the crowd had remained in the area of the miraculous feeding. **Had given thanks** (*eucharistēsantos*) is an aorist participle in a genitive absolute construction. The English term "Eucharist" is a transliteration from this Greek word which in the early church was the favorite designation of the Lord's Supper. It seems as appropriate as the term now currently used.

**24** Here is a resumption and clarification of the statements in v. 22, v. 23 being parenthetical. They went **seeking Jesus.** What a noble quest when done with right motives! Apparently the crowd remained on the eastern shore of the lake, near the site of the feeding, all during the stormy night (v. 22). They had witnessed the departure of the disciples, without their Master, in a larger boat the night before. The language of the ASV suggests that one boat still remained and that they noticed it at daylight. The tense of the indirect discourse in Greek retains the tense of the main verb; hence what they saw could refer to an experience of the evening before rather than what the morning light disclosed.[4] The latter is the interpretation as reflected in the RSV and in the NEB.

Presently another group arrived in little boats from Tiberias. Those that had remained by the shore all night joined the new arrivals in their boats and together the flotilla set out in the direction of Capernaum in quest of Jesus. The excitement throughout the whole region was apparent.

**25 They found** (*heurontes*) **him.** The verb is the same as in John 1:41 where Andrew found his brother Simon and said, "We have found the Messiah!" Here they found Jesus but not to have him

---

Another lesson is apparent in the sudden appearance of Jesus at the height of the storm. The first reaction of the disciples was one of fear, as they thought he was a ghost. But had they shunned his presence presumably the storm would have continued unabated. They welcomed him into their midst, however, and suddenly their troubles were over. Prior to his appearance they had struggled desperately at rowing; with him aboard there was peace and rest. With him present we also can meet every situation. In these days of hyper-tension Jesus' presence brings peace.

A New England poet, in the tense years before the Civil War, discovered this truth.

*We may not climb the heavenly
   steeps
   To bring the Lord Christ down;
In vain we search the lowest deeps,
   For him no depths can drown:*

*But warm, sweet, tender, even yet
   A present help is he;
And faith has still its Olivet,
   And love its Galilee.*

    \*    \*    \*    \*    \*    \*

*O sabbath rest by Galilee! O calm
   of hills above,
Where Jesus knelt to share with Thee
   The silence of eternity,
Interpreted by love!*

---

[4] Cf. D-M, p. 296; J. H. Greenlee, *op. cit.*, p. 74.

26 Jesus answered them and said, Verily, verily, I say unto you, Ye seek me, not because ye saw signs, but because ye ate of the loaves and were filled.

27 Work not for the food which perisheth, but for the food which abideth unto eternal life, which the Son of man shall give unto you: for him the Father, *even* God, hath sealed.

28 They said therefore unto him, what must we do, that we may work the works of God?

29 Jesus answered and said unto them, This is the work of God, that ye believe on him whom he hath sent.

---

become their Savior. To hear him and to witness what he did for people was the greatest experience of all their lives. No doubt as long as they lived they often narrated to others what Jesus had said and done, even though it is unlikely that many of them became believers. **Ye saw signs** (*sēmeia*); with these words Jesus administered a mild rebuke to the seekers. He accused them of coming not for further evidences of his deity but for free food. "Sign" is John's characteristic designation of a miracle by means of which Jesus authenticated his claims.

27 **Work not** (*ergazesthe*). As in the discussion with the Samaritan woman (John 4:14), working for food or drink is contrasted with receiving them as God's gift. The contrast in both places is two-fold: between earning and accepting, and between material and spiritual goods. The main emphasis is on the superior value of spiritual over material blessings. Here the seekers, with considerable self-esteem, are eager to get to work. Jesus replies that they should stop working for material food and begin working for the eternal food that lasts and satisfies forever, an appro-

priate command for people today. The spiritual food comes from the Son of man who has been approved, attested ("sealed"). In the term "sealed" (*esphragisen*) John may have had in mind the statement of Matt. 3:17; Mark 1:11; Luke 3:2: "This is my beloved Son in whom I am well pleased." The term is sometimes used of the sealing of a tomb for security (Matt. 27:66), a means of identification (Rev. 7:3), or an eschatological seal (Ezek. 9:4; Isa. 44:5). It refers also to the incorporation of the believer into the body of Christ by the seal of the Spirit (Eph. 1:13 cf. 4:30). It corresponds to the rabbinic practice of stamping approved meats as *kosher,* officially endorsed for use. Jesus presented himself thus with the Father's seal of approval; he was *kosher.*

29 **This is the work of God** (*to ergon tou Theou*). Jesus here interprets how we may receive eternal life, not by working for it, as v. 27 might imply, but by depending upon Christ alone for salvation. Thus we work for God when we become his life-time servants. Salvation is always a gift, but appreciation for it

---

*Drop Thy still dews of quietness, Till all our strivings cease;*
*Take from our souls the strain and stress, And let our ordered lives confess*
*The beauty of Thy peace.*[b]

### c. Works or Faith? (6:22-29)

The argument in this section over the relative merits of faith and works recalls the *sole fidism* of the Protestant Reformation. In order to counteract the legalism of the Pharisees, the N. T. evangelists stressed the factor of faith alone (e.g., Eph. 2:8). In other contexts, however,

the importance of good works is emphasized (Jas. 2:14-26; Matt. 25:31-46). It is even found where least expected (Rom. 2:6; Gal. 6:7-10), in the midst of an emphasis on salvation by faith alone. The paradox of faith and works, of freedom and bondage was a major concern of Paul and of the Reformers (cf. Gal. 5:1, 13). This emphasis on faith rather than good works was never more sorely needed than now in this age of activism. It is needed to counteract the widespread assumption that the way to become a Christian is to get busy with "church work," and the implication often voiced at funer-

[b] J. G. Whittier, in *Hymns of the Living Faith,* p. 396.

30 They said therefore unto him, What then doest thou for a sign, that we may see, and believe thee? what workest thou?

31 Our fathers ate the manna in the wilderness; as it is written, He gave them bread out of heaven to eat.

---

is expressed in service to God and to others. The Work of God is placed in contrast to their own self-effort, on which they had based their hopes (v. 28), and then defined as belief (*pisteuete eis*) on Jesus as the one sent by God. The use of the present tense here suggests that Jesus meant a trust in him for salvation that is more than an isolated act of faith. It is rather a life of faith and service, a life-time relationship. The emphasis on belief is consistent with the over-all theme of this Gospel.

**30 They said therefore unto him, What then doest thou for a sign . . . what workest thou?** *Therefore* (*oun*) can better be translated "in reply" here; it has "responsive" connotations about thirty times in this Gospel.[5] **Believe** (*pisteusōmen*) has the force of "come to" or "begin to believe."** In order to justify their present attitude of being non-committal, the Jews challenged Jesus to give them further evidence as a basis for their belief. The challenge to do something comparable to bringing manna from heaven, as Moses did, is

rather strange in view of the fact that he had just provided for their hunger the day before. This may have been the voice of an articulate minority, which served as the occasion for the long discourse on the bread of life. Here, and on similar occasions, the theme is driven home that unbelief is not due to lack of evidence; it persists in spite of the evidence (cf. Luke 16:31).

This demand for signs is paralleled in the Synoptic accounts by a similar request from the Pharisees (Mark 8:12; Matt. 12:38; 16:1-4; Luke 11:29). Jesus did not accede to their demand since it was not sincere (Mark 8:11). Instead he replied that his coming was as truly a "sign" as was the coming of Jonah to the Ninevites.

**31 Our fathers ate manna in the wilderness, as it is written.** This is a reference to Exod. 16:15 and perhaps a quotation from Ps. 78:24. It brings into focus another important chapter in Old Testament history. As indicated earlier, this background is distinctive and emphatic in

---

als that the basis for hope of life eternal is "good works."

### d. The Bread of Life (vv. 30-59)
#### (1) *Life Available* (vv. 30-40)

It is characteristic of this Gospel that attention centers in the person of Jesus. In the O. T., God, as Provider of his inheritance, sends bread to relieve hunger. As with the discussion in ch. 4 where Jesus said he was the source of life-giving water, here Jesus is the source of food. Here he not only gives bread but he is himself the "bread of life." This is characteristic of the Fourth Gospel. Jesus not only *teaches* the truth but *is* the truth; he not only *shows* the way but *is* the way.

The similitude is a striking one. Bread is still the staple diet of Palestinians, indeed in most of the world it is still the "staff of life." It is a fitting analogy

therefore because it is important to so many. Here "bread" is meaningful because it is related to Life. Colwell and Titus point out that this chapter, like other "signs" moves in three stages.[c] There is first the *historical* occasion. This leads them to follow Jesus further and to demand that he become their king. The second stage is the *assertion* by Jesus that he is himself the bread of life and that they must eat of him in order to have life. They interpret this *literally*. Lastly, the *spiritual* significance is set forth: "It is the spirit that giveth life; the flesh profiteth nothing: the words that I have spoken unto you they are spirit and they are life" (John 6:43).

In contrast to the manna that came from God and satisfied only a day's hunger, Jesus declares that he is the real, spiritual bread that can satisfy the hunger of a lifetime.

---

[5] D-M, p. 254.  The same may be said for vv. 32, 34, 35, 53.
[c] E. C. Colwell & E. L. Titus, *The Gospel of the Spirit* (New York: Harper, 1953). pp. 52-58.

32 Jesus therefore said unto them, Verily, verily, I say unto you, It was not Moses that gave you the bread out of heaven; but my Father giveth you the true bread out of heaven.

33 For the bread of God is that which cometh down out of heaven, and giveth life unto the world.

34 They said therefore unto him, Lord, evermore give us this bread.

35 Jesus said unto them, I am the bread of life: he that cometh to me shall not hunger, and he that believeth on me shall never thirst.

---

John's presentation of the Gospel. The important part that such "mighty acts" of God played in the theology of the Israelites is illustrated in the historical psalms such as Pss. 78:24 and 105:40. This demand of the Jews is the more significant when related to a widespread belief then current that the Messiah would outdo Moses in performing miracles. This belief is reflected in later rabbinic sayings to the effect that as the former redeemer caused manna to descend so the latter redeemer will cause manna to come down (as in Ps. 72:16).[6] He gave them bread (Ps. 78:24) has God the Father as the antecedent of "He." In the light of v. 32, however, the implication is that these Jews regarded Moses as having given the manna. In any case their point in making the challenge was that anyone claiming to be the Messiah should provide something comparable to the heaven-sent manna of Moses' day.

32 Jesus therefore (oun) said. (Oun is better translated "in reply" here and also in vv. 34, 35, 53.) Jesus' purpose in pointing out that the manna really came from "my Father" was to set Moses in proper perspective. The implication is clear that the same God who gave food from heaven in Moses' day is doing it also at the present time. The people reply that this is what they want (v. 34).

35 I am the bread of life (egō eimi ho artos tēs zōēs). In contrast to the manna that came from God but satisfied only a day's hunger, Jesus declares that he is himself the real spiritual bread that can satisfy the hunger of a lifetime.

He that cometh and he that believeth are translations of present participles, denoting not a single act of coming or believing but a continuous coming and believing. Thus lifetime faith is implied. This "bread" is significant because it comes down from heaven, that is, it is a miraculous gift of God in contrast to ordinary food. The "coming down from heaven" (v. 33) recalls the conversations with Nicodemus (3:13) and Nathaniel (1:51). Jesus seized upon the reference to heaven-sent manna and said in effect, "you now have something even better than heaven-sent manna; what is your response to this miracle?" The combination of coming and believing is characteristic of this Gospel.

---

(2) Real Manna (vv. 41-51)

The protest voiced by the multitude arose out of familiarity. It supports the assertion made earlier (4:43) that a prophet has no honor in his own country. This statement is, in the Synoptic accounts, attributed to those who heard his parables (Matt. 13:55) and to the Nazarenes who heard him preach in their synagogue (Luke 4:22 cf. John 7:27). "Familiarity breeds contempt" and the Galilean's reaction to Jesus was no exception to the "rule." In reply the Master warned them not to repeat the sin of their ancestors who murmured in the wilderness in spite of the God-given manna. Gradually Jesus leads up to his main assertion: "I am the bread of life." Jesus as he presents something even better than water from the patriarchal well so he is a gift from God more precious than the life-giving manna their forefathers ate. Jesus is asking them to give the same recognition to the miracle occurring in their midst that they are willing to give to the manna of Moses' day.

Some people are much more ready to have faith with reference to the past than they are with reference to the present. They tend to assume that God's "mighty

---

6 S-B, II, 481; JHB, I, 194.

36 But I said unto you, that ye have seen me, and yet believe not.
37 All that which the Father giveth me shall come unto me; and him that cometh
to me I will in no wise cast out.

---

Indeed "coming" is roughly the equivalent of "believing." It indicates more than intellectual acceptance of a belief; it denotes personal commitment, an "existential" believing.

36 Ye have seen me and believe not recalls the words of the risen Savior to Thomas (John 20:29), "blessed are they that have not seen, and yet have believed." The term "I am" (*ego eimi*) coupled with a predicate is one of the most important characteristics of John's Gospel. The expression occurs 38 times in the Fourth Gospel as compared with 14 occurrences in the other three together. In the Johannine usage there are 8 similitudes in which this expression occurs.[7] The term *"ego"* occurs 134 times in John as compared with 29 occurrences in Matthew, 17 in Mark, and 23 in Luke. As used by John the term "adds dignity and impressiveness to the sentence" as in Sirach 24 where Wisdom makes her majestic claims. (JHB, I, cxvii).

In the Old Testament the *ego eimi* (LXX) "is the divine word of self-revelation and command" (CKB, p. 242). The phrase is impressively associated with Jehovah as speaker as in Gen. 17:1; Exod.

3:6, 17; 15:26; 20:2; Ps. 35:3; Jer. 3:12; 23:23; Isa. 61:8. In Isa. 51:12 and 43:25; the phrase is doubled for emphasis. New Testament passages reflecting the language of the O. T. also use the term, as Rev. 1:8, 17; 21:6; 22:13; (cf. Isa. 41: 4; 44:6; 48:12).[8]

Numerous parallels in contemporary pagan cultures have been noted, especially in connection with the worship of Isis in Hermetic writings.[9] The significance of these literary parallels, as Deissmann points out, is that John wrote in a style familiar to the people of his day, the common people. Also significant is that to Jesus' listeners the repeated "I am" (*ego eimi*) would have the connotations of deity, whether theirs was a Hebrew (cf. Pro. 8:12-31) or a Greek background. As used here it seems unlikely that any sacramental symbolism is involved.

37 All that (*pan ho*) is a phrase which illustrates that collective use of the neuter singular. It is a classic idiom, also found in 6:39; 17:2, 24; I John 5:4. I will in no wise cast out (*ou me ekbalo exo*) uses a strong double negation, such as occurs twice in v. 35. Jesus thus emphasized that he would never forsake the *faithful* be-

---

acts" are limited to past ages and recorded in a sacred record and hence they are not in a frame of mind to expect or accept miracles in the present. This requires a faith that is not rigid, a spiritual tone that is alert and perceptive, rather than merely traditional and repetitive. The people had not known of miracles for so long that they assumed that the age of miracles was past. They were slow to recognize God at work. This same attitude of spiritual lethargy hinders Christ today.

### (3) *"A Hard Saying"* (vv. 52-59)

The Jews misunderstood Jesus' statement about eating his flesh and drinking his blood. Likewise Christians today have diverse interpretations for these verses, which admittedly contain "a hard saying" (v. 60). The literalness of Jesus' reported language perplexed Nicodemus (John 3:4) and now offended many of his hearers. Some commentators see in this discourse an explanation of the Eu-

---

[7] 6:35, 41, 48, 51, "I am the bread of life."
8:12, "I am the light of the world." (cf. 8:18, 23).
10:7, 9, "I am the door of the sheepfold."
10:11, 14, "I am the good shepherd."
11:25, "I am the resurrection and the life."
14:6, "I am the way and the truth and the life."
15:1, 5, "I am the vine."
[8] Also Rev. 2:23 (cf. Jer. 11:20; 17:10); 22:16 (cf. Isa. 11:1; 60:3). For a full discussion see JHB, I, cvvi-cxxi.
[9] E.g., *"Ego eimi Theou Kynos astro epitellousa* (I am he that raiseth in the star of the Dog god)." Deissmann, *op. cit.*, p. 139.

38 For I am come down from heaven, not to do mine own will, but the will of him that sent me.

39 And this is the will of him that sent me, that of all that which he hath given me I should lose nothing, but should raise it up at the last day.

40 For this is the will of my Father, that every one that beholdeth the Son, and believeth on him, should have eternal life; and I will raise him up at the last day.

41 The Jews therefore murmured concerning him, because he said, I am the bread which came down out of heaven.

42 And they said, Is not this Jesus, the son of Joseph, whose father and mother we know? how doth he now say, I am come down out of heaven?

43 Jesus answered and said unto them, Murmur not among yourselves.

---

liever. It assures the sincere seeker of a welcome "at the Father's house."

**38 I am come down from heaven** (*katabebēka,* perf. tense), signifies a past action (the Incarnation) the results of which still continue (D-M, p. 179). The descent of the Son of Man from heaven to earth is another emphasis characteristic of this Gospel. It is found or alluded to in 1:51; 3:13, 31; 6:38, 42; 62; 12:32. Such passages emphasize the deity of Jesus Christ, contrasting his pre-existent state with his present one (cf. Rom. 10:6; Phil. 2:6). **Not to do mine own will**; the present tense of the verb (*poiō*) denotes continuance, i.e., to continue doing God's will, a noble goal for every Christian!

**39 I should lose nothing** (*mē apolesō*) or, "I should not lose any one of them." The neuter relative pronoun is equivalent to a masculine one here, being of the same gender as *pan* in the independent clause (cf. note on v. 37). Judas was an exception. In John 17:12 Jesus prayed, "I

protected them by the power of thy name, those whom thou hast given me, and kept them safe. Not one of them is lost except the man who must be lost, for the Scripture has to be fulfilled" (NEB).

**40 Believeth** (*pisteuōn;* pres. act. part.) in the present tense denotes faith in Christ month after month and year after year. **I will raise him up** (*anastēsō auton*) not only does the believer become an heir to eternal life when he accepts Christ, but he also has the firm promise of his Lord that he is to experience a resurrection — a present realization plus a guarantee of a new and everlasting body.

**41 Therefore** (*oun*) is best rendered "now" in this context. It introduces the reaction of the murmuring Jews to Jesus' claim that he was the bread of God.

**42 How does he now say** (*pōs nyn legei*)? they know Jesus only as the son of Joseph and Mary. Consequently they have real difficulty in accepting him as the Son of God. People of succeeding

---

charist.[d] Others view it as only spiritual and symbolic (BFW, II, 256).

Ch. 6 illustrates well a characteristic of the Fourth Gospel, that of moving from the literal and physical meaning to the spiritual. This movement is noticeable in ch. 3. There Jesus told Nicodemus, "ye must be born again," or "from above." Nicodemus took these words literally and hence thought them absurd. Next Jesus called attention to himself as the one who comes "from above." The final phase was that in which the ultimate issues of life and death were discussed (John 3:16, 17). The pattern is repeated in ch. 4. There is the statement by Jesus

that he is living water. The woman of Samaria, thinking in physical terms, wonders how Jesus can obtain this water, since the well is deep. Then Jesus identifies himself personally with the water. The final stage goes from Jesus' personal involvement to the basic issues of life. The scene in ch. 6 repeats this sequence. There is first the statement by Jesus that "the bread of God . . . comes down from heaven and gives life to the world" (v. 33). The Jews, taking his words literally, request this bread as the Samaritan woman asked for water (v. 34). Jesus then tells them that he is talking about spiritual bread and that he is himself the "bread of

[d] P. J. Temple, "The Eucharist in St. John 6," CBQ, Oct. 1947, p. 450; Hoskyns, p. 298.

44 No man can come to me, except the Father that sent me draw him: and I will raise him up in the last day.

45 It is written in the prophets, And they shall all be taught of God. Every one that hath heard from the Father, and hath learned, cometh unto me.

46 Not that any man hath seen the Father, save he that is from God, he hath seen the Father.

47 Verily, verily, I say unto you, He that believeth hath eternal life.

48 I am the bread of life.

49 Your fathers ate the manna in the wilderness, and they died.

50 This is the bread which cometh down out of heaven, that a man may eat thereof, and not die.

---

generations, because of Christ's teaching, life, miracles, and resurrection have far less reason to be skeptical.

**44 Except the Father draw him** (*ean mē helkysēi auton*). Jesus, after commanding the Jews to cease murmuring, states, that unless God takes the initiative, not one can be saved. In v. 37 human response to Christ is stressed; here the stress is on the necessity of depending on the divine drawing of a person. Prayer is therefore necessary if we are to witness souls accepting the Savior. This is what the theologians call "prevenient grace."

**45, 46 It is written** (*estin gegrammenon*); literally, "it has been and remains written," an intensive use of the periphrastic perfect passive (D-M, p. 202). **He hath seen the Father** is in contrast to John 1:18, "no one hath seen God at any time." There and here the contrast is between Jesus Christ and other human beings. Only Christ has really "seen" the Father.

**47 He that believeth has eternal life** (*ho pisteuōn echei zōēn aiōnion*). Here the participle is used as a substantive. The one who continues believing continues having eternal life. Faith *in* and faithfulness *to* are inherent in the noun (*pistis*) and the verb (*pisteuō*). A good example of what John meant by believing is given in John 3:36, when, after saying belief brings eternal life, he states that disobedience to the Son brings on the wrath of God. Thus, if one's faith is not deep and permanent enough to result in obedience it does not bring eternal life. If there is a new nature it will express itself in faithfulness and obedience to God.

**48-50** In a second reference to the manna of Moses, Jesus again presses home the contrast between the heavenly food then and at the present. They ate manna, but they still eventually died. Now they can partake of the "manna" which conquers death. By these sweeping assertions Jesus hoped to provoke them into inquiring

---

life." Finally Jesus indicates that partaking of this spiritual bread is the condition of eternal life.[e]

In this paragraph we see the "stupid" remark, "How can this man give us flesh to eat?" followed by Jesus' reiteration of and emphasis on the assertion. The statement was deliberately provocative and enigmatic. Like many of the parables spoken to the multitude, its meaning was obscure. It was difficult for his enemies to take hold of such a cryptic statement and use it against him. It was necessary for him to explain the inner meaning to his disciples after the multitude was dis-

missed (cf. Mark 4:11: "Unto you is given the mystery of the kingdom of God: but unto them that are without, all things are done in parables"). So it was here; the enigmatic words, which sounded like cannibalism, were spoken to the crowd in the synagogue, and later the spiritual significance was explained to the disciples (vv. 60-69). Jesus was often deliberately obscure and provocative, his pedagogical purpose being to arouse interest and incite inquiry into his real meaning. Those who were interested could be helped; those not interested were left untouched, and those hostile were frustrated in their attempts to record evidence against him.

[e] Colwell and Titus have noted this dialogue pattern in the Fourth Gospel, e.g., "Occasion: 'What sign have you to show us for doing this?' 2:18. Cryptic remark: 'Destroy this temple,' etc., 2:19. Stupid remark: 'It has taken forty-six years to build this temple,' etc., 2:20. Development: 2:21, 22." *Op. cit.*, pp. 52-58.

51 I am the living bread which came down out of heaven: if any man eat of this bread, he shall live for ever: yea and the bread which I will give is my flesh, for the life of the world.

52 The Jews therefore strove one with another, saying, How can this man give us his flesh to eat?

53 Jesus therefore said unto them, Verily, verily, I say unto you, Except ye eat the flesh of the Son of man and drink his blood, ye have not life in yourselves.

---

about what he had to offer that was superior to the offering in the time of Moses.

51 **My flesh** (*hē sarx mou*) is clearly a reference to Christ's giving up his earthly life and dying on behalf of humanity. Taken literally, the words "I give my flesh for the life of the world" are unpleasant and do not make sense. The hearer (and reader) is thus challenged to seek a meaning that is other than literal. Only in this way can we partake of his flesh. "'Flesh' describes human nature in its totality regarded from its earthly side. . . . The life of the world in the highest sense springs from the Incarnation and the Resurrection of Christ" (BFW, p. 106).

52 **The Jews strove with one another** ("disputed violently," CKB). The imperfect tense implies continued action and the word literally means "to fight." Here it is used metaphorically as in II Tim. 2:24. They fought only with words. This indicates that some Jews were openly espousing Jesus as Messiah; this is not surprising in view of the fact that "he spoke

as none ever had" (cf. 7:46) and served humanity as none ever had. **How can this man give us his flesh?** they demanded an absurdity which reminds one of Nicodemus' question (John 3:4, 9). To take the words literally would mean that Jesus demanded that they be cannibals. Here, as elsewhere, the metaphorical imagery of the Fourth Gospel is conspicuous.

53 **Except ye eat . . . and drink** (*ean mē phagete . . . kai piēte*). As in the Synoptic Gospels, Jesus uses ambiguous words in speaking to hostile unbelievers. "The only possible meaning is the spiritual appropriation of Jesus Christ by faith (v. 47)" (WPNT, V, III).

In spite of the fact that John had not mentioned the Lord's Supper prior to this chapter, many believe that he was writing about partaking of Christ in a communion service, that the elements are channels of divine life and develop Christian character in those that partake. Says Craig, "No other evangelist [John] goes so far in insisting upon the necessity of the saving sacrament of the church."[10] But most

---

### e. The Words of Life (vv. 60-71)
#### (1) *Disciples Offended* (vv. 60-65)

Because of these "hard" sayings, Jesus' auditors were divided into three groups. The unbelievers, who listened to him in the synagogue (v. 59), were now no longer in the audience. The believers consisted of two groups — the larger group of the perplexed (v. 60), and the "hard core" who survived the defections of those offended by the "hard sayings" (v. 66). Included in this last small remnant were the twelve, later called the "apostles." Jesus' public ministry now enters a new phase. The height of his popularity occurred at the feeding of the multitude, but we now see a sifting process at work.

Jesus' strategy appears to be not to build up a huge popular following as he could easily have done (vv. 14, 15). Instead, he was training a small group, an "elite corps," who would share his sufferings and his spiritual ideals, and who would later be his witnesses.

Following the crowd, or wanting to do as others do, sways young people more than any other motivation. In a confidential questionnaire responded to by over one thousand high school and college students, most of them stated that their biggest problem was to avoid the wrongs that others were doing, whether cheating, stealing, lying, smoking, drinking, etc. But this potential urge to follow the crowd can be capitalized on by guiding individ-

---

[10] Clarence T. Craig, *Journal of Biblical Literature*, LXIII, Part I, pp. 31-41.

54 He that eateth my flesh and drinketh my blood hath eternal life; and I will raise him up at the last day.

55 For my flesh is meat indeed, and my blood is drink indeed.

56 He that eateth my flesh and drinketh my blood abideth in me, and I in him.

57 As the living Father sent me, and I live because of the Father; so he that eateth me, he also shall live because of me.

58 This is the bread which came down out of heaven: not as the fathers ate, and died; he that eateth this bread shall live for ever.

---

Protestants interpret these verses as not referring to the Lord's Supper. Westcott's view is representative: "By the 'flesh' in this narrower sense, we must understand the virtue of Christ's humanity as living for us; by the 'blood' the virtue of His humanity as subject to death" (BFW 11, 107). The view of Marcus Dods is similar, as reflected in his comments on vv. 53, 54:

"The difficulty of the statement disappears when it is perceived that the figure of speech is not to be found in the words 'flesh' and 'blood' but in the words 'eating' and 'drinking' . . . and the 'eating' and 'drinking' can only mean the complete acceptance of Him and union with Him as thus manifested" (EGT, I, 758). Others stress the metaphorical language of this Gospel as the clue to the interpretation of this passage: "The metaphor stands for dwelling in constant union with Christ, as the allegory of the true vine will show in ch. 15" (WFH, VIII, 573). In vv. 54-58 there is reiteration of the mystical teaching in v. 53, which Jesus really introduces in v. 35 when he said, "I am the bread of life." One of the most emphatic

rejections of the eucharistic interpretation is voiced by A. T. Robertson: "To me that is a violent misrepresentation of the Gospel and an utter misrepresentation of Christ. It is a grossly literal interpretation of the mystical symbol of the language of Jesus which these Jews also misunderstood" (WPNT, V, 172).

After the public meeting in the synagogue at Capernaum, Jesus, addressing his disciples, gave his own interpretation of what he had been saying to the mixed group (vv. 63): "It is the spirit that giveth life; the flesh profiteth nothing; the words that I have spoken unto you are spirit, and are life." In other words, even if one could actually eat a part of Jesus' flesh it would not help him spiritually. Only as our whole personality is dedicated to and becomes subject to Christ are we feeding upon Christ and abiding in him, "the Bread of Life."

The doctrine of transubstantiation, that one actually eats of the body of Christ and really drinks of his blood in serving the Lord's Supper, was unknown until the late Middle Ages. The church historian Philip Schaff wrote: "The church through-

---

uals into the fellowship of groups that are wholesome and constructive, such as Christian groups where not only the influence is good but also the noblest and highest ideals for character building are taught regularly. Many young people wrote that the way they solved their problem of meeting the bad influence of others, as well as avoiding embarrassment of having to refuse to do as others did, was to change crowds. "Bad company ruins good morals" (I Cor. 15:33); but the reverse is also true, good company fosters good morals. The disciples, since they were in the company of Jesus, were in the best company possible. The same holds true for present-day Christians.

### (2) Peter's Profession (vv. 66-71)

The sixth chapter presents a shifting process in discipleship. At the height of Jesus' popularity the multitude was seized with an impulse to make him king and thus fulfill the messianic hopes of a second David, hopes that had been flickering for centuries. This movement Jesus checked before it really got started. This conception of a political Messiah was the prevailing conception of that day and drew its inspiration from Old Testament passages such as Isaiah 1-39. In this section of Isaiah the passages of the child-king (ch. 9), the righteous ruler (11:1-10; 32:1), the one on the throne of David

59 These things said he in the synagogue, as he taught in Capernaum.

60 Many therefore of his disciples, when they heard *this,* said, This is a hard saying; who can hear it?

61 But Jesus knowing in himself that his disciples murmured at this, said unto them, Doth this cause you to stumble?

62 *What* then if ye should behold the Son of man ascending where he was before?

---

out the world, down to the period of the unhappy change of doctrine in the Western church in the eleventh and twelfth centuries, never worshipped either the consecrated elements on account of their being the body and blood; nor again either Christ Himself as supernaturally present by consecration or the presence of His divinity; neither have the churches of God to this hour, with the exception of those of the Roman obedience, any such custom."[10]a At the close of the apostolic period, Schaff continues, these three views were current: "the mystic view of Ignatius, Justin Martyr and Irenaeus; the symbolic view of Tertullian and Cyprian, and the allegorical or spiritualistic view of Clement of Alexander and Origen."[11] Since there was no trace of the sacramental view in the post-apostolic period we may well assume that there was none in the apostolic period itself. Unless one has put his trust in Christ for salvation and is earnestly seeking to please him, baptism and communion are of no avail. If they were, one would be saving himself by works; and that concept is denounced frequently in the New Testament (cf. Eph. 2:8).

60 Hear (*akouein*) means "understand" as in Acts 22:9 and I Corinthians 14:2. This is a usual meaning of the word in classical as well as Hellenistic Greek. **Giveth life** (*zōopoioun,* v. 63) is a present tense participle with an article preceding it, meaning, "the spirit is the one who continues to make alive."

Here even Jesus' disciples murmured in perplexity at the apparent absurdity of his statements. The term "hard" (*sklēros*) has the connotation of "rough," "harsh," "unpleasant," "difficult." Although they did not express this to Jesus he "knew" (*oida*) their thoughts (cf. 1:48; 2:24; 6:64).

These sayings of Jesus caused them to "stumble" (v. 61). The same Greek term is translated equally well by three English words: "stumble," "offend," and "scandalize." Peter was an "offense" (*skandalon*) to Jesus (Matt. 16:23). Jesus warned his disciples against things which might cause them to "stumble" (Matt. 18:7-9). Paul knew that the idea of a Messiah crucified was offensive and scandalous (I Cor. 1:23; Gal. 5:11) to the Jews. The whole idea of a vicarious atonement was a "stone of scandal," a stumbling stone to "the world." The "scandal" of the cross has its antecedents in Isa. 52:13-53:4 where the idea of a suffering Messiah was "despised and rejected of men." Here, likewise, the idea of eternal life, as conditioned upon devouring the Son of man, was a scandal, an offense, a stumbling block. Here, as elsewhere in the New Testament (except for Hebrews 2:1-18) there is little attempt to soften, to rationalize, or to make the "scandal" more reasonable and hence less offensive. The solution of the impasse is stated to be not rational explanation, but faith (v. 64). The enigma is resolved by the "called"

---

(16:5; 22:22-25), and the "king in his beauty" (33:17) fostered the dream of a powerful and righteous ruler. Jesus rejected this pattern at the beginning of his ministry (Matt. 4:8-10), or rather deferred it, giving priority to the other concept in the book of Isaiah. In these chapters (40-66) the concept of the Messiah as the servant who suffers vicariously for the sins of the people is set forth,

especially in Isaiah 52:13 — 53:12. It is this second messianic role which Jesus chose. His decision is set forth in dramatic fashion in this chapter of John; the political role was rejected and the role of vicarious sacrifice taken and presented here in cryptic, symbolic language. This has rather obvious overtones relative to the Lord's Supper, especially in view of the absence of any other reference to

---

[10]a P. Schaff, *A History of Christianity.*
[11] *Ibid.,* p. 502.

63 It is the spirit that giveth life; the flesh profiteth nothing: the words that I have spoken unto you are spirit, and are life.

64 But there are some of you that believe not. For Jesus knew from the beginning who they were that believed not, and who it was that should betray him.

65 And he said, for this cause have I said unto you, that no man can come unto me, except it be given unto him of the Father.

---

ones in I Cor. 1:24. As with Nicodemus, the dubious are here confronted with the *fait accompli* of the Son of man descending and ascending (v. 62, cf. John 3:13). Apparently the ascension of the Son of man will be a greater tax on their credulity than the statement that they must eat the flesh of the Son of man in order to live (v. 53). What is the connection between eating flesh and the ascending and descending of the Son of man? Relevant texts are 1:14, "the Word became flesh;" 1:51, "ascending and descending upon the Son of man;" 3:13, "he that descended out of heaven." An interpretative paraphrase may help answer the above question. Jesus asked in effect, If this "hard saying" about eating the flesh of the Son of man offends you, what would you say if you saw the Son of man returning to heaven from whence he came? If you doubt that he actually came from heaven and is here now, would you believe in his visible return? The real meaning of this is in the realm of the spirit. Obviously, eating flesh and drinking blood are meaningless if we think only in physical terms; the essential thing is the spiritual counterpart of which these terms are symbolic. "The bread I recently gave you profits little;

the words I have spoken are far more important. The bread gave physical life, but my words give spiritual and hence eternal life. You are in the presence of a miracle greater than that of multiplying the loaves and fish. The appropriate thing for you to do is not to stop with the physical but to press on to the spiritual; not to quibble about literalism but to grasp by appropriating faith the inner, real significance of 'flesh' and 'blood.' It will mean the difference between life and death for you now." Perhaps the statement "the Word became flesh" (John 1:14) is the most important in this Gospel.[12]

65 **No man can come unto me, except it be given unto him of the Father** is to be interpreted with the aid of v. 37, "he that cometh to me I will in no wise cast out" (John 6:37, 65; 17:6). They are similar in that they speak of the Father giving disciples to the Son. The idea is also similar to that voiced at Peter's confession to which Jesus replied, "flesh and blood hath not revealed this unto thee but my Father who is in heaven" (Matt. 16: 17). It suggests the doctrine of "prevenient grace," the initiative of God in influencing the sinner to repent and *desire* salvation.

---

the supper in the Gospel. But to use the literalism of this chapter as Biblical support for the doctrine of transubstantiation is contrary to the entire spirit and purpose of the "Spiritual Gospel." It is refuted in particular in v. 63, which is perhaps the "key-verse" of this chapter.

Summary: This chapter presents the theme of belief as the condition of life with a varied but similar motif. There is the miracle with the resultant discussion. Most of the crowd take Jesus' words literally, as did Nicodemus and the Samaritan woman, while some recognize a spiritual significance in them. From the

physical manna the thought moves to the Bread of Life there incarnate in their midst. The multitude is thenceforth divided, some scandalized by his words which speak of cannibalism if taken literally; others believe and recognize in the same words the source of life eternal (cf. CHD, p. 344).

The connection between word and life (*logos* and *zōē*) is noteworthy in this chapter and will be developed at greater length in ch. 17, after the author's habit of presenting a theme under several aspects, each contributing its share to the total concept in a cumulative fashion.

[12] John's dualism is between flesh and spirit, an ethical dualism. The stress is not upon the ascent but upon the descent — "the Word became flesh" — the reverse of contemporary Hellenistic notions. Heaven and earth are united in the Son of man. See E. M. Sidebottom, "The Ascent and Descent of the Son of man in the Gospel of St. John," *Anglican Theological Review*, April, 1957, pp. 115-222.

66 Upon this many of his disciples went back, and walked no more with him.

67 Jesus said therefore unto the twelve, Would ye also go away?

68 Simon Peter answered him, Lord, to whom shall we go? thou hast the words of eternal life.

69 And we have believed and know that thou art the Holy One of God.

70 Jesus answered them, Did not I choose you the twelve, and one of you is a devil?

71 Now he spake of Judas *the son* of Simon Iscariot, for he it was that should betray him, *being* one of the twelve.

---

66 **Walked no more with him** (*ouketi met' autou periepatoun*). The use of the imperfect tense denotes that these half-hearted disciples, who wanted material benefits more than spiritual ones, stopped walking with or following Jesus. They had only been outward, part-time disciples.

67 **Would ye also go away?** (*Mē kai hymeis thelete hypagein*). "You do not also want to go away, do you?" The *mē* in the question indicates that a negative answer was expected. Jesus did not ask because he doubted their loyalty but to evoke from them, at this time of crisis, a reaffirmation of loyalty.

68 **To whom shall we go?** (*pros tina apeleusometha*). Peter, as spokesman for the disciples, gave expression to a profound and vital truth when he asked this question and then answered it himself, by saying, "Thou hast the words of eternal life." He indicated a truth that generations of believers share: Jesus alone, of all the people in the world then and now, has the authoritative and God's **approved** teachings by which our lives should be guided.

69 **We have believed** (*hēmeis pepisteukamen*, perf. act. ind. of *pisteuō* "be-lieve") means literally, "We have come to believe and still believe." The Greek word for "know" (*ginōskō*) is also in the perfect tense, connoting "we knew and still know." Thus Peter stressed the continuity between the initial belief of the twelve and the conviction that now sustained them. **Thou art the Holy One of God** (*sy ei ho hagois tou theou*), i.e., "you are the Messiah, the only Savior, and sent directly from God." This confession on the part of Peter is similar to, but at the same time uttered at a different time from that recorded in Matt. 16:16-18. That was made at Caesarea Philippi; this in Capernaum. "Here the confession points to the inward character in which the apostles found assurance of life; there the confession was of the public office and theocratic Person of the Lord (BFW, p. 111).

70 **One of you is a devil.** Only twelve, and one of them became a traitor! When church members cease serving Christ to-day, we may seek comfort in the realization that one-twelfth of the first disciples deserted Christ also. Later John reports that Satan entered into Judas (John 13: 27). In Revelation 12:9, for the first time Satan and the devil are explicitly identified.

---

## EXCURSUS

## CONCERNING REVERSING THE ORDER OF CHAPTERS 5 AND 6 IN JOHN'S GOSPEL:

### SHOULD 7:15-24 FOLLOW 5:47?

Many problems are encountered in dealing with the chronology of the Fourth Gospel. Why, for example, does John present Jesus as going at least three times to Jerusalem during his public ministry, while the Synoptic Gospels mention only one such visit? Why is the cleansing of the temple placed at the close of the public ministry in the Synoptics and at the be-ginning in John? The chronological difficulties are not limited to differences with the other three Gospels; there are also problems within the Fourth Gospel itself. Among the more noteworthy attempts to rearrange the materials of this Gospel are those of J. H. Bernard (*ICC*) G. H. C. MacGregor (*Moffatt N. T. Commentary*), Bultmann (*Johannes Evangelium*), Fr. R. Hoare ("The Original Order and Chapters of St. John's Gospel," *BOW*, 1924), A. E. Garvie (*Abingdon Commentary*) and W. F. Howard (*Interpreter's Bible*). The proposal to reverse the orders of chs. 5 and 6 dates at least from the fourteenth century when voiced by Ludolphus of Saxony. It was repeated by J. P. Norris in the last century (*Journal of Philology*, 1871, p. 107). In this study attention is limited to the proposal that the events of ch. 6 occurred before those related in ch. 5 and, specifically, that 7:15-24 should follow 5:47.

As they now stand the transition between 5:47 and 6:1 is very abrupt. Ch. 5 reports the healing at the Pool of Bethesda and ends with a discussion of belief. Ch. 6 begins with these words: "After these things Jesus went to the other side of the Sea of Galilee." There is no mention of going from Jerusalem to Galilee nor is there any indication of the place of departure to the "other side" of the lake. Ch. 4, however, ends with the healing in Capernaum and the transition to ch. 6 is smooth; they are still in Galilee and leave Capernaum for the opposite side of the lake. In addition 6:2 becomes more meaningful. The people, according to 6:2, were attracted by "the signs which he did on the diseased." If the "signs" refer to the healings in Capernaum, including that recorded in John 4:53, the meaning is clear; but, in the present order, the last "sign" reported occurred in far-off Jerusalem several months earlier. Also, in John 7:23, Jesus wonders why they are indignant because he healed on the Sabbath day, an obvious reference to John 5:1-10. Would he speak thus if the events of chs. 6:1-7:14 had occurred between the healing and the argument of 7:15-24?

Advocates of the proposed change point to several chronological factors as justification of the change. First, it would be more in harmony with the Synoptic accounts of Jesus' itinerary in which movement is from Galilee to Jerusalem. Under this proposed rearrangement we would find Jesus in Samaria and Galilee (John 4), later going about Galilee (6:1-7:14), and then departing for Jerusalem (5:1-47; 7:15-24). This would eliminate one of the Passovers, shorten the public ministry of Jesus by one year and thus bring it more in line with the Synoptic accounts (JHB, I, xviii).

Another chronological factor involves the reference to John the Baptist in 5:35. There, Jesus says, "John was a lamp, burning brightly, and for a time you were ready to exult in his light." (NEB) The past tense ("was," *ēn*) implies that John was dead when Jesus was in Jerusalem for the Feast of the Tabernacles. However, the Synoptic accounts state that John's death occurred shortly before the following Passover and the feeding of the multitude, hence about six months later. (Matt. 14:3-21; cf. John 6:5) Reversing the placement of chs. 5 and 6 would clarify the apparent discrepancy, by having the expression of 5:35 come last. It is stated in 7:1 that Jesus remained in Galilee because the Jews wanted to kill Him. The first mention of the Jews' desire to kill Jesus is in 5:18. Would it not be better, say some, to assume that the events of ch. 6, which show Jesus' popularity at an all-time high, had occurred before these two passages rather than between them?

In further support of the view that 7:15-24 follows directly after 5:47 is the fact that Jesus asks the Jews, "Why do you seek to kill me?" in John 7:20-23. Their acute hostility is shown in 5:18ff., following the healing at the pool to which Jesus specifically alludes in 7:21, 22. Thus, should not 7:15ff. immediately follow the events of ch. 5, which ends with a discussion of Moses? Ch. 7:15ff. follows with the statement, "Did not Moses give you the Law?" (John 7:19 NEB) The entire paragraph (7:15-24) follows closely the theme of 5:1-47 on the subjects of Moses, circumcision, Sabbath observance, judgment and persecution. Unless 7:15-24 is changed to follow 5:47 there is an additional problem in 7:31 when the people refer to many miracles, while 7:21 refers to only "one deed." Again, the paragraph 7:15-24 seems to have occurred sometime previous. Some scholars make the transition without explanation while others make the change and seek to justify it.[f]

While the proposed change helps answer some questions it raises others at least as great. By retracing our steps we can see

---

[f] MacGregor justifies the transposition thus: "Although spoken in October" particular reference is made (7:21) to the effect produced by 'one deed' and performed at the Feast of Pentecost the previous May, since when Jesus has been absent in Galilee (7:10). The emphasis again on *one* miracle (7:21) seems inconsistent with the people's testimony to Jesus' *many* miracles (7:31). Finally, 7:20 ('Who wants to kill you?') seems incongruous if placed immediately before 7:25 ('Is this not the man they want to kill?'). G. C. MacGregor, *The Gospel of John: Moffatt N. T. Commentary* (New York: Harper, 1928), p. 188.

some of the additional difficulties raised by the proposed "solutions."

1. The most ardent advocates of re-arrangement cannot point to any text in which such an arrangement is reflected. Even the earliest extant text of John, the recently discovered Bodmer Papyrus II (P66), from the third century, has the traditional sequence.g To most scholars this fact in itself is decisive against the proposed changes. Even Bernard, after citing Irenaeus, Origen and Tatian thinks it unlikely that they knew any except the traditional order (JHB, I, xviii).

2. An additional complication is the fact that the transition from ch. 4 to 6 would be smoother, but the resulting transition from 5 to 7 would be more difficult. Ch. 5 ends in Jerusalem; while ch. 7 begins, "After this Jesus went about in Galilee; he would not go about in Judaea, because the Jews sought to kill him" (RSV). The verb *peripatein* (used twice) in 7:1 means to "walk about" within a given locality rather than to move from one locality to another. If John had had in mind a journey from Jerusalem to Galilee he probably would have used the verb *poreuesthai,* meaning "to go from one place to another."h The contrast is not between leaving or remaining at Jerusalem, but between walking about in Galilee rather than in Judaea; hence no sudden exodus from Jerusalem is implied. Thus the transition from ch. 6 to 7 is smoother than from 5 to 7. Bernard meets this objection by placing 7:1-14 after 7:15-24. But the re-arranging of materials is quite subjective and can easily be carried to extremes.

3. An additional factor favoring the traditional arrangement is its alleged harmony with the Synoptic parallels. The abruptness with which ch. 6 opens can be explained by assuming that John was aware that his readers were familar with the Synoptic narratives and that he selected the account of multiplication of the loaves from this material for a didactic purpose. If, however, 7:1 follows 5:37, there is no room to insert the Synoptic material; it is covered only by the meager statement

that "Jesus went about in Galilee" (in semi-retirement — 7:4).i

While one of the more convincing reasons for the change is the reference in 7:23 to the healing of 5:1-18, even this is less compelling than it seems. The conversation of 7:23 took place in the fall while the healing in ch. 5 occurred more than six months earlier. It is quite possible that the miracle at Bethesda was still in the minds of the people. Since this was Jesus' first appearance in Jerusalem after this miracle, it could have been a common topic of conversation.j

4. The assertion that the rearrangement is more consistent with the Synoptics is cancelled by some other considerations. The reference to the Passover (6:5) may be due to John's interest in associating the multiplication of the loaves with the Eucharist, rather than with a temporal sequence. F. C. Grant actually brushes aside attempts at chronological rearrangement to fit geographical locations with the remark, "His geography is spiritual, not physical."k It is somewhat inconsistent to take the chronology so seriously and yet to go ahead and rearrange without textual justification.

5. The reference to John's "light" (5:35) need not be a reference to his death. As many commentators point out, his light was no longer shining when he was imprisoned in Herod's fortress at Machaerus (Jos. *Ant.,* 18. 5. 2). A lamp (*lychnos*) that is put under a meal-tub or in a cellar (Luke 11:33 NEB) is no longer shining.l He was out of the public eye and inaccessible to all but close friends.

6. In reply to the assertion that the threat to Jesus' life, voiced in 5:18, must be placed closer to the same threat in 7:20, it may be noted that there is also a reference to this danger in 7:1 which, in the present order, would explain 7:20. The point seems to be that the threat to Jesus' life is seen not in chronological but geographical pattern. The threat of 5:18 and of 7:1 was present during the events of ch. 6. The danger lay in Jerusalm, but not in Galilee. It was the same with Paul later; he was comparably

g V. Martin, *Papyrus Bodmer II, Evangile de Jean,* p. 18.
h Albert Powers, "The Original Order of St. John's Gospel," CBQ, p. 400.
i *Ibid.,* p. 404.
j *Ibid.,* p. 401.
k Grant, F. C., *The Gospel of John: Harper's Annotated Bible Series* (New York: Harper, 1956), I, 42.
l Powers, op. cit., p. 402.

safe outside of Judaea but was arrested in Jerusalem during the Passover (Acts 21:11; 27).

7. In answer to the proposal to have 7:15-24 follow 5:47 because of similarity of themes, it would follow that many more such transpositions would have to be made in order to be consistent. This is what Bultmann and Moffatt have done very extensively. The changes are based upon the assumption that John's mode of thought and presentation is built on the mental habits of the Occident. John's thought is cyclical. A few themes are mentioned, left, taken up later, and elaborated. (For example, John the Baptist is mentioned three different times in ch. 1 instead of having an entire section devoted to him.) John's style is deliberately repetitious. It is unwise and unnecessary to force the Fourth Gospel into patterns of thought like our own, especially in the absence of any textual variants to justify doing so.[m]

Titus has pointed out numerous instances of cross references and repetition.[n] In 4:46, for instance, the evangelist recalls that it was in Cana that Jesus had turned water into wine (2:1-11). In 5:33 Jesus refers to the delegation from Jerusalem which visited John the Baptist (John 1:19). In a similar manner Jesus' reference to "one miracle" (John 7:21) is probably a reference to 5:1-12, not necessarily because this was the only miracle done in their presence, but because it was related to the Sabbath and hence more controversial. This seems confirmed by the fact that later, while still in Jerusa-

lem, Jesus mentioned "many miracles" known to them (John 10:31).

8 In contrasting the reference to "signs" in 7:31 with "one deed" in 7:21, it should be noted that Jesus spoke in 7:21 while the people spoke in 7:31. Jesus asked the reason for their hostility to the Bethesda cure. Not all of the crowd was hostile. The reactions were varied. One group was favorably impressed and commented, "Would any Messiah do more miracles than this man?" They were summing up all the miracles of His public ministry. The remark came from a different section of the crowd than that addressed in 7:21; the difference was in the multitude, not necessarily in the time.

## IN SUMMARY

The two most convincing reasons supporting the proposed revision are the abruptness with which ch. 6 opens if it follows ch. 5 and the similarity of John 7:15-24 to 5:1-47. If, however, the principles which are used to justify these changes should be applied to other sections as well, the distinctive patterns of the Fourth Gospel would be changed to conform to western habits of logical thought. John is more interested in presenting a convincing thesis relative to belief (20:31) than he is in setting forth the sequence of events "in order." This does not mean the chronology of this Gospel is not trustworthy. It only means that chronology is secondary; any rearrangement of the text should be made with caution if at all. There seems to be insufficient evidence for any proposed rearrangement.

m "Topographical considerations are of less moment than the fact that the existing arrangement of chapters corresponds to the movement of thought: ch. vi presupposes the position established in ch. v. and makes a definite advance upon it." CHD, p. 340.

n Colwell and Titus, *op. cit.*, p. 68. Other repetitions include 7:50 cf. 3:1; 11:8 cf. 10:31; 13:33 cf. 7:33. See also B. P. W. Stather Hunt, *Some Johannine Problems* (London: Skeffington, 1958), p. 48.

# CHAPTER VII

And after these things Jesus walked in Galilee: for he would not walk in Judaea, because the Jews sought to kill him.

2 Now the feast of the Jews, the feast of tabernacles, was at hand.

## EXEGESIS

1 **The Jews sought to kill him.** The use of the imperfect tense implies that the Jews had been seeking to kill Jesus for some time. John reiterated the fact of the deadly hostility of the Judean Jews, which first became apparent in ch. 5 and increases in intensity through ch. 12.

2 **The feast of the tabernacles was at hand.** This was the most popular of the annual feasts, as it permitted camping in open-air shelters for a week and hence was something of a "vacation." Tabernacles (*skēnopēgia*) means "tent-fastening," i.e., *skēnē* (tent) plus *pēgia* (fastening). The fact that the attendants were supposed to sleep in booths or tents made the affair an adventure, as this simulated the experience Moses and his countrymen endured in the wilderness after the Exodus. It also made lodging inexpensive. The feast began on the 15th day of the month Tishri (Sept. 13-30) and lasted eight days (Deut. 16:13-15; 23:33-36; Nah. 8:18). This feast was orginally seven days in length to which an eighth day was later added (Lev. 23:35-36). Next to the Passover it was, in the words of Josephus, "the most sacred and most important feast of the Hebrews" (Jos. *Ant.*, viii. 100). It combined thanksgiving for the annual harvest and a reminder of God's providence during the years between Egypt and Canaan.

1 **After these things** may refer either to the controversy arising from healing of the cripple at Bethesda (ch. 5) or to the defection of some disciples in Galilee (ch. 6); the same phrase introduces ch. 5 and 6. Some scholars believe that the events related in ch. 7 follow ch. 5. In favor of changing the order of chs. 5 and 6 are these considerations: (1) it would avoid the abrupt transition between chs. 5 and 6 — from Jerusalem to Galilee; (2) it would make 7:1 more significant

## EXPOSITION

3. AT THE FEAST OF TABERNACLES (7:1-52)

   a. Confusion Concerning Jesus (vv. 1-13)

   (1) *His Brothers' Skepticism* (vv. 1-9)

**Jesus walked** — the words are a reminder that Jesus conducted a very informal "school" for his disciples (learners). The word used here is the same as that which gave its name to the school founded by Aristotle in Athens — the Peripatetics. To be a disciple or pupil of Jesus (or Aristotle) was to walk with the Master. Thus the greatest teacher of all time had no classroom, no teaching aids, no salary, and he charged no tuition. It was person-to-person encounter.

3 Much of John and indeed of the New Testament is a sobering recognition of the fact that "he came unto his own and his own received him not" (John 1:11). Their negative reaction to Jesus is not difficult to understand. It seems that his youth in Nazareth had been rather natural and ordinary, causing his neighbors to remark in bewilderment, "Is not this the carpenter's son? Is not his mother called Mary? and his brethren James, and Joseph, and Simon, and Judas? And his sisters, are they not all with us? Whence then hath this man all these things? And they were offended in him" (Matt. 13:55-57).

They could not reconcile the ordinary craftsman they had known as a neighbor with the messianic stature he had gained abroad; it placed too great a strain on

3 His brethren therefore said unto him, Depart hence, and go into Judaea, that thy disciples also may behold thy works which thou doest.

4 For no man doeth anything in secret, and himself seeketh to be known openly. If thou doest these things, manifest thyself to the world.

5 For even his brethren did not believe on him.

6 Jesus therefore said unto them, My time is not yet come; but your time is always ready.

---

(why say "walk in Galilee" since Jesus was already in Galilee in 6:71?); (3) ch. 6 seems to follow more naturally and smoothly from ch. 4 than from ch. 5. However, the advantages gained from such a transposition are more than cancelled by the disadvantages: (1) there is no warrant for such a change in any extant text; (2) if ch. 7 follows ch. 5 it makes little allowance for getting to Galilee between the events of 5:47 and 7:2; (3) the transition from 5 to 6 is more easily harmonized with the Synoptic accounts than the transition from 5 to 7.[1] Conclusion: the proposed transposition would create as many problems as it would solve. There seems to be no compelling reason for altering the order of all extant texts.

3 His brethren were sons of Joseph and Mary, hence half-brothers to Jesus. Opinion differs as to the real attitude of these brethren of Jesus. Some think their

comment indicates skepticism as to Jesus' power (Bernard); others interpret the words as acknowledging Jesus' miraculous power and challenging him, as the devil did at the temptation (Matt. 4:3; Luke 4:9), to show his power to a wider audience (Hoskyns, Westcott, Bauer, Chrysostom). In the light of vv. 5-7 it seems apparent that they were not yet believers in his divinity and were ridiculing Jesus, urging him to expose himself to the wrath of the Jerusalem Jews. That Jesus' mother and brothers were not in full rapport with him at this time is also implied in the Synoptics (Matt. 12:46-50; Mark 3:31-35; Luke 8:19-21 cf. Mark 3:21).

6 My time is not yet come. The word for time here is kairos and appears only three times in this Gospel. The other synonym for time is chronos and appears five times in John (i.e., 5:6; 7:33; 12:35; 14:9). While chronos refers primarily

---

their credulity and they "stumbled at the stumbling-stone." Jesus explained this as an illustration of the principle that a prophet is more readily accepted in other countries than at home. It is consistent with our proverb, "Familiarity breeds contempt." This "scandal" of unbelief on the part of those who should know better was anticipated in Isaiah 53:2, 3 — "he grew up . . . as a root out of dry ground . . . and we esteemed him not."

6 Several contrasts are noticeable here: the contrast between Jesus and his brethren, between "my time" and "your time," between Jesus and "the world." The spiritual hostility between God and the world, shown in the analogy of light and darkness, is a prominent theme of this Gospel. It appears in the Prologue (1:5, 10), in ch. 3 (3:19-21) and is implied in 5:35-38. The same hostility is

later explained to the disciples — "because ye are not of the world . . . therefore the world hateth you" (John 15:19). In an apparent paradox the disciples are warned against loving the world (I John 2:15), and yet it is stated that God loves the world (John 3:16). Obviously the "world" has a different connotation in each passage. The "world" (kosmos) is one of John's characteristic words, occurring seventy-five times in the Fourth Gospel and a total of thirteen times in the other three.[a] In John's usage the term has about eight different meanings. In these two passages the term means respectively, the moral element in the inhabited earth that is hostile to God, and the mass of humanity in need of redemption.

Jesus' brothers, here depicted as more in accord with "the world" than with Jesus, were later converted, according to

---

[1] In both John (5:33 cf. 6:3) and the Synoptics (Luke 7:24 cf. Luke 9:7, 13) the discussion concerning the Baptist is followed by feeding the five thousand.

[a] E. A. Abbott, Johannine Vocabulary: A Comparison of the Words of the Fourth Gospel with Those of the Other Three (London: Adam and Charles Black, 1905), p. 239.

7 The world cannot hate you; but me it hateth, because I testify of it, that its works are evil.

8 Go ye up unto the feast: I go not up unto this feast; because my time is not yet fulfilled.

---

to duration, *kairos* usually denotes an event, a period within *chronos*. *Chronos* connotes continuity while its synonym indicates the punctuation of that continuity by a specific incursion. *Chronos* stresses the horizontal aspect of history, while *kairos* is often found in an eschatological context with a stress on the vertical aspect of God coming into history.[2] John's usual word for this period is *hour,* which occurs some twenty-six times in this Gospel. Fourteen of these refer to "the hour" of the passion. That the pre-occupation with the coming passion dominated the latter portion of Jesus' public ministry is reflected in the "up to Jerusalem" motif in Luke and the words "my time" and "my hour" in John. Jesus disagreed with his brothers both as to when he would attend the feast and why. Jesus may have meant the day of his crucifixion by this remark. Sometimes a day, an hour, or even a minute may mean the difference between life and death. The Master explained that he was hated because he taught that people need to repent — that the "works" of the world are evil.

8 Various methods have been suggested to solve the apparent contradiction in vv. 8 and 10, in which Jesus stated that he would not go to the feast and later did so. There is an almost equal division among the best Greek manuscripts as to whether Jesus said "not" (*ouk*) or "not yet" (*oupō*). The 1928 edition of Nestle's Greek text has *oupō* and the 1960 edition has *ouk*.[3] A. T. Robertson (WPNT, p. 119), C. K. Barrett (CKB, p. 258) and W. F. Howard (WFH, VIII, 580) advocate the reading of "not" (*ouk*) on the ground that it is the more difficult reading. The text was altered, they think, in order to fit the general context; Jesus meant that he was not going with the caravan but privately a few days later. While none of the manuscripts mentioned above was written before A.D. 300 the recently discovered Bodmer Papyrus II (P[66]), dated about A.D. 200, has the reading *oupō*. This reading has the added advantage of being more favorable to the veracity of Jesus. Perhaps the confusion may be accounted for by the fact that, in making manuscripts, sometimes one person would read and

---

Christian tradition.[b] The events of Jesus' life and death, the testimony of eye-witnesses, and the purity of his daily life must have convinced them that he was indeed the Savior of the world. This is not the last instance when it has been easier for strangers to believe than those of one's household.

This paragraph (vv. 1-9) seems to focus on two things: Jesus' deliberate timing and an additional instance of unbelief. The dominant motif of this Gospel is belief and unbelief. This dialogue between Jesus and his brethren is mentioned in none of the other three Gospels; it shows Jesus virtually alone. In the preceding chapter several of his disciples left him (6:66). Hostility in Judaea was so

bitter that a visit to Jerusalem was extremely hazardous. Even in his boyhood home Jesus found criticism, unbelief, and even cynicism. Jesus did not condemn his unbelieving brothers but patiently explained the different relationship he sustained to "the world." It is evidence of Jesus' poise and magnanimity that he was gentle rather than vindictive in his reply to the brothers' challenge. This may have been a factor in their subsequent conversion.

### (2) *Perplexity in Jerusalem* (vv. 10-13)

At most of the annual festivals of the Jews, when pilgrims gathered in Jerusalem,

---

[2] See data in AG, under these words. Both terms appear together in Acts 1:7 and I Thess. 5:1 in schatological contexts. Cf. J. Manfk, "The Biblical Concept of Time and Our Gospels," NTS, 1956, 6:45-51.
[3] *Ouk* occurs in manuscripts Aleph, D, old Latin, Vulgate and many MSS. of lesser importance. *Oupō* is found in B, W, L, and Theta, and WFH, VIII, 580.
[b] Hegesippus, quoted by Eusebius (*Hist. Eccl.* III, xx, 1-6), states that James, the Lord's brother, succeeded to the government of the Church" and that the grandchildren of another brother, Jude, "ruled the churches, because they were witnesses and were also relatives of the Lord."

9 And having said these things unto them, he abode *still* in Galilee.

10 But when his brethren were gone up unto the feast, then went he also up, no publicly, but as it were in secret.

11 The Jews therefore sought him at the feast, and said, Where is he?

12 And there was much murmuring among the multitudes concerning him: som said, He is a good man; others said, Not so, but he leadeth the multitude astray.

13 Yet no man spake openly of him for fear of the Jews.

14 But when it was now the midst of the feast Jesus went up into the temple, an taught.

---

several scribes would write down what was read to them. Since both words begin with *ou,* some may have failed to understand correctly the consonant. Certainly John did not intend to cast any doubt on Jesus' veracity.

9 **He remained** is a translation of *emeinen,* which is in the aorist tense. Usually this tense was used to express a single act (punctiliar action), whereas the present and imperfect tenses expressed action or progress or repeated action, as in a moving picture. However, a few Greek words were linear in their roots and did not require the present or imperfect tenses to express action in progress. *Menō,* present tense of the above word, is a word of that type; also is *zaō* ("live"). Hence, the term implies continuity here even though the aorist is used.

10 **Not publicly but in private** (RSV). Had Jesus traveled with a crowd, his popularity would have caused complica tions. It certainly was less strain on him to travel, not with his sneering brother and other unbelievers, but with his ow believing and friendly disciples.

12 **And there was much murmurin concerning him.** Again, as in ch. 6, is stated that the Jews were divided i their estimate of Jesus. He was popula with the masses but increasingly unpopula with the two most influential groups o religious leaders, the Pharisees and th Sadducees. Both groups of leaders wer afraid that their influence and authorit over the people were being undermine by Jesus' popularity, so their oppositio continued relentlessly until his death.

14 **The midst of the feast** would b about Wednesday; he would still hav four days to teach the pilgrims gathere there. These would be more open-minded less prejudiced than the people of Jerusa

---

there was something exciting going on. This one was no exception. Jesus was "the talk of the town." According to both John and the Synoptic accounts, the mid-point of Jesus' ministry was a time when almost everyone was wondering about Jesus' identity (Mark 8:28). Here the questioners seem less concerned about relating Jesus to Old Testament prophecy than evaluating the moral impact he was making. Some, viewing Jesus from the stand-point of his good works, made the pragmatic test and said, "He is a good man." Others, more concerned with the theological implications, professed to believe that he was misleading the people, a false Messiah. Widespread perplexity was, therefore, the dominant mood of this feast and the main theme of this chapter.

This was Jesus' *anabasis,* his "going up" to Jerusalem. Hoskyns thinks Jesus' word in 7:8 have a double meaning, that he sai in effect, I do not ascend to the cross o to heaven yet, even though I will go u to this feast. It is true that "to ascend or "to go up" is a very important concep in John's presentation, but it is doubtful i Jesus' language here is that subtle. Ho else could he have expressed himself?

In all of the excitement at the feast there was not only perplexity as to Jesus identity but also fear of expression. I times of tension it is difficult to be neutral Here was pressure. The voice of con science and the voices of the rulers de manded that a position be taken concern ing Jesus' claims. In view of Jesus words and works, the unsophisticate wanted to follow their instincts and ac knowledge his lordship. But in view o

c Hoskyns, p. 313. He notes that the verb *anabaino* denotes going up to Jerusalem (2:13; 5:1; 11:55 12:20), Jesus' ascent to the Father (3:13; 6:62; 20:17; cf. 1:52) and is cognate with the verb t "lift up" (3:14; 8:28; 12:32, 34).

d Hegesippus, quoted by Eusebius (*Hist. Eccl.* III, xx, 1-6) states that James, the Lord's brothe

15 The Jews therefore marvelled, saying, How knoweth this man letters, having never learned?

16 Jesus therefore answered them, and said, My teaching is not mine, but his that sent me.

17 If any man willeth to do his will, he shall know of the teaching, whether it is of God, or *whether* I speak from myself.

---

lem. The Jews of the Dispersion were always more liberal and open-minded than those of Palestine.

**Jesus went up into the temple and taught.** Jesus' ministry was four-fold: preaching, teaching, healing and the casting out of demons. The "teaching" (*didachē*) was normally for the believers, and the preaching (*kērygma*) for the others. Here, however, the teaching was to the auditors, most of whom were unbelievers. They naturally compared the words and methods of this migrant expositor with the rabbis whom they were accustomed to hear at their home synagogues.

**15 How knoweth this man letters (*grammata*) having never learned?** Such was the initial reaction of those in Jerusalem who heard Jesus for the first time. It was a reaction similar to that caused in the synagogues of Galilee (Mark 1:22). Perhaps the thing that puzzled them most was the fact that Jesus had not attended either of the rabbinical schools (semi-

naries) in Jerusalem. There was to be a similar reaction toward the preaching of Peter and John (Acts 4:13) when they were sized up by their hearers as "uneducated, common men" (RSV). Evidently the wisdom, method of speaking, and the fervor, so manifest in Jesus, became noticeable also in his disciples. The term "letters" as used here in Acts 26:24 is "a general term for *scriptural* and *Rabbinical* learning" (MRV, II, 422).

**16 My teaching is not mine but his that sent me.** In case any were disposed to assume that Jesus' superior teaching was due to his being self-taught, he took pains to inform them that such was not the case. God had given him these teachings.

**17 If any man willeth to do his will, he shall know of the teaching, whether it is of God, or whether I speak from myself.** In these words the master teacher told his audience then, and people ever since then, how they can ascertain for themselves whether his teachings are from

---

the silence and known hostility of the leadership, such impulses were stifled for reasons of expediency. Probably the majority were undecided and wished to remain neutral and anonymous "for fear of the Jews." None of the evangelists etches the inner tensions of the populace quite so incisively as John.

### b. Jesus Teaches in the Temple (vv. 14-24)

14 Only John records the fact that Jesus taught openly in the temple prior to passion week. His teaching on this occasion was a bold thing to do, in the light of prior statement that it was dangerous for Jesus even to be in Judaea. The pilgrims at the feast were surprised at his audacity (v. 25). While Jesus did not stride into Jerusalem with fanfare and a glare of publicity, as his kinfolk had urged, he did not sneak in furtively. Rather, here, as

always, he spoke openly and publicly in accordance with the claim he made at his trial (John 18:20).

The people were surprised that Jesus was so conversant with the Scriptures and so facile in argument. It was obvious to them that Jesus had had little or no formal schooling. Reared a carpenter and without professional training, he still surpassed the best educated rabbis in the use of their own methods of instruction (cf. Luke 2:47). In those days, of course, there was no such thing as popular education. Only a few could read and write.

Jesus' exposition of the Scriptures impressed both the educated and the uneducated for its clarity, independence of thought, and familiarity with the Old Testament. The scribes and rabbis normally spoke with a second-hand authority. They often quoted interpretations and applications of earlier rabbinic authorities.

18 He that speaketh from himself seeketh his own glory: but he that seeketh th glory of him that sent him, the same is true, and no unrighteousness is in him.

19 Did not Moses give you the law, and *yet* none of you doeth the law? Wh seek ye to kill me?

20 The multitude answered, Thou hast a demon: who seeketh to kill thee?

God or not. Only by determining to do God's will, and by continually doing His will, can one learn that Christ is really God's mouthpiece. The word "willeth" (*thelē*) and the word "to do" (*poiein*) are both in the present tense, one subjunctive and the other infinitive. Thus they both denote continued willing and doing, not a single action but a permanent decision to do God's will.

15-18 The theme of these verses is the source of Jesus' teaching (*didachē*). Jesus' assertion of the identity of his words with those of his Father was occasioned by the exclamation of the Jews in v. 15. It is not necessary to suppose with Bacon, Bernard, and Bultmann that 7:15 follows immediately after 5:47.[4] This verse follows naturally after 7:14 where Jesus is teaching in the temple. It also (v. 19) presupposes the hostility reflected in 7:1. "John's chronological connections are at least tolerable, and his theological connections are in perfect order. The latter can hardly be mended, the former only slightly, and that at the expense of the latter" (CKB, p. 262).

Four contrasts are given here: "mine cf. "his that sent me"; "from myself cf. "of God"; "his own glory"; cf. "glor of him that sent him"; and "from himself cf. "the same is true." In each case th contrast is between man and God, mo specifically between human authority an the self-revelation of God the Fathe Jesus insisted that his words are not contrast to but identical with the words the Father.

19 The accusation here is that all of th Jews had violated the law of Moses. Th is a sweeping assertion, but it is support by Stephen's accusation (Acts 7:51), Peter at the Jerusalem Council (Acts 1 10), by Paul (Rom. 2:12-24), by th author of the letter to the Hebrews (He 10:1), and even by the Psalmist (Ps. 5 2-4). Among the rabbis of that day was believed that obedience to the la was theoretically but not practically po sible.[5]

20 **Thou hast a demon** was equivale to saying, "You are crazy," or "You a a fanatic" (8:48; cf. Luke 7:33).

It was a dogmatic, authoritarian, didactic, transmissive type of teaching. While unrivalled in their claim to be orthodox and definitive, they were often unconvincing. Jesus' mode of teaching was unprecedented and unique. He used neither the pedantic homilies of the rabbis nor the ecstatic utterances of the prophets, nor yet the apocalyptic visions of the seers. It was, rather, a combination of fresh insights into the interpretation of the law, an appreciation of the prophets, and a bold application of both to contemporary issues.

17 How can one be sure of Jesus' teaching? What is the source of religious certainty? How can one distinguish true teaching from the false? The answer is stated succinctly in v. 17, and it is an

emphasis characteristic of the Fourth Go pel. The pathway to spiritual knowled lies through the will as well as the inte lect. There is a moral condition to on grasp of divine truth.

Knowledge is a very important conce in John's Gospel. The "know" of v. is *oiden*, meaning a knowledge whi stresses perception and insight. T "know" of v. 17 is *ginōskō* which has t 'connotation of knowledge of God, knowledge gained by personal experien (John 17:3; I John 3:24). Jesus is sa ing to his perplexed and largely skepti audience that if they really want to kn whether Jesus' claims are true they shou earnestly set themselves to *do* the will God. Commitment to existing "light" the condition for gaining more "ligh

[4] For reasons why John 7:15-24 is thought to follow John 5:45 see JHB, I, xvii-xix, and Excur following chapter six.

[5] S. Schechter, *Aspects of Rabbinic Theology* (New York: Macmillan, 1909), pp. 216, 217, 2

21 Jesus answered and said unto them, I did one work, and ye all marvel because thereof.

22 Moses hath given you circumcision (not that it is of Moses, but of the fathers); and on the sabbath ye circumcise a man.

23 If a man receiveth circumcision on the sabbath, that the law of Moses may not be broken; are ye wroth with me, because I made a man every whit whole on the sabbath?

24 Judge not according to appearance, but judge righteous judgment.

25 Some therefore of them of Jerusalem said, Is not this he whom they seek to kill?

26 And lo, he speaketh openly, and they say nothing unto him.  Can it be that the rulers indeed know that this is the Christ?

27 Howbeit we know this man whence he is: but when the Christ cometh, no one knoweth whence he is.

---

21 **I did one work.** This is a reference to the healing at Bethesda (5:5).

22 As a specific instance of their failure to follow Moses' law precisely, Jesus cited their inconsistency of circumcising a boy on the Sabbath day.  They break the Sabbath themselves in their insistence on circumcision on the eighth day; now they are accusing Jesus of Sabbath desecration simply for making a man whole, the opposite of injuring one by circumcision. Consequently they are inconsistent and do not "judge righteous judgment."  They are so degraded in their perversity and sin, Jesus said, that they even plan to kill him, in spite of the fact that there

was "no unrighteousness in him."  What a scathing accusation!  *Kai* (and) is used adversatively, meaning "but" or "and yet" in vv. 19, 20.

27 **No one knoweth whence he is.**  There is evidence that there was a general tradition that no one would know who the Messiah was or where he came from prior to his sudden appearance.  This is stated in IV Ezra 13:51 — "Even so can no man upon earth see my Son, or those that are with him, but in the time of his day."[6] G. F. Moore has noted that the common literature of "popular Judaism," such as Enoch, made a greater impression on the common people than it did upon the

---

and assurance.  The Jews were always asking for more evidence before committing themselves in Jesus' favor.  They demanded further "signs" (Mark 8:11; John 6:30) as the condition of belief.  In response Jesus emphasized that their trouble was not lack of evidence (John 5:47; Luke 16:31) but hardness of heart.  They, in fact, were less responsive to evidence than the people of Nineveh or the Queen of Sheba (Matt. 12:41, 42).  While John's emphasis on knowledge has some affinities with Greek thought of the day, it is more like the emphasis on knowledge of God in the Old Testament, especially in Hosea. To Greeks like Aristotle knowledge came through the five senses.  The Platonists were nearer to the New Testament emphasis when they conceived of knowledge as the reward of disciplined meditation (Plato: *Republic* VII, 533; cf. *Timaeus*

51).  While Plato, like most moderns, thought of knowledge, conviction, and assurance as the reward of native ability disciplined to the acquisition of information, Jesus, as interpreted by John, taught that knowledge of God is given on the condition of commitment.  Wesley made a distinction between a knowledge of the natural world mediated through the senses and a knowledge of the things of God mediated through faith, the "eyes of the soul" (J. Wesley, *Appeal to Men to Reason and Religion*).[d]  Jesus indicated that motive was a decisive factor in his own mission as well.  He was aware of the danger of seeking his own glory and of the importance of seeking the glory of God.  In the end he can truly say, "I have glorified thee" (John 17:4) and make this fact the basis of his own petition. The highest act of which man's will

6 Cited in R. H. Charles, *Apocrypha and Pseudepigrapha of the Old Testament*, II, 619.  So also Justin, *Thypho* 8, I Enoch 48:6.
d Cited in G. A. Turner, "John Wesley as an Interpreter of Scripture," *Inspiration and Revelation* (Grand Rapids: Eerdmans, 1957), p. 100.

28 Jesus therefore cried in the temple, teaching and saying, Ye both know me, and know whence I am; and I am not come of myself, but he that sent me is true, whom ye know not.

29 I know him; because I am from him, and he sent me.

30 They sought therefore to take him: and no man laid his hand on him, because his hour was not yet come.

31 But of the multitude many believed on him; and they said, When the Christ shall come, will he do more signs than those which this man hath done?

---

rabbis.[7] This judgment is substantiated by the Dead Sea Scrolls. This would help explain v. 27.

28 **Therefore** (*oun*) is better translated "in response." Of its 196 occurrences in John's Gospel it should be translated "therefore" only about 55 times; as adversative ("but" or "however") 30 times; as intensive or emphatic ("really" or "indeed") 5 times (John 6:62; 9:10; 16:22; 19:25; 20:30); as responsive ("in reply" or "in response") 27 times (John 7:6, 16, 28, 47) as resumptive or continuative ("then," "now") 79 times.[8]

29 **I know him; because I am from him and he sent me.** These are plain but strong and graphic words! Jesus came from God and was sent by him. The hostile Jews were altogether wrong in their estimate of him. "Their syllogism was as follows:

Major premise — No one will know where the real Messiah comes from.

Minor premise — We know where Jesus comes from.

Conclusion — Hence, Jesus cannot be the real Messiah."

(Wm H, II, p. 17).

Since their premises were faulty, so was their conclusion. John reiterated the statement that Jesus came from God (1:14; 6:46; 16:27; 17:8) and that he knew God intimately (1:18; 8:55; 17:25).

31 **Many believed on him** (*polloi episteusan eis auton*). The verb **believed** is in the aorist tense. Had John wanted to emphasize that they continued believing, he would have used the imperfect tense. If he had desired to imply that they were then believing on Christ and remained in that relationship, he would have used the perfect tense. The aorist simply states the fact that at that particular point of time they believed on or in him. The only ground mentioned for their belief is the miracles performed by him. "Do"

---

is capable is the renunciation of self will. As Tennyson expressed it, "Our wills are ours, we know not how; Our wills are ours, to make them thine." To "will to do his will," then, means a basic and all-inclusive decision to renounce self-will and to choose God's will. Such a person can say, "I delight to do thy will, O God, yea, thy law is within my heart" (Ps. 40:8).

20 **Thou hast a demon** is the same as saying today, "You are a fanatic." They had said the same concerning John the Baptist because of his ascetic habits (Luke 7:33). They may also have meant that Jesus would have to be in touch with the occult world in order to suspect his hearers of murder. They may have thought Jesus was morbid and suspicious — they were quite unaware of the *secret* decision of

their leaders to do away with Jesus (cf. John 5:15; 7:1).

21 The controversy over Sabbath desecration, touched off by the healing recorded in ch. 5, remains in the background here. The point seems to be this: The Jews were angered because Jesus restored an infirm man to soundness, health, and wholeness on the Sabbath. Among the rabbis, physical wholeness and health were kindred ideas. They sanctioned circumcision on the Sabbath day even though it made the person temporarily unsound and unhealthy (cf. Gen. 34: 25; Josh. 5:8) but they criticized Jesus for making one whole on the Sabbath. There is a play upon words here; literally it means to "make a whole man sound and healthy." The contrast between apparent legality and righteous judgment is

---

[7] G. F. Moore, *Judaism* (Cambridge: Harvard University Press, 1927), I, p. 127.
[8] D-M, pp. 252-58. *Oun* can well be translated "now" in John 7:11, 15, 40, 45 and "then" in 7:25, 33.

32 The Pharisees heard the multitude murmuring these things concerning him; and the chief priests and the Pharisees sent officers to take him.

33 Jesus therefore said, Yet a little while am I with you, and I go unto him that sent me.

34 Ye shall seek me, and shall not find me: and where I am, ye cannot come.

35 The Jews therefore said among themselves, Whither will this man go that we shall not find him? will he go unto the Dispersion among the Greeks, and teach the Greeks?

36 What is this word that he said, Ye shall seek me, and shall not find me; and where I am, ye cannot come?

---

or "perform" (*poiei* — present tense) instead of "hath done" (*epoiēsen* — aorist tense) is found in several important old manuscripts.[9]

32 **The Pharisees**, only about 7,000 in number due to restrictive membership, were the most influential religious leaders in Palestine. The chief priests, the Sadducees, were the official political as well as religious leaders.[10] With such a combination of opposition against Jesus, his doom was virtually assured. The unorganized masses, who heard him gladly and enjoyed witnessing the miracles he performed, could not have saved Jesus from execution without staging a successful revolt against powerfully entrenched forces.[11]

33 The **little while** that Jesus said he would be with them was only about six months, approximately from October to April.

34 **Where I am ye cannot come** refers to his presence with the Father where they could not come after death since they had rejected God's Son. "No one cometh unto the Father, but by me" said Jesus on another occasion (John 14:6).

35, 36 The Jews discussed among themselves what Jesus had just said, but they did not come to a correct conclusion. The **Dispersion** apparently meant all Jews not living in Palestine. **The Greeks** could mean proselytes, but in John's vocabulary it very likely meant Gentiles. Through his disciples, a few years later, Christ did go to the Dispersion and also to the Greeks with results far exceeding his success among Palestinian Jews.

---

stressed (v. 24). In so saying Jesus challenged them to discernment between the good and the best. "The good had become the enemy of the best."[e]

24 Here, as on so many occasions, the Pharisees and Jesus had contrasting ideas of holiness. They thought that less activity made the Sabbath more hallowed. Jesus believed that the sanctity of the day does not exclude an act of God's grace. Abraham's circumcision (Gen. 17:10-27) was linked with the call to perfection, to blamelessness, or wholeness (Gen. 17:1); the opposite of being maimed or blemished. To Jesus the making of a man whole on the Sabbath was a fulfillment or perfection of the Law, not something contrary to it. Jesus, then, was not liberalizing the

interpretation of the Law but rather fulfilling it (CKB, p. 265). This contrast between appearance and essential righteousness is one vhich Jesus constantly emphasized. Hence he challenged them to judge on sounder principles.

### c. Jesus' Origin, They Say, Proves He is not the Messiah (vv. 25-36)

25-36 The question of this paragraph is Jesus' identity, but it is related closely to his place of origin. The author skillfully shows here the interplay of forces swirling around the controversial figure of Jesus. He was now known outside of Galilee, and the Jews in Jerusalem, natives and pilgrims, were trying desperately to "size

[9] E.Q., Aleph D., Theta, Phi, Old Latin, and the Vulgate.
[10] For the classic description of the Pharisees and Sadducees see Jos. *Ant.*, XVII, ii, 4ff.; and Jos. *War*, II viii, 2ff.
[11] As G. A. Smith (*Jerusalem*) has pointed out however, the *vox populi* was influential, hence, before the crucifixion, the leaders maneuvered to have the mob demand, "Crucify him."
[e] The good excludes not only the bad, but also the better. Cf. Paul Tillich, *Systematic Theology* (Chicago: University of Chicago Press, 1957), p. 279.

37 Now on the last day, the great *day* of the feast, Jesus stood and cried, saying, If any man thirst, let him come unto me and drink.

38 He that believeth on me, as the scripture hath said, from within him shall flow rivers of living water.

39 But this spake he of the Spirit, which they that believed on him were to receive: for the Spirit was not yet *given;* because Jesus was not yet glorified.

37 **The great day of the feast.** According to the Old Testament (Lev. 23:39), this may have been the 7th day, or according to later practice, on the 8th day (Macc. 10:6). "They kept the feast eight days with gladness" (cf. Jos. *Ant.*, III. x. 4). The Old Testament festival ended on the seventh day (Lev. 23:39, 41), the eighth being a day of rest and rejoicing. Josephus (Jos. *Ant.*, III. 245). II Maccabees, and Rabbinic tradition speak of it as an eight day feast. If, as Strack-Billerback believe (S-B, II, 799-812), the "great day" was the seventh, it would coincide with the practice of a water libation on this day.[12] According to rabbinic tradition and practice, on the seventh day a procession of priests drew water from the pool of Siloam and poured it out at the base of the altar of burnt-offering as a reminder of the time when God gave water to the thirsty multitude in the wilderness. Whether on the seventh or eighth day, on this climactic "great day," Jesus offered eternal

quenching of spiritual thirst to all who accepted him as the true Messiah. The expression, "he that believeth," is a translation of a present participle (*pisteuōn*) and denotes a continued relationship of trust in Christ.

38 **Rivers of living water** is interpreted by John to mean the presence of the Holy Spirit in the lives of God's people. In Isaiah 58:11 a similar statement is made about God's people being like a "watered garden." "The saying in John 4:14 is so similar that it seems preferable to understand it in the same sense" (EGT, I, 768). The passage, however, to which this is the most similar is John 3:5, "born of water even the Spirit." Most translators render this "born of water and the Spirit," but the *kai* ("and") had the regular meaning "even" as well as "and." Since John has used water as a symbol of the Spirit in 4:14 and here in 7:38, 39, why not assume that he also did in 3:5? Speaking of water in v. 34 he said, **This spake he of the Spirit**

him up." The reactions were varied. This confusion and curiosity came to its height during the middle period of Jesus' public ministry as all four Gospels bear witness. Public perplexity is reflected by the six questions in this paragraph. These questions can be summarized into three. Since the rulers are seeking Jesus' life, why do they permit him to teach here in the temple unchallenged (vv. 25, 26)? Will the true Messiah perform more miracles than Jesus has done (v. 31)? Where will Jesus go that we cannot follow him (vv. 35, 36)? Out of the perplexed multitude two diverse reactions crystallized. *Some believed* on the basis of Jesus' words and works (v. 31). *Others* remained *unconvinced* because of professed uncertainty concerning his origin (v. 27). Confronted as they were by Christ and his demands, none could ever be the same afterwards.

This is still true today. No one confronts Jesus Christ today and remains unchanged.

The Pharisees' reaction at this point was one of indecision about procedure. At first they were slow to apprehend him while he taught boldly in the temple (v. 26). These rulers were finally galvanized into decisive action because of the converts Jesus was winning (v. 32). Even then, however, they seemed to delay final action. Later they were to decide, in conjunction with the Sadducees, that they would arrest Jesus secretly rather than openly.

28 Jesus' assertion was directly contradictory to their profession. Whereas they professed knowledge of God but ignorance of the Christ, the Master states that the reverse is true. They know him but do not know the Father (v. 28).

[12] Dodd, Hoskyns and Barrett argue for the eighth day on the grounds that the observance did not cease until the very last day and that the ceremony of the pouring of water did not necessarily coincide with Jesus' proclamation.

40 *Some* of the multitude therefore, when they heard these words, said, This is of a truth the prophet.

41 Others said, This is the Christ. But some said, What, doth the Christ come out of Galilee?

42 Hath not the scripture said that the Christ cometh of the seed of David, and from Bethlehem, the village where David was?

which those that believed on him were about to receive. Spirit-filled people are a blessing to those around them just as water on fertile soil produces *life*. Every person who is "born again" possesses, to a certain degree, the Holy Spirit. "No one born of God continues sinning (Gk. present tense), for God's seed, (Spirit) abides in him, and he is not able to continue sinning (pres. inf.) because he is born of God" (I John 3:9). When one stops sinning, he thus becomes a worthy example and a powerful, fruitful witness for Christ. (See Exegesis on John 3:5.)

40 At least three divergent views of Jesus now came to expression. Some said he was the prophet (cf. John 1:21), a probable reference to Deuteronomy 18:15, where a prophet like Moses is promised — "The Lord thy God will raise up unto thee a prophet from the midst of thee, like unto me." Another group now concluded, This is the Christ, this group voicing a similar but more explicit conviction than the first group. It is not surprising that this invitation should suggest to some the Messiah. John does not say that Jesus spoke of the Spirit to the multitude explicitly. The linking of the Spirit to the water is the Evangelist's editorial comment. The Spirit is associated with the Lord's Anointed several times in the O.T. (e.g., Isa. 61:1-3; 35:6; 41:18; 44:3). Both viewpoints were highly complimentary to Jesus (cf. Matt. 16:13-16 where some called Jesus "a prophet," but Peter said he was the Christ or the Messiah). But a third group sneeringly asked, "The Christ does not come out of Galilee, does he?" (note the force of the negative *mē* in the questions). Does not the Scripture say that the Christ comes from Bethlehem? Jesus did indeed come from Bethlehem but it was obviously not generally known. Had

The point is that they knew his human origin, as Jesus of Nazareth, but refused to acknowledge that he came also from God. The difficulty of reconciling the human and divine natures of Jesus Christ remained as a major theological problem in the church for centuries. It is understandable that his contemporaries found it difficult. But Jesus stresses here that they could more easily believe if they were closer to God in spirit.

### d. Jesus' Invitation to Partake of the Spirit (vv. 37-44)

37-39 Two of the great affirmations attributed to Jesus by the Fourth Gospel use images that are simple and universally understood: "I am the bread of life," and "I am the water of life." The attention given to water in chs. 3 and 4, as typifying life in the Son, now receives additional emphasis. The occasion of this great invitation, If any man thirst let him come unto me and drink, was a dramatic one. The great, joyous feast of the tabernacles was nearing its climactic close. Arguments about whether or not Jesus was the expected Messiah were inconclusive and indecisive. During the eight-day observances the people were dramatically reminded of the wilderness sojourn of their ancestors. The highlight of these observances was the moment when the high priests poured out the water from the pool of Siloam, thus reminding the people of the time water emerged from the rock under Moses' command (Num. 20:11).

At this moment, it seems Jesus appeared with his invitation and challenge: He that believeth on me, out of his innermost being shall flow rivers of living water.f Living water, in contemporary contexts, means "running water."g The intimate

f Jos. *Ant.*, XIII. xiii. 5; cf. Edersheim, *op. cit.* II, pp. 156-160.
g *Didache*, vii, 1. 2.

43 So there arose a division in the multitude because of him.
44 And some of them would have taken him; but no man laid hands on him.
45 The officers therefore came to the chief priests and Pharisees; and they said unto them, Why did ye not bring him?
46 The officers answered, Never man so spake.
47 The Pharisees therefore answered them, Are ye also led astray?
48 Hath any of the rulers believed on him, or of the Pharisees?
49 But this multitude that knoweth not the law are accursed.

they asked him he very likely would have set them right in the matter, but they would have found some other excuse for not accepting him as the Messiah.

43, 44 **There arose a division . . . and some wanted to arrest him** (*piasai*); **but no man laid hands on him.** Divine providence intervened until Christ had finished his ministry. Repeatedly in this Gospel the reader is reminded that all was going according to plan, that the tragedy of the passion was not a disruption of the divine purpose, but rather its fulfillment.

45-49 The officers sent to arrest Jesus (v. 32) now return without their man. The officers were sent out, according to verse 32, by "the chief priests and the

Pharisees." The Sadducees are not prominent in the four Gospels. They are mentioned only ten times, not at all by John, as compared with about 95 references to Pharisees. There are 20 such references in John. But, as Josephus says, while the Sadducees were far less numerous than the Pharisees, they wielded an influence far greater than their numbers would suggest. They were of the aristocracy and firmly entrenched in the priesthood. As such they had many vested interests. They had come to terms with the Romans and were interested in maintaining the *status quo*. It seems certain, therefore, that when John mentions "the chief priests," the Sadducees are involved. When the two rival religious sects joined

connection between water and life can scarcely be appreciated except by one who lives in an arid or semi-arid region. In such places green vegetation is limited to oases, springs, or streams where there is a constant supply of water. This phenomena is perhaps most clearly marked in Egypt, a land where the rainfall is about two inches annually. Egypt is a vast desert except for the long winding green strip which is the Nile. The entire population of 22 million is dependent upon this one "river of life." In the later prophets the connection between water and the Spirit is equally intimate, as in Isaiah 32:15 — "until the Spirit be poured upon us from on high, and the wilderness become a fruitful field" — "wilderness" here meaning an area devoid of vegetation. In Isaiah 44:3 — "I will pour water upon him that is thirsty, . . . I will pour my Spirit upon thy seed." The connection between the water and the Spirit is indicated again in Ezekiel 36:25-27 as life-giving waters emerge from the temple to give life to the arid Negeb. In ch. 4 the Spirit which Jesus gives is likened to a well-spring of water (cf. Jer. 2:13; 17:13).

But in ch. 7 the figure is much more bold; the spring becomes a river and is adequate not only for the individual consumption but for all. The eschatological overtones are unmistakable here. As envisioned in Joel 2:28 and as fulfilled in Acts 2:16, the historical out-pouring of the Holy Spirit coincided with the day of Pentecost a few months after Jesus uttered these words. It is at least possible that the figure was also suggested by Ezekiel's vision of the life-giving river emerging from the temple area (Ezek. 47:1-12). In what sense was the Spirit not given before Jesus' "glorification" (v. 39)? This must be understood in a relative sense, in the sense of Joel 2:28 and Acts 2:16. Certainly the Spirit of God ministered to the saints before and during the earthly ministry of Jesus, and hence, prior to Pentecost. The difference seems to be this: in Old Testament times through the ministry of John the Baptist, the Spirit was given to only a few individuals and then for special service — such as for judging or prophesying. In the New Covenant the Spirit is to be poured out upon "all flesh" not only for specialized tasks,

50 Nicodemus saith unto them (he that came to him before, being one of them),

51 Doth our law judge a man, except it first hear from himself and know what he doeth?

52 They answered and said unto him, Art thou also of Galilee?  Search, and see that out of Galilee ariseth no prophet.

---

forces in an effort to destroy Jesus, it is not surprising that their combined efforts were successful.

**46 Never man so spake.** In this judgment the "officers" evidenced much sounder judgment than those who sent them.  The reaction of these men was similar to that of those who heard Jesus in the synagogues of Galilee — "he spake as one having authority and not as the scribes" (Mark 1:22).  The common people heard Jesus gladly.  The leaders had little appreciation of the opinion of the common people.  Disdainfully they exclaimed, **This multitude which knoweth not the law are accursed.**  The term was formerly applied to the "people of the land" (*am ha-aretz*) and later acquired, in the minds of the religious aristocracy, a connotation of contempt.[13]

**50-52** The mounting hostility among these religious leaders seemed prejudiced and unjust to at least one of their number.  Nicodemus came to the defense of Jesus, insisting that a man is not guilty until sufficient evidence is presented against him in court.  It was his conviction that the Pharisees, who claimed to know the law, were deliberately disobeying the law in seeking to silence and kill Jesus when his guilt had not yet been legally determined.  By his outspoken word of caution Nicodemus brought on himself instant suspicion and hostility.  Caustically they

---

but also for moral renewal and re-creation.  It has occurred to many commentators that the "well of water" in ch. 4 implies the birth of the Spirit, while the "rivers of water" of ch. 7 implies that Spirit-filled and empowered life which has an outflow for others, so that the believer becomes a channel of blessing.  The progression here is noteworthy — from being "born" of the Spirit (3:5) to being "filled" with the Spirit (7:38).  The Spirit-filled life is normative for the Christian (Eph. 5:18).

**40-44** The effect of Jesus' dramatic assertion and invitation must have been sensational.  The reaction was immediate and diverse.  Again and again our author points out that reaction to the same stimulus could be diverse and was often in contrast.  It is a reminder of the truth taught in the Parable of the Soils (Mark 4:2-9), that men react to the same gospel message in a variety of ways.  The thought of the Messiah coming out of Galilee would naturally encounter a deep-seated prejudice.  The men of Jerusalem and Judaea thought of the Galileans as second-rate Jews at the best, and at the worst, as Judaized pagans.  Furthermore, they had been deeply influenced by the rabbinic expositions of Micah 5:2, which is probably the earliest interpretation of Isaiah 7:14.  The passage from Micah, the rural contemporary of Isaiah, hails Bethlehem as the city from whence comes the Messiah-ruler of Israel.  The people, not aware of Jesus' birth in Bethlehem, found it almost impossible to reconcile a Galilean Messiah with either their prejudices or with their Old Testament.

How may v. 42 be reconciled with v. 27?  One says that no one knows the place of the Christ's origin in advance, and others say that he will originate in Bethlehem.  Howard suggests that, in v. 27, the reference is to a rabbinic tradition based on Malachi 3:1 — "the messenger of the Covenant shall suddenly come to his temple" — which stressed the suddenness of the messianic advent from an unknown source (WFH, VIII, 586).  In v. 42, the allusion is to the belief based on Micah 5:2.  It is quite possible that both traditions were current: two rival theories about the Messiah's advent, similar to rival theories concerning the details of his second coming today.  Since he is a descendant of David, it would be appropriate that the Messiah come from the city of David.  John does not tell his readers that Jesus was born in

---

[13] Ezek. 12:19; later applied to non-Jews (Ezra 10:2); cf. S-B, II, 494.

53 [And they went every man unto his own house:

---

demanded, *Are you also of Galilee?* as if that would be the only reason he demanded justice.

**Search and see that out of Galilee ariseth no prophet.** If this is the correct reading, the Pharisees were betraying their ignorance of the Scriptures. Jonah and possibly Hosea came out of Galilee (II Kings 14:25 cf. Jonah 1:1). Another reading places the definite article before "prophet" (*prophētes*), with the resultant reading: "The prophet does not rise out of Galilee." This reading is very fitting in this context.[14]

Verse 53 is omitted in the best manuscripts as well as vv. 1-11 in ch. 8.

---

Bethlehem before becoming a resident of Nazareth. He may assume that his readers are familiar with this from the other Gospels or he may wish to stress the point that the Christ came from God (John 1:14; 3:13; 5:30; 6:33; 7:28 — Hoskyns, p. 323).

### e. Nicodemus Calls for Justice (vv. 45-52)

The henchmen of the high priests paid a marvelous tribute to Jesus. They had orders to arrest him, but what he did and said overwhelmed them to the extent that they deliberately disobeyed. **Never man so spake.** Why arrest the best speaker ever heard, especially when he was innocent? They took a sensible attitude. But the self-righteous rulers ridiculed the report of the officers. **Has any ruler or Pharisee believed on him? This multitude which does not know the law is accursed.**

It may be that these Pharisees had been influenced by the fact that often the populace would flock to hear an eloquent rabbi expound the Law in the synagogue and forsake a more learned scribe or doctor of the law in a nearby synagogue. They may have learned to distrust the judgment of the populace.[h] It is more likely, in this instance, that it was a reflection of the Pharisees' contempt of the common man (the *hoi polloi*) who was less precise about the legalistic niceties of the traditions of the elders. Comparable to the sophists of Athens, who were conscious of their intellectual superiority to the common people, the Pharisees, as the religious elite, thought of the common people as too far removed from the temple to really fulfill the Law and too ignorant of its contents to meet its demands. They were perfectionists in Law observance and regarded all non-specialists with disdain. Because Jesus lacked their fastidiousness in Law observance, because he appealed to the essential spirit of the Law, the common people sensed in him a kindred spirit and "heard him gladly." Seen in this perspective, "the century of the common man" was the first century no less than the twentieth.

50-52 Was Nicodemus a secret believer? Can any true believer remain a secret one? The three pictures given of Nicodemus in the Fourth Gospel are consistent. He came during the night for a private interview with Jesus; of no one else was this said. After Jesus' death he defied prevailing public opinion by providing the victim's body a decent burial, an important factor in Bible lands. In this passage he risked his status as a "ruler of the Jews" by counseling fairness in dealing with Jesus. In this emotion-charged atmosphere one could scarcely be objective; he would be either hostile to Jesus or a partisan of his cause. This much is obvious: Nicodemus did not share their prejudiced view of the teacher from Galilee. Unlike them, he did not regard Jesus as a dangerous impostor, and he had courage to call for fairness when it would expose him to ostracism. It is clear that Nicodemus was doing his own thinking and speaking. It is tragic that his sense of justice did not find an echo in other members of the Sanhedrin. The conclusion may be tentatively drawn that the one man who urged giving Jesus a fair hearing was a sympathizer with Jesus and, possibly, a disciple. To have done more than he did would have meant exclusion from the Sanhedrin with

---

[14] Bodmer Papyrus II (P66, 200 A.D.) has the definite article *O* before *prophētes*. This reading would indicate that the Messiah does not originate in Galilee, rather than a blanket assertion that no prophet ever arose in Galilee.

[h] Edersheim, *Life and Times of Jesus the Messiah* (New York: Longmans, Green Co., 1899), I, p. 447.

no opportunity to influence his colleagues. Perhaps he was too cautious, but at least he was courageous.

In summary we may observe that here, to a greater extent than in any other chapter, the crucial issue is the identity of Jesus. Out of the conflict of fact and rumor, deed and word, there are crystallized three different identifications of Jesus: some thought him an impostor, some a God-sent prophet, and others the Christ. There were also three types of reaction to him. Some became more openly hostile, others were perplexed and non-committal, and others believed. Nicodemus appears again as one who apparently believed but did not openly espouse the cause, typical of many who secretly admired Christ.

In many nations today, where anti-Christian pressure is severe, there are many who "believe" but do not confess Christ openly. During the early days of the Protestant Reformation, there were many groups of secret believers in central Europe. The Bible gives no encouragement to such caution. Today, the millions who "live and move and have their being" under these conditions need sympathy and prayer.

As a remedy for this hostile world, with its temptation to compromise, the promise of Christ, that to believe is to be filled with the Spirit, is offered to all. The disciples accepted this challenge and made possible the writing of the Acts (Acts 4:31).

# CHAPTER VIII

But Jesus went unto the mount of Olives.

2 And early in the morning he came again into the temple, and all the people came unto him; and he sat down, and taught them.

## EXEGESIS

This interesting story is not part of the text, but it is included in the footnotes in Nestle's Greek New Testament, in the RSV, and in the NEB. It is omitted completely in C. B. Williams' translation, with this footnote: "vv. 1-11 not in best mss." Goodspeed omitted it without even a footnote; however, J. B. Phillips has it in his translation of the New Testament. A. T. Robertson (WPNT, III, 135) has stated that it "is certainly not a genuine part of John's Gospel. The oldest and best manuscripts (Aleph, A B C L W) do not have it. . . . Some manuscripts put it

at the close of John's Gospel and some place it in Luke. It is probably a true story for it is like Jesus, but i does not belong to John's Gospel." B. F. Westcott's view (BFW, p. 125) wa similar: "This account . . . is certainly no a part of St. John's narrative. The evidence against its genuiness . . . is overwhelming but on the other hand it is beyond doub an authentic fragment of apostolic tradi tion." C. K. Barrett does not include o comment on it in his splendid critica commentary. Bodmer Papyrus II (P⁶⁶) the oldest extant copy of this chapter does not include vv. 1-11. However since this passage represents the magnani

## EXPOSITION

### 4. THE WOMAN TAKEN IN ADULTERY (7:53—8:11)

#### a. Textual Problems

The episode of the woman taken in adultery is one of the few instances of the inclusion of deutero-canonical material in the text of the New Testament. The evidence against its having been written by the author of the rest of the Gospel is convincing enough to most scholars.[a] It has a certain intrinsic merit, a consistency with the well-attested words of Jesus, which sets it somewhat apart from the "sayings" of the New Testament Apocrypha. The story does appear consistent with what is known of Jewish practices at that time and of Jesus' characteristic attitude. The story creates interest because of the skillful sequence of plot, suspense, and surprising climax in which the accused is forgiven, the villains vanquished,

and the hero glorified. The story is both wholesome and edifying. The history o its insertion in some texts is quite uncer tain.[b]

#### b. The Test Question (vv. 1-6)

1 Why did Jesus go to the Mount o Olives at this time? It was probably for rest and for prayer; it is reported tha Jesus often went there for retiremen (John 18:2). This pattern of retiring fo rest and prayer was practiced in Galile (Mark 1:35; Luke 6:12; John 6:15), an prayer at this critical time would be consistent with the Master's habit. Ther is a tradition that it was on one of thes seasons of retirement on the Mount o Olives that Jesus taught the disciples the model prayer (Luke 11:1). The larg Carmelite convent and church of th *Pater Noster* now commemorate the in cident.

---

[a] It is absent from the oldest codices of the second, third and fourth centuries: Bodmer P⁶⁶, Sinaiticus Vaticanus, Washington and Koridethi and Alexandrinus, but is found in Bezae (5th cent.), O.L., the Vulgate and later Greek MSS. No Greek commentator before the twelfth century cites it, but among the Lati fathers Ambrose, Augustine, and Jerome quote from it. It has been suggested that its insertion here ma be due to a contrast between judging on the basis of externals and on the basis of essentials in 7:24 an 8:15 (Hoskyns, p. 564).

[b] See F. A. Schilling, "The Story of Jesus and the Adulteress," ATR, XXXVII (1955), p. 91-106

3 And the scribes and the Pharisees bring a woman taken in adultery; and having set her in the midst,

4 they say unto him, Teacher, this woman hath been taken in adultery, in the very act.

5 Now in the law Moses commanded us to stone such: what then sayest thou of her?

6 And this they said, trying him, that they might have *whereof* to accuse him. But Jesus stooped down, and with his finger wrote on the ground.

7 But when they continued asking him, he lifted up himself, and said unto them, He that is without sin among you, let him first cast a stone at her.

---

mous spirit of Christ, and has early tradition (Papias) favoring it, it is included in this commentary.

**4 Woman taken in adultery** — While Jesus was teaching hundreds of people in the temple, he was interrupted by hostile Jewish leaders, who had arrested a woman guilty of adultery. The purpose was simply to entrap Jesus; they had a court and judges for such cases.

**3, 4 Moses commanded us to stone such, however** (adversative use of *oun*), **what do you say?** If Jesus did not concur with Moses' teachings, he would lose favor with the masses. He would be discredited as an orthodox teacher, and thus the public would more readily consent to his execution. Instead of answering as they hoped, he simply wrote on the ground. It has been conjectured that he wrote the name of each questioner who was guilty of the same sin or of some other equally great sin.

**7** What a surprise to his accusers! Jesus did not act contrary to the law of Moses. Instead, he made the execution

---

**3 The woman taken in adultery . . . in the midst.** According to this story, this was a thinly disguised maneuver to present Jesus with a dilemma like that of the Herodians when they asked whether or not they should pay tribute to Caesar (Mark 12:13-17). The death penalty to which the plotters referred is commanded in Leviticus 20:10 — "The adulterer and the adulteress shall surely be put to death," and in Deuteronomy 22:22 — "they shall both of them die, the man . . . and the woman; so shalt thou put away evil from Israel."

The matter of severity in punishing those who broke the Law was a subject of debate among the Jews at this time. The Law seemed more harsh in punishment than the majority of people felt appropriate. For example, the Law of Moses plainly states that the blasphemer is to be stoned (Lev. 24:10-16). But in the Judaism of the New Testament period, this rigorous law was interpreted so that it was applicable only for a few months after children reached the age of thirteen, and the parents had to be the witnesses. This,

in effect, nullified a law deemed to be too harsh.[c] Thus the "oral tradition" made the written law "of none effect." Jesus had accused them of evading the Torah by legalistic interpretations in many areas (Mark 7:13). Their problem in trying to recognize the law as fixed and unchangeable and yet trying to harmonize it with a world of changing mores. Their answer was to interpret and qualify it to such an extent that it was no longer operative. This solution seemed to them better than either ignoring the Law or obeying it to the letter. Had Jesus insisted on stoning he would have incurred criticism as being too severe; if he had not insisted on the death penalty he would have been accused of encouraging the breaking of the Law. It seems likely also that to have recommended the death penalty would have brought him into conflict with Roman law, which forbade capital punishment by Jews (RHL, p. 347). Yet, since the subject was debatable, the inquiry they made of Jesus had the appearance of being an innocent search for truth.[d]

**6 And this they said trying him, . . .**

---

[c] H. A. Wolfson, Harvard Lectures on Judaism, February, 1944.
[d] The passage was a problem in some of the ancient churches because they felt Jesus had dealt too leniently with the woman. Basil required 15 yrs. penance, the Council of Ancyra 7 years and the Council of Eliberis (Spain) 5 years (Bingham, *Antiquities*, XVI, ch. 11, cited by P. Schaff in Lange's *Commentary*).

8 And again he stooped down, and with his finger wrote on the ground.

9 And they, when they heard it, went out one by one, beginning from the eldest, *even* unto the last: and Jesus was left alone, and the woman, where she was, in the midst.

10 And Jesus lifted up himself, and said unto her, Woman, where are they? did no man condemn thee?

11 And she said, No man, Lord. And Jesus said, Neither do I condemn thee: go thy way; from henceforth sin no more.]

12 Again therefore Jesus spake unto them, saying, I am the light of the world: he that followeth me shall not walk in the darkness, but shall have the light of life.

of it a personal and spiritual matter rather than merely a legal affair. So penetrating and searching were Jesus' words that the consciences of the accusers were awakened.

**9 They went out one by one.** Jesus and the woman were left alone. A sense of guilt made each leader feel unworthy to punish the guilty woman. But the crowd in the temple still was present, and it witnessed the defeat and chagrin of the accusers. What a tremendous relief that must have been to the adulteress; one moment expecting death and the next being set free!

**11 Neither do I condemn thee.** The accusers, out of shame, did not punish her; but Jesus, out of infinite compassion for her, refused to condemn her. He stood ready to forgive her sins. At the same time, he cautioned her: **from henceforth sin no more.** Such mercy and tenderness must have made a powerful impression on the embarrassed and distraught woman. It is likely that she later on became a Christian. Certainly she could not help feeling grateful to her liberator!

**12** *Oun* in v. 12 means "now"; in vv. 21, 22, 28, and 31 it is also used transition-

**but Jesus . . . wrote upon the ground.** Three contrasting figures are in this drama: (1) the woman, guilt-ridden and defenseless, (2) her accusers, caring little for Law as such and less for the women, eager to use her to embarrass Christ, and (3) Jesus, refusing to be pushed to a hasty decision. He did not assume a posture of defense. He calmly ignored both the accusers and the accused and, with his fingers, scratched Hebrew or Aramaic characters in the dust — the only known instance of his writing. "The scraping or drawing figures on the ground with a stick or the finger has been in many countries a common expression of deliberate silence or embarrassment" (EGT, I, 769). The silence was awkward and increasingly embarrassing to the Pharisees, who waited the Master's reply first with confidence, and then with growing impatience.

### c. The Answer (vv. 7-11)

**7 They continued asking.** Both the word "asking" itself (*epimenō*) and its tense (imperfect) stress the persistence with which they pressed Jesus for an answer.

**He that is without sin.** The word "without sin" (*anamartētos*) is found in the New

Testament only here and rarely elsewhere. The root, however, is the usual term for sin and probably does not imply the specific sin of adultery (WFH, VIII, 593). Once again Jesus repeated the operation; he stooped to write with his finger in the dust. Something in Jesus' words and actions, something in his attitude, must have penetrated the consciousness of these evil-minded men so that they saw themselves. They began to realize that more was at stake than trying to trap Jesus. They may even have recognized the evil in their real motive, which was not to uphold the law or to deal justly with the sinful woman, but rather to find an occasion against an innocent and influential man. Jesus' refusal to fall into their trap, his refusal to enter into an argument with them, lifted the matter to a higher plane. They realized that Jesus saw through their snare; they had met their master in the area of jurisprudence and morals. Rather than face the issue they departed, mortified and silent.

This episode is very similar to the account recorded in Luke 7:40-50. In both accounts the sinful woman is in contrast to the self-righteous Pharisees. Jesus re-

13 The Pharisees therefore said unto him, Thou bearest witness of thyself; thy witness is not true.

14 Jesus answered and said unto them, Even if I bear witness of myself, my witness is true; for I know whence I came, and whither I go; but ye know not whence I come, or whither I go.

15 Ye judge after the flesh; I judge no man.

16 Yea and if I judge, my judgment is true; for I am not alone, but I and the Father that sent me.

17 Yea and in your law it is written, that the witness of two men is true.

18 I am he that beareth witness of myself, and the Father that sent me beareth witness of me.

19 They said therefore unto him, Where is thy Father? Jesus answered, Ye know neither me, nor my Father: if ye knew me, ye would know my Father also.

20 These words spake he in the treasury, as he taught in the temple: and no man took him; because his hour was not yet come.

---

ally but is properly rendered "then"; while in vv. 13, 19, 25, and 57 the preferred translation is "in response." The present participle in Greek, **he that follows me,** implies a continuance in following (*akolouthōn*). The use of the double negative (*ou mē*) makes very emphatic the statement: **"he will never walk in darkness but he will have the light of life."** In other words, Christ will always bring light into his life and never at any time permit darkness to overwhelm him. Christ will always be present: cf. "Though I walk

through the valley . . . thou art with me" (Ps. 23:4).

13-18 To the charge on the part of the Pharisees that his witness concerning himself was not true, Jesus replies that the charge is false. He insists that what he says is dependable not only because he says so, but also because God, who sent him, says so. **Your law says the witness of two men is true** (Deut. 17:6).

19, 20 **If you knew me, ye would know my Father also.** "Know" (*eideite* — pluperfect) is used in both clauses here in

---

bukes the hypocrisy of the Pharisees and shows mercy and forgiveness to the woman. In these instances both Jesus' concern with righteousness and his compassion are stressed. In striking contrast is the false idea of righteousness or holiness held by the Pharisees, the idea that righteousness is exclusive and not redemptive, this idea that stressed status and privilege rather than evangelism.

11 **Neither do I condemn thee . . . sin no more.** Did Jesus let the woman off too easily, so easily as to minimize her sin? For a time in the eastern church, this story was passed over in silence. Parallel passages are John 5:14 (where he bade the healed man to "sin no more"), Luke 7:48 ("thy sins are forgiven"), Luke 19:10 (to Zacchaeus: "salvation has come to this house") and Luke 15:2 ("this man welcomes sinners" — BV). The fact that Jesus said, "sin no more" means that he did not minimize her sin. He did lift the doctrine of repentance and forgiveness into new prominence.

### d. Significance of the Story

This episode is consistent with the New Testament emphasis on grace. The story teaches that (1) repentance and forgiveness are available to all, (2) righteousness is more than outward conformity to the Torah (Law), (3) mercy is not inconsistent with a concern for holiness, and (4) professed concern for legal exactitude is no substitute for a concern for persons as ends in themselves.

### 5. THE LIGHT OF THE WORLD (8:12-9:41)

#### a. Its Source in God (vv. 12-20)

12 **I am the light of the world.** This is another of the great "I am" passages and also an elaboration of another breathtaking metaphor of the Master. The memory of the sojourn in the wilderness is echoed faintly here. The "light" recalls the "pillar of fire by night" which symbolized the presence and protection of God. The word "light" (*phōs*) occurs 76 times in the New Testament, of which,

21 He said therefore again unto them, I go away, and ye shall seek me, and shall die in your sin: whither I go, ye cannot come.

22 The Jews therefore said, Will he kill himself, that he saith, Whither I go, ye cannot come?

23 And he said unto them, Ye are from beneath; I am from above: ye are of this world; I am not of this world.

---

a contrary-to-fact sentence. Since they did not recognize Jesus for what he was, they did not know God. This agrees with the statement in 14:9, "He that hath seen me, hath seen the Father." The most reliable and adequate picture of God is Jesus Christ. Again, John repeats the statement: No one arrested him, because his hour was not yet come. Although Jesus taught in the temple, over which his bloodthirsty enemies had supervision, he remained free to continue his ministry. God was able to make, "the wrath of man to praise him" (Ps. 76:10).

21-24 Jesus very frankly and boldly states that those who do not accept him as Savior will die in their sin (singular in v. 21; plural in v. 24). The reason given for judgment upon them is, you do not believe that I am he. The expression ego eimi ("I am he") definitely means "the Messiah" here. It occurs also in 4:26,

---

23 occurrences are found in John's Gospel. The metaphorical usage, meaning spiritual illumination, is a prominent feature of the Fourth Gospel and yet is found also in the Sermon on the Mount ("Ye are the light of the world" Matt. 5:14-16; and elsewhere, Matt. 4:16; Luke 2:32). As previewed in the prologue (John 1:4-9) and amplified in this passage, the concept of "light" harks back to the Genesis account of creation. Jesus Christ created the light (John 1:3; Col. 1:16; Heb. 1:2) and yet is himself the light. Among the highest forms of pagan religions was the worship of the sun,[e] which was popular at Heliopolis in Egypt, in Asia Minor, in Lebanon (Baalbek), and especially in Persia (Zoroastrianism). The Aztec Indians are a notable example of sun worship with their famous "Pyramid of the Sun." In the New Testament, God the Father is spoken of as Light (e.g., Jas. 1:17; I Tim. 6:16; I John 1:5, 7; 2:8). In spite of messianic connotations of the term "light" and the audacity of the claim itself, there is no indication that the hearers branded the assertion as blasphemous. Instead they merely challenged the validity of his witness, since it lacked collaboration.

13-18 In these verses the argument passes from a discussion of light to the kindred theme of judgment, another prominent feature of this Gospel. The kinship between light and judgment (krisis) is close. This relationship was clearly pointed out in 3:19 — "and this is the judgment, that the light is come into the world and men loved the darkness rather than the light. . . ." The Greek word "to judge" (krinein) means "to separate," or "to discriminate." It is usually used to translate the Hebrew shaphat which means "to decide to judge, to establish" or "to govern" and "to condemn."[f] In John 3:17 it is stated that "God sent not the Son into the world to judge the world" while in John 5:22-28, Jesus says, "Neither doth the Father judge any man, but he hath given all judgment unto the Son" because "he is a son of man." Again in John 5:30 Jesus says, "As I hear I judge: and my judgment is righteousness." In John 8:16 Jesus says paradoxically, "I judge no man. Yea and if I judge my judgment is true." How can these apparent contradictions be harmonized? First, Jesus is the natural one to judge because, having a human nature, he can sympathize. Second, while judgment is committed to him his primary role is that of Savior rather than that of judge. Punishment is not from an arbitrary decree but from the inherent necessity of a moral universe. Isaiah's portrait of the future Messiah welcomes him as one whose judgments are characterized by righteousness (Isa. 11:4) in contrast

---

[e] H. Leitzmann, *History of the Christian Church*, tr. by B. Woolf (New York: Scribner's, 1933), II, 43, 49, 55.

[f] Cf. Gen. 19:9; I Sam. 3:13; 8:20.

24 I said therefore unto you, that ye shall die in your sins: for except ye believe that I am *he,* ye shall die in your sins.

25 They said therefore unto him, Who art thou? Jesus said unto them, Even that which I have also spoken unto you from the beginning.

26 I have many things to speak and to judge concerning you: howbeit he that sent me is true; and the things which I heard from him, these speak I unto the world.

27 They perceived not that he spake to them of the Father.

---

8:27, and 13:19 with the same meaning, but it is also found in 6:20; 9:9; and 18:5, 6, 8; meaning only, "I am he." It is reasonable to believe that Jesus' use of the phrase may have had some connection with that term in Deuteronomy 32:39 — "see that I am he, and there is not a God except me" — and in Isaiah 43: 10 — "I am he. Before me there was not another God, and after me there will not be."[1]

25 In answer to the question "Who are you?" Jesus reiterates his claim to be the Messiah. The phrase *tēn archēn* has various translations. In the R.S.V. and Phillips it reads, "Even what I have told you *from the beginning.*" In Weymouth, Goodspeed, and Williams it reads, "Why do I even talk to you *at all?*" A more plausible and literal translation for *tēn archēn* in this context is "the supreme one" (meaning Messiah). *Archē* is rightly translated "ruler" in the R.V. and the R.S.V. in Luke 12:11, and with similar connotations, "principality," in Romans 8:38, Ephesians 3:10; 6:12; and Titus 3:1. It is translated "ruler," "commander," or

---

to contemporary kings and judges. It should be remembered that the Messiah (Christ) means the Lord's Anointed and that among the first of these Spirit-anointed charismatic leaders were the judges of ancient Israel. The role of the Messiah as judge was anticipated in the early judges. The judgment which Christ administers will not be only in a future apocalyptic setting (e.g., Matt. 25) but is also going on in the present. By their reaction to the light, life, and love of God, men secure their own justification or condemnation (judgment) — cf. John 3:19. The general judgment of the future will be only the public announcement of judgment which men have already invoked by their acceptance or rejection of the light (John 3:18). This is one of the most powerful insights of the New Testament. A hint that sin brings its own punishment may be seen in Amos ("I will not turn away the punishment thereof" — 1:3, 6, 9, 11, 13).[g] Perhaps no one has grasped the combined role of Christ as judge and Savior more clearly or expressed it more poignantly than a medieval

saint named Thomas as he pondered the "day of wrath" predicted by Zephaniah:

> *The Judge ascends his awful throne;*
> *He makes each secret sin be known,*
> *And all with shame confess their own.*
>
> .    .    .
>
> *Thou mighty, formidable King,*
> *Thou mercy's inexhausted spring,*
> *Some comfortable pity bring,*
>
> .    .    .
>
> *Thou who wert moved with Mary's grief,*
> *And by absolving of the thief*
> *Hast given me hope now give relief!*[h]

Another paradox is Jesus' statement in 5:31, "my witness is not true," while in 8:14 he says, "my witness is true." In 5:31 he seems to mean — "If I were the only one bearing witness it would not demand credence because two witnesses are normally required and because I am personally involved." In 8:31 he seems to mean that he is in a unique position to speak the truth about himself because they do not know much about him, es-

---

[1] In the Nestle Greek text *egō eimi* is in parenthesis, indicating a variant reading. But it occurs in P⁶⁶, the oldest codex of John extant.

g The recognition of a basic moral law in the universe was also voiced by Heraclitus about 500 B.C. — "The sun will not overstep his measures, else would the Erinnyes, the handmaids of Justice find him out" ("Fragment," 94, *Elegy and Iambus,* I, Loeb Library).

h Thomas of Celano, tr. by W. Dillon, cited in Schaff & Gilman, *A Library of Religious Poetry* (New York: Funk and Wagnalls, 1889), p. 902.

28 Jesus therefore said, When ye have lifted up the Son of man, then shall ye know that I am *he*, and *that* I do nothing of myself, but as the Father taught me, I speak these things.

29 And he that sent me is with me; he hath not left me alone; for I do always the things that are pleasing to him.

30 As he spake these things, many believed on him.

---

"king" 32 times in non-biblical, Hellenistic Greek literature.[2] Similar usage is seen also in the New Testament. The contexts in Rev. 3:14 and Col. 1:18 also call for this type of translation. "The *ruler* of the creation of God . . . who is the *ruler*, the first born from the dead." Where several translations have "beginning," Barrett prefers "from the beginning" for *archē* in John 8:25 (CKB, pp. 283f.).

28 **When ye have lifted up** (*hypsōsēte*) **the son of man.** A more literal rendering (due to the use of the aorist subjunctive) is "whenever you lift up the Son of man," meaning the crucifixion. This was to be the ultimate act of Jesus' complete obedience to God, obedience even to the ignominious and torturous death on the cross. The statement (v. 29) **I do always the things that are pleasing to him** corroborates the preceding verse. No mere human being could honestly make a statement like that!

30 **Many believed on him.** The aorist indicative, *episteusan*, used here could mean either that they were superficial, temporary believers or genuine, permanent believers. The fact that Jesus es-

pecially about his origin. The fact that his hearers are ignorant of his origin and destination (heaven) renders them incapable of evaluating or refuting his testimony. Consequently, they have to take his word for it (cf. John 3:11-13). Thus, the different contexts seem to account for the apparent contradiction.

20 Jesus is still in the temple teaching without molestation, in spite of attempts to arrest him (7:44). The evangelist explains this as providential — "his hour" had not yet arrived.

b. Its Destination: "to the Father" (vv. 21-30)

21 **I go away.** This clause seems to be repeated in John more often than in the other Gospels. He mentions his departure to the Jews several times (8:14, 21, 22; 12:31-37), the stress being on the temporary character of his sojourn upon earth and the fact that his native habitat is with his Father in heaven. The same emphasis on departure is seen in conversation with his disciples (13:1, 33, 36; 14:2, 3, 19, 25, 28; 16:5, 7, 10, 17, 28; 17:11). Jesus' emphasis on his departure was a source of perplexity, bordering on annoyance both to the "world" (8:22) and to

his disciples (14:5; 16:17). The emphasis of the Fourth Gospel seems to be on Jesus' supra-mundane and supra-temporal status. He is not so much the prophet of Nazareth, the wonder-worker, as the heavenly visitor, as the eternal *Logos* now become flesh. The phrase **die in your sin** recalls Ezekiel 3:18; 18:18 and possibly Proverbs 24:9 (LXX). His solemn assertion is repeated in v. 24, with the condition that if they believe they will live. In Ezekiel life for the sinner is conditioned on repentance and reformation; here upon repentance and faith.

22 The assertion that they would die in their sin (singular here; plural in v. 24) seems to have interested the Jews less than the statement, **Whither I go ye cannot come.** Their reaction was quite different from that in 7:35 to the same statement. There they wondered if he contemplated a ministry among the Dispersion; here they wonder if he contemplates suicide. The mysterious prediction appears to have aroused their curiosity more than their concern. The "natural man" is usually more given to curiosity and speculation than to repentance and transformation.

---

[2] E.g., "He held the greatest and the most perfect position as a *ruler*" (Plutarch, *Morals*, II, 151, F); "They were altogether lacking in a *commander* of great reputation" (Plutarch, *Lives*, VIII, *Sertorius* 10); "For it is not fitting for the *Ruler* and Lord of all to listen to anyone" (Plutarch, *Morals*, V. 75, E); "Him the multitudes take for a king" (Didorus Siculus, II, Bk 3, 5, 1); "for the sake of being a *ruler* with governors . . . Amalek, the *ruler* of the nations" (Philo, *Allegorios*, III, 58, 66).

31 Jesus therefore said to those Jews that had believed him, If ye abide in my word, *then* are ye truly my disciples;

32 and ye shall know the truth, and the truth shall make you free.

---

plained to them what was involved — continuous obedience to his teachings — could be interpreted either way. The words which follow — **we are Abraham's seed** — seem to imply that they were still depending on their Jewish heritage and not sufficiently on Christ.[3]

**31, 32** This important promise of Jesus hinges on the words "If . . . *then*." The words were addressed to those of v. 30

who believed. Apparently theirs was an initial credence which was not well grounded.[4] The author's report that "many believed" is stated also in 7:31; 10:42; and 12:11, 42. While the noun "faith" (*pistis*) is not found in this Gospel (and only once in I John 5:4), the verb "believe" is found about 103 times here and 10 times in I John. The condition laid down by the Master is that they "abide"

---

**23, 24** There follows a series of contrasts between Jesus and "the Jews" of increasing incisiveness and acrimony. They are "from beneath" and from "this world"; Jesus is "from above" and not "of this world." In his accusations against the Jews, Jesus moves progressively in his indictment from "ye judge after the flesh" (v. 15) to the statement that they: do not like the Father (v. 19), will die in their sin (vv. 21, 24), are of this world (v. 23), are potential murderers (v. 37), are children of the devil (v. 44), and are liars (v. 55). In the course of the argument, they also become increasingly belligerent. A brief interlude is afforded in v. 30 where we are told that "many believed on him."

**24, 28** When Jesus said **I am he,** what did it mean to his hearers? In the light of v. 25, it apparently only perplexed them. Hence their rejoinder, "Who art thou?" They had been wondering where Jesus came from (6:42), where he was going (8:21, 24), and now they demand to know his identity. Jesus' constant concern is to make them recognize that he comes from God and works in harmony with the Father. He wants them to recognize the Father in him. Accordingly, in v. 28, he states that after they have lifted him up, they will know his origin, destiny, and identity. The "lifting up" (*hypsōsēte*) is pregnant with meaning. It is used in 3:14 — "as Moses lifted up the serpent, so must the Son of man be lifted up" and again in 12:32 — "if I be lifted up

from the earth."[1] It means to exalt, to lift up on high, raise up, and it passes easily to the figurative meaning of exalt to opulence and prosperity, fame, power, fortune, and the like. As applied to Christ its scope includes the crucifixion (John), the resurrection, and the ascension (Acts 2:33; 5:31). It is comparable to the "received up" of Luke 9:51, which applies to the ascension. Later the apostles made the resurrection and ascension the major point in their assertion of Jesus' messianic claims (cf. Acts 3:15; 17:31; Rom. 1:4).

**29 He that sent me is with me.** These words reflect the Master's inner consciousness of the Father's presence. Again he affirms his intimate relationship to the Father and, yet, his subordination as one who is "sent." He is here in the role of an ambassador who speaks according to instructions from his superior (v. 28). It has never been easy for the church to grasp the full scope of Jesus' person and relation to the Trinity. Consequently theologians have oscillated between the extremes of an exclusive stress on his diety (docetism) and the opposite stress on his humanity (unitarianism). In John's Gospel, as in the Epistle to the Hebrews, his full humanity ("Jesus wept") is set forth along with his full deity ("The Word was God") with little attempt at rational harmonization. We find here, then, the raw-material of "Biblical theology" from which "systematic theology" is de-

---

[3] The "believe" of v. 30 is aorist with *eis* and the accusative while the "believe" of v. 31 is perfect with the dative and "should probably be translated 'had believed.'" Cf. R. V. G. Tasker, *The Gospel According to St. John* (Grand Rapids: Eerdmans, 1960), Tyndale N. T. Commentaries, p. 121.

[4] The problem is this: Those addressed in v. 31 seem to be the "believers" of v. 30 (cf. 7:31 etc.), yet the "believers" of v. 31 later seek to kill Jesus (v. 37).

[1] Cf. the heave-offering — Lev. 7:14, 32; Num. 18:24, 26; Deut. 12:6.

33 They answered unto him, We are Abraham's seed, and have never yet been in bondage to any man: how sayest thou, Ye shall be made free?

---

(aor. subj. of *menō*), a characteristic word in John's vocabulary.[5] This important declaration of Jesus may thus be analyzed:

The Condition —
"If ye abide in my word" —
DOCTRINE (v. 31)

The Consequences — "then"

1) "Truly my disciples"
DISCIPLINE

2) "Know the truth" — discovery
DISCERNMENT

3) "Be made free" (from sin, v. 34)     DELIVERANCE

There is a paradox here. Insight and freedom follow from a pattern of belief (doctrine) and practice (discipline). Bondage is the condition of freedom! Again, this is characteristic of John and of the New Testament generally. This paradox is also expressed by the Psalmist — "I keep thy law continually . . . and I will walk at liberty" (Ps. 119:44, 45). The paradox may also be noted in nature: The dam that impounds the waters of a mighty river, like the Columbia, restrains and limits the freedom of the water, but, in so doing, the energy of the river is released by turbines, and electric power is made available over a wide area. Nature, re-

---

veloped. We need not glory in the paradoxes, as did some disciples of Luther, and be content with irrationalism. At the same time, it ill becomes us to insist that all of the paradoxes be reduced immediately to rational explanations. **I do always the things that are pleasing to him.** The Gospels witness unanimously that God had a Son in whom he was (and is) well pleased. One of the greatest miracles of the Bible is the perfect character of the Lord Jesus Christ. Friends, enemies, and neutral witnesses all agree that in him there was "no fault."[j] In another context Jesus said, "Every disciple who is perfect (*katērtismenos*) shall be as his master" (Luke 6:40). This, along with passages like Matthew 5:48, indicates that God's children should be like their Heavenly Father, that Jesus' disciples should be like their Master. In other words, they should be perfect. Whatever else it may mean, "Christian perfection" means being "well-pleasing in his sight." The idea is developed at some length in the Epistle to the Hebrews, where it is said of Enoch that "he pleased God" (11:6).[k] Only Jesus could say, "I do always the things that are pleasing to him," but no child of God may be content with anything less than the type of living that is "well pleasing in his sight" (Heb. 13:21).

O for a lowly, contrite heart,
Believing, true and clean,
Which neither life nor death can part
From him that dwells within.
A heart in every thought renewed,
And full of love divine;
Perfect and right and pure and good,
A copy, Lord, of thine.

(C. Wesley, 1707-1788)

c. Its Mission: Freedom through Truth (vv. 31-38)

The Jews resented Jesus' statement that they would be free if they became disciples of his because of the implication that they were not really free at the time. Out of their racial and religious pride they affirmed, "We are descendants of Abraham (RSV). To say, however, that they had never been in bondage was something less than the truth. Their ancestors had been bond-slaves in Egypt for four centuries. Later they had been enslaved by the Philistines. Six centuries later they had been enslaved by Nebuchadnezzar, and in the second century B.C., the Syrians had oppressed them. Now they were in bondage to Rome, as the presence of Roman soldiers and tax collectors reminded them. Jesus had touched upon a sore spot when he reminded them of their lack of freedom. As usual they inter-

---

[5] The verb occurs about 40 times in this Gospel (cf. 12 times in the Synoptics), and is applicable "to someone who does not leave the realm or sphere in which he finds himself" (A-G).
[j] For an excellent treatise on this subject consult Ullmann, *The Sinlessness of Jesus.*
[k] Cf. Heb. 11:5, 6; 12:28; 13:16, 23.

34 Jesus answered them, Verily, verily, I say unto you, Every one that committeth sin is the bondservant of sin.

35 And the bondservant abideth not in the house for ever: the son abideth for ever.

36 If therefore the Son shall make you free, ye shall be free indeed.

37 I know that ye are Abraham's seed, yet ye seek to kill me, because my word hath not free course in you.

38 I speak the things which I have seen with *my* Father: and ye also do the things which ye heard from *your* father.

39 They answered and said unto him, Our father is Abraham. Jesus saith unto them, If ye were Abraham's children, ye would do the works of Abraham.

---

strained at the Grand Coulee Dam, makes possible freedom from nature in factories and farms of the state of Washington. Truth always emancipates. Jesus himself is the truth (John 14:6) and to learn from him is to know the truth which brings freedom — spiritual (v. 34), intellectual, and, ultimately, political.

34 To the Jewish claim that they were not in bondage, he replies, "Everyone who continues in sin is a slave of sin."[6] Jesus did not teach that a single act of sin made one a slave of sin, but rather that continuance in it did. This statement is similar to that in I John 3:8, 9: "He that goes on sinning (pres. part.)

is of the devil . . . the one born of God does not practice (pres. ind.) sin . . . he is not able to continue sinning" (pres. infin.)." An excellent human heritage is not enough; one needs a spiritual "heritage" to be a child of God through divine adoption (Rom. 8:16). Verse 38 can be translated with better adaptation to its context: "What I have seen from the Father I am speaking. However (adversative use of *oun*) are you also doing what you heard from the Father?" The definite article, not a pronoun, precedes "Father" in both instances. However, most translators render the first article "my" and the second article "your." The

---

preted his words in a temporal and, hence, political sense. His meaning was spiritual; he was referring to the bondage of sin.

There are several contrasts in this paragraph: Freedom and bondage; "your father" and "my father"; "your deeds" and "Abraham's deeds"; "born of fornication" and "born of God." It is the same contrast made in I John 3, between good and evil, children of God and of the devil, sinning and not sinning. John speaks of spiritual relationships in biological terms, in terms of life. While Paul used forensic terms — justification and the like, John speaks of generation and regeneration.[1]

d. Its Antiquity:
(1) *Abraham's True Children* (vv. 39-47)

"Born of fornication" may be an allusion to apostasy, for in the O.T. idolatry was often likened to immortality (Hos. 4:12; Jer. 3:1; Ezek. 16:15). More

likely, it is an allusion to gossip about the birth of Jesus. It seems unlikely that the metaphor would so abruptly change from the relation of son and parent to that of husband and wife (JHB, II, 312). It is more likely a subtle allusion to the virgin birth.[m]

44 "Your will is to do your father's desires" (RSV). Throughout this passage the contrast is between God and Satan, good and evil, truth and falsehood. The sanction of Abraham is claimed both by the Jews and by Jesus. The "lusts" (*epithymia*) are not necessarily sexual desires but desires in general. The picture brought before the mind is the Genesis account of the Fall of man. I John 3:4-10 is the most relevant commentary — "the devil has sinned from the beginning." It was the devil who not only tempted Eve but also led Cain to kill Abel. John recognized that the basic conflict between good and evil leads to envy and often to murder (I John 3:12;

[6] Present participle denotes action — *poiōn tēn hamartian.*
[1] See Henry Drummond, *Natural Law in the Spiritual World.*
[m] "John is subtly bringing out by implication what he believes to be the truth regarding the birth of Jesus, who, though the circumstances might to the uninitiated suggest fornication, was in fact born of no human act but of God (John 1:13)" (CKB, p. 288).

40 But now ye seek to kill me, a man that hath told you the truth, which I heard from God: this did not Abraham.

41 Ye do the works of your father. They said unto him, We were not born of fornication; we have one Father, *even* God.

42 Jesus said unto them, If God were your Father, ye would love me: for I came forth and am come from God; for neither have I come of myself, but he sent me.

43 Why do ye not understand my speech? *Even* because ye cannot hear my word.

44 Ye are of *your* father the devil, and the lusts of your father it is your will to do. He was a murderer from the beginning, and standeth not in the truth, because there is no truth in him. When he speaketh a lie, he speaketh of his own: for he is a liar, and the father thereof.

45 But because I say the truth, ye believe me not.

---

following context is not at all foreign to such a translation, since Jesus states that their father is the devil (v. 44).

**40 I have spoken the truth to you which I heard from God.** A similar declaration occurs in 5:30; 7:16, and 8:26. Why did Jesus address Jews "that had believed him" as murderers, "ye seek to kill me"? He was addressing Jews, like those named in 2:23, 24, who saw his miracles and believed but to whom Jesus did not commit himself.[7]

**42 If God were your father, you would love me** (contrary to fact condition). They hated Jesus enough to kill him (a statement repeated several times), but if they were God's children they would have the opposite attitude and love Jesus. Since

---

cf. Matt. 27:18; Mark 15:10). Jesus is pointing out that these Jews, who eventually are to murder him, follow the precedent of the devil and of Cain consistently. They are hostile to all those aligned with goodness and truth, if for no other reason, because of their genealogical antecedents. It is a case of "like father, like son." The message of the Gospel (implicit here and explicit in the conversation with Nicodemus) is that, by an act of God's grace, one who is now in the spiritual lineage of the devil can be transformed and transferred to the lineage of God. This is the emphasis of the New Testament generally. Paul calls it justification by faith; in II Peter 1:4 it is called partaking of the divine nature; James refers to it as receiving by faith "wisdom from above" (Jas. 1:5; 3:17); and in the Apocalypse the change is described as being "freed from our sins" (Rev. 1:5 — RSV). The folly of assuming that, because one can claim the ancestry of Abraham, he is automatically in the kingdom was emphatically refuted by John the Baptist, ("God is able of these stones to raise up children unto Abraham," Matt. 3:9), Paul (Rom. 2:28, 29), and John (John 1:13; 3:6, 7).

**46 Which of you convicteth me of sin?** Here the master makes a direct challenge. It is interesting to contrast Jesus' consciousness of sinlessness with the consciousness of sin on the part of the self-righteous (John 8:1-9, 10). Jesus Christ is unique among the men of history in that no one ever found him exhibiting any sin. On the contrary friends, enemies, and neutral witnesses were unanimous in witnessing to his sinlessness. Of no other person in history, not even Socrates, may this be said.[n] One of the greatest miracles of the Bible is the sinlessness of Jesus. As E. Stanley Jones has emphasized, we believe in Jesus and hence have no difficulty in believing in the miracles, since the character of Jesus himself is the greatest miracle of all.

*Fair is the sunshine,*
*Fairer still the moonlight,*
*And all the twinkling starry host:*
*Jesus shines brighter,*
*Jesus shines purer*
*Then all the angels heaven can boast.*[o]

(2) *Jesus' Priority to Abraham*
(vv. 48-59)

58 The answer that infuriated the Jews

---

7 Cf. John 7:31; 11:45; 12:11, 42, 43 and Hoskyns, p. 388.
n Cf. Zeller, *Stoics, Epicureans and Skeptics,* p. 275.
o Crusaders Hymn, *Hymns of the Living Faith,* p. 150.

46 Which of you convicteth me of sin? If I say truth, why do ye not believe me?

47 He that is of God heareth the words of God: for this cause ye hear *them* not, because ye are not of God.

48 The Jews answered and said unto him, Say we not well that thou art a Samaritan, and hast a demon?

49 Jesus answered, I have not a demon; but I honor my Father, and ye dishonor me.

50 But I seek not mine own glory: there is one that seeketh and judgeth.

51 Verily, verily, I say unto you, If a man keep my word, he shall never see death.

---

they do not love him but hate him instead, they are of the devil (v. 44), who is "a liar" and "the truth is not in him."

**47 He that is of God hears the words of God.** This is a fundamental axiom, reiterated in various statements throughout the Bible. The word "hear" means "heed" or "obey" in this sentence, as it does in many places in the New Testament.[8] In Hebrew 5:9 a word that always means to *obey* (*hypakouō*) is used: "He (Jesus) became to all that *obey* him the author of eternal life." These passages make it clear that the genuine Christian has faith deep and permanent enough to result in obedience and faithfulness to Christ.[9]

**48 Thou art a Samaritan and hast a demon.** The Samaritans were looked upon by Jews as the lowest and most worthless type of people. Obviously the connotation in the popular mind is clear — being a Samaritan is closely akin to being indwelt by a demon. Jesus ignored the statement about being a Samaritan but he disclaimed being demon-possessed. When hostile people become angry, they are inclined to use extravagant language in defaming those that disagree with them.

---

so much that they tried to lynch Jesus on the spot was the apparently enigmatic statement, **"Before Abraham was I am** ($\dot{\epsilon}\gamma\omega$ $\epsilon\dot{\iota}\mu\dot{\iota}$). It is important to notice the distinction here between the two verbs "was" (*genesthai*) and "am" (*eimi*). Abraham was mortal and temporal, Jesus was immortal and eternal. Hence, "before Abraham was born," or "came into existence" is correct (CGT, p. 202). In this context the "I am" has the connotation of absolute, timeless existence as in John 1:3 and 7:34. The expression seems to have its origin in Exodus 3:14 and in Isaiah 43:10 — "in order that ye may know . . . that I am he" (LXX). In Exodus 3:14 the verb *hayah* ("to be") is connected with the tetragrammaton, the four-letter personal name of Israel's God (יהוה) transliterated *yhwh* and pronounced "Jahweh" or "Jehovah." Thus Jesus seems to identify himself with the Eternal One, whose existence is timeless and, hence, not only prior to Abraham but "prior" to time itself (cf. Deut. 32:39; Isa. 41:4; 43:10; 46:4; 48:12).[ᴾ] The Jews in-terpreted his words as claiming equality with God and hence as blasphemy. Without further ado they seized stones to kill him in the traditional way (Lev. 24:16). But Jesus, probably shielded by sympathizers, eluded them and disappeared in the crowd.

Ch. 8, therefore, is not only important for its reference to Jesus as the true "Light" and for its comparison of Jesus with Abraham, but also for its reinforcement of one of the cardinal doctrines of the New Testament. It teaches that membership in the kingdom is essentially based on grace rather than on genealogy and privilege. It implies a "universal" rather than a "limited" atonement, since it is not limited to the physical posterity of Abraham. The making of the kingdom available to non-Jews on the same basis, that is by faith, was the "glorious mystery" which thrilled the Apostle Paul (Eph. 3:3-6) and infuriated the proper Palestinians (Acts 22:21, 22).

It appears probable that the events reported in chs. 7 and 8 all occurred at the

---

[8] Cf. John 5:24, "He that heeds (obeys) my word and believes him that sent. me, has eternal life"; John 10:3, "The sheep *obey* his voice"; John 10:8, 16, 27, "The sheep did not *obey* them . . . But my voice they will *obey* . . . My sheep *obey* my voice and I know them and they continue following me and I give unto them eternal life"; Acts 4:19, "Whether it is right before God to *obey* you . . ."
[9] Other passages where *akouō* means to *heed* or *obey* are Matt. 17:5; Mark 6:11; Acts 3:22; Gal. 4:21; Rev. 1:29; 3:20; cf. Deut. 30 for emphasis on obedience.
[ᴾ] For an excellent study of $\dot{\epsilon}\gamma\dot{\omega}$ $\epsilon\dot{\iota}\mu\dot{\iota}$ ("I am"), see JHB I, cxviii-cxxi, and CHD, pp. 349f.

52 The Jews said unto him, Now we know that thou hast a demon. Abraham died, and the prophets; and thou sayest, If a man keep my word, he shall never taste of death.

53 Art thou greater than our father Abraham, who died? and the prophets died: whom makest thou thyself?

54 Jesus answered, If I glorify myself, my glory is nothing: it is my Father that glorifieth me; of whom ye say, that he is your God;

55 and ye have not known him: but I know him; and if I should say, I know him not, I shall be like unto you, a liar: but I know him, and keep his word.

56 Your father Abraham rejoiced to see my day; and he saw it, and was glad.

57 The Jews therefore said unto him, Thou art not yet fifty years old, and hast thou seen Abraham?

58 Jesus said unto them, Verily, verily, I say unto you, Before Abraham was born, I am.

59 They took up stones therefore to cast at him: but Jesus hid himself, and went out of the temple.

---

53 Jesus defended himself in the face of the ridicule of the Jews: **Are you greater than Abraham and the prophets who died?** In reply Jesus stated, "You have not known and do not now know (perfect tense) God, but I know him. And if I should say I do not know him I would be like you a liar," — a scathing denunciation and a point-blank defense.

56 **Abraham rejoiced to see my day.** This was Jesus' defense. In these words Jesus made clear the contrast between the Jews' profession of affinity with Abraham and their hostility to the fulfillment of Abraham's vision. While Abraham was a "friend of God," these descendants of his were enemies of God — so much so that they were plotting to kill God's Son. Thus they denied the essence of their ancestral heritage, retaining only a hereditary connection with the patriarch. Here, as elsewhere in the Fourth Gospel, the contrast is stressed between the outward and inward, the peripheral and essential, the cultic and the moral, the flesh and the spirit, the devil and the Lord.

57 The expression, **fifty years,** is a "round number and no more is intended than to stress the contrast between a short life-time and the great interval separating Jesus and Abraham" (CKB, p. 292).

58 **Before Abraham was I am** was an affirmation that Jesus antedated the existence of the father of the Jewish nation. It was also a unique way to declare his own eternal existence and deity. This claim angered the Pharisees beyond self-control. They had been frustrated in every debate with Jesus. They failed to overcome with words; so they resorted to trying to eliminate him with stones. But Jesus outwitted them even in that attempt by suddenly disappearing. The Greek (*ekrybē* — aor. pass.) says, "he became hidden." No doubt friendly people gladly helped Jesus escape as he left the temple.

---

Feast of the Tabernacle (CHD, p. 350). There are some seven dialogues here which Dodd has identified; they coincide with the paragraph divisions of the ASV.

| Dialogue | Reference | Theme | Speakers |
|---|---|---|---|
| I | (7:14-24) | Moses compared to Christ | Jesus and "the Jews" |
| II | (7:25-36) | Is Jesus the Messiah? | Jesus and "People of Jerusalem" |
| III | (7:37-44) | Jesus' Invitation to Partake of the Spirit | Jesus and the people |
| IV | (7:45-52) | Behind the scenes with Nicodemus and the Pharisees | |
| V | (8:12-20) | Jesus, Light of the World | The Pharisees |
| VI | (8:21-30) | The Challenge of Jesus to the Jewish Leaders | |
| VII | (8:31-59) | Abraham's "Seed." | "Believing" Jews (v. 31) |

The merit of this arrangement is that the above shows the continuity in these controversial dialogues; however, it fails to show that chs. 8 and 9 are united under the theme of light. Here, as in ch. 10, the topical and chronological divisions do not seem to coincide.

# CHAPTER IX

And as he passed by, he saw a man blind from his birth.

2 And his disciples asked him, saying, Rabbi, who sinned, this man, or his parents, that he should be born blind?

3 Jesus answered, Neither did this man sin, nor his parents: but that the works of God should be made manifest in him.

4 We must work the works of him that sent me, while it is day: the night cometh, when no man can work.

---

## EXEGESIS

1 **Blind from his birth.** This indicates the *hopelessness* of any cure as far as medical treatment is concerned. John may have had also in mind, as he recorded this story, how mankind is spiritually blind from birth and not naturally receptive to spiritual light.

2 **Who sinned?** There was a general assumption that sin was the cause of blindness. "This was a common belief in Judaism; see e.g. *Shabbath* 55a: There is no death without sin (proved by Ezek. 18:20) and no punishment (i.e. suffering) without guilt (proved by Ps. 89: 33)" (CKB, p. 294). The book of Job counters the above assumption. **That** (*hina*) **he should be born blind** or "Why was he born blind?"[1]

3 Jesus denied that sin brought blindness to this man, and he explained that it was permitted so that the **works of God**

---

## EXPOSITION

e. Its Remedy For Physical Blindness: The Fifth "Sign" (vv. 1-34)

In order to gain perspective the relationships within this chapter may thus be displayed:

This chapter continues the theme of light introduced in 8:12. In the synagogue at Nazareth Jesus had claimed the power to forgive sin *before* healing a crippled man (Mark 2:5-11). The miracle of healing which followed substantiated a claim which, by its nature, could not be self-evident as could the power to heal.

| Para-graphs | LIGHT VERSUS DARKNESS | | | | |
|---|---|---|---|---|---|
| | Physical blindness 1 remedied | Questions of the Pharisees | | | Spiritual blindness 35 persists |
| | | Man 13 Questioned | Parents 18 Questioned | Man 24 Cross-questioned | |
| Para-graph analyses | Disciples' Query Jesus' claim Sight restored Neighbors wonder | Pharisees' dilemma: a) God's servant would not break the Sabbath b) Only God's servant could do a miracle | Parents' dilemma: a) If we approve; excommunication b) If we do not: ingratitude Hence: "neutral" | Two types of assurance: Dogmatic: "We know he is a sinner." Experiential: "I know he cured me." | The man (believer): "I believe" The Jews: "Your sin remaineth" |
| | Who? | How? | Whose? | | |
| Questions: | of theology 6 | of man's identity | of method 16 | of Jesus' power | "Are we blind also?" 27 |

[1] *Hina* introduces a result, not a purpose clause here (D-M, p. 249).

5 When I am in the world, I am the light of the world.

6 When he had thus spoken, he spat on the ground, and made clay of the spittle, and anointed his eyes with the clay,

---

might be manifested in him (cf. John 11:4).

5 I am the light of the world. By this statement John relates the miracle causally to the divine light (sight) that emanates from the Lord Jesus (cf. John 1:4, 7, 9; 5:35; 8:12; 11:9; 12:35, 36, 46). *Phōs tou kosmou* (*light for the world*) is an objective genitive construction such as we have in Matthew 5:13, 14, "salt for the earth . . . light for the world."

6 The clay put upon the blind man's eyes was not to function as a medicine but to bolster the man's faith.[2] The going to the pool to wash was a test of obedience. A similar instance is that of Naaman dipping himself in the Jordan River seven times before his leprosy left him (II Kings

---

In this instance Jesus had said, "I am the light of the world" (8:12) and now provides evidence to support this tremendous assertion.

#### (1) *The Blind Man Healed* (vv. 1-12)

It is always instructive to observe the contrast between the reaction of Jesus to a given situation and the reaction of the disciples. In this instance they passed out of the temple (to escape enemies, 8: 59) and saw a man blind from birth. In Palestine and the Orient, then and now, the sight of blind persons in public places is very common. Often they are beggars using their blindness as an additional appeal to the sympathies of the passers-by. To the disciples the sight of another blind man evoked little compassion but served only to pose a theological question. The disciples did not think of this particular blind person as an individual with personal problems and possibilities. They saw him only as another representative of his class. (The Pharisees, in a similar manner, thought of the one Jesus healed only as a Sabbath breaker, not as a person who had received the gift of sight.) The disciples shared the common belief that the one afflicted physically was being punished by God. That is, he was not only a sick man, but a sinner as well.

The belief that health and prosperity were evidence of divine favor, while disease and penury were evidences of divine displeasure was perhaps rooted in Deut. 27, 28. In these chapters the rewards

for obedience were spelled out in great detail while the consequences for disobedience were also specific — disease, crop failure, natural calamity, captivity, and death. The same correlation between virtue, on the one hand, and physical and financial well-being, on the other, are deeply engraved in the consciousness of many religious groups. This same attitude (the "orthodox" attitude) is repeatedly stated by Job's volunteer counsellors. They were insistent that all affliction is from God (or with his permission), that such affliction is the result of sin, and that the only sure way to find relief is to repent and get right with God. As Bildad put it, "If thou wert pure and upright: Surely now he would . . . make the habitation of thy righteousness prosperous" (Job. 8:6). This "orthodox" view Job challenged because it was not in accord with his own experience. But the Book of Job did not provide the full answer to the question, "Why do the righteous suffer?"[a]

In Ezekiel's day it was considered axiomatic that the sins of the fathers were "visited upon their children," that in the words of the parable, "the fathers have eaten sour grapes and the children's teeth are set on edge" (Ezek. 18:2). The answer given in the prophecy of Ezekiel is one of the most distinctive features of the New Covenant. Ezekiel announced in God's name that this proverb is no longer in effect. Rather, the one who sins, he alone, not his kinfolk, will bear his iniquity. It was an announcement of in-

---

[2] Early expositors (e.g. Iren. *Adv. Hear.* 5. 15. 2) saw here a reference to Gen. 2:7 and interpreted the clay as a symbol of re-creation, i.e., restoration of sight.

[a] A partial answer was given when Jehovah appeared and Job was speechless: attention was directed from his problem to God's presence (Job 42:5, 6).

7 and said unto him, Go, wash in the pool of Siloam (which is by interpretation, Sent). He went away therefore, and washed, and came seeing.

8 The neighbors therefore, and they that saw him aforetime, that he was a beggar, said, Is not this he that sat and begged?

9 Others said, It is he: others said, No, but he is like him. He said, I am *he*.

10 They said therefore unto him, How then were thine eyes opened?

---

5:10). Divine power in each case worked the cure.

7 **Siloam** (Heb. "to send") may be a symbol of the Messiah who was "sent."[3]

The reaction of the neighbors to this miracle is depicted in considerable detail. They had difficulty believing that it was the same beggar until he was questioned, and then they were amazed over the way sight had come to him.

8 **Is not this?** The *ouch* expects an affirmative answer. In v. 10 *elegon oun autōi pōs oun* is "Then (*oun*) they were saying to him, How *really* (*oun*)." *Oun* is continuative in the first instance and emphatic in the second.[4] The cured beggar

---

dividual responsibility, the change from group to personal morality (Ezek. 18:19, 20, 30-32). However, this insight did not gain wide acceptance until the time of Jesus. The question of the disciples was therefore quite natural.

It is the "unorthodox" attitude of Jesus, not the attitude of the disciples, which was impressive because it was so unusual. Unconventional as it was, it was quite characteristic of the Master Teacher. An awareness of the worth of the individual is characteristic of Christianity. Jesus was concerned with this man not merely as "exhibit A" in the display of God's works, but he was also interested in him as an end. Jesus considered people not as means to ends, as in totalitarian regimes, but as ends in themselves.

Jesus reaction to the blind man's affliction was similar to his reaction to the report of Lazarus' illness (John 11:4). In each instance the overall purpose was the glory of God. For this reason Jesus was able later to look back over his ministry and say, "I glorified thee on the earth, having accomplished the work which thou hast given me to do" (17: 4). Another respect in which Jesus' reaction here was similar to his reaction to Lazarus is his mention of being busy during the hours of daylight. The connection between light and healing here is obvious. In connection with Lazarus, it is less obvious, but it probably is simply a reaffirmation of the need to "work, for the night is coming." In this instance the remark echoed the declaration of

8:12 — **I am the light of the world.** The manner in which the theme of light is interwoven in the fabric of the narrative is intriguing indeed.

The varied reactions to the miracles of healing are similar to the mixed reactions to Jesus at almost every turn, such as on the visit to Jerusalem recorded in ch. 7. Here the problem is one of identification of the blind man as it was the identification of Jesus in 7:25-31. This whole chapter focuses attention on the problem of reaching a conclusion on the basis of evidence; it is the problem of the light overcoming the darkness. The readiness with which Jesus' physical initiative was met with a ready response in the realm of the physical is not duplicated in the realm of the spiritual. It was relatively easy to perform the miracle of physical healing but more difficult to open the spiritual eyes of the understanding, the things that Paul wanted done for his readers in Ephesus (Eph. 1:17, 18). The contrast between the uncertainty of the neighbors and the certitude of the ex-blind man himself is noteworthy, especially since a similar contrast is made later in the narrative (vv. 20-28).

The sequence of *obeying* and then *seeing* is consistent with several other places in this Gospel where the same sequence may be observed. In John 1:39, 46 the coming or obedience is rewarded by "seeing" Jesus. In John 5:40 Jesus told the Jews, "ye will not come to me, that ye may have life." So this Gospel repeatedly calls attention to something in humans that conditions

---

[3] See RHL, pp. 202, 03; cf. John 4:10, 14; 7:38.
[4] *Oun* means "then" also in verses 15, 17 and 24.

11 He answered, The man that is called Jesus made clay, and anointed mine eyes, and said unto me, Go to Siloam, and wash: so I went away and washed, and I received sight.

12 And they said unto him, Where is he? He saith, I know not.

13 They bring to the Pharisees him that aforetime was blind.

14 Now it was the sabbath on the day when Jesus made the clay, and opened his eyes.

15 Again therefore the Pharisees also asked him how he received his sight. And he said unto them, He put clay upon mine eyes, and I washed, and I see.

16 Some therefore of the Pharisees said, This man is not from God, because he keepeth not the sabbath. But others said, How can a man that is a sinner do such signs? And there was a division among them.

---

knew who healed him and the details of the process, but he did not know where Jesus could be found.

**11 Go . . . and wash . . . I washed.** Both words for wash (*nipsai*) are aorist denoting a single washing; the cure was instantaneous.

**13** Evidently, because the miracle had occurred on the Sabbath, the beggar was taken to the Pharisees by hostile Jews as evidence against Jesus.

**15 Again therefore.** The question of v. 10 is repeated.

**16** Some Pharisees immediately concluded that Jesus **is not from God, because he does not keep the Sabbath.**[5] Their legalism blinded their understanding. But some of them were discerning enough to

---

them to resist the true light that enlightens all.

This intractable element in human nature was recognized in the Old Testament, especially in books of the later kingdom period. Jeremiah speaks repeatedly of the perversity and stubbornness of the people. Ezekiel predicts the era in which the "stony" heart will be entirely removed and replaced by a "heart of flesh" (Ezek. 36:25-27). This chronic perversity is a special concern of the authors of II Baruch and IV Esdras where general pessimism prevails and little immediate hope is held out for deliverance.[b]

Paul did not use the O.T. term "evil imagination," which was stressed by the rabbis but expressed a similar idea in Rom. 5:12 and laid the foundation for the doctrine of Original Sin. In his defense Stephen reflected a similar appraisal of the quality in his forefathers which "did always resist the Holy Spirit" (Acts 7:51). A consistent theme through the Scriptures is this chronic perversity recognized in the antediluvians (Gen. 6:5; cf. 8:21).

Twentieth century thought has rejected the idea that man is essentially depraved and pre-disposed to evil. However, the monstrous forces of evil let loose in two major wars and the mass killings and deportations of the totalitarian regimes in China and Russia have caused the classical doctrine of Original Sin to be revived and refurbished. A new awareness of the social solidarity of the races is now linked in the minds of many with a new awareness of the universality of sin.[c]

### (2) *Opposition Encountered* (vv. 13-17)

Why were the Pharisees brought into the picture? Unlike the situation in the Galilean synagogue (Mark 3:1-8) or in Jerusalem (John 5:1-18), when healings occurred on the Sabbath, in this case the Pharisees did not take the initiative in the role of opposition. Apparently the bystanders thought the healing was of sufficient importance that it should come to the attention of the religious authorities. The Pharisees had more influence with the people than did the other major party,

---

[5] *Oun* ("Therefore") in verses 16, 20, 25, and 26 means "in reply."

[b] II Baruch 23:4; 48:42; IV Esdras 3:20; 4:30, 31. R. H. Charles, *Apocrypha and Pseudepigrapha of the Old Testament* (Oxford, 1913), II, cited in G. A. Turner, *The More Excellent Way* (Winona Lake: Light and Life Press, 1952) pp. 54, 58. The date of these is probably later than the composition of the New Testament.

[c] Reinhold Niebuhr, *The Nature and Destiny of Man* (New York: Scribner's, 1941).

17 They say therefore unto the blind man again, What sayest thou of him, in that he opened thine eyes? And he said, He is a prophet.

18 The Jews therefore did not believe concerning him, that he had been blind, and had received his sight, until they called the parents of him that had received his sight,

19 and asked them, saying, Is this your son, who ye say was born blind? how then doth he now see?

---

ask how a sinful man could perform such miracles. Soon a schism (*schisma*) developed among them, a phenomenon noted repeatedly in this Gospel and in the Book of Acts. The same evidence produced opposite results.

17 When asked, the beggar replied that he believed Jesus to be a prophet.

18 **The Jews however** questioned his parents as to whether this was really their son.[6] They confirmed that he was their son and that he was born blind, but refused to commit themselves as to how he received his sight. They knew that they could be excommunicated if they were suspected of faith in Jesus as the Mes-

---

the Sadducees, even though the latter were more influential with the Roman authorities (Jos. *Ant.*, XVIII. i. 3. 4).

The reluctance of the Pharisees and others to draw the appropriate conclusion from the evidence presented is demonstrated in great detail in this event. It helps explain the general problems of belief and unbelief that are so central in this Gospel. With a repetition that almost becomes monotonous and amusing, they demand a reiteration of the story and yet are reluctant to act upon it. The familiar pattern of struggle over evidence is set forth in this paragraph. The man whose blindness was cured on the Sabbath day is brought before the Pharisees, probably officials of the temple area. The religious leaders questioned him about the alleged miracle. They were divided in their reactions, a division which one encounters throughout this Gospel. Some started from the main premise that God does not do things of this kind on the Sabbath, therefore God had nothing to do with this alleged miracle. Others were inductive in their reasoning rather than deductive. They reasoned that a real miracle has occurred; only God's power makes such a miracle possible, therefore Jesus must be in harmony with the will of God. In the hope of resolving the difference of opinion that prevailed among them, they asked the once-blind man for his explanation. Since he was convinced that a miracle had occurred and that God was involved, he concluded that Jesus

was a prophet and approved by God. This rather natural conclusion they could not bring themselves to accept. "A man convinced against his will is of the same opinion still."

### (3) Parents Non-committal (vv. 18-23)

The resort to the man's parents was ostensibly to establish identity. It was a device to postpone the time when they would have to make a decision relative to the "sign." As the record stands there were not careful and competent investigators, but rather a group of men confronted with the necessity of coming to a conclusion on something about which they had already formed a prejudgment. They were so prejudiced that normal, rational processes were not operating. The parents were non-committal for reasons of expediency. They were fearful of losing status, of being excommunicated from the synagogue.

Nevertheless, because of their relationship to the former blind man they were called to be witnesses. They could have taken this opportunity to lend effective confirmation to their son's testimony and extend the influence of Christ. But, because of "vested interests" in the religious mores of the day, they wanted to play it safe.

As elsewhere in John, so here, there is an emphasis on "know." The parents "know" that he is their own son; they also "know" that he was born blind. Be-

---

[6] *Oun* is adversative in verse 18 — "however."

20 His parents answered and said, We know that this is our son, and that he was born blind:

21 but how he now seeth, we know not; or who opened his eyes, we know not: ask him; he is of age; he shall speak for himself.

22 These things said his parents, because they feared the Jews: for the Jews had agreed already, that if any man should confess him *to be* Christ, he should be put out of the synagogue.

23 Therefore said his parents, He is of age; ask him.

24 So they called a second time the man that was blind, and said unto him, Give glory to God: we know that this man is a sinner.

---

siah. They were afraid, but their son was honest and fearless enough to speak favorably of Jesus and say that he was a prophet, i.e., a spokesman for God, not a sinner.

21 **We know not** (*oidamen*). The word "know" occurs 11 times in this chapter alone. In each instance, *oida* is used. It is used frequently in John to express a lack of spiritual apprehension.[7]

24 The expression **Give glory to God** means "do not lie to us but in the sight of God tell the truth" (cf. Josh. 7:19). The exasperated beggar did exactly that.

---

yond that they do not know and are unwilling to express an opinion. Instead they throw the responsibility upon their son — "ask him; he is of age; he shall speak for himself." The fact that the parents were called before this tribunal placed them in a difficult position, but their failure to express wonder and gratitude puts them in the category of uncommitted inquirers or neutrals. The New Testament is not very tolerant of those professing a "benevolent neutrality." Jesus said, "He who gathers not with me scatters abroad" (Matt. 12:30). Those who are "neither cold nor hot" are particularly offensive (Rev. 3:16).

#### (4) The Man's Witness Rejected (vv. 24-34)

Ostensibly to secure all the evidence and complete a thorough investigation, the inquisitors called the man that was blind a second time and asked him to repeat his story. This is the most dramatic and fascinating part of the entire story. Seven times the word "know" is used. The Pharisees are quoted as saying that "we know this man is a sinner" (v. 24); "We know that God hath spoken by Moses" (v. 29); "We know not" where Jesus came from (v. 29). The blind man acknowledged that he did not know (theoretically) whether or not Jesus was a "sinner," but affirmed that he was certain that his sight

had been restored (v. 25). He marvelled that the Pharisees still professed ignorance of Jesus' origin when it was a matter of common knowledge that God does not work miracles through sinners (v. 31). He wondered that they refused to draw the obvious conclusion: **If this man were not of God he could do nothing.** Here is the chief center in the Gospel for the elaboration of the theme that "signs" are the basis for belief and that, while the "signs" are fully adequate, they do not always result in faith. The principle announced in the prologue (1:5), and elaborated several times thereafter (e.g., 5:44), that one must be willing to be convinced, here receives its fullest elaboration in narrative form. The central point of the thesis is that faith should be based upon adequate evidence and that, because of prejudice and sin, subjective factors prevent the persons from drawing the appropriate conclusion — that of faith. Thus, the battle between faith and doubt remains a perennial problem.

33 The conclusion drawn by this witness was simply unanswerable. **If this man were not from God, he could do nothing.** The man had concluded that there are two miracles now to be considered: the miracle of his sight and now the **marvel** (*thaumaston*, v. 33) of their unbelief. The men who were unwilling to walk in the light had no answer at all. Instead they refused to follow this logic

---

[7] E.g., John 4:22; 4:32; 20:9, 14; 21:4. See De la Potterie, "*Oida et ginoskō;* les deux modes de la connaissance dans le Quatrieme Evangile," *op. cit.,* p. 720. See also footnote following 4:42.

25 He therefore answered, Whether he is a sinner, I know not: one thing I know, that, whereas I was blind. now I see.

26 They said therefore unto him, What did he to thee? how opened he thine eyes?

27 He answered them, I told you even now, and ye did not hear; wherefore would ye hear it again? would ye also become his disciples?

28 And they reviled him, and said, Thou art his disciple; but we are disciples of Moses.

29 We know that God hath spoken unto Moses: but as for this man, we know not whence he is.

30 The man answered and said unto them, Why, herein is the marvel, that ye know not whence he is, and *yet* he opened mine eyes.

---

Furthermore, he not only reiterated his former testimony but also defended Jesus' action and, by implication, his character.

25 **Whether he is a sinner, I know not: one thing I know, that whereas I was blind, now I see.** This is perhaps the most impressive statement in the chapter; it has the ring of authority arising from experience.

27 **Ye did not hear.** "You did not listen" (*ēkousate*) or "heed what I told you." In the question, **Would ye also become his disciples?**, the negative *mē* im-

plies an expected negative answer: "You do not wish to become his disciples, do you?" Evidently the beggar knew that some people actually believed Jesus was the Messiah.

28 That question provoked anger and ridicule: **They reviled him** and accused him of being a disciple, which he was not at that time.

30 **Why, herein is the marvel** (*thaumaston*). Of the seven synonyms for miracles in the N. T., the most frequent in order of prominence are *sēmeia* (c.

---

further and restored to an entirely different defense, the *ad hominem* argument. They attacked his character on the basis of this pre-natal blindness, which ˇ (they assumed) indicated sin, and refused to listen to him further. In so doing they asserted their *personal* superiority to him and refused to acknowledge that his *argument* was superior to theirs.

### f. Its Exposure of Spiritual Blindness (vv. 35-41)

35 **Jesus found him.** This is one of the most touching scenes in the whole New Testament. We see Jesus, the divine Lord of Light and Life, looking up an ordinary beggar, a person at the bottom rung of humanity's ladder, who had just been excluded from membership in his synagogue. Jesus offered him the pardon, peace, provision, and presence that only Heaven can provide. Here was Jesus doing "follow-up work" in the task of personal evangelism. The Master was not interested in doing a miracle for display purposes, nor only for the relief of physical suffering; his main concern was for the man's soul. It was not the parents apparently, nor sympathetic neighbors but

the Lord of life who sought until he found the courageous witness. From this we also learn that we must not deny love and fellowship to a person on the threshold of faith. Jesus did not ask him to subscribe to an elaborate creed. What the title "Son of man" meant to the man is hard to say. The context makes it clear that to the man it connoted deity, the Messiah, since he worshipped (*proskyneō*) Jesus afterwards.

The question **Dost thou believe?** was a question of recognizing the Messiah, of identifying the individual who would correspond to current messianic expectations.

In contrast to the Pharisees, the man had already demonstrated his ability to accept the conclusion towards which the evidence led. He was not one of those who "could not believe because they loved the praise of men more than the favor of God" (cf. John 5:44). John is constantly stressing the subjective factors which facilitate or hinder belief.

39 It is characteristic of this Gospel to emphasize that every person who is exposed to the light and rejects it places himself under judgment (*krisis*, 3:19, A-G, p. 452). The impenitent, unbelieving

31 We know that God heareth not sinners: but if any man be a worshipper of God, and do his will, him he heareth.

32 Since the world began it was never heard that any one opened the eyes of a man born blind.

33 If this man were not from God, he could do nothing.

34 They answered and said unto him, Thou wast altogether born in sins, and dost thou teach us? And they cast him out.

---

80 times, 17 in John), *terata* (14 times, 9 in Acts) and *dynameis* (virtue, power, wonder, e.g., Matt. 7:22). The term marvel (*thaumaston*) occurs only 6 times in the N. T. The RSV is more emphatic, "Why this is a marvel!" The man viewed this blindness on their part as unprecedented reluctance to draw the obvious conclusion. Their blindness was as much a mystery as was his new sight.

31 The remark, **we know that God heareth not sinners,** needs to be interpreted in its context. The statement was made in defense of Jesus. An unsaved man, not an inspired writer, made the declaration. If God did not hear sinners, no one could be saved. The prayer of penitence is as music to God. But it is also true that the persistent sinner is not likely to get special favors from God when

he prays. The noble defense the beggar made for Jesus vexed and incensed the Pharisees so much that they had him excommunicated.

34 They declared that he had been **born in sin,** due to his former blindness, and they scoffed at his presumption in attempting to teach them. Their false premise was that Jesus was an imposter. Consequently, regardless of the facts, they would not concede that God was working miracles through him. Prejudice always blinds one to the truth. "Whoever would draw nigh to God must believe that he exists and that he rewards those that seek him" (Heb. 11:6).

**They cast him out.** This was not a formal excommunication from the synagogue (*cherem*) since that could be done only by the Sanhedrin. This was a lower

---

person, therefore, lives out his days under condemnation. On the other hand the one who repents and believes and obeys is no longer under judgment but has passed "from death unto life." Judgment is therefore an important theme in John and *krisis* is a key word. It is a key word not so much in the relative abundance of the times it is used but in the usage itself. This is especially seen in chs. 5 and 16.

The Pharisees overheard Jesus making this comment to the new confessor and asked, **Are we blind also?** They got the point. In his answer Jesus indicated that theirs was a spiritual, self-imposed blindness. Had their blindness resulted from the absence of light, they would have been guiltless. Since it was acquired by resistance to the light, they were guilty and Jesus had to say, **Your sin remaineth.** As the old adage correctly states, "There are none so blind as those who will not see." Because of his physical blindness this early confessor received both physical and spiritual illumination. Because of their

prejudice the Pharisees' light was turned into darkness.

This chapter ends on a note similar to Paul's emphasis in Rom. 1:18-32. There the Apostle argues that when the Gentiles rejected the revelation of God through nature and conscience, their whole nature became perverted, values were inverted, and their perversity ended in a "reprobate mind" which could not distinguish good from evil or right from wrong. This is the ultimate in apostasy. Likewise, in the Synoptic Gospels, Jesus warned that a chronic rejection of light could lead to the "blasphemy against the Holy Spirit" for which no forgiveness would be possible (Mark 3:28-30). This is the same situation that Jesus had in mind when he said, "Thou hast hidden these things from the wise and understanding and revealed them to babes" (Matt. 11:25 NEB). Such is the irony of the judgment of God; those who prefer darkness to light will have darkness as their punishment.

It was pride which prevented the Pharisees from being teachable and welcoming

35 Jesus heard that they had cast him out; and finding him, he said, Dost thou believe on the Son of God?

36 He answered and said, And who is he, Lord, that I may believe on him?

37 Jesus said unto him, Thou hast both seen him, and he it is that speaketh with thee

38 And he said, Lord, I believe. And he worshipped him.

39 And Jesus said, For judgment came I into this world, that they that see not may see; and that they that see may become blind.

---

court or committee and they merely thrust him out from their presence and fellowship.[8]

35 **Dost thou believe on the Son of God** is "Son of man" in ASVm, RSV and NEB.[9] When Jesus made clear to the outcast beggar that he was the Son of Man he immediately responded **I believe, Lord.** Then **he worshipped him** (v. 38). The narrative having been completed, an application is made. This new convert and humble believer is contrasted with the proud, hostile, unbelieving Pharisees who claimed they had the light of God in themselves.

39 **For** (eis) **judgment** (krima) **came I into** (eis) **this world, that they that see** (professed to see) **may become blind.**[1] This is not a reference to the Great Judgment but rather the personal, existential crisis in which everyone who encounters Christ finds himself. Under the Mosaic

---

the light. The three hardest words to utter are, "I am wrong." Four distinct classes are depicted in this chapter, judged from the standpoint of their response to the evidence and the light. An old Arabic proverb reads:

He who knows not, and knows not
    he knows not,
He is a fool; shun him.
                    (the Pharisees)
He who knows not, and knows he
    knows not,
He is simple; teach him.
                    (the blind man)
He who knows, and knows not he
    knows,
He is asleep; waken him.
                    (the neighbors)
He who knows, and knows he knows,
He is wise; follow him.
                    (the confessor)[d]

In the section on light (8:12—9:41) Jesus made the announcement that he was the world's source of light. This led to an argument as to the veracity of this testimony concerning himself. In the course of this dialogue Jesus identified himself as being in the spiritual lineage of Abraham while his accusers were in the spiritual lineage of the devil (8:44). This accounted for their murderous intentions. In the course of eluding them, he encountered and healed the blind man and thus demonstrated his power to give light. In the debate which followed, the consequences of welcoming the light are portrayed, the judgment which follows its rejection is illustrated, and the dilemma faced by those who try to remain neutral is exemplified in the parents. Thus, this section spells out in great detail the general principle stated in 1:5 and 3:19, namely that while light is generally diffused, one's reaction to it differs because of subjective factors.

The inter-relationship of light and life is also illustrated here. In 1:4 life leads to light; here light leads to life. In John's thought, life is more basic al-

---

[8] Wm. Temple, *Readings in the Fourth Gospel* (London: Macmillan, 1950), p. 159. Cf. the phrase "put out of the synagogue" in John 9:22; 12:42; 12:2; cf. Luke 6:22; Matt. 5:11; 24:9. Hoskyns thinks that earlier persecutions did not include this formal excommunication and that the expression in John reflects a later practice by the Jews (Hoskyns, p. 356). Excommunication was a serious matter for it led to loss of employment and other social, political, and economic liabilities (RHS, p. 220). See also Schürer, *The Jewish People in the Time of Jesus Christ*, II, ii, 60-62; K. L. Carroll, "The Fourth Gospel and the Exclusion of Christians from the Synagogues," *British Journal of Religious Literature*, XL:1 (1957), pp. 19-22. Edersheim, *Life and Times of Jesus the Messiah* (New York: Longmans, Green Co., 1899), II, p. 183.

[9] The MSS. Aleph, B.D. and P[66] have "Son of Man" instead of "Son of God" (Theta, Omega, Old Latin, Vulgate). So the weight of evidence is decidedly for the former.

[10] *Krima* (verdict, condemnation) is found only here in this Gospel. Its synonym *krisis* occurs eleven times and connotes separation (See A-G).

[d] Cited in F. N. Peloubet, *Suggestive Illustrations on the Gospel of John* (New York: E. R. Herrick 1895), p. 286f.

40 Those of the Pharisees who were with him heard these things, and said unto him, Are we also blind?

41 Jesus said unto them, If ye were blind, ye would have no sin: but now ye say, We see: your sin remaineth.

---

Law (Old Covenant) the Law presented the individual Israelite with a choice: to obey the Law meant life while disobedience meant death.[11]

40 To the Pharisees' question, **Are we also blind?**  Jesus answered that, if they were blind (had not seen and heard the Son of God), they would have no sin; but because they had seen and rejected the Light of God, Jesus informed them, **Your sin remaineth.**[12]

---

though the terms are really different aspects of the God-head.  Life may be said to be the principle of action while light represents the intellectual and moral aspect of life.  Light is the medium through which life comes.[e]  Collateral reading on this relationship may be found in I John 1:5-5:20.  The chief point of this passage is that divine light brings both privilege and responsibility.  The important thing therefore is to "walk in the light" and thus have rapport ("fellowship") with God and experience deliverance from sin as a result (I John 1:7).

Not only Jesus but the men of Qumran were convinced that the Pharisees, Sadducees and their followers were "Children of Darkness" while they themselves were the "Children of Light."[f]  The latter considered themselves exiles while the early Christians thought of themselves as the "light of the world" (Matt. 5:14-16; Eph. 5:8; Col. 1:12; Phil. 2:15).  The dualism of John's Gospel is not the metaphysical dualism of the Greeks (between matter and spirit), nor the eschatological dualism of the Essenes of Qumran (present and future) but the moral dualism which presents every man with a personal crisis (*krisis*) of judgment.

[11] Compare the doctrine of "the two ways" in Deut. 30:15; Amos 4:4, 5; Jer. 6:16; Matt. 7:13, 14; Did. I. p. 1; cf. 1 QS, iii. 13.

[12] The word "sin" used here (*hamartia*) occurs 214 times in the N. T., the most frequent of several synonyms for sin.

[e] See J. P. Weisengoff, "Light and its Relation to Life in St. John," CBQ, Oct. 1946, pp. 448-51.

[f] See T. H. Gaster, *The Dead Sea Scriptures* (New York: Doubleday Co., 1956), pp. 281ff.

# CHAPTER X

Verily, verily, I say unto you, He that entereth not by the door into the fold of the sheep, but climbeth up some other way, the same is a thief and a robber.

2 But he that entereth in by the door is the shepherd of the sheep.

3 To him the porter openeth; and the sheep hear his voice: and he calleth his own sheep by name, and leadeth them out.

4 When he hath put forth all his own, he goeth before them, and the sheep follow him: for they know his voice.

5 And a stranger will they not follow, but will flee from him: for they know not the voice of strangers.

6 This parable spake Jesus unto them: but they understood not what things they were which he spake unto them.

7 Jesus therefore said unto them again, Verily, verily, I say unto you, I am the door of the sheep.

8 All that came before me are thieves and robbers: but the sheep did not hear them.

---

## EXEGESIS

1 **Verily, verily.** This is a translation of *amēn, amēn,* meaning, "it is dependably true." Jesus repeated this word frequently to prepare the minds of his hearers for very vital and important truths, he was about to proclaim. As Jesus introduced the metaphor of the sheepfold and the thief, he must have had in mind the example of the bad leadership of the Pharisees (shepherds) over the Jews (sheep) (cf. 9:40, 41). Among the Rabbis, Moses was often referred to as the "faithful shepherd."[1] Jesus' use of the comparison may have been occasioned by the Jews' assertion that they were disciples of Moses (9:28). Judas was a "thief" (*kleptēs*); Barabbas was called a "robber" (18:40).

2 Reference is first made to the customary procedure of the shepherd walking ahead of his sheep through a gate into a fenced enclosure called a sheepfold. At night the gate was locked. If a thief wished to enter, he would have to climb over the wall.

3 **The porter openeth.** The **porter,** (*thyrōros* from *thyra*: *door,* and *hora*: *care*), was possibly an undershepherd (MRV).[2] The sheep recognized and obeyed the voice of their shepherd (**the sheep hear** ["heed"] **his voice**). The shepherd knew each sheep so well that he gave each one a name.

4 **Put forth** (*ekbalēi*) implies a reluctance on the part of the sheep to leave the fold. **And the sheep follow** (i.e. "continue following," present tense) **him** implies customary and continuous obedience. By contrast they will not follow a stranger (v. 5), but rather flee from him.

6 The word *paroimia* (parable, v. 6) is defined (A-G), "In Johannine usage *dark saying,* figure of speech, in which especially lofty ideas are concealed" (cf. John 16:25, 29).[3] John states that the hearers did not get the significance of Jesus' prolonged metaphor, because, as inferred previously, they did not want to believe what they heard.

7 Jesus begins a detailed explanation of the general figure of the shepherd and the sheep, by calling himself the **door** (*thyra*) **of the sheep.**

8 The statement **All that came before me are thieves and robbers** needs interpretation. As it reads, it puts all people from Adam through John the Baptist in a

[1] *Mekita* 13d 14a, cited in Hugo Odeberg, *op. cit.,* p. 139 (cf. Heb. 3:5).
[2] The word designates a male door keeper in Jos. *Ant.* II, 108; Mark 13:34 and a female door keeper in Jos. *Ant.* 7, 48; John 18:16. Is God the Father the doorkeeper? Wesley, *Notes.* Acts 14:27, 16:14; Col. 4:13; Rev. 3:8.
[3] In the N. T. παροιμιαν occurs only here and in John 16:25, 29; II Pet. 2:22. It also means "proverb" as in Sip. 6:35 — "Proverbs of Understanding."

bad category. The preposition *pro* ("before"), in classical Greek usage, in addition to meaning "before," also was used to mean "in behalf of" or "claiming to be." The context clearly implies the latter meaning for it here. "Jesus refers to false messiahs and self-appointed leaders who made havoc of the flock" (ATR, V, 176). "All who came before me, claiming to be what I am and to give the sheep what I give" (BFW, p. 789). **But the sheep did not heed them (RSV).**

## EXPOSITION

6. TRUE AND FALSE SHEPHERDS (10:1-39)

This important section needs to be seen in perspective: this analysis may help provide this.

### THE ANALOGY          THE REACTION

| Para-graphs | "I AM" | | Opposition | | |
|---|---|---|---|---|---|
| | "the DOOR" | "the good SHEPHERD" | division | "the CHRIST" | "SON OF GOD" |
| 1 | | 11 | 19 | 22 | 31    39 |
| Para-graphs | The "Parable" or "Figure" | | Resulting controversy (because of) | | |
| | stated | explained | "these words" | alleged blasphemy | |
| Place | Jerusalem | | 22 Solomon's porch | | |

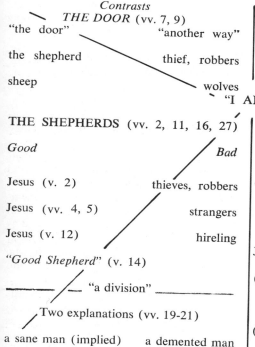

*Contrasts*

**THE DOOR (vv. 7, 9)**

"the door"                    "another way"

the shepherd              thief, robbers

sheep                    wolves

"I AM"

**THE SHEPHERDS (vv. 2, 11, 16, 27)**

*Good*                         *Bad*

Jesus (v. 2)                thieves, robbers

Jesus (vv. 4, 5)              strangers

Jesus (v. 12)                 hireling

"Good Shepherd" (v. 14)

———— "a division" ————

Two explanations (vv. 19-21)

a sane man (implied)    a demented man

a God-endorsed man      a demoniac

*Dialogue*

Jews' Question: "Are you *the Christ?*"
Jesus' Answer: by implication, "yes":
  (1) The miracles are in God's name.

(2) The miracles attest Jesus' messianic claim.

(3) The disciples (sheep) bear witness to this.

(4) The explanation is that "I and the Father are one."

The Jews' Reaction: (vv. 31, 33, 39)
  (1) Attempt to stone him.
  (2) Charge of blasphemy.
  (3) Attempt to arrest him.

Jesus' Rebuttal (vv. 34-38)

(1) In O.T. men are called "gods."
  (a) They were chosen by *men*.
  (b) They were called *"gods."*
  (c) This was not blasphemy.
(2) Jesus is called *"The Son of God."*
  (a) He was sanctified by the *Father*.
  (b) He is called *"Son* of God."
  (c) Is not this less blasphemous?
  (d) "Judge me not only by what *I say* but by what *God does* through me."

9 I am the door; by me if any man enter in, he shall be saved, and shall go in and go out, and shall find pasture.

---

9 I am the door. In ancient Greece some people visualized entering heaven by a door. Similarly the idea was expressed in Jewish literature: "the gate of heaven" (Gen. 28:17); "the doors of heaven" (Ps. 78:23). In Luke 13:24 is quoted: "Strive (exert yourself to the limit) to enter by the narrow door; for many . . . will seek to enter and will not be able." The same combination of shepherd and door in rabbinic sources (Mek. 13d. 14a) is noted by Odeberg (op. cit., p. 315), By me, if any man enter in, he shall be saved. The emphasis, due to

---

### a. The "Parable" of the Good Shepherd (vv. 1-6)

Where should this chapter begin?

Nestle's Greek text begins this division with 9:40 rather than with 10:1. There is merit in both divisions. In favor of beginning the chapter at 9:40 is the consideration that 10:1ff is addressed to the Pharisees mentioned in 9:40. In favor of making the transition at 10:1 is the fact that here the imagery shifts from light to life, from the blind man to the shepherd. But the Pharisees are in the background of both chapters. After solemnly telling the Pharisees that they are not only blind but sinful, Jesus goes on to compare them to hirelings who are unfaithful in dealing with the "sheep" under their care. He then contrasts the hirelings with the Good Shepherd.

The theme of sheep and shepherd is the basis for a large area of Biblical literature and Christian art and letters. Jesus, as the Good Shepherd, was the favorite theme of early Christian artists. This is reflected in the catacombs and in other early evidences of Christian life and thought. Parallels to this figure may be traced throughout the Old Testament and even in Greek mythology, in which Orpheus is the good shepherd. The tending of sheep is one of the most widespread of occupations, so that this analogy speaks a universal language. It is especially relevant to central Palestine where the rugged terrain and limited rainfall make grazing a major "industry." Even to this day, in the vicinity of Bethlehem, Hebron, Jerusalem, Ramallah, and elsewhere, the sight of flocks of sheep and goats is a common occurrence. Sheep-raising is surprisingly extensive and is not limited to pastoral peoples. This writer was astonished, upon arrival at the Berlin airfield in 1955, to see a shepherd grazing a large flock of sheep on the airfield of a metropolis of four million.

Because the Bible utilizes word-pictures with a wide application, it has a universal appeal. Because of the wide variety of terrain, flora, and fauna in Palestine, it is a microcosm, a little world in itself, and hence uniquely suited to be the origin of a world religion, the theatre of a divine revelation intended for the whole earth.

In the Old Testament the "Shepherd" often stood for God and sometimes for the leaders, while the sheep represented Israel. This concept received its finest expression in the twenty-third Psalm. It is found also in Micaiah's message to Ahab (I Kings 22:13-18) where the "shepherd" is the king. The "shepherd" meant any leader, such as the prophets (Jer. 23:1-11), or the princes (Nah. 3:18; Ezek. 34:1-16), or priests (Zech. 10:2), or leaders in general. The most frequent use of the analogy was made by the Exilic prophets — Jeremiah, Ezekiel, and Zechariah. In contrast to the unfaithful, selfish leaders, God himself is pictured as the Good Shepherd (Ezek. 34:15). David is also remembered as the good shepherd (cf. I Sam. 17:34-36), and the Messiah is described as the Good Shepherd, like David (Ezek. 34:24; 37:24-27). The portion of the O.T. which most closely resembled John 10 seems to be Ezek. 34 where the contrast between the true and false shepherds is brought out, and David is promised as the coming Good Shepherd, precisely as in John 10. It is noteworthy that Israel's greatest leaders — Moses and David — were both shepherds. Because they were faithful in small things, they qualified for greater responsibilities (cf. Matt. 25:21).

10 The thief cometh not, but that he may steal, and kill, and destroy: I came that they may have life, and may have *it* abundantly.

---

word order, is on by me. He is the only door to salvation (cf. John 14:6). But Jesus offered much more than salvation or "eternal security." He also offered freedom from fear and sin's guilt and power, as well as liberty to go in and out, symbolizing protection while in the enclosure at night and provision while in the pasture during the day. The shepherd is present to see that the needs of the sheep are supplied.

10 This thought is further developed and amplified by the direct statement: **I came that they may have life, and have it abundantly.** By contrast the figure of a thief is given as one who comes to steal, kill and destroy. He takes advantage of the sheep and exploits them, whereas Christ does just the opposite; he protects them and provides for them. Jesus may have had in mind the Pharisees and Sadducees of his day whom, at one time or

---

Travelers in Palestine and among the Basques of Spain report scenes which, even today, have a remarkable similarity to the details of this parable. The shepherd thrusting the sheep out of the fold, leading them to pasture, defending and nourishing them, seeking the lost (Luke 15:4), calling them by name, and separaating the sheep from the goats — all these are everyday occurrences in many lands. It is difficult for urbanized people, or even modern mass production herdsmen, to realize how intimate is the relation between man and beast in more primitive pastoral economies. It is this sense of personal intimacy which makes the twenty-third Psalm and the picture of Jesus as the Good Shepherd so appealing.

### b. The Parable Explained (vv. 7-18)

This is the first parable mentioned in John's Gospel. As was often the case, Jesus explained the parable after telling it. Often the explanation which followed was occasioned by a question from a disciple as to the meaning of the parable (Mark 4:10). The parable was frequently made deliberately enigmatic so that the multitude could not use it as a weapon against him. Yet it evoked inquiry and clarification among his more sympathetic followers (e.g., Matt. 13:10-16). The parables in this Gospel, however, differ from the typical parables in that they are extended metaphors, a com-

parison which is not stated to be such. "I am the door," "I am the vine" — these are metaphors in which the comparison is not stated. The typical parable begins with a simile — the "kingdom of heaven is like unto . . . ," in which the comparison is explicit. This is neither a parable nor an allegory but a "symbolic discourse," in which a picture is given followed by a statement of its significance. Here the discussion centers in Christ rather than the kingdom as such. "John finds in the person of Jesus himself that which the Synoptists find in the kingdom of God" (CKB, p. 307).

**The door** is not *either* the door by which the shepherd enters (v. 7) *or* the one by which the sheep enter (v. 9); it is both.[a] The sheepfold had only one door (*thyra*) for maximum security. It is rather surprising that the similitude is complicated by the additional thought of Christ as the door as well as the shepherd. Yet, upon reflection, both analogies are seen to be appropriate. As the door, in contrast to the "other way," Jesus is the proper way of access to the sheep. If the fold symbolizes the church or heaven, then the one mode of entrance through Christ is appropriate. Jesus is often referred to as the Gate or the Door in early Christian literature.[b] The "door" of a Palestinian sheepfold is not the gate which closes the opening; it is the opening itself. The point here is that Jesus is the only way into the sheepfold, into the Father's

---

[a] "When He is conducting us to His Father, He calls Himself a door, but, when He is caring for us Himself, He calls Himself a shepherd." Chrysostom, *Saint John Chrysostom: Commentary on Saint John the Apostle and Evangelist*, Homilies 1-88, tr. Sister Thomas Aquinas Goggin, S.C.H. (New York: Fathers of the Church, Inc., 1957), vol. II, P. 126.
[b] E.g., Clem. Rom. I *Cor.* xlviii; Ign. Phila ix. I; Hermas *sim.* Eus., H. Eccl., ii. 23. 8; Acts of John, 95; Chrysostom interprets "the Door" as meaning *the Scriptures* (*op. cit.*, II, 124).

11 I am the good shepherd: the good shepherd layeth down his life for the sheep.

12 He that is a hireling, and not a shepherd, whose own the sheep are not, beholdeth the wolf coming, and leaveth the sheep, and fleeth, and the wolf snatcheth them, and scattereth *them*:

13 *he fleeth* because he is a hireling, and careth not for the sheep.

14 I am the good shepherd; and I know mine own, and mine own know me,

---

another, he accused of stealing, killing and destroying. They stole from people in connection with worship at the temple; they were guilty of having Jesus killed; they were hindering genuine worship; and they were later guilty of destroying Christian leaders.

11 Here the metaphor returns from the *door* back to the figure of the *shepherd*

(vv. 2-4). **I am the good shepherd: the good shepherd layeth down his life for the sheep.** The idea of shepherd is repeated again in v. 14; and the statement of laying down his life in v. 15. In between vv. 11 and 14, there is a return to the subject of false and selfish leaders of the sheep (people). When danger comes, they flee and forsake the sheep,

---

presence, into the kingdom of God. This is the consistent theme of the New Testament: "No one cometh unto the Father but by me" (14:6); "neither is there any other name under heaven, that is given among men, wherein we must be saved" (Acts 4:12). This exclusive mode of legitimate entrance is also implied in 5:40 and 6:68 where life comes only through Christ, and in 14:6 where only *one* way is implied.

This is often regarded as narrow provincialism and bigotry. Many adherents of other world faiths resent this intolerance and consider exclusiveness a hindrance to Christian evangelism. But, as in the Old Testament, so in the New, there is only one true God, one Savior, and one true faith. All lines converge in Christ. The ways that are broad and attractive at first lead to destruction, while only the "narrow portal" leads to life (Matt. 7:13, 14). Attempts to limit this sweeping exclusiveness fail to do justice to the Biblical evidence. It was not the author's intention to say that only certain leaders, prophets, Hellenistic cults, or elements of Jewish leadership were false. He includes *everyone* except the Old Testament heroes (Hoskyns, pp. 374f). Some modern commentaries and Bible study guides soften this exclusiveness to read "*a* Door" or "*a* Good Shepherd." These reflect, not the influence of the Bible, but rather, the religious eclecticism of the age. Jesus Christ is not to be by-passed; he is not *a*

way but *the* Way; this is the consistent emphasis of the Fourth Gospel.

The **thieves** and **robbers** refer primarily to the leaders condemned for willful blindness in 9:41, but not to them exclusively. They include also the false shepherds of the Old Testament — kings, priests and prophets — who perverted the truth and led the people astray.[c] The contrast is the point being emphasized, not so much to single out false shepherds for condemnation but to call attention to the one Good Shepherd. The contrast extends to the motives of the true and false shepherds. As in Ezekiel's classic description, so here, the "thief" is motivated by a desire to exploit the sheep, hence he comes to **steal**, **kill** and **destroy,** to deprive the sheep of life. The Good Shepherd, in contrast, comes to give and preserve life. The terror that "the thief" inspires in the flock is reflected in **seeth** (*theōrei*), meaning to gaze upon in horror.

Jesus presents himself as the way of access in and out of the fold. It has been well stated that herein lies an important distinction between the laity and the clergy. The laymen have to go in and out of the church into the world. The clergy remain within the "fold" and hence tend to become isolated from the world in which their parishioners live.[d]

The **good shepherd** employs an unusual term for **good** (*kalos* rather than *agathon*). It has the connotation of "winsome" or "attractive" as well as "virtuous." Few

---

[c] The false political Messiahs admired by the Herodians may also be included in this condemnation cf. Acts 21:38).

[d] Wm. Temple, *Readings in St. John's Gospel* (London: Macmillan Co., 1950), p. 163.

15 even as the Father knoweth me, and I know the Father; and I lay down my life for the sheep.

16 And other sheep I have, which are not of this fold: them also I must bring, and they shall hear my voice; and they shall become one flock, one shepherd.

---

but in contrast Christ remains with them and protects them, even to the extent of providing for their eternal welfare by his sacrificial death.

16 The **other sheep** mentioned are all those who would believe and be redeemed in the vast future that lay ahead, those of that generation, of our generation, and of the final and last generation when

Christ returns to earth (cf. Matt. 8:11 and Luke 13:28f). Was the *primary* reference to Jews of the Dispersion, to Gentiles, or to future believers of all nations? In this context it certainly included Samaritans (John 4) and Gentiles (7:35; 12:20). The transition from narrow Jewish exclusiveness to the inclusion of Gentiles in the covenant is one of the cardinal doc-

---

portraits of Jesus are more appealing than that of him in his role of shepherd. In this case the good and the beautiful are merged in the figure of Christ. The goodness of this shepherd is such that he spares not himself in behalf of the welfare of the sheep. As David risked his life to protect his charges (I Sam. 17:34-37), so this Son of David not only risks his life but also surrenders his life for the people. God who "spared not his own Son," reflected Paul, will spare no pains to give us what is needed (Rom. 8:32). The important thing to note is that Jesus' sacrifice was *voluntary;* because it was vicarious and free, it is efficacious. Herein lies the central and most unique doctrine of the Christian faith. Other religions have great teachers, heroes, even martyrs, but no other religion thinks of its founder as having died for his followers, much less for the whole world.

The **hireling** differs from the good shepherd not only in the service he performs, but also in his motive. He is not interested in the sheep as such; he is interested in the sheep as a means to an end, the end being his wages. Because of inadequate motivation, he fails to meet the crisis.

A similar scene is graphically described in Homer:

*As the lion who has leaped*
*Into a fold — and he who guards the*
*   flock*
*Has wounded but not slain him —*
*   feels his rage*
*Waked by the blow; — the affrighted*
*   shepherd then*
*Ventures not near, but hides within*
*   the stalls,*

*And the forsaken sheep are put to*
*   flight,*
*And huddling, slain in heaps, till*
*   o'er the fence*
*The savage bounds into the fields*
*   again.*
—*Iliad*, v. 136-142.

David, as a good shepherd in his day, was more heroic. Jesus, as the Good Shepherd, is now predicting the fate that will befall him soon in the line of duty. He could not save himself and save the "sheep" at the same time; he could not accept the challenge "Come down from the cross" (Luke 23:35), and accomplish the Father's purpose. Thus the Good Shepherd is placed in contrast both to the thief who destroys, and the hireling who is more concerned with his own safety than with the welfare of the flock. When the hireling is most needed, he is of least value. One reason for the protection given by the Good Shepherd is the personal concern he has for individuals in the "flock." This note is sounded repeatedly in this Gospel (13:1, 34; 17:6, 24).

The laying down of the Shepherd's life is mentioned several times here: in vv. 11, 15, 17, 18, and is, of course, a prediction. It is noteworthy that:

(a) The *purpose* of the laying down of his life is that the flock may have life (v. 10, 11).

(b) The *beneficiaries* of this laying down of life include "other sheep" as well (v. 16).

(c) The *consequence* of the surrender of life is the Father's love (v. 17).

17 Therefore doth the Father love me, because I lay down my life, that I may take it again.

18 No one taketh it away from me, but I lay it down of myself. I have power to lay it down, and I have power to take it again. This commandment received I from my Father.

---

trines of the New Testament (see Eph. 3:1-20).

17 **Therefore doth the Father love me.** The Father loves Jesus because of his perfect obedience and complete, effective sacrifice, which culminated in death for "the world."

18 **No one taketh it away from me.** Jesus gave up his life voluntarily. I have power (*exousia* — "authority") **to lay it down, and I have power** (authority) **to take it again.** This idea of authority is reflected in the NEB rendering — "I have the right." God had thus provided for his beloved Son to die at a time when Jesus chose and then to rise from death also. Jesus' assertion of his own prerogatives in the matter is again linked with

---

(d) The *efficacy* of this self-sacrifice lies in the fact that it is voluntary (v. 18). The emphasis on knowledge continues in vv. 14, 15. Here the word is *ginōskō* (experiential knowledge) rather than *oida* as in ch. 9.

The relationship between Father and Son is developed further in this paragraph. By implication the Son is left in charge of the Father's flock (cf. 5:26; 6:44; 17:6). In order that the flock might be preserved from enemies, and have not only life but life in abundance, the Shepherd-Son finds it necessary to lose his life to save the lives of his flock. With the Father's knowledge and consent, he makes the supreme sacrifice for the sake of others. The beneficiaries of his death are not only the flock under his immediate care (Jews) but others also (Gentiles). This self-sacrifice pleases the Father. From the Father the Shepherd-Son receives authority to lay down his life and also to retrieve it. His death is the prelude to resurrection. The full authority (*exousia*) exercised by the Son is set in juxtaposition to his subordination to the Father's commandment. The Christological problem of the two natures in the Son had not yet arisen, but there is a hint here that the problem of the Son's freedom and simultaneous subordination was acknowledged. The sacrifice had to be voluntary and hence contingent and, yet, it had to be in the framework of divine foreknowledge and sovereignty. The Son was equal with the Father in his choice of self-sacrifice; he was subordinated to the Father in accepting the Father's command-

ment in this regard. The paradox is best left where it is left in the Fourth Gospel.

### c. The Sheep Heed Only the Good Shepherd (vv. 19-30)

#### (1) *Divisions Again* (vv. 19-21)

This is one of several instances reported in the Fourth Gospel where divided reactions to Jesus are noted. While the entire Gospel is preoccupied with the fact that the same Light (the same evidence) evokes contrasting reactions, the latent tension comes to a head in several specific places. The divided reactions of the public are given in anticipation in 1:11, 12 and implied in 2:23, 24. The basic principle is stated more precisely and fully in 3:19-21 and 9:39 in the metaphor of reaction to light. To believe or not to believe is the question noted in 3:35, 36. Overt hostility is first reported in 5:17, occasioned by healing on the Sabbath. The consequences of this for the people are predicted in 5:29, 40 and many places thereafter. It is the issue of life or death, the same issue on which the Mosaic Covenant focused (Deut. 30: 15). The same divided reaction followed the miracle of the loaves and the ensuing discourse (6:60-67). It became even more pronounced at the Feast of the Tabernacles in Jerusalem (7:25-31, 47). The healing at Siloam evoked even more dramatic and significant divisions, not only in the public at large but among the Pharisees (9:8, 16, 35:41). This is the second instance in which the actual "division" (*schisma*) is recorded, the first

19 There arose a division again among the Jews because of these words.
20 And many of them said, He hath a demon, and is mad; why hear ye him?
21 Others said, These are not the sayings of one possessed with a demon. Can a demon open the eyes of the blind?
22 And it was the feast of the dedication at Jerusalem:

---

his subordination to the Father — "This charge (*entolē*) I have received from my Father" (RSV, NEB).

**20 He hath a demon and is mad.** This really constitutes one accusation, namely, that he was mad due to demon possession (cf. 7:20; 8:48; Mark 3:21f., 30). **Why hear ye him** means "why are you continuing to listen (*akouete*, present tense) to him?" Slandering people is a very ancient custom.

21 Some then (and many now) were open-hearted and open-minded enough to realize Jesus was all he claimed to be. They asked: "A demon cannot open the eyes of the blind (force of *mē*), can he?"

22 Manuscript evidence favors *tote* (*then*) over *de* (*and*) at the beginning of verse 22.[4] The feast of dedication came about three months after the feast of tabernacles (7:37). Both lasted for eight days. It was instituted by Judas

---

being the reaction to the healing of the blind man (9:16). It is the third time that Jesus was accused of having a demon (cf. 7:20; 8:48). The accusation took three forms. After casting out demons (not mentioned in John's Gospel), he was accused of being in *league* with the "prince of *demons*" (Mark 3:22). In other words, since they were compelled to acknowledge that his was a supernatural power, and since they refused to believe that this came from God, they illogically concluded that it was from the devil. The second form of the accusation connoted *malice*, and evil intention. It was the equivalent of accusing him of being demonic, diabolical, and evil (8:48). In the other instances, here and in 7:20 (cf. Mark 7:33), to have a demon is the equivalent of being *crazy*, of being a fanatic; it is said with more scorn than fear.

This division was repeatedly predicted and explained by Jesus. It is rather startling in our generation to learn that he said, "Do you think that I have come to give peace on earth? No, I tell you, but rather division" (Luke 12:51 RSV). It is the prevailing assumption of contemporary Christianity that all division is to be deplored. Honest Christianity realizes that regardless of how painful it is, the presentation of the rugged truths of the Gospel will not win general acceptance and the divisions are inevitable. The call to accept the Good News carries with it the challenge to "come out from among

them and be separate and touch not the unclean thing" (II Cor. 6:17, 18) as the condition of sonship. Only a soft "cultural Christianity" assumes that "the world" is favorable to the truth of God, and that "peace" can be purchased by the avoidance of moral issues. The "peace" which Jesus gives is not a surface tranquility precariously maintained by a compromise of truth. It is the poise and stability that comes as a result of a complete surrender to the will of God. The modern preacher-prophet can no more hope to avoid controversy than did John or Jesus. Pugnacious inclinations are, of course, to be deplored and repudiated, but loyalty to the faith sometimes involves contention, now as then (Jude 3).

(2) *The Security of the "Sheep"*
(vv. 22-30)

**22 It was the Feast of Dedication . . . and it was winter.** Although Bernard and others think there is a chronological misplacement here, the evidence cited by Hoskyns in support of the existing sequence seems convincing enough. The burden of proof lies on the one proposing any rearrangement, especially in the absence of any textual witnesses to the proposed alteration. Bernard has v. 30 follow v. 18 immediately on the assumption that the author should move in some occidental thought pattern whereas there is abundant evidence that this author does not end one subject before beginning an-

---

4 *Tote* with BLW, P⁷⁵, some versions, and, oldest of all, P⁶⁶.

23 it was winter; and Jesus was walking in the temple in Solomon's porch.

24 The Jews therefore came round about him, and said unto him, How long dost thou hold us in suspense? If thou art the Christ, tell us plainly.

25 Jesus answered them, I told you, and ye believe not: the works that I do in my Father's name, these bear witness of me.

---

Maccabeus in December, 164 B.C., when the temple was cleansed and rededicated, after it had been profaned by pagan foes from Syria (I Macc. 4:36-59; Jos. *Ant.,* XII. vii. 7).

24 Once more an account is given of caustic questions and a hostile attitude toward our Lord. By asking the question, If thou art the Christ, the expectation was that Jesus would incriminate himself by

whatever answer he gave. If he denied that he was, he would disappoint all who believed in him. If he confessed that he was, he would incur further the wrath of the religious rulers who were plotting to kill him anyway. His answer was, in effect, an affirmation.

25 I told you and you believe not . . . Ye believe not, because ye are not of my sheep. The meaning is not that they

---

other, but has a habit of referring again and again to a favorite theme. Apparently, therefore, the theme which dominates this section is a continuation of the preceding section. The analogy of the sheep and shepherd continues, the reference in v. 33 to a "good work" goes back to 9: 1ff., the charge of blasphemy connects v. 33 with v. 30.

The emphasis gradually shifts from light (chs. 8 and 9) to life (chs. 10 and 11). The words My sheep know my voice, and I know them, and they follow me; and I give unto them eternal life are focal in that they point backward to the parable (10:1-6) and forward to the miracle (11: 17:44) (Hoskyns, p. 383).

The Feast of Dedication followed the Feast of Tabernacles by about three months. It was added to the Jewish calendar in post-biblical times because of an event in the Maccabbean struggle for independence. In the attempt by the Syrians to wipe out the Jewish religion, the city of Jerusalem was captured and the sacred altar desecrated by an offering of swine's flesh (cf. Dan. 11:30-32; I Macc. 1:37, 47, 54; 4:36-59; Jos. *Ant.,* XII. vii. 7). One of the first things that was done after the recapture of the city was the purification and rededication of the sanctuary. This was a service beginning on the 25th day of Chislev — or December (I Macc. 4:59) — and continuing eight days. It was a time of great rejoicing. On the first night of the feast a lamp was lighted, on the second night two lamps were kept burning, adding

one lamp a day until the climactic eighth day when all eight lights were burning. For this reason it was also called the Festival of Lights (*phōta*) as indicated by Josephus (*Ant., XII.* 325). The significance of this Festival of Lights recalls Jesus' claim to be the "Light of the world." The Feast of Dedication is also relevant to Jesus' dedication of himself as stated in the passage which follows (vv. 36-38). The winter weather probably led to the shelter of Solomon's porch, a portico on the eastern side of the Temple area (Jos. *War,* V. 184; *Ant.,* XV. 396-401; XX. 220).

The demand on the part of the Jews who gathered around that Jesus be more explicit about his messianic claims was not an expression of a sincere desire for truth but a reflection of hostility.

In characteristic fashion Jesus' answer was indirect. The implied affirmation that he was the Christ was substantiated by the evidence of the "works." The "works" that he did were the strongest possible evidence of his messianic claims. In his appeal to Isa. 61:1ff at the synagogue in Nazareth, the correspondence between the prophecy and its fulfillment in Jesus was so remarkable that the light "blinded" the hearers (Luke 4:22-30). By stating that their unbelief arose from the fact that they were not his "sheep," Jesus expressed the principle that genealogy (cf. 8:54, 55) conditions response to the truth. It is not that because they are in a certain category, they are automatically denied the privilege of sonship. Belief is not something of which they are

26 But ye believe not, because ye are not of my sheep.

27 My sheep hear my voice, and I know them, and they follow me:

28 and I give unto them eternal life; and they shall never perish, and no one shall snatch them out of my hand.

---

were incapable of belief but rather that unbelief led to their exclusion. Unbelief was not the effect but the cause. As long as they were unwilling to be convinced, belief was impossible (cf. 5:44).

**27 My sheep hear my voice, and I know them, and they follow me; and I give unto them eternal life; and they shall never perish. My sheep hear** (obey) . . . **and follow me.** Both verbs in Greek are in the present tense and therefore denote

continued action. (See 8:47 for discussion on *akouō*). In ancient times herds of sheep were usually small, and they followed the shepherd wherever he went. There is no difficulty in believing in the "eternal security" of believers *if* they are consistent in obeying and following Christ. The difficulty arises when so-called believers claim they are saved, but do not manifest obedience to Christ nor unselfish service to others. "By their fruits

---

incapable. It is rather that, by one or more choices with reference to divine revelation, they have placed themselves outside of the divine-human fellowship. This idea is echoed repeatedly in this Gospel. They are blind, not as a result of predestination or determinism, but as the consequence of their reaction to truth and light. In brief, committal to God's revelation in his Son is the condition of religious certainty and of life (cf. 7:17; 8:31, 32). Previously Jesus had told them that if they were truly descendants of Abraham they would accept him (8:39-44). The fact that they reject him is evidence that they are actually children of the devil. He is saying the same thing again here but in different words. He is pointing out once more that the works they have already witnessed are adequate evidence of the truth of his claims. Further mighty works would not help them even if they included a resurrection from the dead (Luke 16:31). It has well been said that: "A belief into which a man is bludgeoned by some ocular demonstration which leaves him no course but to submit, has none of the moral quality of that faith which avails to the saving of the soul."[e] No book of the Bible exposes the subjective factors which condition belief so profoundly.

The eternal life which Jesus gives to his "sheep" is something of which no combination of outward circumstances can deprive them. It is in line with Paul's ringing and triumphant challenge —

"What shall separate us from the love of Christ?" (Rom. 8:35-39). This is the logical conclusion to be drawn from the fact that the Good Shepherd is faithful to his task and, unlike the hireling, remains to protect the flock from danger (vv. 11-14). This does not, of course, mean an unconditional "eternal security." But it does mean that "eternal security" is a glorious reality to that believer who abides in Christ. The subordination of the Son to the Father is implied once more in v. 29; the believer is in the Father's "hand." There was a strong element of determinism in the teachings of the Pharisees and the Dead Sea Scrolls, but in the Gospels the emphasis on human responsibility as well as divine sovereignty is balanced. The eternal life is not only something promised for the future; the present tense indicates that the giving is present and continuous.

d. Jesus Escapes Stoning for Alleged Blasphemy (vv. 31-39)

Bitterly, and with a touch of irony, Jesus asked for which of the many good deeds he was being stoned. They had started to stone him before, as reported in 8:59, hence the again of v. 31. Stoning was the normal punishment for blasphemy. In defense of his claim to deity, Jesus resorted to typical rabbinic exegesis as he did when arguing for the resurrection (Luke 20:27-38). This was a mode of exegesis well understood and acceptable to his hearers. Paul followed a similar

---

[e] W. F. Howard, *Christianity According to St. John* (Philadelphia: Westminster, 1946), p. 160.

29 My Father, who hath given *them* unto me, is greater than all; and no one is able to snatch *them* out of the Father's hand.

30 I and the Father are one.

31 The Jews took up stones again to stone him.

---

you shall know them . . . not everyone who says to me 'Lord, Lord' shall enter the Kingdom of heaven, but he who does the will of my Father who is in heaven" (Matt. 7:20, 21).

**29 No one is able to snatch them out of the Father's hand.** Paul gave expression to this teaching in a more detailed manner: "God is faithful, and he will not let you be tempted beyond your strength, but with the temptation will also provide the way of escape, that you may be able to endure it" (I Cor. 10:13, RSV, cf. Rom. 8:35).

---

strategy in arguing for the inclusion of Gentiles in the Abrahamic covenant (Gal. 3:16). The quotation is taken from Ps. 82:6:

> Elohim standeth in the congregation of God,
> Among the elohim doth He judge.
>
> .    .    .    .
>
> I have said; Ye are elohim,
> And sons of the Most High are ye all.
> Yet as men shall ye die,
> And, as one of the princes shall ye fall.[f]

Jesus, by means of an *argumentatio a minori ad majus,* argues that if an Old Testament judges temporarily invested with divine prerogatives, are called "gods," why should one who gives his whole life and service and who was sent from God for that purpose, be accused of blasphemy for designating himself "Son of God"? (S-B II, p. 543; Bultmann, p. 297).

His second defense was another appeal to the evidential value of his miracles as proofs of God's endorsement. God would not endorse a blasphemer, he argued, by working miracles through him. In the Synoptic accounts and in Revelation, the possibility of miracles occurring from some other source is recognized, but there is none of this in the Fourth Gospel.[g] In this Jesus put the issue rather objectively, saying in effect, "If you find me personally objectionable then do not let that prejudice you; instead look at the good deeds and draw your conclusions as to whether these works are characteristic of the predicted Messiah." But looking objectively at the evidence and drawing the logical conclusion was the last thing his critics were prepared to do. They had now gone far beyond the point where they would consider the matter without bias. Their minds were already made up, their wills were set. Once again he eluded them as they prepared to close in and capture him by force. There is more than a hint here that divine providence made possible his escape, as had been the case more than once before.[h]

This marks another climax of opposition in John's account. In the section on controversy (ch. 5-10) they rejected the living water (7:44). Next they rejected the Light of the world (8:59; 9:34-41), and now they have rejected the Good Shepherd by whose death the world finds life available. In chs. 8-10 the movement is from light to life.[i] Light, as the symbol of God, is "the medium through which we receive life."[j] Both concepts are basically the same in that they represent God's presence and power available to the believer. They are different aspects of the same divine reality. Life may be said to be the more basic inasmuch as life is the principle of activity while light is the manifestation of this activity. The rejection and subsequent loss of light leads to the forfeiture of life itself (cf. Rom. 1:24-28; II Thess. 2:10, 11).

---

[f] F. Delitzsch, *Commentary on the Psalms,* tr. by F. Bolton (Edinburgh: T. & T. Clark, 1877), II, p. 400.

[g] Mark 3:22; Matt. 10:25; Rev. 13:12-15; cf. Exod. 7:11; 8:7.

In Nazareth (Luke 4:30); in Jerusalem (John 8:59) where some ancient witnesses add, "and going through the midst of them went his way and so passed by."

[i] In I John the emphasis on light and life is even more pronounced. To have the light means to love our brothers (I John 2:9-11), to avoid sin (I John 1:9; 2:2), to keep the commandments (I John 2:2-5), to imitate Christ (I John 2:6), and to combat evil (I John 2:15-17).

[j] J. P. Weisengoff, "Light and its Relation to Life in St. John," CBQ, Oct., 1946, p. 449.

32 Jesus answered them, Many good works have I showed you from the Father; for which of those works do ye stone me?

33 The Jews answered him, For a good work we stone thee not, but for blasphemy; and because that thou, being a man, makest thyself God.

34 Jesus answered them, Is it not written in your law, I said, Ye are gods?

35 If he called them gods, unto whom the word of God came (and the scripture cannot be broken),

---

The Jews reacted with hostility and violence to the claim of Jesus to deity (33), accusing him of blasphemy; the penalty for it was stoning (Lev. 24:16). There is an example of the connative or tendential use of the present tense (32) in the verb *lithazete*. They picked up stones *with the intention* of throwing them at Jesus. Jesus defended himself by quoting Psalm 82:6, and in doing so met the rabbis on their own ground in a thoroughly Jewish way. "Ye are gods, and all of you sons of the most high" (Ps. 82:6). Judges, as God's representatives, were called gods in Ex. 21:6; 22:9, 28 (cf. KJV, ASV, RSV; Ex. 7:1).

32 *For which of these works*: not "which one" (*poion*) but, "what is it about these works" (cf. RSVm, KJV, ASV, RSV, Ex. 7:1).

---

Paralleling this is the movement of a remnant of believers toward the light. In each case where a division (*schisma*) is recorded, some emerged as believers (6:68, 69; 7:40; 8:30; 9:38; 10:21). While more attention is given to the many who disbelieved than to the few who believed, it is the latter for whom the whole drama of redemption is presented.

Since Jesus was content to win them, not so much by mass movements as by ones, twos, and threes, his servants today should not despair of the multitudes that are largely indifferent or even hostile. We may well be thankful if God is pleased to add to his church the relatively few who experience the light and go on to receive life.

With the attempt to arrest Jesus, reported in 10:39, the section dealing with Jesus as the Light of the World comes to a close. The announcement that he was the Light of the World, expressed in 8:12, was followed by a miracle in which a man hopelessly blind from birth received sight instantly. In the crisis which this miracle evoked, the tables were reversed: the one regarded as not only blind but sinful had sight both physical and spiritual. He was ejected from the fellowship of "the Jews" but welcomed by Jesus into the Kingdom of God. It is the Pharisees who are really blind. The influence of this event extends into ch. 10 with its Parable of the Good Shepherd, for the people continue to ask, "Can a demon open the eyes of the blind?" (10:21). Jesus continued to emphasize his intimate relationship to his Father and the charge of blasphemy, voiced in 5:18, was resumed with greater bitterness than ever. The spiritual kinship of Father, Son, and believer is stressed here in contrast to the children of darkness. The hostility of the world and the dangers surrounding the "sheep" are not of sufficient strength to make precarious the position of the believer. He is secure in the "fold" because of the Good Shephard's vigilance and his Father's omnipotence. The death of the Christ, as the condition of the life for the believers, is again the focus of attention as it was in chs. 1, 3, and 6. Only here is the Messiah pictured as the Shepherd who welcomes death for the sake of the sheep. The Father's sanctification of the Son is an elaboration of the pregnant assertion of the Prologue: "The Word became flesh and dwelt among us;" it is another evidence of the pre-incarnate existence of the Christ.

The section moves from the emphasis on light to an emphasis on life, the two being different facets of the central idea of God as the source of all truth and reality. This is mediated to man by one means — Jesus the Christ. Life is available on no other basis. Such is the recurring emphasis of this Evangelist.

In nature the connection between light and life is immediately apparent. Most vegetation deprived of sunlight dies. Fish

36 say ye of him, whom the Father sanctified and sent into the world, Thou blasphemest; because I said, I am *the* Son of God?

37 If I do not the works of my Father, believe me not.

38 But if I do them, though ye believe not me, believe the works: that ye may know and understand that the Father is in me, and I in the Father.

39 They sought again to take him: and he went forth out of their hand.

40 And he went away again beyond the Jordan into the place where John was at the first baptizing; and there he abode.

41 And many came unto him; and they said, John indeed did no sign: but all things whatsoever John spake of this man were true.

42 And many believed on him there.

---

36 The sanctification (*hagiazō*) of the Son by the Father means not moral purification but separation for divine service or dedication. It is used in the same sense in 17:19 — "I sanctify myself" — an act of consecration.

38 Jesus challenged his audience to believe the works (deeds) which he had performed as evidence of his claims since they were unwilling to accept his statements. Then as they sought to stone him he managed to escape. The manner of escape is not stated.

---

which swim in dark underground rivers are sightless. Donkeys compelled to work underground in the dark eventually lose their eyesight. By using such universally-understood analogies, the Fourth Gospel has earned the title, "The Spiritual Gospel." Its message is beamed to the entire world.

Plato's famous analogy of the cave serves to illustrate a similar kinship between light and life. In this "mythus," prisoners in a cave have as the only illumination a large fire behind them. These prisoners can only look straight ahead where the fire casts on the wall in front of them shadows of people who pass behind the prisoners (between them and the fire). The prisoners, unable to see the figures, think the only reality is the shadow cast by the figures. If a prisoner escapes and emerges into the sunlight outside the cave, he can for the first time distinguish between shadow and substance.

He will be dazzled by the brightness of the true light. If he returns to the interior and reports his discovery to the prisoners, they greet his testimony with skepticism and derision. The contrast stressed by Plato between the philosopher and the common people is similar to the contrast here between the enlightened, emancipated believer and those who prefer to remain in spiritual darkness, mistaking shadow for substance, form for content.[k]

Behind the picture of the gentle Shepherd's solicitude for the sheep is the aspect of cool courage. The conditions under which these words were spoken matched the words themselves. The love that caused the shepherd to lay down his life for the sheep rather than purchase a cheap "peace" from the enemy is more than a sentiment, more than an emotional thing. It is virile and robust, a calculating, informed and joyous love, which counts the cost and then pays the price of victory.

[k] Plato, *Republic*, VII. 514-520, *Dialogues of Plato,* tr. J. Jowett (New York: Random House, 1937), I, pp. 773-779.

# CHAPTER XI

Now a certain man was sick, Lazarus of Bethany, of the village of Mary and her sister Martha.

## EXEGESIS

1 In ch. 11 the reader approaches the climax of a series of "signs" which unify the public ministry of Jesus (chs. 2-12). Ch. 11 contains what is not only the most striking miracle story in the Gospel of John, but is also the longest account of any miracle in all of the New Testament. This "sign" furnishes additional evidence that Jesus had the authority (*exousis*) and power (*dynamis*) to give healing and even life to whomever he chose. It is also an earnest or token of what is to occur on the last day when Christ returns (I Thess. 4:13-18).

The sentence structure indicates that the author's primary interest here is not the Bethany family as such but the miracle itself; hence, he begins, "a certain man was sick." Lazarus was a common name among Hebrew families, hence the identification, of Bethany. This Hebrew name means, "God helps"; its Greek form is Eleazar. Some scholars identify this Lazarus with the Lazarus of the parable (Luke 16:19-31), for no adequate reason. According to tradition (Epiph. *Haer.* 66) Lazarus lived thirty years after his resurrection and died at the age of sixty.

Bethany. This town is mentioned in all four of the Gospels and is located on the southeast slope of the Mount of Olives,

## EXPOSITION

7. RETIREMENT TO JUDAEA AND BETHANY (10:40-12:11)

a. "Beyond Jordan" Again: Many Believe (10:40-42)

This section shows Jesus in relative retirement from the public. It is the period between the controversy in Jerusalem (following the healing of the blind man) and his triumphal entry into Jerusalem before the Passover. The reason for the retirement was either to escape a premature death or to establish contact with the disciples of John (Hoskyns) or both. In the light of 10:39, 40; 11:8, 16, 53; 12:10, it would appear that the main reason was survival — his "hour had not yet come."

One of the most convincing evidences that John had done his work well was the reception Jesus received from John's disciples near the scene of John's labors. Apparently most people in that area had heard John and knew him well but had not yet committed themselves. When they heard Jesus and saw him doing the miracles they had learned to expect from one claiming to be the Messiah, they readily believed and became followers. There were three areas in which Jesus was generally accepted: in Galilee, in Samaria, and now in Perea. When it became apparent that he would be accepted in Jerusalem also (following the resurrection of Lazarus), the authorities took steps to get rid of him (12:10).

John had lived up to his own preaching: "I must decrease but he must increase." John's task was not to make himself indispensable but rather the opposite. The best leaders are those who prepare the way for their successors so that their work may be continued. It is noteworthy that Jesus was more readily accepted here in Judaea than in Nazareth, his home town. Two factors explain it: John's preparatory work and the fact that at Nazareth the new light was too sudden and hence too dazzling.

b. Recalled to Bethany (11:1-53)
(1) *"Lazarus Is Sick"* (vv.1-4)

The comparative seclusion and security of this haven were not to last long. As in Galilee his attempts at retirement were

2 And it was that Mary who anointed the Lord with ointment, and wiped his feet with her hair, whose brother Lazarus was sick.

3 The sisters therefore sent unto him, saying, Lord, behold, he whom thou lovest is sick.

---

about two miles east of Jerusalem (v. 18). The road from Jerusalem passes over the Kidron and winds south and east around the base of Olivet, passing the villages of Siloam (Silwan) and Bethphage, en route to Bethany. It was, and still is, a residential suburb of Jerusalem.

2 Mary· is identified as not only the sister of Martha and Lazarus but also as the one who **anointed the Lord with ointment,** as reported in 12:1-8 and in Mark 14:3-9. This Mary of Bethany is not the unnamed sinner who anointed Jesus' feet in Galilee (Luke 7:36-50). Both sisters are mentioned as having entertained Jesus in their home previously (Luke 10:38-42). They were apparently a family of some

affluence, with a wide circle of friends, not only in Bethany but also in Jerusalem (11:18, 19). Jesus seemed to have been at home here while in the Jerusalem area. Stress is laid upon the friendship which Jesus found in this home; it must have been a haven for the Master, and he must have appreciated a home where he found not only lodging but affection.

3 The word **Lord** is vocative in this passage. Sometimes it designates only respect (e.g., 4:11, 15); sometimes reverence and devotion (6:68; 14:22), as here. **He whom thou lovest** (*phileis* — "you are fond of") **is sick,** a persuasive way to urge Jesus' immediate concern and presence. It reminded Jesus that he, as well as the

---

interrupted with requests to meet human need (Mark 1:3-39), so here. Jesus was never one to turn a deaf ear to a request for help. This request was of unprecedented urgency — his closest friend was seriously ill. More than most people, the Bethany sisters would feel they had a personal claim on Jesus' services and solace, for he had been their house guest more than once and a recipient of their bounty. Moreover, a special bond of affection existed between Jesus and this family of three. Jesus' reaction gives the clue to all that follows. The Master saw in this apparent catastrophe an opportunity for God to be glorified and the cause advanced. Many would have been depressed or maybe even irritated by the report, but Jesus accepted it with resignation and with a confidence that "all things work together for ultimate good."

### (2) *"Lazarus Is Dead"* (vv. 5-16)

In spite of Jesus' affection for the family and the urgent request for help, Jesus made no move for two days. This caused no restiveness on the part of the disciples for they did not want to be exposed again to danger. To the anxious sisters in Bethany, the two days of delay must have caused excruciating pain. Many a saint

has had to learn the lesson of patience in the face of unanswered prayer. Many have had to realize that God does not run at every beck and call. They have learned the significance of waiting on the Lord. Thus, "patience has her perfect work." Perhaps the days of agonized waiting helped prepare the sisters for the miracle which followed. Little did they know that while the delay seemed to deepen the tragedy it was really the prelude to a greater victory.

Two ways of life are again presented here: walking in the light and walking in the dark. Jesus used this occasion to state one of the most basic truths of the Scriptures and a dominant conviction of the Evangelist. Paul likewise stressed the fact that the "children of light" have no business trifling with the devious ways of the "children of darkness" and urged that we "walk as children of light" (Eph. 5:8). Once more the theme of light is mentioned in this Gospel (12:35, 36). These two contrasting ways were well understood by the Essenes of Qumran, who were also in the wilderness of Judaea at this time. As mystics they formulated their convictions in imagery familiar to readers of the Bible in general and of the Fourth Gospel in particular. Said they, "The origin of truth lies in the Fountain of Light and

4 But when Jesus heard it, he said, This sickness is not unto death, but for the glory of God, that the Son of God may be glorified thereby.

---

sisters, had a personal interest in bringing relief to Lazarus. In this context, *phileō* (v. 4) and *agapaō* (v. 5) are apparently used synonymously, both denoting affection in person-to-person relationships (cf. 21:15-17). Obviously these were among Jesus' warmest friends, and how natural it was that in this crisis they should immediately send for Jesus. That they would send so far indicates the serious character of Lazarus' illness.

4 **For the glory of God.** The word glory (*doxa*) is a prominent one in this Gospel. It occurs 19 times in the 21 chapters. It connotes the power and compassion of God. In the LXX, it normally translates *kabod,* the term for "honor, prestige, repu-tation, radiance." In usage similar to this context, the miracles done prior to the Exodus were for the glory of God (Exod. 7:5; 9:14, 16; Rom. 9:17). In the N.T. generally it means "radiance" (e.g., Luke 9:32), "majesty" (Rom. 1:23), "renown" (I Thess. 2:20), "praise" (John 9:24), "God's presence" (Luke 24:26; I Pet. 1:11).[1] In Johannine usage, parallels to this passage are to be found in Jesus' reaction to a man's blindness — "that the works of God may be manifest" (9:3). In a similar fashion the death and resurrection of Jesus are viewed as that which glorifies both Father and Son (12:28-33; 17:1). So Jesus sees in Lazarus' illness not only the misfortune of a friend

---

that of perversity in the Wellspring of Darkness. All who practice righteousness are under the dominion of the Prince of Lights and walk in ways of light. . . . The God of Israel and the Angel of His truth are always there to help the sons of light. It is God that created these spirits of light and darkness and made them the basis of every act."[a] This is another evidence of the particular symbolism encountered in this Gospel. It speaks a language well understood then as now.

In the War document the Sons of Light, now in exile, return to something comparable to the battle of Armegeddon, a final and successful struggle against the Children of Darkness. In the manner of apocalypses this one envisions the ultimate victory of the Children of Light over the Sons of Darkness in which "His exalted grandeur will give light, shedding on all the Sons of Light peace and blessing, gladness and length of days."[b] They are enabled to gain the victory by the Angel of Light, and they give him the credit.[c] While the Qumran salvation army was summoned to a holy war against the Children of Darkness, helped by the Angel of Light, Jesus demands that as individuals we follow him in the path of light.

This is language well understood by mystics and devout people of all ages. Few, if any, in the history of the church laid greater stress on the "Light" than George Fox, leader of the Friends. In his *Journal* he reported: "As the light appeared, all appeared that is out of light: darkness, death, temptations, the unrighteous and the ungodly; all was manifest and seen in the light. After this a pure fire appeared in me; then I saw how he sat as a refiner's fire and as fuller's soap; — then the spiritual discerning came into me . . . . I saw also that there was an ocean of darkness and death; but an infinite ocean of light and love, which flowed over the ocean of darkness. In that also I saw the infinite love of God, and I had great openings."[d] Thereafter, to Fox and his followers the "Light of the world" and the "openings" became the central point of faith.

Walking in the light, therefore, as I John 1:5-7 emphasizes, is the Christian's daily concern. It may be noted that:

(1) To walk in the light involves a basic *commitment* to the Light of the World. When the light comes to "every man," he is confronted with a crisis of decision whether to accept or reject the

---

[1] See also R. B. Lloyd, "The Word 'Glory' in the Fourth Gospel," *Expository Times,* 43, 1932, pp. 546-548.
[a] *Manual of Discipline* (1QS), iii. 13-iv. 26 (tr. by T. Gaster, *op. cit.,* pp. 43f).
[b] *Wars.* (1QM) i. 5 (Gaster, *op. cit.,* p. 282).
Ibid., xiii. 1 — xiv. 1.
[d] George Fox, *Journal,* abridged by P. L. Parker (London: Pitman & Sons, 1906), pp. 16f.

5 Now Jesus loved Martha, and her sister, and Lazarus.

6 When therefore he heard that he was sick, he abode at that time two days in the place where he was.

7 Then after this he saith to the disciples, Let us go into Judaea again.

8 The disciples say unto him, Rabbi, the Jews were but now seeking to stone thee; and goest thou thither again?

---

but an occasion for God's name to be exalted and the Kingdom advanced.

**5 Now Jesus loved** (*agapē,* the imperfect tense signifying continuance). His was a permanent, self-sacrificing devotion. The same word for "love" is used for Jesus' regard for his disciples prior to the last supper (13:1) and to designate the bond between Father, Son, and believer in the Lord's prayer (17:26).

**6** *Oun* — "however" here. **He abode at that time two days** beyond Jordan before departing for Bethany, called by Hoskyns

"a provocative delay." This delay was in spite of his deep affection for the family. Later events demonstrate the reason for the delay.

**8 The Jews were but now seeking** (imperfect — continuing action) **to stone thee.** To the disciples it seemed suicidal to return so soon to the place from which Jesus had just fled for his life. To them survival was the paramount consideration; to Jesus the most important consideration was "the greater glory of God." They felt justified in ignoring the message

---

light (3:18). Life henceforth depends on this decision.

(2) Such a walk is a *continuing operation.* The initial basic decision must be implemented by small daily decisions consistent with the basic one. One must choose constantly his reading matter, his line of inquiry, the things his eyes dwell upon. His continuing status as a "child of the light" depends upon this constant choice of the light and the rejection of darkness.

(3) There is *progression* in this "walk." As he continues his pursuit of light, he becomes more and more conformed to the Light of the World. He discovers that the light shines "more and more unto the perfect day" (Prov. 4:18).

(4) He finds himself a *partisan* of "The Way." He is in mortal combat with the forces of darkness and seeks to point his fellow travelers to the true Light. He possesses a moral concern for the outcome of the struggle and for the conversion of his fellows. This concern leaves no room for spiritual complacency.

(5) He thus finds the kingdom of God *within.* He learns that before he gets to heaven he must have heaven in his own soul. Heaven becomes not only a destination or a place but also a present condition of existence.

*Light of life, seraphic fire,*
*Love divine, thyself impart:*
*Every fainting soul inspire,*
*Shine in every drooping heart;*
*Every mournful sinner cheer;*
*Scatter all our guilty gloom;*
*Son of God, appear, appear!*
*To thy human temples come.*[e]

After the discourse on the necessity of walking in the light, Jesus announced that Lazarus had **fallen asleep.** The disciples' initial assurance soon turned to consternation as they learned that the Master really meant that Lazarus was dead and, worst of all, that Jesus purposed to go to him. It is then that Thomas's courage became apparent. **Let us also go that we may die with him.** Thomas had more loyalty than faith. He was a realist by making up in loyalty what he lacked in faith and hope. In 14:4 Thomas complained that they were in the dark as to Jesus' destination and means of reaching it. He is seen, in this context, to be demanding clarity; he wanted little left to the imagination. Later, he demanded objective, tangible evidence before he believed the companions' report that they had seen Jesus alive. In this instance, he appeared at his best; he was ready to commit himself to Christ even though lacking confidence in victory. He possessed Ignatius' willingness to die

---

e  Charles Wesley, "Light of Life," *Hymns of the Living Faith,* p. 305.

9 Jesus answered, Are there not twelve hours in the day? If a man walk in the day, he stumbleth not, because he seeth the light of this world.

10 But if a man walk in the night, he stumbleth, because the light is not in him.

---

from Bethany. Jesus felt that the call to service took priority over considerations of personal safety.

**9 Twelve hours in a day** indicates the popular, not legal, mode of reckoning time. The period of daylight varied with the season, hence the "hours" of fall and winter were shorter than those of the spring and summer. Clocks and other devices to measure time with precision were relatively unknown. **He stumbleth not** (*proskoptō*). The literal meaning of this term is to "strike against something" (Matt. 4:6; 7:27), hence to stub one's toe, "to stumble," as a blind person (Jer. 13:16; Prov. 3:23; Tob. 11:10). Used figuratively, as here, it means "to take offense at, feel repugnance for, reject, give offense" (A-G), as seen in Romans 9:32; I Peter 2:8. Jesus may be quoting a proverb, such as our "Make hay while the sun shines," in justifying the hazardous trip. His point is that opportunities for service such as these are limited and that what is done must be done quickly before his "hour" arrives (cf. 13:1; 17:1), when further action will be impossible. This was the third time Jesus had spoken thus. His brothers had challenged him to "walk in the light" as they prepared to go to Jerusalem for the Feast of Tabernacles (7:3-8, 13). The Evangelist apparently reported this exchange to call attention to another facet in the underlying conflict between light and darkness. A closer parallel is that in which Jesus prepared to heal the blind man (9:4, 5), by saying, "The night cometh when no man can work." Here "the light of *this* world" means natural light in contrast to "the Light of the world" (cf. 8:12; 9:5). As long as the disciples walk with Jesus, the

---

for his faith without Ignatius' hope in a resurrection.[f] Love and loyalty with a minimal creed was voiced by Whittier as he wrote,

*No offering of my own I have,*
*Nor works my faith to prove;*
*I can but give the gifts he gave,*
*And plead his love for love.*
*I bow my forehead in the dust,*
*I veil my eyes for shame*
*And urge, in trembling, self-distrust*
*A prayer without a claim.[g]*

### c. The Sixth "Sign" (vv. 17-53)

#### (1) *Jesus Greeted by Martha* (vv. 17-27)

The interview with Martha is perhaps the most important portion of this chapter because it deals with the basic issue. Upon Jesus' arrival at the edge of town, he learned that Lazarus had been entombed four days. There is a hint that he learned this upon arrival (in contrast to his supernatural knowledge of Lazarus' death, v. 11). Martha apparently wanted to converse with Jesus without the throng of friends being present and so went to meet him. Although deeply disappointed at Jesus' failure to come earlier and prevent the death of her brother, she still had confidence in him. She did not indulge herself in the temptation to doubt, bitterness, and disillusionment. To her, the thought uppermost was that Jesus had come too late to prevent the death of her brother. To Jesus, the over-all objective was the glory of God.

The faces carved in stone on Rushmore Memorial in the Black Hills of South Dakota are among the most impressive sculptures extant. These granite faces of Washington, Lincoln, Jefferson and Theodore Roosevelt are startling in their lifelikeness, except for size. The heads are proportionate to figures more than four hundred feet in height. To the workmen who hung for days on the face of the cliff, patiently carving the features of these patriots out of solid granite, only a few yards of rock were visible. They saw only the little irregularities, the chisel marks, the minute imperfections. Doubtless, they were bored with the tedium of

---

[f] Ignatius, "To The Romans" IV. I, *The Apostolic Fathers*, Loeb (N. Y.: Putnam, 1930) I, 231.
[g] *Hymns of the Living Faith*, p. 410.

11 These things spake he: and after this he saith unto them, Our friend Lazarus is fallen asleep; but I go, that I may awake him out of sleep.

12 The disciples therefore said unto him, Lord, if he is fallen asleep, he will recover.

13 Now Jesus had spoken of his death: but they thought that he spake of taking rest in sleep.

14 Then Jesus therefore said unto them plainly, Lazarus is dead.

15 And I am glad for your sakes that I was not there, to the intent ye may believe; nevertheless let us go unto him.

---

Light, they will not be in the dark. To those not possessing the indwelling light (1:9; I John 1:7), stumbling is inevitable.

11 The announcement Lazarus is fallen asleep is another evidence of our Lord's supernatural knowledge (cf. 1:42, 38; 2:25; 4:16, 49-53; 5:6; 6:64). As usual, the disciples interpreted Jesus' words literally rather than figuratively or spiritually, as had been the case when he spoke of birth (3:3, 4), water (4:16), food (4:32), bread (6:34), and destination (7:35). The term fallen asleep (kekoimētai) was used by pagans, Jews, and especially by Christians as a symbol of death (cf. II Macc. 12:45; Matt. 27:52). Later it became commonplace for Christians to speak of physical death as "sleep" (cf. I Thess. 4:13). The early Christians apparently preferred this word because of their belief in eternal life. The resurrection was likened to awakening from sleep (I Thess. 4:13-15).[2] Because the disciples interpreted his words literally, they were optimistic, thinking, He will recover (sōthēsetai — "be saved"). Then Jesus had to tell them bluntly, Lazarus is dead (from apothnēiskō — "to die"); since they failed to catch the higher significance, he must again resort to plain speech.

---

their task. Yet when one stands at a distance of several hundred or even thousand of feet away, the awe-inspiring majesty and near perfection of Borglum's massive sculptures become apparent. The same is true, on a lesser scale, in any large portrait; the close-up view is one of a series of smears, while at a distance the whole is pleasing. The marvel is that each workman could relate his little task so well to the finished masterpiece in the mind of the master sculptor. So to Martha, in her grief, the over-all purpose was not apparent until afterwards. There would have been no resurrection had Lazarus not died. Lazarus would not have died had Jesus been present, for as Bengel put it, "We read of no one having died while the Prince of life was present." Lazarus' resurrection made possible the climax of the "signs" reported by John, and resulted in many conversions in the Jerusalem area.

Martha and her companions had passed through days of great tension. The body of Lazarus had been washed and prepared for burial by winding sheets around the body, probably with arms and legs bound together, after the manner of Egyptian burials. Spices had been intermingled with the cloth to retard decomposition and to help cover the resulting odor. Burial had been on the same day as the death, as was the universal custom, because of rapid decay in the warm climate and because the corpse was considered ritually unclean (Num. 19:11-14). Although the Bible prohibited the extreme measures used by the heathen in mourning (Deut. 14:1), the mourning customs then, as in Eastern lands generally, were much more elaborate than in the West. In addition to the grief-stricken family and friends, mourners would often be hired to supplement the genuine expressions of grief (Joel 1:8; Matt. 9:23; Jer. 9:17; Amos 5:16). This mourning would sometimes include a formal lamentation or dirge (e.g., Isa. 14:4) and loud wailing (Micah 1:8); often the name of the dead was repeated over and over with great emphasis (II Sam. 18:33; I Kings 13:30; Jer. 22:18). Women showed the most extravagant emotions, rending their garments,

---

2 Acts 7:60; 13:36; I Cor. 7:39; 11:30; 15:6, 51; II Pet. 3:4; I Clem. 44:2. It was used as a euphemism for death on both Jewish and Christian graves (A-G). Ancient tomb inscriptions reflect the contrast between the "general hopelessness of the pagan world in the presence of death" and the hope of the Christian — M-M, p. 350.

16 Thomas therefore, who is called Didymus, said unto his fellow-disciples, Let us also go, that we may die with him.

17 So when Jesus came, he found that he had been in the tomb four days already.

18 Now Bethany was nigh unto Jerusalem, about fifteen furlongs off;

19 and many of the Jews had come to Martha and Mary, to console them concerning their brother.

20 Martha therefore, when she heard that Jesus was coming, went and met him: but Mary still sat in the house.

---

16 The importance of belief is brought out in this verse. Jesus' absence and the consequent death of Lazarus would provide a greater demonstration of the power of God and hence establish a stronger basis for the disciples' faith. Without specifically stating his strategy, Jesus challenged them to follow him into danger. Thomas, concerning whom little is reported outside of this Gospel, rose to herculean heights of courage and loyalty by urging his fellow disciples to follow Jesus regardless of the consequences.

17 In the tomb four days already; apparently it had taken Jesus and the disciples two days to arrive at Bethany. Lazarus died perhaps two days after the messengers left, soon after Jesus had received them. Jesus remained there two days and was two days en route, traveling perhaps twenty miles daily. It was customary to bury one, if at all possible, on the day that he died. There was the general belief among the Jews that one's spirit hovered near the body three days after death. A resurrection on the fourth day would be the more impressive because all hope for a restoration of the corpse to life would be gone after the third day.[3]

19-22 Many of the Jews had come to Martha and Mary, to console them. Evidently, the family had a wide circle of friends. Martha first went out to meet Jesus while Mary remained in the house. It was characteristic of Martha to take the lead (cf. Luke 10:38). Lord, if thou hadst been here (contrary to fact condition). A gentle reproof is implied in her address

tearing their hair, covering their heads with mud or dust, beating their bared breasts repeatedly and wailing the eerie death wail. Sometimes (as in Japan) the dead were addressed as if alive. Sometimes the tears of these mourners were caught in little bottles and kept as prized possessions (Ps. 56:8). Such tear bottles are on display now in the Palestine Archaeological Museum in Jerusalem (Jordan).[h] This writer noticed an Egyptian woman coming down the highway near Assiut, accompanied by a few other women. She was shrieking hysterically, her clothes and hair were disheveled; with both hands she held a black cloth or veil which she raised and lowered, accompained by a writhing of the body, her voice periodically rising and falling in apparently uncontrollable grief. Such practices are still prevalent, not only in the Middle East but in Ireland, Latin America, and elsewhere. In India, for example, similar customs prevail among the Hindus and even among nominal Christians. Among real Christians, however, these extravagances are lacking as they "sorrow not as those who have no hope." It may safely be assumed that mourning for Lazarus was more subdued, but it probably contained many of the features common to Eastern burial customs. It seems that Lazarus was not an avowed believer at the time of his death; otherwise, "the Jews" would not have attended his funeral; instead they would have rejoiced over the death of an apostate to the Jewish faith.

It was with Martha that the basic issues of the resurrection and the life were faced. She was apparently the oldest of the three and the head of the household. Jesus sought to transform her nominal faith in a general resurrection to a personal acceptance of resurrection faith centered in himself.

The belief in the resurrection was a cardinal doctrine of the Pharisees but was

---

[3] Hoskyns, pp. 199f.

[h] Some archaeologists challenge this use of the "tear bottles."

21 Martha therefore said unto Jesus, Lord, if thou hadst been here, my brother had not died.

22 And even now I know that, whatsoever thou shalt ask of God, God will give thee.

23 Jesus saith unto her, Thy brother shall rise again.

24 Martha saith unto him, I know that he shall rise again in the resurrection at the last day.

25 Jesus said unto her, I am the resurrection, and the life: he that believeth on me, though he die, yet shall he live;

---

to Jesus. Doubtless the two sisters had said this to themselves and to each other over and over again during the past four days. It reflects a sad conviction that things could have been different, that this need not to have happened — if only the Master had been in Bethany instead of beyond Jordan! Yet her faith seems without bounds — even now Jesus has access to the Father's bounty. Her faith was in Jesus' faith and the efficacy of his prayers. Her attitude was something like that of Jesus' mother at Cana (2:3-5) — there was expectancy without the voicing of a specific request. This is in contrast to Bartimaeus at Jericho who was asked to be specific in his request (Mark 10:51).

24 Jesus' assurance to Martha, Thy brother shall rise again, gave only a small amount of comfort because she thought only of a general resurrection with little personal about it and nothing immediate. Her belief was that of the Pharisees, in contrast to the Sadducees, a belief in a general resurrection. Belief in the resurrection was a very live issue at that time, a fact which Paul cleverly exploited when arraigned before the council (Acts 23:6-9).

25 I am the resurrection and the life. As he had done when discussing water (4:14), bread (6:35), and light (8:12), Jesus now turns a doctrine into an embodiment of the idea. Attention focuses upon the affirmation, "I am," with which Jesus confronted Martha. In Christ, ab-

---

denied by the Sadducees. The latter could point to O.T. passages which indicated no expectation of life after death (e.g., Job 7:9, 10, 21; 10:20-22; 14:7-12; 16:22; 17:13-16; Ps. 6:5; 30:9; 88:11-12; 115:17; Eccl. 9:10; Isa. 38:18). On the other hand, the Pharisees, who believed in the resurrection, could point to other O.T. passages in which there were either clear "intimations of immortality" (e.g., Job 19:25-27; Ps. 16:10, 11; 49:15; 86:13; 73:24; 23:6) or an explicit assurance of a resurrection of the body (Isa. 26:19; Dan. 12:2; 2 Macc. 7:9, 11, 14; 12:42-45; Enoch 22:9-13; 103:1-4; Test. Benj. 10:6-9; Ps. of Sol., 3:16.). It is true that some Christian scholars find nothing in the Old Testament that supports a doctrine of eternal life. Other scholars, however, find in the O.T. a basis for a vague doctrine of life after death, which arose in a large part from the conviction that the next life would equalize the injustices of the present life (cf. Pss. 37, 49, 73), and that this, supplemented by further reflection during the inter-testa-

mental period, led to the doctrine of resurrection which Martha had accepted.

On the premises of Scriptures the only logical way in which the Jews could conceive the fulfillment of God's promises to the righteous was that they should live again upon earth in the golden age to come and share in the salvation of Israel. The resurrection seems, indeed, so necessarily the consequence of the whole teaching of Scripture concerning the salvation of the righteous and their great reward that it is not strange that the Pharisees found it explicit or by intimation in all parts of their Bible.[1]

Martha's confession of faith was similar to that Nathaniel, of the Woman of Samaria, of Peter, and of the man born blind. It was not a fully developed Christology but a developing one — Martha was "walking in the light." The Lord seldom demanded his loyal ones to subscribe to a creedal statement as the condition of discipleship. At the outset, he was content with their initial commitment and continuance in his word (8:30). "First he

---

[1] G. F. Moore, op. cit., II, 313f.

26 and whosoever liveth and believeth on me shall never die.  Believeth thou this?

stract truths are personified, as here. Jesus not only gives the bread of life but *is* that bread; he not only brings the light, he *is* the light; he not only tells the truth, he *is* the truth; he not only provides life, he *is* life. Such is the consistent emphasis of the Fourth Gospel. Jesus is saying that the resurrection is not only in the future but a present reality. The words **and the life** are absent from some ancient witnesses but are appropriate to the context. In these words Jesus is pointing out that union with him means participation in the benefits inherent in him. Because he rose from the dead and has life beyond death, the believers also will rise and experience life with him in heaven.

This teaching illustrates the characteristic of this Gospel — to introduce a theme and then develop it gradually throughout the book. Thus, Jesus claimed to give life after the healing at Bethesda. The raising of the dead is said there to be a divine act in which Father and Son share (5:21, 25, 28, 29). "The hour cometh in which all that are in the tombs shall hear his voice, and shall come forth" is the statement Jesus made then; now he claims to be the resurrection itself. While 5:29 speaks of the future double resurrection of good and bad, the raising of Lazarus is a proof of Jesus' claim and a prophecy of what is to come.

25 **Though he die, yet shall he live** means that even if the believer dies physically, he shall live spiritually. The relevance to the decomposing corpse nearby is obvious, so that in this context the "living" is also physical. She is assured that Lazarus will rise again, but she does not anticipate an immediate resurrection.

26 **Whosoever liveth and believeth on me shall never die,** or with the NEB — "no one who is alive and has faith shall ever die." (The omission of "in me" — *eis eme* — seems to lack justification.) The double negative (*ou mē*) denotes emphasis — "there will never be spiritual death." **Believest thou this?** Jesus' challenge to Martha's faith here is consistent with the emphasis on faith as the condition of divine blessing in all of the

wrought and afterwards he taught." Faith was not something suspended in thin air.[j] It was not a self-generating faith. Evangelical faith was based upon fact, upon experience, or rather a sequence of experiences of Jesus the Christ (I John 1:1-3).

*The healing of his seamless dress*
*Is by our beds of pain;*
*We touch him in life's through and*
*    press,*
*And we are whole again.*

*O Lord and Master of us all,*
*Whate'er our name or sign,*
*We own thy sway, we hear thy call,*
*We test our lives by thine.*[k]

### (2) Jesus Welcomed by Mary
### (vv. 28-37)

This scene is one of the most emotional of the Gospel. Even the crucifixion scene is more restrained than this. Mary, summoned by the Master, quickly arose to meet the Master where Martha had been conversing with him. The mourning friends accompanied her, assuming that she was returning to the grave. Obviously Jesus was not far from the grave, or it was at least in the same direction from the house. The fact that Mary echoed the words of Martha implies the frequency with which these thoughts had come to mind since their brother's death. Jesus did not ask of Mary an expression of faith, apparently deciding that the time for decisive action was at hand.

Vincent calls attention to the contrast between these two mourning sisters of the Gospel and the Greek maidens featured in Sophocles' tragedies, "Antigone" and "Electra." Antigone had hope that she would be reunited to her dead brother, a product not of theology, but of wishful thinking. Electra had no such hope —

[k] Neo-orthodox theologians and Tillich's philosophical theology in particular are vulnerable to this criticism. See G. H. Tavard, *Paul Tillich and the Christian Message* (New York: Chas. Scribner's Sons, 1962), pp. 49-51.
[j] J. G. Whittier, "Immortal Love, Forever Full," *Hymns of the Living Faith*, p. 123.

27 She saith unto him, Yea, Lord: I have believed that thou art the Christ, the Son of God, *even* he that cometh into the world.

28 And when she had said this, she went away, and called Mary her sister secretly, saying, The Teacher is here, and calleth thee.

29 And she, when she heard it, arose quickly, and went unto him.

30 (Now Jesus was not yet come into the village, but was still in the place where Martha met him.)

Gospels. The implication is that an expression of this higher, more immediate and more personal confession of faith is a condition of the ensuing miracle. Martha had to be spiritually prepared for the miracle.

27 **Yea, Lord; I have believed.** Martha's confession of faith was similar to that of the woman of Samaria (4:25), except that Martha's was fuller and more specific. Apparently Martha did not get the full significance of Jesus' words. She voiced a general confession without drawing from it any specific faith regarding her deceased brother. Her faith was centered in the Christ and she committed all to him in confidence. The force of the perfect tense (*pepisteuka*) denotes a permanent belief which had begun in the past and was still in effect at the time of speaking.

28 **She went away and called Mary her sister secretly, saying, The Teacher is here.** Does secretly modify called or say-ing — that is, did Mary steal away secretly or did Martha whisper something to her which the bystanders did not hear? Did the secrecy refer to Martha's calling of Mary or to the message she brought to Mary? The ASVm, RSV, and NEB agree against the KJV and ASV that the message was secret. This is borne out by the fact that the guests knew of Mary's departure but did not know the purpose (v. 31).

28-30 To avoid the crowd that always flocked to him, Jesus evidently paused at the edge of town where Martha came to meet him (v. 20). Mary, the more passive type, waited to be summoned. As she left, the friends rose to accompany her, assuming that she was going to the grave again to weep. In the Middle East and the Orient, the expression of emotion, especially in the presence of death, is considered desirable, so much so that professional mourners were often hired. The O.T. reflects much of the

---

*If thou suggestest any hope from
  those
So clearly gone to Hades, then on me,
Wasting with sorrow, thou wilt tram-
  ple more.*

. . . .

*What! shall I ever bring the dead to
  life?
I meant not that: I am not quite so
  mad* (832-34).[1]

Electra was motivated by a desire to have her brother assist her in avenging a grievance. She did receive her brother back, as though from the dead, but it was only to lead him into multiple murders. In contrast to pagan drama of suicide and murder is the picture of Jesus sorrowing with his friends. They look to him with speechless, helpless grief, expecting that with his arrival relief will somehow come. Then, as always, faith had its reward.

Their prayers were to be answered "exceeding abundantly above all that they could ask or think."

#### (3) *Lazarus Lives Again* (vv. 38-44)

The stage was now set for the greatest "sign" of all. The dramatic tenseness of the situation was comparable to that on Mt. Carmel when Elijah was challenging the prophets of Baal and calling on the God who answered by fire. Like Elijah's, the prayer of Jesus was short and calm. Jesus' apparent calmness in prayer was in contrast to the strong emotions he had just registered. He had gained the victory over death even *before* Lazarus emerged from his tomb.

There can be little doubt that the Evangelist had in mind much more than the description of another miracle. This one involved the issue of life and death —

[1] M. R. Vincent, *op. cit.*, II, 208.

31 The Jews then who were with her in the house, and were consoling her, when they saw Mary, that she rose up quickly and went out, followed her, supposing that she was going unto the tomb to weep there.

32 Mary therefore, when she came where Jesus was, and saw him, fell down at his feet, saying unto him, Lord, if thou hadst been here, my brother had not died.

33 When Jesus therefore saw her weeping, and the Jews *also* weeping who came with her, he groaned in the spirit, and was troubled,

34 and said, Where have ye laid him? They say unto him, Lord, come and see.

35 Jesus wept.

36 The Jews therefore said, Behold how he loved him!

37 But some of them said, Could not this man, who opened the eyes of him that was blind, have caused that this man also should not die?

---

practice of loud and prolonged lamentation at funerals (cf. Gen. 50:3; I Sam. 1:17ff.; Ezek. 27:2ff.; Nah. 3:7).[4]

32 Mary went immediately to Jesus and, unlike Martha, **fell down at his feet.** Her first words, uttered while weeping, were exactly the same as Martha's (v. 21) and reflected the same sense of disappointment at Jesus' absence. She manifested more emotion and a greater depth of sorrow, or at least expressed it more freely than did Martha. Evidently her weeping was contagious, for the record stated that the Jews wept with her and that even Jesus wept. He had genuine sympathy and shared their sorrow.

35 **Jesus wept** (*edakrysen*) or "burst into tears" (Moffatt). Famous as the shortest verse in the Bible, this statement emphasizes Jesus' true humanity. The generalization is often made that in the Fourth Gospel the deity of Jesus Christ is stressed so much that he seems to have poise without compassion, but verses such as this prove that the Evangelist lays stress on both his deity and humanity. The ASV calls attention to the distinction between Jesus' weeping and that of the others. Theirs was the loud wailing (*klaiontas*) of those who have no hope, his the expression of grief.

36 So obvious was Jesus' grief that the Jews were moved to comment, **Behold how he loved him.** The remarkable thing is that Jesus knew that soon their mourning would be turned to joy; his grief therefore must have arisen purely out of compassion for their grief, not for the cause of their grief. It underscores Jesus' real humanity. There is no more Docetism in John's Gospel than in the Epistles which bear his name (cf. II John 7).

37 **Could not this man** have prevented this untimely death, the Jews wonder as they recall the recent miracle of giving sight to the blind. They all believe that Jesus could have avoided the tragedy had he been present; the sisters hope that he

---

the ultimate in human experience. Previously Jesus had shown himself to be the Lord in the realm of disease and deformity, in the realm of nature (on the sea) and in meeting the demands for food and beverage; now the issue was whether or not he was conqueror over man's most dreaded enemy, death. The potential for good or bad was vast. If Lazarus failed to return from the realm of the dead, all would be lost; if death could be defeated, it would be an irrefutable evidence that his claim to be "the resurrection and the life" was valid. In response to Jesus' loud summons Lazarus appeared, a miracle within a miracle

(Basil). He was not only restored to life but came forth *bound* in graveclothes.

44 **Loose him and let him go,** commanded Jesus after Lazarus appeared at the mouth of the tomb, much the same as he commanded to give food to the girl he brought back to life (Mark 5:43). Before Lazarus' resurrection could be completed, he had to be restored to the fellowship of the community; the people had to accept him. This called for a decisive response on the part of his relatives and neighbors. One may imagine the shock of fear and revulsion which the crowd must have experienced as they heard the command to unwrap the shroud

---

[4] George B. Eager, "Burial," *ISBE,* I, 530.

38 Jesus therefore again groaning in himself cometh to the tomb. Now it was a cave, and a stone lay against it.

---

may yet do something (v. 22); but no one expected him actually to bring Lazarus back to life.

**38 Jesus therefore groaning** (*embrimōmenos*) **in himself** (or "deeply moved" A-G); the present participle denotes progressive emotion which lasts for some time. Was the groaning in anger or in grief? If in anger, as the verb indicates elsewhere (Lam. 2:6), was he angry at the unbelief of the Jews, at the temporary victory of Satan and of death, or at himself for being so emotional? Hoskyns argues at length for the last interpretation, which is also advanced by Bultmann, Bauer, Plummer, Tasker, and others. Still others (e.g., Bernard, Howard) consider the groaning mainly an expression of great grief, occasioned either by the distress of the mourners or by the presence of death itself (Westcott, Lenski). The suggestion that Jesus was indignant at the necessity of performing a miracle that would soon terminate his ministry (Barrett) seems unsustained by the context or by the character of the Master.

This is one of the most difficult passages in the N.T. The verb *embrimaomai*, used in vv. 33 and 38, is found in Daniel 11:30; Psalm 7:11; Isaiah 17:13 (LXX) and in Matthew 9:30; Mark 1:43; 14:5. It always indicates a combination of strong feeling and emphasis but not always of anger (Matt. 1:43; 9:30). Perhaps the context should be decisive here, since other evidence leads to no clear conclusion. Here anger would seem inappropriate, as would extreme grief. It seems adequate to interpret the word as Jesus' capacity for empathy, for entering into the situation of his friends, but it must also include the spiritual struggle akin to that which he experienced in Gethsemane or when he beheld an impenitent Jerusalem (Luke 19:41), or akin to that of Paul when he thought of unrepentant Israel (Rom. 9:2)

---

of the man who had been dead four days. The command of Jesus was a command to brave contact with one who a few moments before was a lifeless corpse. Obedience meant to overcome doubts that the restoration to life was actual and not a dream or hallucination. It meant venturing to the borderline between life and death, so dreadful to normal people. Faith on the part of Martha and her friends must now be followed by obedience. Their part was not only to view Lazarus but to welcome him to their love and fellowship.

Many a person who has been "quickened" after being dead in trespasses and sins has experienced difficulty at this point. After the conversion of Saul of Tarsus in Damascus the disciples in Jerusalem still found it difficult to forgive and forget; Barnabas had to intercede for him and introduce the transformed Saul to the group he had been persecuting. The church of the redeemed needs today not only to pray and work for the resurrection of many a "Lazarus" in the community, but also to welcome into fellowship the redeemed and tranformed person whose past life has been bad. Some Christians need more of Christ's spirit at this point.

One is left to imagine the feelings and words exchanged in the household as Jesus shared with the family the joy of the restoration. Next to Jesus, Lazarus became the most discussed man in the Jerusalem area.

It is difficult to overestimate the importance of the doctrine of the resurrection among the early Christians, as witnessed in the N. T. Every sermon reported in Acts features the resurrection of Christ. It forms a prominent feature of Pauline theology and ethics. When urging converts to live righteously Paul reminds them that they have experienced a spiritual resurrection from the dead and that henceforth they should walk in newness of life (Rom. 6:1-6; Col. 3:1-10; Eph. 2:1-8). The "Ephesians" are assured that resurrection power is available to them personally (Eph. 1:19-23).

On an Easter Sunday morning, in a small church in the Appalachian highlands, two men sat near the front giving every evidence on their faces that they had just experienced "the power of his resur-

39 Jesus saith, Take ye away the stone.    Martha, the sister of him that was dead,
saith unto him, Lord, by this time the body decayeth; for he hath been *dead* four days.
40 Jesus saith unto her, Said I not unto thee, that, if thou believedst, thou shouldest
see the glory of God?

---

or when he wrestled against the "prince of the powers of the air" (Eph. 2:2; 6:12). It is likely that an inner spiritual conflict preceded the outward calm and poise Jesus showed before the tomb as the convulsions of Gethsemane preceded the calm of Calvary. An anonymous commentator of Christ may have had such instances in mind when he reported that "in the days of his flesh" he "offered up prayers and supplications with strong cryings and tears unto him that was able to save him from death" (Heb. 5:7). The *tō pneumati* (in the spirit) of v. 33 is the equivalent of *en eautōi* (in himself) of v. 38. Both signify the *location* of his grief rather than its *object*.

**Came to the tomb** (*mnēmeion*), the word signifying "token of remembrance." It is further described as a cave (*spēlaion*). Unlike the Romans and Indians, the Jews, and later the Christians, with others of the eastern Mediterranean area, buried their dead. The doctrine of the resurrection reinforced this practice. For tombs, natural caves, which abound in Palestine, were used, and also chambers hewn out of the rock. This tomb appears to have been a natural cave, perhaps adapted to family use as a sepulchre. Only the wealthy could afford to buy such places (cf. Gen. 23:4). Whether this tomb was vertical or horizontal is not stated. The traditional "Tomb of Lazarus" is now thirty steps below the level of the street and hence vertical. Most tombs in the vicinity of Mt. Olivet, dating from the Roman period, are horizontal with an opening about two feet square into which a square stone cover can be set. Some of the more costly tombs, such as the tombs of the Herod family and the tomb of Queen Helena ("Tombs of the Kings"), have a rolling stone set in a groove for ease of handling.

39 **Take away the stone.** As so often in the "signs" of Jesus, an act of obedience precedes the miracle itself. The shock of surprise which the group must have experienced finds expression in a mild protest by Martha. She did not wish the memory of her brother to be marred by an unpleasant stench or sight. The RSV ("There will be an odor") and the NEB ("stench") versions are truest both to the Greek and to good English.

40 **See the glory of God** is a specific reference to the resurrection of Lazarus. It recalls Jesus' interpretation of illness and also his prophecy voiced when news of Lazarus' illness first reached him (v. 4). There is no other record of his

---

rection" in their own lives. The older man had recently been converted from a life of sin. The younger man had conferred with the preacher on the previous evening about matters involving his own future life and service. One, with most of this life behind, the other with most of his life ahead — both had been raised from "death" into "newness of life." Likewise, in a rural church in South Dakota, when an interdenominational group gathered for spiritual fellowship, a middle-aged man in the front row arose to bear his testimony. Said he, "The person you see here is not the old Oli Soccerson; this is the new Oli Soccerson." Since he had been one of the most dissolute characters in the community, and since all who knew him could attest the miraclous transformation, his words carried conviction. There was not a dry eye in the audience when he finished speaking. In that rural community a "Lazarus" had been truly raised from the dead.

There are some problems here. Why was not this greatest of miracles reported in the Synoptic accounts? Why is it that in this Gospel the raising of Lazarus appears to have been the immediate cause of Jesus' arrest while in the other accounts it was the cleansing of the temple? How could the spirit return to re-activate a body so long dead? Some think of this as "a Christian midrash" (R. H. Strachan), a story told for a homiletic purpose. Others think that although we do not know what

41 So they took away the stone. And Jesus lifted up his eyes, and said, Father, I thank thee that thou heardest me.

42 And I knew that thou hearest me always: but because of the multitude that standeth around I said it, that they may believe that thou didst send me.

43 And when he had thus spoken, he cried with a loud voice, Lazarus, come forth.

44 He that was dead came forth, bound hand and foot with grave-clothes; and his face was bound about with a napkin. Jesus saith unto them, Loose him, and let him go.

45 Many therefore of the Jews who came to Mary and beheld that which he did, believed on him.

---

having said this recently to Martha, an indication that not all of the conversation was recorded. It points to the element of contingency here. Was the outcome still dependent on Marth's faith? What would have happened had Jesus found no faith at all in the sisters?

41 **Father I thank thee.** This prayer was not so much for Jesus as for the spectators. It was comparable to sanctifying the name of God before the performance of a "mighty act." Moses publicly acknowledged the name of God before the plagues of Egypt, and even the heathen magicians were compelled to sanctify the name of the Lord by acknowledging, "This is the finger of God" (Exod. 8:19). When Moses neglected this, giving the impression that it was he who miraculously produced water from the rock, he was rebuked and disciplined (Num. 20:12). The real praying had been done prior to this time, probably while Jesus remained in Perea; this was the formal invocation to make clear that God the Father was recognized as the

source of power, that the multitude might believe (v. 42).

43 **Come forth** (*deuro exō*), literally "hither forth" (MRV), or "come out" (RSV).

44 **He that was dead came forth, bound hand and foot with grave-clothes.** The words **dead** and **bound** are perfect middle participles in Greek, indicating a state of being dead and bound for some time. **Grave-clothes** is from *keiriais,* meaning "bandages"; it occurs nowhere else in the N. T. (A-G). In 19:40 and 20:5, 7 *othonia* — "linen bands" — is the term used for wrapping the dead. His face and head were apparently covered with a different type of cloth — a **napkin** (*soudariō*). This was a cloth (Luke 19: 20), such as was used to wipe off perspiration (MRV). Apparently the body of Lazarus was prepared for burial in the same manner as the body of Jesus, using the narrow winding sheet for the torso and a separate cloth for the head.

45 The impression created by this "mighty act" is easily imagined. It made

---

actually happened, it is sufficient to know that Jesus is the resurrection and the life (Barclay). Still others are convinced that the conviction that Jesus is the resurrection and the life is on far sounder ground if he actually performed what he claimed. John the evangelist and the New Testament writers generally were careful to give historical facts as the basis for faith. They did not expect belief to be self-generating and self-perpetuating. In spite of the difficulties, the acceptance of the story at face value presents fewer problems for faith than attempts at rationalization. Like Martha, the modern reader is summoned to a faith which involves committal and venture.

(4) *Divided Reaction: Many Believed, Some Report to the Pharisees* (vv. 45-53)

The same evidence left some believers and other doubters. It was subjective factors that made the difference. Faith is the result not only of experiencing the evidence but of responding to it. Repeatedly in the Gospel the point is stressed that one's own attitude and motive are the determining factors in belief (3:19; 5:44; 7:17; 8:44; 9:22). With the possible exception of 6:65, these passages emphasize that the responsibility for unbelief is not with God but with the people, not with the revelation but with the re-

46 But some of them went away to the Pharisees, and told them the things which Jesus had done.

47 The chief priests therefore and the Pharisees gathered a council, and said, What do we? for this man doeth many signs.

48 If we let him thus alone, all men will believe on him: and the Romans will come and take away both our place and our nation.

49 But a certain one of them, Caiaphas, being high priest that year, said unto them, Ye know nothing at all,

50 nor do ye take account that it is expedient for you that one man should die for the people, and that the whole nation perish not.

---

so profound an impression that many believed on him (the aorist indicates a complete act of faith). On the other hand, not all the witnesses were convinced. Instead, they reported what had happened to Jesus' enemies who, because of it, became all the more determined to have Jesus killed. The contrast, here as elsewhere in this Gospel, is between the "many" who believe and the "but some" who did not.

47 The chief priests (mostly the Sadducees) and the Pharisees were now thoroughly aroused and united in opposition to Jesus. The Sadducees were the legal leaders, the Pharisees the religious leaders of the people. Jesus' popularity was endangering their own position of leadership and influence. Having been called together they asked themselves, "What are we going to do?" (futuristic present). Jesus was actively winning more and more people while they were losing more and more influence with the common people.

48 They frankly expressed their fears — all men will believe on him and the Romans will come and take away both our place and our nation. Jealousy was now turning to envy and fear to hate. They were thinking of their own interests and security rather than the welfare of others or the kingdom of God as a whole. The injustices and misrule which they tolerated or practiced produced the result they feared in A.D. 66 when the Romans brutally crushed a revolt. This meeting of the Sanhedrin made a decision which vastly influenced not only their own fate and that of their nation, but also the history of the world. They sought to preserve vested interests and lost all. The Sadducees, whose "kingdom" was "of this world," lost totally and finally in A.D. 70 Phariseeism, however, lives on in modern Judaism.

50 One man should die for the people. Thus they solemnly decreed that the most loving, perfect and powerful person that

---

cipients of it. The problem is not inadequate evidence but refusal to accept evidence — such is a major thesis of this Gospel.

There are many problems of interpretation which come from the account of the meeting of the council and the speech of Caiaphas. On the surface the Sanhedrin is deciding the issue on the basis of cold expediency. Its concern is not with truth or justice but only with its own security. The Sadducees in particular held their offices and position under the patronage of the Roman occupation authorities. The Sanhedrin, with its control of religious affairs, was the only semblance of home rule and independence which was left in the region governed by the procurator, who was responsible only to the emperor

and the governor of Syria. Thus, this religious aristocracy believed that some authority is better than none at all.

Perhaps Caiaphas was proposing to use Jesus as a scapegoat. If members of the Sanhedrin did nothing, he argued, things would go from bad to worse; they would lose the support of the people and the confidence of the Romans. If, on the other hand, they prosecuted a man who could be represented as a rebel, as a would-be king, they would demonstrate their loyalty to Roman rule by their repudiation of a local leader hostile to that rule. The twofold objective of eliminating their own rival and ingratiating themselves with the Romans, however cynically it was proposed, presented a temptation which they could not resist. Caiaphas may have made

51 Now this he said not of himself: but being high priest that year, he prophesied that Jesus should die for the nation;

52 and not for the nation only, but that he might also gather together into one the children of God that are scattered abroad.

53 So from that day forth they took counsel that they might put him to death.

54 Jesus therefore walked no more openly among the Jews, but departed thence into the country near to the wilderness, into a city called Ephraim; and there he tarried with the disciples.

55 Now the passover of the Jews was at hand: and many went up to Jerusalem out of the country before the passover, to purify themselves.

56 They sought therefore for Jesus, and spake one with another, as they stood in the temple, What think ye? That he will not come to the feast?

57 Now the chief priests and the Pharisees had given commandment, that, if any man knew where he was, he should show it, that they might take him.

---

ever lived should perish. Plato, after observing that the Athenians executed their best citizen, became embittered and distrustful of the people. The for (hyper) of vv. 50, 52, 53 means "instead of" or "on behalf of" here as in Galatians 3:13; Romans 5:6; II Corinthians 5:14, et al. It indicates substitution. The idea of Jesus dying to gather together into one the children of God is probably the Evangelist's interpretation of Caiaphas' prophecy. The reference is probably to Jews of the Dispersion and Gentile believers in the true God. From that day forth their whole strategy was concentrated on bringing about Jesus' death. The Evangelist's concern with chronology is again apparent here as well as his characteristic attention to details.

54 Jesus therefore walked no more openly (periepatei is imperfect tense, denoting continued action) but returned to the wilderness (erēmou), a dry and sparsely settled country. Areas which were arid and hence unproductive were then, as now, the unpopulated areas. This is applicable still to the vast areas east and south of Jerusalem. The location of Ephraim is not known but it could well be identified with the modern Et-Taiyibeh, four miles northeast of Bethel, hence some fifteen miles north of Jerusalem (CKB). It would thus be in the territory of Ephraim and adjacent to the "wilderness of Judaea."

55 Meanwhile the Jews began to assemble in Jerusalem, prior to the beginning of the Passover to purify themselves — that is, to immerse themselves in water, to wear freshly laundered clothes, etc. (Exod. 19:10-15; Num. 9:9-14; II Chron. 30:17, 18). This was a prerequisite to entering the temple grounds for worship.

56 He will not come to the feast? The question with the double negative assumes a negative answer. They do not expect Jesus to attend the Passover because of the danger. The leaders of the Pharisees gave strict orders that if anyone knew of his whereabouts he should report it. Thus Jesus had become something of a "public enemy number one." The Passover was always a time of excitement, of political and religious tensions; this one would be no exception!

---

the proposal purely on the basis of expediency, but the Evangelist apparently saw that Caiaphas inadvertently spoke more wisely than he knew. What they intended as murder for self-interest the Evangelist recognized as part of divine providence — Jesus was the scapegoat who bore the sins of the nation into the wilderness (Lev. 16:20-28). The Evangelist speaks of a substitutionary atonement, a vicarious sacrifice (v. 51), in language similar to 1:29, 36.

d. Retirement near Ephraim (vv. 54-57)

Jesus' retirement to the relative security of Ephraim was not the result of cowardice but of prudence. He was waiting for "the hour" to arrive. While he could be secure in the Father's providence anywhere, he did not "tempt" the Father by recklessly exposing himself. In popular parlance a certain fatalism leads some to conclude that no matter what they do the outcome will not be affected. Their attitude often is, "What is to be will be and I can do nothing about it." The Japanese have a popular adage reflecting the same fatalism — "*shakategnay*" — meaning, "what is to be will be." Such an attitude encourages carelessness and irresponsibility. In this mingling of caution with courage, Jesus is our exemplar. He avoided the extremes of paralysis and presumption by living on the level of faith, an open-eyed faith which included insight, foresight, resignation, and courage.

In summary, it may be noted that this climactic "sign" is the seventh and last of the report series. The result of "so many signs" was both positive and negative. From now through ch. 19, the negative forces of unbelief and destruction gain the ascendancy and culminate in the death of Christ.

# CHAPTER XII

Jesus therefore six days before the passover came to Bethany, where Lazarus was, whom Jesus raised from the dead.

## EXEGESIS

Some of Jesus' closest friends (with the exception of the apostles) lived in Bethany. In addition to Lazarus, Mary, and Martha, they included Simon the Leper in whose home Jesus and his disciples were honored with a supper (Mark 14:3). Probably Simon had been cured from his leprosy by Jesus and wanted to express his appreciation. Since Lazarus had been raised

## EXPOSITION

### e. The Anointing at Bethany (12:1-11)

Ch. 12, taken as a whole, presents itself as an elaboration of the theme "Life from Death" focused in the great threefold affirmation at the "heart" of the chapter (vv. 24-26). In these three verses Jesus says the same thing in three different ways. First, he presents an analogy from nature: death of the parent-seed grain makes possible a harvest of much grain.

Second, the application of this principle in the spiritual realm means that self-preservation leads only to death while self-denial leads to life eternal. The third statement is that those believers who follow Jesus in his humiliation will ultimately share his glory, bestowed by the Father. This threefold statement appears to unify the entire chapter. For further elaboration of the relationship of parts to the whole in this chapter note the accompanying chart.

SYNOPTIC VIEW:     LIFE FROM DEATH

| | GOD ACTS | | | | MAN REACTS | | | |
|---|---|---|---|---|---|---|---|---|
| Theme | LIFE | | | | 34      LIGHT: seeing is believing (?) | | | |
| Para-graphs | Mary Anoints 12:1 | Lazarus' Testimony 9 | Triumphal Entry 12 | Bitter-"sweet mystery of life"; | "Who is Son of man?" 34 | Unbelief Explained 36b | Jesus' Last Appeal 44      50 | |
| Life | Shared (v. 2) | Demonstrated (v. 9) | Witnessed (v. 17) | Life from death in nature v. 24 in grace v. 32 | To Be Welcomed v. 36 | Rejected | in Jesus v. 45 | Light |
| Death | Predicted v. 7 | Sought v. 10 19 | | 20      33 | Threatens v. 35 | Penalty for Unbelief | Defeated v. 46 | Darkness |
| Prophecy of | Death v. 7 | Reign v. 15 | | Glory v. 28 | Skepticism | | Last Judgment | |
| Segments | Witnesses: Mary Lazarus | | Predictions of Kingship of Atonement | | Reactions: To Light of Perplexity          v. 34 of Rejection      vv. 37, 42, 47 of Acceptance          v. 42 | | | |
| | Close of Public Ministry | | | | Summary 36b | | | |

from the dead, he and his two sisters were invited by Simon to share in the honoring of Jesus at the banquet.[1]

One of the major problems in chronology is the sequence of events here as compared with the report given in the other Gospels. Luke does not report this episode but instead reports a sinner anointing Jesus' feet in the home of Simon the Pharisee in Galilee (Luke 7:36-50). Matthew and Mark report this supper as occurring in the house of Simon the Leper in Bethany but make no mention of Mary, Martha and Lazarus by name, and the woman who does the anointing is not named. The first two Gospels state that the anointing occurred two days before the Passover (Matt. 26:2; Mark 14:1), while in the Fourth Gospel it is said to have occurred six days before the Passover (John 12:1).[2] In the first two Gospels the head was anointed while in the accounts of Luke and John the feet were anointed. In Luke's report the significance of the act was a forgiven sinner's expression of gratitude in contrast to the host, Simon. In the other three accounts the anointing is a prophecy of Jesus' death rather than a useless waste of money, as charged by Judas (John 12:4-6) and the disciples (Matt. 26:8; Mark 14:4). In spite of the many explanations for those

similarities and differences, none thus far has met with general acceptance. Many critics have assumed that Luke's account of the tearful woman in Galilee is the historical event and that John has altered the story to suit his purpose. This conclusion grows out of their general assumption that John is more concerned with doctrine than with history. Many others follow the tradition of the Western church that Mary Magdalene is the sinner of Luke's story and also Mary of Bethany. This view is defended at some length by Bernard (*op. cit.*, II, 409-414). His conclusion is based upon the testimony of the Fathers — Clement of Alexandria, Tertullian, Origen — and the tradition of the Roman Church since Gregory the Great, which teaches that Mary Magdalene was a great sinner (Luke 8:2; Mark 16:9) who became the great saint who washed Jesus' feet with tears (Luke 7:38), sat at his feet while her sister served (Luke 10:39) and later anointed him in Bethany (John 12:3). Bernard finds that this identification explains Jesus' statement that the Bethany anointing is prophetic of the anointing at the grave, *viz.*, Mary of Bethany anointed Jesus before the Passover and "Mary Magdalene" visited the tomb for that purpose after the crucifixion — this argues for the identification.

---

### (1) *Mary's Lavish Devotion* (vv. 1-8)

Mary was criticized not for her devotion as such but for her extravagance in it. Many there are who are tolerant of those who are not "righteous over much" but are hostile to those whom they regard as "extremists" in piety. Often tolerance is acquired at the price of being only moderately concerned. Those who are deeply concerned are an irritant (often unconsciously) to those who are indifferent and complaisant. The crusader, who really works as if he expected to see changes is never popular with those who prefer the *status quo.*

The principle figures in this story are five. Martha, characteristically, served. She conceived of her task as that of mak-

ing each guest comfortable, of taking over-all responsibility for the success of the occasion.[a] This role is quite consistent with the picture of Martha given by Luke (10:38, 40). Were it not for dedicated and efficient persons like Martha life would often be chaos. Yet both in Luke and in John devout Mary is the heroine to a greater extent than practical Martha. A great poet observed this with a touch of cynicism.

### THE SONS OF MARTHA

*The Sons of Mary seldom bother, for*
*they have inherited that good part,*
*But the Sons of Martha favor their*
*mother of the careful soul and*
*the troubled heart.*

---

[1] *Oun,* meaning "now" introduces v. 1 and functions similarly in 12:2, 3, 9, 17, 21.

[2] The solution proposed is that the "two days" of Matthew and Mark do not refer to the time of the anointing (which follows) but to the apocalyptic discourses (which precede).

[a] For a hostess's joy in sharing, cf. Elsa Maxwell, "How to Do It," *Best in Books* (Garden City, N. Y.: Doubleday, 1958), pp. 283-293.

2 So they made him a supper there: and Martha served; but Lazarus was one of them that sat at meat with him.

3 Mary therefore took a pound of ointment of pure nard, very precious, and anointed the feet of Jesus, and wiped his feet with her hair: and the house was filled with the odor of the ointment.

4 But Judas Iscariot, one of his disciples, that should betray him, saith,

---

This, says Bernard, does not mean that the anointing described by Luke is the same as that described by John; as a sinner Mary anointed Jesus in Galilee at the house of Simon the Pharisee and as a saint Mary anointed Jesus in Bethany at the house of Simon the Leper.

It appears to the present writer that there are two anointings; one in Galilee by a harlot, reported by Luke to commend gratitude for God's love for penitent sinners, a favorite theme of Luke (cf. Luke 14:15-24; 15:1-32; 18:9-14; 19:1-10). The two Simons are different persons; the name being a very common one. There seems no adequate reason for assuming that Mary of Magdala (in Galilee) who, with several others, accompanied Jesus from Galilee to Jerusalem (Luke 8:3) was the same Mary who sat at his feet and anointed him in Bethany.[3] There is justification for the conclusion that the anointing in Bethany by the unnamed woman mentioned by Matthew and Mark is the same event as that reported by John. That the Johannine report is a bungled mixing of traditions (WFH) also appears to be an unjustified charge. If the use of

hair in the drying of feet could be regarded as the expression of great love and gratitude on the part of a sinner (Luke 7), why would it not be appropriate also in a saint? Edersheim (and Godet) think Mary anointed Jesus' head (as reported in Matthew and Mark) and then his feet (op. cit., II, 359), a very likely way of harmonizing the details of the three accounts.

2 **Martha served** (diēkonei — imperf. — "was serving"), a role consistent with the dinner scene reported by Luke (10:40). Mary created a sensation by opening an alabaster bottle containing a litra (twelve ounces) of very expensive perfume and anointing Jesus' feet with it. It was made from the roots of an Indian plant and imported into Palestine (A-G). The juice was probably hermetically sealed in an alabaster flask (nardi ampullae), the alabaster being a translucent stone such as was used for exquisite vases, flasks and candelabra.[4] The **ointment** (myron) was a highly aromatic unguent used for embalming.[5] The myron is the generic term for all liquid perfumes while **nard**

---

*And because she lost her temper once, and because she was rude to the Lord, her guest,*

*Her sons must wait upon Mary's Sons — world without end, reprieve or rest.*

*It is their care in all the ages to take the buffet and cushion the shock,*

*It is their care that the gear engages; it is their care that the switches lock;*

*It is their care that the wheels run truly; it is their care to embark and entrain,*

*Tally, transport and deliver duly the Sons of Mary by land and main.*

*And the Sons of Mary smile and are blessed — they know the angels are on their side,*

*They know in them is the grace confessed, and for them are the mercies multiplied.*

*They sit at the Feet — they hear the Word — they know how truly the Promise runs,*

*They have cast their burden upon the Lord, and — the Lord he lays it on Martha's Sons.[b]*

---

[3] Cf. A. R. C. Leaney: "The popular identification of 'the woman who was a sinner' with Mary Magdalene is without foundation." Gospel According to Luke (N.Y.: Harper, 1958), p. 147.

[4] On display in the National Museum in Cairo are beautiful artifacts in alabaster from the tomb of King Tutankhamen (13th century B.C.).

[5] From P Oxy IV. 736:13 — "perfume for the dispatch of the mummy of the daughter of Pharaoh." — (M-M, op. cit., p. 419).

[b] Rudyard Kipling, "The Sons of Martha," Carolyn M. Hill, ed., op. cit., pp. 617f.

5 Why was not this ointment sold for three hundred shillings, and given to the poor?
6 Now this he said, not because he cared for the poor; but because he was a thief, and having the bag took away what was put therein.

---

is its most costly species (Godet). It is here, and in Mark's account, designated pure (*pistikos*), a word found nowhere else in the O. T. or in classical Greek before Plato (Gorg. 455A); it was derived from *pistos* (faithful, trustworthy). It was applied to a trusted shipmaster (M-M) and to a faithful wife (by Artemidorus — c. 150A.D.) and was a term used to designate an ointment used by women of luxury.[6] Since nard was often adulterated, this adjective probably indicates a perfume which is genuine, unadulterated, and not a counterfeit (Godet). As a further evidence of its value the word *polytimou* (**very precious**) is added. The offering thus was extravagant both in quality and in quantity. Judas is quoted as having estimated its cost as three hundred denarii, about $60.00 in our money. Since a *dēnarion* was the average pay for a day's work (Matt. 20:10) one readily realizes how expensive this perfume was. Had it been sold, it could have provided for the needs of a family for at least three hundred days! John gave a disparaging dig here at Judas by stating that he was more interested in lining his pockets with money (*kleptēs*, thief) than in helping the poor. In retrospect John suspected him of pilfering from the money box (*glossokomon*) which he, as treasurer of the group, carried (*bastazein*). The verb has a twofold meaning: "to carry," and "to pilfer" or "to steal." The author may have intended this double meaning as a pun, with a touch of irony. Our use of the term "shoplifter" is analagous; the "lifter" is a thief. The "money box" apparently was not a bag or a purse but a box for the receiving of offerings which were thrown in, hence (*ta ballomena*) "what was thrown in." If so, it would resemble the begging bowl of Buddhist or Christian monks. The

---

Lazarus, next to Jesus, was the honored guest. His very presence was a living witness of the truth of Jesus' declaration, "I am the resurrection and the life." The occasion, in the home of Simon, brought together not only the invited guests but also an unusually large number of the "common people" who wanted to catch a glimpse of Lazarus, the man who had lain in his grave four days. The presence of uninvited "guests" on such an occasion was commonplace. Hospitality was perhaps the most mandatory of virtues in the Near East from Asia Minor to India. Travelers in this area have been recipients of oriental hospitality given on a most lavish scale. Indeed the typical host (or hostess) regards himself as the recipient of the highest honor. One traveler speaks of the tears of joy which his host, an impoverished Turkoman, shed at the realization that he was privileged to have a stranger as a guest. In such homes the guest was often regarded as a representative of deity. Even a murderer who found himself in the home of the relatives of the one he had murdered would be safe, the law of hospitality taking precedence over the tribal law of the avenging of blood.[c] There are many instances in the Gospels (two in this one) of Jesus' participating in feasts. He apparently enjoyed wholesome company of this kind.

Judas and Mary are contrasted in this paragraph. She was lavish in her expression of devotion; Judas was scornful of such "waste." There is, of course, some justification for Judas' *alleged* concern for the poor. In many lands the wealth of the country rests in some costly temple or church while the people are in abject poverty. The Mogul emperors of India lavished wealth on mosques which testified to their piety, but while they built monuments to their own piety the peasants were starving by the millions. South Ireland and Latin America present many communities in which churches, as depositories of great wealth, abound in startling contrast to the squalid living conditions of the worshippers. Most people would agree that this type of "devotion" is not pleasing to God. Judas *professed* to represent the practical-minded

---

[6] Wetstein, cited in E. A. Abbott, *Johannine Vocabulary*, p. 252.
[c] H. C. Trumbull, *op. cit.*, pp. 97ff.

7 Jesus therefore said, Suffer her to keep it against the day of my burying.
8 For the poor ye have always with you; but me ye have not always.

---

"box" may have been placed conveniently for the reception of offerings rather than kept concealed on one's person (cf. II Chron. 24:8).

Mark and Matthew state that Mary anointed the head of Jesus. John does not contradict this but supplements it by magnifying Mary's utter love, devotion and humility by portraying her as anointing his feet and wiping them with her hair. In the play *The Wasps* (607), by Aristophanes, the daughter anoints the father's feet as a gesture of respect and love. **The house was filled with the odor.** A rabbinic comment on Ecclesiastes 7:1: "A good unguent goes from the bedroom to the dining room; so a good name goes

from one end of the world to the other" (S-B, II 547). Patristic writers sometimes compared this to the spreading influence of the Gospel.[7]

7 When the disciples (Matthew and Mark) and/or Judas (John) protested what they regarded as extravagance, Jesus defended Mary by explaining that this was a very exceptional circumstance — she was doing this in anticipation (*proelaben*, Mark 14: 8) **for the day of his burial.** The word *tērēsē* (keep) can be translated "to observe" in this context: "Let her observe the last rite now, with a view to the day of my burial" (CKB, p. 345).

Matthew and Mark mention Christ's prophecy that Mary's act of devotion

---

humanitarian who believes that love to God should be balanced by love for mankind. Completely in agreement with this sentiment is I John 3:17: "If any one . . . sees his brother in need, yet closes his heart against him, how does God's love abide in him?" (RSV) But the real reason for this outburst of Judas was different from the ostensible one. As the author tells us, in the bitterness of disillusionment, Judas' real reason for being indignant was his avarice, his materialistic set of values. Not only this, but he was an embezzler, making personal gain from his official position. A few church treasurers, unfortunately, have followed Judas' example. The practice in many churches of having two persons responsible for handling funds removes temptation and protects the honest person from suspicion.

In saying, "the poor ye have with you always," Jesus was not encouraging pauperism — tolerating poverty with little concern for remedying its cause. In Medieval Europe and now in Hindu countries poverty is regarded by the devout as an occasion to incur divine favor by almsgiving. The beggar feels neither embarrassment about begging nor gratitude for donations, because he knows the gift was for selfish purposes — to acquire merit rather than relieve distress. Where the Spirit of Christ prevails today giving

arises from a spirit of compassion, of love. What Jesus meant, in this instance, was that this was an exceptional time and in an exceptional time extraordinary measures are justified. Mary's lavish generosity was justified therefore because it was an opportunity which would never come again.

But love is always lavish; it seldom counts the costs. Where love exists the greater the gift the greater the joy to the giver. So Mary's act does not encourage lavish gifts as ends in themselves, or as a means of acquiring merit, but as demonstrations of devotion that is uncalculating and recklessly generous. In an Indian village in recent years money and materials were on hand to build a new church; all was in readiness, except — a building lot could not be obtained. Finally a man spoke up and said he knew where land was available. He then led them to his own house and lot. At his insistence, they tore down his residence to make room for the church. His giving was lavish.

### (2) *Lazarus Threatened* (vv. 9-11)

Through no fault of his own Lazarus' life was now in danger. Earlier the religious leaders plotted Jesus' death in

---

[7] Clement of Alexandria, "The Instructor," II, viii, *The Ante-Nicene Fathers* (New York: Scribner's, 1903), II, 253.

9 The common people therefore of the Jews learned that he was there: and they came, not for Jesus' sake only, but that they might see Lazarus also, whom he had raised from the dead.

10 But the chief priests took counsel that they might put Lazarus also to death;

11 because that by reason of him many of the Jews went away, and believed on Jesus.

---

would be recounted wherever the Gospel is known. Westcott observes that it is remarkable that John's is the only account which names the woman and yet is the only account which omits mention of the honor which will come to her.

9 The common people (*ho ochlos*) is the usual LXX translation of '*am ha'arets* ("the people of the land"), that is, the outlanders, the peasants, often despised by the religious and political aristocracy. A great crowd, hearing that Jesus was in Bethany, gathered there to see him and also that they might see Lazarus. Lazarus could testify just by acting natural, by being himself! One can easily imagine the sensation which these eyewitnesses would cause when they returned to the homes to report what they had heard and seen at Jerusalem — seeing not only the resurrected man but the Messiah who had called him back to life! It was customary

in those days for poor people and others to attend the banquets of the rich to receive leftovers (cf. Luke 14:25; 15:1). Feasting (by the rich) and fasting (by the poor) was and is widely practiced in the Orient. This time the spectators came for something other than food.

10 The chief priests took council (*ebouleusanto*) to execute Lazarus as well as Jesus, because his witness was so extremely effective. While Lazarus could testify eloquently just by being alive and healthy he doubtless explained his experience repeatedly to the many inquirers. The leaders concluded now that nothing less than immediate and drastic action would avert a general conversion to the "Stranger from Galilee." Their fear of Lazarus was not, of course, because of his antisocial behavior, but simply because the people "were believing (imperf. — *episteuon*) on Jesus."

---

spite of the fact that a man born blind had received sight. For the Pharisees the blessing of sight was of less consequence than the religious implications of the act. Now the fact that a dead man had received back life was to them of little consequence compared to the threat to their position which Jesus' increasing influence produced. Recently three Near East nations were considering a treaty to utilize the fresh water of the Jordan River for irrigation. None doubted the economic advantages of the plan but two of the nations rejected the plan because acceptance would involve the official recognition of the third nation. An emotionally charged issue often distorts perspective. Prejudice blinds. Lazarus may have considered it better to have been still in his grave than be subject to violent death as an alleged traitor to his community and his religion. Discipleship is not only exacting but sometimes dangerous. The reason for the influence of Lazarus' testimony on the uncommitted multi-

tude is easy to imagine. Although silent, he was the most eloquent witness of Jesus' absolute command over death in the entire New Testament. In the old Puritan graveyards in New England the "King of Terrors" was often cited on the tombstones. This is more an Old Testament concept than a Christian one (Job 18: 14). In Christ, the "King of Terrors" has been conquered completely.

### 8. JESUS' LAST PUBLIC APPEARANCE (12:12-50)

#### a. His Triumphal Entry (vv. 12-19)

As noted in the exegesis, John's account makes clearer than do the other Evangelists the reason for the popular enthusiasm which greeted Jesus' arrival in Jerusalem for the Passover. It was basically an expectation of a kingly Messiah, accentuated by the recent raising of Lazarus. By taking a donkey for a mount Jesus confirmed their expectation of the

12 On the morrow a great multitude that had come to the feast, when they heard that Jesus was coming to Jerusalem,

13 took the branches of the palm trees, and went forth to meet him, and cried out, Hosanna: Blessed is he that cometh in the name of the Lord, even the King of Israel.

14 And Jesus, having found a young ass, sat thereon; as it is written,

---

12 **On the morrow** was probably the first day of the week (Sunday). If the Passover occurred on Friday, then six days before the Passover would place the day of his arrival in Bethany on Friday night. After resting on the Sabbath, Jesus and his disciples held the dinner immediately after the Sabbath (sundown), that is on Saturday night. **A great multitude** (*ho ochlos polys*) is in most texts the same phrase as the common people of v. 9 and hence would normally be translated the same. The NEB interprets the phrase in v. 9 as local citizens and the same phrase in v. 12 as newly arriving pilgrims. Lenski concludes that both groups were pilgrims. A distinction seems indicated, however, in the context: the *ochlos* of v. 9 was a gathering in Bethany occasioned by the opportunity to see Lazarus, probably consisting of local people and their acquaintances among the pilgrims. The crowd of v. 12 is identified as those in Jerusalem for the feast. The RSV preserves the ambiguity of the Greek text by translating "great crowd" in both instances. This great throng of people, including those from Galilee who knew of Jesus either personally or by hearsay, together with local people who knew of Lazarus' resurrection and other "signs" went forth to meet him, bearing palm branches, which could easily be obtained from trees along the way from Olivet to the Holy City.[8] **Hosanna** is derived from Hebrew and means "save now."[9] In the language of Psalm 118:25, 26, the throng continued the quotation, **Blessed is he that cometh in the name of the Lord** — and other excerpts from the great processional Psalm. This Psalm was the last of the Hallel group and was sung at each Passover (CKB). They added, even (*kai*) the king of Israel.[10]

14 **Jesus found a young ass.** According to tradition the place where he mounted the ass was at Bethphage on the southeast slope of Olivet. A church stands on the site with a colorful mosaic over the apse, depicting Christ with his mount. Others identify the site as on the summit of Mt. Olivet near the present Russian hospice and Chapel of the Ascension. At either site there is a good panoramic view of the city to the west. Jesus did nothing to

---

king and yet repudiated their concept of the kingdom. Instead of an elegant steed Jesus chose a lowly burro or donkey, one of the most common and least admired of domesticated animals. Today in the Near East a mild form of cursing is to call the object of one's enmity a "donkey." (The writer heard his taxi driver in Turkey shout this epithet in anger at a truck driver who had blocked his passage.) Jesus accepted the role of king but at the same time did so in a manner which was the opposite of popular expectations. In the older days only the more affluent could afford a mount; most of the people walked. One of the most memorable things about the thirty sons of Judge Jair was the fact that each had his own ass (Judg. 10:4; cf. 5:10). From the time of Solomon on (I Kings 1:33) the typical king would have entered on a horse, the horse then as now being the symbol of pride and strength (cf. Isa. 31:3).

In contrast to the manner in which Jesus entered the east gate of the city is the manner in which Kaiser Wilhelm II of Germany entered the west gate of Jerusalem (the Joppa Gate) in 1898. In those days, and for centuries preceding, highways were constructed for the use of kings.[d] For weeks before the arrival of the Kaiser, men worked on the Jerusalem-Jaffa road to have it fit for a king. Upon his arrival

---

[8] Palm branches were associated with nationalistic aspirations of victory since Maccabean times (II Macc. 10:1-9); see W. R. Farmer, "Palm Branches in John 12:13," *JTS*, Apr., 1952, pp. 62-66.
[9] It anticipates victory and is more than a secularized "hurrah." Cf. Eric Werner, "Hosanna in the Gospels," *JBL*, June, 1946, p. 99.
[10] That *kai* is translated "even" as well as "and" may be illustrated also in John 3:5.
[d] H. C. Trumbull, *op. cit.*, pp. 219-236.

15 Fear not, daughter of Zion: behold, thy King cometh, sitting on an ass's colt.

16 These things understood not his disciples at the first: but when Jesus was glorified, then remembered they that these things were written of him, and that they had done these things unto him.

17 The multitude therefore that was with him when he called Lazarus out of the tomb, and raised him from the dead, bare witness.

18 For this cause also the multitude went and met him, for that they heard that he had done this sign.

---

restrain the masses from recognizing him as the long-looked-for Messiah of Jewish hope and prophecy (cf. Zech. 9:9).

**16 When Jesus was glorified.** It was only after the Savior's death that the disciples saw in this event the fulfillment of this prophecy. The expression **was glorified** is another occurrence of this expression so characteristic of this Gospel. It occurs also in 7:39; 12:33; 13:31 and embraces the death, resurrection, and ascension.

**17 The multitude** (*ho ochlos*) is named for the third time and is here identified as the crowd which witnessed the raising of Lazarus several days before. This group has now joined the company of *witnesses* so important in John's report.

**18 The multitude** (*ho ochlos*) **went and met him.** The fourth occurrence of this term apparently identifies a group of inquirers, as distinct from the witnesses of the preceding verse. The *multitude* which consisted of pilgrims (v. 12) and witnesses of Lazarus' resurrection (v.17), who were accompanying Jesus as he went toward the city, were now met by another *multitude* (v. 18) of inquirers or seekers coming from the city. The entire demonstration of enthusiasm was obviously

---

in state in Jerusalem the monarch of Germany disdained to dismount from his carriage in order to enter the city through the narrow gate. Then they tore down part of the wall so that Wilhelm could proudly *ride* into the Holy City. The hole in the wall remains to this day, a testimony to the "pomp and circumstance" befitting the world's conception of a king. Jesus, "meek and having salvation, riding upon an ass," is the antithesis of this concept of a conqueror. To those who insist that the *mighty shall inherit the earth*, and almost demonstrate it, Jesus says, and is demonstrating the fact, that "the *meek shall inherit the earth*" (Matt. 5:5).

This entrance of Jesus into Jerusalem was, in a sense, a *parousia* (an appearing or advent). Indeed, this is the original basic meaning of the arrival of the king.[e] Numerous instances in the eastern Levant of the arrival of a sovereign are illustrated in papyrus fragments publicized by Deissmann and others. The importance of a visit by a king or emperor to a city is seen in the fact that local history was dated from this event, that special highways were constructed for use by the

king, that coins were struck in his honor and that sometimes a triumphal arch was built for the occasion. An arch built to honor the *parousia* or advent of the Emperor Hadrian (A.D. 117-138) still stands in Athens, and another, in a fair state of preservation, honors the same Emperor at Jerash (Gerasa) in the Jordan valley. A third-century B.C. papyrus reports a collection taken to provide a crown of gold for the king at his advent. The excitement which the coming of a king in a provincial city evoked helps us understand the enthusiasm of the crowd which welcomed Jesus to Jerusalem at this particular Passover occasion. The Greek term *parousia* became in Latin *adventus,* the basis for our English "advent," which is now applied both to the First Advent of Christ (Christmas) and to the Second Advent in the future. Deissmann reports an inscription at Tegea which was dated "in the year 69 of the first parousia of the god Hadrian in Greece."[f] As Egyptian peasants worked diligently in preparation for the advent of their king, so Jews had been waiting for the advent of their Messiah. Christians today wait, work, and watch for the second advent or parousia

---

e See Deissmann, *op. cit.,* p. 368, where Zech. 9:9 and Matt. 21:5 are cited.
f Deissmann, *op. cit.,* p. 372.

19 The Pharisees therefore said among themselves, Behold how ye prevail nothing; lo, the world is gone after him.

20 Now there were certain Greeks among those that went up to worship at the feast:

spontaneous and included pilgrims who accompanied him from Galilee, local people converted by the resurrection of Lazarus and others who wanted to see and hear for themselves. In the Synoptic accounts the triumphal entry took place several days before the anointing in Bethany. This Gospel alone, by showing the prior conditioning of the populace by the sensational news of Lazarus' resurrection, gives a reason for this demonstration. In this account it becomes evident that the entry was not stage-managed but was spontaneous.

The Pharisees, watching this demonstration of uninhibited, heartfelt enthusiasm were helpless to stop it: Behold, how ye prevail nothing! After asking the people to report Jesus' whereabouts so they could arrest him, they now find, to their consternation, that he is the center

of attraction and the object of honor bestowed only on kings. In their chagrin they exclaimed, Lo, the world is gone after him. If this fickle multitude had displayed a similar enthusiasm and loyalty on the day of Jesus' crucifixion, Pilate might have reversed his decision. Even in totalitarian regimes, the vox populi is often decisive.

20 Certain Greeks (Hellēnes tines) asked to see Jesus. Only John mentions this delegation. Whether they were actually believers (proselytes) who came to worship or only accompanied those who did is not made clear. Our author was more interested in Jesus' reaction than in the Greeks themselves. These were not Greek-speaking Jews of the Dispersion, for "Hellenes in the N. T. always means Gentiles or heathen" (CGT, p. 177). In KJV the term is translated "Gentiles"

of the King of kings and Lord of lords (Mark 13:33-37) of which Jesus' triumphal entry on the first Palm Sunday was only a preview.

Four reactions are noticeable here: the disciples were a bit perplexed; earlier they had expected death would face Jesus and themselves when they arrived in Jerusalem. The eyewitnesses of Lazarus' resurrection constituted a second large group. The third group were those who believed the report of the eyewitnesses and the fourth group were the unbelievers who reacted negatively to the whole proceedings. The Evangelist may have wished to underscore the fact that those who hear and accept the report of the eyewitnesses are equally blessed (cf. 20:20-29). The detailed and specific account of Jesus' advent into Jerusalem probably reflects the recollection of a participant in the occasion.

#### b. The Rationale of Jesus' Death (vv. 20-36)

##### (1) The Greeks' Inquiry (vv. 20-22)

This chapter begins with three prophecies, not in words but in actions. Mary's

act of devotion was prophetic both of Jesus' burial and of the devotion he would excite for millennia in the future on the part of millions. The triumphal entry was an act prophetic of the time when the "kingdoms of this world shall become the kingdom of our Lord and of his Christ" (Rev. 11:15). The inquiry of the Greeks was prophecy in action of the accession of Gentiles to the Christian church, one of the major themes of the Pauline Epistles. The reaction of Jesus to this indicates that he saw it in this light. The older N.T. criticism regarded Jesus as a Galilean peasant-reformer whose teachings Paul transformed into a world faith. They pointed to such passages as Matthew 15:24 to prove that Jesus had no intention beyond evangelizing his fellow Jews. In recent years the contrast between the "Christ of faith" and the "Jesus of history" has diminished among these liberal critics and there is a greater recognition that the two are essentially one. Vestiges of this view, however, remain with contemporary neo-orthodoxy and existentialism. The Johannine view is that the "Christ of faith" is nothing unless based upon the "Jesus of history." Here, Jesus, by implica-

21 these therefore came to Philip, who was of Bethsaida of Galilee, and asked him, saying, Sir, we would see Jesus.

22 Philip cometh and telleth Andrew: Andrew cometh, and Philip, and they tell Jesus.

23 And Jesus answereth them, saying, The hour is come, that the Son of man should be glorified.

---

in 7:35, and here "Greeks." Thus, they are not just Greek-speaking Jews of Jerusalem (Acts 6:1) but Greeks, like those in Antioch (Acts 11:20). After witnessing the wild display of enthusiasm for Jesus, they sought an interview with him. The depicting of Greeks as inquirers is consistent with the characteristic of the Athenians as those who "spent their time in nothing except telling or hearing something new" (Acts 17:21 → RSV). It has been observed that "the Greek mind inquired while the Hebrew mind affirmed."

**These therefore** (*oun*) **came to Philip.** The **therefore** hints that their approach to Philip was more than a coincidence; perhaps because his was a Greek name or because he spoke Greek. Philip was reticent to take full responsibility and enlisted the help of Andrew who had previous experience in bringing men to Jesus (1:41). These two had been associated before, in the feeding of the multitude (6:8). Andrew has been dubbed "the contact man."

23 **The hour is come that the Son of man should be glorified.** Several times previously Jesus had said, "My hour (*hōra*) has not yet come" (2:4; 7:6; 8:30). Once he used the same idea but a different word, the word for "time" (*kairos*) — 7:6.[11] Now, for the first time, he said, "My hour is come." This he repeated later several times (13:1; 17:1). On three occasions he used words very similar — "The hour cometh and now is" (4:23; 5:25; 16:32). Twice he referred to "his" hour as "this hour" (12:27). Of the six instances in which the phrase "my hour" is repeated, three occur before this instance and three follow. Obviously, Jesus now, for the first time, states that the long-awaited "hour" has at last arrived. What bearing did the inquiry of the Greeks have upon this?

---

tion, anticipates the ingathering of the Gentiles as he did more explicitly elsewhere in this Gospel (10:16; 17:20). In introducing this universal note, Jesus, as reported by this Evangelist, was consistent with the genius of Judaism, for monotheism itself, by its very nature, calls for a world faith.[g] The world-mission of the Gospel is intrinsic to its belief in one God who revealed himself in an only Son. In a sense Jesus was hidden in Israel before his manifestation to the Gentiles as he was hidden in the grave before his resurrection appearance to the disciples.[h] Out of death came life.

24 The analogy expressed in the terms **Except a grain of wheat die** may have been Jesus' way of establishing rapport with the Greeks. When presenting the Gospel to those familiar with O. T. imagery, Jesus can be presented as the "Lamb of God" whose expiatory death takes away the sin of the nation. This would have little significance to non-Jews.

To the Greeks and other non-Jews of the Near East the annual vegetative cycle was woven in with religion. The mystery religions of Greece, such as those centered in Eleusis, were founded on a myth of the reproductive cycle in nature. According to this myth, which goes back at least to Homer, Persephone the goddess of grain and the harvest was abducted by Hades or Pluto, god of the underworld. Her mother Demeter mourned her loss, the earth mourned with her, and vegetation died (in the winter). Zeus persuaded Pluto to let Persephone return from the underworld to her mother in the spring. As a result, the vegetation revived and the earth rejoiced. This sequence is repeated yearly; the time Persephone is in the underworld with her husband coincides with the winter season when vegetation dies. These myth and mystery religions (from the sixth century B.C. on) and fertility cults were the religion of the masses throughout lands adjacent to the eastern

---

[11] *Kairos* denotes conceptual time: *chronos* indicates time that is perceptual, fixed and orderly.

[g] G. F. Moore, *op. cit.*, I, 228.

[h] Cf. B. Weiss, *Das Johannesevangelium* (Berlin: Trowitzsch & Son, 1912), p. 238.

(24) Verily, verily, I say unto you, Except a grain of wheat fall into the earth and die, it abideth by itself alone; but if it die, it beareth much fruit.

(25) He that loveth his life loseth it; and he that hateth his life in this world shall keep it unto life eternal.

(26) If any man serve me, let him follow me; and where I am, there shall also my servant be: if any man serve me, him will the Father honor.

---

The answer is not clear. Perhaps he saw in this evidence of his widening influence a signal that his personal witness was now adequate and that he must be ready to present his body as a vicarious sacrifice.

**24 Except a grain of wheat . . . die, it abideth by itself alone; but if it die, it beareth much fruit.** By this analogy, so familiar to tillers of the soil, Jesus showed the relationship between his own death and the life for the world which would ensue — life available to Jews and Gentiles alike.

**25 He that loveth his life (psychē) loseth it; and he that hateth his life (psychē) . . . shall keep it unto life (zōē) eternal.** The use of two synonyms for life is probably not accidental. The same type of paradoxical statement is found in Luke 12:15,22. In 12:15 Jesus said, "a man's life (zōē) consisteth not in the abundance of things which he possesseth," meaning spiritual life or real life. In 12:22 Jesus said, "Be not anxious for your life (psychē), what ye shall eat; nor yet for your body," obviously meaning earthly,

temporal, physical life. Likewise, here in John, Jesus is saying that placing the things of this physical life in highest esteem will result in the forfeiture of life. On the other hand, he who **hates,** despises, or loves less the temporal, physcial phase of life shall by so doing discover life (zōē) that lasts forever — the real life. It was apparently a generalization for the disciples. Christ suffered; disciples are also to be ready to do likewise. By absolute loyalty to Christ, cost what it may, one becomes rich in abundant living in eternity, viz., he **keeps,** in the sense of safeguarding, his life hereafter.

**26 If any man serve** (diakonē, pres. subj. — "goes on serving") **me, let him follow** (akoloutheitō, pres. imper. — "continue following") **me.** Whether the inquiring Greeks heard these words is unknown. Service is comparable to self-denial implied in the preceding expression and is rewarded by being honored by the Father. The disciple must be prepared to share the role with his Master who was even now en route to the indignity of the

---

Mediterranean.[1] Jesus may have thought that this analogy would be particularly meaningful to Greeks familiar with this approach to death and resurrection. The analogy is also familiar to the Hebrews, as well as to anyone with an agricultural background. Paul used the same analogy in explaining the resurrection to the Corinthians (I Cor. 15:36-38).

The principle may be illustrated in countless lives of sacrifice. Robert Moffat "buried" his life in Africa. His friends thought he was throwing his life away when he left "all" in England. But after his first converts others followed and the success of his pioneer mission became assured. When he returned to England years later, as son-in-law of David Livingston, and a pioneer missionary in his own right,

he was the most honored man in England. He had "lost" his life only to receive it back multiplied a hundredfold.

### (2) The Relationship of Death to Life (vv. 23-26)

The paradox which Jesus expressed here, as a rationale of the cross, is one of the few places in the New Testament where the philosophy of the plan of salvation is given. Another place is Hebrews 2:4-18, another Philippians 2:5-11, and a hint is given in Mark 10:45. The raison d'etre of the cross as here stated may be rephrased as "death must precede life." In support of this fundamental principle Jesus makes three statements which are identical in meaning: (a) in the vegetable realm of nature unless the parent seed dies no fruit will result (v. 24); (b) in human life

---

[1] See "Persephone," in Encyclopedia Britannica (Chicago: 1959), XVII, 540.

27 Now is my soul troubled; and what shall I say? Father, save me from this hour. But for this cause came I unto this hour.

28 Father, glorify thy name. There came therefore a voice out of heaven, *saying*, I have both glorified it, and will glorify it again.

29 The multitude therefore, that stood by, and heard it, said that it had thundered: others said, An angel hath spoken to him.

30 Jesus answered and said, This voice hath not come for my sake, but for your sakes.

31 Now is the judgment of this world: now shall the prince of this world be cast out.

---

cross. **Honor,** in verb form appears in 5:23; 8:49; 12:26, and as a noun in 4:44.

**27 Now is my soul** (*psychē*) **troubled,** is expressed by *tetaraktai*, a perfect passive form, implying a previous state that was still in existence. Here Jesus' "soul" is not his earthly life, as the term connotes in v. 25, but his emotions, i.e., his "heart," or anxiety, anguish, dread (*Angst*); cf. 14:1, 27; Gen. 41:8 (Bultmann, p. 327). Facing the grim prospect of being put to death by torture as a criminal was naturally revolting to contemplate. **Father, save me from this hour** can be read as a petition as in KJV and ARV, or as a question, as in RSV, NEB, and ARVm. The context would indicate that the later versions and commentaries are correct in putting this in a form of rhetorical question which is followed by an instant and emphatic denial. The question is put in the form of a petition in the Synoptic accounts of Jesus in Gethsemane where he

prays, "Let this cup pass from me," but follows with self-resignation — "Nevertheless not my will, but thine be done" (cf. Luke 22:42).

**28** In response to Jesus' request, **Father, glorify thy name,** a voice from heaven responded, **I have both glorified it and will glorify it again.**[12] The voice from heaven was thus given at the beginning, at the middle, and now at the end of his public ministry. As on many other occasions, the same evidence did not evoke the same response from the crowd: some thought it natural, others supernatural in origin. It is the same contrast between the physical and spiritual, the natural and supernatural which is seen in the dialogue with Nicodemus and nearly all subsequent "signs."

**31 Now is the judgment** (*krisis*) **of this world.** There are certain apocalyptic overtones in this statement but it would be consistent with the entire tenor of this Gospel to think of this as primarily a per-

---

only the one who surrenders his hold upon this life will have real life (v. 25); and (c) discipleship requires the same type of self-denial that Jesus experienced (v. 26).

There is something about self-denial that excites admiration. Kagawa, the Japanese social worker and evangelist was described by the Rev. W. P. Merrill, who introduced him to a New York City audience in 1935, as "the most Pauline man of this generation." This eulogy was not because of his theology, his writing, his lectures or his reforms alone, but rather because he shared his tiny room with a beggar and as a result almost lost his eyesight. The world honors Albert Schweitzer for "burying" his life in Africa because he gave up so much to do so. The selfless missionary service of C. T. Studd was the more inspiring because he

gave up so much — his athletic career and his wealth — for others.

On the other hand, self-centered, egotistical people are often unhonored and unloved in the end. Napoleon ended his life in exile, and his passing was unmourned. Herod the Great died in agony, with none to mourn his passing. His mammoth sepulcher atop Mt. Frank near Bethlehem is unvisited and unmarked. The strident, swaggering Mussolini ended his course as a whimpering coward whose body was later desecrated. Hitler, the megalomaniac "superman," ended his career by a self-destruction and cremation so drastic that there remains not even a repository for his ashes.

**27 If any man serve me . . . him will the Father honor.** This continues the thought of v. 26 and makes the principle relevant to daily discipleship. From the

---

12 See Mark 1:11, at the baptism, and Mark 9:7, at the transfiguration, for similar occurrences.

32 And I, if I be lifted up from the earth, will draw all men unto myself.

33 But this he said, signifying by what manner of death he should die.

34 The multitude therefore answered him, We have heard out of the law that the Christ abideth for ever: and how sayest thou, The Son of man must be lifted up? who is this son of man?

---

sonal moral crisis, of response to evangelical truth. **Now shall the prince of this world be cast out** has language similar to Revelation 12:9 where Satan was cast out of heaven. **The prince of this world** is mentioned three times in this Gospel — here and in 14:30 and 16:11. Paul spoke of "the princes of this world" as secular rulers among men (I Cor. 2:6, 8) and of "the prince of the power of the air, the spirit that now worketh in the children of disobedience" (Eph. 2:2 KJV). This may be the same as the "anti-christ" of I John 2:18,22; 4:3. Jewish apocalypses abound in descriptions of this malignant spiritual force.[13]

**32 And I, if I be lifted up** (*hypsōthō*) **from** (*ek*) **the earth will draw all men**

unto myself. This prophecy recalls the remark about the "lifting up" of the serpent on the pole (3:14) and "lifting up" which Jesus attributed to his enemies in 8:28. The meaning "depart" is ruled out by v. 33.[14]

33 To avoid any possible misunderstanding as to the meaning of this third occurrence of the term the Evangelist explains that it is an allusion to the crucifixion. Thus, the serpent-in-the-wilderness analogy runs throughout the book.

34 Although the Evangelist finds it necessary to explain the statement about "lifting up" to his *readers*, Jesus' *hearers* did not question this statement but rather wanted to know about the identity of the Son of man. That the hearers understood

---

American Civil War comes the story of an incident in the triumphal march following victory. A relatively incompetent general was slated to lead the parade because of seniority. The other general, who really won a decisive battle, felt that he was the one entitled to the place of honor. To his protest General Grant replied, "You can afford to let him take the credit because you are a Christian." The Christian general reluctantly agreed. Later he found himself riding in the same carriage with General Grant — "he that humbleth himself shall be exalted." For the thousands of devoted servants of Christ now "bearing his reproach" a day of triumph is coming in which the victors will be crowned.

### (3) *The Lifting Up of the Son of Man* (vv. 27-36)

**32 If I be lifted up.** The meaning here is apparently threefold in application. It probably means "lifted up on the cross"; this is its meaning elsewhere in John (3:14; 8:28). The term **lifted up** means "the height of opulence and prosperity" (Thayer). Its basic meaning is the cross,

for John habitually dwells on the *glory* of the crucifixion, not its *shame*. He meant that Christ's suffering would attract and win converts. To make sure the reader understood this meaning John added v. 33. The second meaning is the "exaltation to glory," the ascension. This is the meaning of the term in Acts 2:33 and 5:31, where it refers to the "exaltation" of Jesus to the Father's right hand.

A similar usage is seen in Isaiah 52:13 (LXX). The conviction that Jesus was in heaven victorious over death caused the disciples to return to Jerusalem with rejoicing (Luke 24:52). The ascension is a dominant motif of Luke's Gospel (cf. 9:51; 18:31; 24:51; Acts 1:2). The third meaning is "spiritual." It means that when Christ is extolled in thought, sermon, or song, people are attracted to his person and message.

*Not a mere priest to tend an altar flame,*
  *He led the spirit like a battle-cry;*
*He shunned the sage's and the warrior's fame;*
  *Free to resist his foreknown doom, or fly,*

---

[13] Cf. "Angel of darkness" of the Qumran writings (IQS 3:25).
[14] See C. C. Torrey, "When I Am Lifted Up from the Earth," *JBL*, 51 (Vol. 4, 1932), pp. 320-22.

35 Jesus therefore said unto them, Yet a little while is the light among you. Walk while ye have the light, that darkness overtake you not: and he that walketh in the darkness knoweth not whither he goeth.

36 While ye have the light, believe on the light, that ye may become sons of light. These things spake Jesus, and he departed and hid himself from them.

37 But though he had done so many signs before them, yet they believed not on him:

38 that the word of Isaiah the prophet might be fulfilled, which he spake, Lord, who hath believed our report? And to whom hath the arm of the Lord been revealed?

39 For this cause they could not believe, for that Isaiah said again,

the meaning of "lifted up" is indicated by their surprise that he was not to "abide forever."[15]

Jesus did not answer directly but implied that if they were willing to accept the evidence around them they would have their answer.[16]

35 **Walk while ye have the light** was almost the last public utterance of Jesus on the subject (cf. 12:46; cf. John 1:5, 14; 3:21; 8:12; 9:5, 59; 11:9, 10; IQS 1:9; 3:20). The expressions "walk in the light" and "sons of light" occur several times in the extant Mandaean literature.[17]

36b **Jesus departed and hid himself.** After Jesus' last public utterance (with the possible exception of that recorded in 12:44-50), he was next seen by the public

when he was a condemned man sentenced to death. Some exegetes think that v. 36b is misplaced, and that if omitted it would explain Jesus' final public statement in 12:44-50.[18] Bengel, supported by Lenski, interprets vv. 44-51 as a general summary of Jesus' claims without reference to time.[19]

37 **In spite of so many signs . . . they believed not on him.** The explanation for this chronic skepticism is sought in Isaiah, in one of the most frequently quoted passages of the Old Testament.[20] The primary reference is to Isaiah's vision of Jehovah in the temple as reported in ch. 6, but it also cites the famous "suffering servant" passages (Isa. 52:13-53:12). The Evangelist is pointing out

> He chose the inner voice and per-
> ished by
> The utmost torture of a felon's
> shame.[j]

### c. Explanation of Unbelief (vv. 37-43)

One of the hardest things the Evangelists had to explain in presenting the Good News was that the Light was not more readily welcomed, especially among those of the homeland. One classic explanation is that God did not intend that all should hear it, that the atonement was limited in its provisions.[k] Such language as John 12:40 (a quotation from Isa. 6:

10) is often cited in support of a limited atonement — **He hath blinded their eyes and hardened their heart.** Literalists say that since the "Bible means just what it says" the meaning is that God renders people incapable of believing and having life. But this is so far removed from the over-all picture of God in the Bible that most Christians conclude that this cannot be the correct interpretation.[l] The other view is that in the O.T. prophecy of Isaiah unbelief was predicted. In order that the Scripture might be fulfilled and in order that God might not be found a liar, unbelief on the part of the Jews of Jesus' day was caused by God, or at least God

---

[15] See W. C. Van Unnik, "Quotation from the Old Testament in John XII:34," *Novum Testamentum,* 3 (Oct., 1959), pp. 174-179.

[16] The Phrase "Son of man" occurs at least eighty times in the Synoptics and eleven times in the Gospel of John where it probably meant Servant" (Sidebottom, *op. cit.,* p. 80).

[17] H. Odeberg, *op. cit.,* pp. 335f.

[18] J. A. Findlay, *The Fourth Gospel* (London: Epworth Press, 1956), p. 104.

[19] Lenski, *op. cit.,* p. 891.

[20] Its influence is noticeable in Matt. 13:14; Mark 4:12; Luke 8:10; Acts 8:26; Rom. 11:8.

[j] C. W. Stork, "Falterings Toward the Unknown God," *Lyra Mystica,* C. C. Albertson, ed. (New York: Macmillan, 1932), p. 443.

[k] John Calvin, *Commentary on John,* tr. by W. Pringle (Grand Rapids: Eerdmans, 1948), II, 41.

[l] For an evaluation of this interpretation see J. Wesley, "Free Grace," *Standard Sermons* (Nashville: Lamar and Barton, agents, n.d.), I.

40 He hath blinded their eyes, and he hardened their heart; Lest they should see with their eyes, and perceive with their heart, And should turn, And I should heal them.

41 These things said Isaiah, because he saw his glory; and he spake of him.

42 Nevertheless even of the rulers many believed on him; but because of the Pharisees they did not confess *it,* lest they should be put out of the synagogue:

---

that the amazing failure of the Jews to accept their long-awaited Messiah should not be surprising to one familiar with the Old Testament, where Israel's chronic skepticism is repeatedly condemned.

42 **Nevertheless, even of the rulers many** believed (*episteusan*; aor. ind. — believed for the moment on him). **But because of the Pharisees they did not confess him** (ARVm). Fear and cowardice prevented their letting others know how they felt about Christ. They were in the same dilemma as the parents of the one born blind — unwilling to face the social, economic, and religious reprisals they knew would follow an acceptance of Christ. According to Matthew 10:32, 33, they were not "saved," even though they "believed" Jesus' claims were true. They loved the glory of men more than the glory of God. They responded more readily to human opinions and standards than to God's. Thus three groups of people are portrayed in this Gospel, corresponding to three typical reactions to the experience of confronting Jesus the Christ. Some believed, others disbelieved, while the rest were convinced but not converted, not committed.

## EXCURSUS ON CONFESSION

An untranslated meaning of the Greek term *homologeō,* which is regularly translated "confess" in the N. T., throws con-

siderable light on what Christ expected of his followers. In 127 contextual usages, observed in first-century Greek outside the N. T., it has the meaning of "agree" 97 times, while it means "to confess" only 30 times. It is common in Greek papyri contracts, meaning "to agree" as in P Oxy II, 275: "Tryphon and Ptolemaeus *agree* with one another. . . Tryphon to apprentice his son to Thoonis for one year." Even when the context demands the translation "acknowledge" in papyri (in business documents) it refers to an agreement implied or specified. An example occurs in Cat. of Gk. P. 162: "She, the acknowledging (*homologousa*) party, has, in accordance with this agreement (*homologian*) sold the half-share of a house and yard."

Although *homologeō* should regularly be translated "to acknowledge or confess" in practically every passage in the N. T. where it occurs, it is well to remember that the basic meaning is "to agree" and that the expression of acknowledgement or confession is rooted in and dependent upon an agreement, either implied or made by the individual concerned. In other words, the confession is supposed to spring from a genuine experience of decision to conform to the will of Christ or of God. In all the papyri usages, even where the correct translation is "acknowledge," the contexts always imply that an agreement

---

left them in their unbelief.[m] Still another view is that the people, because of prior conditioning, of prejudice, and a preference for the "darkness" (John 3:19) hardened their own hearts against the light. If the last view be the correct one, how is one to account for the language of v. 40? The answer seems to lie in the manner in which O. T. writers expressed the activity of God. The sovereignty of God was emphasized to the extent that natural phenomena were often attributed to the direct intervention of God, as in Isaiah 45:

7, "I form the light and create darkness; I make peace and create evil," or Amos 3:6, "Shall evil befall a city, and Jehovah hath not done it?" Even today a natural calamity is legally termed "an act of God." The main concern, in such instances, was to prove God's power and providence, God's goodness not being considered the problem.

The problem of unbelief is no less real now than then. Sometimes unbelief arises from the reluctance to renounce sin (cf. 3:19). With others it is due to a basic

---

m Calvin, *op. cit.,* II, 42-44.

43 for they loved the glory *that is* of men more than the glory *that is* of God.

44 And Jesus cried and said, He that believeth on me, believeth not on me, but on him that sent me.

45 And he that beholdeth me beholdeth him that sent me.

is being made public or recorded. In Acts 7:17, for example, "And as the time of the promise drew near which God had agreed (*hōmologēsen*) to Abraham (cf. Gen. 17:1, 2 [LXX] where *diathēkē* is used to mean "agreement"), the people grew and multiplied in Egypt." There is more of this emphasis in Matthew 10:32 than most readers are aware: "Everyone who shall *agree* with me (*homologesei en emoi*) before men, I will agree with him (*en autōi*) before my Father who is in heaven." Or, in other words, if we will represent Christ before men, he will represent us before God the Father. The prepositional phrases are not translated at all in current translations.

When Paul in Romans 10:9 says, "Because if thou shalt confess with thy mouth Jesus as Lord," he evidently meant that nothing short of a willingness to agree to make Christ Lord of one's life is a condition of salvation. The rulers (John 12:42) were unwilling to pay the price of championing Jesus at such a cost to themselves.

(End of Excursus)

44 Jesus cried and said, He that believeth on me, believeth . . . on him that sent me. In the statement that belief in

himself was equivalent to belief in God, Jesus was proclaiming his deity. The same claim is made in the verse following and in 14:1, reiterated in 14:9, "He that hath seen me hath seen the Father." If God is as compassionate and full of love as Jesus, what a marvelous heavenly Father we have! Since "God so loved the world that he sent his only begotten Son," we have positive biblical evidence of the compassion of both.

46 I am come a light into the world, is a statement reverting for the last time in John's account, to a theme which characterizes this Gospel and I John. This concise statement includes the doctrine of the Incarnation and the evangelistic message of spiritual light being available to all who receive the "Light of the world." As previously noted, the analogy of light as applied to God would be meaningful to those influenced by the O.T. The challenge of the contrast between light and darkness would be equally meaningful, or perhaps more so, to those in the Near East not influenced by Hebrew literature. Evidence for this is abundant in non-canonical Hebrew literature (e.g., O.T. Pseudepigrapha, Dead Sea Scrolls).[21] Equally abundant is the non-Hebraic literature of the first three centuries of our era,

rebellion, an unwillingness to be convinced. In some cases it is due to defective witnesses — a major cause of current skepticism. With still others it may be due to the slow erosion caused by the "acids of modernity," leaving only a nostalgic memory of an earlier faith. Thomas Hardy may illustrate this last type:

### THE IMPERCIPIENT

*That with this bright believing band*
*I have no claim to be,*
*The faiths by which my comrades stand*
*Seem fantasies to me,*
*And mirage-mists their Shining Land*
*Is a strange destiny.*

*Why thus my soul should be con-*
*signed*
*To infelicity,*
*Why always I must feel as blind*
*To sights my brethren see,*
*Why joys they've found I cannot find,*
*Abides a mystery.*[n]

d. Jesus' Summary of His Relationship with the Father (vv. 44-50)

In this closing paragraph of the "Book of Signs" Jesus compresses in one paragraph several facets of themes which were developed at considerable length throughout the preceding twelve chapters. Upon

21 See "Excursus on Light," Introduction, pp. 28-30.
n Thomas Hardy, "The Impercipient," in C. Hill, ed., *op. cit.*, p. 396.

46 I am come a light into the world, that whosoever believeth on me may not abide in the darkness.

47 And if any man hear my sayings, and keep them not, I judge him not: for I came not to judge the world, but to save the world.

48 He that rejecteth me, and receiveth not my sayings, hath one that judgeth him: the word that I spake, the same shall judge him in the last day.

49 For I spake not from myself; but the Father that sent me, he hath given me a commandment, what I should say, and what I should speak.

---

passages in which the opposition of the darkness to light is prominent.[22] The same emphasis is found in I John 1:5 — "God is light and in him is no darkness at all."

**47 I came not to judge the world but to save the world,** a restatement of the declaration made earlier (3:17). Men were already sinners and condemned before Christ came in the flesh. He came to bring acquittal from judgment. But since God has entered humanity, clothed in human flesh, in the person of Jesus, man has greater guilt and a more severe judgment, if, in spite of this revelation, he rejects Christ.

**48, 49 He that rejecteth me** is in direct contrast to **if any man hear my sayings** of the preceding verse. **The word that I spake, the same shall judge him in the last day.** Judgment will certainly come, not from an arbitrary and vindictive Christ but from the Torah itself, the very Word of

God. To the Jews this was a shocking statement. They were brought up to believe that they would be judged by the words of Moses. The basis for the claim of Jesus that the words he spoke would be the basis for their condemnation was that his words were actually God's words. This fact gave a certain objectivity to the judgment administered by Jesus. They will be judged not so much by their reaction to a person but rather by their reaction to the truth which he embodied. He made clear that he was simply the mouthpiece for God; **He hath given** (perf. tense, meaning, an abiding authority) **me a commandment, what I should say.** His message and God's were identical; "It is particularly striking that John ends his final summary of the public ministry on this note. Jesus is not a figure of independent greatness; he is the Word of God, or he is nothing at all" (CKB, p. 362).

---

close examination this paragraph falls into three main segments or themes:

(vv. 44-46)  1. The consequence of believing in Jesus' REVELATION of the Father.
   a. The Unity of Jesus with the Father (cf. 5:17-29).
   b. The basic fact of revelation to the world (cf. 8:12).

(vv. 47, 48)  2. The consequences of not believing is JUDGMENT.
   a. The unbeliever is not judged by Jesus personally (cf. 3:17).
   b. The unbeliever is judged by the truth revealed by Jesus (cf. 5:45).

(vv. 49, 50)  3. The purpose of the commandment is LIFE.
   a. Jesus' words echo the Father's voice (5:37-44).
   b. The Father's commandment gives life eternal (6:65, 68; 8:31-36).

The central affirmation of this paragraph, its key idea, seems to be v. 46 (cf. 3:19) — **I am come a light into the world, that whosoever believeth on me may not abide in darkness.** In this paragraph there is combined the prophetic and the messianic consciousness of Jesus. As a prophet he spoke the words of God so perfectly that his words are the *ipsa verba* of the Father (vv. 44, 45, 49, 50). So authentic are these words by which Jesus expressed

---

[22] In the Leiden Papyrus (2nd or 3rd century) — Moulton & Milligan, *op. cit.*, p. 680. See also H. Odeberg, *op. cit.*, pp. 286-292.

50 And I know that his commandment is life eternal; the things therefore which I speak, even as the Father hath said unto me, so I speak.

**50 His commandment is life eternal.** The rabbis taught that life everlasting came from a study and observance of the Law, or the Torah. The new element in Jesus' teaching is that the Word of God is no longer confined to a scroll but is embodied in a Person. Unless the Jews are able to make the transition from the written Word to the living Word, they will forfeit all the benefits which the Torah provides (cf. 5:47). In this sense, revelation is progressive; if they refuse further light, they will lose what light they possess. Life is conditioned on their response to the Light.

In this paragraph almost all that Jesus said earlier is recapitulated:

"Every single utterance [of this paragraph] occurs in some form or other in the preceding [chapters]: the Unity with the Father, the Son doing the Father's work, the Light and the Darkness, the Belief, Hearing [Jesus'] words, Salvation-Judgment, Eternal Life."[23]

The "book of signs" thus comes to its climax; the public ministry is now over and the ministry of consolation to the disciples begins. As the first section of the book of Isaiah (chs. 1-39) stressed judgment and the latter (chs. 40-66) comfort, so in this Gospel judgment of the nation is dominant in chs. 1-12 and comfort for the fellowship in chs. 13-17.

the Father's thought (1:1) that they constitute the basis on which man is to be judged. The purpose of the revelation is that men may avoid judgment and dark-

ness and receive the light and life (cf. 3:14-17). There was nothing more to be said or done; the witness was adequate; the response to the witness was not.

[23] H. Odeberg, *op. cit.,* p. 336.

# CHAPTER XIII

Now before the feast of the passover, Jesus knowing that his hour was come that he should depart out of this world unto the Father, having loved his own that were in the world, he loved them unto the end.

---

## EXEGESIS

The phrase **before the feast of the passover** may be understood in two ways: either *before* or *on* the first day of the eight-day festival, which began on the 15th of Nisan. The Synoptists make it clear that the supper was *on* the first day of unleavened bread which was the day of the Passover. Thus Mark says, "On the first day of unleavened bread, when they sacrificed the passover. . ." (Mark 14:12; cf. Luke 22:7; Matt. 26:17). Is the supper described by John the passover meal or an earlier supper? In support of the latter, C. K. Barrett (*op. cit.*, p. 364) has written: "That John means in fact the day *before* the Passover is shown by 18:28; 19:14, 31, 42. By this note he clearly distinguishes between the last supper and the Jewish Passover." If

Barrett is right, then either John is right and the Synoptic writers are wrong, or vice versa.[1] Matthew (26:17), Mark (14:12) and Luke (22:7) clearly state that Jesus and his disciples ate the passover supper at the prescribed time for it, and that he died on the same day (the Jewish day began at sunset). Since John, when properly interpreted, is not in conflict with the Synoptic authors as to other events that occurred on that Friday, why not give him the benefit of the doubt and assume that he was in agreement with them as to the time of the eating of the Passover supper unless the evidence proves otherwise? The alleged problem is easily solved by having the phrase **before the feast** understood with the Greek participle *eidōs* (knowing), thus: "Now Jesus, knowing before the feast of the passover that

---

## EXPOSITION

### III. PRIVATE CONFERENCE WITH DISCIPLES (13-17)

#### A. THE PASSOVER MEAL (13:1-38)

##### 1. INTRODUCTION (vv. 1-3)

This section of the Gospel forms a unique and very important contribution made by the author of the Fourth Gospel. The discourses during Jesus' Jerusalem ministry, as reported by the other three evangelists, were, with the exception of the discourse on the last days, delivered to the groups which sought to ensnare him in his talk. John reports nothing of this, and the Synoptists say nothing similar to the contents of chs. 14-17 in this Gospel. Chs. 13-17 are perhaps the

most important in John's account — they are certainly the most unique. New Testament theology would be far less rich than it is without this contribution. The whole section is cast in the lengthening shadows of the cross, in a note of perplexity and apprehensions on the part of the disciples, balanced by an increasing poise and assurance on the part of the Master. There are three main sectors within this chapter: one dealing with the washing of the feet by Jesus (vv. 1-17), another with the identification of the traitor (18-30) and, lastly, the new commandment. The relationship of the part to the whole is indicated both in the analytical outline and by the accompanying chart.

[1] Others who believed the Synoptists and John disagree with one another as to the date of the supper are G. Dalman, F. C. Baur, D. F. Strauss, J. H. Bernard, M. Dibelius, E. Hoskyns, A. E. Rawlinson and H. Windisch.
[2] A. T. Robertson, *Harmony of the Gospels*, pp. 279-284; *Word Pictures in the N. T.* (New York: Harper, 1932) V, 235.
David Smith, *In the Days of His Flesh*, Appendix VIII.
Wm. Hendriksen, *op. cit.*, II, 221.
J. W. Shepherd, *The Christ of the Gospels*, p. 536.

his hour was come. . . ." Several respected scholars hold to this interpretation.[2] According to this translation Jesus' *realization* of the "hour" came before the Passover, rather than that the supper itself came before the Passover. Thus Phillips: "Before the festival of the Passover began, Jesus realized that the time had come. . . ." Such a translation violates no grammatical rule and at the same time is consistent with this and other contexts in the Gospel of John. Cognizance will be taken later, at the appropriate places, of interpretations of John other than the one here adopted. The Passover lamb was killed and prepared on the Jewish Thursday (Luke 22:7, 14) Nisan, and then eaten after sunset, at the beginning of the Jewish Friday, which day was also called Preparation Day (*paraskeuē*), John 19:14, 31, 42.

The translation, **He loved them unto the end** can also be translated "to the limit," or "to the uttermost."[3] The word *telos* means both "end" and "limit" (the end of a board is also its limit). When one is speaking of degree, as we here interpret it, it means "limit." If Jesus meant that he loved them only until he died, the proper rendering would be "end."[4] The boundlessness of Jesus' love is illustrated by the incident John is about to relate, the washing of the disciples' feet. To magnify the uniqueness of the event, John points out that Jesus was infinitely greater than a human being: **the Father had given all things into his hands . . . he came forth from God, and goeth unto God.** In spite of the vast difference between him and the disciples, nevertheless Jesus stooped to the level of a slave, the lowest level of human existence, and did the work of

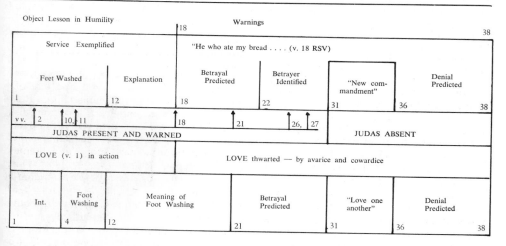

In view of the importance of the Eucharist and of its early origin, it is strange that John does not mention it at all.[a] The nearest thing to the sacrament in this Gospel occurs in connection with the feeding of the multitude and the discussion about eating and drinking (6:33-58). The view that 13:1-3 was designed as an introduction to chs. 13-20 and that these chapters may have been written before 1-12 is at least plausible.[b]

The Evangelist, in his introduction to this esoteric phase of Jesus' ministry, dwells upon two characteristics of Jesus — his knowledge and his love. He states that Jesus knew the end from the beginning, an emphasis seen in Jesus' supernatural knowledge of Nathaniel, of all men (2:24), of heavenly things (3:11), of the woman at the well (4:19), and continuing throughout. Jesus' superior knowledge did not make him haughty,

[3] B. F. Westcott, *op. cit.*, p. 189.
[4] Other meanings of *eis telos* are "forever, decisively, extremely, fully, altogether" (A-G). Beeckman and Jouon are among those who say that the idea of termination is more in harmony with the context than the idea of extent. See P. Beeckman, *L'Évangile selon Saint Jean* (Bruges: Beyart, 1951), p. 289.
[a] It is mentioned by Paul (I Cor. 11:23-26) and by the Synoptists (Mark 14:22-25; Matt. 26:26-29; Luke 22:17-20).
[b] R. A. Knox, *A New Testament Commentary* (London: Burns, Oats & Washbourne, 1955), p. 246.

2 And during supper, the devil having already put into the heart of Judas Iscariot, Simon's *son,* to betray him,

---

the slave in washing the feet of the disciples. It was customary in Palestine to have the feet of a guest washed when he entered the home of the host. Thus Lot invited his two guests to "tarry all night and wash your feet" (Gen. 19:2)[5] In Luke 7:44, where Jesus was a guest in a Pharisee's home, he is reported as having said, "Water for my feet you did not give, but this (woman) with her tears wet my feet." Disciples were expected to perform menial acts of service for their rabbis (cf. S-B, II, 557). The point in this passage is that the natural relationship and custom is reversed by an act of unprecedented and striking humility. When Abigail, widow of Nabal, accepted David's proposal of marriage, she did so in language intended to express the ultimate in humility. Said she, "Thy handmaid is a servant to wash the feet of the servants of my lord" (I Sam. 25:41). Jesus condescended to the lowest level of service to teach by his example that the disciples were to consider no act of unselfish service too menial for them to render. Luke tells us that there was a strife on this occasion as to who was the greatest among the disciples (22:24-27), perhaps a recurrence of an earlier argument (Mark 9:33-35). If this argument occurred on this occasion, as Luke states, it would give additional justification for the object lesson in humility.

**2 And during the supper the devil ....** is mentioned twice by John (v. 27). Apparently John could find no other explanation for the act of Judas. It was so contemptible, so demonic that only a demon-possessed man would be capable of such treachery — it was "supernatural." John probably is reviewing the situation in

---

aloof, distant, "superior," or smug. To Aristotle and the sophists the ideal of humanity was the man of superior knowledge; a man was admired to the extent that he was informed. To the Christian the right kind of knowledge is important but less important than love (I Cor. 13:1-3). Jesus embodied a knowledge mixed with sympathy and love as extensive as the knowledge; in him both were balanced. The Roman philosopher Lucretius, in *De Rerum Natura,* speaks of a philosopher as one who can calmly view from a hilltop a wreck at sea and be passive, calm, and unconcerned. In contrast a missionary on Awagi island, Japan, tells of the anguish with which during a typhoon he witnessed a large ferry carry scores of passengers to their death in the five-mile channel which separates the island from the mainland. The missionary was no more personally involved than the pagan philosopher, but, because of the Spirit of Christ, he had far more sympathy.

It is remarkable that the generous love of Jesus for "his own" did not permit the presence of a villain, in the person of Judas, to divert or stifle that love. Jesus must have been tempted to become cynical and embittered as he realized that one of the "elect" would turn against him. But he did not permit bitterness to enter his heart but "loved his own to the uttermost." It should be kept constantly in mind that the dominant mood and theme of this chapter is love (vv. 1, 34). The love of Jesus for his disciples is comparable to the love of Mary for her Lord in the preceding chapter; in both cases the love was uncalculatingly lavish and did not count the cost. While Mary's love and magnanimity is comparable to that of Jesus, Judas' lack of love is in the sharpest contrast. Another contrast within the chapter is the asserted loyalty of Peter and the silent treachery of Judas. Many have been christened Peter, but no one has ever been named Judas since this night.

Not only did Jesus love them to the uttermost, and without limit, he also loved them without ceasing. His love for Judas did not cease when he knew of the traitor's intent but he made repeated attempts to reclaim him. He did not cease loving Peter when basely denied by the one who

---

[5] See also Frants Buhl, "Roads and Travel (in O.T.)," HBD, V, 375.

3 *Jesus*, knowing that the Father had given all things into his hands, and that he came forth from God, and goeth unto God,

4 riseth from supper, and layeth aside his garments; and he took a towel, and girded himself.

retrospect rather than asserting that at that moment the plot was formulated by Judas.

**3 Jesus knowing** (*eidōs*) **. . . that he came forth from God. . . .** The author takes this occasion to emphasize again that the events which he is about to relate did not occur without a prior knowledge of the Master. Jesus, far from being a helpless victim of forces and passions beyond his control, was in command of the situation from the outset. Jesus knew the issues and the forthcoming events; he was not taken by surprise. Instead, he committed all to the Father and went on

unafraid. His calmness here is in contrast to his agitation prior to the raising of Lazarus, and at the inquiry of the Greeks (12:27; cf. 13:21).

**4 He took a towel and girded himself.** The foot-washing, or *pedilavium*, took place *during* the supper according to John and apparently after the discussion about who was the greatest among them. It is fair to assume that none wanted to accept the role of a slave (*doulos*) by washing the feet of the others, hence the dispute. They probably felt that the one who thus humbled himself would be inviting upon himself a lower status.[6] The

so recently and so loudly had professed loyalty. In Jesus was exemplified the virtue described by Southey:

> But love is indestructible;
> Its holy flame forever burneth:
> From heaven it came, to heaven returneth.
> Too oft on earth a troubled guest,
> At times deceived, at times oppressed,
> It here is tried and purified,
> Then hath in heaven its perfect rest;
> It soweth here with toil and care,
> But the harvest-time of Love is there.[c]

The constancy of Jesus' love in contrast to that of Judas and of Peter is one of the messages the Evangelist wished to convey.

> And who saith, 'I loved ONCE'?
> Not angels — whose clear eyes love, love foresee,
> Love through eternity,
> And by To Love do apprehend To Be.
> Not God, called Love, His noble crown-name casting

> A light too broad for blasting!
> The great God, changing not from everlasting,
> Saith never, 'I loved ONCE.'
>
> O, never is 'Loved ONCE'
> Thy word, Thou victim Christ, misprized friend!
> The cross and curse may rend,
> But, having love, Thou lovest to the end.
> This, man's saying — man's. Too weak to move
> One sphered star above,
> Man desecrates the eternal God-word Love
> By his No More and Once.[a]

The table was probably like other tables about one foot in height. Around the outside edge were placed thirteen pillows on which the guests reclined on the left side, leaving the right hand free for conveying food to the mouth. Apparently the thirteen were placed in such a manner that, as one faced the open end of the U, John, the beloved disciple, would be nearest on the left while Peter was at the opposite end of the table, directly across from John. Jesus

[6] Taking the four Gospels into account, Bernard thus reconstructs the order of events: (a) the supper begins, (b) dispute about precedence, (c) Jesus washes the disciples' feet and rebukes self-seeking, (d) Jesus announces the traitor, (e) the disciples inquire as to the traitor's identity, (f) Jesus identifies the traitor as the recipient of the sop (13:25), (g) Judas receives the sop (13:26) and realizes that Jesus knows of his intention (Matt. 26:25), (h) Judas departs (13:03), the Eucharist instituted (Mark 14:22, Matt. 26:26; Luke 22:19; cf. John 6:51-58), (i) the Eucharist in heaven envisioned (Matt. 26:29; Mark 14:25; Luke 22:18; cf. John 13:31-35; 15:1-13), (j) Peter warned.
[c] Robert Southey, "Curse of Kehama," in F. L. Peloubet, ed., *op. cit.*, p. 359.
[a] Elizabeth Barrett Browning, "Loved Once," *ibid.*, p. 359.

5 Then he poureth water into the basin, and began to wash the disciples' feet, and to wipe them with the towel wherewith he was girded.

6 So he cometh to Simon Peter.   He saith unto him, Lord, dost thou wash my feet?

outer garments were laid aside to facilitate freedom of movement.  The details of the report imply the work of an eyewitness to the events (EGT).  The verb (*tithēmi*) used to describe the "laying away" of his garments was used also in 10:15 to denote his "laying down" of his life for the sheep.

**5 He began to wash the disciples' feet.** The *basin* (*niptēra*), found only here in the N. T., is from the verb "to wash."  It is unlikely that it was a basin for dipping the feet into the water.  In the East to this day water is poured from a container onto the hands or feet and caught in another receptacle or, more likely, allowed to run onto the ground. This would require the assistance of a servant to do the pouring (cf. II Kings 3:11).  In India

today, for example, after the meal a servant pours water over the hands of those who have eaten.  Food is eaten with the fingers and no napkin is necessary. The disciples would be lying prone on the left side, after the Palestinian custom of the day, their feet extending away from the table. The feet therefore could be easily washed with no interruption of the meal.  After the washing, he dried each foot with the towel which hung at his side.  This whole procedure was quite customary, but not for the Son of God.

**6 Lord, dost thou wash my feet?**  As usual, Peter was the most outspoken of the group, hence when Jesus began to wash his feet he asked his question.  The two pronouns, *sy mou,* placed together indicate emphasis: "Do *you* wash *my* feet?"

was situated at John's left, between John and Judas, the latter having the place of honor at Jesus' left.   Such an arrangement would permit the conversation among Jesus, John, Peter and Judas as here described.[e]  The strife as to who would be greatest probably involved the seating arrangement as well as who would act as a servant to the rest (Luke 22:24-27).  Apparently they seated themselves without washing their feet because no servant was available. It was difficult for each to wash his own feet and no one was willing to assume this task as it would imply his inferiority to the group.  After they were seated and the task remained untouched they bickered over protocol and stood "on their dignity."  Jesus arose and did the work of a household slave. Protocol in such matters is less demanding in the more practical West than in the Orient.

In India, for example, a teacher stood at the garden gate.  Because of his high rank, he refused to open the gate and enter but waited until a servant came from a distance to open the gate.  The physical task of opening was beneath his dignity. Likewise, a clerk in a bank, while seated at his desk, dropped his pen on the floor.

Instead of stooping to pick it up, he beckoned to a "servant" from across the office and directed him to pick it up. When baseball was introduced into one of the oriental countries the crown prince was at bat.  After hitting the ball he had his servant run around the bases because it was beneath the monarch's dignity to thus exert himself.  Pictures of Japanese noblemen of feudal times almost invariably picture them seated in flowing robes with a fan.  A "great man" does not serve but is served — such is the world's concept of greatness.  When Jesus exalted the role of servant he was going "against the grain," contrary to all their training and culture.

6-9 The foot-washing was interrupted by the dialogue between Peter and Jesus occasioned by Peter's objection.  On an earlier occasion Peter had voiced a very human protest to Jesus, one which the others probably felt but did not express. After hearing Jesus say that he was about to go to Jerusalem to die, Peter registered a vigorous protest, saying that this was no way for a Messiah to act (cf. Matt. 16: 23).  Peter, in effect, was saying that the messianic role which Jesus envisioned was scandalous, and entirely inappropriate.  In

e Edersheim, *op. cit.,* II, 494.

7 Jesus answered and said unto him, What I do thou knoweth not now; but thou shalt understand hereafter.

8 Peter saith unto him, Thou shalt never wash my feet.   Jesus answered him, If I wash thee not, thou hast no part with me.

---

(CKB). After Jesus explained that the full significance of the act would not be understood until later, Peter again blurted out in his impetuous manner: "You will never (*ou mē*) wash my feet forever (*eis ton aiōna*)." This was the most forceful language available to register his protest. He thought too much of his Master to permit this! But when Jesus said, "Unless I wash you, you do not have a part with me," Peter's resistance melted immediately and he replied, "Not my feet only but also my hands and my head!" (RSV). "A moment ago he told his Master he was doing too much; now he tells him he is doing too little" (EGT).

7 **Thou knowest** (*oidas*) **not now . . . thou shalt understand** (*gnōsēi*) **hereafter.** Unlike most of the modern versions the KJV recognizes no distinction between the two Greek terms for knowing. Westcott

elaborates, "Knowledge as absolute and complete (*ouk oidas*) is contrasted with the knowledge which is gained by slow experience (*gnōsēi*), 'thou shalt learn' or 'understand' " (*op. cit.*, II. 148). This complete understanding began with v. 12 but was not complete until Pentecost (CGT). The opposite transition, from *oida* to *ginōsko,* is seen in 7:26 and 8:55.

8 **If I wash thee not.** Jesus did not mean that the application of water to Peter's feet would be the condition of Peter's continuing in the apostolic fellowship. He probably meant that unless Peter was willing to humble himself and submit to Jesus' ministration the fellowship between them would be broken. It was a lesson in humility and service to which Peter must submit along with the others. Seen in that light Peter instantly agreed to an act which seemed to be so

---

reply Jesus counter-charged Peter with being a tempter, with being out of line, or being a *skandalon* (Matt. 16:23), that is, an "offense," a "stumbling block," a "scandal." Here two diverse concepts of propriety clash, as they did when Jesus announced his passion in Jerusalem; Jesus representing God's idea of greatness and Peter representing the world's concept of greatness. Peter protested that Jesus' way was scandalous and Jesus said that Peter's attitude had no place in the Kingdom. Essentially the same "scandal" is found in Isaiah 53:1-4 (cf. Gal. 5:11; I Cor. 1:23).

10 "He who has bathed (*leloumenos*) does not need to wash (*nipsasthai*), except for his feet, but he is clean (*katharos*) all over (*holos*)" (RSV). This rendering sets off by commas the phrase which is lacking in some of the oldest manuscripts, — the phrase, "except for his feet" (*ei mē tous podas*).[f] In controversies of the ancient Catholic Church it was widely as-

sumed that **bathed** referred to baptism and was used to prove that there was no need for a reclaimed backslider to be baptized. It also figured prominently in the Donatist controversy with reference to whether those baptized by heretics needed to be baptized the second time. Most Catholics and some Protestants, such as B. Weiss, F. Spitta, and Lagrange, rule out this possibility.[g] Among the ancients Cyril was one of the few who believed that the meaning of baptism was excluded. The two things needed, he said, are a conscience purified by love, and sanctification in the Spirit by baptism.[h]

Lagrange and Zahn suggest that the ancient Western church adopted the shorter text to strengthen the argument for one baptism, especially in the light of their eagerness to prove that the apostles had been baptized (MJL, p. 354).

Among those who interpret the contrast between the "bathing" and the "washing" as spiritual rather than physical is Calvin

---

[f] It is omitted in Sinaiticus, Origen and O. L. MSS. It is omitted in the Vulgate of Wordsworth and White and by Pope Gregory I (A.D. 490-604) in a letter to Theoctista.  Its omission, says Westcott, places greater emphasis upon the words "needeth not."
[g] N. M. Haring, "Historical Notes on the Interpretation of John 13:10," *Catholic Biblical Quarterly,* Oct., 1951, pp. 355-380.
[h] Cyril of Alexandria, *op. cit.,* IX, 13:8.

9 Simon Peter saith unto him, Lord, not my feet only, but also my hands and my head.

10 Jesus saith to him, He that is bathed needeth not save to wash his feet, but is clean every whit: and ye are clean, but not all.

---

incongruous, much the same as John protested administering the rite of baptism to Jesus and then consented (Matt. 3:14).

10 Some ancient texts omit "except his feet" (*ei mē tous podas*) but the phrase is found in most of the manuscripts, including the oldest extant (Bodmer II), and it is consistent with the context. **He that is bathed** (*leloumenos* — perfect middle or passive participle) "does not have need except to have his feet washed" (*nipsasthai*). The **bathed** indicates a cleansing of the whole body (cf. Acts 9:37; II Pet. 2:22); **washed** denotes a cleansing of a portion of the body, a partial cleansing (cf. Matt. 6:17). In physical terms a guest who had bathed before leaving home needed only a washing of the feet upon arrival at the home of his host. Bathing was part of the preparation (cleansing) necessary for "eating the passover," and the disciples probably had met that requirement. **Is clean every whit** (*katharos*

*holos*): the term *katharos* is found elsewhere in John only at 15:3, where it means spiritual cleansing. The conversation changes from physical cleansing but his spiritual condition was such that he could betray his best friend. It has been suggested (by Loisy, Bauer, and others) that there is an allusion to baptism here, that the **bathed** refers to this initiatory rite which need not be repeated. Alford, followed by Hovey and Hendriksen, suggests that the subsequent washing of the feet (repeated as needed) symbolizes daily sanctification from recurring pollution. In other words, the one whose sins are forgiven "needs only *one* thing, namely sanctification, here especially (though not exclusively) that work of God within the heart whereby the believer attains constantly renewed and ever-growing humility and day-by-day willingness and eagerness to render service to others in gratitude for all the benefits received" (WmH, II, 238).

---

who thus comments on v. 10: "The children of God are not altogether regenerated on the first day . . . but, on the contrary, the remains of the flesh continue to dwell in them, with which they maintain a continued struggle through their whole life . . . . for, if the Holy Spirit occupied every part of us, we would no longer have anything to do with the pollutions of the world. . . . What is here spoken of is not the forgiveness of sins, but the renewal, by which Christ, by gradual and uninterrupted succession, delivers his followers entirely from the sinful desires of the flesh."[1]

Wesley's comment on vv. 8-10 is characteristically terse; he paraphrases: "If I do not wash thee in My blood, and purify thee by My Spirit, thou canst have no communion with Me, nor any share in the blessings of My kingdom. . . . And so ye, having been already cleansed, need only to *wash* your *feet* — that is, to walk holy and undefiled."[1]

Bernard cites vv. 13-16 to indicate that the primary meaning is not cleansing but a lesson in humility. It has been suggested that "bathed" is an allusion to baptism which symbolizes one's acceptance into the Christian fellowship and does not need to be repeated, and that "washed" is a reference to the Eucharist (which John omits), which is designed to remove the spiritual stains which result from one's daily contacts with a sinful world. The words **ye are clean but not all** does not mean that they are only partially cleansed from defilement; rather, as v. 11 indicates, it means that they are now clean (cf. 15:3) with one exception — Judas.

We conclude that Jesus is using the literal physical meaning to teach a spiritual truth. The person who leaves home bathed and hence clean all over still needs the additional washing of the feet upon arrival at his destination because of contact with defilement en route. Likewise, one who experiences the grace of regeneration needs

---

[1] John Calvin, *Commentary on the Gospel According to John,* tr. by Wm. Pringle (Grand Rapids: Eerdmans, 1949), II, 59.

[1] John Wesley, *op. cit.,* p. 361.

11 For he knew him that should betray him; therefore said he, Ye are not all clean.

12 So when he had washed their feet, and taken his garments, and sat down again, he said unto them, Know ye what I have done to you?

13 Ye call me, Teacher, and Lord: and ye say well; for so I am.

What Jesus in effect said to Peter was that what Peter needed was not more water, but more humility. The point of the object lesson was not to teach hygiene; it was an object lesson in humility. The "washing" needed by Peter was mental and spiritual, a change of attitude toward greatness. A deeper meaning, suggested by Hoskyns, that the cleansing connotes the spiritual cleansing by the "blood of the lamb" (I John 1:7; Rev. 1:5, 7:14; cf. Rom. 6:1-3; I Cor. 10:16) seems justified by the larger context. The word clean appears again in the analogy of the vine and branches (15:3).

11 Judas was, of course, excluded from the declaration ye are clean. John again testifies to Jesus' omniscience by noting that he knew Judas' character all the time. As an eyewitness the author recalled the contrast between the näiveté of the disciples' understanding of Judas and their Master's awareness of what was going on.

12 The details of Jesus' movements — washing, putting his garments back on, and reclining again — suggest again the report of one who witnessed the event and recalled the details vividly. Know (ginō-skete) ye what I have done. The verb form is the same whether indicative or imperative; hence it means either a command or an inquiry. Here it probably means a question as the Greek text and most translations indicate: "Do you realize the significance of what I have just done?"

13 Ye call me, Teacher (didāskalos), and Lord (kyrios). As W. Bauer points out (op. cit., p. 170), John quotes the disciples as addressing Jesus as "Master," or "Teacher" in 1:38; 11:8; cf. 11:28; 20:16. Nicodemus (3:2) and "the Jews" (8:4) also addressed him thus. Jesus applied the same term to Nicodemus (3: 10). John twice explains for the benefit of his Greek readers that this is the same as the Hebrew term "rabbi" (1:38; 20: 16). As noted earlier, the term "Lord" applied both to God and to men as it is in English today. The rabbis often used

subsequent cleansing by the Word (15:3; 17:17; I John 1:2) as the need arises. That this is the significance of the washing for the recipient seems confirmed by v. 8. However, this is only part, the more subtle part, of the meaning. More obviously the effect upon the one doing the "washing" is indicated in vv. 13-16 where the meaning is humility in service. Thus, Bernard and Lagrange are right in insisting on the primary meaning of humility, but the idea of spiritual cleansing should not be excluded.

3. The Meaning of the Washing (vv. 12-20)

The tenseness of the time when Jesus was washing the twelve pairs of feet was now replaced by the silence which followed Jesus' resumption of his place at the table. The embarrassment at seeing their Master perform so menial a task finally had found expression in Peter's vigorous protest. In societies long ac-customed to democracy it is difficult to comprehend the deference disciples have for their teacher or vassals for their lord. For centuries the Jews had learned to respect their rabbis and the scribes as men of learning. In the Far East the sage has been held among the most highly respected men in the community. Today in Japan the sensei (teacher) is a term of highest respect. It would be unthinkable in such a society for the teacher to walk while the disciple rode or for the teacher to carry a book or any other burden if a disciple were near. Students consider it an honor to be a servant of the sensei. The same is true throughout the Orient. A seminary student from the Orient was shocked to see the writer, his teacher, washing his own automobile; the student considered it highly improper. To the disciples of Jesus nothing could have caused greater pain and chagrin than to submit to their Master's ministrations of this kind. This lesson and others on the subject (cf. Mark 10:

14 If I then, the Lord and the Teacher, have washed your feet, ye also ought to wash one another's feet.

15 For I have given you an example, that ye also should do as I have done to you.

---

the two terms synonymously.[7] Previously some rabbinic scholars supposed that John's equation of the Aramaic term "rabbi" with *didaskalos* was an anachronism, since the Aramaic term was of the second century A.D. However, the discovery of this term on bone cases (ossaries) of the first century disprove this theory and indicate that the term was correct in the first century.[8]

**14 Ye ought also to wash one another's feet.** If it is appropriate that I, your Lord and Master, wash your feet, how much more appropriate that you be willing to wash each other's feet! There could be no argument against that; he, the divine Lord, and they, mere human beings! In an Oriental setting the message carries even greater conviction and emphasis than in the West.

**15 I have given you an example:** "What I did for you you are to continue doing (*poiēte*, pres. subj.) for one another." Did Jesus mean by his act and words to establish another ordinance in addition to baptism and the Lord's Supper? There is no such teaching elsewhere in the New Testament. Neither is there any record of churches in the first or second century observing such an ordinance. This rite (known as the *pedilavium*) was practiced in some Western churches later, including churches in Milan, Gaul and Ireland (Hoskyns, *op. cit.*, pp. 443-446). Augustine, with most others, considered it not an additional sacrament but a means of humility.[9] Among the Eastern churches, however, the rite can be traced as far back as the fifth century. It is still practiced in the Greek Orthodox Church on certain occasions. In Jerusalem a Western observer during the British Mandate (1918-48) reported that the archbishop in gorgeous attire entered the church with

---

35-45) left a deep impression on the Christian church, so much so that in lands influenced by the heaven of Christianity "the serving man" is a respected member of the community, quite a contrast to the status of a servant in Plato's *Republic*. In modern times Mahatma Ghandi challenged the mores of his generation in a manner similar to that employed by Jesus; indeed Ghandi borrowed his idea of service from the New Testament. In the Ashrams conducted by Dr. E. Stanley Jones (with indebtedness to Ghandi), each member is compelled to serve, with the highest ranking person performing the most menial tasks of all. This idea of greatness is grasped in a soliloquy by George MacDonald.

### LONELY SERVICE

*Methought that in a solemn church I stood;*
*Its marble acres, worn with knees and feet,*
*Lay spread from door to door, from street to street.*
*Midway the form hung high upon the rood*
*Of him who gave his life to be our good.*
*Beyond the priests flitted, bowed, and murmured meet.*
*Among the candles, shining still and sweet,*
*Men came and went, and worshipped as they could.*
*And still their dust a woman with her broom,*
*Bowed to her work, kept sweeping to the door.*
*Then saw I, slow through all the pillared gloom,*
*Across the church a silent figure came:*
*"Daughter," it said, "thou sweepest well my floor."*
*"It is the Lord!" I cried, and saw no more.*

---

[7] Jehoshaphat is quoted as greeting a teacher affectionately with the words "my teacher, my teacher, my lord, my lord." Strack-Billerbeck, *op. cit.*, II, 558.
[8] W. F. Albright, *Archaeology of Palestine* (Baltimore: Penguin, 1954), p. 144.
[9] The *pedilavium* was not used at Rome and apparently disappeared among churches of the West as the influence of the Roman Liturgy spread. See Hoskyns, *op. cit.*, p. 445.

16 Verily, verily, I say unto you, A servant is not greater than his lord; neither one that is sent greater than he that sent him.

17 If ye know these things, blessed are ye if ye do them.

18 I speak not of you all: I know whom I have chosen: but that the scripture may be fulfilled, He that eateth my bread lifted up his heel against me.

---

twelve priests and re-enacted this scene. After the archbishop washed the feet of the twelve his full vestments were donned and he was seated on his throne. The liturgy includes not only the idea of humility but of sanctification as well,[10] yet this never became established as a sacrament in the churches. Jesus simply gave a graphic and unforgettable object lesson in humility. His disciples were expected to serve one another regardless of the cost to their pride. They were to do any necessary act of service. Timothy was advised that this act of gracious hospitality is to be especially commended (I Tim. 5:10).

16 Verily, verily: this repetition of *amēn* always introduces an important declaration. A servant (*doulos*) is not greater than his lord, an axiom designed to bring home the lesson with greatest emphasis. The *doulos* was a household slave, a domestic. Gibbon estimated that two-fifths of the population of the Roman Empire were slaves. "Neither is the one sent (apostle) greater than the sender." By this obvious truth Jesus drove home the dignity of service (cf. Luke 22:27, "I am among you as one who serves").

17 If ye know (*oidate*) . . . blessed are ye if ye do (*poiēte*). . . . Knowledge must lead to decision, to commitment, to action. The path to glory is not a six-lane highway but it is rough, tough, and hard going, with frequent stops to help wrecked and unfortunate travelers.

18 I speak not of you all, a repetition of the thought of vv. 10, 11, indicating that Judas is excluded from the fellowship of the "blessed." What is being said has no relevance to the traitor. I know (*oida*) whom I have chosen. This statement, together with similar statements in 2:24, 25; 6:64, 70, seems to indicate that Jesus knew Judas's character before he chose him and that the betrayal was foreseen by Jesus from the beginning. He was chosen with this in view in order that the Scripture might be fulfilled (RHL, *op. cit.*, p. 274).

---

It was this awareness of the importance of service which caused Pope Gregory the Great to call himself, "Servant of the servants of the Lord," a title which the Roman pontiff carries to this day.

14 Ye ought also to wash one another's feet. Are these words to be taken literally? Some think so and practice footwashing as a solemn part of the public worship service at stated intervals, something similar to a sacrament. They reason: "The Bible plainly states this as a command; why not obey it, since the Bible always means exactly what it says." This attitude is admirable in some ways but is it not a slavish literalism? It is hazardous to build an institution upon one text of Scripture and to assume that there is only one correct interpretation (our own). Certainly the modern disciple should be willing to perform this or any comparable service. Soon after S. L. Brengle, a gifted clergyman with a bright prospect, felt led to leave this prospect and join the Salvation Army, he was given his first assignment. It was hardly the kind of service for which he had been prepared by his previous training. He was asked to black the boots of the officers. Brengle inwardly revolted at this "degrading" task and was tempted to think that a man of his standing should be shown a greater respect. But he obeyed and submitted to this discipline of the spirit. He "that humbleth himself shall be exalted" and before long Brengle became known as one of the Army's greatest leaders — Commissioner Brengle. Booker T. Washington, the noted American Negro educator, when he was a student, reported for work at the college he was to attend. He was asked to clean a room. He

---

[10] H. C. Luke, "Eastern Ceremonies in Jerusalem," *The Times*, March 17, 1924, cited by Hoskyns, *op. cit.*, pp. 445f.

19 From henceforth I tell you before it come to pass, that, when it is come to pass, ye may believe that I am *he*.

20 Verily, verily, I say unto you, He that receiveth whomsoever I send receiveth me; and he that receiveth me receiveth him that sent me.

21 When Jesus had thus said, he was troubled in the spirit, and testified, and said, Verily, verily, I say unto you, that one of you shall betray me.

Jesus now chose to expose the traitor and foretell his act of treachery so that the disciples' faith would be strengthened when they saw the fulfillment of the prediction. The apologetic value of predicting an event and having it fulfilled was fully realized in Isaiah 45:21; 46:10. This evidence of Jesus' prescience would also help offset the shock to the disciples' faith when they saw him captured and tortured.

20 **Verily, verily** appears again to introduce another important declaration. It elaborates on what was mentioned in v. 16. If it is true that the sender is greater than the one sent (v. 16), it is also true that the one sent is no less important than the one he represents. The sender bestows upon his representative a status equal to his own so far as the mission is concerned. His statement here is similar to statements in the Synoptics (Matt. 10:40; Mark 9:37; Luke 9:48).

The solemn "I am" of v. 19 emphasized his union with the Father, and now he emphasizes his intimate relationship with the disciples. It is a preliminary statement of the tri-unity of Father, Son and believer which is elaborated at greater length later (17:18-26). The contrast between these chosen to represent him and the one chosen to betray him is developed further in the paragraph which follows.

21 **He was troubled** (*etarachthē*) **in spirit,** that is, in his own human spirit or emotions. The word **troubled** occurs now for the fifth time in John. It was used to describe his feeling as he approached the tomb of Lazarus (11:33) and his feeling after likening himself to seed grain (12:27), a sadness which he wanted to spare his disciples (14:1, 27). The trouble **in spirit** here, and "in soul" (12:27), are probably only different ways of expressing inner emotion. The **in spirit**

cleansed it thoroughly and finished before the time allotted. Rather than spend the remainder of the period in idleness he "cleansed" the room the second time. His superior, pleased at the young student's resourcefulness and industry in "little things," gave him greater responsibilities and young Washington's rise was rapid.

The practice of ritual foot-washing has persisted in some Western nations in both church and state. It was practiced by the nobility of England until 1731, King James II being the last monarch to perform this ceremony (EGT). As late as 1896 it was practiced in the Austrian capital of Vienna. An English visitor left an impressive description of the annual *'Fusswaschung'* on Maundy Thursday in the splendid royal palace. On the morning of this day the hall began to fill with the highest dignitaries in gorgeous costumes, and the royal box above with the ladies of the court. After the clergy entered the room and took places at a

raised platform in the hall twelve of the poorest old men of Vienna entered. The emperor laid aside his royal regalia and, assisted by the clergy, one with basin and another pouring water, the emperor washed the feet of the twelve destitute men. The queen was accustomed to do likewise to twelve of the poorest women of the city. After the service the poor were returned in royal carriages to their homes, laden with gifts from the emperor.[k] Such was the way in which Jesus' command was obeyed in strict literalness; the obedience was impressive but also superficial and legalistic.

18 **He that eateth my bread lifted up his heel against me** is a quotation of Psalm 41:9. The Psalmist commends the person who is considerate of the poor and complains of his own miserable condition. One of the most painful experiences known to man is to be betrayed by a friend. Shakespeare grasped this point clearly when describing the assassination of Julius Caesar:

[k] *The Springfield Republican*, April, 1896, cited in F. L. Peloubet, *op. cit.*, p. 362.

22 The disciples looked one on another, doubting of whom he spake.

23 There was at the table reclining in Jesus' bosom one of his disciples whom Jesus loved.

24 Simon Peter therefore beckoneth to him, and saith unto him, Tell *us* who it is of whom he speaketh.

---

is instrumental dative, but this instrument is here the aspect of soul by which and in which the subject is affected (cf. 11:33 — "he troubled himself" — MJL, p. 359).

**One of you shall betray me.** What a surprise and shock that statement must have produced! Only twelve of them with intensive training for three years and now one of them is a traitor (cf. Mark 14:18; Matt. 26:21; Luke 22:21)! **Betray** is from *para* ("beside") and *didōmi* ("to give"), hence, "to give over" or "to deliver up." The term is regularly used of turning one over to the custody of police, or to arrest (A-G). It may also mean to give oneself over (e.g., to death).

23 **The disciple whom Jesus loved** is designated thus for the first time but is repeated in 19:26f.; 20:2; 21:7, 20. He was reclining **in Jesus' bosom**, that is, on his left arm in front of Jesus (also thus reclining) and could readily lean

his head back against Jesus' chest. It was a position of honor and intimacy, as the same term in 1:18 indicates — "The one who was in the bosom of the Father, has declared (exhibited) him." The phrase is intended to denote the closest intimacy. This favored disciple was probably the apostle John.

If Peter had been appointed as viceger-ent, as some interpret Matthew 16:18, 19, why was he not in this position of honor and intimacy? John is here represented as being in the same relationship to Christ as Christ was to the Father (cf. 1:18). That this "beloved disciple" was closer to the Master than Peter is also seen in the fact that Peter had to ask him to inquire of Jesus as to the identity of the traitor.

24 Instead of **Tell us who it is of whom he speaketh** some of the oldest manuscripts read "Enquire who it may be concerning whom he spoke."[11] The latter is less

---

*For Brutus, as you know, was Caesar's angel!*

.     .     .

*This was the most unkindest cut of all;*

*For when the noble Caesar saw him stab,*

*Ingratitude, more strong than traitor's arms,*

*Quite vanquished him; then burst his mighty heart.*[1]

So Jesus was "tempted in all points as we are, yet without sin" (Heb. 4:15).

The eating of bread in the home of one's host is a form of sacred covenant. When Jael gave Sisera the asylum of her tent, and in addition gave him *leban* (sour milk) she entered into a covenant to protect him as a guest (Judges 5:25). When Laban and Jacob made a solemn covenant they ratified it by the eating of bread (Gen. 31:54). It was bad enough for

Judas to betray Jesus under any circum-stances, but to do so right after sharing a meal together made it the more heinous. In addition to being detestably diabolical Judas had a complex character; a mixture of passions must have swayed him, as was true of Socrates' friend Alcibiades who later betrayed his native city to her enemies. He said of Socrates, "I have felt as if I could hardly endure the life which I am leading . . . and I am conscious that if I did not shut my ears against him, and fly as from the voice of the siren, my fate would be like that of others, — he would transfix me, and I should grow old sitting at his feet. For he makes me confess that I ought not to live as I do, neglecting the wants of my own soul, and busying myself with the concerns of the Athenians; there-for I hold my ears and tear myself away from him. And he is the only person who ever made me ashamed. . . . For I know that I cannot answer him or say that I

---

[11] The latter reading (*pythesthai tis an eiē peri hou eipen*) is that of D, P66, etc. Both are combined in Sinaiticus.

[1] Wm. Shakespeare, "Julius Caesar," III. ii. 185, *Shakespeare* (New York: Scott, Foresman, 1934), p. 680.

25 He leaning back, as he was, on Jesus' breast saith unto him, Lord, who is it?
26 Jesus therefore answereth, He it is, for whom I shall dip the sop, and give it him.
So when he had dipped the sop, he taketh and giveth it to Judas, *the son* of Simon
Iscariot.

---

simple and less Johannine than the former.
Because of his reclining position in front
of Jesus the beloved disciple could whisper
to Jesus and get his reply by simply turning his head back and up.

**26 When he had dipped the sop . . .
he giveth it to Judas.** Recently in Egypt
the writer was invited to a chicken dinner. The host, proud of his privilege,
stood and with bare hands wrenched the
fowl in pieces, distributing the choicest
morsels to the guest of honor first and then
giving portions to the other guests. In
many countries of the Mid-East it is
considered a courtesy of the host to
distribute the food to the guests by hand,
as T. E. Lawrence and others have reported. For the guest to refuse is considered base ingratitude, a breach of etiquette. Among the Arabs especially the
guests are seated on the floor around a
huge platter heaped with rice, bread, meat,
and vegetables, topped with gravy. All
eat from a common dish. The Passover

meal consisted of unleavened bread, and
the central vessel was filled with lamb
and bitter herbs. The **sop** (*psōmion*)
means a "morsel" or "piece" of food, hence
"to nourish." The term survives in modern
Greek and means "bread" (A-G). Eastern versions translate this by a word for
bread, perhaps because they associated this
meal with the Eucharist, but, in this passage, it could have been either bread or
meat ("bread" — NEB). The definite
article before the noun implies that Jesus
had it in his hand with the intention of
handing it to Judas before John asked the
question.[12] By this act Jesus singled out
Judas as a recipient of special favor (cf.
Ruth 2:14); perhaps in a final effort to
dissuade him. The significance was
known only to John, however, and apparently he did not convey this to Peter
(cf. v. 28). While dipping a morsel of
food in a dish and giving it to a guest was
a friendly act, in this case it served to
identify the traitor.

---

ought not to do as he bids, but when I
leave his presence the love of popularity
gets the better of me. And therefore
I run away and fly from him, and when
I see him I am ashamed of what I have
confessed to him. Many a time I have
wished that he were dead, and yet I know
that I should be much more sorry than
glad, if he were to die: so that I am at
wit's end."[m]

*And all men kill the thing they love,*
*By all let this be heard,*
*Some do it with a bitter look,*
*Some with a flattering word,*
*The coward does it with a kiss,*
*The brave man with a sword!*[n]

If we are not literally to wash one
another's feet as a ritual, if a crass
literalism is not the soundest exegesis, how
is one to interpret and apply the key verse
of this paragraph, "ye also should do as
I have done unto you (v. 15)? Certainly,

the modern disciple must be willing to
serve; he must not consider himself too
good or too exalted in status to perform
the most humble form of service. In the
Orient so great is the influence of caste
or status, that even converts to Christianity often refuse to do the work normally
reserved for "outcasts," such as cleaning
the bathroom. But the Christian should
be characterized by rejoicing in service.
Paul glorified in his chosen status of a
"slave" of Jesus Christ. No task is too
menial for the servant of Christ if thereby he can advance the welfare of his
fellow men and glorify God. This has
been well expressed in a poetic idealization
of the servant of Christ.

*There, where a few torn shrubs the*
*the place disclose,*
*The village preacher's modest man-*
*sion rose.*
*He was to all the country dear,*

[12] Lagrange, *op. cit.*, p. 362; also Lenski, *op. cit.*, p. 948.
[m] Plato, "Symposium" 216, *Dialogues of Plato*, tr. B. Jowett (New York: Random House, 1937) I, 339.
[n] Oscar Wilde, "The Ballad of Reading Gaol"; W. A. Briggs, ed., *Great Poems of the English Language* (New York: Tudor Pub. Co., 1933), p. 1139.

27 And after the sop, then entered Satan into him.  Jesus therefore saith unto him, What thou doest, do quickly.

28 Now no man at the table knew for what intent he spake this unto him.

29 For some thought, because Judas had the bag, that Jesus said unto him, Buy what things we have need of for the feast; or, that he should give something to the poor.

30 He then having received the sop went out straightway: and it was night.

31 When therefore he was gone out, Jesus saith, Now is the Son of man glorified, and God is glorified in him;

---

27 **Satan entered into him.**  The diabolical plan conceived earlier (13:2) was now to be executed.  The judges of Israel were strengthened by the Spirit of God in times of national crisis and thereby enabled to do exploits otherwise impossible.  In a similar manner Judas seems to have been demon-possessed and thus enabled to carry out a deed otherwise repugnant and loathsome.  John could explain the enormity of Judas's crime in no other way; only a man inhabited by Satan could have done such a deed.  **What thou doest, do quickly,** directed Jesus, apparently wanting the suspense of the crucifixion to end quickly (cf. Luke 12:50); what a contrast to other men!  **Doest** (*poieis*) is a tendential present; i.e., "What you are planning to do, do it speedily," a command that Judas obeyed exactly as ordered.  If the giving of the morsel was a gesture of friendliness, and if the recipient refused to respond to this last appeal, it would help explain his decision to proceed immediately with his plans for betrayal.

28 **No man at the table knew:**  John thus exonerated the eleven from complicity in Judas's sin.  The observation **it was night** is probably more than the reminiscence of an eyewitness but has a symbolic meaning; the traitor went out into "outer darkness" and the "power of darkness" (Matt. 25:30; Luke 22:53).  He went not only to the priests but also "to his own place" (Acts 1:25), i.e., into the company of Satan and infernal darkness throughout eternity.

31 **Now is the Son of man glorified.**  A fresh sense of the imminence of his passion again gripped Jesus as it had after the inquiry of the Greeks (12:28) and again as the Passover approached (13:1;

---

And passing rich with forty pounds
    a year;
Remote from towns he ran his godly
    race,
Nor e'er had changed, nor wished to
    change, his place;
Unskillful he to fawn, or seek for
    power,
By doctrines fashioned to the vary-
    ing hour;
Far other aims his heart had learned
    to prize,
More skilled to raise the wretched
    than to rise.
Thus to relieve the wretched was
    his pride,
And e'en his failings lean'd to Vir-
    tue's side;
But in his duty prompt at every call,
He watched and wept, he prayed
    and felt for all.
And, as a bird each fond endear-
    ment tries

To tempt its new-fledg'd offspring
    to the skies,
He tried each art, reprov'd each dull
    delay,
Allur'd to brighter worlds, and led
    the way.
At church, with meek and unaf-
    fected grace,
His looks adorned the venerable
    place:
Truth from his lips prevailed with
    double sway,
And fools, who came to scoff, re-
    mained to pray.
His ready smile a parent's warmth
    expressed;
Their welfare pleased him and their
    cares distrest:
To them his heart, his love, his
    griefs were given,
But all his serious thoughts had rest
    in heaven[e]

---

[e] Oliver Goldsmith, "The Deserted Village," C. Hill, ed., *op. cit.,* pp. 371f.

32 and God shall glorify him in himself, and straightway shall he glorify him.

33 Little children, yet a little while I am with you.  Ye shall seek me: and as I said unto the Jews, Whither I go, ye cannot come; so now I say unto you.

34 A new commandment I give unto you, that ye love one another; even as I have loved you, that ye also love one another.

---

cf. 17:1).  The association of "glory" with the death and resurrection of Christ, in the thought of this Gospel, is expressed several times, the cumulative effect of which is quite impressive, even to the casual reader of the Gospel.[13]  As the death of Lazarus had glorified God (11: 4, 40) so the death and resurrection of Jesus glorified God.  Now, with the departure of Judas, Jesus faced the dreadful hours just ahead by talking of the glory in his approaching death in behalf of others.  He was thinking of what his submission to the torture would mean for sinful human beings, and what it would mean to the Father.

32 God shall glorify him in himself is a good translation; another possibility equally good is "God will glorify himself in him."  The latter is to be preferred.  The same pronoun is repeated: *auton en autōi*.  One is used as a reflexive pronoun, but nothing in the spelling indicates which one.  *Autos* is apparently used in a similar manner in I John 5:18 — "He

that was born of God guards himself, and the evil one does not cling to him."  As Jesus had told the Jews (7:34; 8:21; 12: 35; 14:4) so now he tells his disciples that he is leaving them (v. 33) and that they cannot go with him.  They are destined to outlive him and to be his witnesses until death overtakes them also.

34 A new commandment I give unto you, that ye love one another.  From a consideration of his destination, which must remain a mystery to them, Jesus now turns to a matter of immediate concern.  Frequently Jesus had magnified the importance of practicing love both toward God (I John 5:3) and toward others (Luke 10:27).  He even stated that the command of greatest importance was to demonstrate love: "This is the great and first commandment" (Matt. 22:38).  The famous Rabbi Hillel had warned against the practice of hate: "That which is hateful to thee, thou shalt not do to thy neighbor.  This is the whole law: the rest is only commentary" (BFW, II, 162).  Even

---

### 4. The Prediction of Betrayal (vv. 21-30)

Few scenes in the Bible are more charged with emotion than this, although the language is remarkably restrained and matter-of-fact.  Jesus was "troubled" as he contemplated his immanent sufferings and the betrayer in the place of honor on his left.  The disciples were soon to be gripped with a series of conflicting emotions — fear, curiosity, suspicion, self-accusation, and astonishment, Judas likewise was so powerfully moved that he was said to be demon-possessed, or even stronger — taken possession of by Satan.  Many artists have sought to portray this highly-charged scene on canvas.  Of these by far the most famous is that of Leonardo da Vinci in Milan, now being restored to something of its former splendor.  Among the most noted reproductions of Leonar-

do's picture is the one in stained glass in Forest Lawn, near Los Angeles; another is the chapel of "The Upper Room" in Nashville, Tennessee.  Leonardo was a better artist than archaeologist, although in his day none could have known as much about Biblical customs as is known today.  While in Leonardo's picture the thirteen are seated on benches about a table, it seems certain that Jesus and the disciples followed the oriental practice of the time by reclining around a low table in a U-shaped arrangement.[p]

Jesus was troubled both because of the human shrinking from the cross and from grief that one whom he had chosen would betray him.  The Bible is remarkable in its portrayal of real life as it exists; not an idealized picture remote from reality.  That exquisite literary gem, the twenty-third Psalm, was written "in the

---

[13] Cf. John 7:39; 8:54; 12:28-33; 13:31, 32; 17:1, 5.
[p] Edersheim, *op. cit.*, II, 494.

**35** By this shall all men know that ye are my disciples, if ye have love one to another.

---

more remarkable is the advice of "Gad": "Love ye one another from the heart; and if a man sin against thee, speak peaceably to him, and in thy soul hold not guile; and if he repent and confess, forgive him from the heart, and leave to God the avenging."[14] The positive injunction of love is much more far-reaching (as is also the Golden Rule) and certainly much harder to practice. To obey Christ in this respect is to be a pioneer, to take the initiative in showing good will and being kind to others. What did Jesus mean by **a new commandment** (*entolēn kainēn*)? Perhaps no answer is more satisfactory than the one given here — that they should love one another as Christ loved them. Further elaboration of this principle is to be found in 17:23-26; I John 4:7-21. The *newness* of the precept here promulgated is evident from the fact that Jesus requires his disciples to love one another *as he loved them* (WmH, II, 253). That is, the emphasis is upon *the degree* of love that they are to manifest toward fellow Christians. The newness consists in the source and nature of their love (RHS, p. 278). The important thing in the Old Covenant was "obey"; in the New Covenant it is "love."

**35 By this** (*en toutō*, i.e., "by means of this") **shall all men know that ye are my disciples.** The insignia by which Christians are to be identified from others, and definitely known as disciples of Christ, is by the way in which they love one another. How tragic that too seldom is this in evidence among those who profess the name of Christ today! Had this commandment been consistently obeyed the world would have been evangelized long ago. Tertullian (c. A.D. 200) witnesses that the early Christians were distinguished from others by this quality of life. Said he, "The heathen are wont to exclaim with wonder, 'See how these Christians love one another . . . and how they are ready to die for one another.' "[15]

The verb translated "love" here is not the Greek verb *phileō* but rather *agapaō*. It is not possible to express in English the distinction which is in the Greek and corresponding Latin terms. The term *agapaō* like the Latin *diligo*, expresses a more reasoning attachment, of choice and selection,"[16] a sense of obligation, of gratitude. On the other hand, *phileō*, like the Latin *amo*, is more instinctive, more emotional, more human. The Christians chose a relatively scarce and colorless

---

presence of enemies"; the birth of Jesus in Bethlehem was against the background of a vengeful tyrant who ordered the babes of Bethlehem massacred; the love of Jonathan and David was against the background of Saul's murderous jealousy; the repentance of the prodigal son was against the background of the elder son's resentment; Paul's poem on divine love (I Cor. 13) was set in the midst of a letter dealing with such problems as schism, vanity, rivalry and immorality. The visions, the dreams, and the inspiration of saints in the Biblical literature are found side by side with sin and unworthiness. Even Jesus encountered the problem of unbelief and

hostility with his own townspeople. It follows that God can perfect his saints today in circumstances which are anything but ideal. Like Joseph in the O.T., Jesus was betrayed in the house of his friends and like Joseph returned love for hatred, good for evil. Jesus experienced this, and was tempted in all points as we are, yet without sin.

One of the most plausible explanations for Judas' betrayal is that he was a zealot, that is, he expected a political Messiah who would lead the nation in a revolt similar to that of the Maccabees and establish a new kingdom.[q] When he found that Jesus was a "suffering servant"

---

[14] Test. of Gad., 6:3, 7, cited in R. H. Charles, *op. cit.*, II, 341.

[15] Tertullian, "Apologeticus," xxxix. 7; tr. by T. R. Glover; *Loeb Classical Library* (London: Heinemann, 1931), p. 177.

[16] R. C. Trench, *Synonyms of the New Testament*, 7th edit. (London: Macmillan, 1871), p. 39.

[q] Among other explanations of Judas' career are (1) that Judas was a personification of Judah rather than a real person, (2) that Judas "joined the band" with a view of betraying Jesus because Jesus was "unpatriotic," (3) that Judas sought to hasten Jesus' self-revelation by placing him in a situation where he would summon help from the angels and overwhelm his captors, and (4) that since he was foreordained to be a traitor Jesus chose him with this in view.

36 Simon Peter saith unto him, Lord, whither goest thou? Jesus answered, Whither I go, thou canst not follow me now; but thou shalt follow afterwards.

---

Greek term (*agapaō*) and charged it with a new, rich meaning. The better known word for love (*eros*) had associations with paganism which made it less appropriate to express the love of God; it stands primarily for romantic love.[17]

36 *Whither goest thou?* is the type of question one would expect from the talkative Peter. Its Vulgate form, *Quo vadis?*, appears also in the apocryphal story of Peter's death (*Acts of Peter and Paul*, 82). The question was prompted by Jesus' remark in v. 33 that they could not follow him. This subject of Jesus' departure and destination, introduced here, preoccupied the minds of the disciples for the remainder of this discourse (cf. 14:4; 16:28,29). The word translated *follow* may mean "accompany as a disciple"

(Matt. 9:9), or "obey," or "follow in death," as here. Earlier, Jesus' statement that the Jews could not follow him perplexed and annoyed them (7:34). There Jesus was saying that he was going to the Father (7:33) and the unbelievers could not follow him. Here Peter thinks of a journey (perhaps an exile) while Jesus speaks of his approaching death and ascension. Peter cannot follow him in death now because Jesus is going to the cross to make expiation for the sins of the world. He alone can do this for there is only one "Lamb of God who takes away the sin of the world." Afterward, however, Peter and believers may follow Jesus into the presence of the Father (Heb. 4:14, 15). This may also be a prediction of Peter's martyrdom (cf. 21:18,19);

---

rather than fulfilling the conventional idea of a Messiah, he became disillusioned and embittered. That he could have been so crafty and concealed his machinations so well that even the eleven were unsuspecting until the last is amazing. John gives more attention to Judas than do any of the other Gospel writers. Judas's true nature is given in 6:70 ("one of you is a devil"). That he was guilty of embezzling the common fund is indicated in 12:4-6. Matthew (27:3-10) reports Judas's "repentance" and his testimony that Jesus was "innocent." But this change of mind was more of remorse than of true repentance in faith. Instead of faith and hope he had only despair and committed suicide (cf. Acts 1:16-20). Jesus' efforts to win him are reflected in repeated warnings (John 6:70; 13:18,21,26) before abandoning Judas to his chosen course (13:27). Judas is perhaps the least admired man in all history, his name being synonymous with treachery.[r]

### 5. The New Commandment (vv. 31-35)

With the departure of Judas a new phase begins with the last discourses of Jesus with his disciples. He now turns to the

matter of preparing them for his departure. Tenderly he addresses them as "little children" (*teknion*), an expression characteristic of the Johannine literature (cf. I John 2:1,12,18; 3:7,18; 4:4; 5:21). It implies a spiritual genealogy (cf. 1:12; 8:39; 11:52; I John 3:1). The tender solicitude of Jesus for the eleven arose from his announcement of his coming glorification. The passion would terminate the relationship they had known for three years. Henceforth they would no longer "know Christ after the flesh." The joys and sorrows, triumphs and irritations of their three years together would soon be only a memory. They did not yet experience a sense of bereavement and isolation but Jesus knew in advance how they would soon feel and assured them in advance. Often in our Christian experience the Lord prepares us in advance for the unforeseen trials ahead.

Jesus did not make preparation for the physical protection of his disciples. He did not advise them to flee nor to plan a counterattack. His whole concern was an inner fortification. He wanted them spiritually prepared and strong, confident that if the "heart" was sound the body would survive. He did not recklessly expose himself to danger and thus "tempt the

---

[17] Strachan, *op. cit.*, p. 278. See also exegesis following 3:16; 21:17.
[r] He was admired by the Cainites. See C. M. Cerr, "Judas," ISBE, III, 1765-67.

37 Peter saith unto him, Lord, why cannot I follow thee even now? I will lay down my life for thee.

38 Jesus answereth, Wilt thou lay down thy life for me?  Verily, verily, I say unto thee, The cock shalt not crow, till thou hast denied me thrice.

---

Peter apparently interpreted it thus, as his answer implies.

**37 I will lay down my life for thee.** The words were spoken with obvious sincerity but with insufficient self-knowledge. Peter, the extrovert who often spoke before he thought, was over-confident. He must have withered with chagrin at Jesus' reply and prophecy.

**38 Wilt thou lay down thy life?** With God-given foresight Jesus envisioned Peter's cowardice which in a few hours would be painfully evident.  Here he warned Peter and, according to Luke's account, prayed for him (Luke 22:32). Some of the accounts depict Peter as affirming his loyalty *before* the prediction of betrayal (Luke 22:33; John 13:37) and others both *before and after* Jesus' prediction (Matt. 26:33,35; Mark 14:29,31). Peter, like many impulsive people, was quick to express undying devotion; but he was just as quick to surrender to fear in a moment of grave danger. In spite of these characteristics, by grace he eventually became one of the "pillars" in the church (Gal. 2:2).

---

Lord," nor encourage his followers to do so. But his main concern, as was theirs after Pentecost, was that they have strong internal defenses. This inner defense was "love." The kind of love here mentioned was not only an emotion but a quality of life, a discerning and calculated commitment to God who is love.  In the light of this common commitment to *agapē* (love) they will perforce love one another because of a prior love to God. This love is a positive dynamic force which is "stronger than death." It was this factor which led Jesus to live his life and at the appropriate time lay it down for "his friends." It was the same love which later led his disciples to witness by their lives that this quality of life had been imparted to them. It was wonderful for Jesus to exemplify this love; it was a greater miracle to impart this virtue to his followers. "Who follows in his train?"

### 6. THE PREDICTION OF DENIAL (vv. 36-38)

If the prediction of the betrayal by Judas was painful for Jesus (13:21), the prediction of Peter's denial must, if possible, have been even more distressing. Peter had been the leader of the twelve; it was his expression of faith that Jesus said would be the foundation of the church (Matt. 16:18). He was a member of the trio who had witnessed the raising of a maiden (Mark 5:37) and the transfiguration (Mark 9:2) and had been the most emphatic in his expression of loyalty (v. 37). It seems that nothing was lacking to make Jesus' sorrow unprecedented in kind and degree (Isa. 53:3; cf. Lam. 1:12). This kind of suffering must have been even greater than the physical anguish of the passion experiences.

Peter's vacillation was not entirely cured as Paul discovered at Antioch (Gal. 2:11-14), but after he was "converted" he was by contrast a tower of constant strength (cf. Acts 3-4). He was also teachable (Acts 10) and hence influential with his brethren (Acts 15). Because he learned to follow, he earned the right to lead. His repentance was easier than that of Judas because his apostasy was not premeditated, and because he repented in faith rather than lapsing into faithless despair and futility. The capacity to repent and believe is forfeited if rebellion persists too long.

In summary it may be noted that ch. 13 marks something of a transition. It marks the transition from the fellowship of the twelve to that of the eleven, from participation in the normal activities of the public to a withdrawal for the purpose of dealing with the basic issues involved in discipleship. The chapter is replete with predictions — of Judas' action, of Peter's action, of Jesus' departure, and of future understanding on the parts of the disciples. The general atmosphere was that of the "night" in more ways than one, but in the midst of the "night" (v. 30) there was the promise of "glory" and a new light (v. 31). The hope that up to now was so robust in the disciples had to be nourished lest it be entirely ex- tinguished in the tragedies just ahead. The hope of the prophets survived the shock of captivity in the sixth century B.C.; now the hope of the disciples is to survive the shock of the crucifixion, largely because of these "last words" preserved only by this Evangelist.

# CHAPTER XIV

Let not your heart be troubled: believe in God, believe also in me.

## EXEGESIS

The chapter division should really have begun at John 13:36 with Peter's question, "Lord, where are you going?" (RSV) or at 13:31 where Jesus announced his imminent departure to a place where they could not come. This discourse occurred less than twenty-four hours before Jesus' crucifixion. Now he prepares the disciples for the sad and shocking event.

**1 Let not your heart be troubled** (*mē taressesthō* — pres. mid. imper.), i.e., "Don't permit yourself to be troubled," or, as 13:33, 36 implies, "Stop being troubled." This is the sixth appearance of the word "troubled" in the Gospel. On the three previous occurrences of the term it was Jesus who was "troubled" (11:33; 12:27; 13:21). Here and in 14:27 it is the disciples who are troubled or stirred up, and for good reason. In addition to the known dangers, they are now confronted with the announcement of their Master's departure. In the Synoptic accounts Jesus' announcement of his departure by death was given midway in his public ministry (Matt. 16:21; Mark 8:31; Luke 9:22-27). In John's account Jesus' predictions of this event were expressed so enigmatically that his disciples did not understand what he meant.[1]

**The heart** (*kardia;* cf. "cardiac") was regarded in the O. T. as the seat of life (II Kings 18:14) and, "in a psychological sense, the seat of man's collective energies, the focus of personal life, the seat of the rational as well as the emotional and volitional elements in human life."[2] In this context also it was not the physical organ, obviously, but the seat of spiritual

## EXPOSITION

### B. Preparation for Jesus' Departure (14:1—16:26)

#### 1. Reunion assured (vv. 1-7)

In anyone's choice of five favorite chapters in the Bible, this chapter, along with I Corinthians 13 and Psalm 23 would be included. What is it that gives this chapter its appeal and its power? It is similar in many respects to the opening words of Isaiah 40 with its message of comfort, a message which continues through most of Isaiah 40-66. This chapter speaks of home and of heaven, two favorite themes of most Christians. It speaks of prayer, of the Comforter, and of God's presence and help. These valuable chapters (14-17) contain material found only in John and otherwise completely unknown. How much poorer the Christian church would be without these famous "last words." The comfort Jesus gave was given in the calm before the storm. The tension occasioned by Judas and the announcement of a betrayer in their midst was now relieved and the tumultuous hours of the arrest and trial were in the future. They were now in the "eye of a hurricane." The dreams of the kingdom and their place in it were rapidly fading in the minds of the eleven disciples. Instead of vying for the chief places they were now gripped with the realization that nothing was certain. Fears that had occasionally gripped them on previous narrow escapes from the authorities (cf. 11:8, 16) now returned with multiple force. They were startled by the announcement of the betrayal; this alone would have plunged them into deep gloom. Added to this, however, was the realization that they would no longer have their leader with them. What is a movement without a leader? Everything in the Gospel accounts up to this time

[1] John 2:20; 3:21; 6:62; 7:33; 8:28; 10:12; 12:7, 32.
[2] G. Abbott-Smith, *A Manual Greek Lexicon of the New Testament* (New York: Scribner's, 1922), p. 230.

2 In my Father's house are many mansions; if it were not so, I would have told you; for I go to prepare a place for you.

3 And if I go and prepare a place for you, I come again, and will receive you unto myself; that where I am, *there* ye may be also.

---

life, the center of faith and feeling, the innermost being of personality.

**Believe in God** (or, preferably, "you believe in God"), **believe** (*pisteuete*) **also in me.** (Grammatically, "believe" can be either imperative or indicative. Here the first occurrence appears to be indicative, the second imperative.) If they had not believed in God they would not have been chosen as disciples. Now they are urged to put similar faith in Christ.[3]

**2 Many mansions** (*monai*, from *meno*, "to abide") is best translated "abiding places" as in ASVm. The **Father's house** would be similar to our concept of a "mansion" with many apartments or chambers. The RSV and Phillips rendering of "room" is good. The imagery is that of a vast palace, like that in Knossos, Versailles, or Vienna, with over a thousand apartments — plenty of room for all sons and daughters of the king, however numerous they be, besides hundreds of servants

(cf. Godet). Jesus was assuring them that in the Father's "palace" (heaven) there would be plenty of "apartments" with room for all.

**3 And if I go and prepare a place for you** seems less desirable than the RSV — "when I go" — the "if" implies some uncertainty. Lagrange likewise translates the *ean* by *quand* ("when"). Jesus is preceding his beloved disciples and promises to see to it that a place will be reserved and ready for each one of them on his arrival in heaven. He even promises that he will also return and personally escort them to his heavenly home. This can be interpreted to mean when death overtakes each one, or it can happen at Christ's second coming. If only the latter, then the disciples are still waiting to be received by Christ. But if the former (which seems more reasonable), as well as the latter, then each one was welcomed at the gates of death and safely and joy-

---

indicates that the disciples were unprepared for "going it alone." Two of their foremost fellow-disciples were guilty of defecting — both their treasurer and their most articulate spokesman. They sorely needed the comforting, strengthening, illuminating words of these chapters.

Jesus' words were intended for the "heart," that is, for the center of personality. In the Old Testament, as here, the "heart" meant not only the emotional side of one's nature, but his intellectual and volitional nature as well. Jesus could sympathize with them for he also had been "troubled" (11:38; 12:27).

The main theme of the first three verses seems to be reassurance. The basis for this assurance is threefold:

i. *Faith* in God cures anxiety. Anxious care is inconsistent with faith. Repeatedly in the Synoptic teaching comes the exhortation to "be not anxious" (Luke

12:22). This kind of tranquillity is not that which comes from tranquilizers of various kinds; it is not an escape from reality. It is not the kind of relief which comes by ignoring the problems. It is rather confidence in God. This confidence in God's faithfulness, as James Hudson Taylor, pioneer missionary to China, put it, assures one that the final outcome will be good. It may not even be faith that a certain thing will come out as we hope, but rather faith in God, his wisdom and providence, with confidence that the outcome will be satisfactory. To have such faith one must look to God and not to his trouble. When Peter looked at the waves, rather than at his Master, his faith failed (Matt. 14:30). In Christ we find God, according to John 14:9; in God we find Christ, according to John 14:1; it works both ways.

ii. *Security* is in the future of every believer (v. 2). In a winsome word pic-

---

[3] One of the characteristics of the Bodmer Papyrus II of John (c. A.D. 200) is that it often has the verbal ending of -etai when the context calls for etc. Examples occur in 14:1, 3, 7, 8, 11 and 12. This can be accounted for if one assumes that the scribe was writing while another was reading the words to be copied. The pronunciation of these endings was almost identical.

4 And whither I go ye know the way.

---

fully escorted to his eternal home. And since Jesus is impartial, each can claim the same promise for himself. At the second advent believers are assured of a new body, suitable for dwelling on the new earth (Rom. 8:22).

**Where I am there ye may be also.** The fellowship between Jesus and the believer is both eschatological (as here) and personal (as in 14:23; 17:21). "He himself conducts them to Himself" (MRV). The good translation therefore is "I will take you along to myself."

**I come again** is present tense as the ASV indicates, not future as the KJV and RSV imply.[4] The emphasis therefore is upon "his continual coming and presence by the Holy Spirit" (MRV).

**Will receive you unto myself.** The verb *paralēpsomai* (receive) is future as the ASV correctly indicates. As the tense usage here indicates, Christ is continuously present with the believer all through life, he comes again and again; but at the end of this life he welcomes the believer into the presence of his Father.

**4 And whither I go ye know the way** is a literal rendering of the shorter of two alternative readings The KJV and ASVm follow the longer reading in which "know" appears twice; the longer reading is clearer but has less textual warrant. On the longer reading (KJV, ASVm) the meaning would be that the disciples know both Jesus' destination and the way he will take to reach it. The shorter reading probably means essentially the same thing but is less explicit; it seems like an abbreviation. The longer reading may well be a correction of the original text preserved in Bodmer II, B, and Y. "The correction eases the grammar, and explains the double question of Thomas" (Hoskyns, p. 456).

---

ture Jesus portrays the Father as a king in his palace with his crown prince preparing lodging for wayfarers journeying like pilgrims to the celestial realm. In this picture we learn two things: that there are adequate accommodations for all and also that Jesus is preparing an individual lodging for each believer. It is this verse perhaps which most endears this chapter to Bible readers. The imagery is sufficiently specific to be heart-warming and sufficiently vague to leave room for imagination and faith, a happy medium between crass literalism and abstraction. It assures us that although "we do not know what the future holds we can know who holds the future."

iii. *Reunion* with Jesus (v. 3) is assured them. This is the whole goal and climax of redemption: God and man together in at-one-ment. This is expressed in Revelation 21:3, "Behold the tabernacle of God is with men and he shall dwell with them." Because "the Word became flesh and dwelt among us" we have the privilege of dwelling with the Father and with the Son forever. The "place" to which Jesus referred is more difficult to localize in the space age than it was in former generations. Then it was natural to think of heaven as above until we realize that the place "above" is in opposite directions for those in Europe and Australia. When the early Russian astronauts irreverently reported that they found no trace of God or of heaven in space, real Christians were not surprised or disturbed. They realized that heaven is more than a place in the sky, and more real than a city in the distance.

3 "Where Jesus is 'tis heaven there" — this personalizes life in the Spirit and makes it a delightful and eternal fellowship with our dearest friend, our Savior and Lord. He is the "magnet" which draws all true believers to himself (cf. 12:32). Consequently, no true believer needs to fear death, for it is an open door to an infinitely better life. It means dwelling in the midst of, and having intimate and thrilling companionship with, both heaven's and earth's choicest personalities. Rather than fear that experience, we have the sacred and sure promise of Christ that should prompt us to long eagerly for it. We are only weak and transitory

---

4 It has been suggested that this coming again is fulfilled when the believer partakes of the Eucharist; then Jesus returns as "the way, the truth, and the life." Cf. O. A. Piper, "Real Presence: John 14:1-6," *Princeton Seminary Bulletin*, 51 (Oct. 1957), pp. 16-23.

5 Thomas saith unto him, Lord, we know not whither thou goest; how know we the way?

6 Jesus saith unto him, I am the way, and the truth, and the life: no one cometh unto the Father, but by me.

---

5 Thomas' answer seems to imply a justification for the longer text in v. 4. He says in effect, "Since we do not know even your destination, how can we know the way by which you will reach it?" This is the fourth reference to Jesus' destination in the passage beginning with 13:31 (13:33, 36; 14:4, 5). Faced with the imminence of Jesus' departure from their midst they naturally wonder, "Where is he going and how will he get there?" Instead of answering directly, Jesus directs their attention to the way. "The Way" (hē hodos) was apparently the earliest name given to the Christian religion, or rather the designation first used by the Christians themselves. It is similar in meaning to "the way of the Lord" (Matt. 22:16; Mark 12:14; Luke 20:21) and to "the way of God" (Acts 18:26). It was also used in an absolute sense as a name for the Christian faith in Acts 9:2; 19:9, 23; 24:22. John 14:6 is the only passage in which Christ is said to be the way of approach to God (GA-S).

6 I am the way (egō eimi hē hodos). Here we are confronted with another of the great "I am" claims of Jesus. Again Jesus turns an abstract truth into a person-to-person confrontation. When the Jews wondered about the destruction of their temple Jesus said that he was the temple. When the Samaritan woman asked for water Jesus said he was the water. When they asked for a sign comparable to manna from heaven Jesus replied that he was the living bread. When Martha affirmed her belief in a general resurrection Jesus said, "I am the resurrection." Now he answers Thomas's question about the way by saying, I am the way.

Only in this Gospel does one encounter this characteristic of the Master's teaching. It is another evidence of a characteristic "dualism" of the Fourth Gospel, the tension between the physical and the spiritual, the abstract and the personal, the doctrinal and the Christological. While all used the same vocabulary, Jesus gave a spiritual meaning to words which others,

---

travelers here, with no hope of complete satisfaction until we reach our heavenly home. There is a whole cluster of promises in v. 3 any one of which would cause the believer to rejoice: Jesus goes, he prepares a place, he returns and ushers us into his Father's presence and his own "place." He thus holds before the anxious disciples the assurance of a reunion in the future.

### 2. THE TRUE WAY (VV. 4-6)

A natural question to follow a discussion of destination is the way to reach that destination. Thomas comes before us the second time. At first he spoke for the disciples in a manner which indicated that he had loyalty but little faith or optimism — "let us go that we may die with him" (11:16). He then thought Jerusalem and the grave would be the end of the journey but because of his loyalty he chose this rather than to remain in hiding or

renounce the way of the Lord. Now he is perplexed. He can envision little of the spiritual kingdom Jesus speaks of. With a touch of irritation perhaps he asked, "What is this way and how do we get there?" The question was sparked by Jesus' statement in v. 4 that they knew the way. Thomas challenged this statement and in effect denied it. Apparently it was difficult for Thomas to be buoyed up by the conviction of unseen reality (cf. Heb. 11:1). He was not a mystic content with meditating on the realities of the unseen. He was a practical man who was impatient unless he could deal with facts, with tangible evidence, with concrete things rather than abstractions, as his demand in 20:25 indicates. It was not so much that he doubted but that he demanded specific goals and grounds for his faith. With considerable justification he has been characterized as a critic.[a]

Thomas and the eleven apparently had

---

[a]  James H. Dunham, *John Fourteen* (New York: Fleming H. Revell, 1917), pp. 40-45.

whether believers or non-believers, understood only in the physical, literal sense.

In many non-Christian religions there is a sacred "way." In Greece it led from Eleusis to Athens, in Babylon it led through the Ishtar Gate, in Egypt it led from Thebes to Luxor or vice versa. In Egyptian religions the soul of the Pharaoh was conveyed in a sacred boat westward over the river of life (the Nile) towards sunset (Valley of the Kings). In Hellenistic religions there was also the "journey of the soul," in which they were conducted by a leader into the "Kingdom of Light" (RHS, p. 281). Some of the later Gnostic writings mentioned a way into life beyond this one.[5]

There is a rich Old Testament connotation in the term "way" (orach — 28 occurrences; derek — about 600 occurrences). The true and false "way" (orach) is contrasted in Psalm 119:15, 101, 104, 128. This metaphorical meaning is also conveyed in the synonym (derek), as in Deuteronomy. 26:17, in referring to God's commandments as "his ways." The ways of the righteous and sinners are contrasted in Psalm 1:6. God's will is called "the way" in Psalm 25:4, 9, 12; 27:11. The doctrine of "the two ways," set forth in Deuteronomy 11:26-28, cf. 30:15, is elaborated by Jeremiah (21:8) as the way of life and the way of death. Jesus used the analogy in Matthew 7:13, 14, contrasting the "way" leading to life and the "way" leading to death. In the Christian literature of the second century the doctrine of "the two ways" became even more prominent. The contrast between "the way of light" and "the way of darkness" is set forth in considerable detail.[6] The so-called "Teaching of the Twelve Apostles" contains the same contrast.[7]

While the disciples are wondering about the way to God, Jesus is saying that "the Way" is actually embodied in their midst; it was something far more than a thoroughfare.

I am the truth (alētheia). While important in Greek thought truth is also important in Hebrew thought. Aletheia is the common translation (LXX) of emeth (אמת), a term which occurs 126 times in the O. T. (TWNT, I, 233). There it refers to right speech (Deut. 22:20; 13:17; 17:4). This would be its domi-

---

two questions, one uttered, the other unexpressed. Thomas asked where Jesus was going; the other unspoken question was, "What shall we do when you are gone?"[b] Jesus, in his answer, pointed to the way in which they were to go; they were to follow his steps (cf. I Pet. 2:21). All ways which lead to reality converge in the one true way of Jesus Christ. Our destiny is linked with the way of Christ. On the one hand our discernment of the true way is dependent upon its relation to universal ways, all of which converge in one Divine Way. As Hort puts it, "The way of man is known only so far as the way of God is known. To learn by experience the identity of the two ways is to learn the supreme lesson of life."[c] In thus presenting himself Jesus was saying that he was more than a guide, or an example, or a creed, or even a destination; he is actually the portal, the door, the very presence of God. He is the one who reclines as John did, but in the bosom of the Father and manifests the nature of God; indeed he embodies God (1:18).

In the second place we notice that Jesus is the right and true way to the Father. Sophisticated persons often think the way of Christ is antiquated and naïve. Hence they seek truth and reality in more elaborate ways, or in ways which seem more direct and less laborious. The ancient Gnostics did likewise. They thought the simple gospel of Jesus was adequate for the average believer who lived on faith. But for the more sophisticated Gnostics, who lived on the "higher" plane of knowledge, there needed to be something more elaborate than Jesus and his teachings. Modern "Gnostics" likewise often think that Jesus is good, as far as he goes, but that something more intellectually and aesthetically satisfying is needed. Paul knew of such people when he wrote to the Colossians (1:19; 2:9; 17-19). To them he emphasized that God's fullness dwells in Christ and that the believer who has

[5] R. G. Hippolytus, Refut. V. 10; Hermes (M-M, p. 438).
[6] The Epistle of Barnabas, XIX, K. Lake, tr., Apostolic Fathers (Loeb), II, 401-407.
[7] Didache, I. 1, 2; ibid., p. 309.
[b] F. J. A. Hort, The Way, the Truth and the Life (Cambridge: Macmillan & Co., 1938), p. 17.
[c] Loc. cit

nant meaning in any language. The kinship therefore between truth and the *Logos* is at once apparent. In the O. T., truth often means the right way, the way of God (Ps. 25:5, 10; 43:3). Especially interesting is the fact that truth is often personified, as in Psalm 85:10, "mercy and truth are met together" (cf. Isa. 59:14; Ps. 86:11; 89:14). Often truth is linked with mercy (as in Prov. 14: 22; 20:28; Hos. 4:1) and with righteousness (Zech. 8:8).

Truth is one of the great words in John's Gospel, one of its distinctive features. The frequency and importance of this term is one reason why some scholars think the dominant external influence on this Gospel is Hellenistic. The Greeks made much of truth. Parmenides (c. 500 B.C.) wrote in praise of "truth" in contrast to mere opinion.

The view of Bauer and others that "truth" and kindred ideas are taken from Hellenistic and Oriental systems which rivaled or were distortions of Christianity seems not sustained by evidence, especially recent evidence. The parallels are indeed interesting. The Mandean writings do speak of the related ideas of the way, the truth and the life.[8] In a rare usage Isis is called "truth" in a text from Menuthis, a village in northern Egypt.[9]

The recently published "Gospel of Truth" has some similar passages also.[10] In this "gospel," as in other Gnostic writings, the "salvation" sought is not from sin but from ignorance, or, as here, from forgetfulness. The close connection between the Father, the Logos and the Holy Spirit is also seen here: "Truth is the mouth of the father. His tongue is the Holy Spirit, who joins him to truth. . . ."[11] Also, as in other Gnostic systems, "salvation" or "knowledge" is not available to "whosoever will" but only to the "perfect," to the "elect." These parallels are

---

Christ lacks nothing (Col. 2:10). John said the same thing in different words (John 1:14-18). Only in Christ do we encounter "all the fullness (*plerōma*) of God."

Not only is Jesus Christ the Way; he is the *only* Way. Like the monotheism of the Old Testament the way of Christ is not one of several legitimate ways but the only way. No N. T. writer is more insistent on this than John. Both implicitly, as in John 5:40, or explicitly, as in John 10:7, 8, the claim is made that no one comes to the Father except by way of the Son (cf. Acts 4:12). This sounds offensive to many modern ears, conditioned to an easy tolerance in religion. To visitors in the Buddhist temple near Honolulu it sounds very plausible to hear the guide explain that "there are many roads to the top of the mountain; Buddhism is one of them." Why cannot Christianity be this tolerant? Would it not have more influence among the great religions of the Orient if Christianity sought to supplement rather than supplant rival faiths?

The argument is very plausible to many. But Christianity, like the high monotheism from which it came, believes that only one true God implies and requires "one Lord, one faith, one baptism." Polytheistic religions are logically tolerant, monotheistic faiths logically intolerant. The premise of one true God carries with it the corollary of one true faith. The Christian modification of the Buddhist proverb would be, "There are many ways which appear to lead to the top of the mountain but only one reaches it" (cf. Matt. 7:13, 14). It is the conviction that Jesus is the *only Way* which has challenged Christian witnesses to blanket the earth with the gospel. In spite of the apparent handicap of this alleged intolerance, Christianity, while not the oldest of the religions of the world, is the strongest numerically and by far the most influential.

In this paragraph, the concept of *way* seems to be fundamental, truth and life being subordinate ideas. It would be similar to saying "the true and living way"

---

[8] Mand. Liturg. S. 77, cited by W. Bauer, *op. cit.*, p. 180.
[9] Oxyrhynchus Papyri XI, No. 1380, cited by Deissmann, *op. cit.*, p. 76.
[10] "The gospel of truth is joy to those who have received from the Father of truth the gift of knowing him by the power of the Logos, . . . who is in the thought and mind of the Father; he it is who is called, 'The Saviour,' since that is the name of the work which he must do for the redemption of those who have not known the Father. . . . That is the gospel of him whom they seek. . . . He enlightened them [and] gave [them] a path. And that path is the truth which he taught them" — ("The Gospel of Truth," tr. by W. W. Isenberg, in *Gnosticism*, R. M. Grant, ed. [New York: Harper, 1961], pp. 146f.).
[11] *Ibid.*, p. 152.

interesting from the standpoint of comparative religion, but throw little light on the Fourth Gospel. They are much later than this Gospel and perhaps were influenced by it. The significance of these parallels is that they display the author's awareness of both Jewish and Hellenistic currents of thought and his conviction that all the best in both converge in Jesus Christ. In contrast to contemporary thought, "the way" is not a doctrine, or system of ethics or methodology, but a person. The "truth" is not a course in logic but focuses in a person.[12]

"Truth" is linked with grace (*charis*) in John 1:14, 17 and with the Spirit in 4:23; 16:13; 14:17; 15:26; 16:13; I John 4:6; 5:6. In John 1:17 the truth is mediated *through* Christ and here Christ *is* the truth. Thus, truth becomes incarnate in Christ. Both John and Jesus bore witness to the truth (5:33; 8:45; 16:7) and this truth emancipates (8:32). The believer who is acquainted with Christ, by virtue of this fact, knows the truth (8:32) and practices it (3:21). Consequently, he stands in the truth (8:44) and is, in fact, of the truth (18:37; cf.

I John 2:21; 3:19: A-G). All this was beyond the scope of a worldly man like Pilate (18:38). Truth is equated with God's Word which sanctifies (17:17; 15:3). Thus, in Christ Jesus, the Logos of God, and the Truth of God merge and are embodied.[13]

**I am the life.** Life is the ultimate goal. In a journey it is important to find the right way at the outset; it is necessary to continue in the way by means of the truth, and perseverance in this leads to the goal of life eternal.[14] Jesus had made this affirmation before. He said that he came to transmit life from the Father to the believer (3:16); to give life directly (5:25, 40); to surrender his own life that others may have life (10:15; 12:24); and that he was himself the embodiment of life (11:25; 14:6).[15]

**No one cometh unto the Father but by me.** That Jesus is not merely *a* way, but *the* way, the *only* way to God is consistently stressed in this Gospel: "Except ye believe that I am he, ye shall die in your sins" (8:24); "He that obeyeth not the Son shall not see life; but the wrath of God abideth on him" (3:36). The

---

(cf. Heb. 10:20-22). But here the emphasis is more personal; Jesus not only *shows* the way and *leads* the way but he *is* the Way. Such a confrontation should cause one to respond with "a true heart" (Heb. 10:22) and thus find life.

**I am the truth** is one of the boldest affirmations one could make. To thoughtful Greeks nothing was more desirable than the truth. When devout Hebrews thought of truth they thought also of God; when they worshipped God they believed they were loyal to the ultimate truth of the universe. Jesus not only *spoke* the truth, as he had often asserted (8:14, 40, 45; 16:7) but he *is* the Truth. Truth is a unity. There is not one truth in the realm of physical science and another truth in the moral and spiritual realm with no possibility of reconciliation. The device of dividing science and faith into two separate compartments, and abandoning any attempt at reconciliation,

is neither a biblical nor a true solution. The universe is essentially monistic rather than pluralistic and truth transcends the little parochialisms which often seem contradictory. Such a conclusion lies in the realm of faith, rather than in science and is not subject to laboratory demonstration. Instances, however, in which apparent contradictions have been reconciled by further discoveries are so frequent that the confidence that ultimately the unity of truth will be apparent rests on inductive reasoning rather than upon credulity alone.

Truth is higher and more commanding than creed or orthodoxy. All must ultimately yield to truth. How can one find the truth and recognize it when he finds it? Jesus declared simply that in him, and only in him, we find truth or ultimate reality. Those who reject this have not found an acceptable substitute. Those who believe and obey discover the truth of Jesus' words. Not only by the theoreti-

---

[12] D. Th. Heckel, *Wahrheit* (Helsinki: Akateeminen Kirjakauppa, 1944), p. 84.
[13] Vos distinguishes between *veracious*, or conceptual truth (e.g. John 1:9; 4:23; 14:6) and *veritable*, or divine truth (e.g., John 3:33; 4:37): Geerhardus Vos, "True and Truth in Johannine Writings," *The Biblical Review*, Oct., 1927, pp. 507-510.
[14] Heckel, *op. cit.*, p. 179.
[15] See "Excursus" on "Life," Introduction, p. 30f.

7 If ye had known me, ye would have known my Father also: from henceforth ye know him, and have seen him.

8 Philip saith unto him, Lord, show us the Father, and it sufficeth us.

9 Jesus saith unto him, Have I been so long time with you, and dost thou not know me, Philip? he that hath seen me hath seen the Father; how sayest thou, Show us the Father?

---

alternative is consistently held by N. T. writers to be eternal punishment (Matt. 25:46). This exclusiveness receives further elaboration in the next verse.

7 If ye had known me, ye would have known my Father also. Sinaiticus, Vaticanus and Bodmer II read, "If ye have known . . . ye will know my Father also," thus avoiding the impression that the disciples had not known Jesus up to this time.

8 Lord, show us the Father, was Philip's rather natural response to Jesus' concluding remark, ye . . . have seen him. In 1:18 we are reminded that "no one has seen God at any time." The reason for this is given in 4:24, "God is a Spirit." It is not clear in what sense Philip expected this request to be answered. The verb show (deiknymi) is used in connection with apocalyptic visions (Rev. 1:1; 4:1; 17:1; 21:9; 22:1); with making something known (I Cor. 12:31); and with an explanation (Jas. 2:18; Matt. 16:21). It is probable that the latter connotation of the term is the most relevant here;

Philip asked for an explanation or manifestation.

9 He that hath seen (heōrakōs) me hath seen (heōraken) the Father. This is another categorical statement which must have startled the disciples into a vivid realization of the privilege that had been theirs for the past thirty months or more. The statement is consistent with the declaration of the Prologue — one of the profoundest statements of the Gospel — "we beheld his glory, glory as of the only begotten of the Father" (1:14). It is also consistent with the other frequent assertions of the close association of Jesus and the Father throughout this Gospel.

It is significant that the verb for seeing appears twice here in the perfect tense, first as the participle and then as a finite verb. The perfect tense denotes permanency, something that happened and remained that way. Here it signifies a present condition due to having seen the Father. Theirs was not just a glance at Jesus, but repeated sight of him day after day, year after year. So they not only

---

cal test but also by the empirical test Jesus proves to be truth in its ultimate expression.

There seems to be a chronological sequence in the words "way, truth, and life." The pilgrimage to the city of God requires the one right way; this leads to the truth; and this, in turn, gives life. Jesus had given a similar sequence in 8:30, 31. The acceptance and continuance in Jesus' word, that is his doctrine or teaching, leads to the possession of truth. The possession of truth leads, in turn, to spiritual freedom, i.e., to freedom from sin (8:34) and, positively, to spiritual life.

In John prominence is given to the contrast between truth and falsehood, between Christ and the devil. In 8:44 this contrast is very specific and the devil is called "the father of liars" and the father

of Jesus' enemies. In I John 2:4 a liar is one devoid of truth, i.e., the commandments. In Daniel 8:12, as I John 2:20, 27; II John 1, 2, truth is the equivalent of sound doctrine. This revelation of truth comes by Jesus Christ (John 8:40, 45) in contrast to the error which has its source in the devil or the antichrist (8:44; I John 2:22). The Paraclete is he who helps distinguish truth from error (I John 2:27; John 16:13). In Christ therefore one finds the truth and the Holy Spirit helps him abide therein.

It follows that the source of true doctrine is in Christ Jesus and that the Spirit-filled life is essential to maintain a clear grasp of the difference between spiritual truth and error. John does not say that intellect alone can assure a grasp of the truth. Many do not believe that Jesus speaks the truth when he says, "I am the

10 Believest thou not that I am in the Father, and the Father in me? the words that I say unto you I speak not from myself: but the Father abiding in me doeth his works.

11 Believe me that I am in the Father, and the Father in me: or else believe me for the very works' sake.

12 Verily, verily, I say unto you, He that believeth on me, the works that I do shall he do also; and greater *works* than these shall he do; because I go unto the Father.

---

know what he was like but also what God is like. Jesus was and is a permanent picture of the God "who changeth not."[16]

10 The question here, since it is preceded by the negative (*ou*), indicates that an affirmative answer is expected: "You believe (*pisteueis*, pres. ind.), do you not, that I am in the Father and the Father in me?" The thought is further clarified by the statement, **the Father abiding in me doeth his works.**[17] Jesus' critics had attributed these "mighty acts" to an indwelling demon; Jesus attributes them to the indwelling Father-God. Thus the issue was drawn, the same evidence resulted in two contrasting explanations, the true and the false.

11 As if to clinch the preceding statements Jesus said, **Believe me . . . or else believe me** (*pisteute*, pres. ind., "keep on believing") "on account of the works themselves" (*auta*). In these statements

Jesus reflects sorrow that belief is not forthcoming more readily. He challenges them to believe first on the basis that he said it, and second, in the light of the evidence provided by "the works." The latter probably includes the miracles primarily but also his total manner of life — he was constantly "going about doing good" (Acts 10:38). The good deeds were not limited to the miraculous, but it was the miracles which had the greater apologetic and evidential significance; they afforded evidence that Jesus was not only a good man but God's man.

12 **Greater works than these shall ye do.** The expression **greater works does not necessarily mean greater in quality** but rather greater in quantity, as evidenced by the results of Peter's preaching in Jerusalem and Paul's effectiveness in city after city on his mission tours. Jesus' converts were numbered by the scores,

---

truth." They think acceptance of Christ and a creed will hinder them from an "unbiased" grasp of the "truth." They fear committal lest they become "prejudiced." They wonder on what grounds the claims of Jesus are more valid than those of Mohammed, Joseph Smith, Buddha or Karl Marx, and fear that once they commit themselves they cannot find out. By attempting to be open-minded, unbiased, and objective they refuse commitment. The fallacy in this is that they unconsciously commit themselves to something else; no mind remains in a vacuum. They become rebels. Jesus claims that commitment to him, far from prejudicing one

and fencing him in intellectually, will actually illuminate and emancipate him (John 8:32, 36). But the commitment must *precede* illumination and emancipation; the sequence, as set forth repeatedly in this Gospel, is come and then see. The kind of intellectual honesty demanded by Jesus is that we welcome the light and ratify it by self-involvement, by "walking in the truth" (II John 3) or "in the light" (I John 1:7). The result is not blind prejudice, or bondage in intellectual and creedal fetters, but a clear-eyed, fearless, inquisitive mental and moral attitude toward truth in its totality. This quest for truth should be centered, not

---

[16] The use of the perfect tense in the Fourth Gospel is somewhat unusual. "For John there is an average of 3.64 perfects to a page. Of the other three gospels Matthew has .71 per page; Mark 1. 13 per page; Luke 1.44 per page. . . . Thus it would appear that John's fondness for the perfect was above the average." M. S. Enslin, "The Perfect Tense in the Fourth Gospel," *Journal of Biblical Literature*, Vol. LV, Part II (June, 1936), pp. 121-131. Enslin rightly interpreted the distinctive force of the perfect tense by pointing out that "it stresses the existing result" of an action or deed. He gave John 18:37 as an example, where Jesus, in talking with Pilate, said, "I have come (*elēlytha*, perf. ind.) into the world." "His coming was not transient but unending." John evaluated and stressed the abiding results of Jesus' teachings, deeds and death by his exceptionally frequent use of the perfect tense. The use of *anabebēken* (ascended) is interpreted correctly by Enslin in its context: "No one has ever gone up to heaven to abide there."

[17] This is an instance where the participle may be used to express instrumentality or means.

13 And whatsoever ye shall ask in my name, that will I do, that the Father may be glorified in the Son.

14 If ye shall ask anything in my name, that will I do.

---

the apostles' converts were numbered by the thousands. The explanation for this lies in the fact that Jesus went **unto the Father.** The risen and ascended Christ is able, through the Holy Spirit, to release infinite life-changing power through his devoted followers. He directs his campaign for world redemption from the very presence of God as is stated in Matthew 28:20.

The theme of Jesus' *destination* is again mentioned here. In 8:14, 22 he had told the Jews that he was going where they could not follow. In 13:33, 36; 14:2-5 he tells the disciples that he is going to the Father and that they are to follow him there. His departure means that (1) he will be there to receive them when they arrive and (2) meanwhile his presence there will make it possible for them to do "greater works" even than he did. The church "is not promised 'tasks equal to its power, but power equal to its tasks!'"[18]

**13 Whatsoever ye shall ask in my name, that will I do.** This sweeping promise should be linked, in the mind of the reader, with the implication that the petitioner must be fully yielded and at the disposal of Christ. *He is able if we are* willing. If these conditions were met the answers to prayers "in his name" would be more frequent. The condition is a continuous self-surrender, on the negative side, and, on the positive side, obedience. The formula **in my name** is similar to the Father's name mentioned in 5:43; 10:25 (Bauer, *op. cit.,* p. 181). Apparently, as Jesus did his works in the name of the Father, so the disciples are to pray and work in Jesus' name. The phrase in these contexts means "by the authority of" or "in harmony with the will of," or "by the sanction of." It is far more than a conventional suffix to one's prayer (cf. 16:24, 26; 15:16). It is characterized and conditioned by our abiding in him and our being filled with the Holy Spirit.[19]

---

primarily in a creedal formula, but in a Person. When Christ is the central, dominant Object of our quest, other things will fall into proper perspective and relative importance.

**I am the life.** Jesus not only *gives* life, he *is* the life. The primary meaning is divine life, eternal life, spiritual life. The secondary meaning is everything that is wholesome in human existence. Once Christ is at the center of our lives, all facets of our total existence are properly integrated and correlated. Some values will be subordinated to others; Christ will be the touchstone of values. A warm, personal, vital relationship to the living Christ is the best assurance of knowing the truth and of finding the freedom which results. This is life on its highest level.

As E. Stanley Jones has pointed out, life is on four levels: the level of *instinct,* experienced by animals; the level of *duty,* experienced by most people, including nominal Christians; the level of *grace,* ex-

perienced by those who are born of the Spirit; and the level of *love,* experienced by those Christians who have been made "perfect in love."[d] Jesus came to give such life, and in abundance (John 10: 10). The paragraph ends with another one of Jesus' claims to be the *only* way to the Father. The statement indicates the centrality of *the Way* in this context. As in ch. 10, so here, Jesus is not one of several ways but *the Way.* "Without the way there is no going; without the truth there is no knowing; without the life there is no living. I am the way which thou shouldst pursue; the truth which thou shouldst believe; the life which thou shouldst hope for." Thus spake the greatest of the Brethren of the Common Life.[e]

### 3. UNION OF FATHER AND SON (14:7-11)

In this paragraph Jesus stresses the fact that a knowledge of God the Father and a knowledge of Jesus Christ the Son are

[18] Strachan, *op. cit.,* p. 283 ("Greater works" are also mentioned in 1:50; 5:20).
[19] J. F. Walvoord, "Prayer in the name of Jesus," *Bibliotheca Sacra* (Oct., 1934), p. 463.
[d] Listed in a sermon heard by this writer.
[e] Thomas à Kempis, *Imitation of Christ,* iii, 56.

15 If ye love me, ye will keep my commandments.

16 And I will pray the Father, and he shall give you another Comforter, that he may be with you for ever,

---

15 If ye love (*agapate*, pres. subj.) me, ye will keep (*tērēsete*, fut. ind.) my commandments, or, "If you continue loving me you will continue to keep my commandments." To Jesus love was more than a sentiment; it was rather an expression of loyalty manifested by habitual obedience to him. A similar declaration is seen in I John 5:3, "This is love for God (objective genitive), namely, that we habitually keep (*tērōmen*, pres. subj.) his commandments."

16 I shall pray (*erōtēsō*, "petition, make request of") the Father. There are at least five synonyms for "pray" in the New Testament. By far the most widely used term is *proseuchomai*, one which occurs approximately 86 times in the N. T. and 54 times in the Synoptics, but is not found once in the Johannine literature (M-G). None of the other four appear in the Gospel, Epistles of John, or the Revelation except for one occurrence in III John. This term *erōtaō* appears in John a total of 30 times out of a total of 69 times in the entire N. T. and 23 times in the Synoptics. Another synonym

(*aiteō*) appears in this Gospel 11 times but only of prayer of man to God, not of Jesus to the Father. Of the 30 times *erōtaō* occurs in John it describes Jesus' prayer to the Father in six occurrences. It indicates that Jesus spoke of making requests of the Father as one man would make request of another. But this term was not used of the requests made by the disciples to God. Thus, it connotes intimacy in Jesus' relation to the Father, a point John stresses more than do the Synoptists.

Another Comforter (*paraklētos*). This term, peculiar to John, occurs only five times in the New Testament (John 14:16, 26; 15:26; 16:7; I John 2:1). It is derived from two words, *para* ("to the side of") and *klētos* (called). It was used of an intimate friend who advised one according to his need; it would be to comfort, counsel, or even rebuke. Emperors had "parakletes." Each of our nation's presidents has had several. The Paraclete we have is not only our intimate friend, guiding and counseling us, but also is the intimate friend of Jesus and God. He

---

mutually interdependent. To know the Son is to know the Father, and vice versa.

7 This verse can be paraphrased: "If you have had an experiential (*ginōskō*) knowledge of me, you have had a direct personal acquaintance (*oida*) with the Father also. And from now on you have this experiential knowledge (*ginōskō*) of the Father and will have an abiding mental and spiritual perception (*horaō*) of him." The knowledge learned by experience with Jesus is the basis for a direct, personal knowledge of the Father and this in turn results in an abiding insight or perception of God. This is to be understood in the light of John 1:18 — which states that one cannot see God except as he is manifested in his Son. We have here one of the last glimpses in this Gospel of Jesus as the Light of the World who reveals the Father. Philip was still unsatisfied and blundered into a question which seems innocent enough but which

reflected the slowness of the disciples to grasp what the Master had been saying, not only in the preceding sentence but through the previous three years. In response Jesus repeated what he had said many times to the Jews, namely, that when they saw the Son at work they were also witnessing the Father in action (John 5:17, 19, 36; 9:33; 10:32; cf. 3:2). The same is true of Jesus' words; they are in reality the words of God (cf. 5:37). Thus Father and Son are united in both word and work. This calls for belief (v. 11) and for commitment.

Why were the disciples so slow to perceive this? The answer is that it took some time before their minds could grasp the full implications. Amid the rapidly moving events, they could only with difficulty grasp the full import of the fact that Jesus of Nazareth, their countryman and neighbor, was actually a living demonstration of Almighty God both by what

17 *even* the Spirit of truth: whom the world cannot receive; for it beholdeth him not, neither knoweth him: ye know him; for he abideth with you, and shall be in you.

18 I will not leave you desolate: I come unto you.

19 Yet a little while, and the world beholdeth me no more; but ye behold me: because I live, ye shall live also.

---

mediates God to us, and through him divine help and power are made available to us. While Jesus was on earth only a few years, his successor is always present (*eis ton aiona*, "into eternity"). Only believers have access to his help. The term other (*allos*) is not "other" in the sense of being different in kind (*heteros*). The distinction is well demonstrated in Galatians 1:6 and I Corinthians 15:40. *Heteros* differentiates while *allos* enumerates.[20]

17 **He abideth with you, and shall be in you.** Since he makes his home in our hearts, we are never without heavenly comfort and hope. These words are probably both personal and eschatological. In support of the latter is consistency with the Synoptics and Acts as an interpretation of Joel 2:28, 29 and also John 7:39. There are five of these "Paraclete" passages in this Gospel. They form the heart of what is most distinctive in the Johannine doctrine of the Holy Spirit. (See Introduction.)

18 **I will not leave you orphans, or desolate.** This continues the theme of the Master's departure which was introduced in 13:31. It strengthens the case of those who regard the primary function of the Paraclete as that of bringing comfort or consolation. Noteworthy here is the fact that Jesus and the Paraclete are almost equated in vv. 16, 18. In v. 16 he says another Comforter will come; in v. 18 he says he will come (cf. I John 2:1). The meaning apparently is that Jesus will return in some measure after his resurrection but that at Pentecost, when the Spirit is given in fullness, Jesus will return in full measure to the believer. The connection between Jesus and the Spirit is again illustrated in Peter's message at the house of Cornelius (Acts 10:40-48); when Peter preached Christ the Spirit came upon the believers. At Pentecost Jesus came to the church only; at the Parousia he will appear to the world.

19 **The world seeth** (*theōreō*) **me no more,** an obvious reference to his departure from the public at the cross. His resurrection appearances were not to the public but to believers only (guards excepted). One may wonder why he did not

---

he said and by what he did. After several months exposure Jesus now expected the disciples to believe him.

#### 4. OBEDIENCE, THE TEST OF DISCIPLE-SHIP (14:12-17)

##### a. The Power of Prayer (vv. 12-14)

This is the first of a series of statements about prayer that are almost breath-taking in their sweep. The good works, including the miracles, which Jesus has been doing, need not cease. Jesus and the Father will continue such work through the disciples. The only condition is that they ask in Jesus' name. They are to sanctify his name. Later, Peter did this, and the lame

man was healed at the temple (Acts 3:6); Moses failed to sanctify the name of God on one occasion and was severely punished (Num. 20:11, 12; Deut. 3:26).[†] The Father has committed all authority (*exousia*) into the hand of his Son (cf. Matt. 28:18; John 14:10; Acts 1:7). This is available to the disciples also if they use it in the name of Jesus. It is not an authority, however, which can be simply asserted, but one which must be requested. This means much more than adding the formula "in Jesus' name" as a suffix to our prayers. The "name" is not a tool to be manipulated; rather it stands for a Being who merits our worship and obedience.

---

[20] In much of N.T. usage these adjectives are used synonymously but the distinction made above normally holds true. See E. D. Burton, *Galatians* (ICC), pp. 420-422. With Paul "*heteros* suggested difference of kind more distinctly than did *allos* and the latter, in contrast with *heteros*, signified simply numerical non-identity" (p. 422). Here *allos paraklēton* means "other than yourself," E. A. Abbott, *Johannine Vocabulary*, p. 612.
[†] Chrysostom, "Homily 74," *op. cit.*, p. 297.

20 In that day ye shall know that I am in my Father, and ye in me, and I in you.

21 He that hath my commandments, and keepeth them, he it is that loveth me: and he that loveth me shall be loved of my Father, and I will love him, and will manifest myself unto him.

22 Judas (not Iscariot) saith unto him, Lord, what is come to pass that thou wilt manifest thyself unto us, and not unto the world?

23 Jesus answered and said unto him, If a man love me, he will keep my word: and my Father will love him, and we will come unto him, and make our abode with him.

---

appear in public as Lazarus did and thus win more adherents. Instead, he chose the method of private appearances and the placing of heavy reliance on witnesses. It was this unique opportunity of seeing Christ alive after his public death which gave the apostles their extraordinary power and influence.

20 **In that day ye shall know** (*gnōsesthe*) or "recognize" — the day referring to the time of the general effusion of the Holy Spirit (cf. 7:39) following Jesus' ascension (cf. 16:23, 26). In this Gospel the eschatological aspect is subordinated to the moral and spiritual aspect of "the last day"; the emphasis is not so much on a certain date as upon an imminent spiritual experience.[21] The **know** means spiritual awareness comparable to the knowledge that the apostle prayed might be the experience of the church (Eph. 1:17).

21 **He that hath my commandments, and keepeth them,** (pres. act. part., "continues keeping them") "that one continues loving me"; . . . and **he that reciprocates shall be loved of my Father. Will manifest;** the word **manifest** (*emphanizen*) is found only here in John; his favorite term is the cognate word *phaneroun,* the meaning of which is similar and yet somewhat less emphatic. Note the sequence: obedience demonstrates love and this in turn leads to insight (cf. 7:17).

22 **Judas** was a very common name in Israel; it was the Hellenized form of the name of the patriarch Judah. This was the third expression of perplexity on the part of the disciples (cf. 14:5, 8). Doubtless Judas could not understand the nature of an appearance which would not be observable to non-believers. Thus, the sense is not eschatological, as Judas assumed, but spiritual and inward, similar to the manifestation in v. 21 (cf. I John 3:2).

23 **We will . . . make our abode with him.** The idea of the Father and the Son dwelling in the believer is breath-taking and makes this one of the most precious verses in the whole Bible for the Christian.

---

### b. The Mission of the *Paraclete* (vv. 15-18)

No N. T. writer emphasizes more than does John the extent of God's love for the world (cf. 3:16; I John 3:1). Nor does any writer rival John in the emphasis on obedience as the test of love (cf. I John 3:13-24). As is often painfully obvious, there exists a gap between profession and the practice of love. Under the old covenant the important thing was to obey; under the new covenant the most important word is love. In John we find the synthesis. It is not duty alone or affection alone, but both. The commandments channel love and define it, while love lifts duty above the level of servitude.

The Paraclete apparently is the new factor in the God-man relationship. Under the old covenant this relationship was one of "this do, and thou shalt live"; under the new covenant it becomes "live, and thou shalt do." The promised Comforter, or Helper, will bring love and obedience into fruition. The world will not recognize the Holy Spirit because the natural man receives not the things of the Spirit (I Cor. 2:14; cf. John 3:19; 12:43). The musician can find far more to appreciate at a concert than can a layman who knows little about music. The trained ear can hear sounds which the ordinary ear will miss.[g] So the world will know of the Spirit only through the lives of those in whom the Spirit dwells.

---

[21] E. K. Lee, *op. cit.,* 164-168,

[g] While Bishop J. W. Pickett and his son were walking along a road in India, the boy suddenly stopped and discovered a beetle near the road. He alone heard the beetle because beetles were his hobby.

24 He that loveth me not keepeth not my words: and the word which ye hear is not mine, but the Father's who sent me.

25 These things have I spoken unto you, while *yet* abiding with you.

26 But the Comforter, *even* the Holy Spirit, whom the Father will send in my name, he shall teach you all things, and bring to your remembrance all that I said unto you.

27 Peace I leave with you; my peace I give unto you: not as the world giveth, give I unto you. Let not your heart be troubled, neither let it be fearful.

---

It is similar to the doctrine of the witness of the Spirit (cf. Rom. 8:16). While the Holy Spirit is not mentioned in this passage, the indwelling implies his presence. It is similar to the Pauline phrase "in Christ." Our bodies are temples of God (I Cor. 3:16f).

**24 He that loveth me not,** i.e., does not continue loving, **keepeth not my words,** the negative side of v. 15. This is another of the frequent assertions in John that love will inevitably issue in obedience (cf. v. 15, 21, 23, 24; 15:10; I John 1:6; 2:3-6; 3:7, 17, 18, 24; 4:20). Again also we encounter the oft-repeated emphasis on the close relationship between Father and Son.

**26 The Comforter, even the Holy Spirit.** Here for the first and only time the Paraclete is identified as the Holy Spirit. Here as in v. 15 the Spirit comes from the Father. Jesus Christ was the sent one in 10:36; here it is the Holy Spirit who is sent. Here his function is to teach the disciples and to refresh their minds as to what Christ taught them. Peter, as

an illustration, was taught very definitely in his housetop vision when he was bidden to "kill and eat" unclean animals (Acts 10:9-16). The Holy Spirit also forbade the apostle Paul to preach in the province of Asia (and led him instead to go to Europe [Acts 16:6-10]). No doubt this promise was fulfilled to the letter as the New Testament writers undertook their task of sharing with their readers their recollection of what Jesus said and did, thus preserving the memory for succeeding generations. It is a reminder of 2:22 and provides additional evidence that the coming of the Paraclete was conditioned on the departure of Jesus.

**27 Peace I leave with you.** The legacy of peace is given in a manner comparable to the ordinary custom of saying "farewell" in Bible lands to this day. The Arabs say, *"Mar Salami,"* and the Jews, *"Shalom,"* both meaning, "Peace to you." Peace is said to be one of the fruits of the Spirit in Galatians 5:22, while here it is a gift of Jesus. It is another indication of the intimate connection, both

---

In these words Jesus raised the anticipation of the disciples so that they could be in a frame of mind to seek the fullness of the Spirit. The Holy Spirit is no gatecrasher; he comes only when welcomed. The disciples were being conditioned to expect and to welcome his indwelling. As additional reassurance Jesus explicitly promised to return to them personally. This promise has several fulfillments: he appeared after his resurrection to his disciples; he appeared in the presence of the Holy Spirit at Pentecost; he appeared to Paul and others in times of crisis (Acts 18:9; cf. 27:33); he returns in the Eucharist; he returns to the believer, we believe, at death; and he will return in glory at the end of this age. Is there any reason why his return is not in all of these ways, rather than in one only?

5. THE UNION OF FATHER, SON, PARACLETE AND DISCIPLES (14:19—15:11)

  a. The Tri-unity of Father, Son and Believer (vv. 19-24)

The thought of this paragraph seems to be centered around two foci: love (vv. 21, 23, 24) and unity (vv. 20, 21, 23). The viewpoint is toward the future. This will come to pass when Jesus returns to them (v. 18). It will not be a visible return (v. 19), hence it does not refer to the *parousia* at the end of the age. There is a chonological sequence here: they will *see* Jesus (after the resurrection); in the *life* of his resurrection theirs will be a living faith (I Cor. 15:13-17); and thereafter they will recognize or *know* the reciprocal indwelling of Father, Son (and Spirit). This return of the Lord is mentioned

28 Ye heard how I said to you, I go away, and I come unto you. If ye loved me, ye would have rejoiced, because I go unto the Father: for the Father is greater than I.

29 And now I have told you before it come to pass, that, when it is come to pass, ye may believe.

---

in the writings of Paul and John, between Jesus Christ and the Holy Spirit (cf. Acts 16:6, 7). This peace is set in contrast to the pseudo-peace which the world seeks to give. Because of this Jesus can repeat his assurance, first voiced in v. 1, adding, neither let it be fearful or "cowardly" (cf. Matt. 8:26; Mark 4:40; Rev. 21:8).

**28 If ye loved me, ye would have rejoiced.** If we read only this far we might think the Savior was suggesting to the disciples that they should rejoice over his impending elevation and exaltation. But he hurried on to state: **because the Father is greater than I.** Freed from bodily limitations, Christ could do more for the disciples and humanity as a whole, while in the presence of God, than he could by remaining in the flesh. Only under

such conditions could he say "all authority hath been given unto me . . . and lo, I am with you always" (Matt. 28:18-20). Their rejoicing therefore is to be based on the fact that the Father has greater resources which then will be at the disposal of the Son and through the Son to the disciples (cf. 5:17, 20, 30).

**29 I have told you before it come to pass.** From here to the end of the chapter Jesus seems to be making a summary of the preceding remarks and bringing them to a conclusion. For this reason Bultmann and others place this portion after the content of chs. 15 and 16. However, to do so breaks the continuity of 13:31 — 14:12ff. and creates more problems than it solves. Since it was customary for Jesus to teach while walking, would it not be easier to assume that 14:

---

three times in this paragraph (vv. 19, 21, 23). In this manifestation there seems to be a combination of the post-resurrection appearances (v. 19) with the infilling of the Holy Spirit (vv. 21, 23). Thus it is in harmony with Luke-Acts.

Here, as always in John, the "new commandment," or commandment given with renewed emphasis, is that obedience is on the level of love rather than of mere duty. It does not replace or evade the law, but rather fulfills and implements it. In this its most characteristic note, Christianity is distinctive among religions of the world.

There is no articulated doctrine of the Trinity in this paragraph. Instead, in anticipation of the emphasis of 17:20-26, the union of Father, Son, and believer is set forth. Yet, even here, in the context of two of the Paraclete sayings, the presence of the Holy Spirit is implied, especially in v. 21 (cf. v. 18). John was a mystic. There is no more precious verse in the whole Bible than v. 23! We can be host to the Trinity! Heavenly guests will always be in our homes if we are always keeping Christ's words, i.e., are regularly obedient. Our bodies are, as Paul put it, "temples of the Holy Spirit"

(I Cor. 3:16). The Father is mentioned here three times to drive home the point that the Father and Son are inseparable and that the one in whom the living word of Christ dwells shares in that fellowship.

**b. The Relationship of Son, Spirit, and Believer (vv. 25-31)**

The link between Jesus Christ and the disciples after the departure of Jesus' physical presence is memory plus the Holy Spirit. For believers, other than apostles, this link is the Four Gospels together with the Spirit.

25 Stress is here laid upon the spoken word of Jesus, now preserved in the canonical Gospels. Contemporary theologians who are only slightly concerned with the historical facts of Jesus' life, work and words, have little in common with the convictions of the Evangelists. Early apostolic preaching was largely concerned with "all that Jesus began both to do and to teach" (Acts 1:1). The apostles and their listeners would have had little patience with those who taught that faith need not be based on fact but could be self-generating and self-propelling. It is noteworthy here that the Holy Spirit is not given to provide a short cut to divine revelation, or to bypass "the histori-

30 I will no more speak much with you, for the prince of the world cometh: and he hath nothing in me;

31 but that the world may know that I love the Father, and as the Father gave me commandment, even so I do. Arise, let us go hence.

---

31 marks the termination of his remarks at the meal and that 15-17 is a summary of Jesus' word en route to Gethsemane? Even more probable is the suggestion of Lightfoot that this represents the conclusion of the first of three stages of instruction (the others being 15:1—16:33 and 17: 1-26) corresponding to the three events of the passion facing Jesus. This section would correspond to the passion in Gethsemane (cf. Mark 14:42; John 14:31).[22]

29 I have told you before . . . that ye may believe. Here Jesus speaks in the manner of predictive prophecy. Repeatedly in Isaiah 40—45 Jehovah states that he is the only God because he alone can accurately predict coming events (Isa. 41:23, 26, 28; 42:9; 43:9-12). The same apologetic is seen in John 1:49, where Nathaniel became a believer because of Jesus' prescience; and John 2:22, where the disciples remembered Jesus' prediction; and 2:25, where this is said to be one characteristic of Jesus. The additional miracle would later confirm the faith of the faithful. "I have spoken unto you" (eirēka hymīn) and the memory of my words remains with you." This is the force of the perfect tense in this context. There was an abiding result to his statements, more than any of that generation ever dreamed. His prophecies would soon be fulfilled both as to his cruel death and also his resurrection. Then the disciples, more than ever before, would have grounds for belief in Jesus as the Son of God and the Savior of believing mankind.

30 The prince of this world (archōn kosmou) really means the ruler of the sinful world (not the Creator, the Sustainer of the universe). This is a reference to the devil who has no authority over Jesus. Regardless of the devil and fallen humanity, Jesus would demonstrate his love for the Father by accomplishing his heaven-sent mission, by making atonement for sin by his death on the cross.

31 Arise, let us go hence. Perhaps the discourse (ch. 15-17) was completed in Gethsemane. If so, the prayer recorded by John would have preceded Jesus' agony in the Garden and his prayer "Let this cup pass." As in Ezekiel, so here, an important concern is that "the world may know." As always Jesus' concern was evangelism, and, as always, he linked prayer with action, hence — "let us go."

---

cal Jesus," but rather to underscore the importance of Jesus in the flesh by recalling his words (and deeds). Historically the Reformed tradition stresses the primacy of the written Word, the Quakers stress the primacy of the Holy Spirit, the Wesleyans stress the combination of the two, the Spirit giving illumination against the background of the Bible. The differences are in emphasis only.

27 Peace, as Jesus bestows it, is more than the absence of war, strife, worry and danger. This peace, which comes only from Jesus, is that which, according to Paul, "exceeds all understanding" (Phil. 4:7). It is not merely the absence of trouble but the positive presence of poise, joy, assurance, and calm, even amid storm.

It is one of the many joyful, enriching benefits received as a gift of the Holy Spirit (Gal. 5:22). Few generations have needed this positive possession of peace more than ours, careening as we are from the brink of one atomic holocaust to another. During the Chaldean crisis, Habakkuk found something comparable to this positive peace; he found a joyous assurance of the goodness of God in spite of outward circumstances. This peace works like the giant gyroscope in a battleship; it provides a dynamic type of stability when everything in the environment seems anything but stable. On this note of peace, a legacy underwritten by the Father, Jesus concluded the first phase of his "last words."

---

[22] R. H. Lightfoot, op. cit., p. 266-271, 277. The other sections presumably would correspond respectively to the arrest and trial (John 15-16) and to the crucifixion (John 17). Jesus spoke of these events as having already been accomplished (John 16:33; 17:4).

# CHAPTER XV

I am the true vine, and my Father is the husbandman.

## EXEGESIS

1 **I am the true vine** (*ampelos*), **and my Father is the husbandman** ("vinedresser" — RSV). The latter Greek word (*geōrgos*) means an earth (*gē*) worker (*ergon*), one who works in the ground, a farmer. The vinedresser was the *ampelourgos* (only at Luke 13:7), a subordinate office; but *geōrgos* may mean the proprietor (II Chr. 26:10 LXX), hence appropriate here. Vines and vineyards are plentiful in Palestine, and adjacent areas, and are mentioned frequently in the N. T.[1] "All these parables have in common the fact that the vineyard, or persons connected with it, represents Israel, or a section of Israel" (CKB, p. 293). In the O. T., Israel is often described as a vine.[2] Grape culture was one of the basic industries of the Judaean highlands. Recent excavations at Gibeon, by Pritchard and others, reveal that this city, located some 12 miles north of Jerusalem, exported

wine in considerable quantity. By using this analogy Jesus was not only building on a rich O. T. background but also using an analogy with which everyone was familiar.

In this passage Jesus for the last time (cf. 18:6, 8) uses the notable words "I Am." This is his last parable or analogy in this Gospel. Successively he had said "I am" the bread of life, the door, the shepherd, the resurrection and the life, the way, the truth, and now the vine. This passage represents him as the *"true* vine." The use of "true" here implies acceptance of a cardinal N. T. doctrine, the doctrine that the true Israel is not "Israel after the flesh," but rather believers in Jesus as the Christ. The concept of spiritual life emanating from Christ, just as vegetable life passes through the vine and into the branches, is one easily grasped and unforgettable. The change from the comparison of Israel as the vine to Christ as

## EXPOSITION

### c. The Parable of the Vine (15:1-11)

The emphasis in Jesus' words swings from consolation the emphasis in ch. 14, to productivity and effectiveness in service in ch. 15. The use of the metaphor of the vine here is skillfully used. It is simple, familiar, hence meaningful and unforgettable. The analogy is so apt that it frightens and at the same time fosters faith and devotion. The nation of Israel had again become like a degenerate vine, as in O. T. days.[a] Now Jesus and the Father are to ingraft and transform the old vine and make it productive, with the help of the disciples. Like the analogies of bread, water, door, and shepherd, this is a metaphor, since it

is a comparison without being labelled as such. The gardener is the Father-God, the vinestock is Jesus Christ, the branches of the vine are the disciples and the fruit corresponds to souls won by the disciples. The relation of Christ to the disciples is even more intimate than that between Christ and the Father, if the metaphor is to be pressed. Of course, no metaphor should be too elaborately explicated; like a parable, it is designed to speak one central truth. He spoke of a new relationship. Previously the disciples had been attached to Israel as "the vine of the Lord," as Israel had been depicted on Maccabean coins. Now they are attached to the *true* vine in contrast to this now-false vine of God (cf. Ps. 80:8-16). Each time the believer takes Communion he reminds himself of his union with the

[1] E.g., Matt. 12:1-9; Matt. 20:1-16; 21:28-41; Luke 13:6-9; 20:9-16; Rev. 14:15-20.
[2] Jer. 2:2; Ezek. 15:8; 19:10-14; Ps. 80:9-16; Isa. 5:1-7; Sir. 24:17; IV Macc. 1:29.
[a] Isa. 5:1-4; Jer. 2:21.

2 Every branch in me that beareth not fruit, he taketh it away: and every *branch* that beareth fruit, he cleanseth it, that it may bear more fruit.

---

the vine may have startled those who heard for the first time. Jesus Christ becomes, in this analogy, the true Israel and his disciples members of the new commonwealth.

**2 Every branch in me that beareth not fruit, he taketh it away.** The penalty for barrenness is excision, excommunication. This is seen in all of nature (Gal. 6:7; Heb. 6:7, 8; Rom. 11:21, 22) and in life. "He will . . . let out the vineyard to other tenants who will give him the fruits in their seasons" (Matt. 21:41) is the common custom of both landlords and vinedressers. People who reject the Messiah have as their penalty rejection by the Messiah. Judas, by dastardly deed and impenitent heart, was one of the rejected, broken branches.

**He cleanseth** (*kathairei*) it, is rendered better by "he prunes it" (RSV). The verb is so used in Xenephon[3] and Philo.[4] The verb occurs elsewhere in the N. T. only at Heb. 10:2 (cf. Heb. 9:14) and means "to make clean" (A-G). It also means "to purify," or "make clear" or,

in connection with a vine, "to prune by the removal of superfluous wood" as here (A-G; also GA-S). "In this passage καθαίρειν, 'to cleanse,' can hardly be distinguished from ἀποτέμνειν, 'to prune' " (JHB, II, 479).

There is a play on words between the *airei* ("takes away") and the *kathairei* ("cleanses" or "prunes") which cannot be expressed in English; the useless branches are *removed* while the good branches are *improved*. As Lagrange points out, two different operations are involved. During the winter all branches unlikely to bear fruit are removed; in addition, from the good branches parasitic shoots or suckers are also removed (MJL, p. 402). Likewise "there is a double element in the purification of the disciples: the initial purgation occasioned by the Word of Jesus (6: 63; cf. Eph. 5:26), and its conservation through the maintaining of a permanent union with Him" (Hoskyns, p. 475). Previously he had described them as having been made clean (13:10), referring to their initial union with Christ. The

---

*true* and living Vine, and testifies to his faith (I Cor. 10:16-18; 11:23-27). In this metaphor we find a Christ-mysticism which charms, instructs, invites and warns.

The structure of this paragraph is interesting. Twice Jesus repeats "I am the vine" (1, 5), twice he warns about the consequences of fruitlessness (2, 6) and thrice he exhorts them to "abide," or remain securely, in him (4, 5, 7). It appears that the analogy from nature is set forth in vv. 1-3 and the application to human life is made in vv. 4-8. This may account for the repetition, although this Gospel is not adverse to repetition. The metaphor therefore, graphically portrays the fact that the important thing is for the believer to be united to his Lord and that the consequences of this union or lack of it are fruitfulness or barrenness, life or death.

(1) First to be stressed here is the *condition of fruit-bearing*. Life must touch life, if life is to continue. In the grape-

vine, as with other vines or tree trunks, the vital portion is not the wooden core or the outer bark, but the cambium layer between wood and outer bark. In grafting it is imperative that the cambium layers of vine and branch are united and held thus until the life from the vine enters the branch. In the spiritual realm this involves a confession, a surrender, saving commitment of the soul to Christ who henceforth becomes Lord in every realm of life. This initial union with Christ is followed by the constant coming of the life-energy of Christ into the believer, progressively sanctifying and confirming him in this new relationship.

In the summer of 1962, Boston surgeons replaced an arm which had been broken and completely separated from its owner, a twelve-year-old lad. This involved grafting bone-to-bone, muscle-to-muscle, nerve-to-nerve. At the present writing, this unprecedented feat of surgery is successful and the healing is progressing. The im-

---

[3] *Oeconomicus*. XVIII. 6.
[4] *Agr.* 10; *Somn.* 2. 64.

3 Already ye are clean because of the word which I have spoken unto you.

---

initial cleansing is comparable to justification by which sins are forgiven through the word (15:3; Eph. 5:26) and signified by baptism. The subsequent cleansing is that of the good branches, which involves "the cleansing which follows throughout life in the putting away of all the defilements of the flesh (sanctification)."[5] The first is analogous to the reception of the bread at the Eucharist (6:33) while the second cleansing is analogous to the reception of the fruit of the vine at the Eucharist (Hoskyns, pp. 471, 475). "Having been justified they now receive the grace of daily renewal, until *finally* (the last stage is the most incisive of all), completely sanctified, they reach the shores of heaven" (Baker, II, 298). There is nothing in the text, of course, to indicate that the believer's entire sanctification must be deferred until death. It seems probable that the many commentators who believe this chapter is related to chs. 6 and 13 are correct. The

eating of the bread of the Eucharist is implied in ch. 6 and the drinking of the fruit of the vine suggested in ch. 13; the first gives life, the second enriches life and makes it fruitful (cf. Hoskyns, p. 475).

The purpose of the pruning was that it may bear more fruit. God's people need not only to be good but also good for something. As the witnessing of the disciples was more effective without the traitor Judas, so the life of a Christian is enhanced by becoming more Christ-like.

3 "Now you have already been pruned by my words" (JBP). By three years of intimate fellowship with Christ and by his example and teachings, the disciples had been greatly helped toward future fruit-bearing. The noun *katharoi* ("pruned" or "cleansed") is the same as in 13:10 "and now ye are clean, but not all." They had renounced the world, learned the demands of discipleship, preached Christ to their countrymen and now were facing

---

portant thing in such a union is speed and contiguity. Nothing must separate the two members; the union must be complete. So with Christ nothing must be permitted to intervene and prevent the grace of Christ the vine from entering the "branch."

This conception of direct union of each believer with Christ is much more dynamic than the average church member's conception of Christianity. Too often this average member considers it adequate to attend, even if perfunctorily, the "means of grace," the customary practices at public worship, and some stewardship of time and treasure. Such outward evidences of union with Christ as baptism, church membership, and the partaking of communion are deceptive if they conceal or substitute for a real, living, constant union with Christ.

(2) The *cost of fruit-bearing* is also stressed here. Pruning or purging is indispensable to fruitfulness in the realm of nature. Trees, shrubs, and vines often prune themselves by "forming an abcission layer" so the unwanted member

drops by its own weight.[b] Dense forests, denuded except for the top branches reaching for the sunlight, illustrate this point. The word for "pruning" is found in contexts where the wind winnows and purifies the seed, or where a field is "cleansed" of weed seed before the good seed is committed to the soil. The obvious meaning of the purging is pruning for the removal of unwanted branches. In certain vineyards sour sap collects under the bark and must be released by puncturing the sac before good fruit will result. This cauterization is a good illustration of what is needed in Christians. It is obvious also that this purging is subsequent and separate from the initial union with Christ in conversion. The union is not something static, a mere maintenance of status. Because life is involved, the relationship is dynamic and becomes progressively better or worse. The pruning is a drastic means taken to assure the change will be for the better. To many Christians this purging is both a crisis and a process; a crisis in which the recognition that purg-

---

[5] R. C. H. Lenski, *The Interpretation of John's Gospel* (Columbus, Ohio: Lutheran Book Concern, 1942), p. 1031.
[b] G. S. Hoof, "Physiology of the Vine and the Branches; John 15:1-9," *Lutheran Church Quarterly*, XI; 402-5, Oct. 1938.

4 Abide in me, and I in you. As the branch cannot bear fruit of itself, except it abide in the vine; so neither can ye, except ye abide in me.

---

death with their Lord and Master; consequently, they had been cleansed by God's grace mediated through Jesus' words.

**I have spoken** (*lelalēka*), since it is a perfect tense, suggests the continuing results or nature of Jesus' teachings.[6] "Heaven and earth shall pass away, but my word shall not pass away" (Mark 13:31; Luke 21:33). Time and circumstances have proved the truth of that statement thousands of times. These words are permanent; other things transitory.

**4 Abide in me and I in you.** Although *meinate* ("abide") is in the aorist tense it still denotes continuing action because the root-word is "linear" or denotes continuance in staying, i.e., the *tense* signifies *doing* it ("abide") while the *word* itself indicates continuation in the deed. Our English terms "abide" and "live," as in the Greek, imply on-going action. Christ will reciprocate and remain in us, a marvelous promise! The word "abide" is an important one in this Gospel. It occurs a total of forty times here as compared with only twelve in the other three Gospels

(M-G). It is used to indicate "staying, living, dwelling, continuing, persisting, remaining and awaiting." In John it is used in association with the word of God (I John 2:24), the words of Christ (John 15:7b), the anointing from heaven (I John 2:27), the seed of God (John 3:9), and the love of God (I John 3:17) (A-G). It is similar to the phrase "in Christ," so characteristic of Paul, with emphasis on the permanence of this relationship. However, "even the abiding of Christ is made to depend upon the will of the believer," but cf. v. 16 (BFW II, 199).

"Except you abide in me . . . you cannot bear fruit." Separation from the true vine means lack of sustenance and hence lack of fruit. The fact that "abide" (*menē*) occurs in the present tense here heightens and intensifies the necessity of continuously abiding in Christ. The analogy is a very effective one; as separation in nature leads to death, so separation from Christ leads to spiritual death. This is illustrated in the case of Judas, who after his treachery was "cut off."

---

ing is needed to remove elements in the soul inconsistent with the love of Christ. A recognition of the need for drastic soul surgery and a commitment to the Lord of the vineyard for this purpose results in "more fruit" and eventually in "much fruit." When the need of purging exists and the believer shrinks, refusing to face the issue, disobedience begins, which, if continued, can only lead to separation from the True Vine. This inner renewal and cleansing is not only a crisis but a process as well. After the "crisis" of cleansing, subsequent to union to the Vine at conversion, there needs to be an ever-increasing responsiveness to the Life constantly coming from the Gardener through the Vine. "Much fruit" is the result of this progressive sanctification and growth in grace. *What needs to be pruned?*

(3) *All that is bad* should be pruned. Disease spreads and endangers the whole. Sin likewise should not be knowingly pro-

tected or tolerated in the believer. "He who covers his sins shall not prosper; but whoso confesseth and forsaketh them shall have mercy" (Prov. 28:13 KJV). The Psalmist was aware of the danger of "regarding" or condoning iniquity in his heart (Ps. 66:18). John assured his readers that "If we confess our sins, he is faithful and just to forgive us our sins, and to cleanse us from all unrighteousness" (I John 1:9). The Christian's attitude toward sin should be that of unmitigated abhorrence. No one is capable of loving holiness without a strong aversion to sin. No one can love God without at the same time hating sin whether in himself or in others.

(4) *Much that is good must also be pruned away,* if the maximum potential for fruitbearing is to be realized. This is readily apparent in nature. The skillful vinedresser knows that many healthy branches must be removed if fruit rather than foliage is desired. These are "good"

---

[6] The perfect tense says there is at *present* an abiding result, without necessarily implying anything pertaining to the future.

5 I am the vine, ye are the branches: He that abideth in me, and I in him, the same beareth much fruit: for apart from me ye can do nothing.

6 If a man abide not in me, he is cast forth as a branch, and is withered; and they gather them, and cast them into the fire, and they are burned.

---

**5 The same beareth much fruit.** The repetition in this verse (cf. v. 2) is characteristic of this Gospel (cf. 6:35, 41, 48, 51; 10:8, 9; 10:11, 14). Progress is denoted here by adding the word "much." The unlimited resources of deity and heaven are available to the Christian who "abides." The sequence here is noteworthy: "fruit" (v. 2), "more fruit" (v. 2) and "much fruit" (v. 5), the latter being the result of the "pruning," or the sanctifying effect of remaining "in Christ."

**Without me ye can do nothing.** When the disciples toiled alone they took nothing (21:6), but under Jesus' direction they experienced amazing success. The same truth is exemplified in Luke 5:5-7. Moses recognized that without God's presence success was impossible (Exod. 33:15), something that other Israelites learned after it was too late (Num. 14:25). Paul expressed this truth in paradoxical terms: "when I am weak then am I strong" (II Cor. 12:10). Only when Christians are united to and dependent upon the Vine can they be effective. Christianity is effective to the extent that it lives in constant union with and dependence upon its Founder. This is true in spite of the fact that outward success sometimes conceals a lack of true spiritual vitality.

**6 If a man abide not in me, he is cast forth . . . and they are burned.** The fearful consequences of not abiding in Christ are frankly set forth. The picture of final judgment is consistent through each of the four Gospels, although presented in different contexts and with a difference of language and imagery. The familiar consequences of non-productivity in the natural realm, and its application to the spiritual, are numerous in the N. T. In the parables of the tares (Matt. 13:30) and of the net (Matt. 13:47-50) destruction awaits "the bad." The unfruitful fig tree is finally "cut down" (Luke 13:9). For land which produces only thorns and thistles is in the end cursed and burned (Heb. 6:7, 8). The fate of the doomed is progressive and tragic, for

---

branches in that they are healthy, vigorous, and beautiful, but if they are too numerous they must be severed from the vine the same as the diseased branches. To the novice, this pruning seems much too drastic, too wasteful, but the apparently ruthless vinedresser knows that drastic surgery is imperative if the vine is to bear "much fruit." Thus the pruner, while really taking measures which are apparently cruel, actually does it with tenderness and skill as a means to a greater end — that of productivity. The grape vine is the most useless of plants except for one thing — the bearing of grapes. The wood is useless for fuel; in O. T. days people were forbidden to present it to the temple as an offering for fuel. The wood is also useless as timber. There is little beauty in the grape vine. Its only value to men is the grapes it bears. So Christians are to be useful rather than merely ornamental; they should be fruitful.

There are many "good" things in the life of the normal Christian which often compete with the "better part." Martha's meal was "good" but Mary's eagerness to learn was "better" (Luke 10:42). Many an earnest Christian has learned that the stewardship of time is an important factor in the matter of "fruit-bearing." Reading the newspaper is a good, wholesome activity but if it usurps the time which should be budgeted for the reading of the Bible, it should be "pruned" or disciplined. The television set is not wrong in itself, but it can crowd out something more creative unless disciplined both by the allotment of time and the quality of the program. The indulgence in "harmless" diversion is justified by comparison by the alternatives available. To a Christian who is well-informed and eager to be at his best for the Master, the usual question will not be "What is wrong with this?" but rather, "Will this help make me more Christ-like, more useful in his kingdom?" To the person intent on being "well-pleasing in his sight" many "good" things will be "pruned" to make room for the "best."

7 If ye abide in me, and my words abide in you, ask whatsoever ye will, and it shall be done unto you.

8 Herein is my Father glorified, that ye bear much fruit; and *so* shall ye be my disciples.

"they shall go away into eternal punishment" (Matt. 25:46). Mark 9:43-45 mentions "unquenchable fire" where "their worm dieth not." That this does not result in annihilation is evident here and in Rev. 20:10, 15; Luke 16:23. No New Testament writer denies that there will be eternal punishment for unbelievers, present-day Universalists notwithstanding. The wrath of God remains upon the unrepentant even before the final judgment (John 3:36).

7 **If ye abide in me** . . . **ask whatsoever ye will** . . . . The consequences of remaining united to Christ continue here but are turned from "fruit-bearing" to the more specific result of effectiveness in prayer. The condition for this effectiveness is "abiding." This relationship to Christ is reciprocal: we abide in him and he, or his word, abides in us. By "word" is doubtless meant the written word, the "ingrafted word" (Jas. 1:21 KJV), or the "living word" (John 6:63). It involves "walking in the light" (I John 1:7) and abiding in Jesus' word or doctrine (John 8:31). Thus it is not a static condition but a living, growing, progressive dynamic relationship. The same sweeping promise was conditioned in 14:13, 14 by asking in Jesus' name, here by remaining "in Christ." By having Jesus' words and will within, the petitioner will be guided in his praying, so that prayer will not be the magic genie of Aladdin's Lamp but will represent Christ's own desires clarified and made vital by the Holy Spirit "according to the will of God" (Rom. 8:27). The consecrated and fully dedicated Christian will be praying for what is in keeping with Christ's will. When he does, definite and positive answers will result. Had Peter gone on trusting in his native ability and powers of leadership, had Paul trusted in his powers of logic, or had John trusted in his depth of spiritual insight, all three of them would have been found utterly inadequate and could not have served so mightily as they did.

8 **Herein is my Father glorified**, meaning in vital union with Christ and in fruit-bearing. Glorified (*edoxasthē*), a gnomic or timeless aorist indicative, expressing a general truth — ". . . is always glorified — whenever this happens." **That ye** keep on bearing (pres. subj.) **much fruit**. This stress is on continued fruitfulness rather than on sporadic activity. The goal

The alert believer is always concerned lest "the good become the enemy of the best."

The metaphor of the Vine is an important contribution to the N. T. image of the church. Minear has listed nearly a hundred analogies in the N. T. related to the church. This metaphor of the vine is listed as one of thirty-two "minor images" of the church. Within this list of "minor images," this analogy of the vine is one of the most important.[c] The major images include those of the *body* of Christ (Paul), the *temple* of the Lord (Paul), the new *creation* (Paul), the *new Israel* and the *bride* of Christ. The "minor images" include salt, boat or ark, virgins (Rev. 14:1-4), the Messiah's mother (Rev. 12:1, 2) and guests (Luke 14:16-24). Four of these images are closely related: the vine, the vineyard (I Cor. 9:7; cf. Mark 12:1-9), the fig tree (Luke 13:6-9; cf. Matt. 15:13) and the olive tree (Rom. 11:13-24).

Of these four analogies from nature that of the vine is the most important in defining the church. From it several lessons concerning the nature of the church are obvious. (a) The Church is a community each individual of which is directly connected with Christ; he is a sharer in the life of God mediated through Christ. Peter called this being "partakers of the divine nature" (II Pet. 1:4). To become a member of the true church therefore, it is necessary to be "born again" (John 3:5) and to become a "new creation" (II Cor. 5:17). Henceforth he is "in Christ,"

[c] P. S. Minear, *Images of the Church in the New Testament* (Philadelphia: Westminster Press, 1960), p. 42.

9 Even as the Father hath loved me, I also have loved you: abide ye in my love.
10 If ye keep my commandments, ye shall abide in my love; even as I have kept my Father's commandments, and abide in his love.

is not only fruit but **much fruit**, not only life but life in abundance (10:10), not only thirty-fold but a hundred-fold in productivity (Mark 4:8). God wants a good crop and he stands ready to produce it with the help of fully consecrated workers. This fruitfulness is another badge of discipleship. In 8:31 disciples are said to be those who continue in Jesus' word, in 13:35 disciples are distinguished by their mutual love and hereby their productivity. Paul agreed when he cited his productivity as evidence on his apostleship — "I labored more abundantly than they all" (I Cor. 15:10). Again, Paul said, "the seal of mine apostleship are ye in the Lord" (I Cor. 9:2). Soul-winning is not the only sign of fruitfulness but it is an important one and, above all, it glorifies the Father, even as Jesus glorified the Father by winning men (17:4-10).

9 "Just as (*kathōs*) the Father loved me so also I (*kagō*) have loved (*ēgapēsa*)

you." Repeatedly in ch. 13-17 the love of Jesus for the disciples is compared with that of the Father for the Son, and emphasized to a greater extent than anywhere else in Scripture. The continuity of the Father's love for the Son is expressed in 3:35; 5:20 and 10:17 by the use of present tenses. Here the use of the aorist tense indicates "the whole act of love lavished by Jesus upon his disciples and consummated in his death" (CKB, p. 396). God so loved the world that he gave what was most precious to him — his only Son. The Son so loved the world that he gave his life. In our humanity we can only dimly apprehend the quality and extent of love such as this; but we can know enough to accept it. In view of this, said Jesus, "continue abiding (*meinate* — aorist imperative) in my love."

10 If ye keep my commandments, ye shall abide in my love. Attention is called again to the causal relationship between love and obedience. After telling his

to use a favorite phrase of Paul.[a] The stress is on the direct kinship of the individual to his Lord.

(b) The church is a community of individuals related to each other because of their relation to Christ. The vine has many branches and their unity consists in being united to a common vine. Each is dependent primarily on the vine and secondarily on one another. Unless controlled by spacing and pruning, branches may compete with each other for sunlight and sap. Likewise, in the fellowship of the saints interdependence rather than "playing solitaire" is extremely important. The well-being of the whole is more important than the success of any one part. In his classic analysis of unity and diversity in the church, Paul urged that each member "in honor prefer one another" (Rom. 12:1-21). The fact that the church of Christ is a *corporate unity* is often overlooked by rugged individualists, while the

fact that the church consists of *changed individuals* is often overlooked by those who think the church is primarily a "fellowship." (c) Another truth is that the church is a living and hence changing organism. Relationships are not static but dynamic. The responsive branch will be trimmed and improved while the unresponsive branch will be removed, and no fixed caste will be maintained automatically; precedent will not be determinative in the strategy of the husbandman. One cannot be "in grace" merely by virtue of such externals as baptism, church membership and the like, nor can he remain "in grace" simply by inertia. Rather he must "give diligence to make his calling and election sure" (II Pet. 1:10). (d) The fourth truth about the church taught in this parable is the fact that Christ is central. As the vine mediates between branch and soil so Christ mediates between God — the source of life — and the believers

[a] Here the stress is primarily on the *individual's* relation to Christ, as the *en Christo* implies. However, W. C. van Unnik demonstrates that *meta* ("with" or "among") is the usual term for designating the believer's relationship to Christ, thus implying *corporate*, as well as individual unity ("Dominus Vobiscum," in *New Testament Studies in Honor of T. W. Manson*, Manchester: Manchester University Press, 1959, pp. 287ff.).

11 These things have I spoken unto you, that my joy may be in you, and *that* your joy may be made full.

12 This is my commandment, that ye <u>love one another</u>, even as <u>I have loved you</u>.

disciples to abide in his love he says that the way to do so is simply to obey. This leaves much responsibility to the disciples, as the "if" implies. Jesus had to obey his Father in order to remain in fellowship with the Father; so must the disciples obey their Master (John 8:29; Rom. 15:3). <u>Love and obedience are mutually interdependent. Love prompts and is best expressed by obedience</u> (I John 5:3). "Obedience proves love and secures love in return" (OGT, p. 285).

11 "That my joy may be in you and your joy may be complete" (*plerōthē* — "filled up to the top" — JRM). Joy is mentioned forty-six times in the N. T. Maximum enjoyment is possible only through Christ. In addition to attaining the highest heights of human happiness we also have the rare privilege of enjoying in addition the divine joy which Christ imparts. Real Christians are always joyous. While in prison and awaiting execution Paul wrote to the Philippians of his joy in the Lord (Phil. 1:18; 4:4,

10). To the Galatians he wrote that "the fruit of the Spirit is love, joy, peace" (Gal. 5:22). To the Romans, "the Kingdom of God . . . is righteousness, peace and joy in the Holy Spirit" (Rom 14:17). James agreed that his readers should "count it all joy . . . in manifold temptations (Jas. 1:2). <u>Unlike worldly or merely human pleasure this kind of joy is not conditioned by outward circumstances.</u> In this instance Jesus spoke of the joy of doing the will of God while facing the passion, only a few hours distant. Those Christians who love and serve most diligently are those who are happiest now and will be throughout eternity.

12 "<u>Keep on loving one another</u>" (*agapete,* pres. imp.), in the same manner as Jesus loved his own disciples, is the exhortation here. It could hardly be to the same extent, but it should, by the grace of God, be the same quality of love — divinely inspired love. <u>It is not enough simply to avoid quarreling with other Christians; we are to love them posi-</u>

---

individually and collectively. The church is the Church of Christ. (e) In the fifth place the church is more than an aggregation of individuals. In the true church there is *corporate* unity. As in the vine, the chemical action of soil nutrients, capillary action that raises these to the branches and the action of sunlight on the leaves, transforms the raw materials into fruit and food. The vine is a little factory. So the church which bears fruit is like a factory, each member working with Father, Son and Spirit to transform sinners into saints and earth into paradise. Such a church will reproduce its kind.

There are many churches with large and wealthy congregations that do not reproduce. Young people from many such churches are not challenged to enter the ministry. Many of these large churches do not subdivide and form new congregations; they think of a big church as an end of itself. On the other hand, there are many small, struggling churches from which more than a score have entered the ministry and whose influence is world-wide.

Why the difference? Is it not determined largely by the extent to which Christ is lifted up and his call to consecration honored?

### 6. LOVE, THE DISTINCTIVE QUALITY OF DISCIPLESHIP (15:8-17)

This paragraph begins and ends with the "new commandment" — to love one another. The connection between love and obedience is emphasized throughout. The connection between this paragraph and the previous one is close and the transition smooth. The emphasis on "abiding" (vv. 4-7) continues through vv. 9-10 and thus the two paragraphs are linked together. If we keep in mind the emphasis on union with Christ, the transition does not occur until v. 12; if the emphasis is on love, the transition occurs at v. 9 as here indicated. The disciples are expected to bear fruit, especially the fruit of love, joy, peace (cf. Gal. 5:22-25).

9 The similarity of the relationship between believer and Christ and that between Christ and the Father is again set forth.

13 Greater love hath no man than this, that a man lay down his life for his friends.
14 Ye are my friends, if ye do the things which I command you.

tively. This is a reiteration of the command in John 13:34. It is the cardinal insignia that identifies Jesus' disciples. Everywhere hearts are hungering and living in loneliness waiting and longing for the warmth and satisfaction that love also can bring them. To enjoy it most they must demonstrate it and also be the recipients of it. As rigorous as this demand is, it is consistent with Luke 6:40 — "every one when he is perfected shall be as his teacher." It is also consistent with Matt. 5:45 in which love, even for one's enemies is the mark of a disciple, and the test of Christian perfection (Matt. 5:48). Both in nature and extent this concept of love is in marked contrast to contemporary Jewish tradition.[7]

13 Greater love hath no man .... This statement attempts to measure the extent of this kind of divinely-inspired love. The words to lay down his life are found also in John 10:11, 17, 18 and are "peculiar to John" (Lenski, p. 1049). If the love in the disciples is comparable to that of their Lord it follows that it should make them willing to give up their lives, if necessary, as the Shepherd lays down his life for the sheep (10:15). This sacrifice Jesus freely offered in spite of the torture and ignominy involved. He expressed his love to the utmost degree. As Paul declared: "He died for all that they that live should no longer live for themselves but for him who for their sakes died and rose again" (II Cor. 5:15).

14 Ye are my friends, if ye do (poiēte — pres. subj. — "continue doing") the things which I command you. The privilege of such friendship places the Christian under the responsibility of constant obedience to Christ. The benefits of this friendship are conditional on consistent loyalty and faithfulness to him. Jesus had previously called his disciples his friends (Luke 12:4). The two roles are not inconsistent. Not all servants are friends of those they serve but all who are friends are glad to serve. Henry IV wrote to his friend Sully, "My friend,

Remaining in the vine is the same as remaining in love. The emphasis here is on continuity. The means by which one may remain linked with Christ, in a relation of love, is obedience. Even Jesus Christ remained steadfast in the Father's love through obedience (8:29; 10:18). This tells us by implication that the Son is subordinate to the Father, since he must obey. It tells us also by implication that it is possible for the Son not to obey. The possibilities which such reflections raise are overwhelming and the Bible does not engage in such speculation. Language used to described the divine-human relationship can easily be pressed too far. Certain it is, however, that our relationship to Christ is similar to that which he sustains to the Father; in both the important factor is obedience as a demonstration of love and loyalty.

There is an element of contingency here. The union of the believer to the divine is conditioned on "abiding" and that in turn upon obedience. Can a true believer be severed from Christ after being joined to him? A vigorous denial of this possibility is often voiced. "In no sense whatever do such passages as 15:2 and 15:7 suggest that there is a falling away from grace, as if those who were once actually saved finally perish. This allegory plainly teaches that the branches which are taken away and burned represent people who never once bore fruit, not even when they were "in" Christ. Hence, they never were true believers; and for them the in-the-vine relationship, though close, was merely outward" (WmH, II, 296). On the other hand, fidelity to the analogy of the vine requires that we admit the possibility of a live branch being severed if it fails to produce fruit. This is the whole force of the parable. The cutting off and burning of branches is largely meaningless if limited to what was never actually connected to the vine and the repeated exhortation that the branches "abide" is needless if there is no possibility of being severed from Christ. The fearful consequences of apostasy are set forth in similar imagery in Heb. 6:1-8, where it is made clear that

[7] G. Quell & E. Stauffer, Bible Key Words (Kittel): Love (London: A. & C. Black, 1949), p. 48.

15 No longer do I call you servants; for the servant knoweth not what his lord doeth: but I have called you friends; for all things that I heard from my Father I have made known unto you.

16 Ye did not choose me, but I chose you, and appointed you, that ye should go and bear fruit, and *that* your fruit should abide: that whatsoever ye shall ask of the Father in my name, he may give it you.

---

continue to serve me well" (MJL, p. 407), thus indicating that he felt no contradiction between friendship and service.

15 No longer . . . servants . . . but . . . friends. Here Jesus raises the status of his disciples from learners to sharers. Up to this time it has been enough that they took orders whether or not they knew the purpose of them. From now on they are to understand the purposes. As tested and trusted friends they will be taken into confidence of their Master and know not only the "what" but also the "why" of the commandments. They will be confidants of the Lord, but no less servants, committed to carry out his orders. Previously, they, like slaves (*douloi*) generally did not understand (*oiden*) the direction or purpose of their Lord, but from now on they will acquire insight into (have a revelation of — *ginōsko*) God's purpose in the matter. I have called you friends. Called (*eirēka*) is a perfect tense indicating that since he called them they have continued as his friends. As far as Jesus is concerned, we are chosen to be his life-time friends. We may be disposed to

spurn and sever that relationship, but not so with him.

16 I chose you and appointed you. Here the sovereignty of divine grace is stressed as human responsibility was stressed in vv. 4, 9, 10. Jesus takes the responsibility for his choice; their responsibility is to respond to his choice. The purpose of the Lord's choice was not for themselves alone; it was for others — that ye should go and bear fruit. This verse continues the imagery of the vine and the vintage. The purpose of discipleship and that of the grapevine are identical; both are to produce. Each is to reproduce his kind. This means that by "bearing fruit" we help bring into being other disciples. Furthermore, the effects of our labor and loyalty are to be lasting: your fruit should abide. Those helped by us will enjoy the benefits here and now; and we will continue to enjoy the memory of our service and the rewards for it both here and hereafter. Prayer will assure this result — whatsoever he shall ask. The greatest soul-winners are usually effective in intercessory prayer. Such prayers for success

---

the reference is to those who once were actual participants in the life of Christ. At the same time, it is comforting to know that "final perseverance" is a glorious possibility and that no combination of *external* circumstances can sever the believer from Christ (cf. Rom. 8:35-39; John 10: 28). It is those who abide by loving obedience who never perish. It follows that Jesus was thinking of Christians who became apostates, who heard the message and who accepted it and who fell away, who abandoned their faith, and who became traitors to the Master whom they had once pledged themselves to serve.[e]

Thou art the Vine,
  And I, O Jesus, am a branch of Thine;
  And day by day from Thee
New life flows into me.

Naught have I of my own,
But all my strength is drawn from
  Thee alone.
As, severed from the tree, the branch
  must die.
So even I
Could never live this life of mine
Apart from Thee, O divine Vine;
But Thou dost dwell in me,
And I in Thee!
  Yea, Thine only life through me doth
  flow,
  And in Thyself I live and grow.
          — E. H. Rivall.

By the insistence that obedience is the test of love, Jesus was appealing to the practical rather than to the sentimental. He made it clear that "love" that is only emotional, that does not express itself in

17 These things I command you, that ye may love one another.
18 If the world hateth you, ye know that it hath hated me before *it hated* you.

---

in fruit-bearing are effective to the extent that they are motivated by a desire to glorify God rather than enhance one's own status.

17 The paragraph is summed up by a repetition of the command of v. 12. The repetition of the commandment to love underscores the emphasis Jesus placed upon "the new commandment." Its roots in the O. T. (*ahebh*) connote not the undisciplined *eros* of the Greeks, but the volitional, discriminating love encountered in the O. T. It can mean that which unites husband and wife (Song of Sol. 8:6), the loyalty of friends (I Sam. 20) or devotion to righteousness (Ps. 45:7). It has the quality of jealousy "as strong as death" (Song of Sol. 8:6), and this meaning carries over into a love which enables the Christian to lay down his life for his Lord or for his friends. This love must not be self-centered but Christ-centered and outgoing. It must be fixed not upon the "I" but upon the "Thou" (TWNT, p. 47) .

18 If the world hates you (RSV). The theme of the hostility between the world and the Christian, between the children of light and the children of darkness, comes to prominence here in 15:18—16: 33. There may be here something akin to the sense of "other-worldliness" felt by the contemporary Essenes at Qumran and elsewhere. The polarity is stressed more in John than elsewhere in the N. T. although it is prominent in Paul's letters. As the hostility of the nation's leaders brought on Jesus' death the disciples are warned to expect a similar fate. "If the world is hating you now (*ei* with indic.) you know that it hated me before and its hatred of me still abides" (perf. tense). The cost of discipleship was far from inconsequential. To have Christ's friendship involved having the world's hatred. There are several meanings of "world" in John. Here it does not mean the entire inhabited earth (cf. 3:16) but rather that element in the world which is characteristically hostile to God, because the light of God exposes sin (3:19). It is not primarily an eschatological struggle between cataclysmic forces, as in the War Scroll of the Qumran Covenanters, but a

---

deeds is false. God's love for the world was more than sentiment; it found expression in the fact that he gave his Son for the world: "God commanded his love toward us in that . . . Christ died for us" (Rom. 5:8).

Joy is usually the accompaniment of love. It is not by accident that in the cluster of the fruits of the Spirit, joy is placed next to love (Gal. 5:22). This can be seen in the love of a mother for her child; joy inevitably follows love. Obedience, love and joy are linked in the Ps. 40:6-8 (cf. Heb. 10:5-8): "I delight to do thy will." Times of religious revival in the O. T. were times of rejoicing (II Chron. 30:21; Ezra 6:22). Likewise in the early church, times when the church was most conscious of obeying God were times of special rejoicing (Luke 24:52; Acts 2:46; 8:39; 13:52; 16:34). Paul felt that there was no situation, however difficult, in which he could not rejoice

(II Cor. 1:12, 24; 2:1-4; Phil. 1:4; 4:1, 4; I Thess. 5:16). Joy was also characteristic of religious festivals, not only in Judaism but in contemporary cults.[f] It is perhaps more than a coincidence that in pagan religions joy was normally with the fruit of the vine, and that here the mention of joy follows discussion of the vine. But what a contrast between the false bucolic "joy" of intoxication at wine festivals with the inner soul joy of the one "in Christ"! The contrast here may be deliberate. Paul made the contrast deliberate when writing to some converts (Eph. 5:18). "Other-worldly" joy of which Jesus speaks is the deep inner satisfaction which he experienced in doing the will of God and which he wanted his disciples to share when in similar circumstances (4:34-36; 17:13). Such joy is not a product of environment but rather wells up deep within the person conscious of being in the will of God and being pleasing to his Lord. It

---

[f] R. Bultmann, *op. cit.*, pp. 387ff. This was true in Egypt, as extant wall paintings and sculptures testify, and in Rome as well. Gnostic systems also include references to religious "joy."

19 If ye were of the world, the world would love its own: but because ye are not of the world, but I chose you out of the world, therefore the world hateth you.

20 Remember the word that I said unto you, A servant is not greater than his lord. If they persecuted me, they will also persecute you; if they kept my word, they will keep yours also.

---

personal struggle going on continuously in the soul of every man, one which he, as an individual, wins or loses — rather, one in which he is either on the winning or losing side. This is a major theme of the Johannine literature.

**19 The world would love** (*ephilei*) **its own.** "Love" here is love on the human level, not the divine love of the preceding verses. The verb is imperfect and denotes continual fondness (i.e., "would have been loving"). It is a contrary-to-fact sentence, implying that the disciples were not part and parcel of the world, and that no abiding affection can be expected from non-believers.

**Ye are not of the world . . . therefore the world hateth you.** The verb "to hate" (*miseō*) does not necessarily mean implacable hostility since "hating" one's parents is said to be a condition of discipleship in Luke 14:26.[8] But normally, it means "to hate, persecute, detest, abhor." Jesus had told his brothers that the world hated him because he reported its evil deeds (7:7). This is the reason why Herodias and Herod hated John the Baptist. People are inclined to criticize others who live better than they do as well as those who live worse than they do. Nonconformity is despised. The reason for the hatred of the world is the fact that the disciples are estranged from their natural environment because of their new attachment to Jesus. Previously they had been "of the world" like others (8:21) in that they were from "below." This commitment to God, which necessitates a severance from "the world" makes the world jealous, suspicious, and hostile. Repeatedly the reader of the N. T. is warned that he cannot please God and the world both (I John 2:15; John 8:23, 44-56). To be "of the world" (*ek tou kosmou*) is the opposite of to be "of God" (*ek tou theou*). This contrast is characteristic of John's writings. Jesus was trying to put His disciples into a frame of mind in which they would be prepared to face hostility for no other reason than their love for him.

20 "A servant can expect no better treatment than his master." This is a proverbial saying perhaps; certainly it is axiomatic. Thus the disciples were warned to expect a reception comparable to that

---

is on a different plane entirely from conviviality, pleasure, camaraderie, which is often a by-product of cordial human relationships. This "joy" has its origin in the divine-human relationship. It is noteworthy that the root of the world "joy" (*chara*) is the same as the word "grace" (*charis*); the relationship is ideological as well as etymological.

*Joy is Duty, — so with golden lore*
*The Hebrew rabbis taught in days of yore,*
*And happy human hearts heard in their speech,*
*Almost the highest wisdom man can reach.*

*But one bright peak still rises far above,*
*And there the Master stands whose name is Love,*
*Saying to those whom heavy tasks employ,*
*Life is divine when Duty is a Joy.*[g]

15 Love is that which raised the status of a servant to that of a friend. A servant is valued for his service, a friend is valued for himself. Jesus loved the disciples, not only for the service they would render but for themselves as persons. As friends they are sharers in the project; in its risks and its rewards. They are interested in the project itself and obey not

[8] The meaning of "hate" in the New Testament has received much attention. J. Denney, "The Word 'Hate' in Luke 14:26," *Expository Times*, 1910, pp. 41ff. R. W. Sockman, *The Paradoxes of Jesus*, 1936. A. Carr, "The Meaning of 'Hatred' in the New Testament," *The Expositor*, 1905, pp. 153-60. A-G, p. 524.

[g] H. VanDyke, *Gospel for an Age of Doubt*, cited in Peloubet, *op. cit.*, p. 428.

21 But all these things will they do unto you for my name's sake, because they know not him that sent me.

22 If I had not come and spoken unto them, they had not had sin: but now they have no excuse for their sin.

23 He that hateth me hateth my Father also.

---

afforded their Master, who "came unto his own and his own received him not" (KJV). Today also the world praises Jesus' words, but still refuses to follow him, and makes it difficult for those who do. Why?

21 **Because they know not him that sent me.** Paul also said that the "natural man" is incapable of receiving "the things of the Spirit of God . . . because they are spiritually discerned" (I Cor. 2:14). A spiritual experience of salvation is a prerequisite to understanding and appreciating God's will for our lives. Jesus must have experienced the concern of a fond parent as he realized that his own repeated rejections would be duplicated a thousand-fold in the lives of his disciples in the centuries ahead.

22 **Now they have no excuse** (*prophasis*).[9] Jesus had something similar when he told the Jews that their sin of rejection was the greater because he had brought the light (9:39), one of the grim-

mest statements in this Gospel. Paul recognized the same principle at work as he evangelized. The same gospel that was to its recipients a "savor of life" was to those who rejected it a "savor of death" (II Cor. 2:16). Since Christ manifested himself so strikingly and with so many proofs of his deity, men (then and now) had no excuse for rejecting him.

23 "He who hates me hates my Father also" (RSV). Here, as elsewhere "hate" (*misei*) is set in contrast to "love" (*agapē*). The hostility directed against Jesus by the world, and hence against his disciples as well (v. 20) is at the same time directed basically against God. This might have sounded strange to the average bystander and would have enraged the religious leaders who even then were intent on destroying him. But Jesus had said this in effect to them more than once before (e.g., 8:37-47). He was bold enough to tell them that hostility to him was tantamount to hostility to

---

merely to comply with a demand of the Master as would a slave. It appears that Jesus is eager that the disciples be raised to the very highest level of service and status of which they are capable.

16 They are chosen to serve. The choice is primarily here for service rather than for salvation. The initiative comes from the Lord. It is he who sends forth laborers into the vineyard, but his initiative is linked with human compliance with the command to pray (Luke 10:2; cf. John 4:35). The fact that they were divinely appointed to a specific task was a powerful reason for the disciples' conviction that they would be successful in the task. To this end the privilege and his power of prayer was placed at their disposal. The Lord had promised his presence and his power, but this was conditioned on the disciples' obedience and their willingness to pray. As Jesus found it necessary to pray, so must his disciples, if they are to bring forth fruit that is lasting. Just

why it is necessary to ask God to do what he wants to do has never been fully explained. It is enough perhaps that we have the clear statement as to our responsibility and our privilege in this matter.

**Whatsoever ye shall ask** appears, at first sight, to be too sweeping and unqualified as a statement. Experience shows that it cannot be taken literally. On looking deeper, however, we realize that this promise also is conditioned like the others. Here it is conditioned on abiding in Christ. Because of this the *whatsoever* is a derivative of this union. Actually, therefore, it is the will of Christ expressing itself in the aspirations and petitions of his disciples. It is not merely a "wishing well" or "open sesame" to gratify one's caprice. Prayer is a stewardship with great privileges and with correspondingly great obligations. The prayers that are most likely to be answered are unselfish requests relating to the extension of Christ's in-

---

[9] Cf. Mark 12:40; 23:13; Luke 20:47; Acts 27:30; Phil. 1:18; 1 Thess. 2:5.

24 If I had not done among them the works which none other did, they had no
had sin: but now have they both seen and hated both me and my Father.

25 But *this cometh to pass,* that the word may be fulfilled that is written in their
law, They hated me without a cause.

---

the God whom they professed to serve.
In John's writings there is no middle or
neutral "gray" between light and darkness, love and hate, God and the world,
belief and unbelief." Each is called to
make his own "existential decision" with
regard to this polarity, and the issues of
life and death forever are dependent thereon. In rejecting Christ one also rejects
and "hates" God. "John always insists
that the work of Jesus is unthinkable apart
from the constant activity of God. What
Jesus does is done by God, and every attitude of men to him is an attitude to God"
(CKB, p. 401).

24 "If I had not done among them
the works . . . they would not have sin"
(RSV). It was a sad, grim recognition
of the principle that "light rejected bring-
eth night." After an encounter with
Jesus no man remains the same. The en-

counter always produces a crisis in which
each reacts positively or negatively, resulting in regeneration or degeneration,
life or death.

The works (*erga*) "which none else ha
done" are the good deeds practiced by
Jesus during the past busy months (10
32). The point here is that these miracle
were unique and unprecedented. Instead
of evoking faith they had the opposite
effect. Some saw and believed; other
saw and hated. The witness of the *word*
was rejected (v. 22; cf. 5:31-34) and the
witness of the *works* as well (v. 24). "John
did no miracle" (10:41), reflected the attitude of the multitude, indicating their
recognition of this unique feature of
Jesus' ministry. Others noted that the
miracles were fully adequate to justify
Jesus' messianic claims (7:31). Now
have they both seen and hated. The verb

---

fluence in individuals and in society. In
such prayers we know that we are praying
"according to the will of God" (Rom. 8:
27; cf. I John 3:22).

### 7. THE HOSTILITY OF THE WORLD (vv. 18-25)

This theme is dominant from 15:18
through 16:33. After assuring the disciples
of his presence and power, he warns them
of the hostility to be expected in the environment within which they will be bearing fruit. There is here an allusion to the
analogy of heredity which was introduced
in 1:13; 3:5; 8:37-56 and less explicitly
elsewhere. It relates to the almost cosmic
conflict between light and darkness, flesh
and spirit, good and evil, which is so
prominent in the N. T., especially in John
and in Paul.

Union with Christ not only results in
fruit-bearing but also persecution. Because
of the world's hostility to Christ and because of the believer's union with Christ,
the faithful share with Christ the hostility
of the world.

20 They will persecute you. Persecute
(*ediōxan*) means "put to flight," hence

to "overtake," to "attack," or to "pursue
with hostile intent." The term "persecute"
comes from the Latin *persequor,* meaning
to "follow up, pursue, persecute" (MRV
II, 253). This was literally fulfilled, as reported in Acts, when the Judaizers *pur
sued* Paul from city to city, thus *persecut
ing* him.

When the church is "in the world" and
the world is "in the church," persecution
is unlikely to occur. When the army o
the Lord comes to terms with the enem
and is content with "peaceful co-existence,"
an armistice is in effect. This often hap
pens when the church is in a weak minor
ity in a non-Christian society. The church
often abandons its aggressive evangelisti
outreach then and receives in return
tolerance. Under such conditions the
church usually survives in greatly weak
ened conditions, as was true in Egypt afte
the Moslem conquest. Even in countrie
where the church is relatively strong, i
often accommodates itself to "the world,"
i.e., to the contemporary mores, in th
hope of gaining concessions or status. Both
alternatives are fatal to real fruit-bearing
The fact that the church is a victim o

26 But when the Comforter is come, whom I will send unto you from the Father, *even* the Spirit of truth, which proceedeth from the Father, he shall bear witness of me:

---

(*heorakasin kai memisēkasin*) are in the perfect tense denoting a present attitude and responsibility resulting from their previous experience. "The 'world' and the ecclesiastics (Sanhedrin) had united in this attitude of hostility to Christ and in reality to God" (WPNT, V, 263).

25 **In their law,** cf. 8:17 and 10:34 for similar references to the O. T. It was the Torah to Jesus and his disciples no less than to the Pharisees but their attitude assumed a special prerogative over it. Jesus pointed out that the Law in which they sought to justify their skepticism was in reality the basis for their condemnation. The quotation, **they hated me without a cause,** was taken from Ps. 69:4 (cf. Ps. 35:19). The source of the quotation was probably the lament of a survivor of the Fall of Jerusalem, notably Jeremiah. While there was a sense in which the hatred was uncaused, with both Jeremiah and Jesus there was a cause, although not a justifiable

one. Jesus said the hatred was caused by his exposure of the world's sin (cf. v. 19, 21, 22; 7:7). Jeremiah also was hated because his preaching was not popular (cf. Jer. 26:1-9). Therefore, this quotation is probably to be interpreted not strictly as "without cause" but "without justifiable cause."

26 "But when your Advocate has come" (NEB). This is one of the most important of the Paraclete verses. In this one verse one may find arguments for proving that (1) the Spirit came from the Father *through* the Son (the view of Eastern Orthodoxy) or that (2) The Spirit proceeded from the Father *and* the Son (the Roman Catholic view). This was one of the causes for this historical split between the eastern and western churches — "the Great Schism."[10] In 14:16 Jesus will take the initiative in asking for the coming of the Paraclete but the Father sends Him; here Jesus will send Him. The significance

---

persecution is not in itself an assurance of its spiritual vitality, but the latter seldom exists without persecution. Paul generalized on his own experience when he observed, "all that live godly in Christ Jesus shall suffer persecution" (II Tim. 3:12).

21 "On my account" (RSV). Jesus takes the blame for the world's hostility. Normally the persecution is not the fault of the believer but because of the basic spiritual antagonism in the universe. In contrast to the War Scroll of Qumran, however, this is not a climactic mythological battle in a distant setting, but a moral struggle in which every soul is involved. The older saints recognized this struggle, in the tradition of Paul who warned against conformity to this age (Rom. 12:2). A much-admired analysis of the ways in which a Christian "in the world but not of the world" comes to us from the second century: "The distinction between Christian and other men is neither in country nor language nor customs. For they do not dwell in cities in some place of their

own, nor do they use any strange variety of dialect, nor practice an extra-ordinary kind of life . . . . They pass their time upon the earth, but they have their citizenship in heaven. They obey the appointed laws, and they surpass the laws in their own lives. They love all men and are persecuted by all men. They are unknown and are condemned. They are put to death and they gain life . . . 'They are abused and give blessing,' they are insulted and render honor. When they do good they are buffeted as evil-doers, when they are buffeted they rejoice as men who receive life. They are warred upon by the Jews as foreigners and are persecuted by the Greeks, and those who hate them cannot state the cause of their enmity."[h]

22 Here and elsewhere the reason for the world's hatred is made very clear. As Jesus explained to the Pharisees in 9:39-41, his revelation had the effect of involving them in deeper guilt because they refused the revelation. They did not have the innocence of those who have no opportunity to know right from wrong; because

---

[10] John 15:26a apparently refers to "the temporal mission" of the Holy Spirit, while 15:26b refers to the "eternal procession" of the Holy Spirit; both use *para* — "from the side of" (cf. BFW, II, 213).
[h] "The Epistle to Diognetus," *Apostolic Fathers,* tr. by K. Lake (New York: G. P. Putnam's Sons, 1930), V. 1-17. II, 358-361.

27 and ye also bear witness, because ye have been with me from the beginning.

---

lies not in the apparent contradiction but in the intimacy of the connection between Father and Son. Likewise in 14:26 the sender is the Father but the gift is in the name of the Son and in response to the Son's request as in 14:15. Here, although the Paraclete proceeds from the Father, he is sent by the Son and bears witness to the Son; so the association is very intimate indeed. As in Acts, so here, the function of the Spirit is to bear witness to Christ along with the disciples (cf. Acts 1:8; 4:29-33). (See Introduction on the Paraclete.)

The authority of the apostles lay chiefly in the fact that they had been with Jesus some three years and remembered his words and deeds. This human or natural authority of an eyewitness was tremendously enforced and amplified by the incursion of the Holy Spirit which revivified their memory (14:26), clarified the Scriptures (Acts 2:17-31) and enabled them to press home their relevance with

telling effect (Acts 2:36; 3:25, 26; 4:10-12).

27 **Ye also bear witness** (*martyreite*). A "witness" was often a martyr. In the early days of the church, a witness often paid for his witness with his life as did James, Stephen and a noble host of others. Here the present tense denotes continued witnessing, or perhaps a command to bear witness. Both grammatically and actually, it follows that continuous witnessing is the Christian's obligation. Christ's cause can make rapid progress only when believers become and remain submissive to the Holy Spirit, consistently and boldly witness to what Christ has accomplished for them.

**Because you have been with me from the beginning** (*ap' archēs*) i.e., "you have been with me and still are with me." The book of Acts bears emphatic witness that it was when they were witnessing that the early church was most conscious of the Spirit's dynamic leadership (Acts 4:31;

---

they are enlightened and do not respond, they incur guilt and are "without excuse" (cf. Rom. 1:20).

24 The truth of v. 22 is repeated again by noting that the works wrought by Jesus in connection with the Father were witnessed by "the world" which, after rejecting the evidence, incurred more hatred. Truth that exposes evil hurts unless welcomed. Those who did not welcome the truth ended by hating both the truth itself and the embodiment of it in Jesus Christ.

25 **They hated me without a cause.** This sad comment, echoing the authors of Ps. 35:19 and Ps. 69:4, was part of the "cup" of woe which the Savior drank. Jesus repeatedly placed himself and his disciples in the tradition of the prophets, especially in the negative reaction which most of the prophets experienced. This was summed up in a sweeping generalization by Jesus as he first faced the prospect of his death in Jerusalem, saying, "Go then, finish off what your fathers began . . . . on you will fall the guilt of all the innocent blood spilt on the ground from innocent

Abel to Zachariah" (Matt. 23:32-36 NEB). This was underscored by the fate of John the Baptist and the gathering storm around Jesus as he spoke. A multitude of God's "prophets" since then have experienced this hatred. In 1962, a clergyman in Florida spoke out against what he considered the sin of the white majority to refuse equal rights to the Negro citizens of the community. Later his "Christian" congregation demanded his resignation as pastor.[1] Sometimes the antipathy of people to the truth is transferred almost unconsciously to the bearer of truth regardless of how kindly and graciously the bearer conducts himself. While there is always a cause for hatred, the party to it is often unable to analyze and explain his animosity. A classic example of one who could not explain his dislike for a famous 17th century Dean of Christ Church, Oxford, is thus quaintly expressed:

*I do not love thee, Dr. Fell:*
*The reason why I cannot tell,*
*But this I know and know full well—*
*I do not love thee, Dr. Fell.*[j]

---

[1] J. L. Monroe, "The White Man's Dilemna," *Christianity Today,* Oct. 26, 1962, pp. 71f.
[j] Cited by F. N. Peloubet, *op. cit.,* p. 435.

5:32). When they were exposed to danger during this task of witnessing the Spirit's presence was even more urgently needed and experienced both as advocate (Acts 7:55), counsellor (Acts 10:19) guide (Acts 13:2; 16:6, 7), and activator (Acts 13:9, 52; 20:23). Thus disciples

and the Paraclete share jointly in the privilege of bearing witness to Christ. This was the mighty quartet which confronted legalism on one side and paganism on the other, triumphing over both: the Father, the Son, the Holy Spirit, and the human witnesses.

---

### 8. THE WORK OF THE PARACLETE (15: 26-16:15)

#### a. In Bearing Witness to Christ (15:26, 27)

**26 But when the Comforter is come.** Against the grim prospects of facing a hostile world without the physical presence of their Lord and Master, Jesus holds up the promise of their Advocate's advent. He will be the direct personal representative of Father and Son, their spokesman. His purpose will be that of defending Jesus and also Jesus' disciples when they are under attack. This phase of the Spirit's work is dominant in the passage (15:26-16:15). In this important passage the Paraclete's task will be to provide encouragement and guidance, to reveal Christ, defend the accused, convict the world, bear witness, disclose the future and brings to remembrance (see Excursus). The important ministry in these verses is that of bearing witness. It is not specified here just in what ways the Spirit will bear witness. From elsewhere, however, we gather that the Comforter bears witness by the effecting of miracles, such as blinding the sorcerer Elymas and the consequent enlightening of Sergius Paulus (Acts 13:6-12), inspiring preaching (Acts 2:4, 14-40; 4:8-12), exposing hypocrisy (Acts 5:3-12), rebuking blasphemy (cf. Acts 12:21-24), defending the accused

(Acts 7:51-56), enlightening the believers (Acts 10:19-35), guiding the church (Acts 15:28) and cleansing from sin (Acts 15:9; cf. II Cor. 7:1). All of these together constituted an irrefutable witness to the truth of the *kērygma* (proclamation) and a rebuke to those who opposed it (Heb. 2:4).

**27 Ye also bear witness.** In the Old Testament the prophets were God's spokesmen. In the New Testament the "gift of prophecy" is largely a gift of exhortation. The true successor of the Hebrew prophets is the Christian evangelist. Both are inspired by the same Holy Spirit. This prophetic tradition goes back to the time of Moses and Aaron when God said he would speak through Aaron (Exod. 4:10-15) to his people. But while the Hebrew prophets were authorized to speak new truth, the Christian witness is only a reporter and an exhibit, a "living epistle." This is the chief distinction between an apostle and other Christians. The apostles, like the prophets, were the vehicles of a new revelation, while preachers, since the days of the apostles, are to clarify the revelation once given and applied it to new situations. For modern witnesses the task is not to reveal something new but to apply existing revelation to the changing conditions of each age. In this both the illumination and the strength of the Spirit of truth are needed.

# CHAPTER XVI

These things have I spoken unto you, that ye should not be caused to stumble.

## EXEGESIS

The note of solemnity continued as Jesus proceeded with his task of preparing his disciples for the persecution and social ostracism which were certain to accompany their ministry of witnessing. The words "these things" with which ch. 16 begins are repeated several times in this section.[1] They appear to be a strand which binds the sayings of chs. 14-16 together and casts doubt on the success of attempts to "improve" the order here.

1 These things have I spoken (lelalēka — the effects continuing) unto you, that ye should not be caused to stumble (skandalisthēte) literally "trapped" or "scandalized," or "caught unawares."[2] The last verb (aor. pass.) can mean "to be led

into sin" or "to take offense." From the cognate noun we get the English words "scandal" and "slander" (MRV, I, 41).[3] The term is found elsewhere in this Gospel only at 6:61 in connection with the revulsion of the crowd at Jesus' statement that in order to live they would have to "eat the flesh of the Son of man and drink his blood" (6:53). In that instance many withdrew from his fellowship. Jesus now is trying to prevent a situation in the future when unanticipated persecution might cause them to forsake the faith and give up their allegiance. Paul's thought moved in a similar vein when he urged the Philippians not to be "offended" because he was languishing in prison (Phil. 1:22-30). He emphasized that it is no

## EXPOSITION

### b. Warning (16:1-6)

The emphasis on the hostility of the world, a theme which began with 15:18, continues throughout this chapter. The seriousness of the danger to which the disciples will be exposed, as they witness concerning Christ, will be vastly accentuated by Jesus' departure. Against this two-fold challenge, Jesus presents the promise of the Paraclete's advent as the answer to their anxiety. The third Paraclete saying (15: 26, 27) is now followed by another warn-

ing before the teaching concerning the Spirit is continued in 16:7-15. In this analysis of the chapter, six distinct units of thought are discernible. The first and last paragraphs are concerned with the dual themes of Jesus' departure and the coming persecution. Between these two themes Jesus seeks to bolster their courage by further information about the Paraclete, the resources in prayer and the true source of joy. These relationships may be presented in diagrammatic form:

| JOHN: | Chapter 16 | | | VICTORY ENVISIONED | |
|---|---|---|---|---|---|
| Warning | Accusing World | Guiding Saints | Joy Ahead | Jesus' Departure | "I have overcome" |
| 1 | 7 | 12 | 16 | 25 | 29          33 |
| | PARACLETE | | TENSION (*Angst*) | | |
| WARFARE AND VICTORY | | | | | |

(leftmost label column reads "Paragraph")

[1] Viz., 14:25; 15:11; 16:1, 4, 6, 25, 33.
[2] R. V. G. Tasker, *The Gospel According to St. John* (Grand Rapids: Wm. B. Eerdmans Publishing Co., 1960), p. 181.
[3] Cf. Wycliffe, "If the right eye *slander* thee."

2 They shall put you out of the synagogues: yea, the hour cometh, that whosoever killeth you shall think that he offereth service unto God.

---

disgrace to be imprisoned for Christ's sake. Peter (I Pet. 4:12-16), James (Jas. 1:2-4) and the writer to the Hebrews (Heb. 12: 1-7) all pressed home the same theme, i.e., that while in the eyes of the world it might be a disgrace to experience persecution for one's faith it is not so in the eyes of God. Instead, persecution is one of the occupational hazards of being a Christian and hence nothing about which to be "offended" or scandalized.[4] As Jesus' enemies tried repeatedly to entrap him, ridicule him, disgrace him and eventually bring death upon him, so will they do to his disciples — hence, "to be forewarned is to be forearmed."

2 They will put you out of the synagogue (aposynagogus — lit. "expelled from the congregation"), that is, "they will cause you to be expelled from the synagogues." The word occurs only thrice in the N. T. — John 9:22; 12:42 and here. A prelude to this persecution had already been witnessed by the disciples when the erstwhile blind man's interrogators "cast him out" of their presence (9:34). The man had only dared to speak well of Jesus.

Religious fanaticism is predicted in the statement that whosoever killeth you shall think he offereth service unto God. Opposition is to be so severe that death penalities will be imposed on the ground that God is being served by such diabolical madness. This is the ultimate in the idolatry of the self. James, Stephen, Peter, Paul and most of those who heard these words experienced the fulfillment of this grim prediction. In later history the Spanish Inquisition and the slaughter of the French Huguenots became conspicuous examples of religious intolerance and bigotry.

He offereth service unto God. The rabbinic commentary on the slaughter of an offending couple by Phineas the priest, thus averting divine judgment, illustrates how an assassin can "render God service." "The Midrash on Num. 25:13 (Phineas) made an atonement may serve as a commentary. 'Was this said because he offered an offering (Korban)? No; but to teach them that every one that sheds the blood of the wicked is as he that offereth an offering.' "[5]

---

The chapter begins with a reference to the preceding paragraphs in the words, "I have said all this" (RSV). The things which he had said concerning steadfastness included the warning to Peter (13: 38), the exhortations to believe (14:1-12), to love and obey (14:15-24), to "abide" (15:1-17) and to avoid coming to terms with "the world" (15:18-27). The danger of apostasy was a real one. Judas succumbed, Peter narrowly escaped, earlier some followers had deserted because of "hard sayings" (6:60), and in the centuries to come many would desert in times of persecution. This danger was most fully recognized in the Epistle to the Hebrews and in the Apocalypse where the believers are alternately wooed and warned. Eusebius enumerates ten definite times of persecution during the first three centuries. In each time of stress there

were those who denied the faith to escape persecution. Pliny the Younger writes that in one province of Asia Minor several confessed that they had once been Christians but had ceased to be several years before: "Others, whose names were given me by an informer, first said that they were Christians and afterwards denied it, declaring that they had been but were so no longer, some of them having recanted many years before, and more than one so long as twenty years back. They worshipped your image and the statues of the deities, and cursed the name of Christ."[a]

Pliny, in his letter, continued by saying that these ex-Christians reported to him that before the Emperor's decree outlawing "secret societies," they would gather before dawn "on a certain day" and sing hymns to Christ "as though he were a

---

[4] Cf. Matt. 11:6; 13:21; 18:6, 8; 24:10; 26:31, 33; Rom. 14:21; I Cor. 9:13.
[a] Pliny Jr. to Trajan (Pliny, Epp. X. xcvi) cited in B. J. Kidd, Documents Illustrative of the
[5] Midrash R., cited in BFW, II, 216. Also S-B, II, 565.
History of the Church (New York: Macmillan, 1938) I, 39.

3 And these things will they do, because they have not known the Father, nor me.

4 But these things have I spoken unto you, that when their hour is come, ye may remember them, how that I told you. And these things I said not unto you from the beginning, because I was with you.

5 But now I go unto him that sent me; and none of you asketh me, Whither goest thou?

---

3 **Because they have not known** (aor., *egnōsan* — "never knew") **the Father nor me.** They knew not God nor his Son by personal experience. The verb implies that theirs was a willful ignorance (CGT); it means that "the Jews will persecute the Christians because they failed to recognize God in the person and work of Jesus" (CKB, p. 404). It is another amplification of a generalization expressed several times earlier in this Gospel.[6] Ignorance breeds distrust, suspicion, and hostility. Willful ignorance brings guilt and reinforced opposition.

4 **These things have I spoken** (cf. 15: 11) continues the thought of v. 2, following the parenthetical statement of v. 3. **When their hour comes,** that is the time when the prophecies of persecution will be fulfilled. The phrase echoes the several allusions to the appointed "hour" of Christ's sufferings in this Gospel (e.g.,

2:4; 8:20; 12:23; 13:1). **Ye may remember.** The disciples' faith doubtless was strengthened when they later recalled how Jesus had predicted persecution (Acts 5: 41; 13:52). Previous to this time Jesus had not stressed the prospects of persecution in the future — "sufficient unto the day was the evil thereof." Now, however, in view of his imminent departure, the time has come to forewarn them of what is in store. Although Matthew reports this warning in the early Galilean ministry (Matt. 5:10-12) it was not until after Peter's Confession that Jesus spoke freely about his own suffering and death (Mark 8:31ff.) Gradually he led them to see that their role of suffering for their faith would be similar (Luke 9:23-26).[7]

5 **But now I go unto him that sent me.** Once more Christ announces his impending return to the Father. To allay the grief this caused, he reassured the disciples by

---

god," covenant with each other not to do wrong, and conclude by a meal of "harmless" food. In Pliny's opinion this "offense" was not very serious.

By far the most serious instances of apostasy were the result of the Decian persecution in the middle of the third century. So numerous were the apostates, many of whom repented later and sought re-admission to the churches, that a major controversy developed over what to do about these repentant apostates.[b] Prior to 250 A.D., the matter was of great concern also. The Shepherd of Hermas recommends that such a penitent be given one more chance, but only one.[c] In the Epistle to the Hebrews, however, not even one lapse is permitted but the direct threatenings are uttered against potential apostates (Heb. 6:1-8; 10:26-39).

On the other hand, Christian history is replete with the memory of those who

were faithful, even unto death. Not only did many Christians welcome persecution as an indication of divine favor (cf. Heb. 12:3-17; I Pet. 4:12-19), but they welcomed martyrdom as well.[d] Stephen became the proto-martyr and set a precedent for thousands to follow. Polycarp, while being burned at the stake, prayed for his enemies, and many, such as Ignatius, wanted nothing better than to seal their Christian testimony with their lives. As a result, a distinct type of literature grew up, known as hagiography, accounts of the lives and deaths of the martyrs. This tradition has survived into modern times in works like Fox's *Book of Martyrs,* and in works telling of twentieth-century saints like John and Betty Stam of China and the martyrs among the Auca tribesmen in South America.

These words of Jesus have a remarkable relevance today. From mainland China,

---

[6] E.g., "His own received him not," 1:11; cf. 3:19; 5:37-41; 8:43-45; 12:37.
[7] This theme received much emphasis in the early church (Acts 9:16; II Cor. 11:23-28; II Tim. 2:12; 3:12).
[b] Cyprian, Epistle xx. 3. cited in B. J. Kidd, *op. cit.,* I, 191-2.
[c] *Mand.* IV. iii. 6 (K. Lake, ed., *Apostolic Fathers* — Loeb), II, 84.
[d] Ignatius, To the Ephesians, XXI, 2. Cited in K. Lake, ed., *op. cit.,* I, 195.

6 But because I have spoken these things unto you, sorrow hath filled your heart.

---

the promise that the Holy Spirit is to be his successor and that the Spirit will be able to help them just as much or more than if he were to stay. Jesus often referred to God as the Sender and to himself as the One sent.[8]

None of you asketh me, Whither goest thou? Previous to this, when Jesus mentioned his departure, several questions had been asked, "Whither goest thou?" (13:36) and Thomas had complained that they did not know of his destination (14:5). Then he had explained that he was going to the Father (14:28). Apparently Jesus was disappointed that they did not follow up his announcement that he was going to the Father by further questions. The earlier questions had been self-centered, concerned only with the consequences to them of his departure. Now they appear to have little curiosity about the blessedness, from Jesus' standpoint, of

his return to the Father. If they had loved him they would have rejoiced at his return "home." Instead they only grieved over their own bereavement (16:6). They failed to appreciate the fact that he had predicted the coming of the "Spirit of Truth," who would remain with them as guide and helper, making their witnessing effective (14:16, 17, 26; 15:26).

6 Sorrow hath filled your heart. "Sorrow" (lypē) is grief, pain, affliction.[9] Perhaps "grief" best fits this verse. The use of the perfect (hath filled) here suggests that the disciples were in a state of gloom, as a pervading, lingering condition. All that evening they had been hearing of Jesus' death and departure. To be bereft of his immediate presence seemed to them an irreparable loss. Without him life would be entirely different and the whole matter of the "kingdom" apparently jeopardized. Henceforth their preaching missions would

---

reports filter out of modern persecutions which have caused both widespread apostasy and the development of a virile "underground movement" of Christian witnesses which seems destined to survive. Indeed few persecutions in history have been successful, the most successful perhaps being the virtual extermination of Roman Catholics in Japan during the seventeenth and eighteenth centuries. Thus, daily as we write and read, Jesus' predictions of persecution are being literally fulfilled. One of the fruits of the Spirit, one result of being baptized with the Holy Spirit, is courage to face up to danger and bear witness in spite of personal cost (Acts 4:24-31; 18:9, 10). This facet of N. T. teaching is something "secure" Christians often overlook.

Toward the middle of the first century, when Paul wrote to the Thessalonians, the major persecution was from the Jews (I Thess. 2:14-16). The exclusion from the synagogues was of varying degrees of severity. First came the light punishment (neziphah), the more severe discipline being called the nidduy and requiring exclusion for one month. Offenders who did not respond to these disciplinary mea-

sures were formally and finally banned (herem) from all further fellowship (CKB, p. 299). Like excommunication during the Middle Ages, this action by the Jewish elders was regarded as depriving their victim of eternal life and as well as of acceptance in the community of men. The social and economic penalty of this was often extremely severe. No doubt many of John's first readers knew what this involved by first-hand experience. Similar practices existed soon after the establishment of the modern state of Israel; so-called apostates or renegades from the Jewish faith were feared and detested far more than those who were never Jews. Once a person is convinced that his is the only true position, and that it is very important to espouse this position, tolerance of "heresy" or "apostasy" is difficult. So it was with the ancient Jewish leaders, the Inquisition of the Middle Ages and even with the persecutors of Servetus in Geneva and of Tyndale near Antwerp. Sometimes "tolerance is the child of indifference." True tolerance distinguishes between compulsion and persuasion, between essentials and non-essentials, after the motto of the German pietists: "In

---

8 E.g., 3:17, 34; 5:36, 38; 6:29, 38, 57; 7:29; 8:42; 11:42; 10:36; 13:16.
9 John 16:21; Heb. 12:11; II Cor. 2:3; Phil. 2:27; Rom. 9:2.

7 Nevertheless I tell you the truth: It is expedient for you that I go away; for if I go not away, the Comforter will not come unto you; but if I go, I will send him unto you.

8 And he, when he is come, will convict the world in respect of sin, and of righteousness, and of judgment:

---

seem to be without motive and direction, beset with insuperable problems and difficulties.

7 **It is expedient** (*sympherei* — "profitable" — II Cor. 8:10) **for you that I go away.** An enlightened self-interest would have shown the disciples that Jesus' departure would be mutually advantageous. However, under the circumstances it is easy to see why the disciples were not easily reassured; they could not see how a spirit could possibly replace the man of flesh and blood they knew so intimately and trusted so implicitly. "If I do not go, he will by no means (*ou mē*) come unto you." If, on the other hand, Jesus departs, he will send the Paraclete. The Father sends the Son, the Son sends the Paraclete, and later the Paraclete sends the disciples (Acts 13:2). All three of the "sent" ones are witnesses to the world. The result of the Paraclete's advent was "greater works" (14:12), greater knowledge of God (14:20) and the presence of Christ (14:28). Here again he enumerates some of the benefits that will be derived from the ministry of the Holy Spirit. In 14:26 it is stated that the Spirit will teach the disciples "all things," while here stress is placed on the fact that Jesus' departure is the condition of the Spirit's advent.

8 **He will convict the world.** How could the Spirit convince the world when Jesus' sermons did not carry conviction to all of his hearers? Although Jesus was an historical person who gave ageless incomparable teachings and, by his sacrificial death, made possible peace between God and man, nevertheless, he motivated people by external means of persuasion. From now on, however, "the Holy Spirit is the One whose special task it is to apply the saving merits of Christ to the hearts and lives of believers (Rom. 8; Gal. 4:4-6)" (WmH, II, 323). Westcott suggests the same idea (*in loc.*): "The withdrawal of His limited bodily Presence necessarily prepared the way for the recognition of a universal Presence." The verb *elengchō*, meaning to "expose," to "treat with contempt," or to "reprove, rebuke," to "convict" (e.g., Matt. 18:15 — "show him his fault"), was

*(margin notes: "NOTE", "good!!", "*" )*

---

essentials unity, in non-essentials liberty, in all things charity." The problem is to agree on what is essential!

The challenge presented here is the privilege of sharing in Jesus' experience, even in the experience of his suffering. As the disciples were enjoined to welcome participation in the suffering of the prophets (Matt. 5:12) so they are now welcomed to share in the Master's passion. Paul accepted this sharing with profound soul-satisfaction. Out of the depths of his being he longed "to know him and the power of his resurrection and the fellowship of his suffering" (Phil. 3:10). Only if we share in Christ's passion are we fully qualified or prepared to share in his glory (II Tim. 2:9-13). This spirit is voiced by one of the late Auca martyrs, in saying, "He is not foolish who gives what he cannot keep to obtain what he cannot lose."

### c. The Paraclete Accusing the World (16:7-11)

This paragraph embraces what Windisch terms the fourth Paraclete saying. It is the most difficult of them all to understand. It begins with an announcement that Jesus' departure is for the disciples' own best interests since it makes possible the Spirit's advent. Jesus directed their attention to the unanticipated benefits accruing to them immediately after his leavetaking. It called for the upward and farsighted "eye of faith."

*Yet love will dream, and Faith will trust*
*(Since He who knows our need is just)*
*That somehow, somewhere, meet we must.*
*Alas for him who never sees*
*The stars shine through his cypress-trees!*

9 of sin, because they believe not on me;

used by Greek moralists of the conscience. Philo said the Word was an *elengchos* (*Det.* 146) — a "proof" or a "test" — sent for service to men, convicting their consciences. John has recorded Jesus' statement that the Paraclete will intensify and supplement the function of the conscience. But he does not go into detail as to how this is done. However, elsewhere in the N. T. it is made clear that the Spirit uses internal and invisible stimuli to bring men to conviction, and to use them in furthering God's will. Relevant passages include, "the Spirit of the Father is the one speaking in you" (Matt. 10:20), "the Holy Spirit will teach you in that very hour" (Luke 12:12), "the Spirit is the one who makes alive" (John 6:63 JRM), "they were all filled with the Holy Spirit" (Acts 2:4), "you shall receive the gift of the Holy Spirit" (Acts 2:38 RSV), "then Peter, filled with the Holy Spirit, said" (Acts 4:8), "the Holy Spirit whom God has given to them who make a practice of obeying (pres. tense) him" (Acts 5:32 JHG). The above quotations indicate that

while the Spirit indwells believers, he also uses them to bear witness privately and publicly with telling effectiveness. The truth that Christ alone can save sinners, proclaimed to unbelievers, is used by the Spirit to bring conviction of sin and to lead them to repentance. Since God, through the Holy Spirit, draws the unsaved to himself (John 6:44), Christian workers find the indwelling presence of the Spirit imperative for success in winning men to Christ. No one can be "born again" without the presence and power of the Holy Spirit (John 3:3-7).

9 **Of sin, because they believe not on me.** Before God can reach and use men in his kingdom they must become aware that they are guilty of the cardinal sin of rejecting Christ as Savior and Lord of their lives. "If you believe not that I am he, you shall die in your sins" (John 8: 24 JHM). The Holy Spirit "will convict the world of the fact of sin (in men), of the fact of righteousness (in Christ), and of the fact of judgment. . . .the sin of the world is concentrated in its rejection of

*NOTE:*

*Who, hopeless, lays his dead away,*
*Nor looks to see the breaking day*
*Across the mournful marbles play!*
*Who hath not learned, in hours of*
*  faith,*
*  The truth to flesh and sense un-*
*  known,*
*That Life is ever lord of Death,*
*And Love can never lose its own!*[e]

In John 16:7-11 the ministry of the Spirit to the world at large is stressed. Since it is stated in John 14:17 that the Spirit is not given directly to the world it is implied that the influence of the Spirit on the world is mediated through Spirit-filled believers.

Two English words traslate the Greek *elengcho*: "convict" and "convince." The former has forensic connotations, the latter means persuasion; one is judicial, the other intellectual; the former involves status, the latter attitude.

The work of the Paraclete in indicting and convincing the unregenerate is termed

by the older theologians "prevenient grace," the effect of the Spirit on hearts *prior* to surrender and obedience. Historical examples of this phase of the Spirit's work include the reaction of the crowd to Peter's sermon at Pentecost. After hearing Peter's description of Jesus' life and death, and realizing that they did not believe in him or accept him, many were convinced by the Spirit that their judgment had been wrong, that they had made a tragic mistake in their estimate of Jesus. They were convicted by the Spirit and hence felt guilty. This prepared the way for their repentance and faith and assurance of God's forgiveness and favor (Acts 2:36-41).

There have been other repetitions of scenes like those at Pentecost. One such occurrence is reported among the Moravians in Germany during the eighteenth century. In 1727 at Herrnhut, Germany, among the United Brethren (*Unitas Fratrum*), something similar to this first Pentecost occurred, except that it was

e J. G. Whittier, "Snowbound," in W. A. Briggs, ed., *Great Poems of the English Language* (New York: Tudor Publ. Co., 1933), pp. 722f.

10 of righteousness, because I go to the Father, and ye behold me no more;

---

Jesus . . . . The rejection of Jesus . . . is the type and crown of all sin, and ultimately the sin of the world amounts to the crucifixion of Christ" (CKB, pp. 406f.). Thus the "stone" which the Jewish leaders rejected is also rejected by the world at large in spite of the fact that God vindicated this "stone" by the resurrection from the dead (cf. Acts 3:17; 4:11; Rom. 1:4). Thus, the resurrection became both the central part in the Christian's creed (Rom. 10:9) and the main factor in the world's sin of unbelief.

10 Of righteousness (*peri dikaiosynēs*) because I go to the Father. As the sin of the world was summed up in the unbelief which resulted in Jesus' death upon the cross, so the ascension of Jesus is the event which vindicates Jesus and substantiates his claim to being righteous. The world in its false estimate of "righteousness" brought about Jesus' death; God, repudiating the world's judgment of Jesus, and vindicating Jesus' righteousness, raised him from the grave to a place in heaven at his "right hand" (cf. WmH, II, 326). Jesus' resurrection and ascension together

were God's vindication of Jesus' claim to a share in the righteousness of God.

The whole scope of the coming of Christ to earth — his life, teachings, deeds, death, resurrection and ascension — are the historical works of Christ which make possible righteousness (coming into God's favor) in men. Without faith in Christ as sin-bearer and Savior one does not receive righteousness. The fullest exposition of this truth is in the Epistle to the Romans, focused in 1:16, 17 where there is set forth the "good news" concerning God's method of making bad men good — "for therein is the righteousness of God revealed from faith unto faith." Romans 1-11 explains and illustrates how God in Christ offers pardon, peace and security to those who acquire this God-given righteousness through trust in Christ and his righteousness. The word "righteousness" (*dikaiosynē*) occurs only here (vv. 8, 10) in this Gospel but thirty-two times in Romans and the adjective "righteous" seven times. Here the reference is the righteousness of Christ; in Romans, Paul speaks basically of God's righteousness,

---

limited to believers. The Moravians on this occasion were quarrelling Christian refugees from persecution. They were on Count Zinzendorf's estate as his guests. After some months of Bible study and frequent prayer meetings they were assembled on August 13: "A great hunger for the Word of God took possession of us so that we had to have three services every day, viz., at 5:00 A.M., 7:00 A.M., and 9:00 P.M. Everyone desired above everything else that the Holy Spirit might have full control. Self-love and self-will, as well as all disobedience, disappeared and an overwhelming flood of grace swept us all out in the great ocean of Divine Love."[f]

The account continues by reporting that instead of being critical of each other they were now critical of themselves only, as if alone in the sight of the Savior. Zinzendorf reported in addition that ". . . A sense of the nearness of Christ,

bestowed, in a single moment, upon all the members that were present; and it was so unanimous that two members at work twenty miles away, unaware that the meeting was being held, became at the same time deeply conscious of the same blessing."[g]

All of the members of this congregation were laymen; no clergymen were present. However, from this Pentecostal-type effusion of the Spirit, scores became ministers and missionaries. This gave birth to the modern missionary movement, differing from previous missionary work in that it was not state-sponsored or church-sponsored but arose from the inward convictions of individuals, similar to the inception of the Gentile mission at Antioch in Syria (Acts 13). This impetus fired the heart and mind of William Carey and later the Wesleys, John and Charles. The influence of the Moravians on John Wesley through Spangenberg (in Georgia)

---

[f] Quoted in John Greenfield, *Power From on High* (Atlantic City, N. J.: The World Wide Revival Prayer Movement), pp. 14f.
[g] *Ibid.*, p. 15.

11 of judgment, because the prince of this world hath been judged.

---

which, under certain conditions, can be imparted to man. Neither author intended to teach that the human possessor of this righteousness would necessarily be sinless as a result; but rather that he had come into a saving relationship with God. As a result of this new relationship, however, the Holy Spirit would seek to fully indwell the believer and exclude sin, motivating him to turn to God wholeheartedly and away from all sin, henceforth leading a constructive, useful and unselfish life. When the Holy Spirit comes into one's heart love for God and man overflows — "we know we have passed from death into life because we love the brethren" (I John 3:14). In addition to love, other graces of the Spirit flourish in the Spirit-filled Christian — "joy, peace, longsuffering, kindness, goodness, faithfulness, gentleness and self-control" (Gal. 5:22, 23). Only when this occurs can personality reach its highest level of development.

Closely allied to the term "righteousness" is the word "salvation," a derivative from the Latin *salvus,* meaning "saved,

safe, well." The Greek *sōtēria,* meaning "salvation" is from *sōtēr* or "savior." The former emphasized the results and the latter the advantages of having a savior. The Greek *sōtēria,* like *dikaiosynē,* implies a favorable relationship to God. This was realized fully in Jesus Christ and openly endorsed by God the Father in the raising and ascension of Jesus. Like Job of old, only to much greater degree, Jesus was a living exhibit of probity, and his life and works were validated and vindicated by the mighty acts which culminated in the resurrection and ascension (cf. II Cor. 5:19). Provision for the redemption of all believers was complete when the ascension took place.

11 **Of judgment, because the prince of this world hath been judged** (*kekritai,* perf. pass., i.e., "now stands judged"). This is the third time the world's "prince" or "ruler" (*archōn*) has been mentioned in this Gospel. Victory over this sinister force is predicted both in 12:31 and 14:30. In I John the same essential idea is associated with the "anti-Christ," who is the spirit of the devil in opposing the

---

and Peter Böhler (in London) has often been told. The result was the "strangely warmed heart" of John Wesley at Aldersgate Street in London, the field preaching at Bristol and the world-wide outreach of the Evangelical Revival which became Methodism and its branches.

Another illustration of the Spirit's work in convincing men of sin is seen in the effects of Jonathan Edwards' sermon entitled "Sinners in the Hands of an Angry God." This was an important factor in the revival known to history as the First Great Awakening. In recent times an ordinary chapel service at Asbury College resulted in scenes comparable to Pentecost, in a service that remained in continuous session for 114 hours with the result that some five thousand were converted as a direct or indirect result of this out-pouring of the Spirit.[h] In 1957 the writer of this exposition stood amid thousands on Times Square, New York City, scene of many a half-crazed New

Year's Eve throng, and heard a Spirit-inspired gospel summons which was attended by the deep hush, the solemnity, the silent request for prayer by hundreds of up-lifted hands which bespeaks the conviction of sin which the Spirit brings to the world.

It appears that the Spirit convinces the world that it sinned in rejecting the Savior. The fact that Jesus returned to the Father is evidence that he was not a blasphemer but a righteous man who told the sober truth when he claimed to be the Son of God. Because of these two facts the world is convicted and fears the judgment to come. The world is convinced of its own unrighteousness by its contrast to Jesus' righteousness. Nothing is as apt to convince a person of his own vileness as to contrast his life with something holy. This is seen again after the Spirit-led preaching of the apostles. The report that Jesus had returned to his Father in heaven served to reassure the disciples

[h] H. James, *Halls Aflame* (Wilmore, Ky.: Seminary Press, 1955), *passim.*

12 I have yet many things to say unto you, but ye cannot bear them now.

---

Christ (I John 2:18, 22; cf. 3:8, 10). The "casting out of this ruler" in John 12:31 is similar to the ejection of "that ancient serpent, who is called the Devil and Satan, the deceiver of the world" (RSV), following the war in heaven with the righteous angels (Rev. 12:9). It is comparable also to the struggle between the "Angel of Darkness" and the "Prince of Lights," a struggle which will continue until the time of the Inquisition or the final Judgment.[10] In the Dead Sea Manual of Discipline the conflict continues by God's decree until the consummation of the age while here Jesus announces that the victory is already accomplished. By overcoming death Jesus sealed the doom of Satan, who had power over death. Jesus penetrated into the realm of the "ruler of this world" and dispossessed him of his power over death, thus assuring a victory in which humans can share (I Cor. 15:57). Paul,

likewise, spoke of this *archōn* as "the god of this world" (II Cor. 4:4). In Jesus the Christian has one who has "all authority in heaven and on earth" (Matt. 28:18), and who exercises that authority not only to deliver from death but also from the fear of death since "perfect love casteth out fear" (I John 4:18). This confidence is eloquently phrased by Paul — "I am sure that neither death nor life . . . nor anything else in all creation, will be able to separate us from the love of God in Christ Jesus our Lord" (Rom. 8: 38, 39 RSV).

12 I have many things to say is comparable to the "many things" the writer to the Hebrews was eager to share with his readers but was thwarted by their spiritual immaturity (Heb. 5:11). The Master had already told them things which they had not yet fully assimilated.[11] The remainder would have to await a time in the future

---

that he and his cause were righteous because vindicated by God. Paul used the same argument when writing to the Romans — Christ's incarnation was demonstrably true because consistent with Scriptural promises. The resurrection is demonstrably true because experienced as a God-inspired *fait accompli*. The resurrection of Christ is to the N. T. what the Exodus from Egypt was to the Old Testament — both were viewed as God's accomplished fact, his "mighty act" which vindicates the faith of the elect (Ps. 106: 2; cf. Acts 13:32-41; 17:29-31). The resurrection both substantiated the righteousness of Jesus who was thus vindicated by God's gracious act and exposed the wickedness of the world which had sanctioned Jesus' death by its unbelief.

The third aspect of the Spirit's activity in the world and on the world is convicting men of judgment because the prince of this world has been judged. The victory of God and Christ (by the resurrection) over the ruler of this world means that those not aligned with Jesus but sympathetic with the devil will find themselves involved in the same condemnation with the devil (cf. 3:17-21;

8:44-47). It is the Spirit's prerogative to press home to the consciences of men the fact that they are on the wrong side of the eternal struggle between good and evil, light and darkness, Christ and the "prince of this world." This is clarified by the historical fact that the essential victory was gained by God at the resurrection and ascension. Thus the work of the Spirit is not purely subjective; it is based rather on the objective fact of God's mighty act in Christ and the involvement of the "world" in this fact. There is no room for neutrality in the N. T., much less in the Fourth Gospel and First Epistle of John. Those who are not believers, are, by virtue of that fact, in league with the devil and share in his judgment (5:22-29; 12:31; 14:30; I Cor. 2:6-8; cf. Rev. 20:10, 15). This truth the Spirit brings home to hearts by an appeal to their reason, to their emotions and to their consciences.

One of many instances that could be cited of the manner in which the Spirit convicts the world is reflected in the diary of a Connecticut farmer during the visit of the English evangelist George Whitefield at the time of the Great Awakening in

---

[10] IQS iv. 13 — iv. 26 (T. H. Gaster, *The Dead Sea Scriptures* [Garden City, N. Y.: Doubleday & Co., 1956], p. 43).

[11] John 14:25; 15:11; 16:1, 6, 25, 33.

13 Howbeit when he, the Spirit of truth, is come, he shall guide you into all the truth: for he shall not speak from himself; but what things soever he shall hear, *these* shall he speak: and he shall declare unto you the things that are to come.

---

when the disciples by experience, insight and spiritual growth would be ready to accept them.

13 **He shall guide you** (*hodēgēsei hymas*) **into all truth.**[12] For the third time the "Spirit of Truth" is given as the name of the Paraclete. The same circle of ideas was present in the mind of this author when he wrote to "the elect lady" and to Gaius (II John 1:2, 4; III John 1-4). Opposed to the truth is the deceiver or the antichrist, the antithesis to Truth (II John 7). Among the monks of Qumran also the "Angel of Truth" was expected to assist the "sons of light" to victory over the darkness on the side of the "Prince of Lights" (1QS iv. 1-26). Here the Spirit of Truth leads to Christ. The fact that the Greek article precedes the word for truth suggests that John may have intended to indicate that Christ is the truth (cf. John 14:6). If so, the Spirit of Truth is the same as the Spirit of Christ. The Paraclete does not lead into "all the truth" in the sense of general knowledge; it means rather that he leads into all the truth pertaining to Jesus Christ

(v. 14). The word **guide** (*hodēgēsei*) is compounded of the word for "way" and the word for "guide." It means literally "lead in the way," as in Ps. 25:5. Hermes is one who leads to a knowledge of the light in the Hermetic literature (M-M). Judah is advised that the love of money *leads* one astray. While on the other hand the "spirit of truth" testifieth to all things and accuseth all.[13] In this passage, as here in the Fourth Gospel, the Spirit of Truth also serves as the accuser, as the *katēgoros,* in a role similar to that of "Moses" (cf. John 5:45). Truth is always disturbing, provocative, and hazardous to the exponents of error, as Isaiah so clearly recognized (Isa. 28:17). With a divine leader of infinite knowledge, compassion and power disciples can be assured of adequate guidance "into all truth."

The role of the Spirit is something like that of an ambassador. He does not speak with independent authority but rather relays what he hears from the Godhead. Jesus wanted them to be assured that they would not be under "new management" but that their new guide would give es-

---

New England. In 1740 the farmer wrote that after hearing about the excitement which attended Whitefield's preaching in Philadelphia, "I felt the Spirit of God drawing me by conviction; i longed to see and hear him and wished he would come this way." Whitefield did come to Hartford, Conn., and the farmer and his wife, hearing of it, rushed on horseback from the field to Middletown, arriving just in time to hear the evangelist. In the farmer's own words: "He looked almost angelical a young slim slender youth . . . with a bold countenance . . . for he looked as if he was Cloathed with authority from ye great god and a sweet collome Solemnity sat upon his brow and my hearing him preach gave me a heart wound by gods blessing . . . my old foundation was broken up and i saw that

my righteousness would not save me. . . ."[1] Millions similarly affected by the witnessing of the Spirit-anointed preachers demonstrate the truth of Jesus' prediction on this occasion.

d. Guiding the Believer (16:12-15)

Paralleling the Spirit's ministry to the world is his ministry to the believers who have come "out of" the world. In this passage the term "paraclete" is not used but the Spirit of Truth appears for the third time, an obvious reference to the Paraclete of v. 7. Indeed this may be considered as being in the same passage as 16:1-15. The Spirit's role here is that of a *guide* to the believer. This term as a verb occurs only five times in the

---

[12] Manuscripts Aleph, D, W, Theta and others have "*in* (en) all truth" rather than "into" (*eis*) as here. The former implies a leadership of those already in possession of the truth while the latter implies leading from error into truth; one being a ministry to believers, the other to unbelievers.
[13] Test. Twelve Patriarchs: Judah 19, R. H. Charles, *op. cit.,* II, 321.
[1] From a letter in Yale University, cited by W. W. Sweet, *Religion in Colonial America* (New York: Chas. Scribner's Sons, 1943), p. 286.

14 He shall glorify me: for he shall take of mine, and shall declare *it* unto you.

15 All things whatsoever the Father hath are mine: therefore said I, that he taketh of mine, and shall declare *it* unto you.

---

sentially the same guidance and from the same source as that to which they were accustomed during the past months in his presence. The Spirit of Truth, then, leads specifically "into a complete understanding of and sympathy with that absolute Truth, which is Christ Himself" (BFW, *ad loc.*). New things are in store for the believer who continues to follow the Holy Spirit as the personal representative of Christ; it is a progressive evidence (WPNT, V, 268).

He shall declare unto you the things that are to come. The Paraclete's work is not that of making the disciples oracles, although oracles were prevalent and popular in that day. The Spirit is not a power to be exploited for personal gain, as Simon Magus learned (Acts 8:24). His mission is not to gratify curiosity about future events (Acts 1:7). He is not to be sought even for his own sake. Rather his mission is to supplement and capitalize on the work of Christ. The Spirit would advance "the things already begun concerning the work of the Kingdom (Luke 7:19; 18:

30), not a chart of future history" (WPNT, V, 268).

14 He shall glorify me. As Christ glorified the Father (17:4) so the Spirit is to glorify Christ. The writers of the N. T. are one evidence of how the Holy Spirit glorified Christ through recalling and relating the words and works of Jesus, thus helping create the written Gospel records. The person who is most Spirit-filled is the one most likely to glorify Jesus. The notion that the one who honors the Holy Spirit reflects a higher state of grace, or deeper insight, than the one who honors Christ is not a notion derived from the Scriptures. The teaching concerning the Paraclete, as given in chs. 14-16, urges recognition of the closest possible connection with Father, Son and Paraclete without causing any to lose his identity.

15 He shall take of mine and shall declare it unto you. The promise that the Spirit would reveal Christ is repeated for emphasis. The point being emphasized is that the Spirit will serve as "liaison

---

N. T. and four times as a noun. Parallel uses include the designation of Judas as a guide to the soldiers who arrested Jesus (Acts 1:16) and of Hermes or mind (*nous*) who guides souls to knowledge (M-M). The Spirit of Truth will guide to the One who is the Way and the Truth and the Life. From 8:31 we learn that this truth comes from acquaintance with Jesus and his word. In contrast the Jewish leaders are described as "blind leaders of the blind" (Matt. 15:14; cf. Rom. 2:19). In parallel usages Philip acts as spiritual guide to the Ethiopian eunuch (Acts 8:31), and the Lamb guides the redeemed to "fountains of living water" (Rev. 7:17).

The role of the Holy Spirit as a guide into all truth is represented in a Greek miniature of the tenth century. It depicts King David, praying, "Give the king thy judgments, O God, and thy righteous-

ness to the king's son." On either side of the king are figures representing Wisdom and Prophecy while above is the Holy Spirit in the form of a dove (cf. II Sam. 23:2).[j] David attributed his inspiration as a poet to the Spirit of God, Solomon obtained wisdom, Daniel was given "an excellent spirit," and those who obeyed might "be filled with the spirit of understanding" (Eccles. 39:6) under the Old Covenant. The revelation of divine truth through the Spirit of God to certain men in all generations was a generally accepted belief, as reflected among the Essenes of the first century.[k]

This passage (16:13) reveals the Holy Spirit as the interpreter. He does not speak from himself (*aph' eautou*) or "on his own authority" (RSV, NEB) but speaks of and for Jesus Christ. Thus the closest possible relationship exists between the Son and the Spirit while each retains his

---

j F. N. Peloubet, *op. cit.*, p. 452.
k "To these has He ever revealed His holy spirit at the hands of His anointed and has ever disclosed the truth." Zadokite Document ii, 13, tr. by T. Gaster, *op. cit.*, p. 63.

16 A little while, and ye behold me no more; and again a little while, and ye shall see me.

17 *Some* of his disciples therefore said one to another, What is this that he saith unto us, A little while, and ye behold me not; and again a little while, and ye shall see me: and, Because I go to the Father?

18 They said therefore, What is this that he saith, A little while? We know not what he saith.

19 Jesus perceived that they were desirous to ask him, and he said unto them, Do ye inquire among yourselves concerning this, that I said, A little while, and ye behold me not, and again a little while, and ye shall see me?

20 Verily, verily, I say unto you, that ye shall weep and lament, but the world shall rejoice: ye shall be sorrowful, but your sorrow shall be turned into joy.

---

officer" between God and man. The Spirit's role is authoritative because he has direct access to Christ who in turn has direct access to the Father. John is not attempting to lay the foundation for a doctrine of the Trinity (although that is what he actually did); rather he is quoting Jesus as saying repeatedly and emphatically that his departure does not mean a separation and that in accepting "another Paraclete" they will not be changing leaders. It will be the same leadership through the Paraclete.

16 **A little while and ye behold** (*theoreite*) **me no more** (cf. v. 10), that is, they would no longer gaze upon him in physical form as hitherto. *Mikron* is an adjective meaning "little" or "small," with the implied reference to time. The repetition of this term six times in four verses underscores the fact that the time until Jesus' death was only a few hours away (cf. 7: 33; 13:33; 14:19). Also the period between the death and the resurrection was only from Friday afternoon until Sunday morning. It was natural that the disciples were confused and frustrated by this statement. But, after Easter morning, they looked back upon this as a prophecy fulfilled "above all that we can ask or think" (Eph. 3:20).

20 **Ye shall weep and lament** (*klausete kai thrēnēsete*). Both verbs were used to express loud mourning so customary when death invaded people's homes. Many Hebrews and other Orientals even today are unrestrained in expressing grief when sorrow comes (cf. Gen. 50:3; Nah. 3:7; Luke 8:52). Jesus was predicting their reaction to his death. However, there is

---

separate identity. The revelation comes thus from God and from Christ and is expressed through the Holy Spirit. Again the coordinate relationship of Father and Son is expressed together with the subordinate relationship of the Spirit. These passages are the main source for the doctrine of the Trinity but our author here seems less concerned to specify the precise relationships within the Trinity than to specify the exact relationship of the Paraclete to Jesus Christ. In keeping with this the Biblical writers usually speak of God expressing himself through the Holy Spirit (Wisd. Sol. 7:7, 15, 22; I Sam. 23: 2; Acts 4:25). A possible exception is found in the Epistle to the Hebrews, where it is implied that divine revelation is initiated, rather than echoed, by the Holy Spirit (Heb. 3:7 — "the Holy Spirit saith"). The early church sometimes recognized in the voices of their leaders the influence of the Holy Spirit, as during the first "ecumenical" council at Jerusalem, when the conclusions reached were attributed to the guidance of the Spirit (Acts 15: 28), doubtless a fulfillment of this promise of Christ.

13 **He shall declare unto you the things that are to come.** This was apparently fulfilled in Paul's life when he predicted trouble at sea (Acts 27:10, 21). The author of the Apocalypse believed that it was fulfilled in his inspired visions of things to come (Rev. 1:1, 10). The things revealed are ultimately from the Father (v. 15) and immediately from the Son (vv. 14, 15). There is implied here something akin to progressive revelation. John Robinson, pastor of the "pilgrims" who left Holland for New England in 1620 said to a portion of his "flock" as they sailed away, "God shall yet cause new light to come forth out of his

21 A woman when she is in travail hath sorrow, because her hour is come: but when she is delivered of the child, she remembereth no more the anguish, for the joy that a man is born into the world.

22 And ye therefore now have sorrow: but I will see you again, and your heart shall rejoice, and your joy no one taketh away from you.

---

no record of loud lamentation after Jesus' death; perhaps the shock was too deep for expression. Strong emotion often paralyzes and incapacitates.

21 A woman . . . in travail has sorrow (*lypēn*). "The article is generic; this is the general law" cf. 15:15 (CGT). The common-place agony of a woman in child-birth afforded severals writers of the O. T. with analogies.[14] The point here is not the intensity of pain but the comparative brevity of the pain and the contrast between the temporary discomfort and the joy which follows. The clause **her hour is come** recalls Jesus' frequent references to his "hour" (2:4; 4:21, etc.).[15]

22 **Ye therefore now have sorrow . . . but I will see you again.** Jesus was preparing them for the shock of his death and the surprise of his resurrection. In spite of these bracing words the sequel proves that the disciples were ill-prepared for either the sorrow or the joy of the

resurrection. We may wonder why Jesus did not go into greater detail and become more specific. Apparently the disciples felt likewise (vv. 25, 28, 29). Perhaps, in reporting Jesus' words, the author wished to emphasize the general principles applicable to wider situations than that specific historical event. In the discussion of not seeing Jesus and later seeing him two different verbs are used (vv. 16, 19, 22). When they will not be able to "behold" (ASV) him the word is *theōreō*, but after his resurrection, when they will see him, the word is *horaō*. The former stresses a sustained scrutiny. The latter is often found in contexts reporting a spiritual vision, as in I Cor. 9:1; 15:5; or experiencing something (Luke 3:6). In the LXX it is sometimes used for appearances of the Deity. A fourth-century papyrus uses this verb — "watch the emperor himself acting with so much propriety" — while another (160 B.C.) uses

---

Word." By this he meant, not that they would have a divine revelation of something essentially new, but rather that the revelation given earlier, and preserved in the Bible, would become increasingly clear and relevant to them. The newness would be in their understanding rather than in the revelation itself.

Does God still reveal things to people? Are discoverers and pioneers Spirit-inspired today? The answer varies according to how "liberal" one is in his interpretation. Was Pasteur "inspired" in his discoveries which have been beneficial to humanity? Was Edwin Markham (in "The Man with the Hoe") inspired when he predicted that "judgments of rebellion" will shake the world "after the silence of the centuries," a "prophecy" which has already been fulfilled? Was Kipling "inspired" when he predicted (in "Recessional") that England's pride would be humbled if the nation forgot her Hebrew-

Christian heritage and indulged in foolish boasting?

In the role of serving as interpreter for Jesus the Spirit of Truth may be compared to the *Methurgeman* or *Amora* in the Jewish synagogue. The great Rabbi would deliver his sermon in Hebrew and employ the *Amora* to interpret in the language of the people (e.g., Greek or Latin). At the close of the message the *Amora* might answer questions, as the middle man between the learned Rabbi and the unlearned congregation. In these situations the Rabbi had to be careful lest more attention be given to the interpreter than to himself. Accordingly the Amora would be chosen carefully so as not to outshine the Rabbi; often this meant that the Amora would be at least fifty years of age.[1] In a similar manner the Holy Spirit is not to draw attention to himself but rather to glorify Jesus Christ by taking the things of Christ and revealing

---

[14] Isa. 21:3; 26:17; 66:7; Hos. 13:13; Mic. 4:9.
[15] Papyrus Bodmer II (Supplement) and Codex D have "day" instead of "hour." "Hour" seems more appropriate here and has better MSS evidence.
[1] Edersheim, *op. cit.*, I, 445-450.

23 And in that day ye shall ask me no question. Verily, verily, I say unto you, If ye shall ask anything of the Father, he will give it you in my name.

---

this verb to describe a vision in a temple (M-M, p. 455). As with the woman so with the disciples, grief is to come, but, as after child-birth, they will rejoice when they see or experience Jesus again after the resurrection. Their joy will be permanent, in that it is something inaccessible to outsiders. Men can and do destroy the body and harass the mind, but they cannot touch the source of joy in the Lord. As a result, sometimes their rage increases, while at other times they are chastened and repent. The experience of Saul of Tarsus after witnessing the joy with which Stephen laid down his life suggests that this joy was an important factor in Saul's conversion (Acts 22:20).

23 **Ye shall ask** (*erōtēsete*) **me no question . . . if ye shall ask** (*aitēsete*) **anything of the Father.** It is difficult to express in English the distinction in the two Greek verbs for asking used in this verse. The former is the regular term for making an inquiry, the latter for making a request or prayer.[16] More precisely *erōtaō* in classical Greek means only to interrogate or inquire and implies an exchange between equals. *Aiteō*, on the other hand, like the Latin *peto* "is more submissive and suppliant, indeed the constant word for seeking of the inferior from the su-

perior"[17] (RCT, p. 136). Accordingly when the disciples pray, the term *aiteō* is used (Matt. 7:8; Mark 11:24; Luke 11:13; John 17:23, 24, 26; I John 5:15). But when Jesus prays, the word *erōtaō* is employed (John 14:16; 17:9, 15, 20). With the exception of I John 5:16 *erōtaō* is never used in the N. T. to "express the prayer of man to God, of the creature to the Creator" (RCT, p. 138). In this verse the request (*erōtaō*) of the disciples to Jesus for information will be followed by their petition to the Father (*aiteō*) for help as needed. In Johannine usage *erōtaō* is never used to request some material benefit while this restriction is not observed in the employment of the other synonym. Different situations make one's needs different. Christ has opened the door of access to God the Father and it remains open to all who sincerely approach in the name of Jesus. However, the granting of our requests, as Scripture elsewhere indicates, depends upon the nature of the request and the motives of the one making the requests. "Beloved, if our hearts do not condemn us, we have confidence before God; and we receive from him whatever we ask (*aitōmen*) because we keep his commandments and do what pleases him" (I John 3:21, 22 RSV).

---

them to the believers (v. 14). (See Introduction on Paraclete).

### 9. JESUS' DEPARTURE AND RETURN (vv. 16-33)

#### a. Sorrow Turned to Joy (vv. 16-24)

Three problems lingered in the minds of the disciples, problems which remained from the announcement in 13:33ff. One problem was Jesus' destination, and another was the word (*mikron*, a little while). In addition, they were still perplexed about Jesus going "to the Father." In reply, Jesus turned to another analogy, that of women in child-birth. Their transition from grief to gladness, Jesus prophesied,

would be equally drastic and sudden. This assurance was reinforced by another promise of the effectiveness of prayer (v. 24) as a means of obtaining this "fulness of joy."

16 **A little while** may refer either to time between his burial and resurrection, or between his ascension and the coming of the Holy Spirit. The most obvious meaning is the former but it does not seem to exhaust the meaning of the words. From the parallel passage in 14:19 and here, where the prediction is associated with the advent of the Paraclete, one is led to believe that the meeting with Jesus is best fulfilled at Pentecost and after. This is substantiated by the fact that the resurrection and ascension, so far as the re-

---

[16] *Erōtaō* (to inquire) is used in John 1:19, 21, 25; 9:2, 15, 19, 21, 23. *Aiteō* (to request) is used in John 4:9, 10; 11:22; 14:13, 14; 15:7, 16; I John 5:14.

[17] E.g., Acts 12:20; Matt. 7:9; Jas. 1:5; I John 3:22.

24 Hitherto have ye asked nothing in my name: ask, and ye shall receive, tha your joy may be made full.

---

**24 Hitherto have ye asked nothing in my name,** a reference to their past experience in which they prayed, probably, much the same as they had before they met Jesus. Probably they had been God-fearing men who attended the synagogue and observed the conventional religious practices in their homes. True, during the ministry of Jesus they had expressed a desire to go beyond this in personal prayer (Luke 11:1). But henceforth a new chapter in their spiritual life will be opened, one in which individual personal requests, presented to the Father in the name of the Son, will be honored — quite a contrast to the formal liturgical prayers (or "Eighteen Benedictions") of the synagogue. These public prayers date from at least the end of the first century and included both ascription, petition and praise. The language and ideas expressed are similar to that of the Psalter. The petitions in-

cluded requests for knowledge, forgiveness healing, prosperity, the in-gathering o Israel and for the destruction of "th Nazarenes and the heretics," the latte probably a reference to Christians.[18] is unlikely that Jews applied the nam "Christian" to the followers of Jesus sinc "Christ" means "Messiah." Private praye at least among the rabbis, was not un known, and grace before meals was con monplace.

The prayer in the name of Jesus ma have precedents in the invocation of th name of the patriarchs as seen in the Ol Testament. Thus when Moses intercede for the people of Israel he reminded Go of the covenant with Abraham, Isaac and Jacob as the reason why the re quest should be honored (Exod. 32:11 13). In that instance God did not answe because of the intrinsic merit of the case but only because of the patriarchs.[19]

---

action of the disciples was concerned, were not the climactic events. The disciples were taught to look forward to the coming of the Spirit as the climactic event (Luke 24:49; Acts 1:5; cf. John 20:22). But basically these words of Jesus must be a veiled prophecy of the resurrection, a prophecy incomprehensible to his disciples at the time of its utterance. The disciples questioned each other about his meaning and he cut the discussion short by proffering a further explanation. Often the answers will come sooner if the questions are addressed to Jesus rather than to someone as misinformed as ourselves. Much fruitless discussion could better be spent in prayer and study, searching the Scriptures for light and guidance.

**20 Your sorrow shall be turned into joy** is a prophecy fulfilled on more than one occasion in the N. T. reports. The women were the first to change from lamentation to rejoicing as they left the empty tomb with the news (Matt. 28:8). After Jesus appeared to the disciples that first Easter evening they "still disbelieved for joy and wondered" (Luke 24:41). Again, after the ascension they were filled with joy,

as they returned from Olivet to Jerusalem (Luke 24:53) in spite of the fact that h was not with them.

The analogy of child-birth was an effec tive one. Many women, particularly o the Orient, have but short periods of con finement. A day after the birth of child, many of them can go about thei activities as usual. The period of pain i relatively short, although acute; the perio of rejoicing, especially if the child is boy, is relatively long. To an even greate extent than in western lands the greates treasure of the home are the children indeed, in most homes, they are the onl treasure.

The note of joy is characteristic of th N. T. as of no other contemporary litera ture. The writings of the Jews of th period, such as Baruch and Fourth Esdras are predominantly pessimistic. The sam is true of the Stoics, and other moralists Epictetus took a hard look at suicid and decided against it. Seneca was con vinced that there would never be anothe man as good as Socrates and believe that man's sinful inclinations were in curable. But in the N. T., even the casua

---

[18] G. F. Moore, *Judaism* (Cambridge: Harvard University Press, 1927), I, 291-293.
[19] Cf. Lev. 26:40-43; Deut. 9:25-29; Shabbat 30a (G. F. Moore, *op. cit.,* I, 537).

25 These things have I spoken unto you in dark sayings: the hour cometh, when I shall no more speak unto you in dark sayings, but shall tell you plainly of the Father.

---

Solomon asked for wisdom and based his request on God's promise to his father David (II Chron. 1:9). Later, at the dedication of the temple, he again appealed to the covenant with David as the basis on which to stake his appeal (II Chron. 6:14-17). This same covenant later formed the basis for an appeal for God to intervene in Israel's present plight and bring about a restoration (Ps. 89). Elijah invoked the name of the patriarchs in his prayer at the time of Israel's major spiritual crisis (I Kings 36-38).

It is noteworthy that in each case in which the name of a patriarch is cited as a reason why the prayer should be granted, it is not merely the mention of a name, as in an incantation or magical rite, but rather an appeal to a commitment made by God to them. The petition simply reminds God of his previous commitment and asks him to act now in a manner consistent with this earlier commitment. Christians, authorized to use the name of Jesus, have a much more powerful basis for appeal than those who prayed in the name of the patriarchs. Hence he assures us, Ask (aiteite, pres. imperative, i.e., "be asking repeatedly") and ye shall receive, that your joy may be full, or complete, i.e., "become and remain complete." Christians who habitually ask great things of God and receive them are Christians of deep and abundant joyousness. As they exercise faith for great things, their faith becomes stronger. Out of such daily experiences, Paul wrote, "My God shall supply every need of yours according to his riches in glory in Christ Jesus" (Phil. 4:19). No joy is comparable to that of being instrumental in winning people to Christ. No service is equal to that of bringing people into God's favor. Too few Christians know by experience the unspeakable joy of winning others to Christ.

25 I have spoken to you in dark sayings (paroimiais). This noun may be defined as "1, proverb; 2, in Johannine usage a dark saying, figure of speech in which especially lofty ideas are concealed" (A-G). Veiled truth was often given to un-

---

reader notes the mood of joy and confidence. Those portions of the O. T. which are nearest in spirit to the N. T. (e.g., Isa. 40-66; Ps. 23) are characterized by an undertone of joy. This joy, said Jesus, is something which no combination of circumstances can destroy. It is like the security which believers have in Christ; no outward alien force can deprive them of it (John 10:36; Rom. 8:36-39; I Cor. 15:54-57; Phil. 4:4).

24 Ask, and ye shall receive. Jesus gave three things to the apprehensive eleven to compensate for the loss of his physical presence; his peace (14:27), the Paraclete, and the use of his name in prayer. This is a new teaching on prayer and it is found only in John (14-16). This statement is the fourth in the series on asking in the name of Jesus; in it the same promise is repeated for emphasis, namely, that whatever is asked in Jesus' name will be granted. Later the disciples bore their testimony in Jesus' name (Acts 4:12, 17-21), healings were effected in the name of Jesus (Acts 3:6, 16; 4:7, 10, 30; cf. 19:13), forgiveness of sins was received in his name (Acts 10:43, 48) and prayer in the name of Jesus was answered (Acts 4:30, 31). The proper use of the name in prayer is not that of a magic formula, nor a perfunctory appendage of a petition, but rather a recognition that the blessings from God come to the believer through the Son. What a privilege is thus bestowed upon the believer; what an obligation! The promised joy is both permanent and complete.

The joy of having such a friend as Jesus is one of the choicest treasures one can possess. The believer's status has been lifted to the highest possible level when he becomes an associate of Christ Jesus. The assurances of his concern for his own afford an incomparable satisfaction to the Christian. The assurance of his love and of his eagerness to help in time of need is the believer's unfailing source of peace and joy. Heaven's joy is added to earth's satisfaction so that the Christian actually gets the best of both worlds!

26 In that day ye shall ask in my name: and I say not unto you, that I will pray the Father for you;

27 for the Father himself loveth you, because ye have loved me, and have believed that I came forth from the Father.

28 I came out from the Father, and am come into the world: again, I leave the world, and go unto the Father.

29 His disciples say, Lo, now speakest thou plainly, and speakest no dark saying.

friendly and unresponsive individuals (cf. 10:24; 11:14; Mark 4:12). But even the disciples were often mystified by Jesus' statements, and frequently called for clarification. Predictions of his death, veiled or otherwise, they never did fully grasp until after his resurrection and ascension. However, the time is coming, said Jesus, when he will speak with plainness and openness (*parrēsia*). This was partially fulfilled in v. 29.

26 I will pray (*erōtēsō*, "make request of") the Father for you. This is the fifth and last exhortation to pray in this section (chs. 14-17). After giving assurance that prayer in Christ's name will be answered, the new thought is added that the Father will not need to be informed nor his interest aroused because he is already cognizant of their needs and concerned. The Father loves them and has a personal interest in seeing that their needs are supplied.

27 The perfect tense appears again in "have loved" (*pephilēkate*) indicating a present reality, resulting from a past act of trust and love, hence they love Christ enough to continue living for him. Paul mindful of this kind of discipleship, wrote "He died for all that they that live should no longer live for themselves but for him who for their sakes died and rose again" (II Cor. 5:15). Count Zinzendorf was converted by looking at a painting of Christ on the cross with the statement beneath it: "All this have I done for Thee What has thou done for Me?"

28 I came out from the Father, and am come (*elēlytha*, perf. tense "have come

b. The Disciples Enlightened (vv. 25-33)

25 These things is a reference to the foregoing statements, many of which were enigmatic and obscure. In the future, said Jesus, I shall tell you plainly of the Father. This promise was not long in being fulfilled. In v. 28 Jesus said he had come from the Father into the world and would soon return to the Father. This, replied the disciples, is plain speech (v. 29). In the future, therefore, the disciples can expect a clearer presentation of the things of God. They can also anticipate a more direct access to the Father! Marvelous as it is, the Master is now saying that the Father does not love them simply because of his love for the Son, but that the Father loves them for their own sake, because they believe in the Son. The implication of v. 26 is that the disciples will not really need a mediator to convey their needs to God, because the Father has a personal interest in their welfare.

28 It may be said that the entire Gospel of John can be summed up in this verse: "I came out from the Father (John 1:1-13), and am come into the world (1:14-13:30) again, I leave the world (13:31—19:30) and go unto the Father" (19:31-21:25).

30 Here the disciples indicate an advanced stage in the development of their belief. Although they had been believers already, they now believe more than they did before, or at least have a clearer understanding of what is involved in belief. In practical Christian living it should be generally recognized that there are varying degrees and kinds of faith. Even devils believe (Jas. 2:19), but they do not have saving faith. Some of Jesus' hearers had faith but it was neither deep nor abiding (8:30, 31). On at least one occasion, many of his disciples withdrew their allegiance after initial steps of faith (6:66). Thus "belief" is seldom a "once for-all" decision with permanent consequences; it is rather a conviction leading to a commitment which is subject to constant implementation, growth, and confirmation. What is here reported — by this we believe — is not initial or saving faith, it is the confirmation of that faith

30 Now know we that thou knowest all things, and needest not that any man should ask thee: by this we believe that thou camest forth from God.
31 Jesus answered them, Do ye now believe?
32 Behold, the hour cometh, yea, is come, that ye shall be scattered, every man to his own, and shall leave me alone: and *yet* I am not alone, because the Father is with me.

---

and am now here") into the world (*kosmos*). This is a pithy summary of the incarnation, Christ's life among them, his unequalled teachings and his incomparable deeds. **Again, I leave the world and I go unto the Father.** These two verbs in the present tense are futuristic in function. The immediate future activities of Jesus are thus very briefly stated — his atoning death, resurrection and ascension.

**30 Now we know that thou knowest all things.** The discourses of this night have been reassuring and Jesus has now succeeded in bringing to them real "comfort." Before this, they had believed in Christ's deity but now they have additional confidence that he is like the Father in omniscience. Earlier they experienced evidences of Jesus' knowledge (cf. 1:48;

2:24; 11:14; 16:19) and the cumulative effect of these successive demonstrations of omniscience enabled them now to grasp the fact of his deity anew. It was a step of real progress in their faith.

**31 Jesus** also was relieved and reassured at this expression of confidence which contrasts with his distress at their lack of faith earlier (e.g., 14:9).

**32 The hour cometh, yea, is come** (*kai elēlythen*, perf., "and is now here") **that ye shall be scattered.** *Kai*, in the first occurrence, is used as intensive in function and can be translated "in fact" (D-M, pp. 250f.). What a shock it must have been to the disciples, immediately after their glowing expression of faith, to be told that they would all desert Jesus! This prediction of their fickleness would later

---

brought about by increased comprehension of what is involved in belief.

*So, still within this life,*
*Tho' lifted o'er its strife,*
*Let me discern, compare, pronounce*
*        at last,*
*"This rage was right i' the main,*
*That acquiescence vain:*
*The Future I may face now I have*
*        proved the Past."*[m]

**31, 32 Do ye now believe? . . . ye . . . shall leave me alone.** Peter's profession of loyalty was followed immediately by Jesus' prediction of his apostasy (13:37, 38). Now the disciples' profession of greater faith is followed by Jesus' prediction of their desertion. In the Synoptic accounts this desertion is pointed out as a fulfillment of prophecy (Matt. 26:31; Zech. 13:7). It must have been an unpleasant task for Jesus' biographers to report that his eleven disciples deserted him in the crisis hour. In none of the four Gospels is there a very flattering picture presented of the apostles. The elect ten share with Peter the illusion of

over-confidence in their own fortitude and constancy. Between the extremes of over-confidence and self-despair is the "happy medium" of other-dependence well illustrated by Paul in statements, which, on the surface seem self-contradictory: "I can do all things through Christ which strengtheneth me" (Phil. 4:14 KJV) and "When I am weak then am I strong" (II Cor. 12:10). Paul, not a man given naturally to self-deprecation, had learned on the road to Damascus, and subsequently, the secret that Christ's strength is available to the "weak" (II Cor. 12:9). In a similar mood, a Quaker poet learned to "urge in trembling self-distrust a prayer without a claim."[n] It is such people, rather than the boastful and self-assured, who "from weakness were made strong, waxed mighty in war, turned to flight the armies of aliens" (Heb. 11:34).

**33 In me ye may have peace.** This was the second time that Jesus assured them of peace amid tensions (cf. 14:27). It was not peace *with* the world but peace *in* the world. It was not mere freedom from anxiety obtained by "getting away from it

---

m Robert Browning, "Rabbi Ben Ezra," in C. Hill, ed., *op. cit.*, p. 360.
n J. G. Whittier, "I Bow My Forehead in the Dust," *Hymns of the Living Faith*, p. 410.

33 These things have I spoken unto you, that in me ye may have peace. In th world ye have tribulation: but be of good cheer; I have overcome the world.

---

result in their having a deeper appreciation of Jesus' foreknowledge. Their desertion was also a fulfillment of prophecy — "I will strike the shepherd and the sheep will be scattered" (Zech. 13:7).

**Yet I am not alone, because the Father is with me.** *Kai* is used adversatively here and can be translated "but." As the prophet Micah clung all the more closely to God when he experienced man's unfaithfulness (Mic. 7:1-8) so Jesus found a deeper satisfaction in the Father's continuing presence. With the exception of one short period of crisis (Mark 15:34) Jesus was never without the awareness of the Father's presence and support, but even this was conditioned on Jesus' obedience (John 8:29).

**33 These things have I spoken** (*lelalēka*, perf. tense, "spoken and the words remain") **unto you, that in me ye may have peace.** Peace of mind in the disciples was vastly increased by this intimate dialogue before the passion. Peace, like faith, is inconsistent with worry. When one's peace results from a favorable relationship with God, it is exceptionally well

rooted and hence stabilizes one's entir life. The writer of this exegesis, whil hospitalized following a heart attack, foun great comfort in Isaiah's statement, "Tho dost keep him in perfect peace, whos mind is stayed on thee, because he trustet in thee" (Isa. 26:3). Even though deat should come, the future was "as brigh as the promises of God," and there wa really nothing to worry about.

**I have overcome the world** (*tharseite* pres. imper., "be continually coura geous"). From *nenikēka,* "I have cor quered," comes assurance of victory as present reality. Impending trouble shoul be faced from the perspective of certai ultimate triumph. This is another several instances in which Jesus spoke the future as already past. No doub these words of Jesus were remembere many times by those privileged to hea them, not only during the dark hours the passion, but during the tensions an perils of the next quarter century. Thes words proved to be not only prophec but history as well.

---

all." It was rather a positive and dynamic condition of tranquillity resulting from the indwelling presence of Christ. A poet wrote:

*Give to the winds thy fears; hope and*
*    be undismayed;*
*God hears thy sighs and counts thy*
*    tears, God shall lift up thy head;*
*Thro' waves and clouds and storms,*
*    He gently clears the way;*
*Wait thou his time, so shall this night*
*    Soon end in joyous day.*

*Commit thou all thy griefs And ways*
*    into his hands,*
*To his sure trust and tender care*
*    Who earth and heav'n com-*
*    mands;*
*Who points the clouds their course,*
*    Whom winds and seas obey;*
*He shall direct thy wandering feet,*
*    He shall prepare thy way.*°

**Be of good cheer** (*tharseite*) is foun only once in John but it appears in simila contexts in Matthew 9:2, 22; 14:27; Mar 10:49. In each case the word of er couragement comes in the situation which Jesus' presence and power are t be revealed. In the Synoptic records, th words preceded a change of circumstance for the better, an answer to a heart-fe prayer. The same is true in this instance although the answer is to come as the daw after a dark night of tragedy. These word must have seemed hollow and unrelate to reality as the disciples brooded ove events while Jesus' body was in the grav It must have seemed utterly impossibl for them to reconcile Jesus' brave word "I have overcome the world" with th *fait accompli* of the crucifixion and en tombment. The fact that the eleven wer neither the ones who buried Jesus no the first at the tomb on Easter mornin supports the assumption that their fait

° Paul Gerhardt, tr. by J. Wesley, "Give to the Winds Thy Fears," *Hymns of the Living Fait* (Winona Lake: Light and Life Press, 1951), p. 424.

went into a temporary eclipse at this time. This would account also for their slowness to accept the reports of his resurrection. But once the Easter faith returned, it was made all the more sweet and positive by the "dark night" of testing. After the resurrection and ascension, they could recall the words "I have overcome the world" as a prophecy uttered when its fulfillment seemed on the surface most unlikely. Shelley, in his "Ode to the Skylark," marvelled that a bird, who knew little sorrow, could sing so sweetly, when in normal human experience, it is "the sorrow of the singer which makes the sweetness of the song."

*What objects are the fountains*
  *Of thy happy strain,*
*What fields, or waves, or mountains?*
  *What shapes of sky or plain?*
*What love of thine own kind? what*
  *ignorance of pain?*

*We look before and after,*
  *And pine for what is not:*
*Our sincerest laughter*

*With some pain is fraught*:
*Our sweetest songs are those that*
  *tell of saddest thought.*

*Yet if we could scorn*
  *Hate, and pride, and fear;*
*If we were things born*
  *Not to shed a tear,*
*I know not how thy joy we ever*
  *should come near.*[p]

Jesus did not permit the desertion of the disciples at the critical hour to make him bitter at them. Joseph not only pardoned his brothers but saw their act of treachery as within the benevolent providence of God — "It was not you that sent me hither but God" — (Gen. 45:8). Joseph was benevolent and magnanimous as he looked back; Jesus was magnanimous as he looked forward and upward in the confidence that he would never be without the presence of his Father. The contrast between the spiritual resources of Jesus and those of his disciples is nowhere more striking than here.

[p] Percy Bysshe Shelley, "To a Skylark," W. A. Briggs, ed., op. cit., pp. 569f.

# CHAPTER XVII

$T$ hese things spake Jesus; and lifting up his eyes to heaven, he said, Father, the hour is come; <u>glorify</u> <u>thy</u> <u>Son</u>, that the Son may glorify thee:

---

## EXEGESIS

This, rather than the prayer recorded in Matthew 6:9-13, is really the Lord's Prayer. The other is actually the disciples' prayer, given at their request, as a pattern or model (Luke 11:1). This is by far the longest of the recorded prayers of Jesus. The Synoptic accounts frequently mention Jesus praying but give little of the context of these prayers (Mark 1:35; 6:46; 14:32-39; 15:34; Matt. 14:23; 19:13; 26:36-44; 27:46; Luke 3:21; 5:16; 6:12; 9:18, 28; 11:1; 22:41-45; 23:46). This makes his "high-priestly prayer" the more valuable.

1 **Father, the hour has come.** The supreme purpose for which Christ came into the world was about to be openly displayed. The drama of the world's redemption was ready for the climactic act. Jesus had said these same words before (12:23; cf. 13:1; 16:32). It was the hour of tragedy and triumph, similar to the "day of the Lord" in the Old Testament — the dark and light linked like two sides of the same coin. Here Jesus mentions only the "glory" side.

**Glorify thy Son, that the Son may glorify thee.** The full significance of these words is beyond human understanding. But from the context we ascertain that God's acceptance of Jesus' self-sacrifice for man's release from sin and judgment was glorifying to Jesus as well as to the Father. Also Jesus, by his perfect love and obedience, brought glory to God. This reciprocal glorification is paralleled in 11:4 where it is said that Lazarus's illness "is for the glory of God, that the Son of God may be glorified thereby." In both cases "glory" is linked to death and revival. A magical papyrus of the third

---

## EXPOSITION

We now come to the "throne room," to the "holy of holies" of this "Spiritual Gospel." In no other portion of Scripture, not even in the prayers of St. Paul, does one come so close to the inner counsels of the Trinity as in Jesus' intercessory prayer recorded here. Here one feels like an eavesdropper as he listens in awed reverence to Jesus' heart-cry to his Father. This chapter is to the Fourth Gospel what the central spire is to a Gothic cathedral; it unifies and dominates the whole. Here, more than any other one spot, the reader is truly on "holy ground."

This priceless contribution made by the Fourth Gospel to our knowledge of Christ is quite unique. This is the only full prayer we have reported. In this prayer, as reported by John, Jesus sums up the message of chs. 13-16 and prepares the way for the events of the passion and resurrection. In this prayer we find the climax of the concern for *participation* by the disciples in the life and purpose of Christ which was first expressed at the washing of feet (17:11,21-23; cf. 13:8). Also the new commandment about *love* first announced at the Last Supper (13:34), moves through chs. 14-16 to its climax in this prayer (17:23,26). *Unity* which was emphasized in the analogy of the vine and branches reaches its climax in ch. 17. The conflict with the *world* emphasized in 15:18-16:33, finds an echo in 17:14, 16, 21. *Joy* also is a theme common to all (cf. 15:11; 16:20; 17:13). The mutual indwelling of Father, Son and disciples, first mentioned in 14:7ff., is a major concern of this prayer.

The prayer also looks forward to the ascent of the Son to the Father. The Son's consecration to self-sacrifice (17:19) is followed by the crucifixion. The reunion of Father and Son after the resurrection and ascension is anticipated in

2 even as thou gavest him authority over all flesh, that to all whom thou hast given him, he should give eternal life.

---

century has a similar passage, "Lord Isis . . . glorify me as I glorified the name of thy son. . . ."[1] There seems little justification for placing it in an eschatological context as Bultmann suggests.[2] The Johannine contexts indicate a more spiritual connotation. In this Gospel "glory" is not associated with the end of the age so much as with the spiritual issues of death, resurrection, and glorification in the personal rather than cosmic realm. Thus Jesus prayed that the Father glorify his name (12:28) not by saving Jesus from "this hour" but rather by helping him through it. The "judgment of this world" and the "casting out" of its "ruler" are associated not with the return of the Son of man in glory but rather with the resurrection and ascension. John habitually speaks of Jesus' death, resurrection, and ascension as one event and calls it Jesus' glorification (12:16, 23, 28; 13:31, 32; cf. 21:19). See Introduction, VI, F, pp. 39-41.

There was the glory associated with his death and also the glory associated with the incarnation: "The Logos became flesh and dwelt among us, and we beheld his glory" (1:14).

2 Thou gavest him authority (exousia) over all flesh. Because he became "flesh" Jesus earned the right or authority over all "flesh." In Hebrews 2:14 we learn that God became man in order to deliver man from the power of the devil and of death. In John 5:27 we learn that because the Son of God became the Son of man he has the authority to judge the sons of men. The resurrection gave assurance that Christ's salvation is effective; the incarnation made it available. Here "flesh" has not the moral connotation that it has in Pauline thought; it is rather a Semitism, meaning all mankind, especially man in contrast to God (cf. Gen. 6:3; Ps. 56:4; Rom. 3:20; I Cor. 1:29).

He should give eternal life. In these words is summed up the purpose of

---

17:5, 22, 24. The petition that the disciples eventually share in this glorification (17:. 24) is carried further in 21:19. Thus, this "secret" prayer of Jesus looks back over the dialogue to the Last Supper and forward to their reunion in heaven (cf. Rev. 21:1ff.).

## C. CHRIST'S INTERCESSORY PRAYER

During the observance of the Eucharist or Lord's Supper in the early church the presiding officer offered two prayers, one at the beginning, the other at the close. The closing prayer says in part: "We give thanks to thee, O Holy Father, for thy Holy Name which thou didst make to tabernacle in our hearts, and for the knowledge and faith and immortality which thou didst make known to us through Jesus thy Child. To thee be glory forever . . . . Remember, Lord, thy Church, to deliver it from all evil and to make it perfect in thy love, and gather it together in its holiness from the four winds to thy king-

dom which thou hast prepared for it. For thine is the power and the glory for ever."[a] This prayer, reflecting mid-second-century usage in the church, indicates the influence of this chapter in the expression "Holy Father." It also is consistent with the prayer of John 17 in its petition for protection from evil and perfection in love. Noteworthy also is the fact that this major prayer marked the climax of the Passover meal, just as the above prayer closed the eucharistic meal among second-century churches.[b]

Parallels have been cited in Hellenistic writings, such as the rite of initiation in Poimandres, but these have little in common with John. They may well have been influenced by the Fourth Gospel (CHD, pp. 420-423; CKB, p. 417). The prayer falls into four main parts: Jesus prays for himself (vv. 1-5), for his disciples (vv. 6-19), for other believers (vv. 20-24), and concludes with a summation (vv. 25-26). The specific request may be listed under these headings:

---

[1] P. Lond. 121. 502, Moulton & Milligan, op. cit., p. 169.
[2] R. Bultmann, op. cit., pp. 374-376, cf. John Mark. 8:28; 13:26; Matt. 19:28; 25:31.
[a] Didache, x. 1-5 (K. Lake, edit., op. cit., I., 323-325).
[b] Cf. Strachan, op. cit., p. 299.

Christ's coming to earth and also the theme of the Fourth Gospel. To John eternal life (*aiōnios zōē*) meant more than endless life after death; rather, it meant that quality of life — spiritual life — which one obtains when he is "born again" and is indwelt by the Holy Spirit. Paul expressed the same idea in the words, "If any man is in Christ, he is a new creature" (II Cor. 5:17). He "also sealed us, and gave us the earnest of the Spirit in our hearts" (II Cor. 1:22). In other words, the Christian in this life receives a foretaste of what life will be in heaven. Although we experience but a tiny part of it here, nevertheless it is a sample of what we are to enjoy in fullness and without end in eternity. The "earnest" is a "down payment" and security of much more of the same quality of divine life forthcoming in the future. This concept of life is succinctly expressed in John's First Epistle: "God gave unto us eternal life and this life is in his Son. He that hath the Son hath life; he that hath not the Son of God hath not life" (5:11, 12). This is a quality as that experienced by the believer after the death of the body: "Beloved, now are we the sons of God . . . we shall be like him for we shall see him as he is" (I John 3:2). Paul likewise affirmed that since we are children now in this life, we shall be heirs and even joint-heirs with Christ in the life to come (Rom. 8:16). Eternal life to both Paul and John meant a continuation into eternity of the abundant divine life experienced by the believer while still here "in the flesh" (John 10:10).

However, *aiōnios* ("eternal") was regularly used to mean "eternal" in secular as well as canonical Scriptures. Plato

## JOHN 17   CHRIST'S INTERCESSORY PRAYER

| For Himself 1 | For the Disciples 6 | For Other Believers 20 | Summation 25                26 |
|---|---|---|---|
| Introduction | Preservation        v. 11 | Unity        v. 21 | Jesus knew |
| Source and nature of life vv. 3,4 | Unity        v. 11 | Unity        v. 22 | these knew |
| | Joy        v. 13 | Unity        v. 23 | Father's name made known |
| "Glorify thy Son" vv. 1,5 | Preservation        v. 15 | | divine love |
| Restore former status, v. 5 | Sanctification        v. 17 | View Jesus' glory v. 24 | in Christ |

In distinction from the *requests* are the *motives*. It is noteworthy that the Greek term *hina* ("that") occurs 19 times in this chapter and usually denotes purpose. A survey of these clauses discloses the motive or purposes behind the specific requests of the Master. As Jesus prays for himself his motive is that God may be glorified — "in order that (*hina*) the Son may glorify thee." Another purpose is "that (*hina*) all" believers might have eternal life (v. 2). Another motive in making his request is "in order that they may be one" (v. 11). A motivation which dominates the latter portion of the prayer is "in order that the world may believe" which, of course, is the dominant concern of the entire Gospel. The foregoing represents an attempt to differentiate the specific requests from the motives which prompt the requests. Obviously Jesus' motives were unselfish. The dominant motive in this prayer is the glory of God, as in 11:4 and 13:31. This glorifying of God is associated with the death and resurrection of Jesus (cf. 12:23).[c]

1. CHRIST'S PRAYER FOR HIMSELF (vv. 1-5)

The scene is a very intimate one — Jesus and the eleven chosen ones — in a

c Eduard Schick, *Das Evangelium nach Johannes* (Würzburg: Echter, 1956), p. 148.

3 And this is life eternal, that they should know thee the only true God, and him whom thou didst send, *even* Jesus Christ.

---

used the word in describing God.[3] An ancient inscription uses the term as a synonym for "deathless" in referring to God.[4] In Josephus's works, with few exceptions, the term is equated with that which is everlasting, forever, and eternal.[5] In Romans, Paul used the term twice with reference to God: "the eternal God" (16: 26); "even his eternal power and Godhead" (1:20). The word occurs fifty-one times in the N. T. to connote the endlessness of the future blessedness of the redeemed. John so used it seventeen times. But it should not escape one's attention that *aiōnios* was also used (seven times) to denote the future punishment of the wicked. Most noteworthy is Matthew 25:46 — "these will go away into eternal punishment (*kolasin*) but the righteous into eternal life."[6] The adjective "eternal" is used both with "punishment" and with "life," thus indicating that the punishment of the wicked and the blessedness of the saved are both everlasting. These words,

as Matthew indicates, are from the lips of Christ and have on them the stamp of deity (cf. Matt. 18:8; 25:41; Mark 3: 29; II Thess. 1:9; Heb. 6:2; Jude 7 and especially Luke 16:19-31.

3 **This is life eternal that they should know thee.** Eternal life is here equated with a personal knowledge of God and Christ. The concept that a "knowledge" of God was essential to salvation was common to both Hebrew and Hellenistic thought. Hosea grieved over the fact that "my people are destroyed for lack of knowledge" (14:6), and exhorted, "Thou shalt know the Lord" (2:20). Jeremiah likewise: "I will give them a heart to know me" and "Know the Lord, for they all shall know me" (Jer. 24:7; 31:34). Isaiah pointed out that God's people have less sense than beasts: "The ox knows its owner . . . but Israel does not know [the Lord]" and predicted that "then you will know that I am the Lord" and that "then all flesh shall know that I am the

---

"closet" and alone with God. The words as here recorded are probably as remembered by an ear-witness of the event. There is good reason for assuming with Westcott that this prayer occurred within the temple precincts. He had not yet crossed the Kidron (18:1) but apparently had left the upper room (14:31). A discourse and prayer of this solemnity could scarcely have been uttered on the streets of the crowded city, even after dark. They could well have paused on the temple grounds in a quiet corner for conference and prayer. Proximity to the temple would have been an appropriate setting for what is often called Jesus' high-priestly prayer (BFW, II, 239). But this is only an assumption.

The Master's posture is noted. It is one of confidence, filial love, expectancy — "our pattern for perfect prayer."[d] At the grave of Lazarus also Jesus "lifted

up his eyes," probably for better concentration (11:41; cf. Acts 7:55; Luke 22:41). In contrast to the Master's attitude of confidence is the publican who could not lift up his eyes because of a sense of guilt (Luke 18:13).

While Jesus had previously said "the hour has come" (12:23; 13:1), this time it was even more imminent. A new sense of urgency and solemnity gripped him as he voiced not only the thoughts of the moment but the purpose which had dominated and motivated his entire ministry. Yet it was not the urgency of anxiety but rather of expectancy. The precedent for this prayer is in 12:27, 28, rather than the cry of anguish in Gethsemane (Luke 22: 42).

The manner in which Jesus expected God to glorify the Son was probably fourfold: one was the offering up of the Son of man as a *sacrifice* for the sins

---

3 Plato, Tim. Locr. 96c.
4 Inscr. No. 894, British Museum.
5 Jos. *Ant.* I. xiii. 4; I. xviii. 7; IV. vi. 4, 5; IV. viii. 18; V. i. 27; VI. xiv. 4; VII. xiv. 5; VIII. iv. 2.
6 In the *New World Translation* by Jehovah's Witnesses *kolasin* ("punishment") is translated "cutting off" in spite of the fact that no Greek lexicon has such a definition. Thus, at the sacrifice of objective scholarship, support is sought for a doctrine which, contrary to Scripture, denies the future punishment of the wicked.
d Philip Loyd, *op cit.*, p. 10.

4 I glorified thee on the earth, having accomplished the work which thou hast given me to do.

---

Lord your Saviour" (Isa. 1:3; 49:23,26). The prophets consistently urged their people, "Let us know, let us press on to know the Lord," because of the fact that the important thing is "steadfast love and not sacrifice, the knowledge of God rather than burnt offerings" (Hos. 6:3,6).

But, in the Judaism of John's day, knowledge of God was conceived as coming primarily through study and obedience to the law. Except for a few devout individuals, the idea of a vital, personal faith in God was remote. To John faith, knowledge, and belief were not antithetical but correlated and interdependent. To him having knowledge of God was possible only through faith in Christ (John 14:6, 7). That eternal life comes only from an experiential knowledge of God and that the only way of access to this knowledge is through Jesus Christ is the central message of the Fourth Gospel. It is "a quality of Life which inheres in the Logos, and which He imparts to us here and now."[7]

Here the verb "know" (ginōskō) means "recognize" or "perceive." It is remarkable that here "eternal life" consists in knowl-

edge, or rather the pursuit of knowledge, since the present tense marks a continuance, a progressive perception of God in Christ — that they might learn to know (cf. v. 23; 10:38; I John 5:20; 4:7, 8) (MRV. II, 263). The verb indicates a growing experience of God. The adjective "true" is alēthinon rather than alēthēs; the latter is used to stress a distinction from falsehood (John 3:33), the former to signify the real as distinct from the unreal, shadowy or fanciful, e.g., I Thess. 1:9; Heb. 8:2; 9:24 (MRV, II, 44). Here it underscores the real God in contrast to idols, as in I Thessalonians 1:9. To know God is also to know his representative Jesus Christ; the knowledge of one is inseparable from the other (Lagrange). Here is another emphasis on the fact that Jesus Christ is the one sent from God (8:18; 10:36; 12:45; 15: 21), and the only one.

4 I glorified thee on the earth. Since v. 3 is parenthetical, this verse continues the thought of v. 2. Three of the verbs used here are aorists, used customarily in historical writings unless the writer

---

of the world (13:31), another was the resurrection of the dead (7:39), later the ascension to heaven (12:16), and finally the outpouring of the Spirit (16: 14), as at Pentecost, and ultimately "putting all enemies under his feet at the day of final judgment (5:25-29; cf. 25:31). In Johannine thought "glorify" has a special meaning; it is one of the distinctive terms of this Gospel. God has already been glorified in the Incarnation (1:14, 18; 2:11). This prayer is for the completion of the major emphasis on glorification which characterizes this Gospel, viz., the passion, resurrection, and ascension viewed as one redemptive event. The Son glorified the Father (12:28; 17:4); the Father glorified the Son (through the passion 12:23; 13:31; and the ascension 7:39; 12:16). The disciples glorified both by obedience and fruit-bearing (15:18). See Introduction, VI, F, pp. 39-41.

Jesus well recognized that the path to his own glorification was the path of

execration and suffering (cf. Isa. 53:1-4). The motif of the Suffering Servant is no less prominent in this Gospel than in the Synoptic accounts. While not as explicit as Mark 10:45, it is, if anything, more pervasive. While in the Synoptic Gospels there is a succession of events, one after another, each with its one distinctive period or emphasis, in John's account the end is viewed from the beginning. The rejection is foreseen in 1:5, 11; 3:19; the crucifixion is predicted in 3:14; the resurrection in 2:19-21, and final triumph in 3:35-36; 5:21-23. Thus John does not deal with subjects consecutively but simultaneously, stressing one theme now and another later.

Jesus' prayer for himself, reduced to its essentials, is, "Father, glorify thy Son." It will be helpful to analyze this specific request. Four elements are evident.

(i) The timeliness of the request is given: "the hour is come." For days and months Jesus had been looking forward to

---

[7] G. Tietze, "Knowledge of God in the Fourth Gospel," JBL (Jan. 1954), p. 15.

5 And now, Father, glorify thou me with thine own self with the glory which I had with thee before the world was.

---

desired to emphasize either the continuance (pres. or imperf.) or the finished result (perf. — *dedōkas* — "you have given") of an action or event. Once again Jesus speaks of the future in the past tense. In 5:36 he states that his objective is the completion (*teleiōsō*) of his God-given task (*ergon*); here the work (*ergon*) has been accomplished (*teleiōsas*). But it was not until he was expiring on the cross that he actually achieved the completion (*teleiōthēi*) of his task (19:28) and finally said, "It is finished" (*tetelestai* — 19:30). In a larger sense the work of redemption was not perfected until his ascension, his session at the right hand of the Father, and the sending of the Paraclete. But, strictly speaking, the Son's work was finished at Calvary; the rest was the work of the Father. With his mission accomplished, Jesus was now in a position to make requests. He, the Son, had "learned obedience by the things which he suffered; and having been made perfect" (*teleiōtheis*)

the requests he now voiced were certain to be granted. This verse may have influenced the language of "Thomas": "Lord, I have accomplished thy work and perfected today thy commandment. I have become a bondman; therefore today do I receive freedom."[8]

5 **Glorify thou me** is a prayer for the restoration of the Son's former glory in heaven prior to the Incarnation. **Glorify** (*doxason*) means "to give honor or praise, to clothe with splendor." "It is a favorite term in John, in which the whole life of Jesus is depicted as a glorifying of the Son by the Father (8:54; 12:28; 13:31; 17:1, 4) and, at the same time, of the Father by the Son (13:31: 14:13; 17:1). The glorifying of the Son is brought about by the miracles the Father has him perform 11:4" (A-G, p. 203).

"The glory which I had (*eichon*) with (*para*) thee before the world was made" (RSV). *Eichon* is in the imperfect tense and thus denotes a state in progress in the

---

the time of his being "received up" (Luke 9:51). This Gospel account is clearly divided between the time before "his hour had come" and when "his hour had come." In the Synoptic accounts this occurs after Peter's confession (Mark 8:31). In John's account the transition to "the hour is at hand" is at 12:23, after the inquiry of the Greeks and subsequent to the triumphal entry. In the Third Gospel the imminence of "the hour" is conveyed by the repetition of the phrase "up to Jerusalem." The prayer, "Glorify thy Son" was not so much a request that Jesus be honored, but a request that he be enabled to "drink the cup" from which he shrank at Gethsemane (Luke 22:42). His acceptance of the "cup" is indicated in the question voiced at the arrest, "The cup which the Father hath given me, shall I not drink it?" (John 18:11). Jesus had now "accomplished the work" which the Father had commissioned him to perform and he was now committing himself temporarily to the "prince of this world" deliberately — saying in effect, "This is

your hour, and the power (*exousia*) of darkness" (Luke 22:53). For Jesus' earthly mission was now at the point of completion. The backward look brought great satisfaction, and the forward look gave him a thrill of anticipation. The future was bright because the past had been lived in full conformity to God's will. Would that all could end their lives with such a record and such a hope! The apostle Paul gave expression to something similar to this: "I have fought the good fight, I have finished the course, I have kept the faith: henceforth there is laid up for me a crown of righteousness" (II Tim. 4:7,8). It is not the pleasures enjoyed, nor the honors received, but the knowledge that God is pleased with our lives, and our service to others, that brings the greatest satisfaction when one is at death's door.

(ii) The *basis* of Jesus' request was the fact that his earthly ministry was now finished (v. 4). Thus his ministry was fourfold: preaching, teaching, casting out demons, and healing of the sick. Why

---

[8] Acts of Thomas 167, cited in M. P. James, edit., *The Apocryphal New Testament* (Oxford: Clarendon Press, 1926), p. 436.

**6** I manifested thy name unto the men whom thou gavest me out of the world
thine they were, and thou gavest them to me; and they have kept thy word.

---

past, i.e., "which I was having." *Para*
appears twice and in both instances could
be rendered "in thine own presence" (cf.
RSV). Perhaps the best description of the
contrast between Jesus' pre-incarnate glory
and his humiliation and subsequent exaltation is given by Paul (Phil. 2:5-11).

**6 I have manifested thy name.** It was
Jesus' distinct mission to reveal to the
world at large, and to the disciples in
particular, the nature of the Father.
Hence, the apostle could recall, "we beheld his glory, glory as of the only begotten of the Father, full of grace and
truth" (1:14). Even the casual reader
notes the element of wonder and adoration
in these words. "The 'Name' of God is
equivalent to what a modern writer would
call His 'Providence'; and this, in the N. T.
and especially in John is associated with
the doctrine of God as *Father*" (JHB, II,
568). It was the disclosure of God him-

self (Bultmann, p. 381; cf. John 12:2⁸
17:11, 26). To manifest God's nam
(*onoma*) meant to reveal what God is i
essence. "The belief in the efficacy of th
name is extremely old; its origin goes bac
to the most ancient times and the mo
primitive forms of intellectual and re
ligious life. The period of our literatur
also sees . . . in the name something rea
The piece of the very nature of th
personality whom it designates, that pai
takes in his qualities and his powers
(A-G, p. 574).

**The men whom thou gavest me out o
the world.** Jesus often spoke of the dis
ciples as God's "gift" to him; he realize
that their conversion was not somethin
self-generated but came from the "Fathe
who is in heaven" (Matt. 16:17). Bul
mann and Bernard call attention to
similar passage in the Odes of Solomo
(xxxi. 4, 5): "He offered to Him the son

---

does not John mention the exorcism of
demons? To ask this is to ask why he
omits so many of the miracles described
by the other reporters. It is noteworthy
that while no mention is made of casting
out demons in others Jesus himself is
accused of being demon-possessed (John
7:20; 8:48, 52; 10:10). John mentions the
accusation that *Jesus* was demon-possessed
four times while in the Synoptics emphasis
is placed on *others* being demon-possessed.
But John was selective in his inclusion of
miracle stories and emphasized the controversial phrase of Jesus' ministry. Because
Jesus had completed his work, he was
in a position to "commit himself to him
who judges righteously" (I Pet. 2:23).

The servant of God who has obeyed
his Master's commands in all that he
knows is in a position to commit his way
unto the Lord in confidence. There is an
element of reciprocity there. Jesus glorified the Father by his works and words;
he is thus in a position to ask the Father
to reciprocate by restoring his former
status of "glory" (cf. Phil. 2:11; Isa. 53:
12). Hezekiah used his good behavior as
a reason why the Lord should hear his
prayer and prolong his days (Isa. 38:3).
His prayer was answered.

(iii) The *scope* of the request wa
world-wide in perspective — "thou gaves
him authority (*exousia*) over all flesh" (v
2). In its ultimate outreach this praye
was world-wide, envisioning "all flesh,'
and designed that the world might believ
(vv. 21, 23). To glorify the Son now
would be consistent with what the Fathe
did previously, namely, the giving of al
authority to the Son (cf. Matt. 28:18)
Paul recognized also that all authority ha
been given the Son as a trust. It is hel
by Christ as a gift of the Father and wil
later be yielded up to the Father, "tha
God may be all in all" (I Cor. 15:28)
The Father gives "all things" over to th
jurisdiction of the Son; the Son then re
turns all authority to the Father. Appar
ently the authority of the Son is *derived*
The disciples were regarded as God's gif
to Jesus (vv. 2, 6). A similar idea wa
voiced by Jesus at the great confessior
of Peter as reported by Matthew (16:
17) — the Father had revealed to Pete
the true nature of the Son.

(iv) The *objective* of Jesus' prayer, the
nature of his request, was glorification. In
the light of the foregoing (see discussion
on glory), it is evident that Jesus was no
demanding a restoration of his lost prestige

7 Now they know that all things whatsoever thou hast given me are from thee:
8 for the words which thou gavest me I have given unto them; and they received *them,* and knew of a truth that I came forth from thee, and they believed that thou didst send me.

---

that were in His hands . . . for thus His holy Father had given to Him" (Bultmann, p. 380; Bernard, II, 564). The one baptized in the name of Jesus "becomes the possession and comes under the protection of the one whose name he bears" (A-G, p. 575).

They have kept (*tetērēkan*) thy word (*logon*), contrary to others who began but did not continue (6:66; 8:31-37) in his teaching.

7, 8 Now they know (*egnōkan*) that all things . . . are from thee. They have been so well taught as to Jesus and his relation to the Father while in the flesh that nothing can rob them of the incomparable revelation. The words (*rhēmata*) which thou gavest me I have given unto them. The perfect tense again suggests the continuing influence of the truth once given — it *now abides* with them. The *logon* of v. 6 is the complete message or revelation of God (cf. 5:38; 6:60; 8:43, 51; 12:48; 15:3). The words of v. 8 are

a "detached utterance" or the fragmentary elements in the divine message (cf. 5:47; 6:63, 68; 8:47; 12:47; 15:7 — BFW, II, 247). Usually in John *logos* is in the singular while *rhēmata* is plural. The distinction which Westcott saw in these two synonyms for "word" may not be apparent to all; in 12:48, for example, they appear to be synonymous. The same words of Jesus which will condemn the unbelievers (12:48) will sustain and reassure those who receive them.

They . . . knew of a truth (*alēthōs,* "truly") . . . and they believed. This may be a parallelism since what they "knew" and what they "believed" amounts to about the same thing; to say that Jesus came from God is the same as saying that he was sent by God. The disciples were thoroughly convinced of two profound facts: (1) that Jesus' teachings came from God, and (2) that Jesus also came from God. Little wonder, as later events proved, that they were willing to continue wit-

---

or status. This would be inconsistent with his voluntary self-emptying (Phil. 2:5-9; John 10:17,18). Rather, he was praying that since his *active* ministry was ended his role now was that of a "lamb" about to be offered in expiation for the sins of the world. His role through the tense drama of the arrest, torture, crucifixion, and burial was the *passive* role of a sacrificial victim (I Pet. 2:21-25). It was a prayer of consecration, in which Jesus prayed for the consummation: the ordeal of arrest, trial, crucifixion, followed by the resurrection, appearances, ascension, advent of the Paraclete, and Spirit-inspired witnessing. In a manner similar to that of their Master, Ignatius and Polycarp consecrated themselves to martyrdom.[e] The glorification of the Father and Son is reciprocal: as the Son glorifies the Father by his self-offering so the Father glorifies the Son by "giving him a name which is above every name" (Phil. 2:11). In a similar manner, disciples who let their

light shine (glorify or bring honor) to their heavenly Father (Matt. 5:16). As a result, those who serve Christ will be honored by the Father (John 12:26). Paul expected that this honor would be comparable to that of a victor in games (II Tim. 4:8).

The necessity of vital and personal trust in as well as relationship with God through Christ is thus stated in typical Johannine style. We have a parallel statement of this type in I John 5:3: "For this is the love of God, that we keep his commandments." It is John's unique and intuitive way of presenting the Gospel. Assuming that John was right in saying that eternal life is synonymous with a personal relationship with God, he has, by so writing and by a positive approach, excluded ineffective ways of trying to obtain eternal life. For instance, dependance upon the so-called absolution of a priest or minister or sacraments or church membership or one's own morality or good deeds are all

---

e *Mar. Polycarp,* XIV (K. Lake, edit. Loeb), *op. cit.,* II, 331f. Ignatius, *To the Romans,* II, Roberts and Donaldson, editors, *The Ante-Nicene Fathers* (New York: Scribner's, 1903), I, 74.

9 I pray for them: I pray not for the world, but for those whom thou hast given me; for they are thine:
10 and all things that are mine are thine, and thine are mine: and I am glorified in them.

nessing that Jesus was the Messiah, in spite of a hostile and bloodthirsty generation.

**9 I pray for them . . . not for the world.** Pray (*erōtō*), while used as a synonym for "ask" (*aiteō*), has the special connotation of making a request (ASVm), and the request is focused here upon the disciples only (Trench, *op. cit.*, p. 137). Later on, in v. 20, all those who will believe as a result of their witnessing are included in the prayer. Here Jesus does not come to the Father in abject supplication but as one on equal terms, hence the verb *erōtaō*. This petition is not to be taken to mean that Jesus never prayed for the world; instead, on this particular occasion he was concentrating on his disciples. On the cross Jesus did pray for

"the world" — his executioners. There is no record that he prayed for the Jewish leaders who refused the light. Jesus also prays for the world through the Spirit-inspired intercession of his followers (cf. Rom. 8:26, 27). What a privilege believers have in this ministry of intercession!

**10 All things that are mine are thine, and thine are mine.** This would be a preposterous claim for any human being to make. But it is in perfect accord with many other similar statements uttered by Jesus. The boldness of the statement indicates a "complete mutuality of interest and possession between the Father and the Son" (CKB, p. 423). While true of Jesus' teachings and deeds, it seems to refer to the disciples in this context. Paul voiced something similar in thought "all are

eliminated. Nothing less than the action of a human being putting himself into the hands of a divine being for salvation and for service is implied. To "know" God is a direct experiential knowledge.

2. JESUS PRAYS FOR HIS DISCIPLES (vv. 6-19)

a. His Relationship to the Disciples (vv. 6-10)

This paragraph consists of two subdivisions: the reasons why Jesus is concerned with the eleven men with him (vv. 6-10) and the requests made for them (vv. 11-19). Three times Jesus speaks of the disciples as those given him by God (vv. 2, 6, 9). This sounds somewhat different from the formula often used by evangelicals of so many "decisions" for Christ. The implication in the latter expression is that all depends on man's decision. Christians need to remind themselves that they are not such simply because of their own choice or "decision" but because of God's gracious act of adopting them into the family of God (Rom. 8:16). "By grace have ye been saved through faith; and that not

of yourselves, it is a gift of God" (Eph. 2:8). The problem of God's initiative in grace and man's responsibility in response has occasioned centuries of theological debate. The Christian religion is distinctive in that God rather than man takes the initiative. As A. Deissmann has pointed out, "Christianity is a reacting, rather than an acting religion; God acts in Christ and man reacts. A procedure which trusts in education alone, in information alone, to 'make disciples,' will fail."[f]

Christ indicates that he has done his part, in winning the disciples. He said, "I have manifested thy name" (v. 6) and "the words thou hast given me I have given them" (v. 8). Because he did his part he can now safely commit the disciples to the care of the Father.

The disciples, on their part, had responded in three areas: they received they knew, and they believed. The "seed" of the word had met with four different receptions (Mark 4:1-20). The disciples represented the "good soil" which received the seed and bore a harvest. It is impossible to overstress the importance of receptivity.[g] Jesus' spoken word to the

f Walter Lüthi, *St. John's Gospel* (London: Oliver and Boyd, 1960), p. 244.
g H. T. Kuist, *These Words Upon Thy Heart* (Richmond: John Knox Press, 1947), *passim*.

11 <u>And I am no more in the world</u>, and these are in the world, and I come to thee. Holy Father, keep them in thy name which thou hast given me, that they may be one, even as we *are*.

---

yours; and ye are Christ's; and Christ is God's" (I Cor. 3:22, 23).

**I am glorified in them,** is in the perfect tense, indicating a condition now abiding. It is similar to Paul's statement concerning his converts in Thessalonica: "For what is our hope, or joy, or crown of glorying? . . . For ye are our glory and our joy" (I Thess. 2:19, 20). It seems incredible that any man, even the apostle, could bring credit or honor to Jesus, but such seems to be the import of this passage (cf. v. 22; II Cor. 3:1, 2).

**11 And these are in the world.** This "and" (*kai*) is actually an adversative, as used here, and should be rendered "but." As Jesus contemplates his departure from the disciples he is constrained to pray for their well-being since they remain "in the world" alone. *Holy Father* (*pater hagie*) involves a sanctification of the divine name; it is a recognition of God's holiness comparable to "hallowed be thy name" of the Lord's model prayer. Was Jesus practicing what he preached? To recognize God as uniquely and transcendently holy is true to the genius of O. T. religion (cf. Isa. 6:3; Amos. 4:2). This manner of addressing the most high God was customary in Judaism.[9]

**Keep them . . . that they may be one.** Keep (*tēreson*) is found in the exhortation "keep the word" in 8:51, 52, 55; 14: 23, 24 and is the same as "keep the commandments" (14:21; cf. 5:24). It means to keep the disciples *from* sin and *in* fellowship with God.

**That they may be one even as we** (*hina hōsin hen kathōs hēmeis*). This expression occurs five times in this chapter, an indication of its importance (vv. 21, 22, 23). It means that the disciples should

---

disciples, and his written Word to the church, needs to be received at face value and cherished as a priceless privilege. It is no easy task to acquire the attitude of receptivity — "except ye be converted and become as little children." Often it is easier to teach the untutored and unsophisticated than it is the learned. In the case of the latter many things need to be unlearned before learning can take place. One reason why the common people heard Jesus gladly while the scribes listened with skepticism is that the unlettered multitude had less to unlearn.

The disciples not only *received* the word of Jesus but they also *kept* it. As a result they now knew (*egnōkan*) for certain of Jesus' origin and mission. Most people prefer to reverse the process. They want to know, to be assured, before they receive. In Christianity, and in John's Gospel in particular, the sequence is receive and know, or, "come and see." The "know" in this verse is the same root as that in v. 3 and v. 8. In Paul's religious experience the initial step was submission and a receptive attitude; the "knowledge" of the deeper things came later. The Word of God remains a mystery as long as one's willingness to receive is conditioned on knowing.[h]

In addition to receiving and knowing the disciples had believed. We wonder why the belief follows the knowledge here; would not the reverse be more natural? Perhaps it is a parallelism, the second statement being synonymous with the first. Or perhaps the former refers to their conviction that "this man is of God" (cf. 3:2; 9:29-33). This conviction was based upon the things that they had seen and heard in the presence of Jesus (cf. Luke 7:22). Because of the mounting evidence that Jesus was doing the works of the Messiah they agreed with Peter's confession (Matt. 16:16). Does not the man blind from birth illustrate this sequence? He *knew* his sight had been restored and hence that Jesus came from God (9:25). Later, after learning more about Jesus' identity, he said, "Lord, I believe" (9:38). Existential certainty in a small area leads to belief of the larger concept.

---

9 Lev. 11:44; 19:2; Ps. 71:22; II Macc. 14:36 (*hagie pantos hagiasmou*); III Macc. 2:2; Did. 10 "we give thanks to thee, holy Father").
h *Ibid.*, p. 247.

12 While I was with them, I kept them in thy name which thou hast given me: and I guarded them, and not one of them perished, but the son of perdition; that the scripture might be fulfilled.

be united in purpose, motive, love, and attitude like the unity of the Trinity. It is a personal and functional unity and, as applied to the church, not necessarily an organic union. The prayer is for a unity of desire, purpose, love, and self-sacrifice, such as exists between Jesus Christ and God the Father. This unity of spirit is possible only as believers are indwelt and controlled ˙by the Holy Spirit (Eph. 4: 3). A truly spiritual unity will be a "unity of the Spirit," brought about when God's people are Spirit-filled, both individually and corporately. The motivation and power for such a bond of fellowship is based on faith in Christ, both as Savior and as Lord. Denominational unity, while desirable (other things being equal), is not the underlying thought of this passage. However, to the extent that every individual has been regenerated and lives in full submission to God, to that extent

is organic union possible. The concern for Christian unity and the peril of schism are major doctrines of the New Testament Paul grieved over factionalism in the vigorous church at Corinth and attributes it to spiritual immaturity (I Cor. 1:10-13 3:1-23). Apparently the Corinthians had organizational union but not spiritual unity. To the Ephesians he made a very strong appeal for the unity of the Spirit (Eph. 4:1-16). Peter spoke of brotherly love as the crowning Christian virtue (1 Pet. 4:8). The "Hebrews" were exhorted to a "perfection" which here means corporate unity (Heb. 13:21; Gal. 6:1).

12 I kept them in thy name. Kept (etēroun, impf., continuously "to keep watch over, to protect, or to shield") appears four times in this chapter alone (vv. 6, 11, 12, 15). Virtually all the hope for the Christian church depended on these eleven men being kept steadfast in the

---

### b. Jesus' Actual Request (vv. 9-19)

The requests for the disciples were four in number: that they be preserved from evil and worldliness (vv. 11, 15), that they have unity (v. 11), that they have joy (v. 11), and that they be sanctified (v. 17).

(i) The petition "keep them" has as its background the fact that one of their number was not kept, if indeed he ever was among the "elect." The prayer was fulfilled in that none of the eleven repudiated his Lord although Peter did so rather spontaneously for a time. Peter was "kept" because the Lord had made special request that his "faith fail not" (cf. Luke 22:32). These men had been under a three-year apprenticeship and were now being initiated or inducted into the "new covenant." In the Qumran community, contemporary with Jesus', a major concern was that the members be "kept" loyal. A lapse from the principles of the community, comparable to Peter's denial of his Lord, would mean at least a

two-year probationary period. If a man had been a member of the community for ten years and then suffered such a lapse, he would never be forgiven and received back into fellowship.[1] The readiness with which Peter was received back by both the disciples and by Jesus was gracious by contrast.

The prayer that they be "kept" was answered in the fact that by the end of the generation of the apostles the "good news" had spread from Britain to India and from Africa to the Caucasian mountains.[1] The concern that now prompted Jesus was the same that prompted Paul to pray for the confirmation in the faith of the "saints" he had left at Thessalonica (I Thess. 3: 13). These were not to be removed from temptation. They were not to be withdrawn from the attacks of the "evil one" but rather fortified to resist.

The preservation from the world is not to be sought by external means. The hermits of the third and fourth centuries concluded that the main thing in Christianity was to be "kept" from the evil one. Anthony fled to the deserts of Egypt

---

[1] IQS vii, 18-25.
[1] A. Harnack, *Mission and Expansion of Christianity*, I, *passim*.

13 But now I come to thee; and these things I speak in the world, that they may have my joy made full in themselves.

covenant. Jesus kept them and now that his departure approaches he earnestly asks his Father that they continue to be kept. **I guarded them,** a repetition of the idea "I kept them," but here the aorist tense is used, emphasizing the completed *fact.* The same term is used to describe the "maximum security" with which Paul and Silas were "guarded" while in the jail at Philippi (Acts 16:24). Jude also prayed that the saints be "guarded" and enabled to persevere (Jude 24). With one exception Jesus was successful in "guarding" his apostolic circle. The **son of perdition,** here applied to Judas, refers elsewhere to the antichrist (II Thess. 2:3).

The Scripture, which was fulfilled in Judas' treachery, is seen in the light of 13:18; Ps. 41:9; "He that eateth my bread hath lifted up his heel against me." As noted before, it was considered a gross breach of etiquette to partake of someone's food and then to do anything unkind to

him (cf. WPNT, V, 242). In Acts 1:20 another Scripture is quoted as having been fulfilled by Judas. It is Psalm 69:25, but it refers to Judas' successor. It is not clear which Scripture Peter had in mind in Acts 1:16, whether Psalm 41:9 or 69:25. Whether Judas acted so in order to fulfill the prediction or whether the prediction was made because this outcome was foreseen is not made explicit. But since God transcends time he does not *foresee* a "future" event; he simply sees and describes it (Godet, II, 235).

13 **That they may have my joy made full in themselves.** See comments on 16:22. In this context the joy of Jesus appears to be the awareness of the protection afforded by the Father's constant presence. His joyous confidence he now wants vouchsafed to his disciples in the full measure which he himself experienced. The joy of the Lord was to be their strength.

to pray in solitude. After reading the life of this Christian "athlete," who renounced everything, Augustine of Hippo was convicted and later converted.

The world can be reconciled to God only to the degree that believers live circumspectly and witness frequently and fearlessly, as those did. That God had the world in mind, as the object of his love in sending his Son, is clearly stated in John 3:16. Jesus shared that same concern and affection, but he knew that it could be realized only through those who already accepted and loved him. "How shall they hear without a preacher" (Rom. 10:14).

The Savior then prayed that the eleven "elect" share in their Master's "joy" (v. 13). The note of joy, first voiced in 16:20-24, is echoed here. It is stated that Jesus "for [or in view of (*anti*)] the joy that was set before him endured the cross, despising the shame, and hath set down at the right hand of the throne of God" (Heb. 12:2). This was not simply a "joy" after sorrow but joy in the midst of sorrow. "Sorrow is become joy. The

Christian joy and hope do not arise from an ignoring of the evil in the world, but facing it at its worst. The light that shines for ever in the Church breaks out of the veriest pit of gloom."[k]

Jesus wanted his disciples to share not only his humiliation, persecution, exclusion from the synagogues, etc., but also to share his peace, his joy, his triumph and his glory. The devout Christian knows from experience the deep joy which comes from communion with Christ in the Gethsemane of intercession, in the tears of the seed-time, and in the fires of persecution as well as in the joy of harvest (cf. Phil. 3:10).

The prayer for sanctification is linked here with their relation to the world and to the truth of God's word. Sanctify (*hagiazō*) is another term difficult to put into English. It invariably stands in a religious context. Its basic meaning is *separation*: separation from the sinful and unclean, and positively, consecration unto God.[1] Sanctification, in both O. T. and N. T., includes in its various contexts the following meanings:

k Wm. Temple, *op. cit.,* pp. 295f.
1 G. Turner, *The More Excellent Way* (Winona Lake: Light and Life Press, 1952), pp. 22-31, 82-93.

14 I have given them thy word; and the world hated them, because they are not of the world, even as I am not of the world.

15 I pray not that thou shouldest take them from the world, but that thou shouldest keep them from the evil *one*.

---

**14 I have given them thy word; and the world hath hated them.** Here the prayer reverts to the theme of persecution which was dominant in 15:18-16:33. As Jesus encountered the undeserved hatred of civil and religious authorities so his disciples are destined to experience similar fate. "The disciple is not above his teacher" (Luke 6:40). Paul urged believers to remain faithful, to be "blameless and harmless, children of God without blemish in the midst of a crooked and perverse generation" (Phil. 2:15). The worse the environment is, the greater is the need for consistent Christian living.

**15 . . . Not that thou shouldst take them out of the world** (*ek tou kosmou*). In spite of the opposition to be faced, Jesus did not pray that his followers be spared the risks involved in witnessing to the world. God loved the hostile world enough to send his Son to save it, and Christ loved it enough to "lay down his life for the sheep." Isaiah, although warned that he would face opposition and have limited success, was told to bear his witness (Isa. 6:9). Jeremiah was warned about the hardness of the peoples' heart and was given additional reinforcement to cope with it (Jer. 1:16-19). Ezekiel' commission was to testify to people with a "hard forehead and of a stiff heart" (Ezek. 3:7) but was not excused because of the inherent difficulties of the task. Likewise, the infant church did not pray for an easy way out but rather for more boldness to face the challenge (Acts 4: 29). Consistent with this, Jesus prays not that the warriors be withdrawn from dangers but that they be given strength to overcome them.

**Keep them from the evil one** (*ek tou ponērou*); the phrase can mean either "out of evil" or "from the evil one." Note the

---

(i) Sanctification is man's *recognition* of God's holiness (Lev. 10:3; Num. 20:12; Deut. 32:51; Isa. 8:13; Ezek. 38:16; Luke 11:2; I Pet. 3:15). This recognition should characterize all our praying.

(ii) Sanctification (*qadosh*) is man's act of *dedication* in which the common is separated and transferred to the sacred, such as the Sabbath (Gen. 2:3), the firstborn (Ex. 13:2), the altar (Ex. 29:39), the priests (II Chronicles 29:15), Nazarites (Num. 6:2; cf. Rev. 22:11). This usage is largely limited to the O. T.

(iii) Sanctification is an act of God *setting apart* something or someone for a special service: a war (Joel 3:5), an army (Isa. 13:2, 17), a foetus (Jer. 1:5; cf. Gal. 1:15), an apostle (Rom. 1: 1), or the Son of God (John 10:36).

(iv) Sanctification is an act of God in *imputing* or attributing the quality of sanctity to that which has been separated from the ordinary, and presented to God: sacrifices, such as money (Rom. 15:26); all Christians (I Cor. 1:2, i.e., "holy ones," Rom. 1:7), Christian workers (II Tim. 2:21). In this sense all Christians are set apart or sanctified.[m]

(v) Sanctification is an act of God in which his own righteous nature is *imparted* to those persons (not things) thus yielded fully to him (Eph. 5:26; I Thess. 5:23; Acts 20:32; I Cor. 6:11; Heb. 10:10, 29). In v. 19 Jesus' sanctification of himself obviously falls into the third category — that of dedication to God. Here, as Hoskyns points out (pp. 502f.), the element of sacrifice and consecration is combined. The setting apart for God's exclusive usage, whether of a priest or a victim, involves sacrifice. In this spirit Paul urged his readers to present themselves as a "living sacrifice" (Rom. 12:1). The Father sanctified the Son for this service (10:36). Now the Son concurs by the further sanctification of himself as a vicarious sacrifice ("the Lamb of God"). In v. 17 the primary meaning appears, in

---

m This is the common meaning of the term among Reformation theologians. It means the renewal of our natures by the ingrafted Word, a progressive sanctification. "Entire sanctification" may be defined as "a state possible to Christians . . . in which they can be described as 'unblameable in holiness' . . . and into which they may be brought by the grace of God in this life . . . such is the teaching of I Thess. 3:13; 5:23" (J. V. Bartlet, "Sanctification," HDB, IV, 393). See also Kittel, *op. cit.*, I; Cremer, *op. cit.*, pp. 53ff.

16 <u>They are not of the world</u>, even as I am not of the world.
17 Sanctify them in the truth: thy word is truth. (Gospel)

---

similarity to the phrase *ek tou kosmou* ("but of the world") above. In the light of a similar expression in I John 2:13; 4:4; and 5:18, the meaning is probably evil personified, hence "the evil one."

16 **They are not of the world.** *Ek* ("out of") is frequently used in Johannine writings with the meaning "of." The expression "out of the world" occurs six times in this chapter and three times in I John. It is matched with the phrase *eis ton kosmon* ("into the world"), which occurs four times in this chapter. Jesus came *into* the world and *took* the disciples *out* of the world; now Jesus is going *out of* the world but sending the disciples *into* the world. Thus the disciples are "out of this world," in a spiritual sense, but are commissioned to remain in the world, in a physical sense, and to interpenetrate the world, in a spiritual sense, with the view of transforming it "into the image of the Son." The disciples, now the domain of their Lord and Savior, are free from domination of the "evil one," and are being commissioned to go and bear fruit.

17 **Sanctify (hagiason) them in the truth.** The ASVm "consecrate" was the RSV rendering in the 1946 printing, but in the 1952 RSV printing, the editors restored the KJV and ASV "sanctify." The verb appears also in 17:19 and in 10:36. In two of the three usages of the term in John it refers to Christ "whom the Father sanctified and sent into the world" (10:36). This is one of the few passages in which sanctification is linked with truth. Truth is here equated with God's Word (*logos;* cf. Eph. 5:26). In I Peter 1:2 the readers are "sanctified by the Spirit for obedience" and in 1:22 their souls have been purified by obedience to the truth. In I Peter 1:22 sanctification implies purification. In John 8:32-36 it is the truth which liberates from sin. The term *hagiazo* means, according to its contexts, to "recognize as holy" (Matt. 6:9; I Pet. 3:15; John 17:11), "separation unto God" (I Cor. 1:2), the "consecration or dedication of the Son" (John 10:36; 17:19), a "hallowing by position or relationship" (Matt. 23:17), and "cleansing"

---

this context, to be separation for service in the world. The Father sent the Son into the world (10:36) and now the Son sends the apostles into the world (20:21; 4:38). These men have been made "clean" (13:10; 15:3) through the word of Christ; they are not of the world (v. 16). Now Jesus asks the Father to commission them for their task by confirming the Son's sending of them, reaffirming their appointment and providing that inner cleansing that will fit them both morally and officially for their task. "Since divine consecration must of necessity involve personal moral holiness, he prays that they may not be contaminated by the world, and that they may be preserved from the power of the Evil One" (Hoskyns, *op. cit.,* pp. 501f.). Apparently, therefore, v. 17 should have the word "sanctify" to designate this act of the Father, rather than "consecrate" (NEB), which implies man's actions. The word of God is that which both cleanses (15:3) and sanctifies (17:17).

Jesus did not have the ascetic type of holiness that assumes that the soul is purified in the proportion that the body is tortured. Neither did Jesus have the Pharisaic concept of holiness — that holiness is best served by keeping at a distance from the world. Instead, his was a redemptive type of holiness that welcomed fellowship with publicans and sinners in order to win them. He was not afraid that his sanctity would be rubbed off by physical contact with "the world" and its sordidness. It was not the type that retreats from the world for self-preservation, but in self-sacrifice goes out, like the Salvation Army, "into the hedges and highways" and to cities "where cross the crowded ways of life." A news-reporter recently stated that in one English-speaking nation a census disclosed that two-thirds of the clergymen of one denomination and half of another use intoxicating beverages. The sanctity needed is not so much in clerical vestments or professional zeal, but in living righteously and redemptively (I Thess. 2:1ff.).

18 As thou didst send me into the world, even so sent I them into the world. 19 And for their sakes I sanctify myself, that they themselves also may be sanctified in truth.

*[handwritten margin notes: "PRIESTLY CHARACTER" / "CONSECRATION OF JESUS!"]*

from inner defilement (Eph. 5:26; I Thess. 5:23). Achan represents sanctification by relationship. He took to himself booty which had previously been "devoted" or consecrated to God; his act was sacrilege inspired by covetousness (Josh. 7:18). The meaning of "purify" may be appropriate here in v. 17 since it is followed by the phrase "in the truth." The preposition *en* used here in the Greek frequently means "by" in the sense of agent. The implication of the passage is that God's revelation of himself, as set forth in the Scriptures, is a vital and effective means for developing Christlike character.

**18 As thou didst send me . . . even so send I them into the world."** Send (*apesteila*, "sent," aor. for completed action) is used in both clauses. "Apostle" means "one sent." Jesus was an "apostle" sent from God, as was John (1:6). The Twelve were also "apostles" when they went forth to preach (Luke 9:2), as were the seventy missioners later (Luke 10:1).

So is everyone sent by God to perform a special task. "Apostle" is the Greek term and "missionary" is the Latin term for the same idea — "one who is sent." As Christ represented the Father to the world so now the disciples are commissioned to represent Christ to the world. Their purpose is to witness and to win men to Christ. John Wesley was in harmony with this when he told his preachers, "You have nothing to do but to save souls."

**19 For their sakes I sanctify myself.** One meaning of "sanctify" is "to dedicate as a sacrifice."[10] The meaning of "purify" is excluded here because Jesus did not need to be cleansed from sin. As in 10:36 the clear meaning is separation, dedication, and sacrifice. Clearly Jesus is here referring to the *sacrifice* of himself in behalf of others. The final act of his mission to earth is at hand. He now formally sets himself apart and thus ratifies the sanctification by the Father (10:36). He is about to experience the terrible ordeal that culminates in his being "the Lamb

### 3. JESUS PRAYS FOR FUTURE BELIEVERS (vv. 20-24)

In this prayer for converts of the apostles Jesus' eyes of faith embraced the "other sheep not of this fold" (10:16), other fields "white already unto harvest" (4:35). The petition is a prophecy of events narrated in Acts, reflected in Romans 15:19, and expanded in subsequent church history.

The burden of the Savior's prayer here is for the unity of the church. Mentioned first in v. 11, it is repeated four other times in vv. 21-22. It is viewed here not necessarily as an end in itself but as a means toward world evangelism. The importance of this in modern times is seen best in communities in which Christians are in a minority or non-existent. Distant lands know little and care less about the historical causes of denominationalism in Western Christianity. Consequently, they often find that conflicting appeals of Christian evangelists cancel

each other out. They expect Christ's "sent ones" to speak a common message and they are quite justified in this expectation as Jesus' prayer here indicates. Factionalism among those who bear the name of Christ is nothing new or accidental. Among the greatest problems confronting the church, even during the life of the apostles were church schisms. The acuteness of the problem is reflected in letters to the Corinthians (I Cor. 1, 3), to the Galatians (Gal. 1, 2) to Gaius (III John 9-11) and to others (II Pet. 2:1-22). Sometimes these divisions were among real believers and were caused by spiritual immaturity leading to hero-worship and petty rivalries (I Cor. 3:1-9). The basic cause was spiritual deficiency, especially in the area of love (I Cor. 13). Jesus' prayer was primarily to prevent this kind of disunity. The other kind arose from false teachers (Acts 20:26, 30) or immoral practices (I Cor. 5:9-13). Jesus did not pray for a "unity" which glossed over cleavages of doctrine and discipline. The church, to

[10] As in the LXX Ex. 13:2; 28:41; 29:1, 2, 27; Lev. 16:4; Deut. 15:19. See Hoskyns, p. 503.

20 Neither for these only do I pray, but for them also that believe on me through their word; *NOTE TIME SEQUENCE !!*

21 that they may all be one; even as thou, Father, *art* in me, and I in thee, that they also may be in us: that the world may believe that thou didst send me.

---

of God which takes away the sin of the world." To this objective he had dedicated himself from the beginning. The fruits of this atonement from sin are experienced by all who become genuine believers. Here, as in v. 17, sanctification is "in truth," in reality.

20 Neither for these only do I pray, but for them also. In vv. 20-23 request is made for those who will be believers in the future as the result of the witness of the Eleven. Their word (*logos*) here means their witness. Luke (Acts 1:1) uses this term to refer to his Gospel (i.e., "treatise"). Also in papyrus usage the term is used to designate "book." John used it to designate the Christ (1:1). As used in John, the term means essentially God's message to man, the expression and exhibition of what God is like and of what he offers to mankind. As a result of the witnessing by these eleven in speaking,

writing, and in holy living, multitudes "which no man can number" have by faith partaken of the priceless gift of life eternal.

21 That they be . . . in us; that the world may believe. In this verse the phrase *hen ōsin* ("be one") occurs again for the second and third times. Here the KJV is more accurate, translating "may be one in us." The kind of unity requested for the disciples is that which exists between Father and Son, the closest possible personal, sympathetic working relationship. It is not an alliance merely for the pursuit of common causes, a "marriage of convenience," a partnership of expediency. It is, rather, a unity growing out of spiritual kinship, resulting from the believer's regeneration and incorporation into the family of God. It is a fellowship (*koinōnia*) with the Father and with the Son and with other believers so united to God (I John 1:3). Included in this unity are Father,

---

be truly united, in the sense of Jesus' petition, must have its unity in Christ. The basis for unity is not expediency, such as the consolidation of railroads with declining revenues (for the purpose of self-preservation). The unity Jesus requests is not merely a union of convenience, such as that which united the thirteen original Atlantic colonies (lest they "all hang separately"). It is not a union brought about by the necessity of facing a common foe, a crisis such as united Catholics and Protestants against Moslems in defense of Vienna. It is not a "unity" springing only from mutual desire for friendship, acceptance, and recognition among men and women of good will. The basis of the unity is not humanistic but theistic. More specifically, it is Christocentric. "It is only union with Christ, and through Christ with God, which creates unity among those who have shared this common faith."[n]

There is a widespread idea that the modern ecumenical movement began with the Edinburgh missionary conference in

1910. It is true that the ecumenical movement then became more self-conscious and deliberate from that day to the formation of the World Council of Churches. But the beginnings of the modern movement for Christian unity go back at least to the Pietist movement in central Europe. Casper Schwenckfeld, a younger contemporary of Luther, felt that purity of life and fullness of love was as important as purity of doctrine. The same theme was emphasized by the "Father of Pietism," Philip Jacob Spener, during the latter part of the seventeenth century. Count Nicholas von Zinzendorf tried in vain to unify separate German-speaking communities of Christians in the Atlantic colonies early in the eighteenth century. John Wesley urged ecumenicity in his famous sermon entitled, "On Having a Catholic Spirit." The creed recited weekly affirms belief in "the one holy catholic (universal) church." The Second Great Awakening in America (1801), while it sharpened denominationalism, also led to such ecumenical institutions as missionary societies,

---

° Jean-Louis d' Aragon, "La Notion de l'Unité," *Sc. Eccl.* (1959), p. 119.

**22 And the glory which thou hast given me I have given unto them; that they may be one, even as we *are* one;**

---

Son, the Spirit, the Eleven and future generations of believers. "This unity is not that of a human organization, but is a gift of divine love. . . . This can be perfectly consummated only as its members have fellowship with the Father and his Son" (WFH, VIII, 751). This type of unity among believers has as its basis a unity with God in Christ. The underlying purpose of the unity is world evangelization. The connection between Christian unity and Christian witness has never been adequately recognized in spite of the emphasis of this chapter. Yet some of the best examples of ecumenicity have been brought about as the cause and result of evangelism.

**22 The glory which thou hast given me I have given unto them. Have given** (*dedōkas*) is perfect tense, implying that the gift still abides. In this eagerness, that the disciples have unity with each other and with him, Jesus gives to his followers the same glory which the Father gave him. The Master is not concerned to remain aloof and superior to the apostles; instead he wants the highest degree of unity possible. As in the scene of footwashing Jesus was not concerned with status but rather with unity. The term "glory" (*doxa*) is a complex word, not easily expressed in English. Here the connotation is honor, vindication, and perhaps prestige (cf. 2:11; 11:40). In the Synoptic accounts "glory" is associated with the Son of man who comes back to judge the earth at the *parousia* (Matt. 16:27; 19:28; 24:30; 25:31). The disciples are to share in the glory of Christ's second advent (Matt. 19:28; cf. I Cor. 6:2). We cannot be sure that this is John's meaning, for in this Gospel "glory" is something less eschatological and phenomenal than in the Synoptics and Acts; it is more spiritual in nature (1:14; 12:41). It includes the "glory" associated with the Incarnate Word (1:14), but not with the Eternal Word (v. 24; so JHB, II, 578-80).

**That they may be one, even as we are one.** This is the fourth petition for unity.

---

Bible societies, temperance societies, Sunday-school associations, and reform groups which enlisted support from *all* churches. Other things being equal, organic *union* is the natural and desirable outgrowth of inner spiritual *unity*. However, it should not be assumed that unity cannot exist without union, nor that union in itself assures unity. In many countries where there is the most organic union among churches there is the least amount of vital Christianity. Under conditions of stagnation the adage does not hold true that "in union there is strength." Jesus was praying for inner dynamic spiritual unity in Christ that will bear a consistent witness and thus lead the world to believe on Christ. This comes to its climax in v. 23, a "consummation of unity, the Father and the Son absorbing united Christians in the divine union."º

Jesus had one final request. He wanted his disciples to share with him everything possible that a human being could share with deity. He wanted them to view his heavenly glory. They had seen him in the days of his humiliation — when he was often tired, hungry, dusty, beset by implacable foes and sometimes the object of derision by the multitudes (Mark 5:40).

The Savior now prays that they may see him in his own "natural habitat," in his "native clime." This prayer was fulfilled in part when Paul "saw" and described his reign in glory (Phil. 2:11), and when the apocalyptist described him as above the brightness of the sun (Rev. 1:16), as the "Lion of the tribe of Judah" (Rev. 5:5), as the successful warrior (19:15). What was seen through the eyes of faith in inspiration, and shared by the faithful since, will be realized in full measure when "the kingdoms of this world become the kingdoms of our Lord and of his Christ" (Rev. 11:15). The significant thing here is that Jesus wanted his disciples to share to the fullest possible extent with the divine prerogatives that were his alone. He was not keeping them subordinate, as do many other world leaders, nor was he descending to their level; instead he was bringing them up,

---

º Jean Cadier, tr. by C. Preiss, "The Unity of the Church," *Interpretation* (April, 1957), p. 175.

23 I in them, and thou in me, that they may be perfected into one; that the world may know that thou didst send me, and lovedst them, even as thou lovedst me.

---

23 **That they may be perfected into one,** the fifth petition for oneness in this chapter. **Perfected** (*teteleiōmenoi*) is the perfect participle used with the copula ("may be") and denotes the *state* of completeness of conformity to God's will. This verb occurs with the same meaning in 4:34 ("accomplish his work"), in 5:36 ("granted me to accomplish") and in 17:4. Jesus now prays for the full consummation of unity of Father, Son and believers. Thus Jesus looks ahead and longs for a lasting, vital cohesiveness that will be indispensable to the effectiveness with which the Good News will confront the world. This is the second time that the conversion of the world is linked with the unity of the church.

**That the world may know** (*ginōskēi*), recalls the repeated emphasis in Ezekiel to the effect that Israel, the heathen, the nations, the world "shall know" Jehovah (Ezek. 35:15; 36:36; 37:28; 39:23). There the "knowledge" of God's will and ways would come about through divine *judgment;* here through the *witness* of a united and articulate church; the movement is from Mt. Sinai to Mt. Zion (Heb. 12:20-22). The two things Jesus wants "the world" to know, or to recognize, are that the Son came from the Father and that the disciples are recipients of the same

---

so far as their humanity would allow, to his level. What an uttermost salvation!

#### 4. CONCLUDING SUMMARY (vv. 25, 26)

Jesus closes the prayer in the obvious confidence that his petition will be answered. There is implicit in the wording a note of subdued thanksgiving. There is love implicit in his second direct address to the Father ("O righteous Father"). Again one senses the estrangement of Jesus and his disciples from the world and their alliance with God. To the end there is the acute awareness of one who has been "sent," a missionary.

Even though Jesus knew the disciples would desert him, and not witness the worst aspects of his suffering, he nevertheless wanted them to share vicariously in the restoration to his glory. While the words of this prayer reflect the closest conceivable relationship between Father and Son consistent with a distinction of persons, yet it seems too strong to say with Sidebottom that "the Father and the Son always shared the same character, the same glory."[p] Attention has been called to several passages in which Jesus emphasizes his subordination to the Father equally with his union with the Father (e.g., 10:29). Even with arrest but an hour or so away, Jesus looks beyond to the "glory" which awaits his restoration to the Father's presence in a fuller measure. It is rather paradoxical that Jesus goes to the Father (16:28) and at the same time says that the Father is present with him (16:32). However, Christians experience this paradox daily. Like Paul, they "desire to depart and be with Christ" (Phil. 1:23) and yet they are aware of Jesus' promise, "Lo, I am with you always" (Matt. 28:20), a promise fulfilled through the Holy Spirit.

The prayer appropriately climaxes with the stress upon love that unites Father, Son, and believer. Two things are stressed in the summary: knowledge (v. 25) and love (v. 26); and the greater of these is love. The knowledge resulting from the experience of God in Christ is the basis for the love "shed abroad in their hearts" (cf. Rom. 5:5).

Love is costly. "It costs to care." The great Chrysostom upbraided his sophisticated audience in Antioch, while preaching on this text, urging upon them the application of "the social gospel."[q] Love ought to be the biggest word in the Christian's vocabulary as it is the greatest of the Christian virtues. But we need constantly to remind ourselves that genuine love to God expresses itself in love to man also and that real love to man is content with nothing less than action (I John 3: 17). As incredible as it seems, the same

---

p E. M. Siderbottom, *The Christ of the Fourth Gospel* (London: S. P. C. L., 1961), p. 161.
q Chrysostom, *op. cit.*, XCI, 397.

24 Father, I desire that they also whom thou hast given me be with me where I am, that they may behold my <u>glory</u>, which thou hast given me: for thou lovedst me before the foundation of the world.

25 O righteous Father, the world knew thee not, but I knew thee; and these knew that thou didst send me;

26 and I made known unto them thy name, and will make it known; that the love wherewith thou lovedst me may be in them, and I in them.

kind of love that the Son receives. The love (*agapē*) would be the same in quality but not in quantity.

24 **That they may behold my glory,** i.e., that they may see and, to a degree at least, share the glory *in eternity* that Jesus has within the Godhead. In 1:14 John testifies, "We beheld his glory" (cf. I John 1:1-3), that is, the excellence of Jesus' existence as a man; this is his glory with the Father that he left (17:5) and to which he will be restored. Even this Jesus desires to share. Human imagination is inadequate to visualize the nature and excellence of that "glory." "Eye hath not seen, ear hath not heard . . . what God hath in store for those that love him" (I Cor. 2:9). The foundation of the world is an expression which occurs only once in the LXX (II Macc. 2:29) and nine times in the N. T. (e.g., Eph. 1:4; I Pet. 1:20). It refers to the beginning of creation, the beginning of time (cf. Gen. 1:1). "*Before* the foundation" implies before the creation of the world itself, i.e., from the very beginning.

25-26 The prayer for the disciples is now summarized.

**Righteous Father,** is almost synonymous with "Holy Father" of v. 11, a sanctification of the Name. They have come to know (*egnōsan*) Jesus' relation to God, that he was sent by God and that God had been revealed to them ("I made known unto them thy names"; cf. v. 11 for discussion on "name"). Again Jesus contrasts his knowledge or recognition of the Father with the world's ignorance of the Father (EAA, *Voc.,* p. 125).

The last request of the prayer is for love: "*that the love wherewith thou lovest me may be in them and I in them.*" There is a limitlessness to the love here requested. The type of love God manifested to his Son is sought for the disciples. God loved a sinful world enough to deprive himself of fellowship with Jesus in heaven for over thirty years while Jesus demonstrated God' love and will to men. The prayer is that we have that kind of self-sacrificing love. Such love as manifested in kindness, service, and witnessing to the lost makes a profound and lasting impression. When all else is ineffective, the bestowal of love often breaks all barriers down and opens people's hearts to God. There is no substitute for the love which "never fails."

love which the Father has for the Son is extended to the believer! The God who sends rain upon the just and unjust bids us love both friend and enemy (Matt. 5:44-48). As we respond, we realize or "know" that "love is of God; and every one that loveth is begotten of God, and knoweth God" (I John 4:7). We are warned, however, that love led Jesus to lay down his life (I John 3:16) and the same love in a disciple involves sacrifices also.

# CHAPTER XVIII

W hen Jesus had spoken these words, he went forth with his disciples over the brook
Kidron, where was a garden, into which he entered, himself and his disciples. *Gethsemene*
 2 Now Judas also, who betrayed him, knew the place: for Jesus ofttimes resorted *Synoptic*
thither with his disciples.

---

## EXEGESIS

1 **The brook Kidron** (*cheimarrou tou Kedrōn*) was a winter freshet or stream that flowed only after a shower or rain, a *wadi,* having the name of Kidron. It was located east of the city (II Sam. 15:23). *Kēpos* (garden) occurs also in v. 26, 19:41 and in Luke 13:19. Per-

haps the owner was a friend of Jesus, "for Jesus oft-times resorted thither with his disciples" (v. 2). Mark (14:32) called the place "Gethsemane" as did Matthew (26:36).

2 **Judas, who betrayed him, knew the place.** Judas was a convenient pawn to the Sanhedrin, since he knew where Jesus

---

## EXPOSITION

### IV. THE PASSION NARRATIVE (18:1 — 19:42)

#### A. THE ARREST (18:1-14)

##### 1. THE BETRAYAL (vv. 1-5)

In chs. 18 and 19 the Fourth Gospel moves into an area in which it has most in common with the Synoptic accounts. The large amount of space given to the trial and crucifixion in each of the four biographies indicates the importance of these events in the judgment of the four evangelists. In John's account the material common to the three but lacking here is the prayer in the garden of Gethsemane, a description of the trial before Caiaphas, the fate of Judas (in Matthew), the youth who fled naked (in Mark), the "trial" before Herod, the lamentation of the "daughters of Jerusalem" and the penitence of the thief (in Luke). In John's account alone are recorded: the trial before Annas, in which an officer struck Jesus for what he considered an impudent answer, the refusal of the Jesus' accusers to enter the Praetorium, Pilate's query about truth, Pilate's assumption of the judgment seat at the Pavement, the soldier's casting lots for the seamless robe, the provision for the care of Jesus' mother, and the piercing of Jesus' side. Was John's account designed to supplement the others? In the

judgment of B. F. Westcott, John's account is not designed as supplemental but as "an independent and complete" record. In the record here preserved one notes the arrest (18:1-11), the Jewish trials (18:12-28), the Roman trial (18:29—19:16), the crucifixion (19:17-37) and the burial (19:38-42). Our chief concern here is to note John's distinctive treatment of the narrative.

Better perspective may be obtained by viewing these events with reference to their paragraph sequence. The paragraphs are named and relationships indicated.

18:1 -11 THE ARREST

18:12-14 TO ANNAS

18:15-18 PETER'S DENIAL

18:19-24 TRIAL BEFORE ANNAS

18:25-27 PETER'S 2nd & 3rd DE-
NIALS

18:28-32 JESUS BROUGHT TO
PILATE

18:33-38 PILATE
QUESTIONS JESUS

18:38-40 JEWS DEMAND
BARABBAS

19:1-11  PILATE SEEKS JESUS' RE-
LEASE

19:12-16 PILATE YIELDS TO JEWS'
DEMANDS

3 Judas then, having received the band *of soldiers,* and officers from the chief priests and the Pharisees, cometh thither with lanterns and torches and weapons.

4 Jesus therefore, knowing all the things that were coming upon him, went forth, and saith unto them, Whom seek ye?

5 They answered him, Jesus of Nazareth. Jesus saith unto them, I am *he.* And Judas also, who betrayed him, was standing with them.

---

could be apprehended while away from the crowds. In the daytime Jesus had been teaching the masses openly and was gladly heard by them. Jesus' enemies dared not arrest him openly because Jesus was too popular (Luke 20:19).

**3 Band (of soldiers) and officers from the chief priests and the Pharisees.** *Speira* ("band") literally means a Roman cohort (a tenth part of a legion) which at full strength was about 6000 men. It is possible that John did not use the word in its technical sense. It could then refer to a large number of Jews employed as policemen, who, along with *hypēretas* (ser-vants), functioning as officers of the temple guard and the Sanhedrin, had been dispatched to arrest Jesus. The fact that so many were in the group implies that, due to Jesus' popularity, some resistance on the part of Jesus' friends may have been expected. The band could be seen at a distance since they carried "lanterns and torches."

**4, 5 Jesus . . . went forth and saith unto them Whom seek ye?** Instead of hiding from the officers, who were so plainly visible while he was not, Jesus approached them, thus voluntarily exposing himself to the anticipated arrest. He

---

In John's account much interest centers in Pilate although the dream of Pilate's wife (Matt. 27:19) is not mentioned. Noteworthy also is the fact that John does not stress the original charge of blasphemy which was the basic reason, in the Jewish leaders' thinking, for the execution of Jesus (cf. 19:7).

The betrayal scene is very dramatic. Whether Jesus' intercessory prayer was uttered in the upper room, or near the temple, is not known. But immediately thereafter, about midnight, Jesus and the eleven disciples made their way down into the deep dark ravine of the Kidron and across to the western slope of Olivet. The dark fortress-like walls of "the Holy City" lay behind them, thrusting upwards to what Josephus called a "dizzy height." The city that had welcomed Jesus so joyously a few days before was silent, dark and ominous. Jesus was probably reminding himself of his prophetic words uttered less than a week before — "you did not know the time of your visitation" (RSV, Luke 19:41; cf. 13:34). The disciples were probably reminding themselves of the gloomy resignation of Thomas, "Let us go and die with him" (John 11:16). No doubt the promised Comforter seemed quite unreal and distant at this time. The dark Kidron may have re-minded them of the "valley of the shadow of death" in which the Psalmist found deliverance from his fears (Ps. 23:4). A few hours later they had to recross this gorge, while Jesus was in the custody of his enemies. Only later would "the light" appear and they would realize that, while the Psalmist could expect and experience deliverance, the "Lamb of God" could not. As the jeering watchers at the cross stated correctly, "he saved others, himself he cannot save" (Mark 15:31). They would learn later why God "spared not his own Son, but delivered him up for us all" (Rom. 8:32). If the eleven wondered why Judas was absent so long, their inquiry was not recorded. What John refers to as "a garden" Luke refers to as "the place" (Luke 22:40). The name "Gethsemane" means "oil vat." Today the visitor to that area is shown several sites alleged to be "the place." One site is northeast of Stephen's Gate near the Tomb of the Virgin Mary where the traditional "Grotto of the Agony" is located. Another place alleged to be the authentic site is that within the Church of All Nations with an adjoining garden of ancient olive trees. Up the slope is the more spacious Russian garden of younger olive trees, less frequently visited and more "restful."[a]

a See K. W. Clark, "Gethsemane," *Interpreter's Dictionary of the Bible* (Nashville: Abingdon, 1962), II, 387.

6 When therefore he said unto them, I am *he,* they went backward, and fell to the ground.

7 Again therefore he asked them, Whom seek ye? And they said, Jesus of Nazareth.

8 Jesus answered, I told you that I am *he*; if therefore ye seek me, let these go their way:

9 that the word might be fulfilled which he spake, Of those whom thou hast given me I lost not one.

---

freely admitted that he was **Jesus of Nazareth** whom they were seeking (cf. Acts 24:5, and Mark 14:67).

**6, 7 They went backward and fell to the ground.** Evidently the officers were surprised. Apparently a supernatural fear possessed them for a moment. None wanted to be the first to lay hands on this miracle-worker who claimed to be the Son of God. Jesus was the calmest person in the group. He again asked them, **Whom are you seeking?** John ap-

parently included this in the narrative to illustrate the voluntariness of Christ's surrender. By their answer they put themselves on record that they had come to arrest Jesus only and not his disciples.

**8, 9 Permit these to go their way.** As always, Jesus was concerned about the welfare of others and so asked that his disciples not be arrested. He thus showed himself to be a good shepherd. **Of those whom thou hast given me I lost not one** is a partial quotation of what is recorded

---

John again points out that Jesus was not taken by surprise but knew beforehand what was going to happen (v. 4 cf. 13:1). To Jesus it was simply the unfolding of a series of events which had been long expected and for which he was fully prepared. Jesus, according to this account, did not wait to be seized but stepped out into the light of the torches and asked, "Whom seek ye?" This absense of fear or flight took the arresting party off guard. When Jesus identified himself with the words "I am" (*egō eimi*) there was a violent reaction. It was these words which had infuriated the Jews (8:58) so much that they had attempted to assassinate him immediately. It was these words, in reply to the question, "Are you the Son of God?" which led to the unhesitating verdict of blasphemy (Luke 22:71; cf. John 18:37). It was the statement of an affirmation — "I am the one you seek."

## 2. PETER'S ILL-ADVISED DEFENSE (VV. 6-11)

That the captors literally fell to the ground is indicated in the word *chamai* — "on the ground" or "to the ground" (A-G). The only other N. T. occurrence is in John 9:6, where Jesus "spat upon the ground." Why did the arresting officers

go back and fall down? It may be that the words "I am" (he) carried such a connotation as to awe them before an alleged Messiah. It may be that the boldness and moral grandeur of Jesus made them shrink like creatures in the presence of a strong light. It has been suggested also that is a deliberate allusion to Isa. 28:16 ("a precious corner stone") and Isa. 8:14 ("a stone of stumbling") and consistent with apostolic preaching (Acts 4:11; Rom. 9:33; I Pet. 2:6).[b] If so, the evangelist intended it only as a symbol of national prejudice which led them to reject the "stone" which God later used as the chief corner stone of the building. As the stone of Isa. 8:14 caused unbelievers to fall, so confrontation with Jesus, in this situation caused them to fall in confusion. Jesus himself used the analogy as a prediction and a warning (Matt. 21:42). A related truth is that repentance with reference to this "stone" leads to life; the harsh alternative is being crushed by the stone (Luke 20:18). It is safe to conclude that they were "put to shame" in the presence of innocence and holiness incarnate (Ps. 6:10).

Always solicitous of others, Jesus interceded for the release of the other eleven. He denied himself the natural desire for their companionship and heroically faced brutality alone.

b P. Meine, "A note on John XVIII, 6," ET, 1954, p. 286.

10 Simon Peter therefore having a sword drew it, and struck the high priest's servant, and cut off his right ear. Now the servant's name was Malchus.

11 Jesus therefore said unto Peter, Put up the sword into the sheath: the cup which the Father hath given me, shall I not drink it?

12 So the band and the chief captain, and the officers of the Jews, seized Jesus and bound him,

---

in John 17:12. Another instance of the fulfillment of a prediction of Jesus is found in 18:32.

**10, 11 Simon Peter ... struck the high priest's servant (doulos) and cut off his right ear. Now the servant's name was Malchus.** John, characteristically, is very explicit in relating this incident. He not only gives the name of the wielder of the sword but also states which ear was cut off and whose ear it was. Peter apparently struck horizontally, as if to cut off the servant's head. Malchus dodged sidewise away from the sword, which then grazed the side of his face and cut off the ear. Peter must have struck left-handed. If Malchus had not ducked, his head might have been severed from his body. Peter, impulsive as usual and acting before thinking, felt that the occasion demanded defense for his hero and Lord. He displayed unusual physical courage. However, perhaps only an hour later, he displayed moral cowardice. Peter was commanded to sheath the sword with the explanation: **The cup which the Father hath given me shall I not drink it?** Here "cup" is used symbolically, meaning "the submissive acceptance of whatever God wills for one's life." It refers specifically to the immediate ordeal of humiliation, torture, and crucifixion.

12 John agrees with the Synoptists that there was a trial before the high priest

---

10 Peter's action is strange. How could he expect to make more than a token defense with one or two swords against a well-armed force?[c] Why would he make even a token defense when it could only lead to his own arrest and maltreatment? Why was he so bold here and so cowardly later? Was it an action consistent with previous plans of self-defense (cf. Luke 22:38) or a spontaneous, explosive act of recklessness? Was it over-compensation for the prediction that he would not stand the test (John 13:38)? We cannot say. Jesus' rebuke differs notably from that reported in Matthew, where, in a penetrating epigram, the Master retorted; "They that take the sword shall perish by the sword" (Matt. 26:52). Here is the nearest thing to John's allusion to Jesus' prayer in Gethsemane — **the cup which the Father hath given me to drink.** The cup here is not an allusion to the "cup of blessing" (the Eucharist), nor the "cup of salvation" (Ps. 116:13; Ps. 23:5). It is probably a cryptic allusion to the "cup" of divine judgment mentioned in the prophets.[d] In contemporary Christian literature the "cross" is the equivalent of the "cup" of the O. T. Thus, in the poem "My Rosary," the poet "tries, at last, to kiss the Cross," and in so doing welcomes the chastening rod of God, his "cup of woe." Our cups of woe, in the marvelous alchemy of God, are to turn into cups of blessing.

In the drama of the arrest we learn several more things about Jesus.

(i) He *voluntarily* laid down his life for the sheep (vv. 4, 8, 11, 36). The crucifixion was not the consequence of evil gaining temporary ascendency over good. It was not merely the unhappy and tragic end of a martyr-like career. It was a self-sacrifice of the Lamb of God

(ii) We learn also that Jesus was in full knowledge and command of the situation. He recognized in the events the fulfillment of prophecy (vv. 9, 32).

(iii) He was courageous. Before this he had left the scene of conflict because

---

    c John is the only gospel writer who mentions the presence of Roman soldiers. It has been suggested that since he wrote his gospel later than the three Synoptics, who wrote prior to the Jewish Revolt of 66-70 A.D., he would naturally not have hesitated to include this incident, which might dangerously have tended to "associate Christians with the idea of armed resistance to Roman authority" if it had been recorded and circulated before the Jewish insurrection. Cf. R. A. Knox, op. cit. (London: Burns, Oats & Washbourne, 1955), I, 260.
    d I.e., a "wine cup" which Jehovah compels the nations to "drink," a metaphor of divine judgment. See Jer. 25:15, 17, 28; Ezek. 23:31-33; Hab. 2:16.

13 and led him to Annas first; for he was father in law to Caiaphas, who was high priest that year.

---

and that Peter's denial occurred at that time (cf. Mark 14:53-72; Matt. 26:57-75; Luke 22:54-71).

13 Jesus, seized and bound as a dangerous criminal, was led away. The fact that the word *chiliarchos*, which meant leader of a thousand and is translated captain, is used is some evidence at least that a considerable number of Roman soldiers did participate in Jesus' arrest. Only John mentions this. Led away to Annas first; for he was father-in-law to Caiaphas who was high priest that year. Annas (or Hanan, Ananias, Ananus) wielded unusual power in his generation.

He was high priest from A.D. 7 to 14.[1] Then he was deposed by the Romans, and, after a brief interval, his son Eleazer held the office for one year. After a break of about one year, his son-in-law Caiaphas was appointed to the office by the Romans. Caiaphas ruled until A.D. 36. After that four other sons of Annas held the office.[2] The fact that the high priesthood was in one family so long is convincing evidence that it was very influential with the Roman rulers who appointed the high priests. As long as a former high priest lived, he continued being called a high priest. Annas apparent-

---

"his hour had not yet come" (8:59; 10:39; 11:54). Now that his "hour" had come (12:23; 13:1; 17:1) he boldly faced arrest and torture.

(iv) We note also Jesus' magnanimity in the healing of the ear of Malchus. His justification of this gives further evidence of his submission to the Father's will.

### 3. ARRAIGNMENT BEFORE ANNAS (vv. 12-14)

There are some problems here. Many commentators gloss over them by terming this "trial before Jewish Authorities" without committing themselves to either a trial before Annas, or a trial before Caiaphas, or both. In the Synoptic accounts the trial described is before Caiaphas, while in this the trial before Annas is reported. The Sinaitic Syriac attempts to harmonize the accounts by transposing v. 24 to follow v. 13.[e] If this is done the high priest mentioned in vv. 15, 19, 22 would be Caiaphas rather than his father-in-law Annas.[f] As the account stands in John, Peter apparently made his denial in two different locations, first before the residence of Annas and later at the residence of Caiaphas. Also Peter was warming himself in both places (vv. 18, 25).[g]

Because of a textual variant in v. 24 some (Lagrange and Howard) conclude that v. 24 should follow v. 13. Internal evidence is also cited to justify this change; i.e., it is unlikely that Peter would have continued to follow Jesus after his first denial at the house of Annas and it seems unlikely that John would have referred to Annas as high priest in vv. 15, 19, 22 (WFH, p. 760). While this transposition is quite possible and is considered tolerable by Cyril of Alexandria, Luther and others, the evidence seems inconclusive especially in the lack of good textual support. Also, this proposal fails to account for the differences between the Synoptic accounts of the trial and that of John. It seems better to assume that the existing order is correct for the following reasons. (i) It is the order of all the extant Greek manuscripts. (ii) It seems unlikely that the author would repeat the same statement in two *successive* verses (vv. 18, 25). (iii) It would provide for two supplementary accounts of the dialogue before the high priests rather than two contradictory ones. On this supposition one may reconstruct the sequence of events as follows: After being seized and bound Jesus was led to the high priestly residence, consisting, like

---

[1] Jos. *Ant.* XVIII, 2, 1f.

[2] ·The last of which, also named Annas, had James the apostle put to death and attempted to do likewise with Peter (Jos. *Ant.* XX, 8, 1. Acts 12:1-3).

e Nestle's *Greek New Testament.* MS No. 225 does likewise (Hoskyns, p. 512).

f The following order is suggested by Loisy and others: v. 13, 24, 14, 15, 19-23, 16-18, 25-27.

g This objection is overcome if one assumes that there were two apartments adjoining the same courtyard, a very normal situation in the Near East. See P. Beeckman. *L'Evangile selon Saint Jean . . .* (Bouges: C. Beyaert, 1951), p. 361.

14 Now Caiaphas was he that gave counsel to the Jews, that it was expedient that one man should die for the people.

15 And Simon Peter followed Jesus, and *so did* another disciple. Now that disciple was known unto the high priest, and entered in with Jesus into the court of the high priest;

16 but Peter was standing at the door without. So the other disciple, who was known unto the high priest, went out and spake unto her that kept the door, and brought in Peter.

---

ly had political power, and very likely he had become wealthy as well as influential.

**14 Now Caiaphas . . . gave counsel . . . that it was expedient that one man should die for the people.** This is a reference to what Caiaphas had recommended to the Sanhedrin after Jesus had raised Lazarus from the dead (John 11:47-50). He had argued that the Romans might deprive them of their offices and even further subjugate the Jews, if they did not get rid of Jesus. John, by relating this evidence, indicated what type of character Caiaphas had and also what his diabolical intent was with reference to the Son of God.

**15, 16 Peter followed Jesus, and so did another disciple.** Peter's denial is found in all four Gospels. It constitutes one of the most graphic descriptions in all literature of man's weakness. If "the other disciple" had not been acquainted with Annas and both disciples had not gone in to listen to the proceedings, it could have been avoided. Since they loved Jesus, they naturally wished to be near him.

many oriental palaces, of several apartments facing an inner courtyard. As Peter was admitted to the courtyard he denied any relationship to Jesus. Meanwhile Jesus was being given a preliminary hearing by Annas, who still carried the title "high priest" although not serving officially in that capacity at the time (cf. Luke 3:2; Acts 4:6). He was "high priest emeritus." Annas, after having the satisfaction of seeing Jesus in custody and after questioning him in a semi-official capacity, sent him on to Caiaphas for the official trial before the Sanhedrin, to another part of the residential complex (cf. Bultmann, p. 498). Meanwhile Peter, still warming himself among the other men, twice denied any knowledge of Jesus. John omits the verdict of blasphemy by reason of which Jesus' execution was requested.

The spiritual significance is that Jesus was now in the role envisioned in Isa. 53:7 — he was like a lamb that is led to the slaughter. Previously Jesus' encounters had been with the Pharisees. They were by far the most numerous and highly respected party within Judaism at that time. Jesus encountered the Sadducees only after his bold cleansing of the temple on that Passover week (Matt. 21:23, 45; 22:23). The interest of the Pharisees was primarily religious; they wanted the Law, as they interpreted it, preserved. Their interest was not in politics as such. The Sadducees were the priesthood and although small numerically were very influential, especially with the Romans.[h] Before the Romans came, the high priest was virtually the king; after the Romans arrived in 63 B.C., they appointed the high priest. The priesthood's concern, as in so many other cultures, was to combine political and religious authority. Their concern was to please the Roman authorities and to keep themselves in power. They had vested interests to defend. One of these was the selling of sacrificial animals to pilgrims and it was this that Jesus overturned when he cleansed the temple. It was his decisive and authoritative act of reformation within the temple precincts which led the Sadducees to demand of him, "By what authority are you doing these things?" (Matt. 21:23 RSV). In Jerusalem both Pharisees and Sadducees, in a rare spirit of cooperation, combined against Jesus, for different motives: the Pharisees because of alleged blasphemy, the Sadducees because of the threat to their standing with the Roman authorities (John 11:

h R. H. Pfeiffer, *History of New Testament Times* (New York: Harper, 1949), p. 56.

17 The maid therefore that kept the door saith unto Peter, Art thou also *one* of this man's disciples? He saith, I am not.

18 Now the servants and the officers were standing *there,* having made a fire of coals; for it was cold; and they were warming themselves: and Peter also was with them, standing and warming himself.

19 The high priest therefore asked Jesus of his disciples, and of his teaching.

20 Jesus answered him, I have spoken openly to the world; I ever taught in synagogues, and in the temple, where all the Jews come together; and in secret spake I nothing.

21 Why askest thou me? ask them that have heard *me,* what I spake unto them: behold, these know the things which I said.

---

17, 18 Art thou also one of this man's disciples? He saith, I am not . . . Peter stood with them and warmed himself. Peter had not anticipated such a question and was unprepared for meeting it. The fact that *mē* is used in the question implies that the maid expected a denial: "You are not, are you?" In reply he stated flatly "I am not," perhaps emboldened to deny his Lord by the very form of the question which was put to him. The fact that Peter was in the company of Jesus' enemies and was warming himself with them in front of the fire constituted a greater temptation not to incriminate himself. "Bad company ruins good morals" (I Cor. 15:33, RSV). See comments on John 6:66, 67 for data on the "herd instinct."

19 The high priest then asked Jesus of (about) his disciples and of (about) his doctrine. It could have been either Caiaphas or Annas that did this questioning. But since the account states (v. 24) that Annas later on sent Jesus to Caiaphas, there is likelihood that Annas was in charge of the questioning at this time. He wanted to know apparently how large a following Jesus had, as well as about his teaching.

20, 21 I have spoken openly to the world . . . In secret spake I nothing. Instead of answering directly, Jesus reminded the questioner that his teachings had been proclaimed repeatedly in public and were well known: "Ask them which heard me." The response was appropriate since many people had heard Jesus.

---

48). It is not surprising that Annas, whose dynasty was threatened, would be as eager as the Pharisees to get rid of Jesus. He therefore had the Savior brought in for questioning, prior to the trial, to gloat over his victim as a cat plays with a mouse before destroying it.

4. PETER'S DENIAL (vv. 15-18, 25-27)

Peter had many elements of strength. Not only did he profess loyalty (13:37), but he manifested a reckless courage by undertaking to defend his Master in the garden (18:10). He also manifested loyalty by following Jesus to the place of his trial, in contrast to nine of the others who went into hiding.[1] Like many another person it was his courage and devotion which got him into a difficult situation. If he disgraced himself by denying his Lord while the others did not, it was because he had greater temptations than the less courageous ones. We wonder whether the others would have done better under similar circumstances. How are we to account for Peter's defection? (i) It was basically the instinct of self-preservation. It was not that he had changed his attitude toward Jesus, but rather, on the spur-of-the-moment, a "little" lie seemed the easiest way out of his involvement. (ii) Peter was unprepared for this crisis. In spite of Jesus' emphatic warning (13:36-38) a few hours earlier, Peter apparently had not forseen events as clearly as had Thomas (11:16). (iii) Peter's temperament was impulsive and spontaneous rather than calculating like that of Thomas. He apparently denied his Lord with as little pre-meditation as he had previously sought to defend his Master with his sword.

What were the steps in Peter's downfall? (i) He was overconfident (13:37). Sometimes optimism is not an asset if it

[1] Chrysostom, *Commentary on Saint John the Apostle and Evangelist* (New York: Fathers of the Church, Inc., 1957), p. 404f.

22 And when he had said this, one of the officers standing by struck Jesus with his hand, saying, Answerest thou the high priest so?

23 Jesus answered him, If I have spoken evil, bear witness of the evil: but if well, why smitest thou me?

---

Furthermore, witnesses would be necessary to establish legal evidence in any trial. No one was required to give evidence against himself in court.

**22, 23. One of the officers standing by struck Jesus with his hand, saying, Answerest thou the high priest so?** *Rhapisma*, "struck with his hand," is defined as follows: "a blow with a club, rod or whip, a slap in the face" (A-G). However the painful blow was delivered, a deserved rebuke was spoken by Jesus. The substance of the reproach was that the guiltless are not to be treated as the guilty.

Jesus did not encourage the officer to strike him again by turning the other cheek to him. This throws light on what Jesus meant in saying, "If anyone strikes you on the right cheek, turn to him the other also" (Matt. 5:39). Apparently he meant, judging from the Matthean context, not to return evil for evil, but rather to accept mistreatment without physical resistance, as he accepted it in this instance. If we were to make such a protest whenever we are mistreated, by doing so we would help to discourage wrongdoers. Letting people do evil with im-

---

considerably underestimates the strength of the enemy. Socrates is quoted as saying that sometimes fearlessness is due to folly. During the American Civil War the most famous (or infamous) engagement was Pickett's charge at Gettysburg. Bruce Catton explains it as coming about because of General Lee's "habit of winning," which in turn led him to overconfidence and subsequent disaster.[j] (ii) Peter slept when he should have prayed (Luke 22:46). True, Jesus attributed this to the weakness of the flesh rather than of the spirit, but it was a neglect of Jesus' command to "watch and pray." (iii) Peter also lingered with the wrong crowd. His immediate concern was his own physical comfort and he warmed himself by the fire with the captors of Jesus in a situation where it would be difficult to preserve his anonymity or neutrality. He forgot to pray, "Lead us not into temptation." He was too close to "the world" physically at the wrong time and consequently succumbed momentarily to "the world."

That Peter, who was so brave in the garden, would quail before the maiden gatekeeper (cf. Acts 12:14), is one of the

surprises of the story. But it is not unusual that one who resists temptation in times of great danger will succumb in a relatively unguarded moment. Once having denied any knowledge of Jesus, he was at least consistent when he denied twice later. But, while Judas had remorse and despair (Matt. 27:3-5; cf. Acts 1:18) Peter had hope and repented (Luke 22: 61, 62).[k]

This account alone reports that the unnamed companion of Peter was known to the family of the high priest and hence admitted (v. 15). It was by his request that Peter also was admitted to the courtyard of the high priests' residence. There is an interesting suggestion that the son of Zebedee regularly supplied the family of the high priest with fish from Galilee and this explains his access to the premises on this occasion.[l]

A. THE TRIAL (18:19–19:16)

1. PRELIMINARY HEARING BEFORE ANNAS (18:19-24)

The "palace" of the high priest was probably not like a western house facing the street. It was rather a hollow square,

---

[j] Bruce Catton, *This Hallowed Ground* (New York: Doubleday, 1956), p. 254.
[k] Remorse is as the heart in which it grows:
     If that be gentle, it drops balmy dews
     Of true repentance; but if proud and gloomy,
     It is the poison tree that, pierced to the inmost,
     Weeps only tears of poison.
Coleridge, "Remorse," Act I, Sc. 1. Cited in J. D. Robertson, *op. cit.*, p. 173.
[l] Wm. Barclay, *The Gospel of John* (Philadelphia: Westminster Press, 1956), II 268; cf. J. N. Sanders, "Who was the Disciple whom Jesus Loved?" F. L. Cross, ed., *Studies in the Fourth Gospel* (London: Mowbray, 1957), pp. 76f.

24 Annas therefore sent him bound unto Caiaphas the high priest.
25 Now Simon Peter was standing and warming himself. They said therefore unto him, Art thou also *one* of his disciples? He denied, and said, I am not.

punity usually encourages them to take advantage of others; but protesting often has the opposite effect.

**24 Annas therefore sent him bound unto Caiaphas the high priest.** *Oun,* which is here translated "therefore," as if used inferentially, can be better translated "then" as in the RSV. It is used in a continuative sense here (D-M, p. 253). In a street ballad quoted in the Talmud, a complaint is registered against high priests, including Annas, over their illegal use of "clubs, staves, and fists" during court procedures.[3]

**25 Now Simon Peter was standing and warming himself.** Two periphrastic imperfects, as in verse 18, present a vivid renewal of action going on. Peter was still in unfriendly and tempting company. It would have been better to stand alone out in the cold than to be near the fire with the Lord's enemies. Again as in verse 17, the negative (*mē*) is used, which anticipates a negative answer: "You are not one of his disciples, are you?" Such a question made it easier for Peter to say "No." It made the temptation more attractive while at the same time it was

perhaps two stories in height facing the inner courtyard. Entrance would normally be by a gate on the street and a passage was leading between high stone walls to the court within. As in large oriental homes today there would be an attendant on duty night and day to open the gate (to those whose presence was desired). The family of the high priest was of the rich aristocracy and the house itself probably dated from Hasmonean times. Houses of this kind were common in Pompeii (such as the house of the Vettii family). The Azem palace in Damascus (17th century) is like this. The same design was used in the Middle Ages, and is used in modern times, for college quadrangles. It is a construction which permits privacy, lends itself to defense in times of emergency, and, in mild climates, permits indoor-outdoor informal living. Presumably, therefore, while Peter was warming himself by the fire, Jesus was having "an audience" with the patriarchal high priest. Two questions were reportedly put to Jesus by the high priest: "How many disciples have you and who are they; also, what do you teach?" Jesus apparently ignored the question about his disciples, perhaps to protect them and their families. The manner of the question suggests that Annas was putting Jesus in the category of a dangerous character, a public enemy, the ringleader of a group of fanatics, of which there were several in the country.

This inference may be gleaned more from Jesus' reply than from the question itself. There were even then Essenes at Qumran firmly convinced that the entire hierarchy was apostate and under the judgment of God. The Essenes were militant anticlericals, with memories and legends of the Wicked Priest, perhaps a reference to Alexander Jannaeus.[m] There were also political extremists, the Zealots and Herodians, who dreamed of a successful rebellion. The high priests, who wanted to maintain the status quo, were suspicious of all these rebels. Jesus was in one or more of these categories, and Annas wanted to get from his own lips something by which he could classify him and condemn him.

The Savior's reaction to this is important. Concerning his doctrine Jesus made it clear that his was not some esoteric doctrine, spoken to a few fanatics in clandestine gatherings. Jesus was logically and legally right in saying, "I have not attempted to hide my teaching, there is nothing furtive about my methods. For an objective report call in as witnesses those who heard me here in the streets and temple precincts." Jesus was in effect calling for an open hearing, not a private confessional.

When Jesus said, **In secret spake I nothing,** it may sound contradictory to the statement that when he was alone with the disciples he expounded all things

[3] Joseph Klausner, *Jesus of Nazareth,* trans. by H. Danby (N. Y.: Macmillan Co., 1925), p. 337.
[m] E. F. Sutcliffe, *The Monks of Qumran* (London: Burns & Oates, 1960), p. 64.

26 One of the servants of the high priest, being a kinsman of him whose ear Peter cut off, said, Did not I see thee in the garden with him?

27 Peter therefore denied again: and straightway the cock crew.

28 They lead Jesus therefore from Caiaphas into the Praetorium: and it was early; and they themselves entered not into the Praetorium, that they might not be defiled, but might eat the passover.

---

a less direct and more courteous way of asking the question.

**26, 27 One of the servants . . . being his kinsman whose ear Peter cut off saith, Did not I see thee in the garden with him?** This question, introduced by the negative *ouk,* expected an affirmative answer. To answer "Yes" to this question would really endanger Peter. As an assailant of this man's relative, he was subject to arrest and condemnation. So he again said "No." Then the cock crowed (cf. 13:38)! John did not see fit to mention Peter's cursing (Mark 14:71).

**28 Then (*oun*) they led Jesus from the house of Caiaphas to the praetorium** (RSV — governor's official residence, cf. v. 33; Matt. 27:27; Mark 15:16; John

19:9). There is some uncertainty as to whether the palace, or residence, was located in the western part of the city where Herod's palace was, or whether it was located in the area of the fortress Antonia northwest of the temple area. The weight of scholarly opinion seems to favor the latter location. The Fourth Gospel does not give any details concerning the trial before Caiaphas, either the informal meeting at night (Mark 14:53; 55-65— Matt. 26:47, 59-68 — Luke 22:54, 63-65) or the formal ratification session after dawn (Mark 15:1 — Matt. 27:1 — Luke 22:66-71); however, it does give us considerable supplemental information of the trial before Pilate (18:28-40). In Jesus' trial before the Sanhedrin, there were at least two violations of Jewish legal pro-

---

(Mark 4:34). Calvin defends Jesus from the charge of inconsistency by saying that what he expounded to the disciples in private was consistent with and an amplification of his public utterances, not something different.[n]

The fact that the officer struck Jesus and was unrebuked is consistent with reports of similar disorders at what were supposed to be trials before Jewish officials. When Paul was before the high priest he was smitten in a similar manner, and he rebuked the high priest for authorizing it (Acts 23:1-5). This smiting of the accused person was contrary to the Law. In Corinth another instance of violence at the scene of trial was reported (Acts 18:12-17).[o] Here, too the violence was clearly illicit.

It is noteworthy that Jesus did not literally "turn the other cheek." His action is thus a commentary on Matt. 5:39; that verse is to be interpreted as "Do not retaliate." It therefore weakens the purely pacifist position.[p]

### 2. THE TRIAL BEFORE CAIAPHAS (18:24, 28)

In view of John's interest in the cynical and yet prophetic utterance of Caiaphas, it is strange that his account of the trial before Caiaphas and the Council is not more explicit (cf. 11:47-53; 18:14). In the Synoptic account, the charge was blasphemy. This is the charge which was the *official* Jewish reason for seeking to impose the death sentence. The *actual* reason was expressed by Caiaphas (11:38) and by Pilate (Matt. 27:18; Mark 15:10) as envy (*phthonos*). The Evangelist well understood the sinister effects of this type of sin for it was that which occasioned the murder of Abel (I John 3:12).

### 3. THE TRIAL BEFORE PILATE (18:29-19:16)

From the trial before Caiaphas and the Sanhedrin, Jesus was led to Pilate for obtaining sanction for the execution. This

---

n J. Calvin, *Commentary on the Gospel According to John* (Grand Rapids: Wm. B. Eerdmans Publishing Co., 1949), II, 201.

o J. C. Ryle, *Expository Thoughts on the Gospels,* John 10:10 to the End (Grand Rapids: Zondervan, n.d.), p. 488.

p A. J. Gossip, *op. cit.,* VIII, 764-767.

29 Pilate therefore went out unto them, and saith, What accusation bring ye against this man?

30 They answered and said unto him, If this man were not an evil-doer, we should not have delivered him up unto thee.

---

cedure: holding the trial for a capital case at night and voting to condemn on the same day of the trial. The Romans did not permit the Jews to execute a man regardless of how guilty he was. Hence, they asked Pilate to impose the death penalty.

**That they might not be defiled, but might eat the passover.** Entering the house of a Gentile would constitute defilement for that whole day and would require also immersing and bathing in water. It would also prevent the eating of the Passover meal that evening.[4] These Jews were punctilious about ceremonial defilement but were brazen in their determination to have an innocent man sentenced to death.

**29, 30 What accusation bring ye against this man?** This was the proper legal inquiry. **If this man were not an evil-doer.** It was a charge that to them at least Jesus was guilty of some crime. But as the Synoptists have stated, his "guilt" consisted primarily in claiming that he was the Son of God. For this admission (self-incrimination) the high priest declared that he was guilty of

---

procedure was repeated many times in medieval Europe when the church delivered heretics to "the secular arm" for execution.

Where was the **Praetorium**? The name originated in Roman army camps where it designated the tent or residence of the "praetor" or commander of the legion. The praetorium of Jerusalem was the official residence of the Roman procurator when he was in the holy city. This building was probably the magnificent palace built by Herod the Great at the western edge of the city near the present Joppa Gate. As Josephus describes it, it was spacious, exceedingly well fortified and dominated by three great towers named for Herod's brothers and his wife. Another opinion is that the "praetorium" of the Gospels means the Herodian fortress Antonia, adjacent to the temple at its northwest corner. In support of this is the mention by John of the stone pavement adjacent to the praetorium (19:13). Recently archaeologists have uncovered a vast expanse of excellent Roman paving stones about three feet square, under the present street level at the site of the Antonia. This evidence has led Pere Vincent (supported by Albright and others) to conclude that Jesus' trial before Pilate occurred here rather than at the palace of Herod. However, excavations at the latter place may yet discover a pavement like that near the Antonia. Herod Agrippa, in residence in Jerusalem at the time (Luke 23:6-12), was probably lodged at the Hasmonean palace in the center of the city and west of the temple; it is unlikely that he, a visitor, would occupy the more sumptuous Herodian palace while Pilate lodged at the Antonia with the garrison. Nor is it likely that Herod's palace would be unoccupied during the Passover It seems not unlikely therefore that the trial took place outside Herod's spacious palace at the west gate where Pilate with his bodyguard was stationed.[q]

John notes ironically that the captors of Jesus were so "holy" that they would not defile themselves even by entering this "judgment hall." Entering a heathen house made one "unclean" until sundown (Edersheim). Apparently they wished to be ceremonially pure so they could partake of the paschal lamb. At the

[4] A. T. Robertson (WPNT, II, 291) argues that John did not mean merely the eating of the Passover meal, but rather the observance of the seven or eight days paschal festival. "There are eight other examples of *pascha* in John's Gospel and in all of them the feast is meant, not the supper. If we follow John's use of the word, it is the feast here, not the meal of John 13:2, which was the regular Passover meal. This interpretation keeps John in harmony with the Synoptics." Cf. II Chron. 30:22: "And they did eat the festival seven days."

[p] The *praetorium* is mentioned several times in the N.T., in Matt. 27:27; Mark 15:16; John 18:28, 33; 19:9; Acts 23:35; Phil. 1:13. In the KJV it is translated "judgment hall," in the ASVm "palace," in the NEB it is "headquarters," and in the ASV and RSV it is transliterated "praetorium." The meaning of "palace" is unmistakable in Acts 23:35. See G. D. Gealy, "Praetorium," IBD, III, 856; MJL, p. 469; WFH, VIII 767.

31 Pilate therefore said unto them, Take him yourselves, and judge him according to your law. The Jews said unto him, It is not lawful for us to put any man to death

32 that the word of Jesus might be fulfilled, which he spake, signifying by what manner of death he should die.

33 Pilate therefore entered again into the Praetorium, and called Jesus, and said unto him, Art thou the King of the Jews?

34 Jesus answered, Sayest thou this of thyself, or did others tell it thee concerning me?

---

blasphemy and so deserved the death penalty (cf. Matt. 26:63-66 — Mark 14:61-64).

**31, 32 Judge him according to your law . . . It is not lawful for us to put any man to death.** Pilate seemingly complimented the Jews by suggesting that they impose the proper penalty. Then he learned that they wanted the death penalty imposed, which they were legally restricted from imposing. They were not really asking for a fair trial but simply for Pilate's consent for them to kill Jesus. John in 12:32 had recorded Jesus'

prophecy that by being lifted up (i.e. crucified) he would draw (make atonement for) men to himself.

**33, 34 Are thou the king of the Jews . . . Sayest thou this of thyself?** Luke (23:2) states that the Jews accused Jesus of "perverting our nation, and forbidding us to give tribute to Caesar and saying that he himself is Christ a king." Pilate could not ignore such a serious charge of sedition and disloyalty to Rome. The Jewish leaders (Sanhedrin) wanted Pilate to believe that Jesus claimed to be a civil king of the Jews and as such, an

---

same time, the Lamb of God would be expiring on his cross. Thus the enemies of Jesus would fulfill his prediction that "whosoever killeth you shall think that he offereth service unto God" (16:2). This matter of consistency has often received comment — "Consistency, thou art a jewel." It is said of General Stonewall Jackson that although he would not dispatch a letter on Sunday, or even read a letter from his wife if it arrived on Sunday, "he would fight, slay and deliver doom to the enemy if on a Sabbath the enemy looked ready for punishment."[r]

The objectivity with which the entire passion is narrated by each of the evangelists is amazing. They do not indulge in imprecations of Jesus' foes, nor labor to eulogize their Lord. They apparently felt that the bare facts are eloquent in themselves. The matter-of-fact way in which the drama is enacted testifies to the writers' objectivity as reporters. Writers of fiction or legend could not have refrained from embellishing their story with strong adjectives.

a. Pilate Denies Jurisdiction (vv. 29-32)

In deference to their religious scruples, Pilate went out to listen to the complaints

of the accusers. Pilate was a stubborn man and not at all disposed to be conciliatory toward what he and Gentiles generally considered Jewish superstitions. Upon assuming command in Palestine several years previously he had offended the Jews and imperiled his own tenure of office by bringing the Roman eagles or standards, into Jerusalem. When the Jewish delegation indicated their preference of death to toleration of "images," Pilate withdrew his secret orders to slay the petitioners and conceded the point.[s] He was reluctant to arouse them again, especially when he knew that his superiors would not tolerate civil strife under his administration.

In none of the accounts is the weakness of the Jewish leaders' position more apparent than in this one. In answer to Pilate's question about the nature of the accusation against Jesus they would only lamely reply, **If this man were not an evildoer, we should not have delivered him** up. In each of the other accounts, the charge is that Jesus pretended to be a king. This charge is reflected here also in Pilate's question, "Art thou the King of the Jews?" (vv. 33-39). Pilate realized that the nature of Jesus' offense was properly religious and demanded that they

---

[r] Carl Sandburg, *Abraham Lincoln* (New York: Dell Publishing Co., 1960), II, 182.

[s] Jos. *War*, II. 168-71 (Loeb), II. 389.

35 Pilate answered, Am I a Jew? Thine own nation and the chief priests delivered thee unto me: what hast thou done?

36 Jesus answered, My kingdom is not of this world: if my kingdom were of this world, then would my servants fight, that I should not be delivered to the Jews: but now is my kingdom not from hence.

---

illegal pretender. Jesus, however, had only admitted to be the spiritual king of Israel (John 1:49), but he had not made that admission to unbelievers; some ecstatic and zealous enthusiasts had hailed him as "king of Israel" during the triumphal entry (John 12:13). By asking Pilate whether that was his own idea or whether he had heard it from others, Jesus, to a certain extent, put Pilate on trial. He answered Pilate's question by asking one of his own.

35 Am I a Jew? Thine own nation and the chief priests delivered thee unto me: What hast thou done? Pilate showed his disdain and contempt for the Jews by asking "Am I a Jew?" The emphatic negative *mēti* in the question shows that the anticipated answer was to be "No." ("I am not a Jew, am I?" Cf. 4:29 for a similar usage of the negative in a question: "This is not the Messiah, is it?") Pilate answered Jesus' question by stating that the chief priests, acting for the Jews, had

---

dispose of him in accordance with their own religious laws. There was in existence the understanding that the Jewish leaders, the Council or Sanhedrin, had jurisdiction over all matters pertaining to their religion excepting the administering of a penalty of death. The Romans had jurisdiction over civil matters. Thus, there was in effect, a "separation of church and state" which enabled Jesus to say on one occasion, "Render unto Caesar the things that are Caesar's and unto God the things that are God's." This division of authority, Pilate thought, would relieve him of responsibility for Jesus' fate. The Jews then reminded him that only he could authorize the death penalty. Thus Pilate was "on the spot." His dilemma was this. He could obtain the favor of a determined group of Jewish leaders by authorizing the execution of a man who meant nothing to him. Or he could satisfy his conscience, and the Roman standards of justice, by adhering to well-recognized principles of executing only political prisoners and enemies of the state. It seemed impossible to gratify the crafty Jews and satisfy his conscience. The struggle within Pilate's own soul was intense and it is delineated with great detail and skill by the Evangelist. The additional note of John in v. 32, that the death sentence would be the fulfillment of Jesus' prediction, is added as a witness that the crucifixion was not necessarily a victory for the Prince of this world, but rather occurred with God's permissive will. The

prediction to which John refers here is Jesus' statement about being "lifted up" (12:32), there explained as a reference to the mode of his execution. The normal Jewish mode of execution was stoning, a convenient method because stones were plentiful in Palestine. The Roman method was crucifixion, imported to Palestine from the west where trees were more plentiful than in the "holy land." John apparently points out that the placing of Jesus under Roman jurisdiction was evidence of the exactitude of prophetic detail, even with regard to the *mode* of execution.

One often hears the speculation, "What if Jesus had died by some mode other than crucifixion?" Such conjecture is largely fruitless. The *essential* thing in the atonement is the voluntariness with which the shepherd lay down his life rather than in the mode by which death was accomplished. And we must remember that God could have fitted *any* mode of death into the prophecies as well as he fitted the cross into them.

b. Pilate Examines Jesus and Declares Him Guiltless (vv. 33-38)

While Jesus was inside the Praetorium detained by his guard, Pilate was outside conferring with the Jewish leaders about their formal charge. There was no direct confrontation of accusers and accused before Pilate, because of the Jewish fear

37 Pilate therefore said unto him, Art thou a king then? Jesus answered, Thou sayest that I am a king. To this end have I been born, and to this end am I come into the world, that I should bear witness unto the truth. Every one that is the truth heareth my voice.

38 Pilate saith unto him, <u>What is truth?</u>

And when he had said this, he went out again unto the Jews, and saith unto them, <u>I find no crime in him.</u>   *STAMP OF THE ROMAN GOVERNMENT!*

delivered Jesus to him. He then asked Jesus to tell him why. The response he received must have bewildered him: **My kingdom is not of this world.** Jesus amplified his reply by adding that if his kingdom were of this world his servants would fight for him. No armed resistance, in other words, would be forthcoming.

37, 38 To Pilate's question, **Art thou a king then?**,[5] Jesus gave a positive, idiomatic answer: **Thou sayest that I am a**

king, meaning Yes, I am a king. The rest of the verse confirms this.[6] **To this end am I come into the world, that I should bear witness unto the truth.** That is, Christ came into our world of time and space in order to become incarnate here upon our earth, so as to reveal to us the truth about God and to open a way of permanent access to and favor with him (cf. 14:6). **Every one who is of the truth heareth** (akouei — "obey")

of "defilement." Pilate obligingly went in and out of the building in deference to their scruples. The Jews were trying to get Jesus embroiled with Roman authorities on a half-truth, something which Jesus could not deny and which would seem plausible to Pilate. With demonic cunning they accused Jesus of being a "king." They wanted Pilate to believe he was a political king and dangerous to Roman rule. It was up to Pilate to ascertain whether Jesus was actually an aspirant to purely religious leadership and hence not a threat to the peace. When Pilate asked Jesus, "**Art thou the King of the Jews?**" he was probably thinking of Herod the Great and his successors, or the political sect known as "Herodians" who were agitating for the return of a Jewish king to replace the procuratorship.[t] Thus, to Pilate, the charge must have seemed plausible, except for the appearance of Jesus and the absence of any political agitation in his behalf.

In reply, Jesus simply asked a question

as to whether Pilate asked this on his own "hunch" or whether this was the charge brought against him. Apparently nothing had been said about kingship during the trial before the Sanhedrin. Jesus concluded that in committing him to Pilate they had introduced this new charge, previously unmentioned. Jesus was not asking for information, as he did not need to be informed (2:25). He was rather seeking to get Pilate to form an independent judgment rather than depend upon a prejudiced report.

The fact that Jesus had a counter-question, rather than an answer, irritated Pilate. In reply, Pilate demanded information, saying that since he was not a Jew and had no way of knowing the background, he needed to know the facts. "**What has thou done?**" he demanded. Again Jesus did not answer the question directly. Calmly he replied, in effect that he was a king, but not a king of an earthly realm. He pointed out that had he been an earthly king he and his "officers"

[5] *Oukoun basileus ei sy* — "You are a king then, are you not?" *Ouk* in questions anticipates a positive answer. *Oun* is here joined to *ouk* and means "then."

[6] The idiomatic expressions *sy eipas* (*you said*, Matt. 26:64) and *sy legeis* (*you say*, Mark 15:2; Luke 22:70 and John 18:37), are translated literally in nearly all translations, but nevertheless inadequately; for Greek usage both in secular Greek and in the New Testament proves that they simply mean "yes" and are the equivalent of our slang expression "you said it." In Xenophon's *Anabasis*, in the record of the trial of Orontas (I. 6, 7), in answer to a question, this response follows: *Ephē ho Orontas*, which unmistakably means "yes" in the context. In Matt. 26:64 there is also a trial scene, as in John 18:37. When Jesus was put on oath and asked if he were the Christ he answered, "You said." Mark in the parallel passage (14:62) has given Jesus' answer as "I am." This clue in itself should have been sufficient evidence of the idiomatic meaning of "you said." In Matt. 27:11; Mark 15:2; Luke 23:3, *sy legeis* clearly means "yes" as *sy eipas* ("thou saidst") does in Matt. 26:64 ("I am" in Mark 41:62) (WPNT, V, 294).

[t] Herod the Great, with Roman consent, had divided his kingdom and willed it to his sons. To Archaeleus had been bequeathed Judaea and Samaria. Later Archaeleus had been banished and replaced by a procurator, responsible directly to the Emperor, much to the chagrin of patriotic Jews who felt this an insult.

39 But ye have a custom, that I should release unto you one at the passover: will ye therefore that I release unto you the King of the Jews?

40 They cried out therefore again, saying, Not this man, but Barabbas.   Now Barabbas was a robber.

---

my voice.[7]   Politician and materialistically-minded as Pilate was, he must have wondered what type of person he was questioning.   Was he really a divine being, or was he just a lunatic?   To Jesus' reply he responded with skepticism and possibly with a sneer of indifference, **What is truth?**   But to his credit, it must be admitted that he reported back to the accusers, **I find no crime in him.**   *Aitia* means "ground for capital punishment" in this context (A-G).

39, 40 **Will you have me release for you the King of the Jews?**   "They cried out again, 'Not this man but Barabbas!' Now Barabbas was a robber" (RSV). Pilate displayed contempt and irony by saying "the King of the Jews."[8]   If he had really wanted to secure Jesus' release and at the same time keep in the good graces of the Jews, he would not have shown his disdain for Jesus by this designation, nor would he have infuriated the Jews by calling him their king.   "Now

---

(ASVm, cf. 18:3,12,18,22) would have resisted arrest.   Pilate had experienced many surprises since coming to Palestine but this was unprecedented: an alleged "king," leader of an insurrection, yet so docile.   He no doubt marvelled that the Jewish leaders were so determined to kill this mild-mannered, apparently harmless "king" when they were so tolerant of other patriots who were real troublemakers for Rome.

Only John mentions Jesus' reply. Pressed by Pilate for an unequivocal answer, Jesus replied that he was actually a king, but not the kind of king he had been represented as being.   He was tried and condemned falsely on a half-truth. He was "king" in the realm of truth.   In the background again there is the antithesis between light and darkness, truth and falsehood.   He said, **"He that is of the truth heareth my voice."**   Earlier he had expressed the same idea in different language when he said, "My sheep hear my voice."   Jesus presents himself primarily as a prophet, as one who witnesses. To Pilate, Jesus was apparently claiming himself to be a philosopher in the Greek tradition.   The reply, and the manner in which it was presented, opened up an entirely new vista to Pilate.   He murmured, half aloud, as if not expecting an answer, **"What is truth?"**   This hard "man of the world" had caught a fleeting glimpse of something that was real and yet elusive. It set life in a different perspective.   It

presented a different set of values than those with which he was familiar.   Christian tradition has often been inclined to deal gently with Pilate by taking pains to point out that the Jewish leaders had the greater guilt (Acts 3:13).   Christians have realized the tremendous pressures under which Pilate labored.   The study of Pilate's conflict between his conscience and expediency is comparable to Shakespeare's portrayal of Macbeth, murderer of Duncan.

### c. The Mob Prefers Barabbas (vv. 38-40)

Pilate's direct investigation of Jesus convinced him of the latter's innocence. He was not pronouncing judgment about the acceptability or "orthodoxy" of Jesus' religious views; he was only declaring that in civic affairs, affairs that concerned the Roman authorities, he was innocent — i.e., there was no ground for complaint (cf. 19:4,6; cf. Acts 13:28; 28:18).   Three times Pilate repeated his conclusion that there was nothing about Jesus to warrant the death sentence.   In Matthew's report Pilate's affirmation of Jesus' innocence is even more emphatic (Matt. 27:19, 24).

In spite of this judgment of Pilate, the people, led by those impervious to the truth, continued to demand Jesus' death. Although this political establishment was not a democracy, the leaders could not

---

[7] See discussion on John 10:27 for a similar usage of *akouei*.
[8] W. H. Rigg, *The Fourth Gospel and Its Message for Today* (Lutterworth, 1932), p. 271.

at the feast [of the Passover] the governor was accustomed to release for the crowd any one prisoner whom they wanted" (Matt. 27:15). Pilate's suggestion that he free Jesus was rejected and instead they demanded that he release Barabbas, who not only was a robber but also, as Luke states, "Barabbas — a man who had been thrown into prison for an insurrection started in the city and for murder" (Luke 23:18). The Jews had charged that Jesus was guilty of sedition and that he was plotting the overthrow of Roman rule, of which there was no evidence at all. But the same Jews demanded the release of a man not only guilty of sedition but also of murder. Thus John pointed out their inconsistency and indefensible guilt.

---

ignore the *vox populi*. They dared not execute Jesus without some semblance of popular support. Later the apostles would upbraid these people for demanding Jesus' death and issue a ringing call to repentance (Acts 2:36; 3:13-15).

It is interesting that repentance is not mentioned once in the Fourth Gospel or First Epistle although the verb and noun together are found fifty-five times in the N. T. By contrast, repentance is a major theme in the prophetic writings, in the Synoptics, Acts and Epistles, and rabbinic writings. Even "confess," as used in John, does not connote turning from sin, but rather a declaration of one's faith; the one exception to this is I John 1:9.

Pilate thought of another plan for liberating Jesus. He would release him as a political prisoner, an enemy of the state, in accordance with the precedent of gratifying the people on this festive occasion. Since Palestine was an occupied country the ruling power had several political prisoners whose release would ingratiate the rulers with the ruled. He gave them two choices: Jesus, an innocent and apparently harmless man, or Barabbas who, because he was a brigand, was no more popular with his countrymen than with the Romans. Pilate thought they could not with any semblance of truth choose a criminal in preference to a religious "zealot." But Pilate underestimated the malice and blindness of the Jews. They demanded the criminal's release and Jesus' execution. Since Pilate had given them the choice, he could not forestall this unforeseen outcome. The Jewish leaders had gone beyond the place of repentance. William Henley, in his poem "Invictus," reflects the sinner who remains impenitent "with head bloody but unbowed." The late New England poet, Robert Frost, after a lecture to students at Harvard Divinity School on the subject of "Sin," said he would not know what to advise the sinner, whether to sue for mercy or remain impenitent. Charles Wesley, in "Jesus, Lover of My Soul," found "the better way" when he confessed: "False and full of sin, I am; Thou are full of truth and grace."

Jesus dies while Barabbas goes free. This is a parable and a prediction. It is a parable illustrating the fact that all men are, like Barabbas, condemned and under the sentence of death that is well deserved. It is a prediction that the death of Jesus would be a substitution for the death of sinners who believe.

Barabbas, the guilty one, is released while the innocent one dies! Here is real substitution! There are many theories of the Atonement. But the basic element in all Biblical theories of the atonement is that of substitution. The first clear glimpse of this was caught in Isa. 53:5 — "wounded for our transgressions, bruised for our iniquities: the chastisement of our peace was upon him; and with his stripes we are healed" (KJV). In a literal and historical sense, Barabbas was the first man for whom (i.e., in whose place) Christ died. We have much in common with Barabbas. We were (or are) rebellious. (The essential element in sin is rebellion.) We were (or are) robbers — robbing God of time, treasure, talent. Every self-centered person is a "robber." But because of Jesus' self-sacrifice, we go free. The difference between analogous cases lies in the fact that Barabbas had nothing to do with his release. It was not his change of attitude nor the mercy of captors that led to his release; it was rather their hatred of Jesus. With us, repentance and faith are the ingredients of the personal and subjective condition of the release offered.

# CHAPTER XIX

Then Pilate therefore took Jesus, and scourged him.

2 And the soldiers platted a crown of thorns, and put it on his head, and arrayed him in a purple garment;

---

## EXEGESIS

Pilate, according to John, sought to appease the Jews and to soften their murderous intent toward Jesus by having him scourged in the hope that such a painful lashing would modify their demand for his execution. Luke has given considerable detail to Pilate's efforts to release Jesus (Luke 23:1-25). Three times he quotes Pilate as saying that Jesus was not guilty as charged and that he planned to dismiss him. "Why, what evil has he done?" "I have found in him no crime deserving death; I will therefore chastise him and release him" (RSV). But the releasing of Barabbas and the scourging of Jesus did not placate his enemies. They remained as obdurate as at the beginning. No compromise could be effected with

them. Matthew and Mark picture a more deliberate and systematic mockery and mistreatment of Jesus than that described by John (Matt. 27:27-44; Mark 15:16-32).

1 **Then Pilate therefore took Jesus and scourged him.** Pilate's last appeal having failed, he resorted to scourging. Scourging normally preceded crucifixion, according to Josephus (*War*, V, 449). John does not state definitely whether it preceded or followed the sentence. Mark (15:15) places it after the sentence. Apparently Pilate had sent Jesus over to Herod for a hearing prior to the scourging (Luke 23:6-12).

2 **The soldiers twisted thorn twigs into a crown and put it on his head** (Phillips N. T.). (The verb *plekō* meant "to

---

## EXPOSITION

### d. Jesus Mocked as a False King (19:1-11)

The suffering of Jesus now became more brutal. After the Jews demanded and obtained the release of Barabbas rather than of Jesus, Pilate apparently abandoned any real effort to save Jesus from destruction. He directed his soldiers to scourge the Master. In Luke's account Pilate is quoted as saying that since Jesus has been found innocent by both Pilate and Herod he would scourge him and then release him. He apparently intended that the scourging be administered to gratify the angry Jews and be a substitute for execution. In any ordinary circumstances, they would have been satisfied with that, but the Jewish leaders would be satisfied with nothing less than death.

In Roman usage, scourging was in varying degrees of intensity, according to the

status of the offender and the seriousness of his crime. The milder form was beating with rods (*rhabdos;* cf. I Cor. 4:21; II Cor. 11:25; Acts 16:22, 35, 38) Non-Romans might be beaten with a whip (*mastix*) as in Acts 22:24, 25 and John 19:1. The most severe form of Roman flogging was the *flagellation* (cf. *phragellion* as in Matt. 27:26; Mark 15:15; John 2:15).[a] This was the "punishment inflicted on slaves and provincials after a sentence of death had been pronounced on them. So in the case of Jesus" (A-G, p. 873). It was this type of punishment which Paul was spared after informing his captors that he was a Roman citizen (Acts 22:24, 25). Josephus relates that during the regime of the procurator Florus, he "ventured to do that day what none had ever done before, namely to scourge (*mastigōsai*) before his tribunal and nail to the cross men of equestrian rank" (*War*, II, 308). The victim was normal-

[a] M. Greenburg, "Scourging," IDB, IV, 245.

3 and they came unto him, and said, Hail, King of the Jews! and they struck him with their hands.

---

weave.") This was done as an act of mockery and ridicule, since Pilate had, in apparent derision, called Jesus the king of the Jews. The crown must have looked more like a victor's wreath (cf. I Cor. 9:26; II Tim. 4:7, 8) than a royal diadem.[1] The fact that it consisted of thorns made the wearing of it not only humiliating but extremely painful. The soldiers, carrying the cruel ribaldry even further, put a purple robe on Jesus as mock regalia. Purple, because of the costliness of the dye, was normally worn only by people of high estate, such as nobles, generals, and kings (cf. Acts 16:14). In I Maccabees 8:14 mention is made of the Roman rulers in the second century B.C. as not making use of such customary royal insignia: "None of them did ever put on a diadem, neither did they clothe themselves with purple, to be magnified thereby." In I Maccabees 10:20 is a record of Alexander, the king of Syria sending to Jonathan, the high priest of the Jews, "a purple robe and a crown of gold." The author of Revelation (19:13) gives a picture of Jesus returning to earth in glory and in triumph over his enemies rightfully wearing a crown and "a robe in blood." That scene is the reverse of what John has here given us.

3 And they came (ērchonto, impf. tense — continued coming one after another) unto him and said (elegon, impf. — were saying) Hail, King of the Jews. This was being done with derision and mock

---

ly bound to a pillar, his back bared and the lash applied vigorously. Often the leather thongs were interlaced with bits of metal or bone to lacerate the flesh more deeply. Sometimes victims died under this excruciating pain and from loss of blood.

The soldiers were sufficiently bored with life, sufficiently hardened by professional soldiering, and sufficiently contemptuous of all Jews that they enjoyed this sadistic treatment of their prisoner. As though the scourging were not enough, one of them suggested taunting Jesus as "King of the Jews," for they knew of the trumped-up charges of his accusers. Today in the Moslem cemetery near Herod's gate in Jerusalem, there are thorn trees with sharp spikes one inch in length. With these, or thorns like them, the soldiers with fiendish glee fashioned a "crown" and thrust it down brutally on Jesus' head, piercing the scalp in many places.[b] A faded bluish tunic served as a "robe" draped over the prisoner's shoulders. Some knelt in mock reverence derisively chanting, "King of the Jews."

In homeopathic magic, the object of one's hatred, or fear, is often represented by an effigy which is treated as one would wish to treat the real person if possible.

Hanging a person in effigy is a sample of this. In the case of Jesus the Roman soldiers could vent their scorn upon him without inhibition because Jesus represented to them the Jews. In a larger sense, Jesus represented the Light while his captors represented the world headed by the Prince of this world. This perennial latent antagonism, much of it incoherent and inarticulate, found expression in this torture of a "helpless" victim of the world's hatred. As the triumphal entry was, in a sense, a prophecy of the triumphal return of the Son of Man "in power and great glory" so these jeering soldiers, addressing Jesus as "King of the Jews," may be viewed as an inverted prophecy of the time when Christ shall be universally recognized as "King of Kings and Lord of Lords" (Rev. 11:15; 19:16). In Matthew 26:67 Jewish tormentors implied that Jesus was a false prophet; here Gentiles implied that he was a false king. Mark and Matthew add the further detail that they also spat upon Jesus.

4-7 All this was going on inside the Praetorium, no Jews being present. Pilate left the building to report to the Jews a second time, "I find no fault in him." Jesus then came out still attired in the pseudo "robe" and "crown." He must

---

[1] J. H. Greenlee, "Crowns," The Herald (Mar. 21, 1962), p. 17.
[b] This "crown" was probably a caricature of a victor's crown, often seen on coins of that day, which indicated a "divine" ruler. H. S. J. Hort, "Crown of Thorns in John 19:2-5," Journal of Theological Studies, April, 1952, pp. 66-75.

4 And Pilate went out again, and saith unto them, Behold, I bring him out to you, that ye may know that I find no crime in him.

---

reverence. It perhaps was meant to ridicule the Jews as well as Jesus. Many people would at times endure physical punishment rather than extreme ridicule. But Jesus had to endure both! Once again they began beating Jesus, as is recorded in John 18:22, "they kept on striking (imperf) him." Some interpreters think this means slapping with hands (cf. 18: 22). However, Mark (15:19) definitely states: "they were striking his head with a reed, and were spitting upon him and, bending their knees, they were bowing down to him." Of course, the shameful punishment was not necessarily limited to slapping or using switches; some may

also have beaten him with their fists. Whatever the means, it was humiliating in the extreme.

4 And Pilate went out again, and saith unto them . . . I find no crime in him. *Oudemian* is used for "no" as in 18:38. It is an emphatic negative meaning "no, none at all." The shorter form (*ouk*) occurs in Aleph (א) at this verse; the same as in 19:6. There Pilate is recorded as repeating his statement for the third time that Jesus was without guilt. "It is a travesty on justice and dignity, but Pilate is trying by a bit of humor to turn the mob from the grip of the Sanhedrin" (ATR, V, 297).

---

have presented a pathetic spectacle, a sight that would excite the sympathy of anyone with any human kindness existing in him. Pilate presented Jesus to the mob with the words, Behold, the man! From the Latin equivalent *Ecce Homo* comes the name erroneously applied to an arch over one of the streets of Jerusalem. Visitors to Jerusalem during the Middle Ages assumed this arch marked the ancient Judgment Hall. Another portion of this same arch, which dates from the second century Aelia Capitolina, is now incorporated in the church of the Dames de Zion, a French convent near the Chapel of the Flagellation and on the site of the Antonia.

At the sight of their victim the priests and elders, like a group of modern cheerleaders, led the crowd in crying for Jesus' blood — "Crucify, crucify," they shouted "at the top of their voices" (Phillips). With an air of futility Pilate relented and said, "I find him not guilty, but go ahead and crucify him." This was the third time Pilate pronounced Jesus innocent. To justify their demand the Jews said something very meaningful to them but which affected Pilate in a way opposite to what they intended. They said, "He is worthy of death because he claims to be the Son of God." This, to Pilate, was not a cause for "righteous indignation." Since he was a pagan, the idea of gods in the form of men was not at all unusual or reprehensible to him. Whether from genuine piety or superstition, he was suddenly

awed by this declaration. With great apprehension he drew Jesus into the Praetorium again to find out more about this new role as Son of God. He asked a question which the Jews had asked Jesus many times — Whence art thou? (Cf. 7:12; 8:25; 10:24). Again Jesus seemed uncooperative and indifferent to his own fate. "As a sheep before her shearers is dumb, so he opened not his mouth." Exasperated, Pilate demanded an answer, reminding Jesus that he had the power of life or death over his prisoner. Jesus then answered, in a startling manner, stating that Pilate's authority (*exousia*) was really "from above," i.e., from God. With a show of pity for Pilate in his dilemma, Jesus added that the Jewish leaders were more guilty than he. In this statement Jesus implied several things.

(i) He enunciated the principle that ideally the authority wielded by secular rulers is God-given (cf. Rom. 13:1-3; I Tim. 2:1-3). In the so-called Christian nations today this principle is recognized; hence we are said to be a nation "under God."

(ii) Jesus also indicated that he was not really subject to Pilate's will except by permission of the Higher Power. Pilate had less authority than he thought; his was a delegated authority with implied responsibility with regard to the use made of that authority. Because Pilate was responsible to the Roman emperor, this was language he could understand.

5 Jesus therefore came out, wearing the crown of thorns and the purple garment
And *Pilate* saith unto them, Behold, the man!

6 When therefore the chief priests and the officers saw him, they cried out
saying, Crucify *him*, crucify *him*! Pilate saith unto them, Take him yourselves, and
crucify him: for I find no crime in him.

7 The Jews answered him, We have a law, and by that law he ought to die, because
he made himself the Son of God. *TURNING POINT FOR PILATE!*

---

**5 Jesus therefore came out, wearing the crown of thorns and the purple garment.** This was done, of course, in obedience to Pilate's command. To make the scene graphic, each detail of the regalia is mentioned again. "The exclamation **Behold the man!** was probably a rough jest, meaning 'That poor fellow is the dangerous rebel you bring to me for judgment'" (WFH, VIII, 771). "This exclamatory introduction of Jesus, in mock coronation robes, to the mob was clearly intended to excite pity and to show how absurd the charge of the Sanhedrin was, that such a pitiable figure should be guilty of treason" (ATR, V. 297).

**6 The chief priests and the officers . . . cried out, saying, Crucify him, crucify him.** On the "officers" see comment on

18:3. John describes a preplanned riot fomented and directed by the ruling religionists of that nation. A pagan, agnostic governor was trying to save Jesus from death, while the chief priests were clamoring determinedly for his blood. In later generations certain church leaders behaved as Annas and Caiaphas did on this occasion, by condemning Christians to death.

**7 He ought to die because he made himself the Son of God.** The reference is to their law against blasphemy (Lev. 24: 16). Jesus, when put on oath, incriminated himself by admitting that he was the Son of God, according to Mark 14: 61-62; Matthew 26:63-64: "Are you the Christ, the Son of God? Jesus said, I am.' Now for the first time the Sanhedrin gave

---

(iii) By saying that the Jews had the "greater sin" Jesus clearly implied that Pilate was partly responsible and hence subject to guilt and condemnation if he permitted a miscarriage of justice; Jesus did not absolve Pilate of all guilt.

(iv) Jesus' main emphasis was that Pilate's sin was less than that of the Jewish priests. This must have sounded unusual to Pilate, coming as it did from a Jew. Jesus was telling Pilate that the religious leaders of the Jews were guilty of a greater sin than he, a pagan.

12 Pilate then determined to seek Jesus' release. It becomes increasingly clear that it was not so much the trial of Jesus as the trial of Pilate, and, less directly, the trial of the Jewish leadership. Pilate was torn between the counsels of expediency and of principle. The more convinced he became that Jesus should be released, the more unreasoning and insistent were the demands for Jesus' death.

Then the members of the Jewish hierarchy played their "trump card." In

effect they told Pilate that to let Jesus go would be to betray his responsibility to the emperor. The emperor was the aging Tiberius, then on the Isle of Capri, very jealous of his position and suspicious because of constant efforts by scheming politicians to replace him. Pilate could ill afford to have the Jews report that he was tolerant of a potential king. His own political future would then be in jeopardy. (Later, what he feared actually happened. On another charge, leading Samaritans succeeded in getting Pilate recalled and deposed [Jos. *Ant.*, XVIII. iv. 2].) Without further hesitation Pilate yielded to counsel of expediency, stilled the voice of conscience and sat down on the *bēma* or judgment seat outside the Praetorium for final disposition of the case.ᶜ But even then he tried to make it as embarrassing as possible for the obviously insincere Jewish leadership.

14 John is specific as to the place and time of this awesome hour. The place was at the *Pavement* in Greek (*Gabbatha* in Hebrew, probably, although not certainly,

---

ᶜ This was "Caesar's judgment seat" (cf. Acts 26:10) and represented the reputation of the Roman empire for justice. Paul chose to demand justice before such a tribunal; Jesus did not.

8 When Pilate therefore heard this saying, he was the more afraid;
9 and he entered into the Praetorium again, and saith unto Jesus, Whence art
thou? But Jesus gave him no answer.
10 Pilate therefore saith unto him, Speakest thou not unto me? knowest thou not
that I have power to release thee, and have power to crucify thee?
11 Jesus answered him Thou wouldest have no power against me, except it were
given thee from above: therefore he that delivered me unto thee hath greater sin.

Judas

the real ground for their hostility against Jesus, and it was on this ground that they had condemned him.

**8 When Pilate therefore heard this saying, he was the more afraid** (*mallon ephobēthē*). He was apparently already afraid due to the message from his wife (Matt. 27:19). This claim to deity created additional superstitious fears. The Romans believed in myths of gods becoming incarnate. Could this be one? Pilate wondered. Compare the readiness with which the Lycaonians were prepared to see in Paul and Barnabas incarnations of Zeus and Hermes (Acts 14:11-13).

**9-11 Whence art thou? But Jesus gave him no answer. . . He that delivered me unto thee hath greater sin.** The silence of Jesus (cf. Mark 14:60f.) irritated Pilate and was a blow to his pride, as his remarks indicate. Had Jesus wanted an acquittal he very likely would have been more conciliatory. But he had told his disciples the night before that the hour of his departure had come. However, he reminded Pilate that his office and power had been given to him *from above*. That statement implied that Pilate was responsible to God for whatever disposition he made of Jesus. At the same time Jesus

---

at Herod's palace on the west side.[d] It was here that General Allenby addressed the people of Jerusalem in 1917 after his bloodless capture of the city thus terminating four centuries of Turkish rule.

This was one of the most decisive moments in history. It was the time for the preparation of the Passover — that is, the Friday of Passover week. The preparation day, meaning the day in which one prepares for the Sabbath, was the usual designation for Friday.[e] It was now noon. "The Passover lambs are being prepared for sacrifice, and the Lamb of God is likewise sentenced to death" (Hoskyns, p. 525).

**14 Behold, your king!** Pilate must have spoken the words derisively, contemptuously, as if to shame them for pretending that Jesus was a political leader and a traitor to Rome. Normally they would have been shamed and silenced by embarrassment or their nationalist loyalties, usually so volatile, would have been

aroused. But these leaders were now impervious to either truth or ridicule; they wanted only one thing — the death of Jesus.

**15 They deliberately and finally rejected Jesus as King of the Jews.** A few days earlier many of their townspeople had welcomed him to Jerusalem as "king." Earlier, in Galilee, some wanted to force the kingship upon him. Pilate may have intended to divide the crowd by this strategem, i.e., by arousing the nationalists, as Paul once divided an audience later (Acts 23:6, 7). Pilate still tried in vain to play on their nationalism and their sympathies, by asking jeeringly, "Shall I crucify your King?"

History records no more tragic scene than this. The Jews rejected their Messiah; both the Messiah in the role of the "suffering servant," as "meek and having salvation," and also as the Son of David. This was the ultimate in apostasy. Persisting in their blind hypocrisy, and

---

d So Edersheim, *op. cit.*, II, 586 and E. Kraeling, *Bible Atlas* (New York: Rand McNally, 1956), pp. 405f. *Gabbatha* means "high place" — so Pierre Benoit, "Lithostroton et Gabbath," *Révue Biblique*, Oct., 1952, p. 548. This article contains a vigorous defense of the position that Herod's palace, rather than the Antonia, was the Praetorium. Josephus states that at a later time, Florus "lodged in the palace, and on the following day had a tribunal (*bēma*) placed in front of the building and took his seat; the chief priests, the nobles, and the most eminent citizens presented themselves before the tribunal" (*War*, II. 301). Only since the Middle Ages has the trial scene been located at the Antonia (Kraeling). In support of the latter see L. H. Vincent, *Jérusalem de l'AT* (1954), pp. 216-21; W. F. Albright, *Archaeology of Palestine*, p. 245.
e The Greek church also used preparation (παρασκευή) to designate Friday — Mart. Poly. VII, fn. *Apostolic Fathers* (Loeb) II, 321.

12 Upon this Pilate sought to release him: but the Jews cried out, saying, If thou release this man, thou art not Caesar's friend: every one that maketh himself a king speaketh against Caesar.

---

stated that some one, meaning the high priest, was more guilty than Pilate. The latter had already in principle capitulated to the Sanhedrin's demand to have Jesus crucified (v. 6).

12 Pilate sought to release him (ezētei, impf. tense, — he began seeking). He wanted to render justice and liberate Jesus. He knew he should follow his conscience and conviction rather than be swayed by the cruel crowd. Had he been a man of character and high principles he would have done so. His record as procurator over Palestine was far from good during his ten years in office (A.D. 26-36). Luke (13:1) gives an instance of his misrule: "Galileans, whose blood Pilate had mingled with their sacrifices." Josephus has given us a record of how Pilate infuriated the Jews by allowing his soldiers

to bring ensigns, which were considered idolatrous by the Jews, into Jerusalem. Hundreds of Jews surrounded Pilate and refused to move, vowing that they would rather die than permit this. So Pilate yielded to them. (2) At another time Pilate illegally took money from the temple treasury, called corban, and used it to construct an aqueduct to bring water into Jerusalem. When rioters protested, he had his soldiers, dressed as civilians, beat them into submission with clubs.[2] Also Philo tells us how the emperor Tiberius, after an appeal by the Jews, revoked Pilate's order to leave the shields in the palace of Herod in Jerusalem.[3] Had there been no such acts of misrule in his career, Pilate could have defied the Sanhedrin and freed Jesus. To resist and antagonize the Jews on this occasion

---

again speaking more truly than they realized, they protested vehemently, "We have no king but Caesar." This was too much for Pilate, and he surrendered to them completely. They had with fiendish cleverness touched him at a vulnerable spot. If a report reached Tiberius that Pilate had refused to execute an insurrectionist who claimed to be a king, he might not be able to explain it to the satisfaction of the suspicious old monarch. Thus, Jesus was delivered over, as a scapegoat would be led into the wilderness for destruction (cf. Lev. 16:22, cf. John 12:51). From the viewpoint of Caiaphas Jesus died "instead of" the nation, a prediction more significant than he realized. Like a scapegoat, Jesus carried the sins of the nation. Thus, the Jews could demonstrate their loyalty to Rome by demanding Jesus' death, while Pilate could also benefit by ingratiating himself with the Jews. The only losers were the Nazarene and a few followers with no influence — so Jesus' enemies thought. Selfishness led to fear, fear led to blindness, and blindness led to reckless murder, both in the case of Pilate and the Jewish

leadership. The issue was settled here. From the standpoint of Jesus' enemies all that followed was anticlimactic. The Paschal Lamb was led forth to be sacrified for the sins of the world, and his enemies thought they had triumphed.

C. THE CRUCIFIXION (19:17-42)

. 1. JESUS IS CRUCIFIED AND IDENTIFIED BY PILATE (vv. 17-22)

In this paragraph two verses deal with the *via dolorosa* and crucifixion, and four verses deal with the label Pilate placed over the victim. Jesus went out . . . unto . . . Golgotha. With amazing terseness and restraint the Evangelist reports the bare facts — Jesus went out and was crucified! A recent popular description of the proceedings states that the upright part of the cross was probably left in place and that Jesus carried only the cross-beam.[f] There were three kinds of crosses in use among the Romans: the T-shaped cross, the X-shaped cross, and the Latin cross shaped like a dagger. The latter seems to have been the one used here since the superscription was nailed

[2] Jos. Ant. 18. 3. 1-2.
[3] Legotio ad Caium, 38.
[f] Jim Bishop, The Day Christ Died (New York: Pocket Books, 1957) p. 312.

13 When Pilate therefore heard these words, he brought Jesus out, and sat down on the judgment-seat at a place called The Pavement, but in Hebrew, Gabbatha.

14 Now it was the Preparation of the passover: it was about the sixth hour. And he saith unto the Jews, Behold, your King!

could jeopardize his position as procurator. So he decided to conciliate them instead of his conscience.

**12b If you release this man, thou art not Caesar's friend: every one that maketh himself a king speaketh against** (*antilegei* — opposes) **Caesar.** There was progression in the charges brought against Jesus to Pilate. He was first accused of evil-doing (18:30); then of claiming to be king of the Jews (18:33); next the charge of blasphemy (19:7); and finally that of sedition against Caesar. This move shocked Pilate into speedy acquiescence. Rome was quick to put down any form of sedition.

**13 He brought Jesus out and sat down on the judgment seat.** *Bēma* (judgment-seat) occurs in Romans 14:10 and II Corinthians 5:10 as the place of judgment in the presence of God and Christ. Josephus relates how Pilate on another occasion "sat upon his tribunal (judgment-seat) in the open market-place and called to him the multitude."[4] *Ekathise* (he sat); this

verb occurs 49 times in the N. T., but it occurs as transitive only once (I Cor. 6:4) and then with the meaning of electing people to positions of responsibility in the church. Some have conjectured that it is used in a transitive manner here and that Pilate seated Jesus on the judgment-seat. That theory fits the context of verse 14 well since he once more calls Jesus their king. The verb is used transitively in *The Gospel according to Peter* and, strange to say, in depicting Jesus on trial before Pilate and the Jews: "They sat him on a seat of judgment saying 'Judge righteously, king of Israel.'" It was also used by Justin (I *Apol.*, 1,35). But the sentence structure favors the intransitive use, "Pilate sat on the judgment-seat." Furthermore Pilate was in no mood for buffoonery. Pilate now was finally ready, with great reluctance, formally to sentence Jesus to death.

**14 It was the eve of Passover** (NEB) (*paraskeuē tou pascha* — preparation [day] for the Passover, objective genitive).

"over his head" (Matt. 27:37). In John's account, we are spared the details. The practice of execution by crucifixion is said to have originated with the Persians; it was later adopted by the Carthaginians, from whom the Romans learned it. By the Romans it was regarded as "the most cruel and horrifying" way to die (Cicero) and not practiced in Italy. No Roman citizen was thus executed, only slaves and criminals.[g]

The place of the crucifixion was the Place of the Skull (Lat. *cranium*). Where was it? Most scholars are inclined to favor the traditional site, at or near the site of the Holy Sepulchre, the authenticity of which has been claimed since the fourth century when the Church of the Anastasia was erected nearby. It is well inside the present walled city, east of the Joppa Gate, and south of the New Gate, both of which are adjacent to the present Israel-

Jordan "no-man's land." If, as seems probable, the sentencing was done at Herod's palace, Jesus would likely have been led north to the rocky ridge which runs from the temple area, east of the Damascus Gate in a northwesterly direction, culminating in a high knoll north of the Damascus Gate. It was outside the city walls (Heb. 13:12), not far distant from the city and near a thoroughfare (19:20). It could well have been here, for the Damascus road to all points north goes by here. The fact that the Damascus Gate was formerly called St. Stephen's Gate implies that this was the scene of Stephen's martyrdom, a tradition well attested by the Dominican church of St. Stephen near this site. There is reason to believe that the "Third Wall," mentioned by Josephus as having been built by Herod Agrippa II in 42 A.D., is that which has been located between the exist-

4 Jos. *War* 2. 9. 3. The tribunal (*bēma*) was a normal adjunct to the palace (residence) of an emperor or procurator. Caesar had one in his camps on which he sat in judgment. This may be the precedent for the pope's decisions in *cathedra*.
g Wm. Barclay, *The Gospel of John* (Philadelphia: Westminster Press, 1956), II, 291.

15 They therefore cried out, Away with *him,* away with *him,* crucify him! Pilate saith unto them, Shall I crucify your King? The chief priests answered, We have no king but Caesar.

16 Then therefore he delivered him unto them to be crucified.

---

That is, it was Friday of Passover week. *Paraskevē* is used to mean Friday in vv. 31, 42; Mark 15:42; Matthew 27:62; Luke 23:54. And it is still the name for Friday in Greece today. **It was about the sixth hour.** The *New English Bible* has "about noon." The difference of interpretation depends upon whether Roman time or Jewish time was being used by John. If the latter, it was about noon. But since the Romans began counting time from midnight as we do, their six o'clock in the morning would correspond to ours. Mark (15:25), using Jewish time, stated that it was the third hour (9 a.m.) when the crucifixion began. That leaves a period of about three hours between the sentence and the execution. If John wrote after Jerusalem was destroyed (A.D. 70) and

for Gentiles chiefly, it is plausible to assume that he used Roman legal time; so think B. F. Westcott, William Hendriksen, Edersheim and A. T. Robertson. But Marcus Dods, Wilbert F. Howard (IB) and C. K. Barrett argue that John meant noon. That assumption puts Mark and John at variance with one another. (See Introduction on "Time.")

**15, 16 They therefore cried out, Away with him, away with him, crucify him. Pilate saith unto them, Shall I crucify your King? The chief priests answered, We have no king but Caesar.** "Shall I crucify . . .?" ("Is it proper for me to crucify him?"). "King" is in *emphatic* position — "your *king,* of all people?" Israel was established as a theocratic nation. In rejecting Christ as Savior and King, and in declaring that

---

ing north wall and the tomb of Queen Helena. There is also reason to believe that the existing north wall is built over the wall of Hadrian's city Aelia Capitolina and that in turn over the "Second Wall" of Josephus.[h]

Many have noted that Jesus was placed between two robbers (*lēistēs*) and have seen in it a fulfillment of Isaiah 53:9 "and they made his grave with the wicked." All humanity was represented on the three crosses — the penitent, the impenitent and the Savior.

Pilate's sign was trilingual — written in Hebrew, the national language; in Greek, the language of the Near East; and in Latin, the official language of the Romans. The title was consistent with the alleged grounds of the execution. It was astonishing, of course, for every passer-by to see the person officially designated "King of the Jews" dying on a cross between two criminals. It would be amusing to the Gentiles, perplexing to the pilgrims, and embarrassing to every Jew. Only John records the three languages and the

Jew's protest to Pilate. It was a testimony to the three great sources of western civilization: the Hebrews for their monotheism; the Greeks for their science, philosophy and beauty; the Romans for their political administration. In Latin the sign perhaps read

Iesu
Nazarenus
Rex
Iudaeorum

From this comes the insignia often seen on crosses, altar cloths, etc.: INRI.

This inscription infuriated the Jewish leaders and they pleaded with Pilate to change it to read, "The self-styled 'King of the Jews.'" Pilate refused to change the wording. In a sense, this was Pilate's revenge on those who had so ruthlessly exploited Roman justice and capitalized on his vulnerability to political expediency. History has forever associated him with his deed in the words, "crucified under Pontius Pilate." Like the Rosetta stone, whose trilingual inscription unlocked the literature of ancient Egypt, and like the

---

h This view is not the generally accepted one, but it has much to commend it. The recently-named Gordon's Calvary and the adjacent Garden Tomb answer to the Biblical description of the place but lack archaeological confirmation. See Edersheim, *op. cit.,* II, 585; Chas W. Wilson, *Golgotha and the Holy Sepulchre* (London, 1906), Andre Parrot, *Golgotha and the Church of the Holy Sepulchre* (London, 1957), W. F. Albright, "New Light on the Walls of Jerusalem in the New Testament Age," BASOR 81, Feb., 1941.

17 They took Jesus therefore: and he went out, bearing the cross for himself, unto the place called The place of a skull, which is called Hebrew Golgotha:

18 where they crucified him, and with him two others on either side one, and Jesus in the midst.

19 And Pilate wrote a title also, and put it on the cross. And there was written, JESUS OF NAZARETH, THE KING OF THE JEWS. *Drumwright: "This is the actual title written on the cross."*

---

they had no king but Caesar, these religious leaders declared that they had abandoned the faith of their forefathers. And further, they even had rejected their God-chosen King by declaring their supreme allegiance to a foreign potentate, Caesar. Then Pilate turned Jesus over to his enemies for crucifixion. The chief priests and the Sanhedrin finally had authorization to wreak their vengeance upon the best Jew that ever lived (cf. Luke 23:25).

17 Jesus . . .went out bearing the cross for himself unto the place called The place of a skull (Golgotha). A condemned criminal was required to bear the beam of the cross on which he was to be crucified. Jesus once declared, "Whosoever doth not bear his own cross and come after me cannot be my disciple" (Luke 14:27).

Mark tells us that Simon of Cyrene was drafted to bear the cross for Jesus. Apparently the lack of sleep and the severity of the tortures suffered were too taxing on Jesus' strength for him to carry the cross all the way (Mark 15:21f.; cf. Matt. 27:32f.; Luke 23:26).

18 They crucified him. Not only so but they had a robber hanging on each side of Jesus! This could have been devised to identify him with the worst of criminals (cf. Isa. 53:12: "He was numbered with the transgressors").

19 And Pilate wrote a title and put it on the cross . . . Jesus of Nazareth, the King of the Jews. The Jews had charged that Jesus was "making himself king." Pilate was determined, according to John, to call Jesus king of the Jews in spite of their protests.

---

trilingual Behistun inscription of Darius, which unlocked the civilization of Mesopotamia, so Pilate's inscription unwittingly proclaimed to three worlds — the Semitic, Hellenistic, and European — the identity of Jesus. Later, Romantic novelists made of Pilate a Christian saint.[1]

### 2. THE GARMENTS DISTRIBUTED (vv. 23-25)

Only John reports the distribution of Jesus' garments. His interest in this detail probably derives from the fact that he saw in it a fulfillment of prophecy. The soldiers were entitled to the garments of the executed as a "tip" or gratuity for their services in the execution. They divided the garments among the four, according to the wishes of each. The tunic was probably a loose-flowing garment which reached to the ankles, not unlike that worn by Arab men and boys today in Palestine and in Egypt. A similar garment for use by priests is described in Exodus 28:32; it was not to be torn.

Since not all could share in this garment, the sensible thing was to cast lots and to give it to the winner. The soldiers unconsciously fulfilled Psalm 22:18, "They part my garments among them, and upon my vesture do they cast lots." Psalm 22 reads almost as if written *after* the crucifixion. The Evangelists recorded not less than four statements of this Psalm that were literally fulfilled at the crucifixion. To the Evangelist, the close correlation between the O. T. and the actual events witnessed was evidence that the sufferings of Jesus were not the result of the triumph of darkness over the light, or evil over good, nor to a miscarriage of God's plans. They simply afforded additional evidence that all went "according to plan," and hence constituted a solid revelational and historical basis for faith.

### 3. THE VIGIL (vv. 25-27)

25 Who were the watchers at the cross? There were the Roman soldiers and their commander, the centurion (Matt. 27:54),

[1] The Gospel of Nicodemus, or the Acts of Pilate, Appendices, etc. See M. R. James, ed., *The Apocryphal New Testament* (Oxford, 1926), pp. 94-157.

20 This title therefore read many of the Jews, for the place where Jesus was crucified was nigh to the city; and it was written in Hebrew, *and* in Latin, *and* in Greek.

21 The chief priests of the Jews therefore said to Pilate, Write not, The King of the Jews; but, that he said, I am King of the Jews.

22 Pilate answered, What I have written I have written.

23 The soldiers therefore, when they had crucified Jesus, took his garments and made four parts, to every soldier a part; and also the coat: now the coat was without seam, woven from the top throughout.

24 They said therefore one to another, Let us not rend it, but cast lots for it, whose it shall be: that the scripture might be fulfilled. which saith, They parted my garments among them, And upon my vesture did they cast lots.

25 These things therefore the soldiers did. But there were standing by the cross of Jesus his mother, and his mother's sister, Mary the *wife* of Clopas, and Mary Magdalene.

---

20-22 **It was written in Hebrew, and in Latin and in Greek.** Since Rome governed a polyglot nation, it was customary for official documents to be given out in more than one language. During the British Mandate in Palestine the three languages were Hebrew, Arabic and English. When the chief priests asked Pilate to change this title he stubbornly replied, **What I have written I have written.** In Greek his reply consisted simply of two words with one word repeated: *ho gegrapha, gegrapha,* meaning "What I have written stands written" (with the clear implication that it was to remain). The first perfect, i.e., previous action finished; the second perfect "I have written" is intensive (D-M, p. 202). Pilate had yielded to their demands by releasing Barabbas

and by sentencing Jesus to crucifixion. Had he only been stubborn and adamant concerning Jesus! His peevish petulance came too late.

23-24 **The soldiers . . . took his garments,** *himatia* — outer clothes. These they divided into **four parts, to every soldier a part.** So there were four soldiers. But the *chitōn,* the undergarment, which was woven and without seams, they **cast lots for it.** It would have spoiled its value to cut it. John saw in this incident a fulfillment of Psalm 22:18. Therefore (*oun:* now or presently).

25 "Near the cross where Jesus hung stood his mother, with her sister, Mary wife of Clopas, and Mary of Magdala" (NEB). Some believe that John meant to identify only three women in the above

---

"many women" from Galilee (Matt. 27:55), "they that passed by" (Matt. 27:39; Mark 15:29), "the rulers" — i.e., chief priests, scribes and elders (Matt. 27:41; Luke 23:35) — "the robbers" (Matt. 27:44), and the "beloved disciple" (John 19:26). The women singled for particular mention include Mary the mother of Jesus (John 19:25); Mary Magdalene (John 19:25); Mary of Clopas (John 19:25) mother of James and Joses (Matt. 27:56; Mark 15:40, 47; 16:1; Luke 24:10); and Salome, who was probably Jesus' aunt, wife of Zebedee — and hence mother of James and John (Matt. 15:40; 16:1; cf. John 19:25).[1] Only John reports this evidence of Jesus' tender solicitude for his mother even in the last moments of

his life. If, as seems probable, Jesus' mother was John's aunt, it would be another reason for her remaining in his household. According to medieval tradition, Mary remained in Jerusalem and was buried in the Kidron valley where the "Tomb of the Virgin Mary" may still be visited. Her "tomb" is also shown near Ephesus. Mary, the mother of our Lord, was one of the most noble women of Bible times; and no aversion to "Mariolatry" should blind one to that fact. Mary is seen again for the last time in the Biblical record in Acts 1:14, where, with Jesus' brethren (cf. John 7:5) and other disciples, she prayed for the *parousia* of the Paraclete. It may be that she (with John) made her home with the fifth Mary,

---

[1] The identification of Salome as the wife of Zebedee is probable but not certain. It is based upon the observation that four women were mentioned and the assumption that Salome, the wife of Zebedee and Jesus' aunt are the same. See E. P. Blair, "Salome," IDB, IV, 167.

26 When Jesus therefore saw his mother, and the disciple standing by whom he loved, he saith unto his mother, Woman, behold, thy son!

27 Then saith he to the disciple, Behold, thy mother! And from that hour the disciple took her unto his own *home*.

---

sentence. However, it is most unlikely that two sisters in a family would both have the same name. Mary of Clopas could hardly be another name for Alphaeus, who was the father of the apostle James the less (Matt. 10:3).[5] The sister of Jesus' mother must have been Salome, the mother of the sons of Zebedee (Matt. 27:56; Mark 15:40), since she is identified by two Synoptists. This relationship of John to Jesus (cousins) helps to explain the incident which follows. Mary Magdalene is also mentioned by both Matthew (27:56) and Mark (15: 40).

26, 27 **The disciple standing by** (*parestōta*, perf. part.) **whom he loved.** The same descriptive words occur in John 13:23; 21:7, 20, apparently referring each time to the apostle John. Out of modesty

John abstained from mentioning his own name, but at the same time indicated himself as a participant. Being a cousin, as well as a very intimate apostle, he was worthy of the designation. **Woman, behold thy son!** Mary was to regard John as a son, i.e., to reside in his home. This is understandable since the real sons were still unbelievers. **Behold, thy mother!** or "Here is your mother." To John therefore was committed the responsibility of providing for Mary.[6] **And from that hour the disciple took her unto his own home** (Greek, "into his own things" — cf. John 1:11). Since a person's "things," or possessions, normally are at his home, this phrase is used. How long she made her home with him is not known. Since James, Jesus' brother, a few years after this became pastor in Jerusalem she may

---

the mother of John Mark (Acts 12:12).[k] Although, in this context, "house" need not mean a dwelling place but only the love and protection of the family.[l] From this scene come the stirring lines of the Latin hymn, "Stabat Mater." Jesus' solicitude for his mother to the last is as characteristic as it is moving.[m]

### 4. "IT IS FINISHED" (vv. 28-30)

John once again notes that Jesus, even in his dying agony, knew that **all things are now finished.** The same root-word for "finish" here (*teleō*) is used to describe the "fulfillment" of Scripture (*teleioō* — v. 28) — i.e., "to accomplish, perfect, make complete, bring to its desired end." There remained, as the Evangelist viewed it, but one detail to be "accomplished" before "the end" (*telos*). The Scripture which Jesus fulfilled in saying, "I thirst," in Ps.

69:21 where, in a Psalm sometimes attributed to Jeremiah, it is stated "in my thirst they gave me vinegar to drink," thus adding to his misery. Crucifixion is said to have brought intense thirst which in itself could cause intense suffering. Perspiration also results from intense pain, and this would greatly increase the thirst. Add to this the exposure to the blazing midday sun! This is the second time Jesus, in effect, said, "I thirst" (cf. 4:7). In the first instance he offered "living water"; now his intense thirst was part of the price of relieving thirst in others.

Research indicates that in many crucifixions of that time the victims' arms were nailed or tied to the cross beam and the legs flexed and nailed to the upright beam. The victim could hardly breathe if he slumped down to a more relaxed position, and it would throw all his weight upon his arms. Also, he could endure

---

[5] Mary of Clopas is probably the same as Mary the mother of James and Joseph (cf. Matt. 27:56; Mark 15:40, 47; 16:1; Luke 24:10). In Near East customs a woman after motherhood often takes the name of her son. It is possible therefore that this Mary is the daughter of Clopas and wife of Alphaeus. See Eric F. F. Bishop, "Mary Clopas," *Expository Times*, 1954, pp. 382, 383. Hegesippus said Clopas was the brother of Joseph, the Lord's foster father (Eusebius. H. E. III. ii. 2).

[6] Compare the bequest of Eudamidas, "I leave to Aretaeus my mother, to cherish and support in her old age" (Lucian, *Toxaris*, 22) cited in JHB, II, 633.

[k] L. M. Sweet, "Mary," ISBE, III, 2001-2003.

[l] Lange, John and Peter, *Commentary on the Holy Scriptures: John* (Grand Rapids: Zondervan Publishing House, n.d.), p. 586.

[m] W. W. Martin, "Exegesis of John 19:26, 27," *Methodist Quarterly Review*, July, 1927, p. 445.

28 After this Jesus, knowing that all things are now finished, that the scripture might be accomplished, saith, <u>I thirst,</u>

29 There was set there a vessel full of vinegar: so they put a sponge full of the vinegar upon hyssop, and brought it to his mouth.

30 When Jesus therefore had received the vinegar, he said, <u>It is finished</u>: and he bowed his head, and gave up his spirit.

---

have moved to his home. There is no dependable record that she accompanied John to Ephesus and died there.

**28-30 I thirst** (*dipsō,* pres. ind. — I am thirsty). John saw a fulfillment of Psalm 69:21, "For my thirst they gave me vinegar to drink." *Oxos* (vinegar) is defined as "sour wine, wine vinegar; it relieved thirst more effectively than water and, because it was cheaper than regular wine, it was a favorite beverage of the lower ranks of society and of those in moderate circumstances" (A-G). It was "hot vinegar drugged with myrrh (Mark 15:23) and gall (Matt. 27:34), which Jesus had refused just before the crucifixion," (WPNT, V, 304), and which functioned as a sedative. The loss of blood created intense thirst, which intensified greatly the agony of crucifixion. **It is finished** (*tetetestai,* perf. passive — it has been completed and remains finished). The mission which Jesus left heaven in order to accomplish is now at last done! What a painful, ignominious end for the Son of God! And yet what an inexpressibly marvelous and incomparable achievement!

---

only for a few minutes at a time a position in which the legs were flexed in a half-squatting position. Consequently the sufferer was compelled to continually raise and lower himself in order to breathe. Once the legs were broken, he could not raise himself, and death, partly by suffocation, came more quickly.[n]

Execution by means of a cross was universally abhorred among both Jews and Gentiles. To the former, it meant not only the death of a public enemy but also involved ceremonial defilement — "cursed is every one which hangeth on a tree" (Deut. 21:22; I Cor. 12:3). (Had Jesus been stoned rather than crucified, some of the "offense of the cross" would have been avoided.) Among the Gentiles this mode of execution was the ultimate in disgrace and hence seldom used on Roman citizens. When Romans were crucified, as they were in Sicily and Spain, their execution was universally condemned as an outrage. It was a death reserved for the more dangerous types of criminals. Crucifixions were frequent in Galilee. The bearing by the condemned man of the instrument of his own torture was another element in this disgraceful death. Alexander crucified 2000 Tyrians, and Varus crucified 2000 rioters after the death of Herod the Great (Jos. *Ant.,* XVII. x. 10). Titus crucified Jews by the thousands before the fall of Jerusalem during the Jewish Revolt (Jos. *War* V. xi. 1). Under Tiberius this method of execution was used because of the prolonged suffering and the public infamy incurred by the victim.

To Christians, however, what was a scandal or stumbling-block to the Jews and folly to the Gentiles became the cause of their "boasting" (I Cor. 1:18, 23). Believers who share with Jesus this double humiliation of ceremonial defilement and public disgrace are to share also in his "glory." "Thus crucifixion becomes not merely the means of salvation, but the type of that absolute renunciation of the world which characterizes the true Christian life" (Gal. 5:24).[o]

Only John reports the "seventh saying" on the cross, it is finished (*tetetestai*; cf. v. 28). This statement ties in with similar statements in 12:23; 13:1; 17:1; 18:4 and 19:28. John takes pains to show that Jesus was in command of the situation from the beginning to the very end, that his life was not snatched from him in an unforeseen tragic ending, but that the Shepherd voluntarily laid down his life for the sheep — "no one taketh it from me, but I lay it down of myself" (10:18). In John's account, the last meeting

---

[n] Jim Bishop, *op. cit.,* p. 326.
[o] W. Adams Brown, "Cross," HDB, I, 529.

*(handwritten: for The sabbath day of Passover week)*

31 The Jews therefore, because it was the <u>Preparation,</u> that the bodies should not remain on the cross upon the sabbath (for the day of that sabbath was <u>a high *day*</u>), asked of Pilate that their legs might be broken, and *that* they might be taken away.

32 The soldiers therefore came, and brake the legs of the first, and of the other that was crucified with him:

33 but when they came to Jesus, and saw that he was dead already, they brake not his legs:

34 howbeit one of the soldiers with a spear pierced his side, and straightway there came out <u>blood and water</u>.

*(handwritten: MEANING IS NOT CLEAR.)*

31, 32 *Oun* (therefore) introduces an explanatory or resumptive paragraph and means now. It occurs again in verse 32, where it has the force of "then." **The Preparation** (i.e., Friday; see v. 14). It was the 24-hour period between sunset on Thursday and sunset on Friday (cf. Mark 15:42). **For the day of that sabbath was a high** (*megalē*, i.e., great) **day.** That day was the first day of unleavened bread of the Passover week (Exod. 12: 16; Lev. 23:7) and it coincided, on this occasion, with the Sabbath. **Their legs**

**might be broken.** The law of Deut. 21:23 was that the body of a criminal should "not remain all night upon the tree." But the reason given in this context was to have the bodies removed so ceremonial pollution might not defile the Sabbath nor the first day of the Passover. Breaking the legs (*crurifragium*), usually with a heavy bar or mallet, was resorted to to hasten death.

33, 34 **They came to Jesus, and saw that he was already dead** (*tethnēkota*, perf. part., i.e., having died and was now dead).

with the twelve was the beginning of the end (13:1); this was the "end" that began when "the word became flesh and dwelt among us" (1:14).

### 5. BLOOD AND WATER (vv. 31-37)

The breaking of the thieves' legs and piercing of Jesus' side is reported only in this Gospel. The emergence of blood and water from the pierced side of Jesus' body is noted by John as a phenomenon of special significance. For a significant commentary on this, see I John 5:6-8: "This is he that came by water and blood, even Jesus Christ; not with water only, but with water and with the blood. And it is the Spirit that beareth witness, because the Spirit is the truth. For there are three who bear witness, the Spirit, and the water, and the blood: and the three agree in one." Both in the Gospel and in the Epistle this declaration is followed by an emphasis on witnessing. The church fathers tried to supplement John's terse report by explaining the significance of the phenomena. One illuminated manuscript of this Gospel shows John the Baptist and John the Apostle at the foot

of the cross bringing together the former's prediction about the offering of the lamb of God (11:29, 36) and the Apostle's attestation of the offering consummated.[p] Apparently John wanted not only to refute the Docetists who denied that Jesus' body expired on the cross, but also to provide additional bases for belief. It appears thus as a fulfillment of two predictions, the one quoted relative to being pierced (Zech. 12:10), and the reference to the "fountain opened in the house of David . . . for sin and for uncleanness" (Zech. 13:1). This offering of the Paschal Lamb was in fulfillment of two other stipulations in the Torah, "They shall leave none of it (the lamb) until morning" (Num. 9:12) and "neither shall ye break a bone thereof" (Exod. 12:46; cf. Ps. 11:18; 34:20). Some scholars conjecture that the prohibition of bone-breaking is due to reverence for bones as conveyors of life, something like the blood (Exod. 12:46; cf. Ps. 11:18; 34:20).[q]

Augustine (*De Civ. Dei*, xxii. 17) and many other early Fathers regarded the phenomena of water and blood as symbolizing the two sacraments, the water typifying the "washing of regeneration"

---

[p] MS 110 in Pembroke College Library, Cambridge University (Hoskyns, p. 534).

[q] A pyramid text, observed by George A. Barton, states that the bone of the deceased pharaoh in heaven is not broken. G. A. Barton, "A Bone of Him Shall Not Be Broken," JBL, 1930, pp. 13ff.

35 And he that hath seen hath borne witness, and his witness is true: and he
knoweth that he saith true, that ye also may believe.
36 For these things came to pass, that the scripture might be fulfilled, A bone
of him shall not be broken.
37 And again another scripture saith, They shall look on him whom they pierced.

---

With a spear pierced his side. The head
of a Roman spear was as wide as a
hand and was made of iron (cf. John
20:20, 25, 27). Apparently it penetrated
deep into the body for: there came out
blood and water. "The issuing of blood
and water from His side must therefore
be regarded as a sign of life (blood) in
death. It showed both His true humanity
and (in some mysterious sense) the permanence of His human life" (BFW, II,
319). John, apparently to meet the false
teachings of the Docetic Gnostics, who
denied that the Christ died, related this
significant event as an incontrovertible
proof of Jesus' real humanity. What else
he meant beyond that is uncertain and
will remain so. John emphasized the
reality of the death by stating he that hath
seen hath borne witness, and his witness

is true. He was giving an eye-witness
account of a verified historical event of
tremendous significance. "He knows that
he speaks the truth, so that you too may
believe" (NEB).

36, 37 For these things came to pass
that the scripture might be fulfilled. ("Fulfilled" here is *pleroō;* in v. 28 it is *teleioō.*
The two verbs are thus used synonymous-
ly.) John was alert to any Scripture
reference that seemed prophetic of the
life and deeds of the Messiah. A bone
of him shall not be broken — could be
considered as a free quotation concerning
the paschal lamb; "Neither shall ye break
a bone thereof" (Exod. 12:47; Num. 9:
12). But the structure of the sentence
seems clearly to point to Ps. 34:20 (LXX,
Ps. 33:21) where Jehovah is pictured
as taking care of "the righteous." "He

---

in baptism and the blood representing the
Eucharist. Others thought the water represented the baptism with water and the
blood the baptism of martyrdom.[r] To
others the water is symbolic of cleansing
and the blood of new life. Also the water
may represent the initiation of new life
(3:5) and the blood the sustenance of the
new life (6:53-56). In any case these
symbols are presented as three independent witnesses, as God's three-fold witness
concerning the Son (I John 5:9). Blood
is also the cleansing agent in Rev. 1:5
and the basis for eternal life (Rev. 7:14;
12:11). This is the language of metaphor, obviously the reference is not to
Jesus' physical blood, but rather to the
*life* which is presented by blood in both
the Old and New Testaments (Lev. 17:
14). Cowper's great hymn gives the Christian interpretation and application:

*There is a fountain filled with blood,*
  *Drawn from Emmanuel's veins,*
*And sinners, plunged beneath that*
  *flood,*
  *Lose all their guilty stains.*[s]

### 6. BURIAL (vv. 38-42)

Joseph of Arimathaea is here introduced
for the first time in the story. From Mark
we learn that he was a respected member
of the Council or Sanhedrin (Mark 15:
43). From Luke we learn that he was a
righteous man who had not consented to
Jesus' arrest (Luke 23:50-52). Both Mark
and Luke describe him as "looking for the
kingdom of God." Perhaps Joseph was a
disciple of John the Baptist or subscribed
to his preaching. In similar language,
Simeon of Jerusalem was described as
"looking for the consolation of Israel" and
the aged Anna as among those who were
"looking for the redemption of Jerusalem"
(Luke 2:25, 38). Apparently Joseph was
among that number of devout and patient
people who believed that at some time
God would "visit and redeem his people"
(cf. Luke 1:68). When Jesus came,
Joseph accepted him as God's answer
to the ages-long cry of his people. Because of the known consequences, he made
no open profession of his allegiance. Now,
however, he must have felt a measure of

---

[r] Cf. Luke 12:50; Tertullian, *De Modestia,* xii.  See Hoskyns, p. 535.
[s] Wm. Cowper, in *Hymns of the Living Faith,* p. 186.

38 And after these things Joseph of Arimathaea, being a disciple of Jesus, but secretly for fear of the Jews, asked of Pilate that he might take away the body of Jesus: and Pilate gave *him* leave. He came therefore, and took away his body.

keepeth all his bones: not one of them is broken." The same verbal form, *syntribēsetai*, occurs in both Ps. 33:21 (LXX) and John 19:37.

In the second quotation, John quoted Zechariah 12:10 accurately as it occurs in the Hebrew. The LXX used a different verb ("mock") due to the fact that the Hebrew consonants are almost alike in the terms "pierce" and "mock."

**38 Joseph of Arimathaea . . . asked of Pilate that he might take away the body (*sōma*) of Jesus: and Pilate gave him leave.** Mark 15:43 states: "Joseph of Arimathaea, a respected member of the council (Sanhedrin), who was also himself looking for the kingdom of God, took courage and went to Pilate and asked for the body of Jesus" (RSV). John, writing much later, perhaps knew that this eminent man, while having believed secretly for fear of the Jews, later on became an active Christian. Mark states that Pilate first ascertained that Jesus was dead before consenting to the above request (Mark 15:44, 45).

responsibility for Jesus' death, not only because he also was a Jew, but especially because he was a member of the body that sentenced Jesus to death. In Matthew's account he is listed as a disciple, and nothing is said about the erstwhile secrecy of his belief. There were many secret believers then as there are now; later in the N. T. it is reported that "a great company of the priests were obedient to the faith" (Acts 6:7). Joseph was probably among the number of disciples who "multiplied exceedingly" in Jerusalem. That he was a man of means is implied in the fact that he had a rock-hewn tomb for himself, and his wealth is explicitly stated in Matthew 27:57. Arimathea cannot be located with confidence; its identification with Rama, Samuel's home town, some eight miles north of Jerusalem, has been suggested.[t] Eusebius located it at *Rentis,* north of Lydda.[u]

To ask for the corpse required courage, as is indicated in Mark 15:43, more courage than was shown by Jesus' disciples, especially Peter.[v] The disciples (except for John) had gone into hiding, and nothing but a deep religious motivation would have sufficed to embolden Joseph for this action. In addition to asking Pilate, he had to purchase before sundown expensive linen for a winding sheet (Mark 15:46). Only John mentions Nicodemus as assisting in the burial. His part was to

provide the spices — a mixture of myrrh (*smyrna*) defined as "the resinous gum" of the balsam bush with "incense and other aromatic substances" (A-G, p. 766). This spice mixture was found mostly in southern Arabia and had been imported as a luxury since the second millennium B.C. It had been presented to the infant Jesus (Matt. 2:11), and, mixed with wine, it had been offered to Jesus while he was hanging on his cross (Mark 15:23). Aloes (*aloē*) is the "strongly aromatic, quick-drying sap of a tree (Acquillaria), mixed with myrrh . . . used for embalming" (A-G, p. 40). While the Israelites did not practice embalming as did the Egyptians, yet a proper entombment was regarded as very important in the Jewish culture. The use of spices is stressed in the burial of Asa (II Chron. 16:14) as well as in the burial of Jesus. The use of costly spices was probably prompted by a desire to retard decomposition and to mitigate offensive odor. It was also a tribute of appreciation, as flowers are today. Jesus apparently accepted Mary's lavish tribute in this sense (John 12:7). The extent of Nicodemus' generosity may be gathered by comparison with the fact that eighty pounds of spices were used at the funeral of Gamaliel the elder and five hundred for the burial of Herod the Great.[w]

Nicodemus remains as an enigmatic although admirable figure. He was recep-

t M. Miller, ed., *Harper's Bible Dictionary* (New York: Harper, 1952), p. 42.
u E. A. Kraeling, *op. cit.,* p. 407.
v R. Earle, *Mark: The Evangelical Commentary* (Grand Rapids: Zondervan, 1957), p. 187.
w MJL, p. 503; cf. Jos. *Ant.* XVII. viii. 3.

39 And there came also Nicodemus, he who at the first came to him by night, bringing a mixture of myrrh and aloes, about a hundred pounds.

40 So they took the body of Jesus, and bound it in linen cloths with the spices, as the custom of the Jews is to bury.

---

**39, 40 And there came also Nicodemus . . . bringing a mixture of myrrh and aloes, about a hundred pounds.** He also belonged to the Sanhedrin. He it was that came to Jesus at night for that remarkable interview recorded in John 3:1-21. It is possible that, as a result of that interview, he was moved to declare openly his faith (cf. John 7:50-52). "But he who does what is true comes to the light, that it may be clearly seen that his deeds have been wrought in God" (RSV, John 3:21). Having followed in the shadows, and with uncertainty, he now identified himself with

Jesus' friends by spending his money freely to give Jesus a respectable burial. The huge amount of spices for burial must have been very costly. The burial account of king Asa (II Chron. 16:14) states that "the bed was filled with sweet odors and divers kinds of spices prepared by the perfumers' art." A pound (*litra*) consisted of 12 ounces.

**40 So they took the body of Jesus, and bound it in linen cloths with the spices, as the custom of the Jews is to bury.** Linen (*othonion*) was cut or woven into long strips and used in the burial of people

---

tive to new ideas, he wanted to discover things first-hand; hence his nocturnal interview with Jesus. He was not content with accepting second- or third-hand reports about Jesus. His favorable judgment concerning Jesus is reflected in his protest in the Sanhedrin about condemning a man without a hearing, without a first-hand acquaintance with him and his teachings (John 7:51). Now he appears for the third time, in a role perhaps even more heroic. With Jesus' avowed followers absent, he and Joseph, men who had nothing to gain (from a worldly standpoint) and everything to lose by associating themselves with Jesus and his cause, acted on their faith and loyalty. Thus both men faced censure or worse from other members of the council who had demanded Jesus' death. This is one of few bright spots in the passion narrative. The grief of the "daughters of Jerusalem," reported only in Luke, and the burial of Jesus by two rich men, show that not all of Jesus' friends and admirers were cowards. The women who "stood afar off" and later stood at the foot of the cross also add warmth to the picture. With the exception of John, however, none of the eleven were present to encourage Jesus during his hours of agony, to minister to his needs as best they could, or to hear his final words; instead, "they all forsook him and fled."

A question that often recurs is, "Would I have done better in those circumstances?"

The disciples were vulnerable because they were avowedly partisans of Jesus. The women were known to be sympathetic but were not considered troublesome. The two counselors, Joseph and Nicodemus, were cautious in their loyalty, had more standing, and were not likely to be persecuted. They would be regarded with suspicion and hatred, but they were not in much personal danger.

In none of the accounts do the disciples stand out in very commendable light. In contrast, their Master is the hero of the hour and the only one who knows what is involved and accepts the outcome with complete courage. His prayer in Gethsemane was answered, and he was able to accept the "cup" bravely. His intercessory prayer that his disciples be "kept" was answered. What the disciples lacked here in audacity they gained later when they were "endued with power from on high." The overall lesson is one of weak "vessels of clay" becoming mighty witnesses by the grace of God. The ultimate victory reported later was due not to the native competence of the disciples but to the *power* of God in working miracles and the *grace* of God transforming and empowering otherwise mediocre witnesses.

Artists and sculptors have found scenes of this chapter sources of powerful inspiration. Among the most famous sculptures is Michaelangelo's "Pieta," showing the mother Mary holding in her lap the limp

41 Now in the place where he was crucified there was a garden; and in the garden a new tomb wherein was never man yet laid.

42 There then because of the Jews' Preparation (for the tomb was nigh at hand) they laid Jesus.

---

of means. It was expensive. In John 11:44, Lazarus is described as coming out of the tomb "his hands and feet bound with bandages, and his face wrapped with a cloth."

**41, 42 Now in the place where he was crucified there was a garden; and in the garden a new tomb.** Matthew (27:60) relates that this tomb belonged to Joseph and that it had been "hewn in the rock," an expensive operation in those days, since there was no dynamite. Accounts of royal tombs in gardens are mentioned in II Kings 21:18, 26 and Neh. 3:16. It must have been close to 6 p.m. when the burial rites were completed. Since Jesus died about 3 p.m., great haste must have been exercised to finish the sad task of burial by 6 p.m. when the Sabbath began. Matthew and Mark state that a stone (*lithos* — perhaps hewn to fit) was used to close the entrance to the tomb. *Lithos,* as used here, denoted a rock of considerable size.

---

form of the Savior's body, with its pierced side. In Christian art, the scene of the scourging is portrayed with insight in Velasquez' "Christ at the Column" in the National Gallery of London. Rembrandt's "Descent from the Cross" makes effective use of light and shadow, true to the symbolism of John's Gospel and is a good visual commentary on John 19:38-42.[x]

[x] M. Ross, ed., *The Life of Christ in Masterpieces of Art* (Harper, n.d.), p. 106.

# CHAPTER XX

Now on the first day of the week cometh Mary Magdalene early, while it was yet dark, unto the tomb, and seeth the stone taken away from the tomb.

## EXEGESIS

**1 Now on the first day of the week** (*tōn sabbatōn*, genitive plural, the week as well as the Sabbath day in other contexts). "The plural *sabbata* is used with singular meaning for both 'Sabbath' and 'week'" (CKB, p. 467). The same usage is found in Acts 20:7: "On the first day of the week . . . Paul addressed them." The singular form of *sabbaton*, meaning week, occurs in Luke 18:12 and Mark 16:9. The chief reason the Christians began worshipping on Sunday (first day of the week) was because Christ arose from the dead on that day, according to Justin Martyr (c. A.D. 140): "On the day of the sun all in common came together, since it is the first day in which God,

having changed the darkness and the matter, made a world; and Jesus Christ our Saviour on that day arose from the dead. For they crucified him the day before Kronikos (Saturday) and on the day after Kronikos, which is the day of the sun" (Apol. LXVII).

About A.D. 110 Ignatius of Antioch wrote: "No longer observing sabbaths but fashioning their lives after the Lord's day" (Magn. 9).

In the *Didache* (c. A.D. 120) are these words: "Having come together on the Lord's day, break bread and give thanks."[1] The fact, too, that Jesus appeared to the disciples repeatedly on that day may have also influenced the Christians to make that their day of worship. Acts (20:7)

## EXPOSITION

### V. THE RESURRECTION (20:1-21;19)

#### A. THE FIRST EIGHT DAYS (20:1-31)

##### 1. THE FIRST DAY (vv. 1-18)

###### a. Mary's Discovery (vv. 1, 2)

The resurrection of Jesus from the dead is the basic doctrine of the New Testament. The Incarnation of the Son of God and the death-resurrection of Jesus Christ are the two great foci around which all other Christian doctrines gather. The account of the resurrection of Jesus is told, in the Fourth Gospel, with superb insight, pathos, and conviction. In the First Gospel the emphasis is upon the spectacular accompaniments of the resurrection event, the earthquake, the dazzling light and the raising of the bodies of the "saints." Mark's account is characterized by terseness, Luke's is invaluable chiefly for the description of the walk to Emmaus. In John the spiritual and the

physical both come in for special emphasis and synthesis. In this account the emphasis is placed on Mary Magdalene, but this does not mean that she was the only woman present. Matthew mentions two Marys, Luke's use of the plural indicates more than one woman while Mark names three. Here more than one is implied in the plural of Mary's report to Peter and the "beloved disciple" — "*we* know not where they have laid him" (v. 2). John's is the most beautiful account of the resurrection. Here one finds details which imply an intimate first-hand acquaintance with the events. The story is told simply, straightforwardly, artlessly, and yet with persuasive power. There is nothing sensational or superficial added; the event itself is eloquent and convincing. Mary Magdalene and the others (Mary, mother of James and Salome, Mark 16: 1), their spices prepared, steal away into the "garden" before dawn. It has been part of three days since Jesus' corpse had been laid away — not three days, but

---

[1] Did. XIV, K. Lake, tr. (Loeb) *op. cit.*, II, 33.

*Aposte John*

**2** She runneth therefore, and cometh to Simon Peter, and to the other disciple whom Jesus loved, and saith unto them, They have taken away the Lord out of the tomb, and we know not where they have laid him.

---

records their observing the Lord's Supper, the most sacred phase of their worship on that day. Also worshipping with offerings occurred on that day (I Cor. 16:1, 2). Evidently then by A.D. 55, twenty-five years after the resurrection, it had become the customary day of Christian worship.

For an inferential reason why Christians would choose a day of worship different from that of the Jews see *Didache* VIII. 1. Of course, Christians of Jewish descent for a while worshipped on Saturday (Acts 13:14, 44). Had they not, their chances of winning Jews to their faith would have been considerably less.

**Mary Magdalene** must have felt a tremendous indebtedness to Jesus due to the hopelessness of her condition until he healed her: "Mary called Magdalene, from whom seven demons had gone out" (Luke 8:2). Her name occurs more frequently than that of any other woman in the passion accounts, being named by all the Evangelists. She was present during the crucifixion; she tarried at the tomb after Jesus was buried; she went with other women to buy spices for anointing Jesus' body; she went to the tomb very early on Sunday morning and discovered that it was empty; and she it was, of all women, who was honored with a personal appearance of Jesus on the day he arose from the dead. Evidently she had a striking personality and was very popular among Christians.[2]

**She seeth the stone taken away** (*ērmenon,* perf. pass.) from the tomb. It had been and remained removed from the tomb. This was a shock. The first impression very likely was that hostile people had done this.

**2 So she ran, and went to Simon Peter and the other disciple, the one whom Jesus loved** (RSV). Mary did not wait at the tomb as did the other women to whom, after she left, the angels announced Jesus' resurrection (Mark 16:2-8; Matt.

---

"the third day": Friday afternoon, Sabbath and now the "first day of the week"; in Jewish practice it was customary to call *part* of three days "three days." Love and loyalty overcame the natural timidity of these women and impelled them to render their last tribute to the body of their departed Master. They wondered how they would remove the stone; we wonder where the men were who might have helped in this audacious undertaking. Only when one has lived in a non-Christian land can he appreciate what Christianity has done to the status of women. Even in the O. T., a list of the most heroic characters must include the names of Deborah, Hannah, Esther and Ruth. In the N. T. the same is true to an even greater degree and we read of the Marys, of Dorcas, of Eunice, of Priscilla, of Lydia, and "of the chief women not a few" (Acts 17:4). Bunyan observed that "It was a woman that washed his feet with tears, and a woman that anointed his body to the burial. They were women that wept when he was going to the cross, and women that followed him from the cross, and that sat by his sepulchre when he was buried. They were women that were first with him at his resurrection morn and women that brought tidings first to his disciples that he was risen from the dead. Women, therefore, are highly favored, and show by these things that they are sharers in the grace of life."[a] The burial had been hurried because of the approach of the Sabbath, and now these women wanted to complete the last expressions of tribute to the body of the deceased.

**She seeth the stone taken away.** The verb is *blepō,* meaning a glimpse which was enough to inform her that all was not well at the tomb. The women's fear was due to the darkness and the possibility of thieves. Without investigation they ran to tell the men about their alarming discovery.

[2] In Matthew's report, Mary Magdalene was accompanied by "the other Mary"; in Mark's account by Salome also.
[a] John Bunyan, *Pilgrim's Progress,* cited by James Robertson, ed., *op. cit.,* p. 242.

3 Peter therefore went forth, and the other disciple, and they went toward the tomb
4 And they ran both together: and the other disciple outran Peter, and came first to the tomb;
5 and stooping and looking in, he seeth the linen cloths lying; yet entered he not in
6 Simon Peter therefore also cometh following him, and entered into the tomb; and he beholdeth the linen cloths lying,

28:5-8; Luke 24:1-8). But she hastily ran with all possible speed to inform the apostles Peter and John.

**Simon Peter** is a combination of both the Aramaic and the Greek names. The latter may have been given him at Caesarea Philippi when Jesus called him a stone (*petros*, Matt. 16:16-18), due to his loyalty to and correct understanding of the person and mission of Jesus. **Whom Jesus loved** (*ephilei*, imperf. ind. — "he continued being fond of"). Since this is stated of John only, why did not Jesus appoint him as his vicegerent instead of Peter, as some claim? Since John outlived the other apostles (he died about A.D. 97), after their death, at least, he was regarded as the best qualified and most authoritative representative of Christ,

regardless of who was pastor in Rome
3 *Erchonto* (they went), imperf. middl. — "they were going" (to the tomb). It is a scene of men in motion. Preceding this verb is *exēlthen* (aor, act. ind.) implying immediate action, i.e., "went out.

4, 5 And they ran both together: and the other disciple outran Peter. *Etrechon* (imperf. ind.) — "they were running." They started out together but John reached the tomb first, peered in (*parakypsas*), and observed the linen cloths, but for some reason hesitated to enter.

6 **Then Simon Peter came . . . and he went into the tomb.** He had been following; now he preceded John. No sensitive qualms inhibited him! Impulsive, he acted, then thought later on, as so often in the N. T. accounts of him.

All of the other Gospels report the appearance of angels at the empty tomb and the dramatic announcement that Christ had arisen. Matthew reports, in addition, an earthquake and the consternation of the guards. The stone was rolled back, not to permit the Master's exit, but to permit visitors to see where the body had lain and hence get negative evidence of the resurrection (Matt. 28: 6; cf. Mark 16:5; Luke 23:4). Matthew and Mark report a prediction by the angels that they would see Jesus again in Galilee. Only Matthew and John mention the appearances in Galilee (Matt. 28:16; John 21).

The earliest extant written account of the resurrection appearances is found in I Corinthians 15. Paul stresses the appearances while the Gospels stress both the empty tomb and the appearances. In the light of these five reports the following sequence of events can be assembled.

(i) Mary Magdalene, Mary the mother of James, Salome (Mark 16:1) and Johanna (Luke 23:10) set out for the tomb before dawn.

(ii) Mary Magdalene reaches the tomb first, finds it empty, and reports to Peter and John (v. 2)

(iii) The other women reach the tomb at sunrise (Mark 16:2), find it empty, see the angels, and flee in fear, reporting their discovery to the disciples.

(iv) The apostles are incredulous (Luke 24:11).

(v) Peter (Luke 24:12) and John (20: 3-10) run to investigate.

(vi) The first appearance of the risen Christ is given to Mary Magdalene (John 20:11; Mark 16:9).

(vii) The second appearance is to the other women as they return to Jerusalem (Matt. 28:9).

(viii) The Lord then appears to Simon Peter alone (Luke 24:34; I Cor. 15:5).

(ix) The fourth appearance is to disciples en route to Emmaus (Luke 24:13-31).

(x) Next Jesus appears to ten of the disciples (John 20:19-25; cf. I Cor. 15: 5).

(xi) The sixth appearance is to the eleven, including Thomas, one week later (John 20:26).

7 and the napkin, that was upon his head, not lying with the linen cloths, but rolled up in a place by itself.

8 Then entered in therefore the other disciple also, who came first to the tomb, and he saw, and believed. *THAT JESUS IS ALIVE FROM the DEAD!*

---

**7, 8 And the napkin** (*soudarion*) . . . **not lying with the linen clothes** (*meta tōn othoniōn*), **but rolled up in a place by itself.** *Soudarion* is defined in the Arndt-Gingrich Greek lexicon: "*face-cloth* for wiping perspiration, corresponding somewhat to our handkerchief" (cf. Luke 19: 20; John 11:44; Acts 19:12). See comments on John 19:40 for discussion on *othoniōn.* When Lazarus emerged from the tomb he was still "bound hand and foot with grave-clothes (*keiriais*); and his face was bound about with a napkin." In this case the cloths were present but the body absent. And the handkerchief was not only there but even rolled up and separate from the other cloths. To John

this was a clue that Jesus was alive and that he not only had either crawled out of the bandages or else unwrapped them, but also had taken the pains to roll up the handkerchief as he placed it by itself. Could it be that John had witnessed Jesus roll a handkerchief like this again and again after he finished eating a meal? Since Jesus was able to enter a room with the windows and doors shut (v. 19) it is reasonable to assume that he did not have any physical difficulty in emerging from the wrappings. Evidently there had been no theft of the body, nor haste in Jesus' departure from the tomb. And he saw and believed. Without having seen Jesus alive, John concluded that he had *NOTE!*

---

(xii) Jesus appears to seven disciples while they are fishing (John 20:1-13).

(xiii) He then appears to the eleven on a mountain in Galilee (Matt. 28:16-20).

(xiv) The ninth appearance is to "five hundred brethren at once" in Galilee (I Cor. 15:6).

(xv) An appearance to James alone is reported (I Cor. 15:7).

(xvi) All the apostles see him ascend into heaven at Olivet (Luke 24:50; Acts 1:6-11).

(xvii) He is seen last by Paul as "one born out of due time" (I Cor. 15:8; Acts 9:4).[b]

Thus, twelve separate appearances can be listed if we attempt to harmonize all five of the reports. Others insist that the reports are contradictory and cannot thus be harmonized. It is not to be expected that all of the witnesses agree in detail; indeed the diversity implies a certain independence on their part and hence authenticity. The following is clear: the women were first to discover the empty tomb; it was to women that Jesus first appeared; the men certified that the tomb was empty; the later appearances of Jesus were mostly to the eleven apostles; and here is no reported appearance of Jesus to "the world" as was true of Lazarus.

The stone was taken away or "picked up, forcibly removed, carried away" (A-G). The same verb is used of Jesus' corpse (19:38), of John the Baptist (Matt. 14:12), and of the stone sealing the sepulcher of Lazarus. Most well-constructed tombs of Jerusalem of that period were sealed with a large, flat, circular disk, about six inches thick, set in a shallow trough so that it could be rolled back and forth to open and close the entrance. Such stones may be seen in at least three places in Jerusalem today; one is at the tomb of St. Helena ("tombs of the kings"), another near Bethphage on Mt. Olivet, and another at the family tomb of Herod. The trough for a larger stone than these is seen at the Garden Tomb. The verb does not make clear whether the stone was simply rolled back or violently lifted out of its place and laid flat on the ground; the earthquake, as well as the verb itself, makes the latter probable.

Without stopping to examine the grave closely, Mary and the other women ran to report to the disciples. She reported to Peter and the "beloved disciple" that someone had removed the body. There is every indication that no resurrection was expected, but simply that their concern was for the body; perhaps grave-robbers had deprived them even of the

b R. A. Knox, *op. cit.,* I, 269. B. F. Westcott, *op. cit.,* II, 336. F. N. Peloubet, *op. cit.,* p. 514.

9 For as yet they knew not the scripture, that he must rise again from the dead

10 So the disciples went away again unto their own home.

11 But Mary was standing without at the tomb weeping: so, as she wept, she stooped and looked into the tomb;

12 and she beholdeth two angels in white sitting, one at the head, and one at the feet, where the body of Jesus had lain.

13 And they say unto her, Woman, why weepest thou? She saith unto them, Because they have taken away my lord, and I know not where they have laid him.

14 When she had thus said, she turned herself back, and beholdeth Jesus standing, and knew not that it was Jesus.

---

really risen from the dead. ("Peter had more sight, John more insight" (ATR, V, 310).

9 They knew not the scripture, that he must rise again from the dead. Strange to say, John did not follow his usual custom here of quoting the Scripture that he mentioned. He could have had in mind Psalm 16:10: "For thou wilt not leave my soul to Sheol; neither wilt thou suffer thy holy one to see corruption," which was quoted later on by Peter (Acts 2:27). Apparently Jesus' repeated predictions of his resurrection had not been taken seriously (cf. Mark 8:31; Matt. 26:54; Luke 9:22, et al.).

11 Mary was standing without at the tomb weeping. Peter and John had left and had gone home (v. 10); but Mary lingered near the tomb giving vent to her deep sorrow with tears (cf. v. 1). Her tarrying was rewarded: As she wept she stooped and looked (v. 5) into the tomb. Her love for her Lord was so over-powering that she wanted to be near him in death as well as in life.

12 She beholdeth (theōrei, pres. tense used historically) two angels in white. In spite of her blind tears, she was able to see these heavenly messengers. Angels in the N. T. are regularly described as men, wherever any detail is given as to apparent sex, and usually also dressed in white: Mark 16:5, "a young man in white"; Luke 24:4, "two men in dazzling apparel"; Acts 1, "two men in white."

13 Why are you weeping? Because they have taken away my Lord. Mary revealed in this reply how personal her faith was ("my Lord") and also that to her he was divine and the master and guardian of her soul.

14 "With these words she turned round and saw Jesus standing there, but did not recognize him" (NEB). The two disciples on the way to Emmaus did not recognize Jesus at first in spite of prolonged conversation with him (Luke 24:

---

satisfaction of giving proper care to the corpse. Grave-robbery was commonplace, especially in cases where wealth was interred with the corpse, as in Egypt. The Roman emperor Claudius found it necessary to issue an edict threatening punishment for grave-robbers at Nazareth. In this case the motive for robbery would not be the acquisition of wealth (although the spices were very costly) but rather the desecration of the corpse. In the O. T. the ultimate in punishment was the denial of a decent burial, as in the case of Jezebel (II Kings 9:37). It was this which Rizpah determined should not happen to the seven sons of Saul (II Sam. 21:8-10). There were good grounds for believing that Jesus' enemies were eager to deny to the disciples the privilege of caring for the corpse.

### b. Peter and John Investigate (vv. 3-10)

3-10 It is a dramatic picture, that of Peter and John running toward the tomb. One artist has pictured the running of these two men in a manner which suggests the dawning of Easter hope in their countenances. John, the younger man, is portrayed slightly in advance of Peter who is panting to keep up. In both faces the eyes are peering eagerly straight ahead, suggesting that the open tomb is now in sight.[c] The Evangelist, who alone reports the event says, the other disciple outran

c E. Burnand, in C. Maus, op. cit., pp. 430-434.

15 Jesus saith unto her, Woman, why weepest thou? whom seekest thou? She, supposing, him to be the gardener, saith unto him, Sir, if thou hast borne him hence, tell me where thou hast laid him, and I will take him away.

16 Jesus saith unto her, Mary. She turneth herself, and saith unto him in Hebrew, Rabboni; which is to say, Teacher.

17 Jesus saith to her, Touch me not; for I am not yet ascended unto the Father: but go unto my brethren, and say to them, I ascend unto my Father and your Father, and my God and your God.

---

13-35). Apparently he had assumed a slightly different appearance for these occasions so that his resurrection body was not identifiable with his earthly body (cf. Mark 16:12, "in another form"). It could have been that the ordeal of torture, loss of blood, and agony, so recently experienced, had altered his looks. It certainly would in a normal human being. Another possibility is that their capacity to see was affected temporarily, (Luke 24:16).

15 "Jesus said to her, Why are you weeping? Who is it you are looking for" (NEB)? Jesus did not need an answer to his question. He asked it so Mary would state the cause of her grief. Jews, as Orientals generally, were uninhibited in giving expression to their sorrow. Psychologists agree that such expressions are good for a person.

16 Mary (Mariam). Jesus used the Aramaic form of the name — which he may have used customarily in addressing her. This time he pronounced the name so she would recognize him. Much thought and love can be conveyed by a word sympathetically uttered. And Mary responded by crying, "Rabbouni (teacher)," also Aramaic.

17 At this moment of their dramatic reunion, Mary must have given ecstatic expression to her emotions by embracing Jesus. For Jesus mildly rebuked her by saying, "Stop clinging to me" (mē mou haptou). This prohibition in the present tense implies either action in progress prior to the command (D-M, pp. 301f.) or else forbids beginning and continuing an action. Probably Mary was clinging to his feet as in Matthew 28:9 — "they took hold of his feet and worshipped him." This

---

Peter and came first to the tomb. Then he hesitated, waiting for Peter to catch up. He may have deferred to the elder, he may have hesitated in fear, but he waited. While waiting, he stooped down in order to see in. The tomb entrance was probably less than three feet in height, hence the necessity of bending down to see in. Peter, first to enter, was the natural leader again, in command in spite of his recent defection. From outside John had only glanced at the linen cloths within. When Peter entered, he scrutinized carefully the arrangement of the linen cloths in which the body had been wrapped. They were probably in the spiral arrangement normal in such burials, and in the same position as when last seen on Friday evening. Peter may have recalled that when Lazarus came forth he was still encased in grave cloths. Where was Jesus' body? How could the body have been removed without removing the grave cloths also? If the body had been removed and the cloths left

would they not be in a state of disarray? How could they have been left in the same spiral, cocoonlike shape they were in when they encased the body? How could the napkin, which covered his head, still be rolled up? Peter looked intently (theōreō) and wondered. Then John entered, indicating that the tomb was somewhat spacious. Probably they stood on a raised platform and viewed the shallow depression into which the corpse had been laid. There is significance in the different verbs for "seeing" used here. The "single look" (JHT, p. 452) of Mary (v. 1) and of John (v. 5) is indicated by blepō. The more concentrated gaze of Peter (theōreō) inside the tomb took in the arrangement of the cloths, a careful, studied inspection (v. 6). When John entered and looked at the same cloths Peter was scrutinizing he saw and believed. The verb form here is eiden and means "perception, insight, hence to know" (Thayer). It is vision plus a comprehension of the significance of the

NOTE:

18 Mary Magdalene cometh and telleth the disciples, I have seen the Lord; and *that* he had said these things unto her.

---

would have been the most natural mode of expressing her affection and reverence. This is still a posture of reverence in the Orient and may be preserved in the practice of kissing or caressing the toe of St. Peter's statue by pilgrims visiting the basilica of St. Peter in Rome. The NEB correctly translates "do not cling to me." "The prohibition here reminds Mary that the previous personal fellowship by sight, sound, touch no longer exists and that the final state of glory was not yet begun. Jesus checks Mary's impulsive eagerness" (WPNT, V, 312). **For I have not yet ascended** has a verb (*anabebēka*) in the perfect tense which literally translated means "for I am not yet in an 'ascended' condition." Had the aorist tense been used it would have implied that he had not ascended at all. The perfect tense states the continuing results of an action which has occurred. The use of the perfect here does not deny that he had fellowship with God between the time of his death and his resurrection, as Jesus final saying on the cross, "Into thy hands I commit my spirit," seems to imply (Luke 23:46; cf. D-M, pp. 200-204). **But go to my brethren and say to them, I am ascending to my Father and your Father, to my God and your God.** It is likely from the context that "brethren" here means the disciples and not Jesus' blood-brothers. Mary is to announce to them that Jesus is alive but that he will soon depart this earth to return to his home with God.

**18 Mary Magdalene went and said to the disciples, I have seen the Lord.** *Eōraka* (I have seen), being a verb in the perfect tense, emphasizes the lasting impression of having seen Christ. She not only saw him but also held on to him, and furthermore, she talked with him. That experience would remain in her memory all her life as vividly as if it had just transpired. John (I John 1:1, 2), by using

---

vision. This verb combines the qualities of sight (*horaō*, "to see") and knowledge (*oida*, "to know")[d] The verb used of what Peter saw (*theōreō*) means "to behold with the bodily eye" while the verb used of John's seeing means "to see spiritually."[e] *Theōreō* is usually associated with uncomprehending vision of externals (2:23; 4:19; 6:2, 19). On the other hand, *eiden* and *horaō* usually designate spiritual insight, as in 1:39; 1:50 ("thou shalt see greater things than these"); 11:40 ("thou shalt see the glory of God"); cf. 16:16. Thus John uses four verb forms to present the resurrection faith in four stages:

(i) Mary Magdalene noticed (*blepō*) the opened grave and John noticed the cloths before entering (vv. 1, 5).

(ii) Later both John (v. 5) and Mary (v. 11) stooped down so as to peer (*parakyptō*) into the tomb (cf. Prov. 7:6; Sir. 21:23; Jas. 1:25; I Pet. 1:12; Enoch 9:1).

(iii) Peter now entered and thoroughly scrutinized (*theōreō*) the interior but without faith, in the same sense that Mary later "saw" Jesus physically but not spiritually (v. 14).

(iv) John entered the tomb and saw all that Peter did but caught its significance (*eiden*) and believed in the same sense that Mary did after she recognized Jesus (v. 18).[f]

The importance of the relationship of sight to faith is one of John's favorite themes. It appears in the conversation with Thomas — "because thou hast seen (*horaō*) me, thou hast believed" (v. 29). It appears in I John 1:1 — "we have seen (*horaō*) it with our own eyes; we looked (*theōreō*) upon it . . . the word of life" (NEB).

Faith, to John, was not something that is self-generated or originates apart from "the event of Christ." To John, faith is presumption unless grounded in factual data. One of the most serious fallacies in much contemporary theology is the circular reasoning by which it is assumed that faith can flourish apart from fact.

---

d *Oido,* "to know," comes from the same root as eidon ("to see"), and *eidon* is the aorist active of *horao* (A-S).

e E. A. Abbot, *Johannine Vocabulary* (London: Adams & Black, 1905), p. 105.

f Cf. Thayer, ἰδεῖν is much less physical than ὁρᾶν (*op. cit.*, p. 173).

19 When therefore it was evening, on that day, the first *day* of the week, and when the doors were shut where the disciples were, for fear of the Jews, Jesus came and stood in the midst, and saith unto them, Peace *be* unto you.

20 And when he had said this, he showed unto them his hands and his side. The disciples therefore were glad, when they saw the Lord.

---

the perfect tense, emphasized the lasting impressions obtained by the disciples who heard and saw Jesus. And as Mary did, they even "handled" him "with their hands" (cf. Matt. 28:9).

19 **The first day of the week** (cf. discussion on v. 1). The adjective *opsias* ("late") implies "hour," i.e., at a late hour in the day, either before or after sundown (cf. A-G, p. 606). It was the end of the first Easter day (cf. Mark 16:14; Luke 24:36). **When the doors were shut** (*kekleismenon,* perf. pass. participle — had been shut and were now so). **Jesus came and stood in the midst.** In spite of locked doors Jesus suddenly appeared to them, "sufficiently immaterial to pass through closed doors" (CKB, p. 472).[3] **Peace be unto you** was the usual Oriental greeting among friends (cf. v. 21, 26 and Luke 24:36). In John 14:27 is recorded Christ's promise of his

peace for his disciples, the peace that Paul speaks of as indescribably precious — "passes understanding" (Phil. 4:7).

20 **He showed them his hands and his side,** i.e., the wounds made by the nails in his hands and the spear in his side, as incontrovertible proof that it was the same Jesus who died on the cross three days before and was now alive. Naturally **the disciples were glad** (cf. 16:22). The grief and the gloom of the past three days were exchanged for boundless joy. Their leader was alive again and he had vindicated by his resurrection that all that he had said about his being the Messiah, "that takes away the sin of the world" (John 1:29), was true. God was really in Christ "reconciling the world to himself" (II Cor. 5:19). It meant then that they had been chosen to represent the most important Sovereign and Cause that could be represented. For they were in

---

This places the ultimate authority in the individual, rather than in objective grounding on reality. The result is a mystical subjectivism at best; at the worst, it professes unconcern with the historical validity of Scripture and tradition.

9, 10 It does not say just what the beloved disciple believed. His faith had little content or definition, but it was a real resurrection faith in its germinal stages of development. To a person reading this material the story is much more convincing when one realizes that the resurrection faith came slowly and with difficulty. It rules out the likelihood of hallucination because hallucinations come to those with a prior mental tendency in that direction. A fabricated story would likely present the disciples as leaping to a full-orbed faith almost instantly.

The disciples did not relate the empty tomb and the intact grave-cloths to Jesus' predictions of his resurrection or to the O. T. prediction of this event — they knew

not the scripture. The Holy Spirit had not yet been "given" and hence there was no one to take the things of Christ and reveal them unto the disciples. So they went back home baffled.

### c. Jesus' Appearance to Mary (vv. 11-18)

After the brief mention of Mary Magdalene in vv. 1, 2, the author returns to tell in great detail the Master's appearance to Mary. It is one of the most touching and dramatic of the resurrection episodes. After the women reported to the disciples their discovery of the empty tomb, and the two disciples had made a hasty verification of their report, Mary lingered at the opened sepulcher, loath to leave. Probably love constrained her. It is said of her that Jesus had cast seven devils out of her (Luke 8:2; Mark 16:9). Contrary to J. H. Bernard, who thinks she was the same as Mary of Bethany,

---

[3] Some concepts of supernatural existence would suggest that *our* mere three-dimensional world is so "immaterial" that a supernatural being can pass through our walls and doors as naturally as we pass through a shadow or "see into" a drawing of a house on paper.

21 Jesus therefore said to them again, Peace be unto you: as the Father ha sent me, even so send I you.

22 And when he had said this, he breathed on them, and saith unto them, Recei ye the Holy Spirit:

---

fact ambassadors of God. Little wonder that they were glad! Cf. Luke 24:41, "they disbelieved for joy."

21 As the Father hath sent me, even so I send you. Two different verbs meaning "send" occur here, and both apparently are equivalent to each other. The first, *apestalken,* being in the perfect tense emphasizes completion of Christ's mission to earth and its continuing effects. The second, *pempō* (pres. tense) emphasizes that the authoritative commission is now being given to the disciples, by the Son of God. John frequently used these verbs synonymously. Both were used with reference to the Father's sending out Christ (cf. 17:3, 8, 18, 21, 23, 25, *apostellein;* and 14:24; 15:21; 16:5, *pempein*). Likewise both were used for sending out the apostles (cf. 4:38; 17:18; 13:16, 20). As Christ was dependent upon and obedient to God, and as the power of the Holy

Spirit rested upon him, so individual Chri tians, when obedient to God and su missive to the leadership of the Ho Spirit, are not only bearers of Chris message but are also effective witnesses his redemptive, transforming power. Th is the first record of three commissio given by the risen Christ; another w given in Galilee (Matt. 28:16-20; I C 15:6), and still another on the Mou of Olives (Luke 24:44-51; Acts 1:3-11

22 He breathed on them. Just as n tural life was, in the Garden of Ede imparted to a human body, so here t conveying of the new, spiritual life pictured. In ch. 16 John recorded wh Jesus had taught about his sending of t Holy Spirit, who would always be wi them to guide them into all truth a convict the world with respect to si Receive ye the Holy Spirit (*labete pneum hagion*). Here the disciples are con

---

most scholars agree that she came from Magdala in Galilee, a city on the west shore of the Sea of Galilee. It is unlikely that she was the sinful woman of Luke 7:36-50, since she is introduced in 8:2. Mary's devotion was not reserved until this occasion. She contributed service and treasure to Jesus' Galilean ministry (Luke 8:1-3; Mark 15:40, 41) and joined his last pilgrimage to Jerusalem (Mark 15: 41). She was among the last to leave the scene of the crucifixion (Mark 15:40; John 19:25) and first to return to the tomb on Easter morning (Mark 16:1; Luke 24:1-11). Her lingering was rewarded by the appearance of two figures in white sitting in the sepulcher. The two angels asked her the reason for her grief and she replied that the body had been taken to some unknown place. Then turning about, she saw through her tears a figure she thought to be the keeper of the "garden" and asked him about the corpse. When Jesus spoke her name she recognized him at once and was "lost in wonder, love, and praise." As she endeavored to see whether he was flesh and blood (see JHT, p. 70) he forbade

her because of the ascension to t Father. No explanation is given for t prohibition. The fact that Mary showe no fright suggests the primitive nature the account and "may even go back Mary herself" (JHB, VI, 664). One wee later Jesus invited Thomas to touch hi Some conjecture that Jesus ascended the Father in the interval between the fir Easter day and the second appearanc eight days later. Others seek to resol the difficulty by assuming a spiritual rath than physical meaning; in other word Jesus was saying that spiritual access b tween Master and disciple would not free until the ascension of Jesus and th descent of the Paraclete. Bernard an Meyer suggest that the text has bee altered by mistake; that the words *m mou aptou* ("touch me not") originall read *mē ptou* ("be not afraid," cf. Luk 24:37). There is no known manuscri which has this reading, however, and is a pure conjecture — theoretically po sible but in the highest degree improb able. More likely, by linking this pr hibition with the message concerning th ascension, Jesus wished to underscore th

23 whose soever sins ye forgive, they are forgiven unto them; whose soever *sins* ye retain, they are retained.

---

manded to welcome and receive into their hearts and lives the permanent presence and power of God in the person of the Holy Spirit. While Jesus was present with them they had God's guidance for a limited number of months; but now he commits them to the watchful care and sovereignty of his successor, the Holy Spirit, who will guide them and shepherd them for the rest of their lives. The power of the Holy Spirit which came to them is still available to every Christian. Very likely more than the ten apostles were present that night when they received "the Holy Spirit which the Lord hath given to those whose habit of life is to obey him" (Acts 5:32). The presence of his power in our lives is conditioned by consistent, day-by-day obedience. Acts also reveals that there were repeated fillings of the Holy Spirit to meet specific situations, such as initially at Pentecost, during persecution, on Gentiles in the home of Cornelius, etc. (Acts 2:1-4; 4:31; 10:44-47).

23 **Whose soever sins ye forgive** (*aphēte*, aor. subj. — "you may forgive") **they are forgiven** (*apheōntai*, perf. passive — "they stand forgiven"); **whose soever sins ye retain** (*kratēte*, pres. subj. — "you may retain"), **they are retained** (*kekratēntai*, perf. pass. — "they stand retained"). There is some manuscript variation as to whether there should be a present or a future ending for *aphiēmi* (forgive) here instead of the perfect, which has the best attestation. The context also favors the perfect since there is no question as to the reading *kekratēntai*, which balances with *apheōntai*. It is possible that the growing tendency in the second and third centuries toward the doctrine of sacerdotalism (the claim that men can forgive sins in behalf of God) motivated scribes to alter certain manuscripts to agree with their theology. This verse and Matthew 16:18, 19; 18:18, where the disciples were warned that whatever they bound (declare obligatory) "shall stand bound

---

importance of the spiritual intimacy which would be realized when his physical presence was removed to the Father and the Paraclete was sent by him from the Father to remain with them forever.

The important thing here is the ascension. John does not report the visible ascension as does Luke 24:50-52; Acts 1:9 (cf. John 6:62; Mark 16:19). The word **ascend** (*anabainō*) is used in this sense only here, in 6:62 and in Ephesians 4:8 as a translation of Psalm 68:18. It was not until the fourth century that this term became the technical term for the ascension (JHB, II, 668). The idea, however, occurs repeatedly in John 7:33; 14:12, 28; 16:5, 10. To this Evangelist the elevation to the cross, the resurrection, and the ascension are often fused together almost as one event (e.g., John 12:23-34; 14:12; 16:17, 28; 17:1, 5).

17 Jesus never used the term "our Father" in a sense which included his own relationship with the Father together with the relationship of anyone else with the Father. He often used "my Father"

and "the Father," especially in the Fourth Gospel. Even here Jesus does not say, "our Father and our God" but makes a careful distinction: "my Father and your Father, and my God and your God." The significance is that while Jesus and his disciples both were sons of the Most High, Jesus' sonship was unique and quite different from that of believers. He is Son by nature, we are sons by adoption.

18 Mary, therefore, became the first witness of the resurrection. What an honor! Even though she reported, "I have seen the Lord," it was actually his voice rather than sight which enabled her to identify him with certainty. But the two organs of sense were so closely related that she could appropriately place the emphasis on the sight.[g]

Through Mary's errors the Evangelist seeks to drive home to his readers some important truths:

(i) Her first disappointment turned out to be a blessing in disguise. She was grieved to find the tomb empty (v. 1). But is it not infinitely better that Jesus'

[g] E. A. Abbott, *op. cit.*, p. 108.

in heaven" (future perfect passive, not mere future passive as most translations imply), are the foundational passages used to defend the teaching of sacerdotalism. Instead of God's ratifying the decisions of men, these passages teach, rather, that men are to ratify and implement the decrees of God. In John 20:23 the perfect tense is found in both principal clauses. And, according to the unanimous testimony of all Greek grammarians, the perfect tense pictures an action which is past in relation to the time of speaking and writing. In this case it means that before one treats anyone as forgiven, he is doing it on the basis that God has already forgiven that person. Or, to paraphrase the thought, "Forgive those that God has forgiven; refuse to forgive those that God has not forgiven." The emphasis is on preserving the spiritual life of the church. Only those who have accepted Christ as Savior and Lord and who have been regenerated by the Holy Spirit are to be admitted into the fellowship of the church. "The force of the tenses in the two independent clauses must not be overlooked. The perfect is used each time (*apheōntai* — the better supported reading — and *kekratēntai*): 'they have been forgiven'; 'they have been retained.' This implies insight into a granting or withholding of forgiveness already determined in the divine judgment" (W.H, VIII, 798).[4]

Dr. Wilber Thomas Dayton, professor in Asbury Theological Seminary, wrote his doctoral dissertation on "The Greek Perfect Tense in Relation to John 20:23, Matthew 16:19 and 18:18," and in doing so made the most comprehensive study, in this generation at least, of the

---

body was not in the tomb? If it had been there would have been no resurrection and no good news.[h]

(ii) Her first report to the disciples was erroneous; but it is fortunate that she was mistaken. How tragic if it had been true that the body had been removed by thieves as she assumed!

(iii) Her third mistake lay in assuming that Jesus was the gardener (v. 15). How fortunate that it proved to be Jesus rather than the attendant. How thrilled Mary must have been to discover her mistake!

(iv) She erred for the fourth time in assuming that Jesus' resurrection body was the same body which he possessed before his death. She assumed that he had simply reappeared like Lazarus. But the relationship was different. Lazarus had his same body restored and he was still mortal. Jesus had a body which was all new; it would never die and yet had continuity with the old (cf. I Cor. 15:35-50). The good news she brought was even better than she realized at the time. From this it becomes obvious that what may seem an unmitigated tragedy may turn out even better than our fondest hope and dreams. It should be kept in mind that the one to whom this truth was made known was the one who tarried with the patience born of love and the persistence which springs from hope. And Mary, the first to proclaim the gospel, was a woman.

*Not she with traitor's kiss her Master stung;*
*Not she denied Him with unfaithful tongue;*
*She when apostles fled could danger brave,*
*Last at His cross and earliest at His grave.*

— E. B. Browning[i]

d. Jesus' Appearance to Ten Disciples (vv. 19-23)

The second appearance of Jesus on the first Easter Sunday is related by Mark, Luke and John. In Luke's account it occurs after the return of the two disciples from Emmaus. John relates this appearance in greater detail than the other two perhaps because of its bearing on the later appearance to Thomas and

---

[4] A noted grammarian agrees, "The power to forgive sins belongs only to God, but Jesus claimed to have this power and right (Mark 2:5-7). What he commits to the disciples and to us is the power and privilege of giving assurance of the forgiveness of sins by God by correctly announcing the terms of forgiveness. There is no proof that he actually transferred to the apostles or their successors the power in and of themselves to forgive sins. In Matt. 16:19 and 18:18 we have a similar use of the rabbinical metaphor of finding and losing by proclaiming and teaching. Jesus put into the hands of Peter and of all believers the keys of the Kingdom which we should use to open the door for those who wish to enter. This glorious promise applies to all believers who will tell the story of Christ's love for men" (ATR, V, 315).

[h] Walter Lüthi, *op. cit.*, p. 310.

[i] Cited by F. N. Peloubet, *op. cit.*, p. 518.

use of the perfect tense during the first century. In his inductive study of first-century writings, Dayton discovered 621 occurrences of the perfect tense, and all but eleven percent of them, or eighty-nine percent, best fit their contexts when translated literally, which is the regular and normal procedure unless the context definitely indicates otherwise. He summarized his findings by stating: "Therefore, so far as the writer has been able to discover, no conclusive proof has been found of any use of the perfect tense in Greek where due to grammatical considerations the significance of past action was lost. . . . Consequently, it seems safe to say that, so far as any proof to the contrary is concerned, every perfect is, from a strictly grammatical standpoint, a true perfect." His research led him to translate John 20:23, Matthew 16:19 and

18:18 as we have indicated, applying the results of his research to the above passages of Scripture. He wrote: "From every standpoint sacerdotalism . . . is based on a figurative translation that is, at best, highly conjectural grammatically . . . . It is an impossible view theologically and it can find no basis in historical fact."[5]

As evidence that John did not intend to infer that a human being can forgive a sin against God and by doing so establish peace between that individual and God, one needs but to reflect upon some of the statements he has made as to how one can be saved: 3:16, "Whosoever believeth on him should not perish, but have eternal life"; 3:36, "He that believeth on the Son hath eternal life; but he that obeyeth not the Son" (regardless of whether some one says he is forgiven) "shall not see life, but the wrath of God abideth on him";

---

the rest. Four elements are noteworthy in this paragraph: The miraculous entrance, the verification of Jesus' identity, the command to "go," and the impartation of authority.

### (1) The Disciples' Joy at Seeing Jesus (vv. 19, 20)

#### (a) The Miraculous Entrance (v. 19)

John is again very specific. He states that this appearance to the ten occurred on the evening of this first day of the week. It was a day which would never be forgotten in Christian history; for, like the Passover at the time of the Exodus, it was the "beginning of months" or, in this case, days (Exod. 12:2).

The doors were shut for fear of the Jews. John notes this detail to underscore the element of miracle in Jesus' entrance into the room. As he left the grave cloths and the tomb by a miracle, he entered this room in like manner. It was the same body in the sense that it belonged to no one else; but in another sense it was a different body; it was super-physical. But there is a deeper significance here. The door was shut to protect the disciples from "the Jews," i.e., from danger. They were on the defensive, immobilized. In this condition they were not ready to

evangelize the world. They needed to be released from this paralyzing fear before they could be useful. The commission and the bestowal of the Spirit were designed to correct this need. Correction finally came at Pentecost as subsequent events, reported in the Acts, indicate. Today a church primarily concerned with self-defense is of no use to the Kingdom; there needs to be the impartation of the Spirit in power to overcome this paralyzing fear of personal peril — "perfect love casteth out fear" (I John 4:18).

Jesus came and stood in the midst. True to his name Immanuel — "God with us" — Jesus was with his disciples again, to remain with them forever (cf. Isa. 7:14; 8:10; Matt. 1:23; Rev. 7:17; 21:3). What a joyous reunion this was is reflected in v. 20. The greeting given by Jesus was repeated in v. 21. The bestowal of "peace" was given first in the upper room (14:27). This was not a static peace, but inner calm and poise even in times of tumult. It may have sounded a bit unrealistic to the disciples, coming as it did in a situation of extreme danger and tension. But then it is when this kind of peace is most needed and hence most welcome. This dynamic kind of peace is suggested in the story of two artists commissioned to paint a portrait of "peace." One of them painted

5 Unpublished doctrinal dissertation at Northern Baptist Theological Seminary.  Cited in J. R. Mantey, *Was Peter a Pope?* (Chicago: Moody Press, 1949), p. 56.

24 But Thomas, one of the twelve, called Didymus, was not with them when Jesus came.

5:24, "He that heedeth my word, and believeth on him that sent me, hath eternal life, and cometh not into judgment"; I John 1:9, "If we confess our sins, he [Jesus] is faithful and just, and will forgive our sins and cleanse us from all unrighteousness." And there is no statement recorded in the N. T. that implies that any human being is authorized to function as a mediator between God and man. The apostle Paul has very explicitly stated this: "For there is one God, one mediator also between God and men, himself, the man Christ Jesus" (I Tim. 2:5). And Peter (Acts 10:43) has stated the same idea in different words: "To him all the prophets bear witness that every one who believes in him [Christ] receives forgiveness of sins through his name."

**24 Thomas . . . called Didymus was not with them when Jesus came.** Didymus (cf. 11:16; 21:2) was the Greek word for double or twin. He has been described as "the pessimist of the apostolic band" (JHB). Had he been present at that first appearance we would have been deprived of this interesting account of a hardheaded, skeptical believer, who stubbornly insisted on incontrovertible evidence of Jesus' resurrection.

a quiet pastoral scene in which all was at rest — no wind, no danger — a static peace and calm. The second artist pictured an oriole's nest suspended from a tree branch over a waterfall. The wind swayed the nest dangerously over the falls and occasionally spray would drench the fragile nest. But on the nest with its precious eggs sat the mother bird, calm and constant, in spite of the dangers. It was the second artist who received the prize for the imaginative portrayal of a dynamic peace.

### (b) Verification (v. 20)

**20 He showed them his hands and his side.** To assure them that they were not seeing an apparition or a ghost, Jesus offered verification by showing them the hands and the side which had been pierced. This is consistent with this author's concern to show two things: the fact that faith is grounded on tangible, factual, historical evidence; and, second, the truth that while physical evidence is good and necessary it is better not to be dependent upon it (v. 29). In I John 1:1-3 the basis for the author's own faith is said to be this verifiable evidence — "what we have seen, heard and touched." Throughout the Scriptures faith is of great importance, yet patience is always shown to those slow to believe, to those who need to be "shown"; and ample opportunity is given for faith to be verified. This is seen, for example, in the experience of Gideon and his fleece and with Thomas' demand for tangible evidence (Judg. 6:36-40; John 20:25-29). The verb for "showed" is *deiknyō*, meaning "to show, point out, present to sight, demonstrate, declare, prove" (John 2:18; 5:20; 10:32; 14:8, 9). The meaning "prove" is well illustrated by James 2:18; 3:13, as well as in this verse. Luke also records this detail and adds that "a spirit hath not flesh and bones, as ye behold me having" (24:39). This reference in Luke is the only N. T. evidence that the Master's feet also were pierced.

**The disciples therefore were glad, when they saw the Lord.** Jesus had predicted, "I will see you again and your heart shall rejoice" (16:22). The verb translated saw in *horaō*, the same verb that is used of Mary's joyous announcement, "I have seen the Lord" (v. 18), the disciples' announcement to Thomas (v. 25), and John's sudden intuition of truth in the tomb (v. 8). For them, as for John and Mary earlier, it marked the dawn of an Easter faith. In the fullest sense of the term, as it was later defined, they were now for the first time Christians. Later this became the "acid test" of a true Christian (Rom. 10:9).

### (2) *Their Commission* (vv. 21-23)

21 Jesus now reiterated their commission as *apostoloi*, as "sent ones." He had done so earlier when they were sent

25 The other disciples therefore said unto him, We have seen the Lord.   But he said unto them, Except I shall see in his hands the print of the nails, and put my finger into the print of the nails, and put my hand into his side, I will not believe.

26 And after eight days again his disciples were within, and Thomas with them. Jesus cometh, the doors being shut, and stood in the midst, and said, Peace be unto you.

---

**25 Except I shall see in his hands the print of the nails, and put my finger into the print of the nails, and put my hand into his side, I will not believe.** Apparently the disciples in reporting their having seen Jesus alive mentioned having seen both the print of the nails and also the opening in Jesus' side, which had been made by a spear. Thomas was adamant in his refusal to accept their testimony. He had to see these wounds before he would believe. A double negative occurs in Greek (*ou mē*) to emphasize Thomas' insistence upon adequate evidence. It is fortunate for all the generations of believers since Thomas' day that he refused to believe until he had absolute proof. Because he and the other disciples doubted Jesus'

resurrection until Jesus by his repeated appearances to them convinced them of it beyond the shadow of a doubt, we do not need to doubt. They doubted and were reluctant to believe until positive and overwhelming evidence convinced them. They lived in that generation when the resurrection event occurred and when evidence pro and con was available. They literally "staked their lives" on the reality of that fact, so much so that even when their witnessing to the resurrection meant imprisonment and death, for some of them, they never stopped believing and proclaiming it (cf. Acts 4:19).

**26 After eight days,** that is, on the next Sunday evening. (See discussion on 20:1 for data on worship on the Lord's Day.)

---

forth to preach (Luke 9:2; cf. 10:1). Later he said they were appointed to "go and bear fruit" (15:16). In his prayer he affirmed, "As thou didst send me into the world, even so sent I them into the world" (17:18). Now the commission is more formal and more final. Apparently the commission was given only to the ten apostles (cf. v. 24); this seems implied by the note that Thomas, "one of the twelve," was not present (JHB, II, 677). The formal bestowal of "peace" is preliminary to the formal commissioning. Obviously they cannot be good ambassadors for Christ unless they have his peace, the inner assurance that Christ is alive and that God's cause will triumph. Cabot and Dicks, in *The Art of Ministering to the Sick,* emphasize that a spiritual counselor does not always need to articulate his faith; if he possesses it, or rather, if it possesses him, it will be reflected in his countenance and utterances. Such an inward assurance, they add, is indispensable for effective witnessing and counseling.

**22 He breathed on them.** Perhaps the reference is to Genesis 2:7, "God breathed into his nostrils the breath of life." If so, the Evangelist probably is convinced that this marks the creative origin of the

Christian church. The connection between wind, breath, life, and spirit in both O. and N. T. is very intimate (cf. Job. 33:4; Ps. 33:6; Isa. 42:5; Wisd. 15:11; John 3:5-8). The inbreathing here is comparable to the impartation of new life at creation (Gen. 2:7) and the rebirth of the exiled nation of Israel (Ezek. 37: 5-10).

The problem of this passage is twofold. How can the apostles pardon sins when no one can forgive sin but God alone (Mark 2:7)? When Jesus forgave sins it was clearly implied that it would have been blasphemy had he not been the Son of God. The second problem is to relate this giving of the Holy Spirit here to the outpouring of the Spirit at Pentecost. Several suggestions have been made relative to the latter problem. The view that this gift of the Spirit was only a foretaste of the real gift of the Spirit at Pentecost was maintained by Theodore of Mopsuestia (fifth century). Others argue that it is intended to show that the Spirit proceeds from the Son as well as from the Father (Augustine, Lagrange). Others consider this a first installment as a preparation for the complete gift of the Spirit at Pentecost (Godet, Hoskyns). It is significant that this gift

27 Then saith he to Thomas, Reach hither thy finger, and see my hands; and reach *hither* thy hand, and put it into my side: and be not faithless, but believing.

28 Thomas answered and said unto him, My Lord and my God.

---

Once again, as on a previous occasion, it is said, **the doors being shut.** Possibly the appearance also was in the same room as a week before. So the setting was again as the disciples had described it to Thomas.

**27 Then saith he to Thomas . . . be not faithless but believing.** The very words Thomas had used were repeated back to him by Jesus! That Jesus knew what Thomas had said must have startled Thomas. Now he was invited to do what he said he must do before believing. The fact that the present imperative (*mē ginou apistos, alla pistos*) is used suggests that the translation should be: "Do not continue disbelieving but continue believing." *Pistos* also has the meaning of faithful, while *apistos* means faithless. As long as Thomas doubted the resurrection, he was faithless and hence useless as a witness.

**28 My Lord and my God** (*ho kyrios mou kai ho theos mou*). This is an impulsive exclamation of absolute faith in Christ both as Thomas' Lord and also as his God. All doubt is now gone. Instead he has attained to the highest heights of appreciation as to Jesus' deity. "There can be no doubt that John intended this confession of faith to form the climax of the gospel . . . ; it is his final Christological pronouncement" (C-KB., p. 477). "Thomas's sublime, instantaneous confession, won from doubt, closes historically the progress of faith

---

of the Spirit is preceded and followed by the commission given to the Apostles; therefore it must be linked not so much with their personal experience as with their official responsibility as God's representatives on earth. This places this verse in association with Matthew 16:19; 18:18; Galatians 1:8; I Corinthians 5:3, 7, 13 — texts that deal with the administering of discipline — rather than with Joel 2:28; Acts 1:8; 2:4; 8:17; 10:44; 19:9 — texts that deal with the general outpouring of the Spirit in the messianic age.

It follows that the commission to go under the influence of the Holy Spirit includes the responsibility of loosing or refusing to remit sin in those whom God has judged.[j]

This calls for spiritual discernment, comparable to the spirit in which one saint can rebuke another "in a spirit of meekness; considering thyself, lest thou also be tempted" (Gal. 6:1).[k] Is it not likely that this authority was discharged, in the case of Peter, by pronouncing judgment in the name of the Lord, upon

Ananias and Sapphira (Acts 5:3,9) or by Paul's thundering out the condemnation of Elymas the sorcerer (Acts 13:8), or the Elder's threatening with excommunication Diotrephes (III John 10)? On the other hand, apostolic authority to assure the penitent of God's grace of forgiveness is seen in Paul's word to the Philippian jailer (Acts 16:31), in the decision of the Jerusalem council — "it seemed good to the Holy Spirit and to us" — relative to the inclusiveness of the gospel (Acts 15:28), and in the acceptance of Lydia as a Christian (Acts 16:15). If this interpretation be correct, then the decision whether or not to forgive sin rests not with the apostles (or other clergymen) but with God; the ministers of God under the influence of the Spirit of God certify corporately and officially God's endorsement or the condemnation of the individual in accordance with the Spirit-illuminated Word of God. The tense usage apparently supports this interpretation (see exegesis). It is also supported in church practice: baptism officially certifies that in the judgment of God's

---

[j] According to the Council of Trent it is this verse which gives to Roman Catholic clergy the authority to forgive sin. Godet says, "The matter in question is nothing less than giving or refusing salvation to every human being; to open and close heaven — this is their task" (*op. cit.*, II, 422). This is the basis for the *pontifical prerogative* of excommunication which gave the church such power in the Middle Ages.

[k] For rabbinic parallels to absolution and condemnation see S-B, II, 584.

29 Jesus saith unto him, Because thou hast seen me, thou hast believed: blessed *are* they that have not seen, and *yet* have believed.

---

which St. John traces. At first (ch. 1:1) the Evangelist declared his own faith; at the end he shows that this faith was gained in the actual intercourse of the disciples with Christ. The record of this confession therefore forms the appropriate close to his narrative and the words which follow show that the Lord accepted the declaration of His Divinity as the true expression of faith" (BFW II, 355). Deity is attributed to Jesus in 1:1, 18; 5:18; 10:33.

29 **Because you have seen me, you have believed.** Since both Greek verbs are in the perfect tense the emphasis is upon the effects of seeing and believing. **Blessed** (*makarion*) is common in the Psalms and occurs nine times in the Beatitudes (Matt. 5:1-11). **Have not seen but** (*kai*) **believed.** The occurrence of two aorist participles here gives a contrast with the experience of Thomas. The successors in the faith of the apostles believe and continue believing in spite of never having seen the Lord. We do so on the basis of their testimony and due to the witness of what Christian friends have experienced and reported to us. The blessings of all eternity belong to them and us.[6] Peter (I Pet. 1:8) seems to have given us an interpretation of the significance of this passage: "You must continue to love him, although you do not now see him, you

---

representative the candidate has experienced the transforming grace of God. Or the offending member who has broken his covenant with the Lord is judged by the proper authorities in the church and disciplined by exclusion from membership (Matt. 18:16-18). Contrary to Godet (*op. cit.,* II, 422) this exclusion or inclusion is not made by the minister: rather, he acts in the role of a prophet or priest, in announcing or pronouncing God's judgment or his grace. In this passage the judgment is pronounced "in the Spirit" and corporately, not by personal caprice.

### 2. THE FIRST WEEK (vv. 24-31)

#### a. Thomas' Demand for Tangible Evidence (vv. 24, 25)

Thomas is probably presented by our author as representative of those who will never have the opportunity to see, touch, or hear at first hand (cf. I John 1:1, 2) Jesus' resurrection body. The emphasis is here placed on the historicity of the event, its veritability. Thomas was in danger of becoming an unbeliever, of forfeiting his discipleship. The solicitude of the Lord is apparent in taking particular pains to provide Thomas with the demanded evidence. It indicates the patience of the Lord in bearing with those who are "slow of heart to believe." Thomas is usually characterized with some admiration as the "honest doubter."[1] He is here presented not as an ideal, or as an exemplary individual; rather, he is a type of those who live on a lower level and demand physical tests. He remained "in the kingdom," but under less than ideal grounds.

#### b. Jesus Appears to the Disciples with Thomas (vv. 26-29)

26 **After eight days** is generally taken to mean one week after the preceding appearance of Jesus on Easter evening. During these eight days the disciples apparently remained together in retirement and did little else. Perhaps they lived in daily or hourly expectation of Jesus' return. Ideally, Christians now should live in a state of expectancy as servants watch for their master (Mark 13:33-37) and their hourly prayer should be, "Come quickly, Lord Jesus" (Rev. 22:20).

**Jesus . . . stood in the midst.** Once again Jesus appeared in the room without entering the door. For the third time in eight days his greeting was, "Peace." Directing his attention to Thomas, Jesus asked him in dramatic language to put his fingers to the nail prints in his palms and thrust his hand into the large hole in his side

---

[6] The perfect tenses refer to Thomas' being in a condition resulting from having seen and consequently of having believed. The aorists quite logically refer merely to the *fact* of seeing and believing by others (in the future).

[1] Cf. Tennyson, *In Memoriam.*

30 Many other signs therefore did Jesus in the presence of the disciples, which are not written in this book:

31 but these are written, that ye may believe that Jesus is the Christ, the Son of God; and that believing ye may have life in his name.

---

must continue to rejoice with an unutterable and triumphant joy" (Williams trans.).

30, 31 *Oun* (therefore) is used in an explanatory sense here and can be rendered "now." John makes clear that his account has been selective of the numerous teachings and deeds of his Lord. *Sēmeia* (signs) in general usage meant distinguishing and convincing evidence. Thus quite logically in this Gospel the word denotes chiefly miracles that furnished positive proof of Jesus' deity. *Tauta de gegraptai* (but these have been written), perfect tense — "written and now stand recorded." And what an unequaled record it is! It is the acme of all that is spiritually enlightening and fascinating. It certainly is nowhere surpassed and as a gospel it is without peer and unique. **That you may believe** (pres. subj.) **that Jesus is the Christ the Son of God.** John's theological and evangelistic purpose in writing is thus stated. The use of the Greek present tense suggests coming to believe in Christ and then continuing to believe in him. The aorist tense, found in many manuscripts, would place emphasis either upon "coming to believe" or upon one's whole faith considered as a complete unit. "The man named Jesus is identical with the Messiah

---

where the spear had penetrated. In effect Jesus was saying, "You insisted on first-hand, tangible evidence; here it is." Thomas did not need to go this far. The visual evidence was sufficient. There is a mild rebuke implicit in the Master's invitation, a rebuke that Thomas' faith was so weak as to require this type of additional evidence. But he was not speaking to Thomas alone but also for other recipients of the gospel message who would have far more justification for skepticism than Thomas.

So great was the factor of vision as compared with other sensory experiences that Jesus speaks of "seeing" by a touch of the finger — "Reach hither thy finger, and see (*idē*, from *horaō*) my hands" (v. 27). Again, as so frequently in the Gospels, the emphasis is upon belief. This kind of belief is not an uncritical, easy credulity; it is a conviction growing out of experience, out of confrontation with the facts of life. Because Thomas was capable of doubt, his faith was something discriminating and positive. Because it had come with difficulty, it would be the more convincing in witnessing to other skeptics.

**28 My Lord and my God.** This is the climactic expression of faith in this Gospel. The last of the apostles to become convinced voiced his primitive creed. The first articulated "creed" was that which marked Nathaniel's conversion: "Rabbi thou art the Son of God, thou art the king of Israel" (1:49). The last one in this Gospel is even more unqualified, more Christian; it has a higher Christology. Deissmann observes that the combination of "Lord and God" was often heard in the worship of Caesar. Its use here may reflect a defiance of that cult and the determination to make it clear that Jesus alone is both "Lord and God."[m] It may have been influenced by Psalm 85:15; 88:1. The emperor Domitian, who reigned during the last decade of the first century when this Gospel was probably composed, was the first to apply this title to the cult of emperor worship. One can easily imagine the "whole chain of sensations of contrast and protest" which the average person would experience when Christians would use this of someone other than Caesar. One can also imagine the courage which such an affirmation called for when Christians affirmed it exclusively of Jesus. Perhaps the nearest parallel to this in modern times was in Japan from 1930 until 1945. The Christians then living in Japan experienced much of the same tension of living in two worlds and under two rulers as Christians, who wit-

---

m A. Deissmann, *op. cit.*, p. 361.

the Anointed One) as opposed to the Cerinthian separation of the Jesus of history and the Christ (*aeon*) of theology. The Docetic notion of a phantom body or Jesus with no actual human body (refuted in I John) is also proven false: Jesus is the Son of God with all that this high term implies, the Logos of John 1:1-18" (ATR V, 317). *Hina pisteuontes* ("in order that by believing") instrumental

use of the present participle. Again the use of the present tense denotes continuance in believing, not just an initial or merely temporary faith.[7] *Echēte* — you may continue having (pres. subj.). *Zōēn* (life) as used here and frequently in this Gospel denotes God's pardon, peace, presence, power, and eternal favor and can be obtained only by accepting Christ as Savior (cf. John 10:10; 14:6; 17:3).

---

blessed amid the cult of the Caesars, experienced.[n]

29 A special blessing is promised to those who **have not seen and yet have** believed. This is consistent with the closing verses of the Lord's intercessory prayer. The verbs for seeing here are also from *horaō* and indicate physical vision. Here also believing is set in contrast to seeing — not believing because of having seen, as in 1:39, 46-51; 14:9; 20:8, 20, but believing in spite of not having seen with physical eyes. The perfect tense here connotes the present state of Thomas' belief, i.e., "Because thou hast seen me thou art now in a believing condition."

A character study of Thomas may be drawn on the basis of John's portrayal. The importance of Thomas in the early church may be gathered from the literature which bears his name (the Acts of Thomas and the Apocalypse of Thomas) and by the tradition of his mission to India.[o] That Thomas had the quality of phlegmatic courage is seen in his resolution to die with Jesus in Jerusalem (11:16). His willingness to be shown and his need for demonstration are reflected in his rather irritated remonstrance — "Lord, we know not whither thou goest; how can we know the way?" (14:5). This demand for demonstration is stated more emphatically here. However, once the evidence was produced, his faith was asserted quickly and emphatically. He serves here to encourage second-generation believers in

much the same way that proselytes to the Jewish faith were encouraged by the thought that because they lacked opportunities enjoyed by the Jews their faith was all the more valuable (CKB, p. 478).

### c. The Author's Summary of Purpose (vv. 30, 31)

In this brief summary of his book the author states his editorial policy and purpose. His policy is to be selective in the use of materials. His purpose is not to present a full biography of Jesus but rather to choose from among the many words and deeds available to the historian those which would be conducive to belief in Jesus as the Messiah of the Jews and the Son of God for all men. This belief in Jesus as the Christ is a means to an end. The end is life. The reader may have this eternal divine life by giving credence to what is herein written. That is the first step. The second is to believe and appropriate the life of Jesus Christ, thereby finding real life. The author's concern throughout this Gospel is with *life*. This conviction is in harmony with Paul's conviction and strategy — "Belief cometh by hearing, and hearing by the word of Christ" (Rom. 10:17). Mary A. Lathbury caught the point and sang,

*Beyond the sacred page I seek Thee, Lord,*
*My spirit pants for Thee, oh living Word."*[p]

---

[7] This verse constitutes a fitting close for this wonderful book, and John may at first have intended to stop here. But before he published the work he added the Epilogue (chapter 21), which is written in the same style and gives a beautiful picture of the risen Christ with a sidelight on John and Peter (restored to fellowship). (Cf. WPNT, V, 317.)
[n] John Young, *The Two Empires in Japan* (Tokyo: Bible Times Press, 1959), pp. 93-121.
[o] Thomas is called the brother of Jesus in the Acts of Thomas, M. R. James, *op. cit.*, p. 369.
[p] *Hymns of the Living Faith*, p. 182.

# CHAPTER XXI

After these things Jesus manifested himself again to the disciples at the sea of Tiberias; and he manifested *himself* on this wise.

---

## EXEGESIS

The weight of evidence seems to favor the idea that this chapter was added some time after the previous chapters were written. The concluding verses of ch. 20 are strongly indicative of that. However, no long interval apparently existed before the "Epilogue" (ch. 21) was added, since there is no trace anywhere in the ancient manuscripts of a copy of this Gospel without ch. 21.

As to whether the apostle John wrote the chapter there is a difference of opinion, especially on vv. 24 and 25. Bultmann argues against Johannine authorship of the chapter as does C. K. Barrett: "It is difficult to think that an author would wish to spoil the effect of the apostolic mission charge of 20:21-23 by representing the disciples in a later narrative, as having returned to their former avoca-

tion and as unable at first to recognize the Lord when he appeared" (CKB, pp. 479f.).

These reasons for rejecting the Johannine authorship, however, are not decisive. John did not in chs. 1-20 represent the disciples as above weaknesses, nor does he in ch. 21. He also pictured Mary Magdalene as unable to recognize Jesus at first in his appearance to her, even though they were within a few feet from one another, whereas the fishermen were about a hundred yards, "two hundred cubits," from Jesus when he began talking with them. Besides, it was at daybreak (v. 4), when sight was impaired to a certain extent by a measure of darkness. Luke also represents the disciples as unable to recognize their risen Lord either by appearance or by voice (Luke 24:16-31).

---

## EXPOSITION

### B. Jesus' Appearance in Galilee (21:1-19)

#### 1. fishing (vv. 1-8)

##### a. The Night of Failure (vv. 1-3)

In one sense this chapter is anticlimactic. Ch. 20 ends with an emphasis on the blessedness of those who believe on the basis of the testimony of the apostles. It stresses the relationship between the book and belief and life. This chapter is concerned particularly with Peter and secondarily with John, with the other disciples in the background. However, in this chapter are some inspirational, provocative thoughts with insights of a practical nature. It is appropriately called an appendix. Perhaps it was written by the author and added by request of the elders of Ephesus (cf. 21:24, 25).

According to the Synoptic accounts, Jesus had an appointment with his disciples in Galilee in the interval between the resurrection and the ascension (Matt. 28: 7, 10, 16-20; Mark 16:7). Matthew alone reports a reunion on a mountain in Galilee; John alone reports the meeting on the Sea of Galilee. John's designation for this Galilean lake is Tiberias (cf. 6:1). The name was taken from the city of that name on the south-eastern shore, the only shoreline city that survives until the present day. This scene was probably located near Peter's home town of Capernaum. According to an ancient tradition it occurred southwest of Capernaum at el Tabghah, where there is a rock platform forty-five feet in length that leads down to the shore. It is called *mensa Domini* (the Lord's table), from the belief that the cooked fish were placed upon it.[a] The return to the fishing boats

[a] E. Kraeling, *op. cit.,* p. 410.

402

2 There were together Simon Peter, and Thomas called Didymus, and Nathanael of Cana in Galilee, and the *sons* of Zebedee, and two other disciples.

3 Simon Peter saith unto them, I go a fishing. They say unto him, We also come with thee. They went forth, and entered into the boat; and that night they took nothing.

---

Westcott argues for the unity of this Gospel: "It is equally clear that XXI:1-23 was written by the author of the Gospel" (BFW II, 359). Marcus Dods concludes: "There is no reason why this chapter should be ascribed to a different hand. The style is the same as that of the gospel, and although the gospel closed at the end of chapter 20, this supplementary chapter must have become an integral part of the gospel at a very early period. No trace exists of a gospel without it" (EGT, I, 867).

**Manifested himself** (*ephanerōsen heauton*). This Greek verb (aorist here) occurs several times in this Gospel (1:31; 2:11; 3:21; 7:4; 9:3; 17:6). In Mark 16:12, 14 and here only is it found to depict a resurrection appearance. John is unique in reporting appearances both in

Jerusalem and also in Galilee. Matthew mentions only those in Galilee and Luke only those in and near Jerusalem.

2 John has more to say about **Thomas** than does any other writer. He alone mentions **Nathanael** (cf. 1:45-49) and here mentions Nathanael's home town, a hint that this chapter is by the same author as the other. This is the only reference in John to **the sons of Zebedee,** of whom John was one. Perhaps modesty inhibited John from giving their names, since he was one of them.

3 **Simon Peter saith unto them, I go a fishing** (*hypagō halieuein*). The fact that we have a present infinitive of purpose here for "fishing" makes this statement rather significant, because the present tense in Greek regularly denotes action in progress. Had the aorist tense oc-

---

of their parents would not seem unusual to these young men. The fact that only seven are here and the fact that they decided to fish suggests some uncertainty and perhaps demoralization on their part. However, it is significant that Jesus refrained from any word of condemnation. In this account, Peter is still the leader of the group.

The night of fruitless effort is similar to the experience reported by Luke (5:1-11). On that occasion, at the beginning of Jesus' ministry, they obeyed Jesus by letting down their nets after a mild remonstrance by Peter, "We have toiled all night and took nothing!" (RSV). The reaction to the large catch of fish was similar in both cases. Peter shrank from the Lord's presence because of a consciousness of sin, which was prompted by the recognition of God's presence and power in the miracle.

Several inferences may be drawn from this night of fishing.

(i) They found that efforts under human leadership alone are unavailing. There was no lack of competent leadership; they had that in Peter. There was no lack of

experience; many, if not all, were veteran professional fisherman. The circumstances were naturally conducive to success; they fished in a good place at a good time. But they failed.

(ii) Sometimes our defeats open the way to greater victories, which otherwise would have been forfeited. Their failure helped them realize their inadequacy apart from Christ. They were between two worlds: the past which had been shattered and the future still unknown. Their plight reminds one of a great poet's wistfulness as he longs for a faith which once sustained but now eludes him.

> *Wandering between two worlds, one dead,*
> *The other powerless to be born,*
> *With nowhere yet to rest my head,*
> *Like these on earth, I wait forlorn.*
> *Their faith, my tears, the world deride —*
> *I come to shed them at your side.*[b]

Years after these seven disciples were "wandering between two worlds" Matthew Arnold stood on the English channel at night and looked across towards

---

b Matthew Arnold, in "Stanzas from the Grand Chartreuse," cited in J. D. Robertson, *op. cit.,* p. 56.

4 But when day was now breaking, Jesus stood on the beach: yet the disciples knew not that it was Jesus.

5 Jesus therefore saith unto them, Children, have ye aught to eat? They answered him, No.

---

curred here, the implication could have been that only one fishing trip had been in mind. The present tense may mean that Peter was thinking of returning to his former occupation of fishing. If so, this would be a grave situation — not only would he be abandoning the life-work to which Jesus had called him, but also encouraging six others, by his example, to do likewise. Despair over his denial and many other mistakes may have possessed him. Also the fact that Jesus took Peter aside (21:15-19) and probed him drastically as to his love and loyalty may indicate a waning of loyalty on Peter's part. However, John may have had in mind, in his use of the present infinitive (halieuein), only the action involved during the hours of the one night of fishing. It is difficult to conclude that, after Jesus' personal resurrection appearance to him, Peter would so quickly abandon the cause to which Christ had called

him. It certainly was natural for these former fishermen, while they were waiting for Jesus' promised appearance, to enjoy themselves while fishing, and also earn some money for their families by the sale of fish. But they took (epiasan, firs aor. active — "caught") nothing. This verb was used for catching fish and the like.[1] Aristotle stated a generally recognized fact, true now as well as then: "Fishermen, especially, do their fishing before sunrise and after sunset."[2] This is still the custom of commercial fishermen who fish in the Sea of Galilee.

4 But when day was now breaking (prōias ēdē ginomenēs, gen. absolute — "when dawn was coming") — "dawn coming on and still dark" (WPNT, V, 319).

5 Paidia (children), diminutive of pais (child), but used as a term of endearment by Jesus here (cf. I John 2:12, 18, where it is also used of the disciples). Its use argues for the Johannine authorship

---

France. It seemed that to him and to his countrymen as well the faith of the fathers was no longer possible. Said he,

The Sea of Faith
Was once, too, at the full, and round earth's shore
Lay like the folds of a bright girdle furl'd.
But now I only hear
Its melancholy, long withdrawing roar. . . [c]

(iii) The night was a long one. No doubt what had once challenged and satisfied them now seemed empty and meaningless. After they had caught a glimpse of a new life the old seemed less satisfying than before. Their former way of life seemed now to close its door to them.

(iv) The old-time security they had known, of home, toil, nourishment, sleep, and routine, now eluded them — "they

took nothing." They had yet fully to realize the new security of abiding in Christ, within the will of God. The security of faith, known to their ancestor Abraham, was not yet theirs. Their "rest of faith" was not to come until the day of Pentecost.

b. The Morning of Success (vv. 4-8)

There is something appropriate about Jesus revealing himself at dawn. The rising sun and the flooding light coincided with the self-revelation of the "Sun of Righteousness" (Mal. 4:2) and in the splendor of that revelation the disciples found the promised "healing." It was consistent with the earlier chapters also that the "beloved disciple" would be the first to recognize through the morning mist their risen Lord. It is consistent with the other stories also that this disciple and

---

[1] P. Lond, II, 328, 76.

[2] Hist. Animal, VIII, 19.

[c] Matthew Arnold, "Dover Beach," edited by J. W. Bowyer & J. L. Brooks, The Victorian Age (New York: Appleton-Century-Crofts, 1938), p. 493.

6 And he said unto them, Cast the net on the right side of the boat, and ye shall find. They cast therefore, and now they were not able to draw it for the multitude of fishes.

7 That disciple therefore whom Jesus loved saith unto Peter, It is the Lord. So when Simon Peter heard that it was the Lord, he girt his coat about him (for he was naked), and cast himself into the sea.

---

of these verses. It is a colloquial expression like "my boys." **Have ye anything to eat?** (*mē ti prosphagion echete,* or "You do not have anything to eat, do you?") The use of the negative *mē* here, as in 4:29 and elsewhere in questions, anticipates a negative answer, that is, he correctly expected them to reply, "No, we do not" (D-M, 265). *Prosphagion,* from the aorist tense root *phag* - ("to eat") with the prepositional prefix *pros* ("for") occurs only here in the N. T., but it also occurs in the papyri for "food." The disciples reply simply and frankly, "No."

**6 Cast the net on the right side** (*balete eis to dexia merē to diktyon*). An idiomatic nautical rendering of this in the *New English Bible* is: "Shoot the net to starboard, and you will make a catch." Note that the suggestion was definite and specific: on the right (*dexia*) side. They obeyed and were not able to lift the net aboard due to the weight of the fish, or "for the quantity of fish" (RSV). *Apo* ("for") is used here with causal force, or denoting the *source* of the difficulty, as it is also in Hebrews 5:7, Acts 28:3, and elsewhere in first-century Greek writings.

**7 The disciple whom Jesus loved** (see on 13:23). **It is the Lord.** As at the tomb, so here, John was correct in his insight. None but Christ had such knowledge and power. It took fishermen, who had toiled all night without success, to appreciate this miracle. "Peter slipped on

---

Peter were in close association, so close that this disciple could whisper his insight to Peter. The reaction of Peter is also consistent with what we know about him elsewhere, a man of quick decisions and prompt, often impetuous, action.

John's recognition of the figure on the beach as "the Lord" probably was associated with the miraculous catch of fish. The element of miracle lies in the timing — immediately after the command to try again. Also it was now daybreak when the fish usually go to deeper water. In addition, there is reason to believe that the best fishing was on the opposite side of the lake, probably where they had worked during the night. It was probably the catch of fish, as much as the appearance of Jesus, which led John to conclude that the Lord was there on the shore. He reasoned from effect to cause. Nothing less than the presence of Christ could account for such a draft of fish. They may have recalled other instances in which Jesus had demonstrated complete control of nature, including the time he stilled a storm at night (Mark 4:37-41), and the time when he joined them at the height of a storm (John 6:19-21) bringing calm. They may have recalled the other enormous catch of fish under similar circumstances (Luke 5:5-9). Peter clutched his cloak and plunged into the sea. Whether this reflected a sense of guilt when in the presence of his risen Lord is not clear. Some think it was to get to the Lord sooner.[d] It does not appear, however, that Peter rushed directly to Jesus. He drew the net to land (v. 11) and after that there seemed to be no ready rapport with the Lord; instead, "none of the disciples durst inquire him, Who art thou?" (v. 12). Others link this with the rabbinic aversion to nakedness (CKB, p. 483); the rabbis forbade salutations in the bath (in marked contrast to Japanese, and Roman, custom).

To others the central idea is the haste of Peter's departure; hence, he was not naked but simply fashioned a belt around his jacket and leaped overboard.[e] Apparently he donned his jacket (cf. *ependytēs* — I Sam. 18:4, LXX), fastened his belt, and leaped into the shallow water. The boat was approximately ninety-six meters (about a hundred yards) from shore (Bultmann, *op. cit.*, p. 548).

d J. Wesley, *op. cit.*, p. 388.
e Lenski, *op. cit.*, p. 1407. This is refuted by John's statement, "he was naked."

8 But the other disciples came in the little boat (for they were not far from the land, but about two hundred cubits off), dragging the net *full* of fishes.

---

his clothes, for he had been naked, and plunged into the sea" (Phillips). Because he had been handling a wet net it was not unusual for Peter to be naked, at least nearly so. His clothes, before he jumped into the water, may have been about the equivalent of a loin cloth. More than that would have hampered his swimming and also impeded getting his clothes dry after reaching shore. In several other instances "naked" apparently means a minimum of clothes rather than complete nudity (cf. 13:4; Isa. 20:2; Micah 1:8,

11). Because of low elevation, it is hot in this region in springtime. Three verbs here in the aorist tense describe Peter's rapid and impulsive reactions.

8 *Ploiarion* (little boat) is used synonymously with *ploion* (boat, v. 3) here and in John 6:24. **Dragging the net full of fish.** There was far less likelihood of breaking the net by dragging it ashore than there was in lifting it into the boat. A cubit was about eighteen inches, so they moved the net about a hundred yards (cf. 11:18 for a similar use of *apo*).

---

Meanwhile the other disciples approached on the other boat, bringing the net full of fish into the shallow water. Apparently the net was too full of fish to permit emptying the fish into the boat. They had tried that once before (Luke 5:7) and the boat(s) had become so laden that they began to sink. This time, rather than risk the boat's shipping water by reason of being overloaded, they dragged the net toward the shoreline where they could more easily and safely dispose of the 153 fish they had caught. There would be at least four hundred pounds of fish.

### 2. THE THIRD APPEARANCE (AT BREAKFAST) (vv. 9-14)

When they got to the beach they saw Jesus had breakfast already prepared for them. On a fire of driftwood perhaps, which had now become hot embers, fish were cooking.[f] The aroma must have been pleasant to the hungry men. But these details were completely overshadowed by the realization that their Lord was here in person. Once again, as at the Last Supper, he was in the role of a servant.

11 The exact number of the fish is noted. Some interpret this as reflecting the vivid memory of a participant, i.e., the apostle John.[g] Jerome suggested that this number corresponds to the 153 different species of fish and hence symbolizes

the completeness with which the apostles are to evangelize the world (WFH, VIII, 805). Origen thought it symbolized the Trinity (50 times 3 plus 3), Cyril of Alexandria saw in this number 100 pagans, 50 Jews and the Trinity! Augustine and Gregory I found the O. T. (Decalogue) and the N. T. (Isa. 11:2) combined in the number 17, which, when multiplied by 3 times 3, gives 153 (BFW, II, 376). Hoskyns and Davey find that the only satisfactory explanation lies in the mathematical phenomena that 153 is "the sum of the first 17 of the natural numbers: 1, 2, 3, . . . 17 = 153, therefore 153 dots can be arranged in the form of an equilateral triangle . . . with 17 dots on the base line" (*op. cit.*, p. 553), thus symbolizing "a perfect and unique catch of fish" (p. 556).[h] But even the Evangelist, as concerned as he was with symbolism, would probably find such interpretations astonishing; rather, he apparently recorded a remembered detail consistent with his habit elsewhere (e.g., 1:39; 4:6; 6:7; 12:1; 2:11; 4:54; 21:14). The net may signify the church which includes those of all nations.[i]

12 The RSV and NEB rendering, "Come and have breakfast," is a good contemporary translation rather than merely a colloquialism.[j] The words of the gospel song, "Come and Dine," are perhaps a conflation of the invitation of this text and that of Luke 14:17-24 (cf. John

---

[f] Cf. John 18:18, RSV, "charcoal." "Biblical references are not to mineral coal but to charcoal" (W. G. Williams, "Coal," IDB, I, 655).
[g] CGT, p. 351. Cf. John 2:6; 6:9-13, for similar numerical details.
[h] So also R. M. Grant, "One Hundred Fifty-Three Large Fish," HTR (Oct., 1949), pp. 273f.
[i] Barclay, *op. cit.*, II, 331.
[j] Cf. Krister Stendahl, "Distance and Proximity," *Harvard Divinity School Bulletin* (Oct., 1962), p. 30.

9 So when they got out upon the land, they see a fire of coals there, and fish laid thereon, and bread.

10 Jesus saith unto them, Bring of the fish which ye have now taken.

11 Simon Peter therefore went up, and drew the net to land, full of great fishes, a hundred and fifty and three: and for all there were so many, the net was not rent.

12 Jesus saith unto them, Come *and* break your fast. And none of the disciples durst inquire of him, Who art thou? knowing that it was the Lord.

---

9 *Oun* ("so") here means "now." They saw (*blepousin,* historical present) a fire of coals (*anthrakion*) or burning charcoal. "Anthracite" is derived from this word. And fish laid thereon (*opsarion* here means cooked fish; it appears in 6:9; 21:9, 10 and nowhere else in the N. T.) "broiling with bread ready (toast)" (WPNT, V, 320).

10 Christ enlisted their co-operation in preparing the breakfast by asking them to bring (*enengkate,* aor. imperative) some of the fish (*opsarion*) they had just caught. The other word for fish (*ichthys*) is synonymous (cf. Luke 24:42).

11 Peter . . . drew the net to land. It was left in the water so the fish would stay alive. Full of large fish (*ichthyōn megalōn*), one hundred and fifty three. Perhaps this was the largest catch they had ever caught at one dipping of the net. The net was not rent (*eschisthē,* aor. passive — "torn"). One reason for that was the careful handling of the net by bringing it to the beach. Our words "schism" and "schizophrenia" are derived from this verb, *schizein,* meaning "to cleave, or to split."

12 *Deute aristēsate* (aor. active imperative), that is, "Come, have breakfast." "What a delightful breakfast of fresh broiled fish just caught (v. 10) with the hush of joyful surprise in the presence of the risen Lord" (ATR, V, 320). How hungry they must have been, too, after a night of failure and frustration! None

---

2:8; 6:11; Luke 11:37). The word for "have breakfast" occurs only three times in the New Testament.

The reluctance of the disciples to inquire about Jesus' identity recalls a similar reticence when they returned to find him talking with the woman of Samaria (4: 27). It may be explained as due to their awed recognition of him together with uncertainty as to how he had come, where he was going, and the like. They were not yet in sufficient rapport with him to converse freely; as at Sychar they had questions which they dared not voice. They "knew" (from *oida*) it was the Lord; the kinship of this verb with *horaō* ("to see") has been discussed earlier (exposition of 20:8). What they *saw* led to what they now *knew*.

13 Jesus cometh and . . . giveth them bread and fish. The scene must have reminded them of the feeding of the multitude in Galilee when Jesus gave bread and fish to the multitude (6:11). In primitive Christian art, fish were sometimes pictured in the Eucharist instead of wine. But there is no other evidence that the substitution of the fish was ever actually practiced (Hoskyns, p. 556). The purpose of this account is apparently to underscore the reality of Jesus' human nature. This purpose is explicit and clear in Luke 24:39-43 where Jesus showed them his hands and feet, ate some food (fish), and said, "A spirit hath not flesh and bones, as ye behold me having." This author is even more concerned to prove Jesus' real humanity. Evidence sometimes presented to prove that the Jesus of the Fourth Gospel is never more than a phantom is not convincing.[k] On the contrary, this author states elsewhere, "Every spirit which confesseth not that Jesus Christ is come in the flesh is not of God" and "many deceivers are entered into the world, who confess not that Jesus Christ is come in the flesh" (I John 4:3; II John 7, KJV; cf. RSV). Thus, both Gospel and Epistles reflect a strong concern to refute the heresy of Docetism by stressing that Jesus was truly man as well as truly God, even after the resurrection. While the Evangelist does stress the deity of Christ he does so without jeopardizing a recognition of his humanity. That these two emphases may be maintained simul-

[k] E.g., Guy M. Davis Jr., "The Humanity of Jesus in John," *Journal of Biblical Literature,* LXX (June, 1951), pp. 105f.

13 Jesus cometh, and taketh the bread, and giveth them, and the fish likewise.

14 This is now the third time that Jesus was manifested to the disciples, after that he was risen from the dead.

---

. . . **durst** (*etolma,* imperfect indicative, "was daring") **inquire of him, Who art thou? knowing that it was the Lord.** The participle expresses cause: "because they knew it was the Lord." To them "seeing is believing." It was Jesus and they knew it.

13 "Jesus went and took the bread and gave it to them and gave them all fish as well" (Phillips). Not only had the Lord cooked the food, but he also even served it. This is somewhat comparable to his washing the disciples' feet (13:5). It was another never-to-be-forgotten hour in their lives.

14 . . . **the third time that Jesus was manifested to the disciples.** Evidently the appearances in mind were those to groups of disciples, and not those to individuals. John previously had mentioned three appearances, one of which was to Mary Magdalene (20:11ff.). This enumeration is a characteristically Johannine touch (cf. 4:54).

The portrayal of this encounter of Peter with Christ is graphic and challenging. In the scene at Caesarea Philippi (Matt. 16:16-19) Peter rose to great heights in confessing his faith in Jesus as the Son of God. Here again he gives expression to

---

taneously is demonstrated in the Epistle to the Hebrews (e.g., 1:3; 8:1; cf. 2:10; 5:8). If Jesus' humanity is not stressed, men often resort to other mediators, such as the Virgin Mary or other saints. If Jesus' deity is not stressed he is apt to be regarded as a "young and fearless prophet" but little more. By serving the disciples on the beach, Jesus was making another effort to reassure them by demonstration that he was the same Jesus they had known before the crucifixion.

14 **This was now the third time.** The Evangelist enumerates only appearances to the apostles (20:19, 26) and does not include the appearance to Mary Magdalene or the other women. His listing of these is consistent with his enumeration of "signs" (4:54). This continuity in numbering hints at a common authorship in chs. 20 and 21.

3. JESUS' INTERVIEW WITH PETER (vv. 15-23)

a. Questions Addressed to Peter by Jesus (vv. 15-19)

The repetitions in this paragraph include the question about love and the command to take care of the sheep. The Vulgate uses the word for "lamb" in vv. 15 and 16 and the word for "sheep" in v. 17. The Greek (Nestle) uses the word for "lambs" (*arnia*) in v. 15 and for

"sheep" (*probatia*) in vv. 16, 17 as do the KJV, ASV, RSV and NEB versions.[1] The Vulgate and KJV use the verb for "feed" three times. The Greek, supported by ASV, RSV and NEB, indicates a different verb in v. 16; it is *poimaine* and in these modern versions is translated **tend** (or "to herd, lead to pasture, shepherd, nurture" (A-G). The "feed" (*boske*) of vv. 15, 17 means "to supply with food" (Matt. 8:30, 33). "There is a climax" . . . "feeding the sheep is the most difficult of all" (EGT, 354). The familiar metaphor of sheep and shepherd is the same as that employed so effectively in ch. 10 in addition to numerous other places in both O. and N. T. When these fishermen were first invited to follow Jesus they were promised help in catching men instead of fish. Now they are being called to be shepherds of men's souls. The fishermen may not have appreciated the hint of a "demotion" from commercial fishermen to shepherds. As fishermen they would be comparable to evangelists seeking the lost; as shepherds they would be comparable to pastors and teachers, nourishing the converts. In the earlier analogy Jesus was the shepherd and they the sheep. In this one the "sheep" become the shepherds, serving under the "chief shepherd" (I Pet. 5:4). The relationship of the chief shepherd (*archipoimenos*) to the undershepherds is illus-

---

1 Some inferior texts use "sheep" (*probata*) in each of the three verses (see JHB, II, 706).

15 So when they had broken their fast, Jesus saith to Simon Peter, Simon, *son* of John, lovest thou me more than these? He saith unto him, Yea, Lord; thou knowest that I love thee. He saith unto them, Feed my lambs.

16 He saith to him again a second time, Simon, *son* of John, lovest thou me? He saith unto him, Yea, Lord; thou knowest that I love thee. He saith unto him, Tend my sheep.

17 He saith unto him the third time, Simon, *son* of John, lovest thou me? Peter was grieved because he said unto him the third time, Lovest thou me? And he said unto him, Lord, thou knowest all things; thou knowest that I love thee. Jesus saith unto him, Feed my sheep.

---

the depths of his personal love for the Savior.

Two previous experiences of Peter need to be remembered as one begins to interpret this paragraph: (1) Peter's triple denial of Christ just after his arrest and (2) the fact that Peter had just now been fishing.

**15-17 Simon . . . lovest thou** (*agapas*) **me more than these** (*pleon toutōn*)? There are three possible interpretations of "more than these": (1) Do you love me more than you love these disciples? (2) Do you love me more than these disciples love me? (3) Do you love me more than you love this boat, net, and the occupation of fishing? If Peter was being tempted to give up being an apostle and return to his fishing, then the third viewpoint best fits the context. If he was not thus tempted, the first is a reasonable interpretation. Jesus had demanded of his disciples a love for himself beyond that of love even for their kinfolk (Matt. 10:37). In response to Christ's question, "Do you love me. . .?" Peter responded, Yea, Lord; **thou knowest that I love** (*philo*) you. He did not say that he loved Christ more than others, nor more than his former occupation but, rather, he simply affirmed his love for Christ. However, he used a different word for "love" than did Jesus; he used this same word in answer to the next two questions as well. Jesus in the third ques-

---

trated by the relationship between Laban and Jacob (Gen. 29:31), Nabal and his shepherds (I Sam. 25), Absalom and his servants (II Sam. 13:23-29), the apostle and Christian pastors (I Pet. 5:1-4).

We only conjecture why Jesus dealt thus with Peter. Did he single him out because he was the leader of the seven and what was taught Peter was intended for them all? Or did he concentrate on Peter because of his recent lapse? Those who believe the latter point out that Peter's threefold denial is now matched by a threefold affirmation of loyalty and love, something quite appropriate, to say the least. The incident is reported nowhere else in the N. T. The tenderness of the Master's approach is conveyed in the initial address as "children" (v. 5), in the reference to "lambs" (v. 15), and in the prediction of Peter's end (v. 18). Trench notes the use of the two synonyms for "love" in this passage and their rendition in the Vulgate as "*diligo*" (*agapaō*) and "*amo*" (*phileo*) and regrets the obscuring of this distinction in most English translations. The apostle, eager to express his ardent love for Christ, does not answer with the more formal *agapaō* but with the more personal *phileo*.[m] This he does twice. When Jesus asked the question the third time he used (as here reported) the same verb Peter had been using. Perhaps this added to Peter's embarrassment and irritation — Jesus asked again precisely what he had just avowed. The verb *agapaō* connotes a love that is discriminating, purposeful, deliberate. God loves the world; the verb is *agapaō*. "As far as *philein* is concerned, he could only abominate the foul world."[n] Similarly Jesus did not love his enemies in the sense of *philein* ("to be fond of") but only in the sense of *agapan* (*loc. cit.*). But Peter wanted his Lord to know that he not only loved with determination and loyalty but also with personal affection. The repetition here is comparable to the thrice-repeated "I write" of I John 2:12-14. In both

---

m R. C. Trench, *op. cit.*, pp. 40f.
n Lenski, *op. cit.*, p. 1419.

tion used Peter's word *philō,* which has led some people to assume that the two words for love, *agapaō* and *phileō* are synonymous here.

C. K. Barrett, for example, states: "The usage of these verbs throughout the gospel makes it impossible to doubt that they are synonyms; *philein* does not refer to an inferior kind of love" (*op. cit.,* p. 486). Agreeing with that viewpoint are Marcus Dods, J. H. Bernard, Wilbert F. Howard, and several others. Among those who believe that the words are not completely synonymous here are R. C. Trench and B. F. Westcott: "He lays claim only to the feeling of natural love (*philō se*), of which he could be sure. He does not venture to say that he has attained to that higher

love (*agapān*) which was to be the spring of the Christian life" (*op. cit.,* II, 321). A. T. Robertson: "Peter makes no claim here to superior love . . . and does not even use Christ's word *agapaō* for high and devoted love, but the humbler word *phileō* for love as a friend" (*op. cit.,* V, 321). E. J. Goodspeed in *The Goodspeed Parallel N. T.* translates *agapaō* with "be devoted to" and *phileō* with "love."[3]

*Agapaō* is used approximately seven times as often in the N. T. as *phileō* is. The corresponding noun forms are *agapē* and *philia;* the former occurs 119 times in the N. T. to only one occurrence for the latter (Jas. 4:4). Thus, as far as usage in the N. T. is concerned, *agapaō* (and its noun derivative) is without ques-

---

places different ages are envisioned. Here the "lambs" perhaps means young Christians; "tend my sheep" is applicable to the maturing Christians, while the third command refers to the older ones.[o]

Several lessons are implicit or explicit in this threefold exhortation.

(i) The important thing in our relation to the Lord is love. It accords with the strong emphasis in I Corinthians 13 that the one indispensable thing is *agapē* (Lat. *charitas*) or love. Love (*agapē*) heads the list of the fruits of the Spirit in Galatians 5:22. Love (*agapē*) is the climax of Peter's list of exhortations in I Peter 4:8. The loss of this love is a major disaster in one's relationship to the Lord (Rev. 2:4), but this need never happen (Rom. 8:35).

This love needs to be dominant both in the shepherd's relation to his Lord and in his relation to the flock. He can love people without loving the Lord, but he can hardly love the Lord without loving the people. Love is not complete and adequate until it goes in both directions — both towards God and towards man. More precisely it comes from God to man and through man to other men.

(ii) The "sheep" are not a means to another end but are ends in themselves. The sheep do not exist for the shepherd but the shepherd for the sheep. The

members do not exist for the sake of the church; the church exists for the sake of the members. Hence the command to Peter is not to be "domineering over those in your charge but being examples to the flock" (I Pet. 5:3). This quotation is evidence that Peter learned this lesson well. Like the Master, Christian leaders are "not to be served but to serve" (cf. Mark 10:45).

(iii) "Feeding" is hard and painstaking work. The feeding must be both in accordance with the recipient's needs and his capacity. This calls for knowledge on the part of the shepherd, knowledge of the need of his charges and the available resources to meet these needs. It calls also for patience to bear with the "slow of heart to believe" (Luke 24:25). Tenderness is needed to deal with some, firmness with others. Moreover it calls for sacrificial love, the kind that labors in season and out of season. The most effective shepherds and shepherdesses are characterized by these traits. Mary Slessor of Calabar is among the immortals who thus qualify. She "lost her life" for the west-coast Africans and in so doing "found" it.[p] Upon such as Robert Moffat and Mary Slessor comes "apostolic succession" in the truest meaning of that term.

18 **When thou wast young.** In characteristically enigmatic language Jesus con-

---

[3] An effective defense of the view that the terms are synonymous is presented in J. H. Bernard, *op. cit.,* II, 702-704. For a thorough and judicious statement of the view that the terms are not synonymous, see Wm. Hendriksen, *op. cit.,* II, 494-500.

[o] J. A. Bengel, *Gnomon,* translated by C. R. Lewis and M. R. Vincent (Philadelphia: Perkinpine & Higgins, 1862), p. 733.

[p] W. P. Livingston, *Mary Slessor of Calabar* (New York: G. H. Doran Co., n.d.).